Urban History

AMERICAN GOVERNMENT AND HISTORY INFORMATION GUIDE SERIES

Series Editor: Harold Shill, Chief Circulation Librarian, Adjunct Assistant Professor of Political Science, West Virginia University, Morgantown

Also in this series:

AMERICAN EDUCATIONAL HISTORY—*Edited by Michael W. Sedlak and Timothy Walch*

AMERICA'S MILITARY PAST—*Edited by Jack C. Lane*

IMMIGRATION AND ETHNICITY—*Edited by John D. Buenker and Nicholas C. Burckel*

PROGRESSIVE REFORM—*Edited by John D. Buenker and Nicholas C. Burckel*

PUBLIC ADMINISTRATION IN AMERICAN SOCIETY—*Edited by John E. Rouse, Jr.*

PUBLIC POLICY—*Edited by William J. Murin, Gerald Michael Greenfield, and John D. Buenker*

SOCIAL HISTORY OF THE UNITED STATES—*Edited by Donald F. Tingley*

U.S. CONSTITUTION—*Edited by Earlean McCarrick*

U.S. CULTURAL HISTORY—*Edited by Philip I. Mitterling*

U.S. FOREIGN RELATIONS—*Edited by Elmer Plischke*

U.S. POLITICS AND ELECTIONS—*Edited by David J. Maurer*

WOMEN AND FEMINISM IN AMERICAN HISTORY—*Edited by Elizabeth Tingley and Donald F. Tingley*

The above series is part of the

GALE INFORMATION GUIDE LIBRARY

The Library consists of a number of separate series of guides covering major areas in the social sciences, humanities, and current affairs.

General Editor: Paul Wasserman, Professor and former Dean, School of Library and Information Services, University of Maryland

Managing Editor: Denise Allard Adzigian, Gale Research Company

Urban History

A GUIDE TO INFORMATION SOURCES

Volume 9 in the American Government and History Information Guide Series

John D. Buenker

Professor of History
University of Wisconsin-Parkside

Gerald Michael Greenfield

Associate Professor of History
University of Wisconsin-Parkside

William J. Murin

Associate Professor of Political Science
University of Wisconsin-Parkside

Preface by Howard P. Chudacoff

Preston and Sterling Morton Professor of History
Brown University
Providence, Rhode Island

Gale Research Company
Book Tower, Detroit, Michigan 48226

Library of Congress Cataloging in Publication Data

Buenker, John D
    Urban history.

    (American government and history information guide series ; v. 9) (Gale information guide library)
    Includes index.
    1. Cities and towns—United States—History—Bibliography. I. Greenfield, Gerald Michael, joint author. II. Murin, William J., joint author. III. Title. IV. Series.
Z5942.B88   [HT123]   016.3077'6'0973   80-19643
ISBN 0-8103-1479-7

Copyright © 1981 by
John D. Buenker, Gerald Michael Greenfield, and William J. Murin

No part of this book may be reproduced in any form without permission in writing from the publisher, except by a reviewer who wishes to quote brief passages or entries in connection with a review written for inclusion in a magazine or newspaper. Manufactured in the United States of America.

VITAE

John D. Buenker is professor of history and director of the Center for Multicultural Studies at the University of Wisconsin-Parkside. He holds a Ph.D. from Georgetown University and has previously taught at Prince Georges College and Eastern Illinois University. He is the author of URBAN LIBERALISM AND PROGRESSIVE REFORM (Scribner's 1973) and coauthor of PROGRESSIVISM (Schenkman Publishing, 1977), IMMIGRATION AND ETHNICITY: A GUIDE TO INFORMATION SOURCES (Gale Research Co., 1977) and PROGRESSIVE REFORM: A GUIDE TO INFORMATION SOURCES (Gale Research Co., 1980). He has also contributed essays to ESSAYS ON ILLINOIS HISTORY, THE STUDY OF AMERICAN HISTORY, KENOSHA COUNTY IN THE TWENTIETH CENTURY, RACINE: GROWTH AND CHANGE IN A WISCONSIN COUNTY, FLAWED LIBERATION: SOCIALISM AND FEMINISM, and THE DEVELOPMENT OF AN AMERICAN CULTURE. He has written articles and reviews for the JOURNAL OF AMERICAN HISTORY, AMERICAN HISTORICAL REVIEW, NEW ENGLAND QUARTERLY, HISTORIAN, MID-AMERICA, ENCYCLOPEDIA AMERICANA, DICTIONARY OF AMERICAN BIOGRAPHY, ROCKY MOUNTAIN REVIEW, and the state historical journals of Illinois, Indiana, Ohio, Pennsylvania, New York, Connecticut, New Jersey, and Rhode Island. He is the recipient of the William Adee Whitehead Award of the New Jersey Historical Society and the Harry E. Pratt Award of the Illinois Historical Society and of fellowships from Newberry Library, the American Philosophical Society, and the Wisconsin Alumni Research Foundation. He was a Guggenheim Fellow in 1975-76.

Gerald Michael Greenfield is associate professor of history at the University of Wisconsin-Parkside. He received his B.A. from the State University of New York at Buffalo, his M.A. from Brooklyn College, and in 1975, his Ph.D. from Indiana University, Bloomington. A specialist in Latin American and comparative urbanization, his articles have appeared in the LUSO-BRAZILIAN REVIEW, JOURNAL OF LATIN AMERICAN STUDIES, SOUTH ATLANTIC URBAN STUDIES, and ESSAYS CONCERNING THE SOCIO-ECONOMIC HISTORY OF BRAZIL AND PORTUGUESE INDIA.

William J. Murin is associate professor of political science and currently serves as the director of University of Wisconsin-Parkside's Master of Public Service Administration program and its Institute for Local Government and Human Services. He received his B.A. from Kent State University, his N.P.A. from the Maxwell School of Syracuse University, and in 1971, his Ph.D. from the University of Maryland. His teaching

Vitae

and research have focused primarily in the areas of urban administration and management. His writings include MASS TRANSIT POLICY PLANNING (Lexington Books, 1971); URBAN POLICY AND POLITICS IN A BUREAUCRATIC AGE with Clarence N. Stone and Robert K. Whelan (Prentice Hall, 1979); and a book of readings, CLASSICS IN URBAN ADMINISTRATION, POLICY, AND POLITICS (Moore Publishing Co., in press).

CONTENTS

Preface ix
Acknowledgments xi
Introduction xiii

Chapter 1. General Studies 1
    Texts 1
    Readers 14
    The Teaching of Urban History 21

Chapter 2. The Urbanization Process 25

Chapter 3. The City in American Thought 65
    Historiography 82

Chapter 4. Single City Studies 89

Chapter 5. Regional Studies 125

Chapter 6. Colonial Cities and Towns 145

Chapter 7. Urban Institutions 161

Chapter 8. Planning, Architecture, and Urban Renewal . 195

Chapter 9. Class, Ethnicity, and Race 223

Chapter 10. Urban Politics and Government 273

Chapter 11. Bosses, Machines, and Urban Reform 305

Addendum 349

Author Index 367
Title Index 385
Subject Index 397

PREFACE

If history involves the analysis of change over time, American urban history offers one of the most fertile areas for analysis. In 1790 at the dawn of the American republic, only about 5 percent of the nation's population was urban. Today, upwards of 75 percent of the population lives in urban areas. Thus, in less than two centuries, a very remarkable change has occurred in American society. The United States has evolved into an urban nation, and its problems and promises are those of an urban civilization.

As recently as a half century ago, American scholars deemed the nation's cities to be unimportant for historical study because they considered cities as phenomena which became influential only in the modern era. Then, in the 1950s and 1960s, a new generation, caught up in a social ferment that derived from and centered in urban life, began to search the past for sources of that ferment. They discovered that cities and their problems were not new to American civilization and that from the colonial era onward, cities and city dwellers exerted strong influences on national affairs. Over the past two decades, the field of American urban history has mushroomed as increasing numbers of scholars have begun to explore the nation's urban past.

In this volume, John D. Buenker, Gerald M. Greenfield, and William J. Murin have provided the first extensive bibliographical guide to urban historical studies. They have compiled and annotated a listing of 1,921 scholarly works covering eleven topic areas. The studies that they have included span broad chronological and geographical ranges, covering every era of American history and every area of the country. Anyone interested in research or reading in any of these eras or areas is certain to find pertinent literature listed here. Perhaps most impressively, Buenker, Greenfield, and Murin present an interdisciplinary collection that is necessary for a full study of urban development. Thus they include not only historical works but also studies from the fields of anthropology, architecture, economics, geography, political science, and sociology.

In spite of the large number of entries, this bibliography remains a sample. But it is a very representative sample of general works, monographs, anthologies, articles, reviews, and dissertations. With so many urban historical

Preface

studies completed each year, a bibliography like this one cannot hope to remain fully up to date. Dissertations often are published, and articles often are expanded into monographs even while wholly new material appears. Yet, Buenker, Greenfield, and Murin have done an admirable job of including the most important current and past studies and of presenting scholars who will continue to produce significant work.

Finally, this volume is valuable not only as a resource for scholars, students, and interested general readers but also because of the issues it raises. For example, many of the sources listed focus on aspects of urban life that have differentiated it from rural life. Although the editors have chosen not to include studies that analyze anything that takes place in cities--to have done so would have swelled the volume beyond reasonable proportions--they have included numerous works on such topics as ethnicity, race, class, technology, politics, and reform. The authors of these works disagree as to which factors were more differentiating and at which points in time. Others question whether there have been any truly urban factors at all in American history. These and other issues add a provocative feature to this informative and comprehensive guide.

Howard P. Chudacoff

ACKNOWLEDGMENTS

In preparing this volume, the editors were greatly aided by the contributions of many highly capable people. Barbara Doherty and Leann Dillingham spent endless hours searching for the materials to be annotated and keeping track of the bibliography cards being constantly misplaced by absent-minded annotaters. Barbara Filipone Vanderleest and Ellen Duschak McDonald ably divided the typing chores, until Barbara's baby, Ryan Patrick, won his race with the manuscript. Parkside's library staff, especially Nancy Frederick and Fran Austin of the Interlibrary Loan Department, were helpful and cooperative far beyond the call of duty. Our University Archivist Nicholas C. Burckel, himself the co-editor of two volumes in this series, contributed several of the annotations in chapter eleven and gave us expert advice on editorial matters. As usual, Series Editor Harold Shill significantly improved the finished product by his painstaking attention to detail and concept. To all of them, the editors extend profound and grateful thanks, while absolving them of all responsibility for any errors or omissions that may exist.

INTRODUCTION

This volume presents the editors' attempts to collect, organize, and annotate the most important and useful published sources and dissertations on U.S. urban history which existed at the end of 1979. The veritable explosion of scholarly work on the subject in the last decade has presented us with several related problems of selection and organization. In the late 1960s only a handful of path-breaking scholars considered themselves to be urban historians and few colleges and universities offered courses in the field. There were no journals specifically geared to the publication of urban history articles until the 1970s. Most book-length studies were either "biographies" of a single city or examinations of historical subjects in a setting which often seemed only coincidentally urban; there was, as Sam Bass Warner pointed out in 1968, no "scaffolding" for a systematic investigation of urbanization as a historical process. The efforts of hundreds of scholars to meet this challenge has involved the development of new methodologies, the utilization of sources ignored by generations of previous scholars, a focus upon the activities of the typical many rather than the influential few, and a sometimes uneasy marriage with such disparate disciplines as sociology, anthropology, political science, geography, architecture, education, psychology, demography, planning, and public administration. Compressing the results of that vast outpouring of scholarship into a single volume has required the editors to be selective and representative, rather than comprehensive. Accordingly, we have not included works that focus upon the subject of urbanization unless they have a definite historical context. Similarly we have included the work of urbanologists from cognate disciplines only if they viewed the problem at hand in a historical perspective. We have also excluded studies of the urban history of other countries, unless they make explicit comparisons with the U.S. experience or set forth some landmark conceptual framework basic to an understanding of American city development. We also have generally rejected the view that the proper province of urban history is anything that takes place within a city in favor of one that requires the author to address such questions as the nature, growth, organization, and operation of the city, the roles played by urbanization in the development of the United States, the impact of city life on people and institutions, or the changing dimensions of the urban population. Finally, in the case of the two sources by the same author with substantial overlap in subject matter, we have opted in favor of that which is the more comprehensive, accessible, and useful, and we have made a deliberate effort to include the more recent literature at the expense of older works.

Introduction

Similar considerations have impelled us to favor a topical organization over a chronological one. There is no basic agreement on proper periodization for urban history; the nature of the subject matter does not readily lend itself to any existing chronological framework. Moreover, the bulk of the literature on the city deals with the period between the Civil War and the Great Depression, making a very uneven distribution and requiring some further breakdown of works on that period on a topical basis. Only in the case of colonial cities have we adhered to a chronological basis of organization because it is generally treated as such in the literature and because colonial cities confronted a unique range of concerns resulting from their being "cities in the wilderness" and "outposts of empire." Since it is certainly legitimate to quarrel with the categories that we established (indeed we debated them frequently among ourselves), we have tried to ameliorate any difficulties caused the reader by keying the subject index to topics that are interspersed throughout the various chapters, such as individual urban services, a specific city, chronological period, national event, geographical region, or particular ethnic or social group.

Within the above limitations, we have arranged the information sources in this volume into eleven topical chapters. The first contains textbooks, general overviews of American urban history, and readers and anthologies which cover a broad range of urban topics, as well as a section on the teaching of general urban history courses. The second chapter focuses specifically upon efforts to create the "scaffolding" which Warner called for, to delineate a theory and process of urbanization within a historical context, and to the explication of methodologies for doing so. The third chapter contains contributions to the ongoing debate over the place of the city in American life, a controversy which dates at least from Jefferson's time. Chapter four deals with colonial cities, which seem to the editors to form a discrete category for reasons already noted. The next segment contains studies of single cities, especially those which present theories, processes, or methodologies that have possible applications to other cities. We have not attempted to include all of the "urban biographies" which used to constitute the bulk of urban history; these are readily accessible to those with an interest in a particular city and usually are narrative rather than analytical. We have attempted to include those landmark biographies that have tried to move beyond the realm of narrative to that of analysis. Chapter six focuses upon cities in a regional context and upon the question of whether urbanization in the South and the West especially, departs from the national norms, which largely reflect the East and Midwest. The next chapter deals with a broad spectrum of urban institutions, both public and private, which constitute the infrastructure of any city. These include especially the provision of urban public services, as well as religious, educational, and charitable institutions. Chapter eight deals with the closely related topics of architecture, planning, and housing, largely prior to 1960. Readers with an interest in more recent developments in these areas should consult the respective volumes on planning and housing in Gale's Urban Studies Information Guide Series. The ninth chapter is concerned with that phase of urban history "that puts people at the center and that highlights the networks of interaction between urban dwellers and their environment," to quote Howard Chudacoff. Specifically it deals with the adjustment made by a variety of

Introduction

ethnic groups and social classes to the urban environment and to the latter's impact upon their culture and institutions. Consistent with our approach to the issues, we have excluded the vast literature on the urban racial problems of the past two decades, unless there is a sizeable emphasis on its historical origins. The final two chapters deal with government and politics of the American city. Since scholars have lavished a great deal of attention on urban political machines and on efforts at urban reform in the early part of the twentieth century, the editors treat that impressive volume of literature as a unit in the final chapter. The tenth chapter deals largely with the postreform era, with the structure and operation of city governance, and with urban-state-federal relations. An addendum of current sources which were collected too late to be placed in their proper order of inclusion completes the text.

In generating the items which constitute this guide, the editors consulted the bibliographies of most of the standard textbooks and anthologies on urban history. We also consulted all the issues of the JOURNAL OF URBAN HISTORY, URBANISM: PAST AND PRESENT, and the URBAN HISTORY NEWSLETTER, as well as the recent articles and dissertations section of the JOURNAL OF AMERICAN HISTORY. Other valuable sources included WRITINGS ON AMERICAN HISTORY (American Historical Association, 1976-- . Annual), AMERICA: HISTORY AND LIFE (American Biographical Center-Clio Press, 1964-- . Annual), SAGE URBAN STUDIES ABSTRACTS, THE REINTERPRETATION OF AMERICAN HISTORY AND CULTURE (National Council for Social Studies, 1973), the American Historical Association's GUIDE TO HISTORICAL LITERATURE (Macmillan, 1961), and the HARVARD GUIDE TO AMERICAN HISTORY AND LIFE (Belknap Press of Harvard University Press, 1974). For unpublished dissertations we used the COMPREHENSIVE DISSERTATIONS INDEX, 1861-1872, and updates. For related subjects, readers should consult the volumes in the Urban Studies Information Guide Series by Gale Research Co.

Chapter 1
GENERAL STUDIES

TEXTS

1   Adler, Ronald, ed. A COMPARATIVE ATLAS OF AMERICA'S GREAT CITIES: TWENTY METROPOLITAN REGIONS. Minneapolis: University of Minnesota Press, 1976. 528 p.

Examines land use, housing, population, and socioeconomic regions of the nation's twenty largest Standard Metropolitan Statistical Areas (SMSAs) and compares them with respect to physical environments, leisure use areas, housing, transportation, communication, education, public health, socioeconomic segregation, employment, poverty, and urban redevelopment.

2   Chudacoff, Howard P. THE EVOLUTION OF AMERICAN URBAN SOCIETY. Englewood Cliffs, N.J.: Prentice-Hall, 1975. 280 p.

Defines urbanization as a process that affects the entire nation and focuses on the ways in which it has attracted and assimilated migrants, standardized social and economic activities, provided organizational and technological innovations, and revised the methods and effects of human communications. Highlights the changing networks of interaction between urban dwellers and their environment over time.

3   Cook, Ann; Gittell, Marilyn; and Mack, Herb. CITY LIFE, 1865-1900: VIEWS OF URBAN AMERICA. New York: Praeger, 1973. 292 p.

Contains a variety of written and photographic materials designed to raise issues related to living in cities. Includes sections on attitudes toward cities, transportation, newcomers, architecture, hazards of city life, politics, and life-styles.

4   Curran, Donald J. METROPOLITAN FINANCING: THE MILWAUKEE EXPERIENCE, 1920-1970. Madison: University of Wisconsin Press, 1973. 166 p.

Demonstrates that the fragmentation of the metropolitan area

General Studies

into scores of small government entities over the past half century is one of the major root causes of the city's present financial problems.

5   Davis, Walter G. "A Statistical View of American Cities." GUNTON'S MAGAZINE 23 (1902): 297-304.

Examines census data for the 135 cities with over 30,000 population in 1900. Focuses upon their fiscal situation and the cost of providing social services.

6   Deran, Elizabeth. "An Overview of the Municipal Income Tax." PROCEEDINGS OF THE ACADEMY OF POLITICAL SCIENCE 28 (1968): 19-25.

Surveys the evolution of the tax and assesses its impact on the city and upon its overall structure. Contains a chart of the chronological adoption of municipal income taxes from 1939 to 1967.

7   Dickens, Charles. AMERICAN NOTES. Introduction by Christopher Leach. Gloucester, Mass.: P. Smith, 1968. 288 p.

Features Dicken's often testy comments about life in Boston, Worcester, Hartford, New Haven, New York City, Philadelphia, Washington, D.C., Richmond, Baltimore, Harrisburg, Pittsburgh, Cincinnati, Louisville and St. Louis.

8   Futterman, Robert A. THE FUTURE OF OUR CITIES. Garden City, N.Y.: Doubleday, 1961. 360 p.

Examines the causes of the urban crisis and attributes it primarily to lack of planning, governmental inefficiency, the automobile, and racism. Focuses specifically upon sixteen of the nation's large- and medium-sized cities to illustrate the thesis.

9   Galfont, Blanche H. THE AMERICAN CITY NOVEL, 1900-1940. Norman: University of Oklahoma Press, 1970. 289 p.

Uses sociological perspectives to analyze the works of Theodore Drieser, John Dos Passos, and other realistic novelists of the period for their views of city life.

10   Geruson, Richard T., and McGrath, Dennis. CITIES AND URBANIZATION. New York: Praeger, 1977. 233 p.

Surveys the evolution of cities from ancient times to the present, focusing on American cities in three stages of their growth. Concentrates upon the sources of urban growth, the

General Studies

evolving network of cities, and the relationship between internal change and metropolitan ecology.

11 Glaab, Charles N., and Brown, A. Theodore. A HISTORY OF URBAN AMERICA. New York: Macmillan, 1976. 350 p.

Surveys urban growth from the colonial era to the present, combining chronological and topical approaches. Emphasizes the interactions among politics, technology, demography, and economics and the factors making for both continuity and change.

12 Goldfield, David R., and Brownell, Blaine A. URBAN AMERICA: FROM DOWNTOWN TO NO TOWN. Boston: Houghton-Mifflin, 1979. 435 p.

Traces the development of the American city from colonial times to the present, focusing upon the changing patterns of spatial relationships within and between cities. Delineates four chronologically evolving urban place forms--the cluster, the market place, the radial center, and the vital fringe.

13 Green, Constance McLaughlin. AMERICAN CITIES IN THE GROWTH OF A NATION. New York: Harper and Row, 1965. 258 p.

Contends that the refurbishing of old cities and the founding of new ones is a no less significant and dramatic feature of American history than is the pushing back of the frontier. Offers studies of New York City, Philadelphia, Baltimore, Charleston, Boston, Cincinnati, St. Louis, New Orleans, Holyoke, Naugatuck, Chicago, Denver, Wichita, Seattle, Detroit, and Washington, D.C., as illustrations.

14 _____. THE RISE OF URBAN AMERICA. New York: Harper and Row, 1965. 208 p.

Surveys the development of America as an urban nation from colonial times through the First World War. Stresses the economic, social, and political impact of urbanization.

15 Halverson, Frank D., and Halverson, Eva H.T. ORIGIN OF CITIES OF THE UNITED STATES. Salt Lake City: Halverson Co., 1939. 36 p.

Contains dates of settlement, incorporation, and some relevant historical facts for several cities in each state.

16 Hawes, Joseph M. CHILDREN IN URBAN SOCIETY: JUVENILE DELIQUENCY IN NINETEENTH CENTURY AMERICA. New York: Oxford University Press, 1971. 315 p.

General Studies

Views juvenile delinquency as a by-product of the development of cities and the concentration of population. Finds that the general trend was to think of young offenders as individuals in need of help, rather than as members of a stereotyped group despised by society.

17   Hillhouse, A.M. MUNICIPAL BONDS: A CENTURY OF EXPERIENCE. New York: Arno Press, 1975. 579 p.

Surveys the history of municipal bonds with particular reference to the extent of and reasons for defaults. Contains over fifty pages of statistics and laws concerning municipal bonds.

18   Horowitz, Irving L. "'Separate But Equal': Revolution and Counter-Revolution in the American City." SOCIAL PROBLEMS 17 (1970): 294-312.

Compares urban conditions in 1970 with those reported by the National Resources Committee in 1937. Concludes that the problems have intensified in magnitude but not in character, and that the rural-urban polarity of the 1930s has become the suburban-central city face-off of the present.

19   Jacobs, Jane. THE DEATH AND LIFE OF GREAT AMERICAN CITIES. New York: Random House, 1961. 458 p.

Attempts to introduce new principles and values for city planning and rebuilding on a more human scale. Stresses the importance of sidewalks, parks, neighborhoods, diversity of land uses and buildings, the forces of decline and regeneration, and different taxes for refurbishing cities.

20   Kuznets, Simon S., et al., eds. POPULATION REDISTRIBUTION AND ECONOMIC GROWTH, UNITED STATES 1870-1950. 3 vols. Philadelphia: American Philosophical Society, 1957-1964. 759; 239; 367 p.

Presents estimates of change over time in migration patterns, the composition of the labor force, manufacturing activity, and income by state. Analyzes migration and economic data and seeks to quantify and explain their interrelationship.

21   Leiby, James. A HISTORY OF SOCIAL WELFARE AND SOCIAL WORK IN THE UNITED STATES. New York: Columbia University Press, 1978. 426 p.

Traces evolution of notions about social welfare and social work from 1815 to the present. Attributes the modern initiative and momentum for welfare policies to pressures from diverse groups acting from a variety of motives.

22   McKelvey, Blake. AMERICAN URBANIZATION: A COMPARATIVE

General Studies

HISTORY. Glenview, Ill.: Scott, Foresman, 1973. 166 p.

A text which divides American urban history into three periods: an era of foundations to 1860; an "Age of Industrialism, 1860 to 1910"; and an "Age of Metropolitanism, 1910 to the Present"; and analyzes urbanizing forces for each period "in relation to contemporary and comparable developments in other urban societies."

23 _____. THE CITY IN AMERICAN HISTORY. London: Barnes and Noble, 1969. 229 p.

Divided into two parts--a summary essay which stresses the interaction between city and larger society in America from the colonial period on, and original documents keyed to the chronological and thematic subdivisions of the summary essay.

24 _____. THE EMERGENCE OF METROPOLITAN AMERICA, 1915-1966. New Brunswick, N.J.: Rutgers University Press, 1968. 311 p.

Considers changing metropolitan and national relationships, from initial attempts by the cities to confront and solve the problems generated by continuing urban growth to the "Federal-Metropolitan Emergence" of the 1960s.

25 _____. THE URBANIZATION OF AMERICA, 1860-1915. New Brunswick, N.J. Rutgers University Press, 1963. 370 p.

General discussion examining the character of city growth and exploring its relationship to broad trends and developments in American history. General topics discussed include post-Civil War urban growth, building and governing the cities, urban institutions and social tensions, and forging an urban culture. A concluding section assesses and analyzes the fruition of the urbanization process in metropolitan regionalism.

26 McKenzie, R.D. THE METROPOLITAN COMMUNITY. New York: Russell and Russell, 1967. 352 p.

General sociological inquiry into the basic changes occurring in American cities since the adoption of motor transportation. Discusses population trends, the rise of integrated metropolitan communities, structural interrelations among cities, metropolitan expansion, and problems of large cities.

27 McLaughlin, Glenn E. GROWTH OF AMERICAN MANUFACTURING AREAS. Westport, Conn.: Greenwood Press, 1970. 359 p.

Provides a comparative analysis of thirty-three major industrial areas in the United States, based on census records for the period from 1869 on, identifying factors responsible for differ-

General Studies

ential growth trends. Emphasizes, particularly, the Pittsburgh experience.

28 MacMichael, Stanley L., and Bingham, Robert F. CITY GROWTH AND VALUES. Cleveland: MacMichael Publishing Co., 1923.

Published with the approval of the National Association of Real Estate Boards, and authored by a practicing realtor and an attorney; focuses on factors that affect the growth of cities and levels of land values.

29 Miller, Zane L. THE URBANIZATION OF MODERN AMERICA: A BRIEF HISTORY. New York: Harcourt Brace Jovanovich, 1973. 241 p.

Provides an ecological analysis of the evolution of the American city, concentrating on the interactions between city dwellers and their socioeconomic and political systems. Divides urbanization into three major phases--the emergence of the metropolis to 1880, the era of stabilization from 1880 to World War II, and the modern era of renewal and crisis, relying heavily upon case studies of Cincinnati, Chicago, and Pittsburgh.

30 Mitchell, George L. "The Image of the City in the American Film." Ph.D. dissertation, University of Chicago, 1971. 223 p.

Examines the changing image of the city in film and other popular arts, and uses that as a measure of the nation's difficulties in acculturating to urbanization. Focuses especially on the work of D.W. Griffith as a latter-day Populist.

31 Morris, James. CITIES. New York: Harcourt, Brace, 1964. 375 p.

Travelog discussing seventy-four world cities including New York City, San Francisco, Washington, D.C., Chicago, and Honolulu.

32 Mowry, George E. THE URBAN NATION, 1920-1960. New York: Hill and Wang, 1969. 278 p.

Focuses on the evolution of the "urban mind," on the mentality arising from a mass production-consumption economy, its conflicts with older rubrics of thought, and its impact upon institutions as key themes to explain the nation's history between 1920 and 1960.

33 Muirhead, James F. THE LAND OF CONTRASTS. New York: DaCapo Press, 1970. 282 p.

Contains varied information regarding the United States, including its cities, in the 1890s, with one chapter, chapter 11

General Studies

(pp. 190-218), "Certain Features of Certain Cities," specifically devoted to descriptions of New York City, Boston, Chicago, San Francisco, Denver, and Washington, D.C.

34   Mumford, Lewis. THE CITY IN HISTORY. New York: Harcourt, Brace and World, 1961. 657 p.

Presents a comprehensive overview of the development of urbanization and urbanism within Western civilization, focusing mainly on western Europe, indicating the changing forms and functions of cities, and the nature of their relationships to their larger societies. Ultimately develops a virtual philosophy of urbanization.

35   Neff, Frank A. MUNICIPAL FINANCE. Wichita, Kans.: McGuin, 1939. 167 p.

Uses historical, philosophical, comparative, and statistical approaches to discuss the development of municipal expenditures, revenue, indebtedness, finance administration, and practices of some European cities.

36   Newmark, Helen. "A Nineteenth Century Memoir." WESTERN STATES JEWISH HISTORICAL QUARTERLY 6 (1974): 204-18.

Autobiographical reminiscences of a Polish-Jewish immigrant who settled in California. Contains observations about San Francisco, Sacramento, and Berkeley during the latter half of the nineteenth century.

37   Owen, Wilfred. CITIES IN THE MOTOR AGE. New York: Cooper Square Publisher, 1971.

Summarizes and evaluates the results of a 1957 symposium organized by Connecticut General Life Insurance Company to address problems confronting metropolitan areas. Designed for a general audience. Topics include land use, housing, industry, commerce, transportation, and government organization. A concluding chapter presents strategies for change.

38   Peal, Ethel. "The Atrophied Rib: Urban Middle-Class Women in Jacksonian America." Ph.D. dissertation, University of Pittsburgh, 1970. 264 p.

Comments on the insignificant role of married women in urban America during the early nineteenth century, and attributes the failure of Victorian solutions for social dislocations to the male attitude, which also "predetermined the failure of the alternative solution--the feminist crusade for equality."

39   Potts, James H. "The Evolution of Municipal Accounting in the United

General Studies

States: 1900-1935." BUSINESS HISTORY REVIEW 52 (1978): 518-36.

>Compares the relative merits of commercial accounting, as applied to cities, and of efforts to design a peculiarily urban system. Concludes that cities have fluctuated between the two and that commercial accounting may be more adaptable to city needs than is generally supposed.

40   Queen, Stuart A., and Carpenter, David B. THE AMERICAN CITY. Westport, Conn.: Greenwood Press, 1970. 383 p.

>General text using sociological-anthropological approaches. Considers the factors responsible for urban growth, patterns, and processes involved in the localization of activities within in cities, the social life of urban dwellers, and the city's role in social change.

41   Queen, Stuart A.; Carpenter, David B.; and Thomas, Lewis F. THE CITY: A STUDY OF URBANISM IN THE UNITED STATES. Ann Arbor, Mich.: University Microfilms International, 1979. 500 p.

>Text in urban sociology divided into five sections: the rise of cities and urbanism, urban institutions and folkways, distributive and selective aspects of the city, people in the city, and prediction and control.

42   Richardson, James. "The Historical Roots of Our Urban Crisis." CURRENT HISTORY 59 (1970): 257-301, 308.

>Focuses on nineteenth- and early twentieth-century urban development and the problems it generated. Considers city planning, the role of the state, schools as instruments for social control, and impact of the private search for profits.

43   Robson, William A., ed. GREAT CITIES OF THE WORLD. London: Allen and Unwin, 1954. 693 p.

>Considers government, politics, and planning in selected large cities of Europe, Asia, and Australia. U.S. cities discussed in individual essays include Chicago, Los Angeles, and New York City.

44   Roebuck, Janet. THE SHAPING OF URBAN SOCIETY: A HISTORY OF CITY FORMS AND FUNCTIONS. New York: Charles Scribner's Sons, 1974. 256 p.

>Introductory text providing a broad survey of the development of western cities from early communities to the present. Includes chapters on the medieval city, the early modern city, the industrial city, and the modern city.

General Studies

45 Rossi, Peter H. "The Middle-Sized American City at Mid-Century." LIBRARY QUARTERLY 33 (1963): 3-13.

Presents, based on census material, a "collective portrait" of middle-sized cities, and summarizes a number of studies on community power. Draws some comparisons with the Lynds's studies of Middletown.

46 Schlesinger, Arthur M. THE RISE OF THE CITY, 1878-1898. New York: Franklin Watts, Inc., 1971.

The first book-length attempt to study the city and its impact upon American history in systematic fashion. Also contains a lengthy bibliographic essay discussing the existing sources for the study of urban history.

47 Share, Allen J. "British Travellers and American Cities, 1830-1860: Images and Realities." Ph.D. dissertation, University of Toledo, 1973. 369 p.

Investigates British travel literature on New York City, Lowell, Cincinnati, and New Orleans as a means of studying the social evolution of American cities.

48 Steen, Ivan D. "The British Traveler and the American City, 1850-1860." Ph.D. dissertation, New York University, 1962. 352 p.

Relates comments from some eighty published accounts of British travelers on various aspects of mid-century American cities, including hotels, urban residence facilities, educational and charitable institutions, and urban services.

49 Still, Bayrd. "The History of the City in American Life." AMERICAN REVIEW 2 (1962): 20-37.

Presents an overview of urban development in the United States, stressing the factors responsible for urban growth and the impact of that growth upon American society.

50 _____. URBAN AMERICA: A HISTORY WITH DOCUMENTS. Boston: Little, Brown, 1974. 566 p.

Provides a chronological overview of urbanization in the United States through brief introductory essays followed by contemporaneous documents. Broad categories include: "The City in Early America," "Urban Growth 1820-1870," "Urban Expansion in 1870-1920," and, within each, several topics or themes are identified.

51 Strauss, Anselm L. IMAGES OF THE AMERICAN CITY. New Brunswick, N.J.: Transaction Books, 1976. 306 p.

General Studies

Focuses on past and present American attitudes toward the city, detailing the transition from an agricultural vision and its accommodations to the increasing fact of urbanization. Includes regional variations as well as national trends.

52   Sutter, Ruth E. THE NEXT PLACE YOU COME TO: A HISTORICAL INTRODUCTION TO COMMUNITIES IN NORTH AMERICA. Englewood Cliffs, N.J.: Prentice-Hall, 1973. 214 p.

Uses the search for community as a theme in surveying U.S. history from pre-Columbian times to the present. Focuses also on the European settings of discovery and exploration, colonial settlement, the westward movement, the nineteenth-century city, and the development of an urban-rural dichotomy in the twentieth century.

53   Thomlinson, Ralph. URBAN STRUCTURE. New York: Random House, 1969. 335 p.

Text focusing on urban ecology, with chapters ordered in three major groupings: "Setting the Urban Scene," "How Urban Areas Are Arranged," and "How Urban Areas Might Be Arranged." Provides historical background on the nature and rise of cities, urban networks, and principles of city planning.

54   Toll, Seymour I. ZONED AMERICAN. New York: Grossman, 1969. 370 p.

Details the development of comprehensive zoning as an established American legal institution, stressing the combination of reform and real estate which served as background to the pioneer 1913 law in New York City, and the subsequent national promotion of zoning in the 1920s. Considers the changing nature of concern for zoning, and the purposes it was intended to accomplish as reflecting changing sociocultural conditions in the United States.

55   Trollope, Anthony. NORTH AMERICA. Baltimore, Md.: Penguin Books, 1968. 601 p.

Provides a variety of observations regarding social and political affairs in several American cities during the Civil War, including Detroit, Milwaukee, New York City, St. Louis, and Washington, D.C.

56   Tunnard, Christopher. THE MODERN AMERICAN CITY. Princeton, N.J.: D. Van Nostrand, 1968. 191 p.

Presents an overview of the emergence of the modern American city, followed by a series of readings dealing with various aspects of that process.

General Studies

57 U.S. Department of Housing and Urban Development, Office of International Affairs. THE INFLUENCE OF THE FOREIGN HERITAGE ON THE AMERICAN CITY. Washington, D.C.: 1976. 34 p.

Pamphlet discussing the interaction between European and U.S. urban development from the colonial period, stressing the ways in which the United States drew upon the educational and technological expertise of the Old World.

58 U.S. National Resources Committee. Research Committee on Urbanism. OUR CITIES: THEIR ROLE IN THE NATIONAL ECONOMY. New York: Arno Press, 1974. 87 p.

The first major national study of U.S. cities; assesses urban population trends, urban and racial ways of life, industrial centralization and decentralization, model cities, urban planning and housing, urban growth, transport facilities, land policies, urban government, unions of cities, and federal-city relations. Identifies four changes in American society: a rapid and distinct shift to urban life, unprecedented spatial mobility, a centralization of national enterprise in the cities, and the fact that these urban activities have a vital impact on national life.

59 Vernon, Raymond. THE CHANGING ECONOMIC FUNCTION OF THE CENTRAL CITY. New York: Committee for Economic Development, 1959. 92 p.

Presents past patterns and present trends relating to various aspects of the central city, including economic functions and population movements.

60 Wade, Richard C., ed. THE CITIES. New York: Arno Press, 1976. 386 p.

Contains hundreds of articles from the NEW YORK TIMES of the last century, dealing with urban growth, the impact of the automobile, housing, changes in the ethnic and racial composition of city populations, the interaction of cities and suburbs, and the ongoing struggle between political machines and reformers.

61 Warner, Sam Bass, Jr. THE PRIVATE CITY: PHILADELPHIA IN THREE PERIODS OF ITS GROWTH. Philadelphia: University of Pennsylvania Press, 1968. 236 p.

Landmark study using the story of Philadelphia to provide a framework for identifying and developing the tradition of privatism and assessing its impact on America's urbanization process, particularly with regard to the quality of life and level of social concern in cities. Argues that privatism, the

General Studies

"concentration upon the individual and the individual's search for wealth," became increasingly dysfunctional as towns became large cities, and major conflicts between private interest and public welfare emerged.

62 _____. THE URBAN WILDERNESS: A HISTORY OF THE AMERICAN CITY. New York: Harper and Row, 1972. 303 p.

Sees the problems of the contemporary American city as rooted in various peculiarities of the historical process of urbanization in the United States, demonstrating the weight of continuity and indicating the dimensions of choice as reflected in present prescriptions for confronting the urban crisis. Considers the initial American experience with planning and land management, emphasizing the private tradition, and identifies and discusses three types of cities in historical sequence: New York, 1820-70, the engine of private enterprise; Chicago, 1870-1920, the "Segregated City"; and Los Angeles, from 1920 on, symbolizing the "New Freedom."

63 Weaver, Robert C. DILEMMAS OF URBAN AMERICA. Cambridge, Mass.: Harvard University Press, 1966. 138 p.

Considers present problems posed by urbanization, but provides some historical perspective. Topics discussed include new communities, urban renewal, and race. Based on his Godkin lectures delivered at Harvard University in 1965.

64 Weber, Adna F. THE GROWTH OF CITIES IN THE 19TH CENTURY, A STUDY IN STATISTICS. Ithaca, N.Y.: Cornell University Press, 1963. 495 p.

Classic study presenting the results of a statistical investigation of nineteenth-century urbanization throughout the world. Topics discussed include causes and effects of population concentration, urban growth and internal migration, the structure of city population, physical and moral health of city and country, and projections for the future.

65 Weber, Michael R., and Lloyd, Anne, eds. THE AMERICAN CITY. St. Paul, Minn.: West Publishing Co., 1975. 463 p.

A college-level textbook on the American city, compiled from an interdisciplinary perspective and focusing on the development of analytical skills and problem solving. Thirty-six assignments are organized into four main units: the automobile city, the walking city, the streetcar city, and contemporary urban issues.

66 Weiner, Howard R. "The Cinema and the City." JOURNAL OF

General Studies

POPULAR CULTURE 3 (1970): 825-32.

> Surveys the portrayal of the city in films from D.W. Griffith to the present, identifying two overall trends: "the juxtaposition of hope and despair" and "the use of experimental techniques."

67 Weiss, Thomas. "The Industrial Distribution of the Urban and Rural Workforces: Estimates for the United States, 1870-1910." JOURNAL OF ECONOMIC HISTORY 32 (1972): 919-37.

> Presents estimates of the industrial distribution of the workforce in urban and in rural areas and relates "this disaggregated evidence to structural change in the economy," focusing particularly on the service sector, defined as including trade, transportation, utilities, finance, professional and personal services, education, and government.

68 Wilcox, Delos F. GREAT CITIES IN AMERICA: THEIR PROBLEMS AND THEIR GOVERNMENT. New York: Arno Press, 1974. 426 p.

> Examines a variety of topics including crime, utilities, government, and vice in New York City, Chicago, Philadelphia, St. Louis, Boston, and Washington, D.C.

69 Williamson, Jeffrey G. "American Prices and Urban Inequality Since 1920." JOURNAL OF ECONOMIC HISTORY 36 (1976): 303-33.

> Investigates urban distribution trends, as measured by an urban inequality index, for the years 1920 to 1948, noting the structure of names and prices, and associated explanatory models, for various eras within that period. Identifies and explains eras of dramatic changes in urban inequality and explores their impact.

70 Wilson, William H. COMING OF AGE: URBAN AMERICA, 1915-1945. New York: Wiley, 1974. 221 p.

> General text, largely descriptive, which discusses physical changes in cities, the black migration northward, suburanization, urban political reform, attitudes toward the city, varieties of city planning, and the growth of federal-urban relationships.

71 Wortley, Lady Emmeline S. TRAVELS IN THE UNITED STATES DURING 1849 AND 1850. New York: Harper and Brothers, 1851. 463 p.

> Travel account providing descriptions of Latin America as well as of the United States. Presents information on New York City, Albany, Boston, Bridgeport, Philadelphia, Washington, D.C., Louisville, and New Orleans.

General Studies

READERS

72   Cahill, Susan, and Cooper, Michele F., eds. THE URBAN READER. Englewood Cliffs, N.J.: Prentice-Hall, 1971. 416 p.

   Contains nearly one hundred brief pieces, both fiction and nonfiction, illustrating various facets of urban life and urban problems, organized under such topics as life-styles, physical environment, housing and urban renewal, minorities, economies, politics, music, education, art, literature, drama, and the future. Also includes photographic essays.

73   Callow, Alexander B., Jr., ed. AMERICAN URBAN HISTORY: AN INTERPRETIVE READER WITH COMMENTARIES. New York: Oxford University Press, 1969. 674 p.

   A variety of scholars contributed forty essays arranged around several general topics: the city in history, colonial America, the city in transition, the American mind, national affairs, modern times, and the city and historians. Includes topical summaries and an introduction by the editor.

74   _____. AMERICAN URBAN HISTORY: AN INTERPRETIVE READER WITH COMMENTARIES. 2d rev. ed. New York: Oxford University Press, 1973. 684 p.

   Fifty-five historians, political scientists, sociologists, and urban planners contributed essays which are organized around nine major themes: the city in history, colonial America, the era of Manifest Destiny, the age of industry, politics, the life of the newcomer, the American mind, modern times, and the city and the historians. Substantially revised and updated from the first edition.

74a   Davis, Kingsley, comp. CITIES: THEIR ORIGINS, GROWTH, AND HUMAN IMPACT. See no. 102.

75   Dorsett, Lyle W., ed. THE CHALLENGE OF THE CITY, 1860-1910. Lexington, Mass.: D.C. Heath, 1968. 114 p.

   Contains excerpts from the works of contemporaries and historians on the urban crisis of the age. Includes five pieces on the city as a moral and political problem, four on the redemption of the city, three on its hope, and five on urbanization and the shaping of twentieth-century America.

76   Downs, Anthony, ed. URBAN PROBLEMS AND PROSPECTS. Chicago: Markham, 1970. 293 p.

   Contains eleven essays by a variety of scholars dealing with urban growth, race relations, housing, transportation, governmental administration, and education. Concentrates upon the institutions

General Studies

and behavior patterns that have produced crises in these areas.

77   Eldredge, H. Wentworth, ed. TAMING MEGALOPOLIS. 2 vols. Garden City, N.Y.: Anchor, 1967. 1,166 p.

> Contains over fifty selections by a variety of scholars and statesmen on various aspects of megalopolis--what is, what could be, and how to manage an urbanized world.

78   Feagin, Joe R., ed. THE URBAN SCENE: MYTHS AND REALITIES. New York: Random House, 1973. 274 p.

> Contains selections by fifteen scholars that present unconventional or unique treatments of urban life with planning and policymaking implications. Topics include race, slums, middle Americans, the myth of suburbia, poverty, community control, and the future of the city.

79   Finster, Jerome, ed. THE NATIONAL ARCHIVES AND URBAN RESEARCH. Athens: Ohio University Press, 1974. 164 p.

> Contains essays by a dozen scholars based primarily upon research done in the National Archives and organized around the general topics of urban population, transportation, housing, and the impact of federal government activities.

80   Fortune Magazine. THE EXPLODING METROPOLIS. New York: Doubleday, 1958. 193 p.

> Designed as a book for "people who like cities." Contains six essays: "Are Cities Un-American" by William H. Whyte, Jr., "The City and the Car" by Francis Bello, "New Strength in City Hall" by Seymour Freedgood, "The Enduring Slums" by Daniel Seligman, "Urban Sprawl" by Whyte, and "Downtown Is For People" by Jane Jacobs.

81   Friedel, John, and Chrisman, Noel J., comps. CITY WAYS: A SELECTIVE READER OF URBAN ANTHROPOLOGY. New York: Thomas Y. Crowell Co., 1975. 458 p.

> Contains twenty articles by scholars from various disciplines dealing with the scope and method of urban analysis, categories of urban dwellers, specialized communities, the continuity of social relations, and the culture of poverty. Includes both American and non-American pieces.

82   Frieden, Bernard J., and Nash, William W., eds. SHAPING AN URBAN FUTURE: ESSAYS IN MEMORY OF CATHERINE BAUER WURSTER. Cambridge: MIT Press, 1968. 222 p.

> Selections focus on housing issues and policy, new communities, planning, and the role of governments in urban development.

General Studies

83 Geen, Elizabeth; Lowe, Jeanne R.; and Walker, Kenneth, eds. MAN AND THE MODERN CITY. Pittsburgh: University of Pittsburgh Press, 1963. 134 p.

   Contains ten entries presented at a symposium by scholars, politicians, and administrators dealing with various aspects of the relationship between man and the changing urban environment. Deals especially with technology, values, politics, and education.

84 Glaab, Charles N. THE AMERICAN CITY: A DOCUMENTARY HISTORY. Homewood, Ill.: Dorsey Press, 1963. 478 p.

   Includes a variety of documents on city life in different chronological eras ranging from colonial times to 1960. Has its heaviest concentration in eighteenth and nineteenth centuries.

85 Gottman, Jean, and Harper, Robert A., eds. METROPOLIS ON THE MOVE: GEOGRAPHERS LOOK AT URBAN SPRAWL. New York: John Wiley and Sons, 1967. 203 p.

   Includes papers given by a dozen scholars at a conference on urban sprawl held at Southern Illinois University in 1964. General topics include the forces, pressures, and forms of urban sprawl, sprawl and the functioning city, the skyscraper, planning, and the challenge to education.

86 Greer, Scott. THE URBAN VIEW: LIFE AND POLITICS IN METROPOLITAN AMERICA. New York: Oxford University Press, 1972. 355 p.

   Contains seventeen essays written by the author and various collaborators and organized around four basic themes: Los Angeles, city of the future; St. Louis, city with a past; movements to change the city; and some urban futures.

87 Gutman, Robert, and Popenoe, David, eds. NEIGHBORHOOD, CITY, AND METROPOLIS. New York: Random House, 1970. 942 p.

   Contains sixty essays arranged around seven major topics: theory, urban development, urban differentiation, ecology, locality groups, the environment and social behavior, and policy planning.

88 Handlin, Oscar, and Burchard, John, eds. THE HISTORIAN AND THE CITY. Cambridge: Harvard University Press, 1963. 299 p.

   Contains twenty-two essays by a variety of scholars such as Oscar Handlin, Sam Bass Warner, Morton White, Kenneth Boulding, Denis Brogan, and Eric Lampard, organized around the general topics of technological innovation and economic

General Studies

development, the city in intellectual history, the contemporary urban world, the city as artifact, and planners and interpreters of the city. Includes Handlin's widely reprinted essay, "The Modern City as a Field of Historical Study."

89   Hatt, Paul K., and Reiss, Albert J., eds. CITIES AND SOCIETY: THE REVISED READER IN URBAN SOCIOLOGY. New York: Free Press, 1958. 852 p.

Updates the original version done in 1951. Contains twenty-seven new essays, mostly with a statistical, sociological base, which replace essays with a more historical, philosophical, and impressionistic outlook.

90   Hauser, Philip M., and Schnore, Leo F., eds. THE STUDY OF URBANIZATION. New York: John Wiley, 1965. 554 p.

Contains essays by fifteen social scientists based upon the results of a six-year study conducted under the auspices of the Social Science Research Council. Concentrates on the theme of defining the city demographically.

91   Hughes, James W., ed. SUBURBANIZATION DYNAMICS AND THE FUTURE OF THE CITY. New Brunswick, N.J.: Center for Urban Policy Research, 1974. 286 p.

Reader focusing on the processes that contribute to the growth and change of metropolitan areas. Broad topics include: the dimensions of urban change, the process of neighborhood change, racial ethnic dynamics, and the dilemmas of the seventies.

92   Jackson, Kenneth T., and Schultz, Stanley K., eds. CITIES IN AMERICAN HISTORY. New York: Knopf, 1972. 508 p.

Contains twenty-seven essays by scholars from a variety of urban disciplines organized around seven general themes: the city in American history; cities in the New World, 1607-1800; cities in an expanding nation, 1780-1865; immigration, migration and mobility, 1865-1920; the recurrent urban crisis; bosses, machines, and urban reform; and dilemmas of metropolitan America. Essays written originally for this volume are annotated separately.

93   McKeown, James E., and Tietze, Frederick I., eds. THE CHANGING METROPOLIS. Boston: Houghton-Mifflin, 1971. 200 p.

Includes a variety of short pieces dealing with the city "as it is" and "as it might and ought to be." Focuses specifically on schools, the ghetto, the law, poverty, suburbanism, planning, and shifting political power.

General Studies

94   Meadows, Paul, and Mizruchi, Ephraim H., eds. URBANISM, URBANIZATION, AND CHANGE: COMPARATIVE PERSPECTIVES. Reading, Mass.: Addison-Wesley, 1969. 579 p.

> Contains numerous essays by a variety of scholars seeking to classify and define urban terminology and phenomena.

95   Mohl, Raymond A., and Richardson, James F. THE URBAN EXPERIENCE: THEMES IN AMERICAN HISTORY. Belmont, Calif.: Wadsworth Publishing Co., 1973. 265 p.

> Readings examining various institutional forms and effects of urbanization in the United States, touching on such subjects as planning, the black and immigrant experiences, poverty, education, religion, police, suburbanization, bosses and reform, and including summary essays on the preindustrial and contemporary American city.

96   Mohl, Raymond A.; Richardson, James F.; and Betten, Neil, eds. URBAN AMERICA IN HISTORICAL PERSPECTIVE. New York: Weybright, 1970. 426 p.

> Collection of essays on various urban themes ordered into chronological subdivisions: the colonial city, the industrial city, and the modern metropolis. Begins with a historiographical survey.

97   Morris, Margaret F., and West, Elliot, eds. ESSAYS ON URBAN AMERICA. Austin: University of Texas Press, 1975. 147 p.

> Presents four essays that formed the ninth annual Walter Prescott Webb Memorial Lectures in 1974 whose theme was "On Urban America." Robert F. Oaks discusses Philadelphia during its military occupation by the British, 1777-78, focusing on the functioning of civic institutions and reactions of citizens; Bruce I. Anbecher examines the impact of the Bank War on Philadelphia's Democrats; Richard G. Miller surveys Progressive era political reform in Fort Worth, specifically, the movement for charter revision; and Richard C. Wade uses the black and immigrant urban experience to illustrate the dangers of basing public policy on historical analogies.

98   Richardson, James F. THE AMERICAN CITY: HISTORICAL STUDIES. Waltham, Mass.: Xerox College Publishing, 1972. 407 p.

> Includes selections from the work of twenty-two historians and sociologists focusing on the social history of cities, especially racial and ethnic groups, social class, residential mobility, and social structure. Intended primarily for the undergraduate student of urban and social history.

General Studies

99 Schnore, Leo F., ed. THE NEW URBAN HISTORY: QUANTITATIVE EXPLORATIONS BY AMERICAN HISTORIANS. Princeton, N.J.: Princeton University Press, 1975. 284 p.

    Contains eleven essays by scholars who utilize quantitative methods in examining aspects of three major areas: the growth and function of cities, accommodations by newcomers to the urban environment, and economic analysis of urban-historical phenomena.

100 _____. SOCIAL SCIENCE AND THE CITY. New York: Praeger Publishers, 1969. 335 p.

    Contains ten selections by prominent urban historians, geographers, political scientists, and sociologists dealing with broad themes in their fields and techniques for researching them. Concentrates upon urban theory, the assimilation of minorities, social psychology and social welfare, planning, and political culture.

101 _____. THE URBAN SCENE: HUMAN ECOLOGY AND DEMOGRAPHY. New York: Free Press, 1965. 374 p.

    Collection of previously published sociological essays focusing on six areas: human ecology and demography; metropolitan growth and decentralization; functions and growth of suburbs; socioeconomic status of cities and suburbs; changing color composition of metropolitan areas; and studies in urban circulation.

102 Scientific American. CITIES: THEIR ORIGINS, GROWTH, AND HUMAN IMPACT. Comp. and Intro. by Kingsley Davis. San Francisco: W.H. Freeman and Co., 1973. 297 p.

    Contains twenty selections by renowned scholars taken from SCIENTIFIC AMERICAN, supplemented with introductions and bibliographies. Focuses on several major topics: the earliest cities, population, health and city environment, urban transport and city planning, cities of the developing world, and group relations in cities.

103 Smith, Wilson, ed. CITIES OF OUR PAST AND PRESENT. New York: John Wiley and Sons, 1964. 202 p.

    Reader presenting contemporaneous descriptions of American cities within a chronological framework, including: the colonial town, cities for a new nation; the cities mature, the impact of the civil war, life in urban America, urban reform, cities between the world wars, and cities of today.

104 Speizman, Milton D., ed. URBAN AMERICA IN THE TWENTIETH CENTURY. New York: Thomas Y. Crowell Co., 1968. 228 p.

General Studies

Contains original source material from the works of reformers, social scientists, and social workers dealing with urban issues and problems from Lincoln Steffens to Lyndon B. Johnson. Includes introduction and headnotes by the editor.

105   Tager, Jack, and Goist, Park D., eds. THE URBAN VISION: SELECTED INTERPRETATIONS OF THE MODERN AMERICAN CITY. Homewood, Ill.: Dorsey Press, 1970. 310 p.

Includes essays by twenty-five scholars, reformers, and journalists dealing with different phases of urban life in three distinct chronological eras: social reformers and architectural reformers from 1890 to 1915; ecologists, sociologists, and city planners from 1915 to 1945; and the evolution from metropolis to megalopolis between 1945 and 1965.

106   Thernstrom, Stephan A., and Sennett, Richard, eds. NINETEENTH CENTURY CITIES: ESSAYS IN THE NEW URBAN HISTORY. New Haven, Conn.: Yale University Press, 1969. 430 p.

Presents a series of essays which generally evince an interdisciplinary approach, use quantitative material, and display an interest in the "social experience of ordinary, unexceptional people," attributes collectively defining a so-called "new" urban history. Twelve essays consider four main topics: urban class and mobility patterns, urban residential patterns, urban elites and political control, and urban families. Eight of the selections focus on U.S. cities.

107   Trachtenberg, Alan; Neill, Peter; and Burnell, Peter C., eds. THE CITY: AMERICAN EXPERIENCE. New York: Oxford University Press, 1971. 620 p.

Contains scholarly articles, as well as photographs, poetry, and excerpts from novels and short stories on urban themes.

108   Wakstein, Allen M., ed. THE URBANIZATION OF AMERICA: AN HISTORICAL ANTHOLOGY. Boston: Houghton-Mifflin, 1970. 502 p.

Contains selections by over three dozen scholars dealing with several major themes: the historian's search for a concept of urbanization; the growth of community consciousness; the interaction of urban growth and development; and the social, political, and economic impact of urbanization.

109   Warren, Roland L., ed. PERSPECTIVES ON THE AMERICAN COMMUNITY: A BOOK OF READINGS. Chicago: University of Chicago Press, 1968. 618 p.

Reader in urban sociology with fifty-eight articles divided into six sections: basic approaches to the community, metropolis, city and villages; the community's vertical and horizontal patterns; planned community change; citizen participation in community activities; and varied aspects of community life.

110   Wheeler, Thomas C. A VANISHING AMERICA. New York: Holt, Rinehart and Winston, 1964. 191 p.

    Twelve essays discuss the community patterns developed in the small town past of nineteenth- and early twentieth-century America. Towns considered include: Middlebury, Vermont; Pine Grove, Pennsylvania; Holly Springs, Mississippi; New Harmony, Indiana; Maine on St. Croix; Minneapolis; Nacogdoches, Texas; Chimayo, New Mexico; Telluride, Colorado; Choteau, Montana; Red Bluff, California; and Forks, Washington.

111   Willbern, York. WITHERING AWAY OF THE CITY. University: University of Alabama Press, 1964. 139 p.

    Five essays which attempt to describe and speculate about some of the developments in governmental institutions and processes related to changes in urban life: the transformation of the urban community, the metropolitan predicament, responses to the challenge of urban change, creeping transitions in local government, and the urban-political market place.

112   Wilson, James Q., ed. THE METROPOLITAN ENIGMA: INQUIRIES INTO THE NATURE AND DIMENSIONS OF AMERICA'S "URBAN CRISIS." Cambridge, Mass.: Harvard University Press, 1968. 392 p.

    Collection of essays that originated as a set of background papers on urban issues for the task force on economic growth and opportunity of the U.S. Chamber of Commerce. Topics include industrial and occupational patterns, transportation, finance, pollution, race and migration, housing design, crime, riots, schools, and poverty.

THE TEACHING OF URBAN HISTORY

113   Calhoun, Daniel. "The City as Teacher: Historical Problems." HISTORY EDUCATION QUARTERLY 9 (1969): 312-25.

    Contends that the urban environment has had an educative effect independent of formal education but that it has operated as part of a complex of factors. Cautions that people have often debased their perceptions of the city with a heavy admixture of myth.

114   Dewey, Richard E., comp. "Selected Bibliography for the Design of

General Studies

Urban Programs." URBAN EDUCATION 6 (1971): 106-13.

> Contains over one hundred entries organized into five general categories: (1) the university in the urban context, (2) general urban studies, (3) descriptions of graduate programs in urban studies, (4) descriptions of undergraduate programs in urban studies, and (5) journals.

115 Dunn, Frederick R. "The Central Y.M.C.A. Schools of Chicago: A Study in Urban History." Ph.D. dissertation, University of Chicago, 1940. 352 p.

> Examines the evaluation of the YMCA schools as a unique approach to urban education which sought to meet the needs of thousands of Chicagoans. Portrays the schools as an example of institutional adaptation to the changing urban environment.

116 Foster, E.C. "World War II and Living in a Modern City: Two Curriculum Units for Slow Learners." Ph.D. dissertation, Carnegie-Mellon University, 1970. 226 p.

> The chapter on urban living utilizes such diverse materials as readings, biographies, charts, documents, graphs, maps, photographs, government records, slides, and recordings to convey a sense of city dwelling.

117 Goldfield, David R. "Living History: The Physical City as Artifact and Teaching Tool." HISTORY TEACHER 8 (1975): 535-56.

> Surveys the literature and analyzes the methodology necessary to use the physical aspect of the city as a teaching tool for importing many useful insights into urban history. Suggests many practical exercises for introducing teachers and students to the implications of studying the physical city.

118 Keyes, Scott. URBAN AND REGIONAL STUDIES AT UNITED STATES UNIVERSITIES. Baltimore: Johns Hopkins Press, 1964. 127 p.

> Based upon a survey of one thousand research groups at 159 institutions of higher education. Contains annotated bibliographies of relevant research in progress on general and historical studies, economic, demographic, social land use, transportation, and governmental studies.

119 Klebanow, Diana, and Still, Bayrd. "The Teaching of American Urban History." JOURNAL OF AMERICAN HISTORY 55 (1969): 843-47.

> Based upon two surveys, one of four hundred universities and the other of sixty urban studies centers, divides the teaching of urban history into lecture survey courses and advanced

General Studies

seminars. Calls for the integration of urban perspectives into U.S. history courses.

120   Lichtenberg, Mitchell Palmer. "A Model For The Use Of Urban History In Social Studies Education." Ph.D. dissertation, Carnegie-Mellon University, 1976.

Presents a model for transforming recently published research on urban history into curriculum materials for secondary school use, including selection criteria and teaching strategies, as well as reviews of major literature on urban history, local history, and quantitative methodology.

121   Lloyd, Anne S. "The American City: A Curriculum Unit for Community College Students." Ph.D. dissertation, Carnegie University, 1975. 360 p.

Presents a team curriculum project consisting of four major units spanning the years 1800-1975: "The Automobile City," "The Walking City," "The Streetcar City," and "Contemporary Urban Issues."

122   McCarthy, Michael P. "Teaching Urban History with Games: A Review Essay." HISTORY TEACHER 7 (1973): 62-66.

Notes that few games specifically designed for teaching urban history are available and urges teachers to develop their own. Discusses specifically two urban games, one which illustrates the growth of urban centers and another which is a land use simulation, as well as several others concerned with urban-related contemporary problems.

123   Mohl, Raymond A., and Betten, Neil. "The History of Urban America: An Interpretive Framework." HISTORY TEACHER 3 (1970): 23-34.

Argues that schools have neglected the urban dimension of American history and, after summarizing urban development from the colonial era to the present, suggests topics for use in existing high school history courses.

124   Thompson, Marion Brackenridge. "Three Curriculum Units for Slow Learners: Recreation, Transportation, The City of the Future." Ph.D. dissertation, Carnegie-Mellon University, 1972. 290 p.

Details a ninth-grade curriculum for slow learners using the American city as the focus of study. Asserts that the curriculum was proven successful after its implementation in the Pittsburgh public schools.

125   Weber, Michael P. "Quantification and the Teaching of American Urban History." HISTORY TEACHER 8 (1975): 391-402.

General Studies

Discusses the uses which can be made of quantitative methodology to teach such concepts as social mobility in an urban history course for undergraduates. Provides a detailed syllabus and reading list.

Chapter 2
THE URBANIZATION PROCESS

126 Abrams, Charles. THE LANGUAGE OF CITIES: A GLOSSARY OF CITIES: A GLOSSARY OF TERMS. New York: Viking Press, 1971. 365 p.

> Contains definitions of hundreds of terms with particular relevance to students of the city, and places them within an urban context. Deals with housing, planning, land economics, real estate, public administration, architecture, social welfare, transportation, public law, government, race, and other topics.

127 Abramson, Alan V. "Structural Change and Regularity in the American Intermetropolitan Migration Process: 1930-1970." Ph.D. dissertation, University of Minnesota, 1977. 251 p.

> Concludes that there is an intermetropolitan migration process at work but that much further research into life cycles, occupational proclivities, and the relationship between migration and other social changes needs to be done before an adequate picture of that process can be developed.

128 Abramson, Mark, and DuBick, Michael A. "Patterns of Urban Dominance: The United States in 1890." AMERICAN SOCIOLOGICAL REVIEW 42 (1977): 756-68.

> Contends that urban dominance rested not just upon commercial and financial foundations, but upon a complex convergence of the former with intellectual, cultural, and organizational activities, along with transportation and communication. Distinguishes three types of urban dominance during the 1890s and finds substantial historical continuity between 1890 and 1970.

129 Adams, John S. "Directional Bias in Intra-Urban Migration." ECONOMIC GEOGRAPHY 45 (1969): 302-25.

> Contends that intraurban movements are restricted by limited mental maps or images of the city in the minds of city dwellers.

The Urbanization Process

Compares data from 1890s, 1920, and 1940s and finds that most people moved only within a wedge-shaped area in their own part of town.

130 Ainsley, William F., Jr. "Changing Land Use in Downtown Norfolk, Virginia, 1680-1950." Ph.D. dissertation, University of North Carolina, 1977. 304 p.

Concludes that Norfolk is an almost perfect illustration of Burgess-Hawley model of urban growth beginning at the center and proceeding outward in roughly concentric fashion. Examines the interaction of physical, economic and human factors in determining growth patterns.

131 Anderson, Alan D. "Urbanization and American Economic Development, 1900-1930: Patterns of Demand in Baltimore and the Nation." Ph.D. dissertation, Johns Hopkins University, 1973. 261 p.

Contends that urbanization produced increased demands on municipal government for services and greatly increased city spending which, in turn, stimulated economic growth. Feels that attitudes toward increased governmental services, such as demand, resulted from the different demands made upon the city by different segments of society.

132 Angell, Robert C. "The Moral Integration of American Cities, II." AMERICAN JOURNAL OF SOCIOLOGY 80 (1974): 607-29.

Seeks to replicate similar study done in 1940. Finds that in cities over 100,000 people, in the thirty year interval, there has been a significant decrease in moral integration and that the size of these cities has become a greater independent variable.

133 Angle, Paul M. "American City Prints." CHICAGO HISTORY 7 (1963): 51-61.

Describes the city print collection of the Chicago Historical Society and discusses the role played by these prints in town promotional schemes of the early nineteenth century.

134 Anton, Thomas J. "Three Models of Community Development in the United States." PUBLIUS 1 (1971): 11-37.

Compares Lincolnwood, Illinois, at two stages of its growth (1829-1925 and 1928-66) with Levittown, New Jersey, to derive three models of community development. Finds that the democratic model of early days has been replaced by either the mixed bargaining or the administered choice alternative.

The Urbanization Process

135 Armstrong, Edward G. "The Crisis in Urban Sociology." In SOUTH ATLANTIC URBAN STUDIES, edited by Jack R. Censer and N. Steinert, pp. 93-115. Columbia: University of South Carolina Press, 1977.

> Sees urban sociologists as being confronted with an identity crisis fostered by their relationship to other forms of sociology, on the one hand, and to other urban disciplines, on the other.

136 Bain, Donald E., Jr. "The Suburban Wilderness: A Historical Approach to Metropolitan Decentralization." In SOUTH ATLANTIC URBAN STUDIES, edited by Jack R. Censer and N. Steinert, pp. 229-52. Columbia: University of South Carolina Press, 1977.

> Examines the patterns of suburbanization in Buffalo at the turn of the century and attributes the phenomenon primarily to the desires of the emerging middle class to build communities that provided access to the central city while providing sufficient social and fiscal autonomy to avoid its problems.

137 Baltzell, E. Digby. PHILADELPHIA GENTLEMEN: THE MAKING OF A NATIONAL UPPER CLASS. Philadelphia: University of Pennsylvania Press, 1979. 440 p.

> Traces the historical evolution of the city's financial and social elite based upon residency, religion, education, occupation and membership in social clubs. Posits characteristics which have applicability in identifying the elites of large cities in general.

138 Barth, Gunther. INSTANT CITIES: URBANIZATION AND THE RISE OF SAN FRANCISCO AND DENVER. New York: Oxford University Press, 1975. 310 p.

> Sees Denver and San Francisco as the giants of the western urban frontier which formed important terminals for the national transportation network, enjoyed phenomenal growth rates, and suffered from the common problems of making "reluctant citizens" out of transient wealth-seekers. Links urbanization to city building in earlier times and presents it as the common experience of a single generation of nineteenth-century America.

139 Beals, Ralph L. "Urbanism, Urbanization, and Acculturation." AMERICAN ANTHROPOLOGIST 53 (1951): 1-10.

> Attempts to separate factors which are common to all urban places from those that are culturally indigenous to Euro-American cities.

140 Belcher, John C. "The Impact of Urbanization Upon Selected Aspects of Rural Life in the United States, 1940-45." Ph.D. dissertation, University of Wisconsin, 1950. 158 p.

> Develops an index for the impact of urbanization upon rural

areas and concludes that it has a significant effect on the birthrates of farm families and upon their life-styles. Finds little correlation between urbanization and mechanization.

141 Berry, Brian J.L. THE HUMAN CONSEQUENCES OF URBANIZATION. New York: St. Martin's Press, 1973. 205 p.

Contends that urbanization is a composite of several distinct processes emerging from disparate cultures and historical periods, rather than a single, universal phenomenon.

142 Berry, Brian J.L.; Simmons, James W.; and Tennant, Robert J. "Urban Population Densities: Structure and Change." GEOGRAPHICAL REVIEW 53 (1963): 389-405.

Finds that the degree of central density in most cities is a product of their growth history, while their compactness is largely a function of city size. Develops several formulas for predicting the best location for market-oriented servicing units.

143 Beshers, James M. URBAN SOCIAL STRUCTURE. New York: Free Press, 1962. 207 p.

Deals partly with the historical processes of urban structure and development, builds a theoretical model, and examines the consequences for urban social organization.

144 _____. "Urban Social Structure as a Single Hierarchy." SOCIAL FORCES 41 (1963): 233-38.

Suggests a model for studying changes in the urban social structure based upon the combination of status symbols and social relationships. Feels that will lead to the formulation of a notion of single hierarchy.

145 Binford, Henry. "The Influence of Commuting on the Development of Somerville and Cambridge, Massachusetts, 1851-1860." Ph.D. dissertation, Harvard University, 1973.

146 Blood, Robert O., Jr. "Impact of Urbanization on American Family Structure and Functioning." SOCIOLOGY AND SOCIAL RESEARCH 49 (1964): 5-16.

Contends that urbanization has affected urban and rural families in strikingly similar ways and that the waning of traditional functions has been matched by the evolution of new ones. Finds the urban family structurally efficient and functionally significant.

The Urbanization Process

147   Bloomber, Susan E.; Fox, Mary F.; Warner, Robert M.; and Warner, Sam Bass, Jr. "A Census Probe into Nineteenth Century Family History: Southern Michigan 1850-1900." JOURNAL OF SOCIAL HISTORY 5 (1971): 26-41.

> Surveys, in preliminary fashion, the social history of the American family, presenting a quantitative overview of one region that embraced diverse settlement, economic, and ethnic types. Results suggest that the demographic history of modern America cannot be explained through such "broad causative statements of urbanization, industrialization, or natural origin." Instead, the trend toward smaller families resulted from many complex events. Notes also that "the mixed ecological factors of locale with occupation and with place of birth may be a key to family type in the nineteenth century."

148   Blumin, Stuart M. "Mobility in a Nineteenth-Century American City: Philadelphia, 1820-1860." Ph.D. dissertation, University of Pennsylvania, 1968. 189 p.

> Uses a selected sample from four decades of city directories to test occupational and residential mobility. Finds that, by the 1850s, upward and downward mobility seem to have occurred at about the same level of frequency.

149   _____. "Rip Van Winkle's Grandchildren: Family and Household in the Hudson Valley, 1800-1860." JOURNAL OF URBAN HISTORY 1 (1975): 293-315.

> Focuses upon rural-urban differentials in fertility and household structure as an index of whether economic development in the region decreased or increased between city and country. Finds that rural-urban differences were not carried over in any significant manner to family life.

150   _____. THE URBAN THRESHOLD: GROWTH AND CHANGE IN A NINETEENTH CENTURY AMERICAN COMMUNITY. Chicago: University of Chicago Press, 1976. 298 p.

> Uses Kingstown, New York, between 1820 and 1860, as a case study to ascertain the consequences of crossing the urban threshold, both to individuals and to the community as a whole. Relates his findings to the existing body of literature on community formation.

151   Bogue, Donald J. THE STRUCTURE OF THE METROPOLITAN COMMUNITY: A STUDY OF DOMINANCE AND SUBDOMINANCE. New York: Russell and Russell, 1971. 210 p.

> Delineates procedures and techniques for studying metropolitan communities and focuses upon their population structures, retail and wholesale trade, manufactures, and urban services.

The Urbanization Process

152   Booth, Alan. URBAN CROWDING AND ITS CONSEQUENCES. New York: Praeger, 1976. 139 p.

    Examines the effects of various types of crowding on fifty-eight indicators of stress, poor health, and family and social disorganization and finds that congested household conditions affect people more adversely than do congested neighborhoods.

153   Bowden, Martyn J. "Downtown Through Time: Delimitation, Expansion, and Internal Growth." ECONOMIC GEOGRAPHY 47 (1971): 121-35.

    Develops a model and methodology for studying central business districts from cross-cultural, interregional, and international perspectives. Concludes that the type of growth prevelant in any city at any given time depends primarily upon the demand for a central place made by certain linked establishments.

154   Broadman, Anthony E., and Weber, Michael P. "Economic Growth and Occupational Mobility in Nineteenth Century Urban America: A Reappraisal." JOURNAL OF SOCIAL HISTORY 11 (1977): 52-74.

    Uses Warren, Pennsylvania, as a representative city whose growth rate closely paralleled the U.S. nineteenth-century experience, and concludes that skill level, age, and the type of industry affected the chances for social mobility more than did religion, ethnicity, or marital status.

155   Bromley, David G., and Smith, Joel. "The Historical Significance of Annexation as a Social Process." LAND ECONOMICS 49 (1973): 294-309.

    Decries the lack of scholarly studies on the process of annexation as an index of urbanization and uses data over a 120-year period to demonstrate the variance among cities in the amount of annexation and in its temporal patterning.

156   Brumberg, George D. "Geneva, New York: A Community Study, 1786-1860." Ph.D. dissertation, Miami University, 1977. 173 p.

    Uses Geneva as a test case for various community theories. Finds that it substantiates the Warner privatism theory and the Page Smith notion of "cumulative" towns, but raises doubts concerning Whitney Cross's analysis of enthusiastic religions in the burned over district.

157   Brunner, Edmund De Schweinitz. "Village Growth, 1940-50." RURAL SOCIOLOGY 16 (1951): 111-18.

    Contends that the 1950 census returns demonstrate that places of between 1,000 and 2,500 population increased significantly during the previous decade. Speculates upon the reasons and implications.

158   Burton, Ian. "A Restatement of the Dispersed City Hypothesis." ANNALS OF THE ASSOCIATION OF AMERICAN GEOGRAPHERS 53 (1963): 285-89.

   Concludes that the term "dispersed city" is a useful one by which to identify functionally interdependent cities, located in close proximity, but physically separated by nonurban land.

159   Butler, Edgar W. URBAN SOCIOLOGY: A SYSTEMATIC APPROACH. New York: Harper and Row, 1976. 576 p.

   Discusses approaches and research techniques in urban sociology, the growth, location, and typology of urban places, spatial and social differentiation, organizational structure and behavior, urban problems, and planning.

160   Cahnman, Werner J. "The Historical Sociology of Cities: A Critical Review." SOCIAL FORCES 45 (1966-67): 155-60.

   Rejects the notion of the preindustrial and industrial cities as closed and mutually exclusive systems. Contends that urbanization preceded industrialization and that all models must be understood only as ideal types.

161   Carpenter, Niles. SOCIOLOGY OF CITY LIFE. New York: Longmans Green, 1932. 502 p.

   Traces the origin and evolution of cities from ancient to modern times and discusses such topics as city location, physical setting, growth and control, the urban way of life, poverty, vice, and crime.

162   Carter, Harold. THE STUDY OF URBAN GEOGRAPHY. New York: John Wiley and Sons, 1976. 398 p.

   Deals with the process of urbanization, the growth of the city system, urban functions and functional classification, central place theory, the ranking of towns, the analysis of town plans, urban land use, the specific qualities of the central business district, residential areas, and the rural-urban fringe.

163   Chapin, F. Stuart, and Weiss, Shirley F., eds. URBAN GROWTH DYNAMICS IN A REGIONAL CLUSTER OF CITIES. New York: John Wiley and Sons, 1962. 484 p.

   Contains fourteen essays organized around the general topics of economic orientations to urbanization, leadership, decision making, and urban growth, social correlates of urban growth and development, and patterns of urban development.

164 Chudacoff, Howard. MOBILE AMERICANS: RESIDENTIAL AND SOCIAL MOBILITY IN OMAHA, 1880-1920. New York: Oxford University Press, 1972. 195 p.

Finds that neighborhoods in Omaha were characterized by a high degree of residential mobility, an appreciable amount of occupational mobility for some groups, constant change, and little cohesion. Asserts that this high rate of mobility indicates a reasonably open society.

165 Clark, Dennis. "A Pattern of Urban Growth: Residential Development and Church Location in Philadelphia." RECORDS OF AMERICAN CATHOLIC HISTORICAL SOCIETY, PHILADELPHIA 82 (1971): 159-70.

Compares the pattern of housing expansion with that of the construction of Roman Catholic churches in the city during the nineteenth century. Finds the results particularly useful in plotting the residential mobility of Philadelphia's immigrants.

166 Clark, W.A.V. "Migration in Milwaukee." ECONOMIC GEOGRAPHY 52 (1976): 48-60.

Examines patterns of intraurban migration in Milwaukee between 1950 and 1962 and finds that income and housing costs are the primary determining factors of where people move. Uses those variables to develop a predictive model of residential mobility.

167 Cochran, Lillian T., and O'Kane, James M. "Urbanization-Industrialization and the Theory of Demographic Transition." PACIFIC SOCIOLOGICAL REVIEW 20 (1977): 113-34.

Contends that, contrary to the transition theory, there seems to be little or no correlation between fertility rates and economic growth. Finds that high birthrates can sometimes spur urban-industrial development.

168 Comhaire, Jean, and Cahnman, Werner J. HOW CITIES GREW: THE HISTORICAL SOCIOLOGY OF CITIES. Madison, N.J.: Florham Park Press, 1959. 141 p.

Deals with the significance of urban history, the historical typology of cities, their location, ecology, and social stratification, and surveys ancient, medieval, and modern cities.

169 Condit, Carl W. THE RAILROAD AND THE CITY: A TECHNOLOGICAL AND URBANISTIC HISTORY OF CINCINNATI. Columbus: Ohio State University Press, 1977. 335 p.

Deals with the evolution of railroad technology as a functioning whole and explores its interaction with the development of a major city. Views the emerging union terminal as shaping the urban fabric and land use patterns, and serving as "a special kind of urbanistic institution, a microsity mirroring the urban life around it."

170 Conzen, Michael P. "Capital Flows and the Developing Urban Hierarchy: State Bank Capital in Wisconsin, 1854-1895." ECONOMIC GEOGRAPHY 51 (1975): 321-38.

Develops a three-state model for capital flows between large cities and smaller urban centers. Finds that middle-order cities become more significant in regional or state capital flows the larger and more fully developed the economic network becomes.

171 _____. FRONTIER FARMING IN AN URBAN SHADOW: THE INFLUENCE OF MADISON'S PROXIMITY ON THE AGRICULTURAL DEVELOPMENT OF BLOOMING GROVE, WISCONSIN. Madison: University of Wisconsin Press, 1971. 235 p.

Uses quantitative methodology to build a social model for the impact made by a midwestern city on a neighboring farming village. Contends that the city exercized important influence on land disposal and land utilization.

172 _____. "The Maturing Urban System in the United States, 1840-1910." ANNALS OF THE ASSOCIATION OF AMERICAN GEOGRAPHERS 67 (1977): 88-108.

Examines the banking integration of the national urban network under the leadership of New York as an index of the general reorientation of the American economy of this era. Sees the resultant urban system as a "modified hierarchical one with high-level interdependencies."

173 Davies, Edward J. "Elite Migration and Urban Growth: The Rise of Wilkes-Barre in the Northern Anthracite Region." PENNSYLVANIA HISTORY 45 (1978): 291-314.

Examines the characteristics of the city and its elite which enabled it to attract sufficient talent and capital to sustain large-scale industrialization, and how the movement of capital and talent, in turn, shaped the urbanization process.

174 Davis, John. "Transportation and American Settlement Patterns." In AMERICAN ENVIRONMENT: PERCEPTIONS AND POLITICIES, edited by Wreford J. Watson and Timothy O'Riordan, pp. 168-82. New York: John Wiley and Sons, 1976.

The Urbanization Process

Presents an overview of the ways in which varying transportation modes have affected settlement patterns, including the growth of cities, discussing trailways and canoe ways, roadways, railway and canalways, motorways, airways, and pipeways.

175 Decker, Peter R. FORTUNES AND FAILURES: WHITE COLLAR MOBILITY IN NINETEENTH-CENTURY SAN FRANCISCO. Cambridge, Mass.: Harvard University Press, 1978. 336 p.

Finds that the most salient result of the economic and social upheavals in nineteenth-century San Francisco was the speed with which class lines formed and the rapidity with which they were institutionalized through voluntary associations at all levels of society.

176 _____. "Social Mobility on the Urban Frontier: San Francisco Merchants, 1850-1880." Ph.D. dissertation, Columbia University, 1974. 496 p.

Examines the social origins of the city's merchant class, the manner in which they transformed their occupational and financial status into the social fabric of San Francisco, and their eventual displacement by a new industrial elite in the 1880s. Utilizes extensive statistical data to document its thesis.

177 Douglas, Harlan P. THE SUBURBAN TREND. New York: Arno Press, 1970. 340 p.

Insists that the developing suburbs of the 1920s were closely tied to the cities economically, but were still separate entities in most other senses.

178 Doyle, Don H. Nineteenth Century Cities: Evolutionary and Instantaneous." JOURNAL OF URBAN HISTORY 5 (1978): 109-17.

Reviews books dealing with Kingston, New York; Denver; and San Francisco and synthesizes their findings into generalizations concerning such aspects of nineteenth-century urban life as the economic development of cities, the elaboration of transportation and communication networks, and the attendant forces of population growth.

179 Duncan, Beverly. "Evolution of an Empirical Generalization." AMERICAN SOCIOLOGICAL REVIEW 29 (1964): 855-66.

Compares reports on urban residential structure done in 1950, 1958, 1959, and 1964 and finds some apparently significant contradictions. Includes comments by the authors of some of the papers which Duncan criticizes.

The Urbanization Process

180   Duncan, Beverly, and Lieberson, Stanley. METROPOLIS AND REGION IN TRANSITION. Beverly Hills, Calif.: Sage Publications, 1970.

        Identifies the salient feature of a metropolis as its sizeable commercial-financial complex and traces its evolution from colonial times to mid-twentieth century. Seeks to create a "mid-century bench mark" against which to measure future changes in the metropolitan economy.

181   Duncan, Otis D., et al. METROPOLIS AND REGION. Baltimore: Johns Hopkins Press, 1960. 587 p.

        Examines the nature and functions of the metropolis, its relation to its hinterlands, and the structure of its industry. Focuses upon the nation's fifty largest cities and their regional relationships.

182   Dye, Thomas R. "The Local-Cosmopolitan Dimensions and the Study of Urban Politics." SOCIAL FORCES 40-41 (1961-63): 239-46.

        Posits the scale of social environment in which the individual sees himself operating as creating a dichotomy between locals and cosmopolitans. Aligns politicians and lower- and middle-class persons with the local orientation and business and social elites on the cosmopolitan side.

183   Eames, Edwin, and Goode, Judith Gravich. ANTHROPOLOGY OF THE CITY: INTRODUCTION TO URBAN ANTHROPOLOGY. Englewood Cliffs, N.J.: Prentice-Hall, 1977. 344 p.

        Defines urban anthropology, classifies cities according to roles and functions, discusses the major units of integration. Focuses largely on urban ethnography.

184   Earle, Clarke. "Contributions to Urban Growth." JOURNAL OF THE AMERICAN STATISTICAL ASSOCIATION 14 (1915): 654-70.

        Analyzes census data to determine how much of the increase in urban population between 1900 and 1910 was due to immigration, natural increase, or internal migration. Argues that "alien immigration" contributed only about 30 percent of the total.

185   Ermisch, John, and Weiss, Thomas. "The Impact of the Rural Market on the Growth of the Urban Workforce: United States, 1870-1900." EXPLORATIONS IN ECONOMIC HISTORY 11 (1973): 137-53.

        Finds little evidence that the rural market played any significant role in urban growth during the period. Argues that cities produced primarily for an urban market and that rural areas continued to provide themselves with nonagricultural goods and services, despite the rise of cities.

186 Farley, Reynolds. "Suburban Persistence." AMERICAN SOCIOLOGI-CAL REVIEW 29 (1964): 38-47.

   Based upon 1950s data, denies that the socioeconomic differences between cities and suburbs were increasing. Argues that particular suburbs retain their peculiar socioeconomic characteristics for long periods of time, even in the face of rapid population growth.

187 Firey, Walter. LAND USE IN CENTRAL BOSTON. Cambridge, Mass.: Harvard University Press, 1947. 367 p.

   Discusses the role of social and cultural values in the spatial differentiation of the city and focuses specifically upon Beacon Hill, Boston Common, the North End, the retail center, Back Bay, and the South End. Formulates a theory concerning cultural ecology.

188 Fischer, Claude S. "The City and Political Psychology." AMERICAN POLITICAL SCIENCE REVIEW 69 (1975): 559-71.

   Contends that urbanism is very weakly, if at all, independently associated with political psychology, but that it does help to generate a sense of political inefficacy and to produce a national, as opposed to a local, orientation.

189 Fitzharris, Joseph C. "A Model of Urban Growth and Transition: The Twin Cities, 1870-1930." Ph.D. dissertation, University of Wisconsin, Madison, 1975. 258 p.

   Postulates a model of city growth determined by changes in the level of the hinterland population, the number of access routes between city and hinterland, and the labor force of the processing industries and related trades and industries. Provides a statistical picture of the Twin Cities Evolution into a regional capital.

190 Folsom, Burton W. "Urban Networks: The Economic and Social Order of the Lackawanna and Lehigh Valleys During Early Industrialization, 1850-1880." Ph.D. dissertation, University of Pittsburgh, 1976. 352 p.

   Denies that urbanization in eastern Pennsylvania resulted in social disorganization, anomie, individualism, and atomization. Contends that it resulted instead in the formation of economic and social networks and a structural society based upon the need for order and roots.

191 Fox, Richard G. URBAN ANTHROPOLOGY: CITIES IN THEIR CULTURAL SETTINGS. Englewood Cliffs, N.J.: Prentice-Hall, 1977. 176 p.

   Discusses the cultural milieu of cities and compares regal-

The Urbanization Process

ritual, administrative, mercantile, colonial, and industrial cities in a variety of countries.

192 Frisch, Michael. TOWN INTO CITY: SPRINGFIELD, MASSACHUSETTS AND THE MEANING OF COMMUNITY, 1840-1880. Cambridge, Mass.: Harvard University Press, 1972. 301 p.

Uses Springfield as a focal point for studying the process of urbanization and the factors which made a city different from a town. Contends that local orientation remained of central importance to most residents of Springfield, even while they were building city-wide institutions.

193 Funigello, Philip J. "Urban Research." JOURNAL OF URBAN HISTORY 2 (1976): 256-60.

Reviews conferences held on archives and urban research and the two volumes of essays that resulted. Discusses the uses of material contained in the national archives and methodologies for researching in them.

194 Garner, John Sturdy. "The Model Company Town in New England: A Study of Hopedale and the New Town Tradition." Ph.D. dissertation, Boston University Graduate School, 1975.

Uses Hopedale, Massachusetts, as a case study of the founding and operation of company towns in the region during the antebellum period. Ties it to the philosophy which underlay the creation of "new towns."

195 Gilmore, Harlan. TRANSPORTATION AND THE GROWTH OF CITIES. Glencoe, Ill.: Free Press of Glencoe, 1953. 170 p.

Contends that communities can best be classified according to the type of economic and social system of which they are a part and by the role they play in the division of labor within that system. Regards transportation systems as the key to understanding socioeconomic systems.

196 Glaab, Charles N. KANSAS CITY AND THE RAILROADS: COMMUNITY POLICY IN THE GROWTH OF A REGIONAL METROPOLIS. Madison: State Historical Society of Wisconsin, 1962. 260 p.

Concentrates upon the role played by businessmen and real estate operators in the formulation of a transportation policy designed to make Kansas City into a regional metropolis. Analyzes the development of leadership patterns and the political process in a pioneer community.

197 Glaab, Charles N., and Larsen, Lawrence H. FACTORIES IN THE VALLEY: NEENAH-MENASHA, 1870-1915. Madison: State Historical Society of Wisconsin, 1969. 293 p.

The Urbanization Process

Examines the efforts of promoters to create an American version of Birmingham and Manchester on the Fox River. Attributes their failure to urban rivalry, unwise investment, and "the hard fact that industrialization alone was not the road to urban greatness."

198 Goheen, Peter G. "Industrialization and the Growth of Cities in Nineteenth Century America." AMERICAN STUDIES 14 (1973): 49-66.

Portrays industrialization as both a cause and a consequence of urbanization and discusses several interpretations for understanding population growth, industrial productivity, and transportation technology. Calls for a synthetic view that explains the interaction among all these factors.

199 Goldstein, Sidney, and Sly, David F. THE MEASUREMENT OF URBANIZATION AND PROJECTION OF URBAN POPULATION. Liege, Belgium: International Union for the Scientific Study of Population, 1975. 224 p.

Discusses various statistical measurements of urbanization, its degree and tempo, and the distribution, concentration, and dispersion of urban populations. Also investigates methods for calculating urban population growth and for measuring rural-urban migration and commuting which are applicable to American cities.

200 Gottman, Jean, and Harper, Robert A., eds. METROPOLIS ON THE MOVE: GEOGRAPHERS LOOK AT URBAN SPRAWL. New York: John Wiley and Sons, 1967. 203 p.

Includes papers given by a dozen scholars at a conference on urban sprawl held at Southern Illinois University in 1964. General topics include the forces, pressures, and forms of urban sprawl and the functioning city, the skyscraper, planning, and the challenge to education.

201 Graff, Harvey J. "Patterns of Dependency and Child Development in the Mid-Nineteenth Century City: A Sample from Boston, 1860." HISTORY OF EDUCATION QUARTERLY 13 (1975): 129-43.

Analyzes a sample of 500 families and finds that there was a common age for leaving school, for going to work, and for leaving home. Concludes that the urban environment caused parents to prolong the period of dependency to about age twenty, significantly longer than was common in rural areas of that era.

202 Griffen, Clyde. "Public Opinion in Urban History." JOURNAL OF INTERDISCIPLINARY HISTORY 4 (1975): 469-74.

Uses Michael Frisch's TOWN INTO CITY (no. 192) as a springboard for discussion of methodological questions relating to the determination of public opinion regarding urban politics. Challenges community studies historians to develop new methods for analyzing the consciousness of the inarticulate.

203   Griffen, Clyde, and Griffen, Sally. "Family and Business in a Small City: Poughkeepsie, New York, 1850-1880." JOURNAL OF URBAN HISTORY 1 (1975): 316-38.

Argues that, contrary to Talcott Parsons and others, the extended family played an important role in business entrepreneurship, providing financial assistance, partnership, and succession without interfering with personal mobility.

204   Guest, Avery M. "Ecological Succession in the Puget Sound Region." JOURNAL OF URBAN HISTORY 3 (1977): 181-210.

Concludes that the automobile led to the decline of the center within the metropolis while further emphasizing the importance of the center within the region and the fact that life changes are increasingly a function of their community's ecological position.

205   _____. "Neighborhood Life Cycles and Social Status." ECONOMIC GEOGRAPHY 50 (1974): 228-43.

Focuses upon Cleveland between 1940 and 1970 and finds some evidence that neighborhoods either grow or decline in status over time but sees little real significance in the changes. Concludes that neither life cycle status nor distance from the central business district is strongly related to neighborhood social status.

206   _____. "Urban History, Population Densities, and Higher Status Residential Location." ECONOMIC GEOGRAPHY 48 (1972): 375-87.

Examines the concentric distributions of upper class neighborhoods in the prestreetcar, streetcar, and automobile transportation eras. Links neighborhood population characteristics with morphological patterns of American cities.

207   Hagood, Margaret J., and Sharp, Emmit F. RURAL-URBAN MIGRATION IN WISCONSIN, 1940-1950. Madison: University of Wisconsin, 1951. 56 p.

Examines the reasons, both push and pull, for migration from rural to urban areas in the state during the decade. Predicts that the trend of urban increase will continue in the future unless there is a major depression.

208 Haig, Robert M. TOWARD AN UNDERSTANDING OF THE METROPOLIS. New York: Arno Press, 1976.

> Reprint of parts 1 and 2 of an article in QUARTERLY JOURNAL OF ECONOMICS, volume 40, in 1926, focuses upon the economic bases of urban concentration and the assignment of activities to areas in urban regions by planning agencies. See pages 179-434.

209 Hareven, Tamara K., ed. FAMILY AND KIN IN URBAN COMMUNITIES, 1700-1930. New York: New Viewpoints, 1977. 214 p.

> Contains eight original essays dealing with the relationship between family history and that of the wider urban society. Disputes many prevailing views about the impact of urbanization upon fertility, the nuclear family, and familial disorganization.

210 Hart, John F.; Salisbury, Neil E.; and Smith, Everett G., Jr. "The Dying Village and Some Notions about Urban Growth." ECONOMIC GEOGRAPHY 44 (1968): 343-49.

> Questions prevailing interpretations concerning reasons for founding of city sites and for differentials in urban growth. Stresses the role of the entrepreneur in the founding and growth of cities.

211 Harvey, David. SOCIAL JUSTICE AND THE CITY. Baltimore: Johns Hopkins University Press, 1973. 336 p.

> Deals with the general relationship between social processes and spatial forms. Concludes with an extensive essay on "urbanism and the city."

212 Hassler, F.L. "Transportation and Its Influence on Cities." HABITAT 2 (1977): 259-75.

213 Hawley, Amos H. CHANGING OF METROPOLITAN AMERICA: DECONCENTRATION SINCE 1920. Glencoe, Ill.: Free Press, 1956. 177 p.

> Analyzes data on size and annual growth of central cities, distance between cities, relation of the area to nonirrigatible water, manufacturing, industrial location, and regional setting to illustrate the decentralization of metropolitan life since 1920.

214 Hays, Samuel P. "The Development of Pittsburgh as a Social Order." WESTERN PENNSYLVANIA HISTORICAL MAGAZINE 57 (1974): 431-48.

Contends that one of the most significant aspects of Pittsburgh's historical development was the centralization of urban institutions. Suggests a methodology and a body of sources for testing this hypothesis in other locales.

215   Heibrun, James. URBAN ECONOMICS AND PUBLIC POLICY. New York: St. Martin's Press, 1974. 380 p.

    Introduces the reader to basic concepts in urban economics and examines the economic ramification of location analysis, urban systems and hierarchy, land use, transportation, and farm, housing, and the public sector.

216   Henderson, J.V. "The Sizes and Types of Cities." AMERICAN ECONOMIC REVIEW 64 (1974): 640-56.

    Contends that city sizes vary because cities of different types specialize in the production of a variety of traded goods which involve different scale economies and hence support varying densities of commuting and congestion costs.

217   Henry, Nicholas. "Science and the City: Some Political Implications." In SOUTH ATLANTIC URBAN STUDIES, edited by Jack R. Censer and N. Steinert, pp. 137-69. Columbia: University of South Carolina Press, 1977.

    Surveys the evolution of scientific approaches to studying the city and speculates on their future impact upon a number of urban-oriented disciplines. Posits a dichotomy between an environmental and a structural-function approach.

218   Herbert, D.T., and Johnston, R.J., eds. SOCIAL AREAS IN CITIES: SPATIAL PROCESSES AND FORM. New York: John Wiley and Sons, 1976. 281 p.

    Focuses upon the "social map" of the city, how it comes about, how to identify it, and what shape it has. Contains specific sections on social bases, ethnic residential segregation, institutional forces, housing, household locations and intra-urban migration, and residential area characteristics.

219   Hicks, John D. "The Urban Revolution." PACIFIC NORTHWEST QUARTERLY 57 (1966): 181-88.

    Attributes the urban revolution largely to the sincere desire of millions of youths to get away from the farm because of the decline of rural life. Sees a similar decline of urban life in present day America.

220   Higgs, Robert. "Cities and Yankee Ingenuity, 1870-1920." In CITIES

IN AMERICAN HISTORY, edited by Kenneth T. Jackson and Stanley K. Schultz, pp. 16-23. New York: Knopf, 1972.

> Posits a close correlation between urbanization and the number of inventions per capita. Focuses on Connecticut and regards urbanization as a response to the increasing profitability of nonagricultural economic activities.

221 _____. "Williamson and Swanson on City Growth: A Critique." EXPLORATIONS IN ENTREPRENEURAL HISTORY 8 (1970-71): 203-12.

> Criticizes the works of Jeffrey Williamson and Joseph Swanson (nos. 306 and 329a) on urban growth and argues that they fail to test their hypothesis of urban scale economies, base their conclusions concerning the impact of the hinterland on urban growth on only a crude measure of relevant data, and muddle the issue of the relationship of city age to growth.

222 Holland, Reid A. "Urban History and Computer Mapping." HISTORY METHODS NEWSLETTER 6 (1972): 4-9.

> Contends that computer mapping is especially valuable for demographers, social and political historians, studies of urban industrialization and transportation, analysis of voting patterns, residential mobility, and interurban mobility.

223 Hollingsworth, J. Rogers, and Hollingsworth, Ellen J. DIMENSIONS IN URBAN HISTORY: HISTORICAL AND SOCIAL SCIENCE PERSPECTIVES ON MIDDLE-SIZE AMERICAN CITIES. Madison: University of Wisconsin Press, 1979.

> Analyzes the ways in which social and economic forces have influenced urban politics in Eau Claire, Janesville, and Green Bay, Wisconsin, since 1870. Classifies American cities into categories based upon indices of socioeconomic variables and governmental activity.

224 Hoover, Edgar M. "Motor Metropolis: Some Observations on Urban Transportation in America." INDUSTRIAL ECONOMICS 13 (1965): 177-92.

> Asserts that the mass ownership of private automobiles and revolutionary changes in the physical layout of urban areas are more intimately related than is usually recognized. Proposes policy changes to deal with a variety of metropolitan ills through controlling the use of the automobile.

225 Hoyt, Homer. "Recent Distortions of the Classical Models of Urban Structure." LAND ECONOMICS 40 (1964): 199-212.

> Argues that city growth patterns of the post-World War II era

have seriously altered the concentric circle theory of city development posited by Hoyt and E.W. Burgess. Looks at each major sector of the model in terms of those changes.

226 _____. THE STRUCTURE AND GROWTH OF RESIDENTIAL NEIGHBORHOODS IN AMERICAN CITIES. St. Clair Shores, Mich.: Scholarly Press, 1972. 178 p.

Focuses partly on the influence of city growth on neighborhood growth, the form of city growth, changes in urban land uses, and patterns of movement of residential rental neighborhoods. Includes maps and tables dealing with several major cities.

227 Huang, Jui-Cheng, and Gould, Peter. "Diffusion in an Urban Hierarchy: The Case of Rotary Clubs." ECONOMIC GEOGRAPHY 50 (1974): 333-40.

Uses the proliferation of Rotary Clubs in Kansas and Nebraska between 1905 and 1972 as an index of urban diffusion.

228 Hudson, John. "Density and Pattern in Suburban Fringes." ANNALS OF THE ASSOCIATION OF AMERICAN GEOGRAPHERS 63 (1973): 28-39.

Examines growth patterns in the 1960s for the Midwest's nine largest SMSAs and defines density as a level of fifty dwellings per square mile.

229 Hunter, Albert. "Community Change: A Stochastic Analysis of Chicago's Local Communities, 1930-60." AMERICAN JOURNAL OF SOCIOLOGY 79 (1974): 923-47.

Compares two urban ecology perspectives--a static one emphasizing spatial distributions and a dynamic one stressing stages of community change. Presents data to support the contention that these are four stages of community change which occur in sequence.

230 _____. "The Ecology of Chicago: Persistence and Change, 1930-1960." AMERICAN JOURNAL OF SOCIOLOGY 77 (1971): 425-44.

Uses census data on family, ethnic, and economic status and percentage of single-family dwelling units from the 1930, 1940, 1950, and 1960 censuses. Concludes that the ecological structure of the city is becoming more finely differentiated over time.

231 Hunter, Floyd. COMMUNITY POWER STRUCTURE: A STUDY OF DECISION MAKERS. Chapel Hill: University of North Carolina Press, 1969. 207 p.

Analyzes the power structure of "Regional City" and the manner in which it exercises both political and private control over the community.

232   Huth, Mary J. "Effects of the Urbanization Process on the American Way of Life During the Twentieth Century." UNIVERSITY OF DAYTON REVIEW 3 (1966): 100-15.

Traces the urbanization process from the beginning of the century to the 1960s and concludes that Americans have responded to this change by adaptive behavior which has preserved the semblance, if not the reality, of some of the basic social configurations of preurban society.

233   Jacobs, Jane. THE ECONOMY OF CITIES. New York: Random House, 1969. 268 p.

Delineates the evolution of urban economic systems and their relationship to their hinterlands and to the nation. Argues that, contrary to popular belief, rural economies, including agricultural work, are directly built upon urban economies and urban labor.

234   Johnston, R.J. "Regarding Urban Origins, Urbanization, and Urban Patterns." GEOGRAPHY 62 (1977): 1-8.

Contends that the pattern of city sizes can only be understood in a historical context based upon models of how settlement patterns really came about, rather than by positing mechanistic or random processes.

235   Jones, Emrys. TOWNS AND CITIES. New York: Oxford University Press, 1966. 152 p.

Deals with the process of urbanization, the size, and classification of cities, cities and regionalism, and urbanism.

236   Juliani, Richard N. "Church Records as Social Data: The Italians of Philadelphia in the Nineteenth Century." RECORDS OF THE AMERICAN CATHOLIC HISTORICAL SOCIETY IN PHILADELPHIA 85 (1974): 3-16.

Discusses the use of various church records in the reconstruction of ethnic communities within large cities, their size and growth, their duration, occupational structure, Old World origins, infant mortality, and relations with the city at large.

237   Karp, David A.; Stone, Gregory P.; and Yoels, William C. BEING URBAN: A SOCIAL PSYCHOLOGICAL VIEW OF CITY LIFE. Lexington, Mass.: D.C. Heath, 1977. 242 p.

Examines classical conceptions and observations of urban life and then focuses on various aspects of the urban experience, including the rediscovery of community, the social organization of every day city life, life-style diversity and tolerance, and the stratification of power.

238   Kasperson, Roger E. "Toward a Geography of Urban Politics: Chicago, a Case Study." ECONOMIC GEOGRAPHY 41 (1965): 95-107.

Discusses some tentative conclusions concerning the interplay between geography and politics and what strategies political leaders employ to gain the support of different geographical sections.

239   Kassarda, John D., and Redfearn, George V. "Differential Patterns of City and Suburban Growth in the United States." JOURNAL OF URBAN HISTORY 2 (1975): 43-66.

Examines three indices of expansive city growth: relative decentralization in which suburbs grow faster than central cities, absolute centralization, and the degree to which metropolitan centers have deconcentrated as their peripheries have expanded. Concludes that suburbanization has been the dominant trend over the past fifty years and is unlikely to be reversed.

240   Knights, Peter R. THE PLAIN PEOPLE OF BOSTON, 1830-1860: A STUDY IN CITY GROWTH. New York: Oxford University Press, 1971. 204 p.

Examines the changing composition of Boston's population during a period of massive immigration and substantial mobility. Provides extensive tables and charts to illustrate his conclusions concerning residential and occupational mobility and ethnic succession.

241   Krazberg, Melvin, and Pursell, Carroll, Jr., eds. TECHNOLOGY IN WESTERN CIVILIZATION. Vol. 2. TECHNOLOGY IN THE TWENTIETH CENTURY. New York: Oxford University Press, 1967. 772 p.

Selections cover major aspects of twentieth-century technological development, including such urban-related topics as transportation, building, land use resources, and electronics and communications.

242   Kremm, Thomas W. "Measuring Religious Preferences in Nineteenth Century Urban Areas." HISTORICAL METHODS NEWSLETTER 8 (1975): 137-41.

Describes a methodology for determining the religious preferences of nineteenth-century city dwellers by using a combination of parish records and census returns for Cleveland.

The Urbanization Process

243   LaGory, Mark E. URBAN STRUCTURE AND POPULATION GROWTH: AN ECOLOGICAL ANALYSIS OF THE GROWTH OF CITIES AND METROPOLITAN AREAS FOR THE 1900-1970 PERIOD. Ann Arbor, Mich.: University Microfilms, 1979.

         Argues that the question of urban growth cannot be answered in generalized terms but that urban growth varies according to the individual city's size, historical period, and region.

244   Lampard, Eric C. "The Evolving System of Cities in the United States: Urbanization and Economic Development." In ISSUES IN URBAN ECONOMICS, edited by Harvey S. Perloff and Lowdon Wingo, Jr., pp. 81-140. Baltimore: Johns Hopkins University Press, 1968.

         Explores the historical relationship of the rise of cities to national and regional economic development, using a behavioral-institutional formulation of the "functional-structural" hypothesis of differentiation. Stresses the interrelation among the residential, occupational, and socioeconomic attributes of the population.

245   _____. "Historical Contours of Contemporary Urban Society: A Comparative View." JOURNAL OF CONTEMPORARY HISTORY 4 (1969): 3-25.

         Presents an historical summary of the urbanization process, focusing on population concentration, industrialization of the labor force, and socioeconomic change.

246   _____. "The History of Cities in the Economically Advanced Areas." ECONOMIC DEVELOPMENT AND CULTURAL CHANGE 3 (1955): 86-136.

         Appraises the role of cities in the evolution of economically advanced areas, "seeking to differentiate urban and nonurban influences relevant to some conceptual framework of economic progress." Deals with two approaches: urban-industrial growth as q cultural process and as an economic contingency.

247   _____. "The Pursuit of Happiness in the City: Changing Opportunities and Options in America." ROYAL HISTORICAL SOCIETY TRANSACTIONS 23 (1973): 175-220.

         Outlines the urbanization process in the United States from the seventeenth century to the present and examines both the changing structure of opportunities and the development of the options. Concludes that choices have usually been compromises between stronger interest groups at the expense of weaker ones.

248   Lieberman, Richard K. "A Measure for the Quality of Life: Housing." HISTORICAL METHODS 11 (1978): 129-34.

Contends that housing quality is an alternative to occupation for quantitatively measuring social status. Uses data from New York City's East Village neighborhoods in 1899 to illustrate the kinds of questions that can be answered by housing records.

249 Livingood, James W. THE PHILADELPHIA-BALTIMORE TRADE RIVALRY. New York: Arno Press, 1970. 195 p.

Examines the nature of the rivalry and the topographical and other advantages that caused Baltimore to grow faster than Philadelphia did in the first half of the nineteenth century. Based primarily upon city records, newspaper stories, diaries, and other documents.

250 Lowe, George D., and Peek, Charles W. "Location and Lifestyle: The Comparative Exploratory Ability of Urbanism and Rurality." RURAL SOCIOLOGY 39 (1974): 392-420.

Using consumption of alcoholic beverages as the indicator of rural-urban life-styles, investigates whether rural versus urban residence generates attitudinal differences and whether using a composite definition--residence plus life-style--increases the predictive utility of rurality. Results confirmed both hypothesis.

251 Marsh, Margaret Sammartino. "The Transformation of Community: Suburbanization and Urbanization in Northern West Philadelphia, 1880-1930." Ph.D. dissertation, Rutgers University, 1974. 197 p.

Examines the transformation of "city" into "metropolis," noting the differentiation of function, both industrially and residentially, as a dominant feature of the metropolitan area. Attributes the change of the community structure to the change in the city's class, racial, and ethnic residential patterns.

252 Marshall, Leon S. "The English and American Industrial City of the Nineteenth Century." WESTERN PENNSYLVANIA HISTORICAL MAGAZINE 20 (1937): 169-80.

Identifies and describes various parallels and distinctions in the nineteenth-century industrial city, stressing that, despite the existence of strikingly similar problems, key differences between the English and American industrial revolutions produced substantial idiosyncratic developments.

253 Masotti, Louis H., and Hadden, Jeffrey K., eds. THE URBANIZATION OF THE SUBURBS. Beverly Hills, Calif.: Sage, 1973. 600 p.

Nineteen essays consider "various aspects of suburbs and suburbanization, including contemporary issues, economics, government, politics, and social structure and social process. An initial section provides historical perspectives including Gregory H. Singleton's discussion of nineteenth-century trends, Glenn D. Norval's focus on the post-World War II period, and Jeffrey Hadden and Josef J. Barton's reflections on the history of antiurban ideology.

254   Michel, Jerry B. "The Measurement of Social Power in the Community: An Exploratory Study." AMERICAN JOURNAL OF ECONOMICS AND SOCIOLOGY 23 (1964): 189-93.

Argues the need for better techniques to measure social power, and attempts to devise adequate empirical indices through a case study of community level political power.

255   Miller, Richard G. "Gentry and Entrepreneurs: A Socioeconomic Analysis of Philadelphia in the 1790s." ROCKY MOUNTAIN SOCIAL SCIENCE JOURNAL 12 (1975): 71-84.

Uses census and tax-roll data to relate the distribution of real wealth in Philadelphia to the city's socioeconomic groups and concludes that by 1800 social stratification existed and that in addition to a correlation between occupation and wealth "a select number of the city's merchants and lawyers controlled much of the socioeconomic life of Philadelphia."

256   Miller, Zane L. "Scarcity, Abundance, and American Urban History." JOURNAL of URBAN HISTORY 4 (1978): 131-56.

Develops a superstructure for the entire span of American urban history based on the "interplay between a society's attitude toward scarcity and its institutions," and traces a process of successive definition and redefinition of the city, reflecting the changing conceptions of scarcity and abundance.

257   Mills, Edward S. "An Aggregative Model of Resource Allocation in the Metropolitan Area." AMERICAN ECONOMIC REVIEW 57 (1967): 197-210.

Presents a model stressing the properties of production functions for explaining the sizes and structures of urban areas, based on the view that "the basic characteristics of cities are to be understood as market responses to opportunities for production and income."

258   Mitchell, Robert B., and Rapkin, Chester. URBAN TRAFFIC, A FUNCTION OF LAND USE. Westport, Conn.: Greenwood Press, 1974. 226 p.

Relates the movement of people and traffic to land use patterns in the city and produces an analytical model to help predict traffic flow. Focuses primarily upon Philadelphia in the early 1950s.

259 Molotch, Harvey. "The City as a Growth Machine: Toward a Political Economy of Place." AMERICAN JOURNAL OF SOCIOLOGY 82 309-32.

> Speculates that within the contemporary American context, growth constitutes "the political and economic essence of virtually any given locality," and that the desire for growth provides a consensus goal that contains local socioeconomic reform. The functioning of the city as "a growth machine" hence provides a powerful analytical perspective on urban development and problems.

260 Moses, Leon, and Williamson, Harold F., Jr. "The Location of Economic Activity in Cities." AMERICAN ECONOMIC REVIEW 57 (1967): 211-22.

> Presents a theoretical analysis for examining the structure of factor prices and costs within a core-dominated city, highlighting the effects of certain technological lags and transport cost relationships, and the results of three empirical analyses of the manufacturing sector in Chicago for the years 1900-20 and 1950-64.

261 Muller, Peter O. "The Evolution of American Suburbs: A Geographical Interpretation." URBANISM PAST AND PRESENT 4 (1977): 1-10.

> Argues that, viewed as the "sustained growth of city edges at a rate faster than central areas," suburbanization, rather than a recent phenomenon, has been a significant feature of urban settlement patterns. Focuses on the forces, particularly varying modes of transportation, that have affected this process.

262 Murphy, Raymond E. THE AMERICAN CITY: AN URBAN GEOGRAPHY. New York: McGraw-Hill, 1974. 556 p.

> Contains definitions of most of the terms necessary to understand urban geography as well as up-to-date summaries of the major interpretive work in the field as of the mid-1970s.

263 National Resources Committee. OUR CITIES, THEIR ROLE IN THE NATIONAL ECONOMY. Washington, D.C.: Government Printing Office, 1937. 87 p.

> A report in Washington by the NCR's urbanization undertaken at the request of a variety of major urban civic associations. Presents demographic data, analyzes causes of urbanization, projects trends, identifies a large number of urban

problems, and suggests general policy and specific recommendations for their solutions.

264	Natoli, Salvatore J. "Zoning and the Development of Urban Land Use Patterns." ECONOMIC GEOGRAPHY 47 (1971): 171-84.

   Focuses on the experience of Worcester, Massachusetts, during its first zoning ordinance, from 1925 to 1963, to examine the impact of large area and spot rezoning on urban land use patterns.

265	Naumes, Margaret Jane Oyaas. "The Existence and Growth of the Very Large City: The Philadelphia Story." Ph.D. dissertation, Stanford University, 1974. 203 p.

   Uses Philadelphia's suburbs and more distant towns to study the effect of larger city growth on the surrounding communities. Considers variables relating to personal economic characteristics and quality of housing in predicting Philadelphia's influence over its suburbs.

266	Ottensmann, John R. THE CHANGING SPATIAL STRUCTURE OF AMERICAN CITIES. Lexington, Mass.: Lexington Books, 1975. 207 p.

   Longitudinal study examining spatial patterning of population and housing in the United States, especially focusing on Milwaukee, Wisconsin, for the period 1920 to 1950, a time of transition from industrial city to modern metropolis. Concentrates on developing and testing models for descriptive and predictive pruposes.

267	Pessen, Edward. "Fruits of the New Urban History: The Sociology of Small Nineteenth Century Cities." JOURNAL OF URBAN HISTORY 5 (1978): 93-108.

   Reviews five studies of nineteenth-century cities--Milwaukee, Wisconsin; Lynn, Massachusetts; Hamilton, Ontario; Columbus, Ohio; and Warren, Pennsylvania--and attempts to synthesize their findings concerning medium-sized cities in the nineteenth century. Focuses primarily on the topic of residential and social mobility.

268	_____. "The Social Configuration of the Antebellum City: An Historical and Theoretical Inquiry." JOURNAL OF URBAN HISTORY 2 (1976): 267-306.

   Focuses on social class characteristics, relationships, and mobility as ways of appraising influence and power in the antebellum urban community. Argues that stratification became more intense and rigid, and contends that the wealth-holding elite held both socioeconomic and political hegemony.

269 Platt, Harold L. "Urban Public Services and Private Enterprise: Aspects of the Legal and Economic History of Houston, Texas, 1865-1905." Ph.D. dissertation, Rice University, 1974. 308 p.

> Investigates the city building process, the institutions established to direct development, and the way in which urban growth affects patterns of social organization, with particular focus on "comparing public and private sector responses to community needs for essential services and environmental improvements."

270 Pred, Allan. "Industrialization, Initial Advantage, and American Metropolitan Growth." GEOGRAPHICAL REVIEW 55 (1965): 158-85.

> Presents theoretical discussions of the spatial interaction of urban and manufacturing growth, using approaches suggested by locational theory, and develops a model of urban size growth.

271 _____. "The Intrametropolitan Location of American Manufacturing." ANNALS OF THE ASSOCIATION OF AMERICAN GEOGRAPHERS 54 (1964): 165-80.

> Expresses several tentative generalizations for the logical patterning of locational trends, based on an analysis of the ten largest U.S. metropolitan areas which considers historical evolution, local friction of distance, and broad industrial categories expressing similar locational tendencies.

272 _____. THE SPATIAL DYNAMICS OF U.S. URBAN-INDUSTRIAL GROWTH, 1800-1914. Cambridge, Mass.: MIT Press, 1966. 225 p.

> Analyzes and describes the emergence of an urban pattern and structure in the United States, developing and presenting a model of urban-size growth during rapid industrialization, suggesting a typology for the diffusion of industrial innovations, and analyzing the development of the American mercantile city.

273 _____. URBAN GROWTH AND CIRCULATION OF INFORMATION: THE UNITED STATES SYSTEM OF CITIES 1790-1840. Cambridge, Mass.: Harvard University Press, 1973. 348 p.

> Traces the interrelationships between information circulation and the interdependent growth of large cities, attempting to identify the growth processes of systems of cities. Develops an "ideal-typical, non-deterministic model of the processes by which large-city rank-stability set in for the United States system of cities and those of its regional sub-systems," and explores the diffusion of commercial and industrial innovations as related to the model.

274 _____. "Urban Systems Development and the Long-Distance Flow of Information Through Pre-Electronic United States Newspapers." ECONOMIC GEOGRAPHY 47 (1971): 498-524.

> Discusses spatial biases in the long-distance circulation of information by means of newspapers for the period 1790-1840, presents some time-lag surface maps for various cities to describe and analyze the changing characters of "public-informational isolation," and suggests some relationships between information flows and urban system developments.

275 Preston, Howard L. AUTOMOBILE AGE OF ATLANTA. Athens: University of Georgia Press, 1978.

> Examines the impact of the automobile on urban America, focusing on Atlanta, and asserts that the city would have been structured entirely different had it not been for the automobile's influence.

276 Preston, Richard E. "A Detailed Comparison of Land Use in Three Transition Zones." ANNALS OF THE ASSOCIATION OF AMERICAN GEOGRAPHERS 58 (1968): 461-84.

> Detailed discussion of land use characteristics of transition zones in Richmond, Virginia; Worcester, Massachusetts; and Youngstown, Ohio, which assesses and attempts to explain similarities and differences in the three zones, and relate the empirical data to existing transitions zone theory. Findings support the proposition that "despite the historical and functional peculiarity of individual cities, the transition zone is a repetitive geographical phenomenon in middle sized American cities."

277 _____. "The Zone in Transition: A Study of Urban Land Use Patterns." ECONOMIC GEOGRAPHY 42 (1966): 236-60.

> Outlines a technique for delimiting the transition zone--the so-called "gray area" peripheral to the central business district of the city--and "presents a quantitative and cartographic view of its characteristic land use proportions, patterns and associations." Based on data from Richmond, Virginia; Worcester, Massachusetts; and Youngstown, Ohio. Concludes that the transition zone is composed of distinctive land use types and combinations.

278 Putman, S.H. "Calibrating a Residential Location Model for Nineteenth Century Philadelphia." ENVIRONMENT AND PLANNING 9 (1977): 449-60.

> Uses data generated by the Philadelphia Social History Project in an attempt to validate the Disaggregated Residential Alloca-

tion Model. Results suggest "a rather high degree of descriptive validity and consistency with macro-behavioral theories of spatial allocation."

279 Quandt, Jean B. "Community in Urban America, 1890-1917: Reformers, City Planners, and Greenwich Village." SOCIETAS (1976): 255-73.

Contrasts community, a commitment to a specific geographical locale based upon shared residence, with communion, a psychological commonality of feeling based upon personal fellowship. Sees reformers and city planners as primarily concerned with the former and bohemians as oriented toward the latter.

280 Rannells, John. THE CORE OF THE CITY. Westport, Conn.: Greenwood Press, 1974.

Examines the changing patterns of land-based activities within cities, developing the concept of activity systems and their relationships as an analytical tool, and then uses this approach to measure and compare land-based activities and the patterns of their relationships in the central business district of Philadelphia using data for the year 1949.

281 Rhoda, Richard. "Urban Transport and the Expansion of Cincinnati 1858 to 1920." CINCINNATI HISTORICAL SOCIETY BULLETIN 22 (1964): 131-43.

Reviews and assesses the importance of intraurban transportation to the spatial expansion of Cincinnati, presenting data and analyses related to horse cars and electric streetcars. Stresses increased accessibility as a critical factor in promoting urban sprawl.

282 Richardson, James F.; Steglich, W.G.; and Cartwright, Walter J. "A Refined Index of Urbanism." ROCKY MOUNTAIN SOCIETY SCIENTIFIC JOURNAL 6 (1969): 163-71.

Refines an earlier index of urbanism by eliminating some of the overemphasized and weaker indicators. Retains the basic assumption that demographic data are valid indicators of behavior and can be used to differentiate between rural and urban ways of life.

283 Rickert, John E. "House Facades of the Northeastern United States: A Tool of Geographic Analysis." ANNALS OF THE ASSOCIATION OF AMERICAN GEOGRAPHERS 57 (1967): 211-38.

Discusses the utility of house facade analysis for determining the time periods of house construction. Presents descriptions of house construction for eight distinct periods from 1830 to 1960.

284 Robinson, Warren C. METROPOLITAN AND URBAN GROWTH IN THE UNITED STATES 1900-1960. University Park: Pennsylvania State University, Institute for Research on Land and Water Resources, 1968.

> Presents population figures for each census year since 1900 by regions, divisions and states broken down into the following categories: metropolitan and nonmetropolitan rural and urban, metropolitan rural and metropolitan urban, and nonmetropolitan rural and nonmetropolitan urban. Traces these series "with respect to their growth rates relative to the change in total U.S. population and other selected aggregates."

285 Rodwin, Lloyd. NATIONS AND CITIES: A COMPARISON OF STRATEGIES FOR URBAN GROWTH. Boston: Houghton-Mifflin, 1970. 395 p.

> Analyzes theories of urban growth, strategies for coping with or avoiding problems generated by rapid, unplanned urbanization and presents case studies of policy and planning experiences in Venezuela, Turkey, Great Britain, France, and the United States.

286 Rosen, Elliot Alfred. "The Growth of the American City, 1830 to 1860: Economic Foundations of Urban Growth in the Pre-Civil War Period." Ph.D. dissertation, New York University, 1954. 391 p.

> Discusses the rise and growth of cities throughout the United States, identifying and analyzing the major factors responsible for this development and their varying impacts in different sections of the nation. Cites the importance of the expansion of trade and commerce, both foreign and domestic; the transportation revolution; westward expansion; increased technological sophistication; and growth of industrialization.

287 Russell, Emily W.B. "Mt. Tabor, New Jersey: An Environmental History." NEW JERSEY HISTORY 95 (1977): 157-70.

> Examines the problems faced by the community in providing a liveable environment while meeting its needs for economic and physical growth and trying to retain its religious heritage.

288 Sargent, Charles S. URBAN DYNAMICS. Princeton, N.J.: Jones Books, 1977. 168 p.

> Depicts the major forces shaping contemporary urban society using stories from the WALL STREET JOURNAL. Divided into sections on the downtown, traditional neighborhoods, suburbia, urban transportation, municipal financing and services, and the city's future.

289 Sauers, Bernard J. "A Political Process of Urban Growth: Consolida-

tion of the South Side with the City of Pittsburgh, 1872." PACIFIC HISTORIAN 41 (1974): 265-87.

> Argues that Pittsburgh's nineteenth-century growth resulted from its forceful consolidation of adjunct areas which already were incorporated boroughs. Traces the factors responsible for the 1872 consolidation, including city businessmen and boosters and the PITTSBURGH PRESS, and especially the power of the Pittsburgh political machines.

290 Schnore, Leo F. "Municipal Annexation and the Growth of Metropolitan Suburbs, 1950-60." AMERICAN JOURNAL OF SOCIOLOGY 67 (1962): 406-17.

> Measures population changes in urban centers and their metropolitan "rings" for the 212 SMSAs. Controlling for the effect of annexation reveals a far greater amount of suburbanization than indicated by unadjusted data.

291 _____. "Social Problems in an Urban-Industrial Context." SOCIAL PROBLEMS 9 (1962): 228-39.

> Discusses technological, population, organizational, and environmental problems in terms of their relationship with urbanization, stressing the need for a generally comparative approach to urban problems in a social context.

292 _____. "Urbanization and Economic Development: Demographic Contribution." AMERICAN JOURNAL OF ECONOMICS AND SOCIOLOGY 23 (1964): 37-48.

> Presents a demographic approach to the study of urbanization, suggesting its utility, discussing its measurement, and positing research possibilities in a U.S., as well as world, setting.

293 Schwirian, Kent P., and Prehn, John W. "An Axiomatic Theory of Urbanization." AMERICAN SOCIOLOGICAL REVIEW 27 (1962): 812-25.

> Presents a demographic theory of urbanization, which formulates a theoretically enclosed system.

294 Sennett, Richard. FAMILIES AGAINST THE CITY: MIDDLE CLASS HOMES OF INDUSTRIAL CHICAGO, 1872-1890. New York: Vintage Books, 1974. 258 p.

> Analyzes the Union Park area of Chicago from its origins to the World's Fair of 1893 with respect to family life, demographic and social profiles, and social mobility. Argues that middle-class families were not isolated, but developed a subtle, highly civilized network of kinship and neighborhood ties for mutual self-help.

The Urbanization Process

295 Sharpless, John B. "City Growth in the United States, England and Wales, 1820-1861: The Effects of Location, Size and Economic Structure on Inter-Urban Variations in Demographic Growth." Ph.D. dissertation, University of Michigan, 1975. 307 p.

> A comparative study of urban growth in the United States and Britain concluding that spatial location, city size, and economic function offer little explanation of variations in city growth in the early nineteenth century.

296 _____. CITY GROWTH IN THE UNITED STATES, ENGLAND AND WALES 1820-1861. New York: Arno Press, 1977. 294 p.

> Investigates the effects of spatial location, aggregate city size, and local labor force composition on the patterning of demographic growth rates, using published census materials in the United States and Great Britain. Concludes that these three variables have little explanatory power for the nineteenth-century experience, suggesting the need for modifying prevailing urban growth models.

297 Sharpless, John B., and Shortridge, Ray M. "Biased Underenumeration in Census Manuscripts: Methodological Implications." JOURNAL OF URBAN HISTORY 1 (1975): 409-39.

> Discusses the dimensions of error in census manuscripts, the likelihood of bias as a cause for error, its effect upon statistical estimates, and a methdology for measuring the extent of the error. Feels that biased errors may require recalculating data on mobility and other quantitatively based studies.

298 Simon, Roger D. THE CITY-BUILDING PROCESS: HOUSING AND SERVICES IN NEW MILWAUKEE NEIGHBORHOODS, 1880-1910. Philadelphia: American Philosophical Society, 1978. 64 p.

> Describes and analyzes the process of expansion of the city of Milwaukee during the period of its most rapid industrialization. Contrasts Milwaukee's experience with older eastern cities which, because of their age, already had cheap, if inadequate housing for lower-income residents. Studies three peripheral areas of the city through several components: subdivision, services, construction, and allocation of housing in 1905.

299 Sirjamaki, John. THE SOCIOLOGY OF CITIES. New York: Random House, 1964. 328 p.

> Focuses on the impact of the national community on urban communities, particularly with regard to social and cultural changes. Includes chapters dealing with the development of

The Urbanization Process

cities in the ancient, classical, medieval, and industrial eras, and analysis of American cities in terms of economic functions, ecology, population, social stratification, and government.

300 Sjoberg, Gideon. THE PREINDUSTRIAL CITY, PAST AND PRESENT. New York: Free Press, 1960. 353 p.

> Landmark study describing and analyzing the social and ecological structure of the preindustrial city. Contends that the structure and form of such cities, regardless of their geographical or chronological location, share essential similarities, and differs markedly from modern industrial-urban centers.

301 Smith, James B. "Lumbertown in the Cutover: A Comparative Study of the Stage Hypothesis of Urban Growth." Ph.D. dissertation, University of Wisconsin, 1973. 365 p.

> Quantitatively and comparatively studies ninety-four Wisconsin and Michigan cities that were centers of lumber production between 1880 and 1910. Presents an alternative approach to the study of urbanization through the author's innovative methodological processes.

302 Smolensky, Eugene, and Ratajczak, Donald. "The Conception of Cities." EXPLORATIONS IN ENTREPRENEURIAL HISTORY 2 (1965): 90-131.

> Reports on the initial phase of a larger study designed to provide a rational basis for projecting the magnitude, sequence, and timing of investment in city building. Presents a three-stage theory of urban growth, then focuses on the first of these stages, the elemental settlement, using the development of San Diego as test of this concept.

303 Stephenson, Charles. "Tracing Those Who Left: Mobility Studies and the Soundex Indexes to the United States Census." JOURNAL OF URBAN HISTORY 1 (1974): 73-84.

> Evaluates the Soundex Indexes to the population schedules of 1880 to 1900, indicating their utility for studying patterns of geographic and social mobility by tracing the movements of specific individuals over time regardless of location within the United States.

304 Stroud, Rosemary. "Suburban Growth: Some Social Aspects." In THE SUBURBAN ECONOMIC NETWORK: ECONOMIC ACTIVITY, RESOURCE USE, AND THE GREAT SPRAWL, edited by John E. Ullmann, pp. 7-20. New York: Praeger, 1977.

> Identifies factors that promoted the rise of suburbs after World War II, focusing on the New York region and its suburban

counties of Nassau and Suffolk. Indicates the importance of public policy, the private sector, deterioration of cities, and postwar demographic and social changes.

305 Suttles, Gerald D. THE SOCIAL CONSTRUCTION OF COMMUNITIES. Chicago: University of Chicago Press, 1972. 278 p.

Studies the structure and function of community institutions in the modern metropolis, especially those which relate to the lower and lower-middle classes.

306 Swanson, Joseph A., and Williamson, Jeffrey G. "A Model of Urban Capital Formation and the Growth of Cities in History." EXPLORATIONS IN ECONOMIC HISTORY 8 (1970-71): 213-22.

Presents a formal restatement of a theory of urban capital information underlying the authors' THE GROWTH OF CITIES IN THE AMERICAN NORTHEAST, 1820-1870. (Madison: University of Wisconsin, 1966).

307 Taeuber, Irene B. "The Changing Distribution of the Population of the United States in the Twentieth Century." In URBAN STUDIES, edited by Louis K. Lowenstein, pp. 3-52. New York: Free Press, 1977.

Presents and summarizes quantitative information on continuities, danger and transitions in migration and redistribution for the period 1900 to 1970, identifying and analyzing processes of change for different regions and metropolitan areas.

308 Taeuber, Karl E., and Taeuber Alma F. "White Migration and Socioeconomic Differences Between Cities and Suburbs." AMERICAN SOCIOLOGICAL REVIEW 29 (1964): 718-29.

Based upon census data on migration patterns in the twelve largest metropolitan areas. Argues that people of higher status and income tend to be more mobile and that central cities lose more of these residents to migration than they gain.

309 Taylor, George R. "American Urban Growth Preceding the Railway Age." JOURNAL OF ECONOMIC HISTORY 27 (1967): 309-39.

Presents detailed statistics on urban population changes from 1775 to 1890, dividing cities into four major groups: the four great eastern seaports, the small eastern seaports, the eastern interior cities, and the western cities, emphasizing alternatives in their importance, and indicates the impact on city growth of such factors as foreign and domestic trade, changes in agriculture, transportation development, and the growth of manufacturing.

310   Thernstrom, Stephan. "Urbanization, Migration and Social Mobility in Late Nineteenth-Century America." In TOWARDS A NEW PAST: DISSENTING ESSAYS IN AMERICAN HISTORY, edited by Barton J. Bernstein, pp. 158-75. New York: Pantheon Books, 1968.

> Sketches the process by which ordinary men and women were drawn to the burgeoning cities of post-Civil War America, assesses what little we know about how they were integrated into the urban class structure, and suggests how these matters affected the viability of the political system. Notes that the processes that drew the working class into the urban-industrial order encouraged accomodation and made organized protest difficult.

311   Thernstrom, Stephan, and Knights, Peter R. "Men in Motion: Some Data and Speculations about Urban Population Mobility in Nineteenth Century America." JOURNAL OF INTERDISCIPLINARY HISTORY 1 (1970): 7-35.

> Reviews a number of recent investigations indicating the existence of great fluidity in the composition of urban populations, and advances several tentative conclusions as to the nature, implications, and consequences of this geographic mobility.

312   Thomas, Brinley. MIGRATION AND URBAN DEVELOPMENT: REAPPRAISAL OF BRITISH AND AMERICAN LONG CYCLES. London: Methuen, 1972. 259 p.

> Compares the British and American experiences with both internal and external migration and their relationship to such economic indicators as investment, productivity, balance of payments, and consumption.

313   Thompson, Wilbur R. A PREFACE TO URBAN ECONOMICS. Baltimore: Johns Hopkins University Press, 1965. 413 p.

> Relates urban development to such economic phenomena as interurban and intraurban trade cycles and employment curves.

314   Tyler, Elaine. "The Pressure to Provide: Class, Consumerism, and Divorce in Urban America, 1880-1920." JOURNAL OF SOCIAL HISTORY 12 (1978): 180-93.

> Studies divorce samples from Los Angeles in the 1880s and 1920s and from New Jersey in 1920 and finds that rising affluence was at the root of the causes of divorce. Concludes that the affluence of urban-industrial life brought more frustration than fulfillment.

315   Vance, James E., Jr. "Geography and the Study of Cities." AMERICAN BEHAVIORAL SCIENTIST 22 (1978): 131-49.

Presents an overview of the development of urban geography as a scholarly field and the changing nature of its concern, including a discussion of historical urban geography, one of the most recent trends in the field.

316 _____. "Housing the Worker: The Employment Linkage as a Force in Urban Structure." ECONOMIC GEOGRAPHY 42 (1966): 294-325.

Focuses on the spatial impact of the separation between residence and work, surveying former patterns and the initial development of this new employment linkage from the English mill village through the nineteenth-century Lowell experiment and development of the American factory town.

317 _____. "Land Assignment in the Precapitalist, Capitalist, and Post-capitalist City." ECONOMIC GEOGRAPHY 47 (1971): 101-20.

Appraises the economic and social structuring of cities, focusing on the concepts that determined land assignment and use. Argues that the medieval period saw a primarily associational valuation of land, wheras with capitalism, value became a question of accessibility or potential ascription for profit.

318 Wade, Richard C. "Urbanization." In THE COMPARATIVE APPROACH TO AMERICAN HISTORY, edited by C. Vann Woodward, pp. 187-205. New York: Basic Books, 1968.

Compares the evolution of American cities over time with those in other nations. Sees urbanization and metropolitanization as American expressions of a worldwide trend toward modernization of society and nationalization of government and politics.

319 Walker, Richard A. "The Suburban Solution: Urban Geography and Urban Reform in the Capitalist Development of the United States." Ph.D. dissertation, Johns Hopkins University, 1977. 777 p.

Locates the beginning of the suburbanization trend in the Progressive era when the growth of working-class slums discouraged investment capital in the inner city and motivated middle-class citizens to seek refuge in the hinterlands. Dubs this a transition from the implosive to the explosive city.

320 Ward, David. CITIES AND IMMIGRANTS: A GEOGRAPHY OF CHANGE IN NINETEENTH CENTURY AMERICA. New York: Oxford University Press, 1971. 164 p.

Focuses on some of the geographical aspects and implications of U.S. urbanization during the years from 1820 to 1920, specifically the spatial effects of selective urban growth and internal differentiation. Considers regional economic development, urban employment, transportation and suburbanization, and immigrant residential areas.

321 _____. "A Comparative Historical Geography of Streetcar Suburbs in Boston, Massachusetts and Leeds, England: 1850-1920." ANNALS OF THE ASSOCIATION OF AMERICAN GEOGRAPHERS 54 (1964): 477-89.

Examines regional effects of local transportation upon the growth and characteristics of nineteenth-century cities, contrasting the experience of Boston and Leeds, and relating these distinctions to overall differences in the development of British and American cities.

322 _____. "The Emergence of Central Immigrant Ghettoes in American Cities: 1840-1920." ANNALS OF THE ASSOCIATION OF AMERICAN GEOGRAPHERS 58 (1968): 343-59.

Analysis of Boston in the latter half of the nineteenth century indicates that "timing and dimensions of the expansion of the central business district affected not only the location and longevity of immigrant ghettoes, but also the disposition of the distinctive residential quarters which developed beyond the expanding fringe of the central business district."

323 _____. "The Industrial Revolution and the Emergence of Boston's Central Business District." ECONOMIC GEOGRAPHY 42 (1966): 152-71.

Explores the spatial impact of growing industrialization on the size and complexity of Boston's Central Business District. Notes an increase in specialized business and associated activities which not only came to occupy larger areas but also differentiated into functionally distinctive segments.

324 Warner, Sam Bass, Jr. MEASUREMENTS FOR SOCIAL HISTORY: METROPOLITAN AMERICA 1860-1960. Beverly Hills, Calif.: Sage Publications, 1977. 232 p.

Serves as an instructional manual for social scientists in general, and especially for historians, wishing to place past case studies in a national and contemporary framework provided by the Bureau of Economic Analysis accounting system. Also provides descriptive historical information regarding population growth, race, industrialization, urbanization, migration, and fertility.

325 _____. "If All the World Were Philadelphia: A Scaffolding for Urban History, 1774-1930." AMERICAN HISTORICAL REVIEW 74 (1968): 26-43.

Contends that urban history lacks any tradition of systematic study of urban environments and the progression or sequence of urbanization as a process in the United States. Uses Philadelphia as a case study to demonstrate how a systematic arrangement of facts about Philadelphia's population in three time periods, 1774, 1860, and 1930, can produce insights into and evidence of processes of change.

326 _____. STREETCAR SUBURBS: THE PROCESS OF GROWTH IN BOSTON, 1870-1900. Cambridge, Mass.: Harvard University Press, 1978. 208 p.

Analyzes the effect of the street railway system on Boston in transforming it from a commercial city into an industrial metropolis characterized by an inner core of industry and slums and an outer periphery of residential suburbs.

327 Warner, Sam Bass, Jr., and Fleisch, Sylvia. "The Past of Today's Present: A Social History of America's Metropolises, 1860-1960." JOURNAL of URBAN HISTORY 3 (1976): 3-118.

Demonstrates the usefulness of the 1960 BEA system for historical research by applying it backwards in time, in order to delineate long-term underlying contemporary metropolitan social and economic problems. Includes "cook book" directions for those wishing to use the system.

328 Whebell, C.F.J. "Corridors: A Theory of Urban Systems." ANNALS OF THE ASSOCIATION OF AMERICAN GEOGRAPHERS 59 (1969): 1-26.

Defines corridors as "linear systems of urban places together with the linking surface transport media" and traces the development of this major urban system through four cumulative historical stages: initial occupancy, commercial agriculture, railway transport, and metropolitanism. Also posits a "cultural gradient," a sequential pattern for outward diffusions of innovations.

329 White, Dana F., and Crimmins, Timothy J. "Urban Structure, Atlanta." JOURNAL of URBAN HISTORY 2 (1976): 231-52.

Reports on an attempt to create a "usable past" that will aid architects, planners and humanists in their efforts to solve the problems confronting contemporary cities. The Atlanta study displays a two-pronged approach, city systems and area analyses, the former tracing the city's historical development of internal systems, the latter focusing on key locales and neighborhoods.

329a Williamson, Jeffrey G., and Swanson, J.A. "The Growth of Cities in

the American Northeast, 1820-1870." EXPLORATIONS IN ENTRE-
PRENEURIAL HISTORY 4, 2d series, (1966): supplement, 1-101.

> Presents a test of the urban scale hypothesis and explores the
> forces of northeastern urbanization, providing models of the
> city growth along with empirical analysis of demographic and
> aggregative occupational data. Finds that "size distribution
> data by itself calls for a rejection of the urban economics
> hypothesis."

330 Winfield, Gerald F. "The Impact of Urbanization on Agricultural Processes." ANNALS OF THE AMERICAN ACADEMY OF POLITICAL AND SOCIAL SCIENCE 405 (1973): 65-74.

> Focuses on the years from 1930 to 1970, examining the rela-
> tionship between urbanization and agriculture. Notes signifi-
> cant changes in land utilization and the technological trans-
> formation of agriculture, which has moved farm functions to
> the city, as well as a great rise in solid waste production in
> cities and on farms.

331 Wise, David O., and Dupree, Marguerite. "The Choice of the Automobile for Urban Passenger Transportation: Baltimore in the 1920s." In SOUTH ATLANTIC URBAN STUDIES, edited by Jack R. Censer and N. Steinert, pp. 153-79. Columbia: University of South Carolina Press, 1978.

> Examines the transportation needs of Americans in the 1920s
> emphasizing the variables of commuting time for the journey
> to work, transportation cost, and residential land value alter-
> natives. Contends that the automobile provided an economi-
> cally sound alternative to the streetcar, and that its growing
> popularity did not derive, therefore, from irrational factors of
> the type often suggested by social historians.

332 Withey, Lynne E. "Household Structure in Urban and Rural Areas: The Case of Rhode Island, 1774-1800." JOURNAL OF FAMILY HISTORY 3 (1978): 37-50.

> Contends that social structural differences between cities and
> rural towns account for much of the variation in household
> size, but indicates that after the Revolution fertility declined
> in not only the cities, but in all kinds of towns, a decline
> that represented a major change in attitudes and behavior from
> the colonial period.

333 Yeates, Maurice H. "Some Factors Affecting the Spatial Distribution of Chicago Land Values, 1910-1960." ECONOMIC GEOGRAPHY 41 (1965): 57-70.

> Examines the spatial distribution of land values in terms of

clinical land value theory. Notes the declining importance of the central business district over time as a key factor in explaining land value variations and the concomitant increasing importance of sectoral variations.

334 Zimmer, Donald T. "Madison, Indiana 1811-1860: A Study in the Process of City Building." Ph.D. dissertation, Indiana University, 1974. 288 p.

Analyzes the manner in which environment, technology, and leadership contributed to the building of Madison from a small hamlet in 1811 to one of Indiana's leading cities by 1850, how these elements contributed to its decline.

335 Zunz, Oliver. "Technology and Society in an Urban Environment: The Case of the Third Avenue Elevated Railway." JOURNAL OF INTERDISCIPLINARY HISTORY 3 (1972): 89-102.

Focuses on a case of technological innovation and its impact in central cities as an example of the need to "urbanize" population data to differentiate the effects of a specific urban environment from more general processes of social change. Concludes that emigration and continuous population renewal, rather than the elevated railway itself, proved responsible for social change.

336 Zunz, Oliver; Ericson, William; and Fox, Daniel. "Sampling for a Study of the Population and Land Use of Detroit in 1880-1885." SOCIAL SCIENCE HISTORY 1 (1977): 307-32.

Presents a sampling scheme for historical investigations which permits both micro- and macrolevel descriptions of a city.

Chapter 3

THE CITY IN AMERICAN THOUGHT

337 Abbott, Carl. "Civic Pride in Chicago, 1844-1860." JOURNAL OF THE ILLINOIS STATE HISTORICAL SOCIETY 63 (1970): 399-421.

> Defines the Windy City's civic pride as a confidence in its commercial growth and prosperity which enabled its promoters to view Chicago as a "machine whose function was to further the economic development of the West." Presents civic boosterism as the "logical ideology" of urban imperialism.

338 Anderson, Jack. "Frederick Jackson Turner and Urbanization." JOURNAL OF POPULAR CULTURE 2 (1968): 292-98.

> Examines some of Turner's later published and unpublished works and finds that his attitude toward urbanization generally resembled that of Thomas Jefferson. Claims that Turner feared that urbanization would ultimately lead to collectivism and paternalism.

339 Anderson, Nels. THE INDUSTRIAL URBAN COMMUNITY: HISTORICAL AND COMPARATIVE PERSPECTIVES. New York: Appleton Century Crofts, 1971. 438 p.

> Examines the evolution of the industrial city concept in the nineteenth and twentieth centuries, selecting examples from a wide variety of locales and time periods.

340 Aries, Philippe. "The Family and the City." DAEDALUS 106 (1977): 227-35.

> Contends that the decline of community and the deterioration of urban life caused the family to overexpand its influence and to try to satisfy all the emotional and social needs of its members. Feels that families have generally failed in this impossible task, placing great strain upon them.

341 Bedford, Henry F. TROUBLE DOWNTOWN: THE LOCAL CONTEXT OF TWENTIETH CENTURY AMERICA. New York: Harcourt Brace Jovanovich, 1978. 213 p.

Selects the examples of the Lawrence textile strike of 1912, prohibition in Chicago, Detroit during the Depression and World War II, Montgomery during the 1950s civil rights movement, and the Watts riot of 1965 to illustrate the interaction between local events and national history.

342   Bender, Thomas. COMMUNITY AND SOCIAL CHANGE IN AMERICA. New Brunswick, N.J.: Rutgers University Press, 1978. 159 p.

Contends that most historians have ignored the possibility of community in an urbanizing society and that many private social networks continue to constitute community in the metropolis. Relies largely upon diaries, correspondence, and autobiographies.

343   _____. TOWARD AN URBAN VISION: IDEAS AND INSTITUTIONS IN NINETEENTH CENTURY AMERICA. Lexington: University Press of Kentucky, 1975. 277 p.

Examines America's intellectual and institutional responses to urbanization and finds them to be less antiurban than previous scholars have asserted. Argues that there was a positive vision of the city which emerged out of the interplay of earlier agrarian ideals and the modernizing forces of the industrial city.

344   Berg, Barbara J. THE REMEMBERED GATE: ORIGINS OF AMERICAN FEMINISM, THE WOMAN AND THE CITY, 1800-1860. New York: Oxford University Press, 1978. 334 p.

Deals with the condition, perceptions, and activity of urban women in the pre-Civil War era. Contrasts the feminists with the "woman-belle ideal" fostered by male society and finds that feminism flourished in American cities in that era as it flourishes today.

345   Berns, Walter. "Thinking About the City." COMMENTARY 56 (1973): 74-77.

Analyzes the reasons for America's ambivalent attitude toward the city and ties it to the nation's ambivalence about modernity in general. Contends that the latter's emphasis on self-preservation and self-interest as the ends of civil society lie at the root of antiurbanism.

346   Brownell, Blaine A. "The Agrarian and Urban Ideals: Environmental Images in Modern America." JOURNAL OF POPULAR CULTURE 5 (1971): 576-87.

Finds that the agrarian and urban ideals were rarely mutually exclusive ones in the imagery of popular culture and that there has always existed a "genuinely complex spectrum of beliefs, assumptions, and environmental preferences," rather than two absolute ideals.

347 Burgess, Ernest W., ed. URBAN COMMUNITY. New York: AMS Press, 1972. 352 p.

Contains papers read at the 1925 meetings of the American Sociological Society on various methods of conducting urban research.

348 Clark, John G.; Katzman, David M.; McKinzie, Richard D.; and Wilson, Theodore A. THREE GENERATIONS IN TWENTIETH CENTURY AMERICA: FAMILY, COMMUNITY AND NATION. Homewood, Ill.: Dorsey Press, 1977. 529 p.

Views the changes in the nature of community in the United States over the past seventy-five years through the medium of three generations of families residing in towns, cities, and suburbs throughout the county.

349 Cox, Richard. "Coney Island, Urban Symbol in American Art." NEW YORK HISTORICAL SOCIETY QUARTERLY 60 (1976): 35-52.

Examines the work of several artists who regarded Coney Island as a microcosm of the sociopolitical problems of frenetic, machine-age New York and who saw the city as a harbinger of the nation's technological future.

350 Donaldson, Scott. THE SUBURBAN MYTH. New York: Columbia University Press, 1969. 272 p.

Subjects most of the existing literature on suburbia to critical review. Attributes the antisuburban attitude of many writers to the persistence of the agrarian myth.

351 Doxiadis, Konstantinos A., and Douglass, Truman B. THE NEW WORLD OF URBAN MAN. Philadelphia: United Church Press, 1965. 127 p.

Predicts a solution to the urban crisis through the application of social planning and physical engineering.

352 Dyckman, John W. "Some Conditions of Civil Order in an Urbanized World." DAEDALUS 95 (1966): 797-812.

Examines several characteristic forms of contemporary urban growth which are capable of upsetting the established political and social order and impeding an orderly transition from existing institutions to new ones. Sees the ideological unrest of unassimilated groups as more threatening than the technical breakdown of the urban apparatus.

353 Dykstra, Robert R. "Town-Country Conflict: A Hidden Dimension in American Social History." AGRICULTURAL HISTORY 38 (1964): 195-204.

> Contends that the roots of rural-urban conflict are to be understood as much in terms of countless real issues and events at the local level as through sweeping generalizations about the Jeffersonian intellect and the national mood.

354 Elazar, Daniel J. "Are We a Nation of Cities?" PUBLIC INTEREST 4 (1966): 42-58.

> Contends that most pessimistic appraisals of city life as alienating and disorienting are myths. Views cities as collections of neighborhoods whose residents enjoy the economic benefits of city life while maintaining a sense of community through small-scale organization.

355 Fine, David M. "Abraham Cahan, Stephen Crane and the Romantic Tenement Tale of the Nineties." AMERICAN STUDIES 14 (1973-74): 95-108.

> Contends that Cahan's YEKL, A TALE OF THE NEW YORK GHETTO (1896) and Crane's MAGGIE, A GIRL OF THE STREETS (1896) were attacked by critics and readers because both writers refused to conform to the sentimental and romantic assumptions of the popular tenement tale of the day, but that, in so doing, their work brought to American urban fiction a much needed dose of realism.

356 Fischer, Claude S. THE URBAN EXPERIENCE. New York: Harcourt Brace Jovanovich, 1976. 309 p.

> Summarizes current thought concerning the social and psychological consequences of urban life, focusing upon popular and sociological views, the physical and social contexts, secondary and primary groups, states of mind, the urban personality, and the suburban experience.

357 Furer, Howard B. "The American City: Catalyst for Women's Rights." WISCONSIN MAGAZINE OF HISTORY 52 (1969): 285-305.

> Contends that the leadership of the women's rights movement came from urban environments nationwide and that nothing has aided the cause of women more greatly than has urbanization, economically, socially, and politically.

358 Goheen, Peter G. "Interpreting the American City: Some Historical Perspectives." GEOGRAPHICAL REVIEW 64 (1974): 362-84.

Insists that such great historical issues as industrialization, social and geographic mobility, and suburbanization, are best understood after a careful study of the role of urban people and ideas in shaping the progress of national history. Portrays the city as a "mediator" of national history.

359 Goist, Park D. "City and 'Community': The Urban Theory of Robert Park." AMERICAN QUARTERLY 23 (1971): 46-59.

Contends that Park's sense of community was not antiurban, but rather a "double visioned" response to complex social change where one constantly tests the validity of older forms in order to understand the potential of newer forces. Regards Park as the first real urban theorist who produced a valuable and essentially urban-focused contribution to the national quest for community.

360 _____. "The City as Organism: Two Recent American Theories of the City." Ph.D. dissertation, University of Rochester, 1967. 489 p.

Compares the University of Chicago "human ecology" school with the architects and planners who advocated a "garden city regionalism" approach to urban development. Finds them linked by their view of the city as an organism but differing over the "concentric zone" versus nonmetropolitan dominated concept of urban planning.

361 _____. FROM MAIN STREET TO STATE STREET: TOWN, CITY AND COMMUNITY IN AMERICA. Port Washington, N.Y.: Kennikat Press, 1977. 180 p.

Examines the meaning of community in town and city by issues raised in literature, advertising, sociology, social work, journalism, and city planning. Deals with the function of towns as a symbol of ideal community and with the efforts of representatives from a variety of backgrounds to come to grips with urban life.

362 _____. "Town, City, and Community, 1890-1920s." AMERICAN STUDIES 14 (1973-74): 15-28.

Reviews the notion of community which emerged from the writings of Jane Addams, Sherwood Anderson, and Robert Park, and finds that they did not necessarily associate a sense of community with small-town life. Sought to develop a responsible neighborliness "appropriate to life in the emerging metropolis."

363 Green, Martin. THE PROBLEM OF BOSTON: SOME READINGS IN CULTURAL HISTORY. New York: Norton, 1966. 234 p.

Focuses upon George Ticknor and Charles Eliot Norton as preservers of Boston's intellectual and aesthetic heritage in the face of democracy and plutocracy. Feels that high culture may provide the humanism necessary to pull together the nation's fragmenting urban society.

364 Griffin, C.W. "The Frontier Heritage of Urban America." In PERSPECTIVES ON URBAN AMERICA, edited by Melvin I. Urofsky, pp. 23-42. Garden City, N.Y.: Doubleday, 1973.

Charges that America's frontier heritage, with its emphasis on mobility, unbridled freedom, and exploitation of nature, is largely responsible for the nation's failure to come to grips with the urban crisis.

365 Gruen, Victor. THE HEART OF OUR CITIES: THE URBAN CRISIS, DIAGNOSIS AND CURE. New York: Simon and Schuster, 1964. 368 p.

Examines the forces which have made American cities what they are as well as those which have been fundamentally anticity in their effect. Suggests a counterattack, based largely upon curbing the dominance of the automobile.

366 Guterman, Stanley S. "In Defense of Wirth's 'Urbanism as a Way of Life.'" AMERICAN JOURNAL OF SOCIOLOGY 74 (1969): 492-99.

Examines the various criticisms of Louis Wirth's thesis, finds them to be based upon inadequate evidence, and presents data to support Wirth's contention that the size, density, and heterogeneity of urban life fosters alienation and lack of human friendships.

367 Haeger, John D. FROM COMMONWEALTH TO COMMERCE: THE PRE-INDUSTRIAL CITY IN AMERICA. St. Charles, Mo.: Forum Press, 1973.

Analyzes the factors and the social losses which accompanied the change over from the Puritan commonwealth, with its communal-religious basis, to the highly individualistic, materialistic commercial city of the early nineteenth century.

368 Hammack, David C. "Elite Perceptions of Power in the Cities of the United States, 1880-1900: The Evidence of James Bryce, Moisei Ostrogorski, and their American Informants." JOURNAL OF URBAN HISTORY 4 (1978): 397-416.

Finds that many urban reformers professed a patrician elitist theory of political power which held that governance was the province of men of wealth, status and ability. Finds differences between Bryce and Ostrogorski in their attitudes toward the economic order and toward immigrants.

369 Hancock, John. "History and the 'Living City.'" NORTH DAKOTA QUARTERLY 34 (1966): 100-106.

Contrasts the elite city of earlier times with the broad-based metropolis of the mid-twentieth century and emphasizes the need for all urban dwellers to attempt to master the environment in which they live.

370 Hauser, Philip M. "Chicago--Urban Crisis Exemplar." URBANISM PAST AND PRESENT 1 (1975-76): 15-23.

Asserts that America is seeking to meet the urban crisis of the twentieth century with the values, ideologies, and institutions of the nineteenth century. Attributes the crisis to the "social morphological revolution" consisting of population explosion, implosion, displosion, and technoplosion.

371 Holtan, Orley I. "Individualism, Alienation and the Search for Community: Urban Imagery in Recent American Films." JOURNAL OF POPULAR CULTURE 4 (1971): 933-42.

Finds that the portrayal of the city as an inhumane jungle in many films of the late 1960s indicates the death of the agrarian ideal, the failure of the suburban compromise, and a growing revulsion against urban living.

372 Horowitz, Daniel. "The Meaning of City Biographies: New Haven in the Nineteenth and Early Twentieth Centuries." CONNECTICUT HISTORICAL SOCIETY BULLETIN 29 (1964): 65-75.

Examines the biographies of New Haven written in the nineteenth and early twentieth centuries and contrasts them with academic and booster histories of that city and of Kansas City. Finds that the authors had mixed feelings about the changing composition of the city.

373 Howe, Frederick C. THE CITY: THE HOPE OF DEMOCRACY. Seattle: University of Washington Press, 1969. 319 p.

Analyzes urban problems largely from an economic viewpoint and makes the author's case for municipal ownership of utilities and tax reform, based upon his theoretical expertise and his practical experience.

374 _____. THE MODERN CITY AND ITS PROBLEMS. Folcroft, Pa.: Folcroft Library Editions, 1979. 390 p.

Attributes the urban crisis of the turn-of-the-century to legal institutions and political limitations, rather than to bad people. Presents an agenda for urban reform and professes a faith in the future of American urban civilization.

375　Hughes, Paul J.L. "Edward Everett Hale and the American City." Ph.D. dissertation, New York University, 1975. 320 p.

　　Describes the life of Hale and attributes the development of various social agencies and programs to his ideas and influence in urban reform.

376　Huth, Mary Jo. THE URBAN HABITAT: PAST, PRESENT, AND FUTURE. Chicago: Nelson-Hall, 1978. 305 p.

　　Studies man's relationships to the urban environment, the evolution from preindustrial to industrial cities, various sociological and theoretical perspectives on urbanization, and European and American planning policies and programs. Concludes with a proposal for more humane cities through the construction of new towns.

377　Kail, Thomas E. "Urban Visions and Visionaries: Responses to the Rise of the Industrial City." Ph.D. dissertation, University of Toledo, 1975. 309 p.

　　Explores urban attitudes of individuals such as Edward Everett Hale, Washington Gladden, Brand Whitlock, James B. Matthews, Henry C. Burner, and William A. White, showing their enthusiasm for America being on the threshold of an urban age.

378　Kirschner, Don S. CITY AND COUNTRY: RURAL RESPONSES TO URBANIZATION IN THE 1920S. Westport, Conn.: Greenwood Press, 1970. 279 p.

　　Deals chiefly with rural attitudes toward the city in the decade after the United States officially became an urban nation. Focuses on the political manifestations of those attitudes.

379　Klebanow, Diana. "E.L. Godkin, The City, and Civic Responsibility." NEW YORK HISTORICAL SOCIETY QUARTERLY 55 (1971): 52-75.

　　Asserts that Godkin's contributions to the literature of civic reform have been largely ignored by scholars. Contends that Godkin was one of the first writers to recognize that America was becoming an urban nation and to call for increased civic responsibility.

380　_____. "Edward L. Godkin and the American City." Ph.D. dissertation, New York University. 1965. 225 p.

　　Discovers that Godkin devoted many of his editorials to rapid urbanization, city social patterns, and to tensions in the urban environment and that he maintained a generally positive attitude toward city life, despite occasional suggestions for limiting suffrage by property qualifications.

The City in American Thought

381   Kramer, Paul, and Holborn, Frederick L., eds. THE CITY IN AMERICAN LIFE: COLONIAL TIMES TO THE PRESENT. New York: Capricorn Books, 1970. 384 p.

Contains reprints of seventeen essays on different aspects of cities and urban life by many well-known urban historians. Includes several seminal theoretical pieces as well as studies of such diverse cities as Washington; Memphis; Billings, Montana; New York City; and Los Angeles. Contributors include Arthur M. Schlesinger, Sam Bass Warner, Oscar Handlin, Richard Wade, Constance McLaughlin Green, Nathan Glazer, Daniel Patrick Moynihan, and James Q. Wilson.

382   Kristol, Irving. "Urban Civilization and Its Discontents." COMMENTARY 50 (1970): 29-35.

Evaluates the impact of urbanization upon the values and political system of the founding fathers and asserts that it is vital for the nation to evolve a set of values and a conception of democracy that can function as the equivalent of the "republican morality" of the late eighteenth century.

383   McElrath, Dennis. "The New Urbanization." CENTENNIAL REVIEW 10 (1966): 400-413.

Considers the causes and consequences of two new and contrasting types of contemporary urbanization: accelerated city growth in developing and new nations, and in the older industrial nations, "the decompression of an urban population; the creation of a horizontal city; and the development of a new style of life."

384   Mann, Arthur; Harris, Neil; and Warner, Sam Bass, Jr. HISTORY AND THE ROLE OF THE CITY IN AMERICAN LIFE. Indianapolis: Indiana Historical Society, 1972. 65 p.

Three addresses that formed the 1971-1972 Indiana Historical Society Lectures. Mann's "The City as a Melting Pot" discusses key concepts of American nationality and ethnicity. Harris's "Four Stages of Cultural Growth: The American City," traces the changing definitions and impacts of urban culture, while Warner's "An Urban Historian's Agenda for the Profession" presents a critique of the orientation of academic history and, using urban history as an example, suggests ways in which historical study could play a socially useful role and attract a wider following.

385   Margon, Arthur. "Urbanization in Fiction: Changing Models of Heroism in Popular American Novels, 1880-1920." AMERICAN STUDIES 17 (1976): 71-86.

Argues that the demise of the hero as an important theme in popular fiction emerged from "growing reservations about the compatibility of individualism and the public welfare in the industrial city."

386   Marx, Leo. THE MACHINE IN THE GARDEN. New York: Oxford University Press, 1964. 392 p.

Analyzes the works of nineteenth- and early twentieth-century writers and asserts that a good part of our ideas about cities are based upon a view of the good life as a pastoral one.

387   Matthews, Fred H. QUEST FOR AN AMERICAN SOCIOLOGY: ROBERT E. PARK AND THE CHICAGO SCHOOL. Montreal: McGill-Queen University Press, 1977. 278 p.

Investigates Park's early career as a writer and publicist for Booker T. Washington and the Tuskegee Institute and his later focus as a sociologist on the modern city and the interaction of its varied peoples and cultures. Analyzes Park's social theories and his impact upon the developing field of sociology.

388   Monkkonen, Eric. "Socializing the New Urbanites: Horatio Alger Jr.'s Guidebooks." JOURNAL OF POPULAR CULTURE 11 (1977): 77-87.

Native-born white migrants to the nineteenth-century cities held expectations of upward mobility, and the Alger novels may be seen as "how to do it manuals," providing both exhortative and practical advice for achieving success within the city.

389   Morgan, E. FALLING APART: THE RISE AND DECLINE OF URBAN CIVILIZATION. London: Souvenir Press, 1976. 272 p.

Speculates on the history and nature of urban civilization, its impact on human development, factors in the contemporary world structuring the so-called urban crisis, and the possibilities and implications of deurbanization process as the ultimate solution.

390   Moynihan, Daniel P. "The Soulless City." AMERICAN HERITAGE 20 (1969): 4-9, 78-85.

Provides an historical background to the contemporary "urban crisis" by identifying and discussing several key themes in the American urban tradition: violence, migration, the accumulation of great wealth, mobility, antiurban bias, and the "singular ugliness of the average American city."

391 Muller, Dorothea R. "Josiah Strong and the Challenge of the City." Ph.D. dissertation, New York University, 1956. 405 p.

> Discusses Josiah Strong's philosophy of social Christianity and his activities as a religious reformer and organizer, stressing the critical importance of cities in his belief system. Sees Strong as a major figure in helping America adjust to the ongoing urban revolution.

392 Mumford, Lewis. THE CULTURE OF CITIES. New York: Harcourt Brace Jovanovich, 1970. 586 p.

> Far-ranging philosophical and historical inquiry exploring the nature and role of cities in the Western world, the broad forces which have affected their growth, size, socioeconomic structure, and cultural styles, and identifying the changing nature of urban forms, ultimately detailing a social basis for a "new urban order."

393 _____. "Utopia the City and the Machine." DAEDALUS 94 (1965): 271-92.

> Speculations on the possibility of an original archetypal city that in fact constituted the original utopia, the image of which, perpetuated as myth, has underlain all succeeding concepts of utopia.

394 Nevins, Allan, ed. DIARY OF PHILIP HONE, 1828-1851. New York: Dodd, Mead and Co., 1927. Reprint. New York: Arno Press, 1970. 962 p.

> Presents a perceptive, and often sensitive, upper-class view of the impact of urbanization and immigration on New York City in the period by a prominent businessman and mayor.

395 Ogburn, William F. SOCIAL CHARACTERISTICS OF CITIES: A BASIS FOR NEW INTERPRETATIONS OF THE ROLE OF THE CITY IN AMERICAN LIFE. Chicago: International Manager's Association, 1937. Reprint. New York: Arno Press, 1978. 70 p.

> Deals with population traits, occupations, family life, social services, daily living, and regional differences of large cities, and discusses the growing importance and influence of suburbs and satellite cities.

396 Park, Robert E.; Burgess, Ernest W.; and McKenzie, Roderick D. THE CITY. Chicago: University of Chicago Press, 1968. 239 p.

> Contains ten essays by members of the Chicago School of Sociology stressing the themes of human ecology, community, and environmentalism. Includes a bibliography on the urban community by Louis Wirth.

397 Paterson, John. "The Poet and the Metropolis." In AMERICAN ENVIRONMENT: PERCEPTIONS AND POLICIES, edited by Wreford J. Wilson and Timothy O'Riordan, pp. 91-108. London: John Wiley and Sons, 1976.

> Focuses on the poets of the metropolis in America and their writings about New York and Chicago, identifying several common themes, e.g., the city as stimulation, the city as structure, the city as hero,--and painting a brief overview of the city in American life and thought.

398 Quandt, Jean B. "From the Small Town to the Great Community: The Idea of Community in the Progressive Era." Ph.D. dissertation, Rutgers University, 1970. 407 p.

> Examines the views of several progressive era intellectuals who feared the loss of small town values and advocated such social structures as the settlement house, the community center, and the neighborhood to revive them. Feels that they foundered on the impossible task of harmonizing the town meeting ethos with the need for efficiency and expertise.

399 Raleigh, J.H. "The Novel and the City: England and America in the Nineteenth Century." VICTORIAN STUDIES 11 (1968): 290-328.

> Considers images of the city in major English and American novels of the nineteenth century, and discusses the impact of urban growth from a philosophical and literary perspective.

400 Reed, Marvin E., Jr. "Theodore Roosevelt: The Search for Community in the Urban Age." Ph.D. dissertation, Tulane University, 1971. 228 p.

> Intellectual biography contending that the apparently contradictory nature of Roosevelt's thought and policies assumes a coherent unity "in their relationship to his search for community in the urban age."

401 Reid, Bill G. "The Agrarian Tradition and Urban Problems." MIDWEST QUARTERLY 6 (1964): 75-88.

> Explores the roots and nature of the American tradition of agrarianism and antipathy toward urban life, and considers the ways in which this tradition "complicated America's transition from a farming nation to an industrial, urbanized country.

402 Ricciotti, Dominic. "The Urban Scene: Images of the City in American Painting, 1890-1930." Ph.D. dissertation, Indiana University, 1977. 595 p.

> Analyzes the themes and subjects of urban painters and con-

cludes that they expressed varying political persuasions and a generally prourban attitude. Pronounces their work a major expression of a new urban culture.

403   Riess, Steven A. "Professional Baseball and American Culture in the Progressive Era: Myths and Realities, with Special Emphasis on Atlanta, Chicago, and New York." Ph.D. dissertation, University of Chicago, 1974. 387 p.

Examines three cultural myths about baseball: agrarianism, social integration, and social democracy. Argues that the data fails to sustain the validity of any of these three assumptions.

404   Schmitt, Peter J. BACK TO NATURE: THE ARCADIAN MYTH IN URBAN AMERICA. New York: Oxford University Press, 1969. 230 p.

Examines the evolution of the "back to nature" movement in the first three decades of the twentieth century. Dubs it an upper- and upper middle-class movement, which neither rejected the city nor its amenities, but rather sought to graft the values and benefits of rustic living into urban institutions and settings.

405   Schneider, John C. "Community and Order in Philadelphia, 1834-1844." MARYLAND HISTORIAN 4 (1974): 15-26.

Contends that to Philadelphia of the early nineteenth century, the best guarantee of civic order was not governmental action, but public opinion and the volunteer tradition, and focuses on the city's experience with mob violence during the years 1834-44 to illustrate the power of these values.

406   Sennett, Richard, ed. CLASSIC ESSAYS ON CULTURAL CITIES. Englewood Cliffs, N.J.: Prentice-Hall, 1969. 233 p.

Contains essays on city culture by a group of historians, anthropologists, and sociologists, including Max Weber, Robert Park, Louis Wirth, Oswald Spengler, and Robert Redfield.

407   Shideler, James H. "Flappers, Philosophers, and Farmers: Rural-Urban Tensions of the Twenties." AGRICULTURAL HISTORY 47 (1973): 283-99.

Discusses various aspects of the clash between rural agrarian traditions and the rush of modernizing urbanism in the 1920s, indicating philosophical, literary, and political implications and manifestations of the tensions generated by societal change.

408   Siegel, Adrienne. "The Image of the American City in Popular Literature, 1840-1870." Ph.D. dissertation, New York University, 1973. 410 p.

> Reveals the mood expressed in the literature during the turbulent years of urban growth between 1840 and 1870 to be one of optimism and belief in the power of the individual to make his mark in the world.

409   _____. "When Cities Were Fun: The Image of the American City in Popular Books, 1840-1870." JOURNAL OF POPULAR CULTURE 9 (1975): 573-82.

> Surveys popular or mass literature of the mid-nineteenth century, discovering that, in contrast to the philosophical comments of intellectuals, these books frequently portrayed the city in a positive vein, stressing material pleasures and advancement, excitement, and freedom. Suggests that these "pop urban novels" may have played a role in the rural to urban migration of that century.

410   Smith, Page. AS A CITY UPON A HILL. New York: Knopf, 1966. 332 p.

> Pioneer study exploring the historical impact and signficance of the town in America. Focuses mainly on New England towns, discussing religion, economics, politics, social life, and social structure, and the ideology, imagery, and mythology of the town.

411   Stein, Maurice R. THE ECLIPSE OF COMMUNITY: AN INTERPRETATION OF AMERICAN STUDIES. Princeton, N.J.: Princeton University Press, 1960. 354 p.

> Interpretive volume focusing on changing patterns of American community life, based on major sociological field studies of the twentieth century. A concluding section presents anthropological, psychoanalytic, and sociological perspectives on the modern community.

412   Strong, Josiah. THE TWENTIETH CENTURY CITY. 1898. Reprint. New York: Arno Press, 1970. 186 p.

> Expresses concern over the future shape of large cities and their increasingly immigrant-stock populations and proposes increased efforts at evangelizing them by Protestant churches.

413   Szuberla, Guy. "Making the Sublime Mechanical: Henry Blake Fuller's Chicago." AMERICAN STUDIES 14 (1973-74): 83-94.

> Examines Fuller's notion of the "city-scape" as the great liberating environment for the human senses, a man-made

Arcadia. Sees his work as a powerful antidote to the antiurban strain in American literature and thought.

414   Thomas, John L. "Utopia for an Urban Age: Henry George, Henry Demarest Lloyd, Edward Bellamy." PERSPECTIVES IN AMERICAN HISTORY 6 (1972): 135-63.

Contends that a survey of the careers and works of George, Lloyd, and Bellamy reveals "a nearly identical concern with the contradictions involved in adjusting an older agrarian liberal creed to the realities of a new, urban, industrial America."

415   Turner, Ralph E. "Industrial City-Center of Cultural Change." In THE CULTURAL APPROACH TO HISTORY, edited by Caroline F. Ware, pp. 228-42. New York: Columbia University Press, 1940.

Argues that the industrial city served as a focus of technological, political, intellectual, and aesthetic changes and a theater for the transformation of behavior and thought among urban populations. Contends that the realities of urban-industrial existence, particularly the labor market, machine technology, and urban association, overwhelmed traditional or peasant modes.

416   Wade, Richard C. "The City in History--Some American Perspectives." In URBAN LIFE AND FORM, edited by Werner Z. Hirch, pp. 59-79. New York: Holt, Rinehart, and Winston, 1963.

Reinterprets American history from an urban perspective, stressing the important role of cities in shaping American economic, social, political, and cultural life since the Revolution.

417   _____. "Violence in the Cities: A Historical View." In URBAN VIOLENCE, edited by C.U. Daley, pp. 7-26. Chicago: University of Chicago, Center for Policy Study, 1969.

Surveys outbreaks of urban violence, analyzing their origins and consequences, identifying such background conditions as the loose and heterogeneous social structure of American cities with weak internal and external controls, and more direct factors like politics, labor disputes, ethnicity, and race, arguing that the last has been the most persistent source of civil disorders.

418   Walker, Robert H. "The Poet and the Rise of the City." JOURNAL OF AMERICAN HISTORY 49 (1962): 85-99.

A survey of the poetry of the Gilded Age reveals antiurban bias demonstrating the strength of America's agrarian traditions as well as the defensive position of the farmer at the end of the nineteenth century.

419 Weber, Max. THE CITY. New York: Colliers Books, 1962. 242 p.

> Classic theoretical statement on the essential meaning and importance of the city, written from a social-behaviorism perspective. Developed a concept of the urban community as "a total systematic unit of inter-human life distinguished not by a single institution but by an order of institutions."

420 Weimer, David R. CITY AND COUNTRY IN AMERICA. New York: Appleton-Century-Crofts, 1962. 399 p.

> Collection of readings, mainly didactic and analytical, focusing on expressions of agrarianism, urbanism, and regionalism in American thought, drawn from the works of philosophers, authors, architects, and planners whose works have either helped to shape or embodied these positions.

421 Weiner, Howard R. "The Response to the American City, 1885-1919: as Reflected in Writings Dealing with the City in Scholarly and Professional Serial Publications." Ph.D. dissertation, New York University, 1972. 371 p.

> Analyzes the attitudes exhibited toward the city by historians, economists, sociologists, political scientists, educators, and urban affairs experts, as expressed in such journals as MUNICIPAL AFFAIRS, AMERICAN CITY, and NATIONAL MUNICIPAL REVIEW. Avers that their most important response was an abandonment of the traditions of frontier individualism and a call for more governmental action to deal with urban problems.

422 White, Dana F. "The Self-Conscious City: A Survey and Bibliographical Summary of Periodical Literature on American Urban Themes, 1865-1900." Ph.D. dissertation, George Washington University, 1969. 712 p.

> Analyzes the development of urban awareness at the close of the Civil War as experienced and described by its contemporaries. Serves as a "counterbalance to many previous, overly-structured and problem-oriented interpretations of the rise of the city in American life."

423 White, Morton. "The Philosophers and the Metropolis in America." In URBAN LIFE AND FORM, edited by Werner Z. Hirch, pp. 81-89. New York: Holt, Rinehart, and Winston, 1963.

> Details the prevalence of antiurban sentiments in the writings of America's most influential philosophers, contending that they have exalted rural virtues while viewing the city and its inhabitants with mistrust.

424 White, Morton, and White, Lucia. THE INTELLECTUALS VERSUS THE CITY: FROM THOMAS JEFFERSON TO FRANK LLOYD WRIGHT. Cambridge, Mass.: Harvard University Press, 1962. 270 p.

    Landmark study detailing and analyzing the prevalence of antiurban attitudes among American intellectuals as a powerful tradition in the history of American thought.

425 Wiebe, Robert H. THE SEARCH FOR ORDER, 1877-1920. New York: Hill and Wang, 1967. 333 p.

    Locates the unifying theme of the era in the efforts of a new urban middle class of professionals, managers and bureaucrats to impose their values and system upon a society whose old order has been shattered by urbanization, industrialization, and immigration.

426 Wirth, Louis. ON CITIES AND SOCIAL LIFE. Chicago: University of Chicago Press, 1964. 350 p.

    Written by one of the leaders of the Chicago School of Sociology in the 1920s and 1930s; stresses the disorienting impact of urbanization on the social and cultural system of migrants to the city.

427 Wohl, R. Richard. "The 'Country Boy' Myth and Its Place in America Urban Culture: The Nineteenth-Century Contribution." PERSPECTIVES ON AMERICAN HISTORY 3 (1969): 77-158.

    Presents a brief exploration of Wohl's career and interests in urban history followed by the author's explanation of the success theme, as grounded in "the sound realities and ideological sentiments of nineteenth century, urban America," through an analysis of the nature and persistence of the myth of the yeoman in an increasingly urbanizing nation.

428 Yearley, Clifton K. "The 'Provincial Party' and the Megalopolises: London, Paris, and New York, 1850-1910." COMPARATIVE STUDIES IN SOCIETY AND HISTORY 15 (1973): 51-88.

    Discusses modern urbanization in terms of social struggles for control of the dominant institutions of great cities, indicating middle- versus working-class tension, but focusing predominantly on the "provincial party," not a conventional political party per se but typifying those adhering to a traditionalized concept of community threatened by the development of the modern city.

429 Zangrando, Joanna Schneider. "Monumental Bridge Design in Washington, D.C. as a Reflection of American Culture, 1886-1932." Ph.D. dissertation, George Washington University, 1974. 583 p.

Seeks to bridge the separation between art and utility by studying the nature of the aesthetic and functional concerns in the designing and construction of a monumental, memorial bridge in Washington, D.C.

HISTORIOGRAPHY

430 Blumin, Stuart M. "In Pursuit of the American City." JOURNAL OF INTERDISCIPLINARY HISTORY 2 (1971): 173-78.

Uses a review essay of Harold Mayer and Richard Wade's CHICAGO (no. 593) and Sam Bass Warner's PRIVATE CITY (no. 61) to speculate on the possibilities of producing a grand framework of the American urban past and its impact upon American society and culture, comparable to Frederick Jackson Turner's frontier thesis.

431 Breeman, Richard R. "The New Social History and the Search for 'Community' in Colonial America." AMERICAN QUARTERLY 24 (1977): 422-43.

Praises the emergence of the new social history and its focus upon community studies but calls for union of anthropological theory and historical technique in order to fashion these disparate studies into some coherent interpretive pattern.

432 Conzen, Kathleen Neils. "Approaches to Early Milwaukee Community History." MILWAUKEE HISTORY 1 (1978): 4-12.

Discusses the relative importance of a variety of sources, both systematic and impressionistic, for constructing a community study of early Milwaukee. Focuses mainly upon manuscript censuses, city directories, maps, censuses of manufacturers, newspapers, and "mug books."

433 Curran, Donald J. "Historical Approach to a Study of a Metropolitan Area." LAND ECONOMICS 42 (1966): 209-15.

Insists that there are unique and valuable rewards to be had from examining a metropolitan area, such as Milwaukee, from a historical viewpoint, including fresh methodology, the testing of hypotheses, sifting and winnowing of evidence, reliability, forecasting, and policy projections.

434 Davis, Lenwood G. A HISTORY OF URBAN GROWTH AND DEVELOPMENT: A SELECTED BIBLIOGRAPHY OF PUBLIC WORKS ON THE STATES, 1872-1975. 2d ed. Monticello, Ill.: Council of Planning Libraries, 1976. 28 p.

Bibliographical listing of approximately 150 articles and 200 books on urban-related subjects. Emphasizes the status of blacks in the city.

435 Ershkowitz, Herbert. THE PEOPLE OF JACKSONIAN CITY. St. Charles, Mo.: Forum Press, 1973.

Synthesizes most significant recent scholarship on the phenomenon of mobs and violence in American cities in the antebellum period.

436 Finster, Jerome, ed. THE NATIONAL ARCHIVES AND URBAN RESEARCH. Athens: Ohio University Press, 1974. 164 p.

Contains historical and historiographical essays on the literature of urban housing, population, transportation, and federal impact on cities, proposes new directions for future research, and warns researchers of pitfalls to be avoided in using materials in the archives.

437 Glaab, Charles N. "The Historian and the American City: A Bibliographic Survey." In THE STUDY OF URBANIZATION, edited by Philip M. Hauser and Leo F. Schnore, pp. 53-80. New York: John Wiley and Sons, 1966.

Bibliographic essay organized around the themes of the development of urban history, its conceptual framework, the process of immigration, general works, urban biographies, period studies, urban rivalry and transportation, and special themes.

438 Green, Constance McLaughlin. "The Value of Local History." In THE CULTURAL APPROACH TO HISTORY, edited by Caroline F. Ware, pp. 275-86. New York: Columbia University Press, 1940.

Contends that local history should be the life history of a community especially its social and economic aspects. Raises many questions that historians must research at the local level and suggests many possible sources of material.

439 Gutman, Robert, and Popenoe, David. "Urban Studies." AMERICAN BEHAVIORAL SCIENTIST 6 (1963): 4-23.

Surveys the important books on urban studies published between 1952 and 1962, delineates its role as a field of research, and discusses the discipline's relationship to higher education.

440 Haraven, Tamara. "The Historical Study of the Family in Urban Society." JOURNAL OF URBAN HISTORY 1 (1975): 259-67.

Reviews the recent literature on the interaction between the family and the city and finds that the trend is to view the family as an institution interacting with other societal processes and to counteract the notion that urban life had a devastating effect on family life.

441 Hershberg, Theodore. "The New Urban History: Toward an Interdisciplinary History of the City." JOURNAL OF URBAN HISTORY 5 (1978): 41-68.

Faults urban historians for failing to develop a conceptual framework for the study of urban history and suggests one based upon the classification of urban environments and the fruits of the new urban social history. Delineates a plan for the organization of research so as to produce an urban process.

442 Hoover, Dwight W. CITIES. New York: Bowker, 1976. 231 p.

An annotated bibliography of over one thousand books, films, filmstrips and journals dealing with urban-related topics. Divided into two major parts, one dealing with the historical roots of urban crisis, the other with the city as viewed by the practitioners of a variety of academic disciplines.

443 _____. "The Diverging Paths of American Urban History." AMERICAN QUARTERLY 20 (1968): 296-317.

Discusses and analyzes the concepts and approaches of the major urban historians from Arthur M. Schlesinger, Sr., to the late 1960s. Relates their major conceptual frameworks to theories in sociology and human ecology and speculates on the future orientation of the discipline.

444 _____. "Surveying the American Urban Past." JOURNAL OF URBAN HISTORY 1 (1974): 111-15.

Compares Warner's URBAN WILDERNESS (no. 62); Miller's URBANIZATION OF MODERN AMERICA (no. 29); McKelvey's AMERICAN URBANIZATION (no. 22); Still's URBAN AMERICA (no. 50); and Mohl and Richardson's URBAN EXPERIENCE (no. 95). Stresses the differences in emphasis and approach to emphasize the variety of themes in urban history.

445 Hopkins, Richard J. "Mobility and the New Urban History." JOURNAL OF URBAN HISTORY 1 (1975): 217-28.

Compares Peter Knights's THE PLAIN PEOPLE OF BOSTON (no. 240); Howard Chudacoff's MOBILE AMERICANS (no. 164); and Stephan Thernstrom's THE OTHER BOSTONIANS (no. 1407); and finds a common interest in occupational and geographic mobility, but significant differences of emphasis and methodology. Faults all three for failing to make a "full disclosure" of their methodology.

446 Klebanow, Diana; Jonas, Franklin; and Leonard, Ira M. URBAN LEGACY: THE STORY OF AMERICA'S CITIES. New York: New American Library, 1977. 421 p.

Surveys the field of urban history and summarizes the major schools of interpretation for most important questions. Focuses upon community development, the evolution of the metropolis, and the situation of ethnic minorities.

447 Lampard Eric E. "American Historians and the Study of Urbanization." AMERICAN HISTORICAL REVIEW 67 (1961): 49-61.

A critique of historical studies of American urbanization, concluding with a suggestion for two new approaches: "the study of urbanization as a societal process," and "the comparative study of communities in a framework of human ecology."

448 _____. "The Dimensions of Urban History: A Footnote to the Urban Crisis." PACIFIC HISTORICAL REVIEW 39 (1970): 261-78.

Summarizes and criticizes the traditional approaches of urban history and suggests the need for analyses that begin from a more generalized process-oriented perspective.

449 McKee, James B. "Urbanism and the Problem of Social Order." CENTENNIAL REVIEW 10 (1966): 382-99.

Historiographical discussion of urban sociology asserting that "the effort of sociologists to create a theory of urbanism never managed to transcend that intellectual perspective which saw in the city a symbol of social disorder."

450 McKelvey, Blake. "American Urban History Today." AMERICAN HISTORICAL REVIEW 57 (1952): 919-29.

Comments on the state of urban history since the 1930s, emphasizing the awakening interest in the field. Prints a bibliographic essay indicating major trends in scholarship and neglected areas demanding study.

451 _____. "A City Historian's Report." ROCHESTER HISTORY 35 (1973): 1-24.

McKelvey reminisces about his thirty-seven years as a historian for the city of Rochester, providing a perspective on the development of urban history in the United States.

452 _____. "The Metropolis and the Historian." NIAGARA FRONTIER 12 (1965): 77-80.

> Discusses research agendas and opportunities for the urban historian in regard to the development and impact of the twentieth-century metropolis.

453 _____. "The Urban History Group Newsletter." URBANISM PAST AND PRESENT 1 (1975-76): 36-37.

> Discusses the inception of the newsletter, reviews some of the early issues and reports on its transformation into a journal, URBANISM: PAST AND PRESENT.

454 Miller, Zane. "Urban History, Urban Crises, and Public Policy." URBANISM PAST AND PRESENT 1 (1975-76): 1-6.

> Historiographical essay on urban history, keyed to the notion that societal definitions and perceptions of cities influence research agendas. Concludes with a listing of areas demanding research, stressing that information on these topics can have a positive impact on the formulation of public policy to solve the current metropolitan crisis.

455 Schnore, Leo F. "Urban History and the Social Sciences: An Uneasy Marriage." JOURNAL OF URBAN HISTORY 1 (1975): 395-408.

> Presents the author's retrospective account of the development of his professional interest in urbanization, particularly with regard to his belief in the importance of history in studying urban phenomena from various disciplinary perspectives.

456 Schultz, Frederick M. A SELECTED BIBLIOGRAPHY OF THE AMERICAN CITY. Bloomington, Ind.: Indiana University Press, 1967. 71 p.

> Interdisciplinary bibliography representing the initial stage of a larger project to develop a "comprehensive interdisciplinary bibliography of secondary sources in the American city and the process of urbanization." Emphasizes books, and contains about 1,100 entries. No annotations.

457 Sharpless, John B., and Warner, Sam Bass, Jr. "Urban History." AMERICAN BEHAVIORAL SCIENTIST 2 (1977): 221-44.

> Presents an overview of trends in urban history scholarship which summarizes the field as "a series of urban related studies which build on established interests in social and economic reform and its concern for the contrasts among the social circumstances of rich and poor, whites, blacks, and immigrants." Argues that great amounts of data have been amassed, but not used in a social-scientific fashion, and con-

tends that the new urban history is a misnomer, for it demonstrates overwhelming continuity with past conventions.

458 Stave, Bruce M. THE MAKING OF URBAN HISTORY: HISTORIOGRAPHY THROUGH ORAL HISTORY. Beverly Hills, Calif.: Sage Publications, 1977. 336 p.

Contains transcripts of the editor's conversations with Blake McKelvey, Bayrd Still, Constance McLaughlin Green, Oscar Handlin, Richard Wade, Sam Bass Warner, Stephan Thernstrom, Eric Lampard, and Samuel P. Hays. Includes an introductory essay by Stave, notes, and a selected bibliography of works by each historian.

459 Still, Bayrd. "Problems of an Urban Biographer." HISTORICAL MESSENGER OF THE MILWAUKEE COUNTY HISTORICAL SOCIETY 23 (1967): 34-43.

Presents Still's address to the Milwaukee County Historical Society concerning the problems he encountered in writing his history of Milwaukee, a future research agenda for historians of that city, and the changing state of urban history.

460 Thernstrom, Stephan. "The New Urban History." In THE FUTURE OF HISTORY, edited by Charles F. Delzell, pp. 43-52. Nashville: Vanderbilt University Press, 1977.

Contends that "the new urban history is not so new, it should not be identified as urban, and there is some danger that it will cease to be history." Considers the historical roots, present status, and future possibilities for the field, and argues the need for better written and more intelligently conceived works as opposed to relying solely upon quantitative methodology and social science jargon.

461 _____. "Reflections on the New Urban History." DAEDALUS 100 (1971): 359-75.

Discusses some of the inadequacies of the term "new urban history," then reviews some of the positive contributions of its practitioners with regard to studies of urban population fluidity, class and ethnic differentials in spatial mobility, rates and rates and trends in social mobility, and immigration and differential opportunity.

462 Tilly, Charles. "The State of Urbanization." COMPARATIVE STUDIES IN SOCIETY AND HISTORY 10 (1967): 100-113.

Reviews several major works dealing with urbanization in a variety of world areas and suggests the need for synthesis and for a standardization of concepts and terminology.

463 Wade, Richard C. "An Agenda for Urban History." In THE STATE OF AMERICAN HISTORY, edited by Herbert Bass, pp. 43-65. Chicago: Quadrangle Books, 1970.

> Discusses the reasons for the tardiness of historians to come to grips with urbanization as a major theme and suggests several aspects of the topic which require intensive analysis. Regards the first task as description and analysis of urban growth and the second as assessing the impact of urbanization on the development of the United States.

464 _____. "Urbanization." In COMPARATIVE APPROACH TO AMERICAN HISTORY, edited by C. Vann Woodward, pp. 187-205. New York: Basic Books, 1968.

> Presents an overview of the development of urbanization in the United States stressing the importance of the eighteenth-century commercial city and the rise of the modern city.

465 White, Dana F. "The Underdeveloped Discipline: Interdisciplinary Directions in American Urban History." In AMERICAN STUDIES: TOPICS AND SOURCES, edited by Robert H. Walker, pp. 152-70. Westport, Conn.: Greenwood Press, 1976.

> Bibliographic essay surveying the present state of urban history, styled as still an "underdeveloped discipline" but one that shows some promising signs of coming to grips with urbanization as a process. Also comments on classroom and research projects.

Chapter 4
SINGLE CITY STUDIES

466   Abbott, Bernice, and McCausland, Elizabeth. NEW YORK IN THE THIRTIES. New York: Dover Publications, 1973. 97 p.

    Contains almost one hundred black and white photographs of a wide spectrum of New York City scenes during the Depression decade. Includes explanatory notes concerning the significances of the subject matter of the photograph to the life of the city.

467   Abbott, Carl. "Norfolk in the New Century: The Jamestown Exposition and Urban Boosterism." VIRGINIA MAGAZINE OF HISTORY AND BIOGRAPHY 85 (1977): 86-96.

    Contends that New South advocates were every bit as prone to boosterism as were their counterparts in frontier cities. Demonstrates that their concept of urban progress fully justified excluding blacks from civic affairs.

468   _____. "Suburb and City: Changing Patterns of Socioeconomic Status in Metropolitan Denver since 1940." SOCIAL SCIENCE HISTORY 2 (1977): 53-71.

    Compares the five counties which comprise metropolitan Denver with respect to occupational status, income, education, and ethnic composition. Concludes that the city's suburbs continue to demonstrate significant differentiation in status and that older "stranded suburbs" have taken on many of the interests and social characteristics of the central city.

469   Adams, J.S., ed. CONTEMPORARY METROPOLITAN AMERICA. Vol. 1, CITIES OF THE NATION'S HISTORIC METROPOLITAN CORE; Vol. 2, NINETEENTH CENTURY PORTS; Vol. 3, NINETEENTH CENTURY INLAND CENTERS AND PORTS; Vol. 4, TWENTIETH CENTURY CITIES. Cambridge, Mass.: Ballinger, 1976. 354, 314, 507, 350 p.

    Contains short monographs on the physical, natural, and economic development of the nation's twenty largest metropolitan

Single City Studies

areas, with an introductory essay by James E. Vance, Jr. on the American city as a "workshop for a national culture." Volume 1 deals with Boston, New York, Philadelphia, and central Connecticut; volume 2 with Baltimore, New Orleans, and San Francisco; volume 3 with Pittsburgh, St. Louis, northeastern Ohio, Chicago, Detroit, St. Paul-Minneapolis, and Seattle; and volume 4 with Dallas-Fort Worth, Miami, Atlanta, Los Angeles, and Washington, D.C.

470   Aikman, Duncan, ed. THE TAMING OF THE FRONTIER. New York: Minton Balch and Co., 1925. Reprint. Freeport, N.Y.: Books for Libraries Press, 1967. 319 p.

     Contains essays on El Paso, Ogden, Denver, San Francisco, St. Paul, Portland, Kansas City, San Antonio, Los Angeles, and Cheyenne, each by a different author.

471   Algren, Nelson. CHICAGO: CITY ON THE MAKE. Oakland, Calif.: Angel Island Publications, 1961. 148 p.

     A collection of Algren's essays and short stories which examines the cultural conflict in Chicago between the "live-and-let-livers" and the "do-as-I-sayers."

472   Andrews, Wayne. ARCHITECTURE IN NEW YORK: A PHOTOGRAPHIC HISTORY. New York: Harper and Row, 1973. 212 p.

     Contains numerous photographs on the major architectural features of the city.

473   Axelrod, Bernard. "Rocky Mountain Customs Port of Entry." COLORADO MAGAZINE 41 (1964): 126-34.

     Examines the efforts of Denver to get Congress to have it declared a customs port of entry, a development which significantly augmented the city's economic base and made it the center of trade for the entire region.

474   Bach, Ira J. CHICAGO ON FOOT: AN ARCHITECTURAL WALKING TOUR. Chicago: J.P. O'Hara, 1973. 331 p.

     Includes over thirty walking tours of historical sections of Chicago.

475   _____. "Pullman: A Town Reborn." CHICAGO HISTORY 4 (1975): 44-53.

     Attributes Pullman's growth to the careful planning of its founder and to his concern for attracting and maintaining a stable labor force of skilled mechanics and craftsmen.

Single City Studies

476   Bain, Donald E., Jr. "Urban Decentralization: The Process of Growth in Amherst, New York, 1900-1950." Ph.D. dissertation, State University of New York-Buffalo, 1974. 290 p.

    Traces the evolution of Amherst from a rural township to a middle-class suburb of Buffalo and relates its development to the diminishing population and function of that urban center. Focuses primarily on the era of the 1920s and on the response of the middle class to growing urban problems.

477   Barnes, Joseph W. "The City's Golden Age." ROCHESTER HISTORY 35 (1973): 1-23.

    Concludes that Rochester's businessmen and planners overreached themselves in the 1920s and generated a greater debt level and tax burden than the populace was willing to shoulder, but that the civic improvements of the decade were of great benefit to the general populace.

478   _____. "Rochester's Era of Annexations, 1901-1926." Ph.D. dissertation, State University of New York-Buffalo, 1974. 280 p.

    Finds that Rochester's annexation plans were highly dependent upon the changing political makeup of the state legislature and upon the attitude of suburban residents who balanced higher taxes against the likelihood of better services. Notes that suburbs often delayed annexation by purchasing such services piecemeal.

479   Barrows, Robert G. "The Ninth Federal Cause of Indianapolis: A Case Study in Civic Chauvinism." INDIANA MAGAZINE OF HISTORY 73 (1977): 1-16.

    Argues that civic chauvinism and urban rivalry motivated the political and economic leaders of Indianapolis to take a variety of measures to augment that city's population during a recount of the ninth federal census. Finds that the city actually annexed new lands in order to increase its head count.

480   Barsness, Richard W. "Railroads and Los Angeles: The Quest for a Deep-Water Port." SOUTHERN CALIFORNIA QUARTERLY 47 (1965): 379-94.

    Contends that the efforts of the Southern Pacific to monopolize the harbor facilities severely retarded the city's evolution into a deep water port until the city finally obtained outright municipal control over its harbor facilities.

481   Barton, Thomas F. "Relative Growth of Terre Haute, 1900-1950." PROCEEDINGS OF THE INDIANA ACADEMY OF SCIENCE 60 (1951): 236-38.

Single City Studies

Attributes the city's steady growth between 1850 and 1910 to its location near valuable raw materials and to its favorable transportation nexus. Lists ten reasons for its relative decline since 1910.

482   Beaudet, Paul. "The Growth of Buffalo's Suburban Zone." NIAGARA FRONTIER 18 (1971): 46-63.

Examines the course of suburbanization between 1895 and the 1960s and finds that the period from 1940 to 1960 witnessed the greatest spurt. Relies largely upon population and employment figures to chart its course.

483   Benjamin, Philip S. THE PHILADELPHIA QUAKERS IN THE INDUSTRIAL AGE, 1865-1920. Philadelphia: Temple University Press, 1976. 301 p.

Finds that the Quakers, although a small portion of Philadelphia's population, played a key role as members of the board of banks, corporations, and social agencies. Sees the growing involvement in public service and philanthropy as an attempt to maintain their unique identity.

484   Bigelow, Martha C. Mitchell. "Birmingham: A Biography of a City of the New South." Ph.D. dissertation, University of Chicago, 1946. 294 p.

Deals with the evolution of Birmingham from a cornfield in 1871 to an industrial city of 1910. Focuses upon economic development; government and politics; crime; the laboring classes; health and welfare; civic, professional, cultural, and religious activities; education; and recreation.

485   Bolding, Gary. "Change, Continuity, and Commercial Identity of a Southern City: New Orleans, 1850-1950." LOUISIANA STUDIES 14 (1975): 161-78.

Argues that New Orleans' attachment to the Mississippi River and to its identity as a commercial center prevented it from responding to westward expansion and the technological innovations of the nineteenth century. Concludes that the business community ultimately reconciled the city's traditions with the need for change and insured its prosperity.

486   Brenneman, Bill. MIRACLE ON CHERRY CREEK: AN INFORMAL HISTORY OF THE BIRTH AND REBIRTH OF A NEIGHBORHOOD. Denver: World Press, 1973. 130 p.

Deals with the history, decline, and redevelopment of the area where the city of Denver originated.

487   Brook, Anthony. "Gary, Indiana: Steeltown Extraordinary." JOURNAL OF AMERICAN STUDIES 9 (1975): 35-53.

Single City Studies

Charges that U.S. Steel failed to develop a stable and constructive relationship between the company and the town and that this gap led to a disordered socially divided community. Sees a basic inability to reconcile profit with humanity.

488   Buder, Stanley. PULLMAN: AN EXPERIMENT IN INDUSTRIAL ORDER AND COMMUNITY PLANNING 1880-1930. New York: Oxford University Press, 1967. 263 p.

Presents Pullman as an experiment in town planning and labor relations which was designed to be an agent of fundamental social reform and which failed because its utopian goals gave way to the desire for profit and efficiency and because of the frustrated expectations of its worker-residents.

489   Buehler, Alfred G. "Philadelphia's Experience." PROCEEDINGS OF THE ACADEMY OF POLITICAL SCIENCE 28 (1968): 27-29.

Examines the impact of the city's income tax from its adoption in 1939 and disputes most of the criticisms levied against it. Feels that local taxes have proven easier to levy than have statewide ones.

490   Burgess, Ernest W., and Newcomb, Charles, eds. CENSUS DATA OF THE CITY OF CHICAGO, 1920, 1930. 2 vols. Chicago: University of Chicago Press, 1931, 1933.

Contains breakdown of the data from all the major census categories for each census tract in the city. Includes occupational breakdown, the value of homes by value or monthly rental, and characteristics of families.

491   Burt, Nathaniel. "Philadelphia Plain and Fancy." HORIZON 5 (1963): 5-27.

Focuses upon the city's aristocracy, its residence, and its centers of power. Contains many photographs of the city.

492   Butler, Tod J. "The Cincinnati Southern Railway: A City's Response to Relative Commercial Decline." Ph.D. dissertation, Ohio State University, 1971. 217 p.

Details Cincinnati's unsuccessful efforts to arrest its decline as the "Queen City" of the West by building a municipally owned railroad. Attributes its failure to changes in population distribution, transportation, technology, and marketing techniques.

493   Cable, Mary. "The Marble Cottages." HORIZON 7 (1965): 19-27.

Surveys Newport, Rhode Island, in its salad days as a resort

Single City Studies

area for the elites of Boston and New York. Contains many photographs of prominent residents and residences.

494 Callahan, Helen. "1888--The Flood Threatens Augusta's Efforts to Become 'The Lowell of the South.'" RICHMOND COUNTY HISTORY 7 (1975): 47-60.

Discusses the city's efforts to recover from the disastrous flood and to build a retaining wall to prevent a reoccurrence. Attributes great influence to the New South boosterism of the city's leaders.

495 Chaffee, Eugene B. "Boise: The Founding of a City." IDAHO YESTERDAYS 7 (1963): 2-7.

Attributes the founding of Boise to the efforts of three individuals, a military officer, a surveyor, and a crusading newspaper editor, who attracted capital and settlers and established law and order.

496 Chamberlin, Everett. CHICAGO AND ITS SUBURBS. 1874. Reprint. New York: Arno Press, 1978. 468 p.

Details the growth and development of every Chicago suburb then in existence, and relates their origins to the construction of an urban transportation network.

497 Chapman, Edmund H. CLEVELAND: VILLAGE TO METROPOLIS: A CASE STUDY OF PROBLEMS OF URBAN DEVELOPMENT IN NINETEENTH CENTURY AMERICA. Cleveland: Western Reserve Historical Society, 1965. 165 p.

Attributes Cleveland's extraordinary expansion partly to its favorable location on Lake Erie and partly to its position as seat of the Rockefeller's varied interests.

498 Clark, Dennis. "Invention and Contention in the Quaker City." JOURNAL OF URBAN HISTORY 5 (1979): 265-71.

Reviews four recent books dealing with politics, religion, and technology in Philadelphia in the nineteenth century. Calls for more imaginatively conceived social history projects, such as that in Philadelphia, and for integrative narrative and analytical works to synthesize the findings of the impressive number of monographs that have emerged from such projects.

499 Clark, John G. "New Orleans: Its First Century of Economic Development." LOUISIANA HISTORY 10 (1969): 35-48.

Examines New Orleans' economic development during French

Single City Studies

and Spanish rule and finds it inadequate because the Europeans lacked the physical and technological skills necessary to exploit the untapped wealth of the region.

500 _____. NEW ORLEANS, 1718-1812: AN ECONOMIC HISTORY. Baton Rouge: Louisiana State University Press, 1970. 395 p.

Assigns New Orleans' slow growth in the period to the lack of economic opportunity and to the paucity of goods to trade, both results of the mercantilist policies of the French and Spanish who ruled the city until 1803.

501 _____. "New Orleans and the River: A Study in Attitudes and Responses." LOUISIANA HISTORY 8 (1967): 117-35.

502 Clark, Norman H. MILL TOWN: A SOCIAL HISTORY OF EVERETT, WASHINGTON. Seattle: University of Washington Press, 1970. 267 p.

Traces the development of Everett from its founding as a model town by railroad magnate James J. Hill in 1892 to the massacre during the Red Scare. Stresses the social cleavage between the owners and the workers which spawned the Industrial Workers of the World and led to the massacre.

503 Connors, Margaret E. "Their Own Kind: Family and Community Life in Albany, New York, 1850-1915." Ph.D. dissertation, Harvard University, 1975.

504 Conway, Alan. "New Orleans as a Port of Immigration, 1820-1860." LOUISIANA STUDIES 3 (1962): 1-22.

Emphasizes a combination of economic, commercial, and transportation factors in shaping New Orleans' rise and fall as a port of immigration. Concludes that the advent of the railroad ultimately caused most immigrants to leave the city.

505 Cook, Philip L. "Zion City, Illinois: Twentieth Century Utopia." Ph.D. dissertation, University of Colorado, 1965. 443 p.

Examines the foundation of Zion as a Christian-centered utopia with an economy based upon a skilk factory, a theocratic government, and extensive "blue laws." Concludes that economic failure eventually led to disillusionment and ended the utopian era.

506 Cunningham, Lynn C. "Venice, California: From City to Suburb." Ph.D. dissertation, University of California, Los Angeles, 1976. 303 p.

Single City Studies

        Demonstrates that a change in a community's status from independent municipality to dependent suburb caused little change in the established decision-making pattern, regional planning, or the nature of local conflicts.

507   Curtis, James Robert. "Alviso, California: A Study in Cultural-Historical Geography." Ph.D. dissertation, University of California, Los Angeles, 1978. 305 p.

        Illustrates the settlement dynamics of a small town, its changing land transportation economics, environmental influences, and political and social considerations. Finds that strict enforcement of building codes, changes in zoning, routing of transportation corridors, and other preemptive public policies guaranteed that most of its residents will be forced to relocate.

508   Cutler, Irving. CHICAGO: METROPOLIS OF THE MID-CONTINENT. Dubuque, Iowa: Kendall, Hunt Publishers, 1976. 210 p.

        Looks at Chicago from the viewpoint of an urban geographer--its physical setting, growth, settlement patterns, economy, transportation, development as a metropolis, and its prospects for future growth.

509   Danforth, Brian J. "Hoboken and the Affluent New Yorker's Search for Recreation, 1820-1860." NEW JERSEY HISTORY 95 (1977): 133-44.

        Examines Hoboken's brief career as a resort area for affluent New York City residents. Finds that its proximity to the metropolis was the cause of both its rise and fall, as vacationers eventually sought places farther removed.

510   Davis, Stephen R. "From Plowshares to Spindles: Dedham, Massachusetts, 1790-1840." Ph.D. dissertation, University of Wisconsin, 1973. 457 p.

        Demonstrates how the "village faction" wrested power from the once dominant agrarians, resulting in the ascendancy of the board of selectmen over the town meeting, in occupational specialization and more sophisticated economic organization, and in religious and cultural heterogeneity.

511   Daws, Gavan. "Honolulu in the Nineteenth Century: Notes on the Emergence of Urban Society in Hawaii." JOURNAL OF PACIFIC HISTORY 2 (1967): 77-96.

        Traces the evolution of an urban society and government in the island city during the nineteenth century, forged by the growing economic and cultural dominance over the natives by foreigners.

Single City Studies

512 Dawson, Cole P. "Yankees in the Queen City: The Social and Intellectual Contributions of New Englanders in Cincinnati, 1820-1850." Ph.D. dissertation, Miami University, 1977. 211 p.

> Insists that New Englanders, although never more than one-fifth of the city's population, exerted enormous impact upon Cincinnati's life in the early years, especially in such areas as social welfare, education, literary societies, and the campaign against slavery.

513 Dorsett, Lyle. THE QUEEN CITY: A HISTORY OF DENVER. Boulder, Colo.: Pruett Publishing Co., 1977. 320 p.

> Divides the history of Denver into five periods--"Turnstile Town," 1858-70; "Youthful City," 1870-1904; "The City Beautiful," 1904-23; "Queen City," 1923-World War II; and "Vertical City," since World War II. Focuses primarily on social, political, and cultural institutions and upon their interaction with economic growth.

514 Ebner, Michael H. "Passaic, New Jersey, 1855-1912: City-Building in Post-Civil War America." Ph.D. dissertation, University of Virginia, 1974. 310 p.

> Traces the evolution of Passaic from an island of tranquility with little or no civil strife in the mid-nineteenth century to a national focal point for labor unrest between 1912 and 1926, and an urban crisis center after World War II. Contends that there has been virtually no attempt to understand the causal factors responsible for the change.

515 Ellis, Roy. A CIVIC HISTORY OF KANSAS CITY, MISSOURI. New York: Columbia University Press, 1930. 243 p.

> Deals with the founding of the city, its form of government, transportation system, city plan, industrial enterprises, social institutions, public service corporations, provision of such services as water, fire, police, health, welfare and education, municipal finance, and politics.

516 Ericksen, Eugene P., and Yancey, William L. "Work and Residence in Industrial Philadelphia." JOURNAL OF URBAN HISTORY 5 (1979): 147-82.

> Rejects the model of concentric zones as an explanation for urban development and posits such characteristics as the location of work opportunities, the economics of the journey to work, and available housing supply as the primary determinants of city growth patterns.

Single City Studies

517 Fahey, John. "The Million-Dollar Corner: The Development of Downtown Spokane, 1890-1920." PACIFIC NORTHWEST QUARTERLY 62 (1971): 77-85.

> Argues that the physical pattern and value of downtown Spokane were decreased by land investors who survived the 1889 fire and the 1893 panic, and who built a sterile environment of multipurpose buildings.

518 Farrell, Richard T. "Cincinnati, 1800-1830: Economic Development Through Trade and Industry." OHIO HISTORY 77 (1968): 111-29.

> Focuses on the efforts of manufacturers to create a dual based economy of making industry coequal with commerce and concludes that this diversification equipped the city for the increased specialization and expansion of the next two decades after 1830.

519 Feiss, Carl. "Washington, D.C.: Symbol and City: A Critique of the Physical Plan in its Sociogeographic Setting." In WORLD CAPITALS: TOWARD GUIDED URBANIZATION, edited by H. Wentworth Eldredge, pp. 139-60. Garden City, N.Y.: Anchor Press, Doubleday, 1975.

> Details Washington's problems as a "new town," as a modern city, and as an integrator of diverse populations, and concludes that it is "an excellent capital city with a dynamic, dramatic and distinctive ambiance."

520 Ferdinand, Theodore N. "The Criminal Patterns of Boston Since 1849." AMERICAN JOURNAL OF SOCIOLOGY 73 (1967): 84-99.

> Analyzes arrest records for crimes of violence between 1849 and 1881 and concludes that there has been a notable decline in all categories, except forcible rape. Attributes this largely to structural changes resulting from urbanization--a growing middle class, a more highly urbanized population, and an evolving pattern of social organization.

521 Fine, Sidney. FRANK MURPHY: THE DETROIT YEARS. Ann Arbor: University of Michigan Press, 1975. 608 p.

> Contains information on Detroit in the first three decades of the twentieth century, especially its social makeup and its political patterns. Views Detroit as the premier boom town of the era.

522 Fleming, William F. "San Antonio: The History of a Military City, 1865-1880." Ph.D. dissertation, University of Pennsylvania, 1963. 445 p.

Single City Studies

Attributes the city's growth to refusal to link its economic welfare to the function of supplying goods and services to the military establishment and its consequent search for other income-producing commercial enterprises.

523 Fogelson, Robert M. FRAGMENTED METROPOLIS: LOS ANGELES, 1850-1930. Cambridge, Mass.: Harvard University Press, 1967. 361 p.

Contends that Los Angeles, more than any other major city, succumbed to the disintegrative forces of suburbanization and proliferation to become the archtype of the contemporary American metropolis. Attributes this phenomenon to a mixture of topographical, technological, ethnic, socioeconomic, and political conditions.

524 Foster, Edward H., and Clark, Geoffrey W., eds. HOBOKEN: A COLLECTION OF ESSAYS. New York: Irvington Publishers, 1976. 107 p.

Contains nine essays on various aspects of life in Hoboken from its early days as a resort to its present status. Of particular interest to urbanologists are two essays by Geoffrey W. Clark: "An Interpretation of Hoboken's Population Trends, 1856-1970" and "The Progressives vs. the Political Machine in Hoboken, 1911-1915."

525 Foster, Mark S. "The Model-T, the Hard Sell, and Los Angeles's Urban Growth: The Decentralization of Los Angeles during the 1920s." PACIFIC HISTORICAL REVIEW 44 (1975): 459-84.

Contends that the 1920s was the crucial decade in Los Angeles' commitment to horizontal, as opposed to vertical expansion. Attributes the development primarily to the rise of the automobile, in conjunction with the decade's real estate boom.

526 Funnell, Charles E. "Virgin Stand: Atlantic City, New Jersey as a Mass Resort and Cultural Symbol." Ph.D. dissertation, University of Pennsylvania, 1973. 305 p.

Describes the conflict in desires by Atlantic City to become the "Family Resort of America," offering a pleasurable family setting, and a more vibrant "Pleasure Resort," catering to a faster-paced clientele.

527 Furer, Howard B. "Heaven, Hell, or Hoboken: The Effects of World War I on a New Jersey City." NEW JERSEY HISTORY 92 (1974): 147-69.

Finds that the war and its consequent influx of sailors and government agents led to restrictions on the German popula-

Single City Studies

tion, an influx of Italian and Hungarian immigrants, postwar depression, and creeping urban blight. Concludes that the wartime boom ultimately led to the devastation of the city.

528   Garner, John S. "Leclaire, Illinois: A Model Company Town, 1890-1934." JOURNAL OF THE SOCIETY OF ARCHITECTURAL HISTORIANS 30 (1971): 219-27.

   Proclaims Leclaire as a visual and social success, largely due to intelligent foresight in design and construction. Insists that it provided a decent environment for working-class residents which persisted until its annexation to the larger city of Edwardsville in 1931.

529   Garofalo, Charles. "The Atlanta Spirit: A Study in Urban Ideology." SOUTH ATLANTIC QUARTERLY 74 (1975): 34-44.

   Examines the message of THE CITY BUILDER, an Atlanta magazine, between 1916 and 1935, and finds it to be a mixture of boosterism, togetherness, appeals to civic pride, and nearly religious fervor. Finds the key in the concept of community loyalty which supposedly overcame racial and socioeconomic differences while benefitting the business leadership.

530   Gates, Grace H. "The Making of a Model City: A History of Anniston, Alabama, 1872-1900." Ph.D. dissertation, Emory University, 1976. 536 p.

   Profiles the founders and residents of Anniston, a newly created New South industrial town, using its economic development as a microcosm of the southern industrial revolution.

531   Gazell, James Albert. "The High Noon of Chicago's Bohemias." JOURNAL OF THE ILLINOIS STATE HISTORICAL SOCIETY 65 (1972): 54-68.

   Examines the rise and decay of two of the city's "bohemias," where artists and writers lived and worked. Focuses upon their social institutions and the impact upon their communities of gang warfare during prohibition.

532   German, Richard. "The Queen City of the Savannah: Augusta, Georgia, During the Urban Progressive Era, 1890-1917." Ph.D. dissertation, University of Florida, 1971. 455 p.

   Analyzes the social, political, and economic environment of Augusta during the urban Progressive era.

533   Giannini, Ralph. "San Francisco: Labor's City: 1900-1911." Ph.D. dissertation, University of Florida, 1975. 408 p.

Single City Studies

Examines the rise and the success of the Union Labor party, its dedication to trade union principles, its economic and political goals, and the reasons for its ultimate disappearance.

534 Glen, Grave A. "Old Bay Ridge." JOURNAL OF LONG ISLAND HISTORY 6 (1966): 1-14.

Chronicles everyday life in the Bay Ridge section of Brooklyn during the 1880s and 1890s, up until the consolidation of greater New York in 1898.

535 Goldfield, David R. "Disease and Urban Image: Yellow Fever in Norfolk, 1855." VIRGINIA CAVALCADE 23 (1973): 34-41.

Argues that Norfolk's failure to achieve the economic growth predicted by its boosters resulted from a complex web of bad luck, legislative favoritism, and underdeveloped entrepreneurial skill, but that the yellow fever epidemic was perhaps the single most important factor.

536 Goldman, Mark. "Buffalo's Black Rock: Neighborhood Identity and the Metropolitan Relationship." Ph.D. dissertation, State University of New York, Buffalo, 1973. 230 p.

Finds that physical isolation and separate economic development made Black Rock into an identifiable neighborhood, even though its population was largely native-born American. Observes that Black Rock opposed metropolitan centralization every bit as much as did ethnic enclaves.

537 Gong, Alfred. "Capital of Our Time: Foreign Writers Experience New York, a Literary Montage." AMERICAN-GERMAN REVIEW 30 (1964): 6-14.

Summarizes the impressions of New York City rendered by emigré writers fleeing Nazi Germany. Finds that they were generally critical of the city, although regarding it as a microcosm of the times.

538 Goodall, Elizabeth J. "The Charleston Industrial Area: Development, 1798-1937." WEST VIRGINIA HISTORY 30 (1968): 358-412.

Traces the growth of Charleston from a village of seven houses to a city of 68,000 by 1937 and styles it according to the dominant industry: 1797-1875, the salt period; 1875-1920, the coal, iron, and gas era; and 1920-37, the chemical period.

539 Greb, Gregory A. "Charleston, South Carolina, Merchants, 1815-1860: Urban Leadership in the Antebellum South." Ph.D. dissertation, University of California, San Diego, 1978. 274 p.

Examines the relationships of Charleston merchants with the planter class and with their counterparts in other urban centers.

Single City Studies

Finds that they maintained ties to the plantation system, but also relied upon railroads, maritime development, and banks to be competitive with the commercial elites of the Atlantic seaboard.

540   Green, Constance McLaughlin. HISTORY OF NAUGATUCK, CONNECTICUT. New Haven, Conn.: Yale University Press, 1948. 283 p.

Traces the evolution of Naugatuck from an agricultural village to a Yankee town to an industrial city. Devotes a good deal of attention to the changing relationship between labor and management in response to industrial development.

541   _____. HOLYOKE, MASSACHUSETTS: A CASE HISTORY OF THE INDUSTRIAL REVOLUTION IN AMERICA. Hamden, Conn.: Archon Books, 1968. 425 p.

Presents Holyoke as a deliberately planned and consistently promoted town, designed to be a cotton textile center but emerging instead as a city of diversified industries. Asserts that the city is a microcosm for the study of changing modes of life and adjustments of thought due to industrialization.

542   _____. WASHINGTON: CAPITAL CITY, 1879-1950. Princeton, N.J.: Princeton University Press, 1963. 558 p.

Concentrates much attention upon the differences and interaction between white and "colored" Washington and on the impact of national and international events upon the city's development.

543   _____. WASHINGTON: VILLAGE AND CAPITAL, 1800-1878. Princeton, N.J.: Princeton University Press, 1962. 445 p.

Focuses especially on the plan of the city's founders to have it symbolize the ideas of the new republic, the decay and revival of that dream, and the manner in which the economic dependence of its inhabitants on the federal government affected development. Concludes with the emergence of a "new Washington" as a "national city" under the direction of political boss Alexander Shepherd.

544   Green, Mary Fulton. "A Profile of Columbia in 1850." SOUTH CAROLINA HISTORY MAGAZINE 70 (1969): 104-21.

Finds that Columbia's response to residential dispersion and the increasing need for muncipal services was shaped by the nature of its population, its physical characteristics, its government and politics, its economic development, its social institutions and organizations, and the reaction of its citizens to national affairs.

545   Greenleaf, Richard E. "The Founding of Albuquerque, 1706: An Historical-Legal Problem." NEW MEXICO HISTORICAL REVIEW 39 (1964): 1-15.

Examines the efforts of the city fathers to establish their water

Single City Studies

rights and discusses the lack of documentary evidence to sustain or disprove rival claims.

546   Haeger, John D. "The American Fur Company and the Chicago of 1812-1835." JOURNAL OF THE ILLINOIS STATE HISTORICAL SOCIETY 61 (1968): 117-39.

Argues that the fur trade contributed litte to Chicago's development in terms of investment capital and leadership for political and social life. Concludes that eastern migrants brought the necessary professional knowledge, technical skills, and investment capital to make Chicago an urban center.

547   Hansen, Gladys, ed. SAN FRANCISCO: THE BAY AND ITS CITIES. New York: Hastings House, 1973. 496 p.

Uses material from the 1970 census to update what was originally the result of a Federal Writers Project efforts in the 1930s.

548   Harper, Frank C. PITTSBURGH: FORGE OF THE UNIVERSE. New York: Comet Press Books, 1957. 320 p.

Written by a prominent staff member of the city's chamber of commerce, celebrates Pittsburgh as the "industrial marvel of the modern world" and lauds its renaissance and civic rebirth. Contains some useful biographical and statistical data.

549   Haskell, Henry C., and Fowler, Richard B. CITY OF THE FUTURE, A NARRATIVE HISTORY OF KANSAS CITY, 1850-1950. Kansas City, Mo.: F. Glenn Publishers, 1950. 193 p.

Presents Kansas City as "the most American city," a microcosm of the larger experience of the United States over a century, partly due to its midcontinent location and its largely native-born population.

550   Hessler, Sherry O. "'The Great Disturbing Cause' and the Decline of the Queen City." CINCINNATI HISTORICAL SOCIETY BULLETIN 20 (1962): 170-85.

Attributes Cincinnati's failure to become the great city of inland America to her weak railroad position due to lack of foresight. Denies that its decline was due to whims of nature, technological revolution, or conspiracies of eastern capitalists.

551   Hodes, Frederick A. "The Urbanization of St. Louis: A Study in Urban Residential Patterns in the 19th Century." Ph.D. dissertation, St. Louis University, 1973. 193 p.

Traces the development of St. Louis from small town to urban complex and clarifies the social and economic residential pattern of the city.

Single City Studies

552 Hodges, Margaret. "Pittsburgh: Seven Authors, Seven Views." WESTERN PENNSYLVANIA HISTORY MAGAZINE 56 (1973): 253-79.

    Analyzes the works of seven Pittsburgh authors and finds significant variations in their respective attitudes toward the city.

553 Hoffecker, Carol E. "Nineteenth Century Wilmington: Satellite or Independent City?" DELAWARE HISTORY 15 (1972): 1-18.

    Argues that Wilmington, while manifesting some characteristics of a "satellite city" vis a vis Philadelphia, still was a manufacturing center in its own right and was both a partner and a competitor of the larger city.

554 Horowitz, Helen Lefkowitz. CULTURE AND THE CITY: CULTURAL PHILANTHROPY IN CHICAGO FROM THE 1880S TO 1917. Lexington: University Press of Kentucky, 1976. 288 p.

    Contends that Chicago's business elite founded museums, libraries, a symphony orchestra, and a university as a means of purifying the city, exercising social control, and generating a civic renaissance. Deals with the contrast between commercial-industrial Chicago and the social uplift movement.

555 Hutchinson, William R. "Disapproval of Chicago: The Symbolic Trial of David Swing." JOURNAL OF AMERICAN HISTORY 59 (1972): 30-47.

    Argues that Swing's heresy trial demonstrated that Chicago was a center of religious liberalism which influenced New England as much as the older region affected it. Sees this as contributing to the turn-of-the-century cultural explosion in the Windy City.

556 Jackson, Dorothy B. "The Growth of an Industrial City, Birmingham, 1800-1851." Ph.D. dissertation, Yale University, 1956. 241 p.

    Finds that the city's leaders believed that they had to educate the working and middle classes and provide a decent life for them by building various schools, institutes, and cultural facilities. Sees them motivated by a mixture of self-interest and humanitarianism.

557 James, D. Clayton. ANTEBELLUM NATCHEZ. Baton Rouge: Louisiana State University Press, 1968. 344 p.

    Concentrates largely upon the social and political history of the city, its evolving class structure, the domination of the Federalists and Whigs, and the reaction of the city's people to the worsening crisis over slavery and secession.

Single City Studies

558   Keiser, John H. "Chicago: The Ultimate City." In his BUILDING FOR THE CENTURIES: ILLINOIS, 1865 TO 1898, pp. 256-92. Urbana: University of Illinois Press, 1977.

   Paints a portrait of life in Chicago in the late nineteenth century emphasizing economic, social, and cultural conditions.

559   Kellogg, Paul U., et al. THE PITTSBURGH SURVEY. 6 vols. New York: Russell Sage Foundation, 1909-1914. 440, 345, 380, 292, 554, 582 p.

   Includes volumes on WOMEN AND THE TRADES by Elizabeth B. Butler, WORK ACCIDENTS AND THE LAW by Crystal Eastman, THE STEEL WORKERS by J.A. Fitch, HOMESTEAD'S HOUSEHOLDS by Margaret F. Byington, THE PITTSBURGH DISTRICT CIVIC FRONTAGE by Kellogg, and WAGE-EARNING PITTSBURGH by Kellogg. Contains a great deal of social and economic information about the city and its ethnic working class.

560   King, Moses. KING'S HANDBOOK OF NEW YORK CITY, 1893. Reprint. New York: B. Blom, 1973. 1,008 p.

   Contains profuse illustrations detailing with the architecture and urban design of the city in the late nineteenth century.

561   Kirker, Harold, and Kirker, James. BULLFINCH'S BOSTON, 1787-1817. New York: Oxford University Press, 1964. 305 p.

   Examines the city from the perspective of Charles Bullfinch, the architect of Federal Boston, the chairman of the board of selectmen, and the chief of police. Regards Bullfinch as the leader in the unsuccessful effort to keep Boston culturally British.

562   Klein, Milton M., ed. NEW YORK: THE CENTENNIAL YEARS 1676-1976. Port Washington, N.Y.: Kennikat Press, 1976. 202 p.

   Contains five essays on New York City in different periods of its development: Anglo-Dutch (1676) by Thomas J. Archdeacon, Revolutionary (1776) by Bruce M. Wilkenfield, Centennial (1876) by Albert Fein, Bicentennial (1976) by Bayard Still, and The Greater City (1876-2076) by Kenneth T. Jackson.

563   Klein, Philip. A SOCIAL STUDY OF PITTSBURGH: COMMUNITY PROBLEMS AND SOCIAL SERVICES OF ALLEGHENY COUNTY. New York: Columbia University Press, 1938. 958 p.

   Examines the agencies and institutions that provided social

Single City Studies

and health services under both public and voluntary auspices. Also explores the conditions of life in the Pittsburgh area, focusing upon social and ethnic stratification, physical conditions, social legislation, labor organization, social attitudes, public opinion, pressure groups, and the school system.

564   Knapp, Vertie. "The Natural Ice Industry of Philadelphia in the Nineteenth Century." PENNSYLVANIA HISTORY 41 (1974): 413-21.

Surveys the development of the ice industry in Philadelphia and asserts its crucial role in urbanization by providing a means of food preservation which would allow the city to depend upon more distant farm areas for food.

565   Kopf, Edward J. "The Intimate City: A Study of Urban Social Order, Chelsea, Massachusetts, 1906-1915." Ph.D. dissertation, Brandeis University, 1974. 287 p.

Contends that Chelsea, Massachusetts, maintained a well developed, personalized social life as a result of its various ethnic communities, concluding that isolation and alienation need not be conditions of urban life.

566   Kouwenhoven, John A. THE COLUMBIA HISTORICAL PORTRAIT OF NEW YORK. New York: Octagon Press, 1978. 550 p.

Surveys the evolution of New York City from 1614 to 1953 in hundreds of photographs, with a running commentary that ties the pictures in with aspects of the city's development.

567   Kramer, Carl. "Images of a Developing City: Louisville, 1800-1830." FILSON CLUB HISTORY QUARTERLY 52 (1978): 166-90.

Describes Louisville during a period in which it began to emerge as a leading western river port, focusing particularly on the interaction between changing images or attitudes toward the city held by residents and visitors, and the pace and nature of the city's development.

568   Lafore, Lawrence, and Lippincott, Sarah Lee. PHILADELPHIA: THE UNEXPECTED CITY. Garden City, N.Y.: Doubleday, 1965. 178 p.

Contains eight photographic essays organized around the general theme that Philadelphia is an "unexpected city" because it is so uniquely skilled at absorbing disparate elements.

569   Landesman, Alter F. "The Early History of Brownsville." JOURNAL OF LONG ISLAND HISTORY 4 (1964): 18-27.

Discusses the development of the Brownsville neighborhood in Brooklyn, New York, during the 1850s to 1870s, when it

Single City Studies

remained a small rural village, indicating some of its prominent families and their involvement in land sales and settlement.

570   Lantz, Herman. A COMMUNITY IN SEARCH OF ITSELF: A CASE HISTORY OF CAIRO, ILLINOIS. Carbondale: Southern Illinois University Press, 1972. 236 p.

Focuses on Cairo and the surrounding hinterlands of Little Egypt, to understand the reasons for the failure and decline of cities which began with great promise. Emphasizes interacting political, social, economic, physical, and ideological factors.

571   Lee, Lawrence B. "William E. Smythe and San Diego, 1901-1908." JOURNAL OF SAN DIEGO HISTORY 19 (1973): 10-24.

Although generally known for authoring HISTORY OF SAN DIEGO (1907) Smythe also was a strong booster who believed in the future of San Diego. His speeches and writings called for government ownership of local utilities and federal reclamation of the Imperial Valley, which was opposed by city leaders.

572   Leech, Margaret. REVEILLE IN WASHINGTON, 1860-1865. New York: Harper and Row, 1941. Reprint. Westport, Conn.: Greenwood Press, 1972. 481 p.

Examines the impact of the Civil War on the city that was the capital of the United States, but which had a majority of southern sympathizers among its residents. Contends that Washington really came of age as the nation's capital during these years.

573   Litchfield, Norman, "Blythebourne: A Community That Was Swallowed Up." JOURNAL OF LONG ISLAND HISTORY 4 (1964): 28-39.

The grandson of Blythebourne's developer reminisces about the little community which flourished from 1887 to 1921 as one of the early real estate developments south of the city of Brooklyn.

574   Lofton, Paul F., Jr. "A Social and Economic History of Columbia, South Carolina, during the Great Depression, 1929-1940." Ph.D. dissertation, University of Texas, 1977. 346 p.

Attributes Columbia's survival during the Depression to four causes: (1) the predominance of government and education as major employers, (2) the diversification of other industry, (3) responsible and aggressive civic leadership, (4) southern agriculture and textiles were depressed industries in the twenties, lessening the impact of the Great Depression.

Single City Studies

575 Longstreet, Stephen. CHICAGO: AN INTIMATE PORTRAIT OF PEOPLE, PLEASURES, AND POWER, 1860-1919. New York: McKay, 1973. 547 p.

> Popular descriptive history providing an anecdotal political and social overview of Chicago's developments.

576 Lorant, Steffen, ed. PITTSBURGH: THE STORY OF AN AMERICAN CITY. Garden City, N.Y.: Doubleday, 1964. 520 p.

> Presents a comprehensive narrative of Pittsburgh from its founding on, with separately authored individual chapters on various eras and themes. Profusely illustrated, and includes an extensive chronology of events in the city's history.

577 Lotchin, Roger W. "San Francisco: The Patterns and Chaos of Growth." In CITIES IN AMERICAN HISTORY, edited by Kenneth T. Jackson and Stanley K. Schultz, pp. 143-63. New York: Knopf, 1972.

578 _____. SAN FRANCISCO 1846-1856: FROM HAMLET TO CITY. New York: Oxford University Press, 1974. 406 p.

> Presents a detailed account of San Francisco's first decade of existence, discussing its economy, the nature of its population, government and politics, and the emergence of urban institutions. Stresses the intellectual and emotional adjustments that urbanization requires, as well as the philosophical debates engendered by the need to develop municipal institutions.

579 McClelland, John M., Jr. R.A. LONG'S PLANNED CITY: THE STORY OF LONGVIEW. Longview, Wash.: Longview Publishing, 1976. 288 p.

> Biography of Longview, a planned city founded and developed in the 1920s by private capital as part of the western expansion of the Long-Bell Lumber Company.

580 McClymer, John F. "The Pittsburgh Survey, 1907-1914: Forging an Ideology in the Steel District." PENNSYLVANIA HISTORY 41 (1974): 169-86.

> Uses the Pittsburgh Survey to illustrate the role of an emerging professional class of social engineers who owed both their existence and their technology of social accounting to industrial capitalism. They represented a strain of progressivism that emphasized efficiency and order in the social sphere to match the same characteristics they saw in the business world.

581 McComb, David G. "Houston, The Bayou City." Ph.D. dissertation,

Single City Studies

University of Texas at Austin, 1968. 482 p.

> Focuses on the economic development of Houston from a primarily commercial town in 1836 to an industrial city by 1968, in an effort to explain the reasons for its growth; also covers social, political and cultural affairs.

582 McKelvey, Blake. "The Changing Face of Rochester." ROCHESTER HISTORY 26 (1964): 1-20.

> Presents observations of and historical background on various features of Rochester's urban profile, including vistas, and architectural styles.

583 _____. "East Avenue's Turbulent History." ROCHESTER HISTORY 28 (1966): 1-48.

> Chronicles the changing character of a street which reflects more than any other in the city the different "moods and trends of Rochester's history."

584 _____. "Errata and Addenda: Plus Some Thoughts on the Nature of History and the Rochester Story." ROCHESTER HISTORY 24 (1962): 1-24.

> Listing of some errors in McKelvey's ROCHESTER: AN EMERGING METROPOLIS: 1925-1961, communications from friendly critics pointing to events and personalities omitted from the story, coupled with the author's comments on the nature of urban history in general and on the entire four-volume cycle on Rochester.

585 _____. "The Lure of the City of Rochester in the 1890s." ROCHESTER HISTORY 28 (1966): 1-24.

> Discusses various factors that made Rochester attractive to visitors and new settlers, while exploring some of the experiences of newcomers and the changing nature of the city.

586 _____. "Names and Traditions of Some Rochester Streets." ROCHESTER HISTORY 27 (1965): 1-22.

> Provides a brief historical overview of Rochester's street pattern, and background information on some twenty of the city's thoroughfares, including the origins of their names, and their early character in terms of residents, functions, landmarks, and events.

587 _____. ROCHESTER: THE WATER POWER CITY, 1812-1854. Cambridge, Mass.: Harvard University Press, 1945. 383 p. ROCHESTER: THE FLOWER CITY, 1855-1890. Cambridge, Mass.: Harvard Univer-

Single City Studies

sity Press, 1949. 407 p. ROCHESTER: THE QUEST FOR QUALITY, 1890-1925. Cambridge, Mass.: Harvard University Press, 1956. 432 p. ROCHESTER: AN EMERGING METROPOLIS, 1925-1961. Rochester, N.Y.: Christopher Press, 1961. 404 p.

    Chronologically organized four-volume urban biography focusing on political, economic, and social developments within Rochester, including information on notable citizens.

588   _____. ROCHESTER ON THE GENESEE: THE GROWTH OF A CITY. Syracuse, N.Y.: Syracuse University Press, 1973. 292 p.

    An urban biography of Rochester from its origin to the present which divides the city's history into various eras and attempts to identify dominant problems and responses.

589   _____. "A Sesquicentennial Review of Rochester's History." ROCHESTER HISTORY 24 (1962): 1-40.

    Comments on varied aspects of incidents in Rochester's history prepared for a radio series commemorating the sesquicentennial of the city's permanent settlement.

590   McLear, Patrick E. "William Butler Ogden: A Chicago Promoter in the Speculative Era and the Panic of 1837." JOURNAL OF THE ILLINOIS STATE HISTORICAL SOCIETY 70 (1977): 283-91.

    Traces Ogden's entrepreneurial career stressing the way his business approach--particularly his ability to serve the interests of both easterners and westerners--proved a critical factor in his success.

591   McMullin, Thomas A. "Industrialization and Social Change in a Nineteenth-Century Port City: New Bedford, Massachusetts, 1865-1900." Ph.D. dissertation, University of Wisconsin, Madison, 1976. 295 p.

    Comparatively analyzes the response of several basic institutions--public and private charity agencies, schools, churches, and labor unions--to the economic, ethnic, spatial, and social status changes that occurred in New Bedford during its period of intense industrial development, in order to gauge the social transformation generated by the coming of the factory.

592   Maurice, Arthur B. NEW YORK IN FICTION. 1899. Reprint. Port Washington, N.Y.: Ira J. Friedman, 1969. 231 p.

    Uses excerpts from novels of the period and photographs to present a portrait of turn-of-the-century New York City.

593   Mayer, Harold M., and Wade, Richard C. CHICAGO: GROWTH OF

A METROPOLIS. Chicago: University of Chicago Press, 1969. 510 p.

> Combines the insights of urban history and geography to present a largely visual history of the evolution of the midwestern metropolis through six chronological eras: prairie seaport, 1830-51; railroad capital, 1851-71; second city, 1871-93; the white city and the gray, 1893-1917; war and prosperity, 1917-45; and revival and crisis, 1945-69.

594 Mazzi, Francis J. "City From Frontier: Symbols of Urban Development in Nineteenth-Century San Francisco." Ph.D. dissertation, University of Southern California, 1974. 258 p.

> Focuses on the efforts of the boom town to achieve a sense of permanence and dignity by constructing elaborate and ornate hotels, theatres, and other architectural monuments. Views them as both monuments to its frontier past and as harbingers of San Francisco's coming of age as a city.

595 _____. "Harbingers of the City: Men and their Monuments in Nineteenth Century San Francisco." SOUTHERN CALIFORNIA QUARTERLY 55 (1973): 141-62.

> Investigates the development of theatres and hotels, arguing that to the city's residents, these constituted important and tangible symbols of San Francisco's coming of age as an urban center.

596 Merriam, Paul G. "Urban Elite in the Far West: Portland, Oregon, 1870-1890." ARIZONA AND THE WEST 18 (1976): 41-52.

> Contends that "the experience of Portland's elite, during its formative years, 1870-1890, supports the view that the urban Far West, rather than being open and equalitarian with innovative and unique characteristics, developed quite early a class-conscious, stratified society whose leaders sought to copy old rather than create new societal patterns."

597 Messmer, Charles. "Louisville on the Eve of the Civil War, Part I: 1860: Year of Activity." FILSON CLUB HISTORICAL QUARTERLY 50 (1976): 249-89.

> Comprehensive description of Louisville in the 1850s with particular emphasis on the role of the city's newspaper in the secession crisis.

598 Miller, Rita S., ed. BROOKLYN, U.S.A.: FOURTH LARGEST CITY IN AMERICA. New York: Columbia University Press, 1978. 371 p.

> Contains nearly thirty articles by a variety of contributors on diverse aspects of Brooklyn's history and culture, arranged un-

Single City Studies

der the topics of historical perspectives, symbols and nostalgia, contemporary communities, public education, and the borough's present and future.

599   Miller, William D. "Rural Values and Urban Progress: Memphis, 1900-1917." MISSISSIPPI QUARTERLY 21 (1968): 263-74.

Discusses the role of the southern agrarian myth and associated values in reinforcing the "Memphis sin-center myth" and in contributing to the high rate of violence, particularly murder, in that city.

600   Morgan, Helen M., ed. A SEASON IN NEW YORK, 1801: LETTERS OF HARRIET AND MARIA TRUMBULL. Pittsburgh: Pittsburgh University Press, 1969. 189 p.

Provides a social history of New York City in 1801 as recorded in the observations of two teenaged visitors from Connecticut. Includes an essay by the editor detailing the social, political, religious, and cultural scenes in New York and Connecticut at that time.

601   Myhra, Thomas J. "The Social Significances of Steamboat Men on Early Bismarck." NORTH DAKOTA HISTORY 30 (1963): 72-96.

Describes Bismarck, North Dakota, during the first decade of its existence in the 1870s, stressing the impact of the steamboat trade on the city's development, primarily from a social perspective.

602   Nadeau, Remi A. LOS ANGELES: FROM MISSION TO MODERN CITY. New York: Longmans, Green, 1960. 302 p.

Popular account of Los Angeles' development from its Spanish colonial origins to the present, stressing the city's consistent attempts at boosterism.

603   New York Historical Society. OLD NEW YORK IN EARLY PHOTOGRAPHS, 1853-1901. Intro. and commentary by Mary Black. New York: Dover, 1973. 228 p.

Contains almost two hundred photographs of the city in the last half of the nineteenth century.

604   Nordstrom, Carl. FRONTIER ELEMENTS IN A HUDSON RIVER VILLAGE. Port Washington, N.Y.: Kennikat Press, 1973. 199 p.

Examines daily life in the town of Nyack, New York, and attempts to relate the village's evolution to the frontier thesis of Fredrick Jackson Turner.

Single City Studies

605   Noyes, Richard, and Turner, Howard E. AT THE EDGE OF MEGA-
        LOPOLIS: A HISTORY OF SALEM, NEW HAMPSHIRE, 1900-1974.
        Canaan, N.H.: Phoenix Publishing, 1974. 370 p.

   Local history, basically descriptive, that traces in detail the
   twentieth-century history of Salem, New Hampshire. Contains data drawn from interviews, and an appendix with
   family sketches of leading Salemites.

606   Older, Mrs. Fremont [Cora Older]. SAN FRANCISCO: MAGIC CITY.
        San Francisco: Longmans, 1961. 280 p.

   Presents a wide array of disparate information about twentieth-
   century San Francisco, including sketches of business leaders
   and society figures.

607   Osterweis, Rollin G. THREE CENTURIES OF NEW HAVEN, 1638-1938.
        New Haven, Conn.: Yale University Press, 1953. 541 p.

   Narrative discussion of New Haven's growth from colonial
   village to modern city, emphasizing religion, education, economic development, and civic improvements. Sponsored by the
   New Haven Colony Historical Society.

608   Parker, Margaret Terrell. LOWELL: A STUDY OF INDUSTRIAL DE-
        VELOPMENT. New York: Macmillan, 1940. Reprint. Port Washing-
        ton, N.Y.: Kennikat Press, 1970. 238 p.

   Traces the rise and fall of Lowell as one of New England's
   important industrial towns, emphasizing the insights of historical geography.

609   Parkins, Almon. THE HISTORICAL GEOGRAPHY OF DETROIT.
        Lansing, Mich.: Michigan Historical Commission, 1918. Reprint.
        Port Washington, N.Y.: Kennikat Press, 1970. 356 p.

   Traces the growth of the city and its environs from the days
   of the traders and fur trappers to the early days of the automobile age.

610   Parraga, Charlotte Marie Nelson. "Sante Fe De Nuevo: A Study of
        a Frontier City based on an Annotated Translation of Selected Documents
        (1825-1832) from the Mexican Archives of New Mexico." Ph.D.
        dissertation, Ball State University, 1976. 266 p.

   Provides historical information on New Mexico's political
   system, its prominent people, and the activities of Anglo-
   American trappers and traders.

611   Penna, Anthony N. "Changing Images of Twentieth Century Pittsburgh."
        PENNSYLVANIA HISTORY 43 (1976): 49-63.

Single City Studies

Examines the promotional efforts of Pittsburgh's business elite who attempted to create an image of their city as "the workshop of the world" and to neutralize the notion of a smoky and unhealthy environment. After the Depression, the business elite created a new image, that of the Renaissance city.

612   Petersen, William J. "The El Dorado of Iowa." PALIMPSEST 45 (1964): 401-64.

A history of Dubuque from the 1830s through the Civil War, with a brief closing section on the city since that time.

613   Peterson, Arthur E., and Edwards, George W. NEW YORK AS AN EIGHTEENTH CENTURY MUNICIPALITY. 1917. Reprint. Port Washington, N.Y.: Kennikat Press, 1967. 352 p.

Analyzes in detail the governmental organization of the city of New York and its efforts to regulate trade and commerce and to provide municipal services.

614   Pierce, Bessie L. A HISTORY OF CHICAGO. 3 vols. Vol. 1: 1673-1848; vol. 2: 1848-1871; vol. 3: 1871-1893. New York: Knopf, 1937, 1940, 1962. 455, 546, 575 p.

Emphasizes economic and political developments in the city from its exploration by Marquette and Joliet to the White City of the Columbian Exposition. Focuses upon group life and institutions rather than upon prominent individuals.

615   Pierce, Bessie L., and Norris, Joe L. AS OTHERS SEE CHICAGO: IMPRESSIONS OF VISITORS, 1673-1933. Chicago: Chicago Press, 1933. 540 p.

Presents descriptive accounts drawn from diaries, journals, and magazine articles.

616   Pomerantz, Sidney. NEW YORK: AN AMERICAN CITY, 1783-1803. A STUDY OF URBAN LIFE. New York: Columbia University Press, 1938. Reprint. Port Washington, N.Y.: I.J. Friedman, 1965. 531 p.

Focuses on the impact of the early national period of New York City's development. Discusses city governmental structure and politics, economic development, municipal and social services, finances, and popular and formal culture and recreation.

617   Porter, Philip W. CLEVELAND: CONFUSED CITY ON A SEESAW. Columbus: Ohio State University Press, 1976. 314 p.

Account by a long-time journalist of civic and political af-

Single City Studies

fairs in Cleveland over the past fifty years. Stresses the role of political volatility and fragmentation in determing the evolution of the city's current malaise.

618   Posadas, Barbara Mercedes. "Community Structures of Chicago's Northwest Side: The Transition from Rural to Urban, 1830-1889." Ph.D. dissertation, Northwestern University, 1976.

Examines the evolution of Jefferson Township from a rural frontier community to a complex of suburban villages annexed to the city. Attributes the transition to the interaction of a "community of residence" with a "community of speculation," impelled by extrinsic forces, such as the Great Chicago Fire and the Panic of 1873.

619   Pratt, Edward E. INDUSTRIAL CAUSES OF CONGESTION OF POPULATION IN NEW YORK CITY. New York, Columbia University Press, 1911. Reprint. New York: A.M.S. Press, 1968. 259 p.

Argues that congestion itself was a major cause of the urban crisis of the early twentieth century and attributes a variety of other problems to overpopulation.

620   Quandt, Jean B. "Community in Urban America, 1890-1917: Reformers, City Planners, and Greenwich Villagers." SOCIETAS 6 (1976): 255-74.

Compares the attitude of settlement workers, city planners, and bohemian artists and intellectuals and finds that the two former groups, despite disagreements, both sought to maintain a sense of local community which the latter found too restrictive and sought to replace with a notion of community based upon shared experience or function.

621   Radford, John P. "Culture, Economy, and Urban Structure in Charleston, South Carolina, 1860-1880." Ph.D. dissertation, Clark University, 1974. 366 p.

Asserts that Charleston's domination by the planter elite prevented the city from sharing in the socioeconomic transformations resulting from industrialization that characterized other major cities in the United States. Particularly with regard to residential patterns, the Charleston of 1860 conforms more closely to the preindustrial city than to the industrializing models usually associated with North American cities.

622   Ralph, Raymond M. FROM VILLAGE TO INDUSTRIAL CITY: THE URBANIZATION OF NEWARK, NEW JERSEY, 1830-1860. New York: New York University Press, 1978. 314 p.

Single City Studies

Focuses on the causes of Newark's economic transformation, the impact of urbanization upon the city's population, and the impact of urban growth upon its political leadership. Stresses the interrelationship between technology and urbanization and the importance of transiency and mobility.

623 Rammelkamp, Julian S. "St. Louis in the Early 'Eighties." MISSOURI HISTORICAL SOCIETY BULLETIN 19 (1963): 328-39.

Describes various aspects of St. Louis, including changing spatial patterns, class composition, commercial and industrial developments, and the role of St. Louis' capitalist class, styled as a "conservative and monopolistic oligarchy."

624 Reed, Merl E. NEW ORLEANS AND THE RAILROADS: THE STRUGGLE FOR COMMERCIAL EMPIRE, 1830-1860. Baton Rouge: Louisiana State University Press, 1966. 172 p.

Argues that New Orleans' reliance upon river transportation prevented it from adjusting to the rise of the railroad, thus putting the city at a disadvantage in commercial competition with northern cities.

625 Reeve, Kay A. "The Making of an American Place: The Development of Sante Fe and Taos, New Mexico, as an American Cultural Center, 1898-1942." Ph.D. dissertation, Texas A & M University, 1977. 248 p.

Examines the development of artistic and literary colonies in Sante Fe and Taos, focusing on the environmental, cultural, and promotional factors which fostered the emergence of a new American cultural center in an area so removed from major U.S. cities. Stresses that the elemental character of the physical environment and overlays of Pueblo Indian and Spanish-American cultures proved highly attractive to the Anglo artists and authors, for they represented values that were missing in a dominant American society increasingly characterized by depersonalization and alienation.

626 Richards, Ira D. "The Urban Frontier, Little Rock in the Nineteenth Century." Ph.D. dissertation, Tulane University, 1964. 208 p.

Covers life in a territorial capital founded in 1819, the struggle for commercial success, and the war years, which severed the city's ties with the South and ushered in the boom decade of the last quarter of the nineteenth century.

627 Rickey, Don. "The Old St. Louis Riverfront, 1763-1960." MISSOURI HISTORICAL REVIEW 58 (1964): 174-90.

Traces the changing face of St. Louis' riverfront area, discussing the development of the harbor, warehouses, wharves, and

Single City Studies

dykes, emphasizing municipal regulations and the city's commerce.

628 Rose, William G. CLEVELAND, THE MAKING OF A CITY. Cleveland and New York: World Publishing Co., 1950. 1,272 p.

Standard urban biography tracing Cleveland's development from pioneer days on. Chronological approach, with individual chapters on individual decades from the 1790s through the 1940s; largely descriptive and laudatory.

629 Rosenwaike, Ira. POPULATION HISTORY OF NEW YORK CITY. Syracuse, N.Y.: Syracuse University Press, 1972. 224 p.

Based largely upon census data and vital statistics, traces changes in the city's population in six distinct periods: colonial; national period; foreign city, 1825-60; world's second city, 1860-1900; city of five boroughs, 1900-40; and metropolitan giant, 1940-70.

630 Russell, James M. "Atlanta, Gate City of the South, 1847 to 1885." Ph.D. dissertation, Princeton University, 1972. 401 p.

Studies the rapid growth of Atlanta at a time when most southern cities experienced a stand-still and attributes the phenomenon to two major factors, the completion of the Western and Atlantic Railroad in 1850 and the contributions of local citizens involved in entrepreneurial projects.

631 Sale, Roger. "Seattle's Crisis, 1814-1919." AMERICAN STUDIES 14 (1973-1974): 29-48.

Attempts to "read" the city of Seattle during the critical period which culminated in the General Strike of 1919 by weaving together impressionistic materials of various sorts. Regards the attempts of the I.W.W. and the Central Labor Union to control the city as one of the few authentic attempts at working-class urban governance in American history.

632 Sarver, Phillip M. "Historical Influences on the Economy of Pueblo, Colorado." Ph.D. dissertation, University of Nebraska, Lincoln, 1973. 277 p.

Explores the aspects of growth of Pueblo which helped to influence its initial development, and its present condition. Attempts to determine from the historical factors what implications there are for future growth of the community.

633 Scharf, Thomas J., and Thompson, Westcott. HISTORY OF PHILADELPHIA 1609-1884. 3 vols. Philadelphia: L.H. Everts and Co., 1884. 2,399 p.

Single City Studies

Massive study providing a complete political narrative of events in Philadelphia for the period indicated, as well as descriptive information regarding economic and social affairs.

634 Schlereth, Thomas J. "America, 1817-1919: A View of Chicago." AMERICAN STUDIES (University of Kansas) 17 (1976): 87-100.

Discusses the press, music, architecture and political, economic, and literary developments in Chicago to demonstrate that the city proved a microcosm of late nineteenth- and early twentieth-century American cultural history.

635 Schmid, Calvin F. THE SOCIAL SAGA OF TWO CITIES. Minneapolis: University of Minneapolis Press, 1937. 418 p.

Describes and analyzes selected phases of urban development and community life in Minneapolis and St. Paul, focusing especially upon population trends, housing, and patterns of social and personal disorganization, largely for the years from 1890 to the 1930s. Includes a brief history of the growth of the two cities and several chapters on processes of city expansion.

636 Schnitzer, Henry R. "The Sidewalks of Jersey City." PROCEEDINGS OF THE NEW JERSEY HISTORICAL SOCIETY 83 (1965): 174-202.

Personal recollections of childhood in Jersey City in the early 1900s, providing information about games and amusements, schools, dances, theatres, and other social aspects of urban life.

637 Schoenebaum, Eleanore W. "Emerging Neighborhoods: The Development of Brooklyn's Fringe Areas, 1850-1930." Ph.D. dissertation, Columbia University, 1977. 332 p.

Traces the evolution of Brooklyn, a small commercial community in 1850, into a city in which modern residential suburbs surround a decaying core by 1930, "a prime example of urban failure."

638 Schultz, Charles. "Glimpses into Cincinnati's Past: The Gest Letters, 1834-1842." OHIO HISTORY 73 (1964): 157-79.

Uses letters written to Gest by family and friends to discuss some of the major events animating Cincinnati citizens, including abolitionism, economic depression, and political campaigning.

639 Shambaugh, Benjamin F. "Iowa City Through the Years." PALIMPSEST 48 (1967): 41-80.

Single City Studies

Attributes the founding and growth of Iowa City to the combined efforts of pioneers, promoters, and politicians. Finds that the city's substantial growth was stymied by the Panic of 1857 and by the Civil War.

640   Silvia, Philip T., Jr. "The Position of Workers in a Textile Community: Fall River in the Early 1880s." LABOR HISTORY 16 (1975): 230-48.

Discusses the development of Fall River, Massachusetts, as a one-industry city, the attitudes of workers and employers toward unions and conditions in the mills and comments on tenement construction and living conditions.

641   Simon, Roger D. "The Expansion of an Industrial City: Milwaukee, 1880-1910." Ph.D. dissertation, University of Wisconsin, 1971. 412 p.

Focuses on the physical environment--housing, transportation, street improvements, sewers and water mains--in an examination of the process of peripheral growth in an industrial city and the resulting environment of that growth.

642   Simonds, Thomas C. HISTORY OF SOUTH BOSTON: FORMERLY DORCHESTER NECK, NOW WARD XII OF THE CITY OF BOSTON. 1854. Reprint. New York: Arno Press, 1974. 331 p.

Surveys the growth of the area from colonial times and contains much information concerning streets, bridges, churches, schools, businesses, and voluntary organizations.

643   Somers, Dale A. THE RISE OF SPORTS IN NEW ORLEANS, 1850-1900. Baton Rouge, La.: State University Press, 1972. 320 p.

Sees the years from 1850 to 1900 as the period in which sports gained prominence as a recreational activity in the United States. Focuses primarily on organized and commercial activities which had a distinctly urban nature. Analyzes the impact of sports on urban life in New Orleans and the reasons for growing interest in sports, and discusses such developmental trends as commercialization, professionalism, and the rise of collegiate and intercollegiate athletics.

644   Steen, Ivan D. "Philadelphia in the 1850s." PENNSYLVANIA HISTORY 33 (1966): 30-49.

Reports impressions of British travelers, noting comments on hotels, the appearance of city streets, shops, entertainment and cultural facilities, and various public institutions.

645   Stewart, Roy P. BORN GROWN, AN OKLAHOMA CITY HISTORY. Oklahoma City: Fidelity Bank, 1974. 352 p.

Single City Studies

Popularly written urban biography detailing the development of Oklahoma City from its origin in 1889 to 1974. Focuses on personages and luminaries arguing that the city grew and prospered largely because of the enterprise of its people, and the quality of its civic leadership.

646 Still, Bayrd. "The Development of Milwaukee in the Early Metropolitan Period." WISCONSIN MAGAZINE OF HISTORY 25 (1942): 297-307.

Describes some of the social and political aspects of Milwaukee for the years from 1870 to 1910, contending that it was during this period that the city first perceived and then adjusted to its status as metropolis and discusses the development of Milwaukee's noted "municipal conscience" as a significant part of this process.

647 _____. "The Essence of New York City." NEW YORK HISTORICAL SOCIETY QUARTERLY 43 (1959): 401-23.

Discusses and documents various characteristics of New York City which have been remarked over the years and which taken together constitute the "essence of the city's personality." These include a business orientation, commercial vigor, conviviality, ethnic diversity, and continual physical transformation.

648 _____. "Evidences of the Higher Life on the Frontier, as Illustrated in the History of Cultural Matters in Chicago." JOURNAL OF THE ILLINOIS HISTORICAL SOCIETY 28 (1935): 81-90.

Notes that Chicago, despite its rude physical appearance, already showed signs of "higher" culture. Discusses the theatre, education, popular literature, the lyceum movement, and newspapers, concluding that frontier towns had a continuous link with eastern culture which found concrete expression at an early date.

649 _____. GREENWICH VILLAGE: A BRIEF ARCHITECTURAL AND HISTORICAL GUIDE. New York: New York University, 1976. 32 p.

Pamphlet outlining two walking tours of Greenwich Village and providing brief historical vignettes for various landmarks.

650 _____. "The Growth of Milwaukee as Recorded by Contemporaries." WISCONSIN MAGAZINE OF HISTORY 21 (1938): 262-300.

Uses letters and visitors' accounts from the 1770s through the late nineteenth century to chronicle the growth of Milwaukee and convey some sense of the city's social history.

651 _____. MILWAUKEE, THE HISTORY OF A CITY. Madison: State

Single City Studies

Historical Society of Wisconsin, 1965. 638 p.

> Early urban biography detailing the development of Milwaukee in a chronological-developmental framework of four stages--village; expanding city, 1846-70; emerging metropolis, 1870-1910; and mature metropolis, 1910-40--and discussing political, economic, and social affairs.

652 _____. "Milwaukee 1870-1900." WISCONSIN MAGAZINE OF HISTORY 23 (1939): 139-62.

> Analyzes columns from Milwaukee newspapers as reflections of the city's growing metropolitanization and indicators of the attractive forces of urban centers. Focuses on perceptions of urban problems, concern with planning, and the growing acceptance of the idea of an urbanized society.

653 _____. MIRROR FOR GOTHAM: NEW YORK AS SEEN BY CONTEMPORARIES FROM DUTCH DAYS TO THE PRESENT. New York: New York University Press, 1956. Reprint. Westport, Conn.: Greenwood Press, 1980. 417 p.

> Presents a history of New York's development from its colonial days as New Amsterdam to 1950 based on some six hundred commentaries from visitors and residents. Excerpts from representative commentators are appended to each of the chapters.

654 _____. NEW YORK CITY, A STUDENT'S GUIDE TO LOCALIZED HISTORY. New York: Teachers College Press, Columbia University, 1965. 52 p.

> Provides a brief overview of New York City's development for four periods--Dutch; provincial city; the advancing city, 1783-1860; and the metropolitan era--and for each lists books, objectives for field trips, instructions for walking tours, and brief descriptions of key sites.

655 _____. "The Personality of New York City." NEW YORK FOLKLORE QUARTERLY 9 (1958): 83-92.

> Contends that the habits, attitudes, and activities of its people constitute the most important factor in determining the personality of a city, and traces several key characteristics of New York, concluding that from its earliest days on, the major attributes of the city's personality--commercialism, conviviality, cosmopolitanism, and constant change--have remained essentially the same.

656 Strickler, Carolyn J. "Los Angeles, Profile of a Super City." MANKIND 4 (1974): 10-15, 60-64.

> Presents a descriptive overview of the development of Los Angeles from its Spanish colonial origin.

Single City Studies

657   Thernstrom, Stephan. THE GROWTH OF LOS ANGELES IN HISTORICAL PERSPECTIVE: MYTH AND REALITY. Berkeley and Los Angeles: University of California Press, 1970. 25 p.

>Speculative essay identifying and discussing eight interrelated fallacies concerning Los Angeles' development and the concomitant nature of that city. These include misconceptions concerning rates of population growth, mobility, political culture, and physical and social fragmentation.

658   Troen, Selwyn K., and Holt, Glen E., eds. ST. LOUIS. New York: New Viewpoints, 1977. 220 p.

>Contains 67 documents dealing with aspects of St. Louis' growth divided into three periods: from colonial outpost to frontier town, 1763-1830; from town to city, 1830-1910; from city to region, 1910-75. Includes a brief overview by the editors of these three stages of growth.

659   Tucker, Louis. "Cincinnati: Athens of the West, 1830-1861." OHIO HISTORY 75 (1966): 10-25.

>Contends that Cincinnati did not deserve the image of "Porkopolis" given to it by Francis Trollope in DOMESTIC MANNERS OF THE AMERICANS (1832), and that, in fact, for the period discussed it held a vital position as the leading cultural and intellectual center of the West.

660   Vadasz, Thomas P. "The History of an Industrial Community: Bethlehem, Pennsylvania, 1741-1920." Ph.D. dissertation, College of William and Mary, 1975. 293 p.

>Uses Bethlehem as a case study in the industrialization of the United States, describing its transformation from a religious community into an industrial city and focusing on social change.

661   Walker, Charles R. AMERICAN CITY: A RANK AND FILE HISTORY. New York and Toronto: Farrar and Rinehart, 1937. 278 p.

>Focuses on the development of Minneapolis from a perspective stressing the development of class conflict and labor strife.

662   Ware, Caroline F. GREENWICH VILLAGE, 1920-1930. Boston: Houghton, 1935. 496 p.

>Presents the results of a sociological survey of New York's Greenwich Village. Provides a brief history of the community's development, a discussion of its ethnic groups, and analyses of religion, politics, education, recreation, social welfare, and the family.

Single City Studies

663 Weber, Michael P. SOCIAL CHANGE IN AN INDUSTRIAL TOWN: PATTERNS OF PROGRESS IN WARREN, PENNSYLVANIA, FROM CIVIL WAR TO WORLD WAR I. University Park: Pennsylvania State University Press, 1976. 185 p.

> Examines the social structure and socioeconomic mobility patterns in a small Pennsylvania oil town and finds that upward mobility was related to length of residence, that it came in small steps, that immigrants had a harder time moving up and were more likely to fall, and that rapid, large-scale industrialization adversely affected the status of nearly all workers.

664 Weiner, Ronald R. "A History of Civic Land Use Decision Making in the Cleveland Metropolitan Area, 1880-1930." Ph.D. dissertation, Kent State University, 1974. 383 p.

> Investigates city planning in Cleveland emphasizing city structure, population concentrations and decision making as associated variables. Argues that the industrial revolution and technological and demographic change produced a host of urban problems, preponderantly physical in nature, a fact which seemingly was understood only by the city's socially advantaged. Planning was the natural response to this perception.

665 Wertenbaker, Thomas J. NORFOLK: HISTORIC SOUTHERN PORT. Edited by Marvin W. Schlegel. Durham, N.C.: Duke University Press, 1962. 417 p.

> Focuses upon the commerce and economic life of the town and on the impact of national and international events on the local scene, but also presents information on various aspects of social history.

666 Wilson, William H. "The Founding of Anchorage." PACIFIC NORTHWEST QUARTERLY 58 (1967): 130-41.

> Discusses a unique experiment in federal operation of a frontier municipality, the Interior Department's five-year control over the development of Anchorage, a period during which it evolved from a rough construction camp to an established railroad town.

667 Wohl, R. Richard. "Three Generations of Business Enterprise in a Midwestern City: The McGees of Kansas City." WESTPORT HISTORICAL QUARTERLY 9 (1973): 63-79.

> Examines the concept of enterprise by focusing on the business concerns of three successive generations of businessmen and relating these to the changing nature of growth, opportunities, and institutions in Kansas City, Missouri.

Single City Studies

668 Wurman, Richard S., and Gallery, John A. MAN-MADE PHILADELPHIA: A GUIDE TO ITS PHYSICAL AND CULTURAL DEVELOPMENT. Cambridge: MIT Press, 1972. 104 p.

> Guide book that includes a section describing patterns of growth from the days of William Penn to the present and provides historical background for various places of interest. Concluding section presents city plans for Philadelphia, including Penn's Plan of 1683.

669 Young, James Sterling. THE WASHINGTON COMMUNITY, 1800-1828. New York: Columbia University Press, 1966. 307 p.

> Makes extensive use of statistics and quantitative methodology to examine the interaction between members of the legislature and the executive during the early years of the city's existence. Winner of Woodrow Wilson Award of the American Political Science Association.

670 Zorbaugh, Harvey W. THE GOLD COAST AND THE SLUM. Chicago: University of Chicago Press, 1977. 287 p.

> Describes and analyzes Chicago's wealthy lake-front Gold Coast and its Little Sicily, an Italian ghetto on the lower north side, providing an early example of an urban anthropological approach to the presentation of urban patterns.

Chapter 5
REGIONAL STUDIES

671   Abbott, Carl. "Popular Economic Thought and Occupational Structure: Three Middle Western Cities in the Antebellum Decade." JOURNAL OF URBAN HISTORY 1 (1975): 175-87.

        Examines the popular assumptions of Chicago as a commercial city, Cincinnati as a manufacturing city, and Indianapolis as a center for public and professional services and finds that the statistical data tend to support such conceptions. Suggests that city "boosters" of the era based their impressions upon the best evidence available and made reasonably accurate assessments.

672   Abbott, Collamer M. "New England Money Goes South." GEORGIA HISTORICAL QUARTERLY 49 (1965): 306-19.

        Examines the abortive efforts of promoters to build "New England City" as the future industrial capital of the New South in the 1890s. Attributes their failure to suspicion between northern and southern entrepreneurs.

673   Adkins, Howard G. "The Geographic Base of Urban Retardation in Mississippi, 1800-1840." STUDIES IN THE SOCIAL SCIENCES (West Georgia College) 12 (1973): 35-49.

674   Allen, James B. THE COMPANY TOWN IN THE AMERICAN WEST. Norman: University of Oklahoma Press, 1966. 205 p.

        Focuses upon towns built by mining and industrial firms for their employees, the living conditions, and the resultant difficulties, such as the Ludlow Massacre.

675   Anderson, Gary G. "Moorhead vs. Fargo: A Study of Economic Rivalry and Urban Development in the Red River Valley of the North." NORTH DAKOTA QUARTERLY 42 (1974): 60-77.

        Explores the heated rivalry between the two towns in the 1870s and finds that Fargo generally fared much better be-

Regional Studies

cause of the region and because its business men displayed all the characteristics of "boosterism" while Moorhead's were defensive and suspicious of new ventures.

676 Armstrong, Thomas F. "Urban Vision in Virginia: A Comparative Study of Ante-Bellum Fredericksburg, Lynchburg, and Staunton," Ph.D. dissertation, University of Virginia, 1974. 473 p.

Explores the process of urbanization in the South from the records of three Virginia towns, giving evidence of the similarity of urban growth of both northern and southern cities and noting the dissimilarities in population patterns, attributable to the black population.

677 Bebout, John E., and Grele, Ronald J. WHERE CITIES MEET: THE URBANIZATION OF NEW JERSEY. Princeton, N.J.: D. Van Nostrand Co., 1964. 127 p.

Examines the beginnings of the state's industrial cities, their experiences with rationalization and reform, and the emergence of New Jersey as the most urban state in the union and as one great urban complex.

678 Belcher, Wyatt W. THE ECONOMIC RIVALRY BETWEEN ST. LOUIS AND CHICAGO, 1850-1880. New York: AMS Press, 1968. 223 p.

Demonstrates how the rivalry between the two for water transportation and traffic was eventually decided by Chicago's domination of the railroad network at St. Louis' expense.

679 Bluoin, Francis X. "The Boston Region, 1810-1850: A Study of Urbanization on a Regional Scale." Ph.D. dissertation, University of Minnesota, 1978. 340 p.

Studies Boston as the focal central place in an urban system that involved 219 cities and towns, stressing the economic base which provided a number of linkages among the various urban places in the region, especially transportation networks, banking and credit facilities, and marketing patterns.

680 Borchert, John R. THE URBANIZATION OF THE UPPER MIDWEST, 1930-1960. Minneapolis: University of Minnesota Press, 1963. 55 p.

Analyzes the data on urbanization of the region and concludes that people have tended to center in large trade centers while the rest of the region has stagnated and over half the population is to be found in twenty-nine "urban regions" around large cities.

681 Brown, Richard D. "The Emergence of Urban Society in Rural Massachu-

setts, 1760-1820." JOURNAL OF AMERICAN HISTORY 61 (1974): 29-51.

>Claims that urban society emerged during this era, spurred by the American Revolution, electoral competition, expanded communications, ideologies of expanded self-improvement, voluntary associations, interest groups, commercial development, population growth, and large-scale migration.

682 Brownell, Blaine A. "Birmingham, Alabama: New South City in the 1920s." JOURNAL OF SOUTHERN HISTORY 38 (1972): 21-48.

>Provides an overview of Birmingham's social, economic, cultural, and political development in the decade and finds that the city had the same urban problems and concerns as urban areas in the rest of the United States. Concludes that the city stood between the Old South and the new, the rural and the urban, and the past and the future.

683 _____. THE URBAN ETHOS IN THE SOUTH, 1920-1930. Baton Rouge: Louisiana State University Press, 1975. 238 p.

>Avers that the urban ethos was promoted by a white commercial-civic elite to meet immediate needs, maintain the existing social order, insure urban expansion, and justify conformity to commercial-civic values and goals. Concludes that it failed to generate a metropolitan sense of community, largely because southern cities lacked the necessary socioeconomic base.

684 _____. THE URBAN SOUTH IN THE TWENTIETH CENTURY. St. Charles, Mo.: Forum Press, 1974. 38 p.

>Argues that the South has resembled the rest of the nation more closely than is generally realized in its pattern of urban development and in its experience of urban problems.

685 _____. "Urban Themes in the American South." JOURNAL OF URBAN HISTORY 2 (1975-1976): 139-45.

>Stresses the essential similarities in the urban experiences of the South and the rest of the nation and argues that southern cities took their identity more from their urban-ness than from their section. Emphasizes the importance of regionalism for understanding southern urbanization.

686 _____. "Urbanization in the South: A Unique Experience?" MISSISSIPPI QUARTERLY 26 (1973): 105-20.

>Contends that southern cities were not unique from those in the rest of the nation with respect to economic origins, class struc-

ture, leadership, public policy, demographic patterns, or responses to technology. Concludes that there were also important differences among southern cities in size, geographic circumstances, cultural backgrounds, and economic functions.

687 Brownell, Blaine A., and Goldfield, David R., eds. THE CITY IN SOUTHERN HISTORY: THE GROWTH OF URBAN CIVILIZATION IN THE SOUTH. Port Washington, N.Y.: Kennikat Press, 1976. 228 p.

Contains six essays arranged in chronological order: an overview by the editors, the first two centuries by Carville Earle and Ronald Hoffman, the Old South by Goldfield, 1860-1900 by Howard N. Rabinowitz, 1900-1940 by Brownell, and 1940 to the present by Edward F. Haas. Stresses the importance of the urban experience to the development of the region.

688 Bryant, Keith L., Jr. "Cathedrals, Castles, and Roman Baths: Railway Station Architecture in the Urban South." JOURNAL OF URBAN HISTORY 2 (1976): 195-230.

Contends that southern cities kept up with the rest of the nation's urban centers in constructing railroad stations that were large, technologically sound, and architecturally significant. Concludes that these stations revitalized the heart of southern cities by making the area formerly occupied by railroad tracks available for industrial and commercial use.

689 Carpenter, Charles G. "Southern Labor and the Southern-Urban Continuum, 1919-1929." Ph.D. dissertation, Tulane University, 1973. 342 p.

Evaluates primary sources that include newspapers, union records and personal accounts by strike leaders, to support the contention that southern labor conflicts spanned a continuum with southern traits gradually giving way to urban ones.

690 Clark, Thomas D. "The Modern South in a Changing America." PROCEEDINGS OF THE AMERICAN PHILOSOPHICAL SOCIETY 107 (1963): 121-31.

Identifies urbanization and urbanites as some of the major forces modernizing the region. Feels that demands for reapportionment are destroying the old rural-based, conservative, racist political organizations that have dominated the South for over a century.

691 Cobb, James C. "Urbanization and the Changing South: A Review of Literature." In SOUTH ATLANTIC URBAN STUDIES, vol. 1, edited by Jack R. Censer and N. Steinert, pp. 253-66. Columbia: University of South Carolina Press, 1977.

Regional Studies

Contends that the South experienced urban and metropolitan developments much as did the rest of the United States. Calls for a more realistic study of the measurable efforts and concomitants of the region's urbanization.

692 Cohn, Raymond L. "A Locational Analysis of Manufacturing Activities in the Antebellum South and Midwest." Ph.D. dissertation, University of Oregon, 1977. 230 p.

Finds that differences in regional resource base and distribution of income led to the establishment of a consumer-oriented economy in the Midwest and stifled its development in the South. Also concludes that the degree of urbanization affected the amount of consumer orientation.

693 Conk, Margo Anderson. "United States Census and the New Jersey Urban Occupational Structure, 1870-1940." Ph.D. dissertation, Rutgers University, 1978. 340 p.

Surveys the efforts of the Census Bureau to collect and report occupational statistics during the period, analyzes the data on changes in race, sex, age, ethnic, and occupational categories in the nine largest cities of the New York-New Jersey-Philadelphia region, and explores the relationship between the social and economic dimensions of the above data.

694 Conzen, Michael P. "Local Migration Systems in Nineteenth-Century Iowa." GEOGRAPHICAL REVIEW 64 (1974): 339-61.

Contends that one-fourth of the outmigrants from the state's twelve most populous counties between 1840 and 1895 moved into cities while about one-half moved westward. Sees this as indicative of the emerging dominance of regional cities, even in a heavily agricultural state.

695 Crowther, Simeon J. "Urban Growth in the Mid-Atlantic States, 1785-1850." JOURNAL OF ECONOMIC HISTORY 36 (1976): 624-44.

Examines the development of the New York City and Philadelphia urban regions during this period. Divides the growth pattern into three distinct eras, based upon a changing economic base.

696 Curry, Leonard P. RAIL ROUTES SOUTH: LOUISVILLE'S FIGHT FOR THE SOUTHERN MARKET, 1865-1872. Lexington: University of Kentucky Press, 1969. 150 p.

Demonstrates the rivalry between Louisville and Cincinnati for southern trade continued unabated after the Civil War and the abolition of slavery.

Regional Studies

697 _____. "Summing Up Southern Urban History." JOURNAL OF URBAN HISTORY 5 (1974): 255-63.

    Uses review essay on THE CITY IN SOUTHERN HISTORY (no. 687) edited by Blaine A. Brownell and David R. Goldfield, to discuss the need for constructing a universal framework of urban process in a comparative vein and to suggest the dimensions which it ought to encompass.

698 _____. "Urbanization and Urbanism in the Old South: A Comparative View." JOURNAL OF SOUTHERN HISTORY 40 (1974): 43-60.

    Argues that urban development in the Old South was neither significantly different from nor consistently inferior to that in the rest of the antebellum United States. Urges historians to free themselves from the plantation and agrarian myths and examine southern urbanism.

699 Davis, Ronald L., and Holmes, Harry D., eds. "Studies in Western Urbanization: Location, Transportation, Mining, Agriculture, Mobility." JOURNAL OF THE WEST 13 (1974): 1-119.

    Contains eight essays: the growth of St. Louis; the development of Superior, Wisconsin, as a transportation center; the Seattle Spirit, 1851-93; Las Vegas city boosters; the saloon in territorial Arizona; Colorado cooperative communities; post office frontier in Kansas; and socioeconomic change in Racine, Wisconsin, 1850-80.

700 Doherty, Robert. SOCIETY AND POWER: FIVE NEW ENGLAND TOWNS, 1800-1860. Amherst: University of Massachusetts Press, 1978. 114 p.

    Studies the towns of Pelham, Ware, Northampton, Worcester, and Salem, focusing upon geographic and social mobility, distribution of wealth, and political power and continuity. Divides society into the stable and the transient, and finds society open to the former and closed to the latter.

701 Dunbar, Willis. "The Speeding Tempo of Urbanization since 1950." MICHIGAN HISTORY 35 (1950): 291-313.

    Surveys the development of cities in Michigan over a ninety-year period and compares rural life in 1860 with urban life in 1950. Asserts that the rapid pace of urbanization since 1950 has caused many social and personal dislocations which need remedying.

702 Earnest, Grace E. "City Life in the Old South: The British Travelers Image." Ph.D. dissertation, Florida State University, 1966. 500 p.

Regional Studies

Relies upon about 150 published accounts of British travelers to construct a composite picture of southern urban life. Concludes that they were generally favorably impressed, although expressing reservations about the degree of lawlessness and the lack of enterprise.

703 Eisterhold, John S. "Lumber and Trade in the Seaboard Cities of the Old South: 1607-1860." Ph.D. dissertation, University of Mississippi, 1970. 254 p.

Examines the relationship between the lumber trade, the South's largest industry, and the cities of Savannah, Charleston, Wilmington, Norfolk, Baltimore, Pensacola, Mobile, and New Orleans. Focuses primarily upon the building of transportation networks and the role of white, free Negro, and slave labor.

704 Folk, Patricia A. "'The Queen City of Mobs': Riots and Community Reactions in Cincinnati, 1788-1848." Ph.D. dissertation, University of Toledo, 1978. 466 p.

Examines the causes and course of eleven riots during the period and finds that they arose primarily out of the establishment and growth of an urban center and that they were exacerbated by the city's unique geographical and economic position.

705 Gilchrist, David T., ed. THE GROWTH OF THE SEAPORT CITIES, 1790-1828. Charlottesville: University of Virginia Press, 1967. 227 p.

Contains papers and commentaries from a conference on seaport cities held in 1966. Includes sections on population, foreign trade, trade and manufactures, financial institutions, and economic thought.

706 Goldfield, David R. URBAN GROWTH IN THE AGE OF SECTIONALISM: VIRGINIA, 1847-1861. Baton Rouge: Louisiana State University Press, 1977. 336 p.

Insists that nineteenth century Southern cities exerted a far greater influence than warranted by their small number, whether measured in quantitative terms, the organization of urban life, or in the degree of urban consciousness. Focuses upon the response of Virginia's urban centers to the sectional crisis.

707 _____. "Urban-Rural Relations in the Old South: The Example of Virginia." JOURNAL OF URBAN HISTORY 2 (1976): 146-68.

Contends that relations between urban and rural Virginians mirrored those of other Americans in that they shared a desire for better access to markets, formed a market-oriented agriculture, regarded the countryside as a labor pool, had common memberships in agricultural societies, and were equally influenced by the press, urban rivalry, intraurban animosities, and sectional disputes.

708 Goldin, Claudia Dale. URBAN SLAVERY IN THE AMERICAN SOUTH 1820-1860: A QUANTITATIVE HISTORY. Chicago: University of Chicago Press, 1976. 168 p.

Denies that the decline in the number of slaves in urban areas meant that an urban-industrial environment was hostile to slavery. Attributes the decline to the influx of cheap immigrant labor and the differences in elasticity of demand between urban and rural areas.

709 Gottman, Jean. MEGALOPOLIS: THE URBANIZED NORTHEASTERN SEABOARD OF THE UNITED STATES. New York: Twentieth Century Fund, 1961. 810 p.

Traces the historical evolution of the nation's first and largest "megalopolis," analyzes the "modern revolution in land use" which characterizes it, examines the "patterns of intense living" which affect its residents, and speculates on the future of this expanding phenomenon.

710 Groth, Philip. "Plantation Agriculture and the Urbanization of the South." RURAL SOCIOLOGY 42 (1963-1964): 206-19.

Rejects both the political economy and the eclectic (combination of socioeconomic, topographical, and climatic features) theories for the preponderant rurality of the South. Finds that the plantation economy had little measurable effect in retarding urbanization.

711 _____. "Population Change and the Urbanization and Industrialization of the South, 1910-1970." Ph.D. dissertation, University of Wisconsin, Madison, 1975. 225 p.

Argues that changes in manufacturing and services employment contributed largely to a resegregation of the population in cities and a lessening of residential segregation in more rural areas.

712 Haeger, John Denis. "Eastern Money and the Urban Frontier: Chicago, 1833-1842." JOURNAL OF THE ILLINOIS STATE HISTORICAL SOCIETY 64 (1971): 267-84.

Argues that eastern capital was vital to the development of Chicago in this era and that most successful Chicago entrepreneurs were in partnership with eastern financiers. Credits

Regional Studies

the latter for realizing that the development of frontier cities and the growth of the nation were intimately related.

713 Heale, M.J. "Patterns of Benevolence: Charity and Morality in Rural and Urban New York, 1783-1830." SOCIETAS 3 (1973): 337-59.

Finds vast differences between the philanthropic enterprises in New York's large cities and those in the state's rural and small town areas. Concludes that benevolence became virtually indistinguishable from moral uplift in urban settings.

714 Hoover, Edgar M., and Vernon, Raymond. ANATOMY OF A METROPOLIS: THE CHANGING DISTRIBUTION OF PEOPLE AND JOBS WITHIN THE NEW YORK METROPOLITAN REGION. Cambridge, Mass.: Harvard University Press, 1959. 345 p.

Attributes the significant changes in the distribution of the work force in the region to the influence of the automobile, the expressway, the five day week, the seven hour day, the blurring of the distinction between factory and office, the work ethic, and technological innovation.

715 Hopkins, Richard J. "Are Southern Cities Unique? Persistence as a Clue." MISSISSIPPI QUARTERLY 26 (1973): 121-41.

Disputes the notion that there was anything particularly unique in southern urban development. Asserts that the urbanization process is essentially the same all over the United States and that it has brought the South to the rest of the country in the past century.

716 Hughes, Sarah S. "Elizabeth City County, Virginia, 1782-1810: The Economic and Social Structure of a Tidewater County in the Early National Years." Ph.D. dissertation, College of William and Mary, 1975. 649 p.

Describes the standard of living of the county's inhabitants, including the black majority and women and children, and assesses the general movement of the population in and out of the county.

717 Kipp, Samuel M. III. "Urban Growth and Social Change in the South, 1870-1920: Greensboro, North Carolina as a Case Study." Ph.D. dissertation, Princeton University, 1974. 480 p.

Deals with the interrelationship between economic development and urban population growth and with the various dimensions of urban change in Greensboro. Concludes that southern cities shared certain distinctive traits that separated them from their northern counterparts.

Regional Studies

718   Kirkland, Edward C. MEN, CITIES, AND TRANSPORTATION: A STUDY IN NEW ENGLAND HISTORY, 1820-1900. Cambridge, Mass.: Harvard University Press, 1948. 385 p.

   Analyzes the changing modes of transportation in the region and their role in making it one of the country's most urbanized areas. Devotes substantial space to efforts at regulation of the transportation industry and to its financial and corporate consolidation.

719   Knight, Oliver. "Toward an Understanding of the Western Town." WESTERN HISTORICAL QUARTERLY 4 (1973): 27-42.

   Dismisses the concept of the "urban frontier" as obscuring rather than illuminating the process of western urbanization. Raises a number of questions for consideration and calls for "an understanding of the flesh-and-blood elements that made western towns function in all their dimensions."

720   Landis, Paul H. THREE IRON MINING TOWNS: A STUDY IN CULTURAL CHANGE. New York: Arno Press, 1970. 148 p.

   Focuses on the impact of the mining company's wrath when the Minnesota boom towns of Hibbing, Eveleth, and Virginia sought to finance improved municipal services by increasing taxes on their major industries in 1912.

721   Larsen, Lawrence H. THE URBAN WEST AT THE END OF THE FRONTIER. Lawrence: Regents Press of Kansas, 1978. 173 p.

   Analyzes the process of urbanization in the western United States, focusing on the experience of the twenty-four towns of eight thousand or more people listed in the federal census of 1880. Discusses various municipal services, the impact of technology, efforts to improve the environment, and demography, society, and economics. Uses comparative data to indicate similarities between frontier cities and older American urban centers.

722   Lemon, James T. "Urbanization and the Development of Eighteenth-Century Southeastern Pennsylvania and Adjacent Delaware." WILLIAM AND MARY QUARTERLY 24 (1967): 501-33.

   Explores the relationship between urbanization and several variables of economic development and social change, focusing on diverse settlement types, including backcountry towns, hamlets, transport centers, and processing towns, as well as the role of Philadelphia as a metropolis.

723   Lindsay, George D. "The Municipal Authority in Pennsylvania 1935-1950." DICKINSON LAW REVIEW 55 (1951): 141-57.

Regional Studies

724   Loftin, Bernadette Kuehn. "A Social History of the Mid-Gulf South (Panama City-Mobile) 1930-1950." Ph.D. dissertation, University of Southern Mississippi, 1971. 356 p.

    Studies the inhabitants of the mid-Gulf South, their attitudes, origins, and entertainments, and notes the prevalence of a strong degree of cohesiveness in all three cities.

725   Lohmann, Karl Baptiste. CITIES AND TOWNS OF ILLINOIS: A HANDBOOK OF COMMUNITY FACTS, 1703-1950. Urbana: University of Illinois Press, 1951. 110 p.

    Examines their origins, transportation systems, populations, streets and roads, industrial, commercial, and agricultural centers, public buildings, municipal parks, and community planning.

726   Luckingham, Bradford. "The City in the Westward Movement: A Bibliographical Note." WESTERN HISTORICAL QUARTERLY 5 (1974): 294-306.

    Bibliographic essay detailing major themes that have emerged in the relatively few works that have focused on the role of the city in the westward movement, and stressing the need for more research on this topic.

727   MacDonald, Norbert. "Population Growth and Change in Seattle and Vancouver, 1880-1960." PACIFIC HISTORICAL REVIEW 39 (1970): 297-322.

    Finds a striking similarity in the nature and timing of population growth in Seattle and Vancouver, but identifies certain distinctive population characteristics in each.

728   McLear, Patrick E. "John Stephen Wright and Urban Regional Promotion in the Nineteenth Century." JOURNAL OF THE ILLINOIS STATE HISTORICAL SOCIETY 68 (1975): 407-20.

    Discusses Wright's various promotional and business activities, concluding that as a propagandist he contributed importantly to the development of both Chicago and the Midwest.

729   Martin, Robert R. THE CITY MOVES WEST: ECONOMIC AND INDUSTRIAL GROWTH IN CENTER WEST TEXAS. Austin: University of Texas Press, 1969. 190 p.

    Focuses on the economic forces that contributed to the growth of cities in central west Texas and asserts that historians have ignored or underestimated the importance of urban development in the Southwest. Contends that the region's cities successfully serviced the cattle, farming, and oil industries.

Regional Studies

730 Mawn, Geoffrey P. "Promoters, Speculators, and the Selection of the Phoenix Townsite." ARIZONA AND THE WEST 19 (1977): 207-24.

> Suggests that the birth of Phoenix, rather than being a spontaneous event, followed an evolutionary pattern which also typified other western towns and delineates the relationship between speculators and promoters and economic profit.

731 Meyer, David R. FROM FARM TO FACTORY TO URBAN PASTORALISM: URBAN CHANGE IN CENTRAL CONNECTICUT. Cambridge, Mass.: Ballinger, 1976. 57 p.

> Provides a brief history of urban growth in central Connecticut, an analysis of contemporary patterns and trends in urban development and assesses possibilities for providing a "quality living environment" in the future.

731a Miller, Roberta Balstad. CITY AND HINTERLAND: A CASE STUDY OF URBAN GROWTH AND REGIONAL DEVELOPMENT. Westport, Conn.: Greenwood Press, 1979. 179 p.

> Analyzes the development of Syracuse, New York, and its hinterland and the relationship between this "city-region" and the nation between 1790 and 1860. Focuses upon the impact of the Erie Canal and the railroad upon the region, on migration patterns, and on the response of the hinterland to rapid, large-scale urbanization.

732 Mitchell, Bruce. "Judge Burke's Wenatchee, 1888-1893." PACIFIC NORTHWEST QUARTERLY 56 (1965): 97-105.

> Discusses the activities of Thomas Burke, promoter of Seattle and the Puget Sound region, as townsite entrepreneur and real estate developer, focusing on his interests in the Wenatchee Valley during the late nineteenth century.

733 Muller, Edward K. "Regional Urbanization and the Selective Growth of Towns in North American Regions." JOURNAL OF HISTORICAL GEOGRAPHY 3 (1977): 21-40.

> Proposes a generalized model of selective urban growth in newly settled regions which uses characteristics of circulation and export activity to identify three periods of development. Also emphasizes the interdependence of central place and mercantile bases of urban growth and relationship between the emergence of manufacturing and city size.

734 _____. "Selective Urban Growth in the Middle Ohio Valley, 1800-1860." GEOGRAPHICAL REVIEW 66 (1976): 178-99.

> Focuses on the experience of the middle Ohio Valley to indi-

Regional Studies

cate that a changing locational and hierarchical pattern of nodality within the transportation network can be related to three phases of regional development, during each of which there were distinct patterns of selective urban growth. Identifies these periods as the "Pioneer Periphery," the "Specialized Periphery," and the "Transitional Periphery," characterized by a different stage of economic development and transportation integration and, as a result, distinct type of urban patterns.

735 Nadeau, Remi A. CITY MAKERS: THE STORY OF SOUTHERN CALIFORNIA'S FIRST BOOM, 1868-1876. Los Angeles: Trans-Angelo Books, 1965. 168 p.

Stresses the impact of the railroad in turning a quiet village into a boom town, with all the attendant changes and problems.

736 Napier, Rita G. "Squatter City: The Construction of a New Community in the American West, 1854-1861." Ph.D. dissertation, American University, 1976. 226 p.

Examines the creation and growth of the power structure of Leavenworth, Kansas, by focusing on the nature of power relationships. Concludes that the decision-making process was controlled by wealthy businessmen and professionals with the majority of people not participating.

737 Nash, Gerald D. THE AMERICAN WEST IN THE TWENTIETH CENTURY: A SHORT HISTORY OF AN URBAN OASIS. Englewood Cliffs, N.J.: Prentice-Hall, 1973. 312 p.

Provides a framework for understanding the trans-Mississippi West, emphasizing its development since 1890, first as a "Colonial Society," from 1898 to 1941, and then as "The Pace-Setting Society," 1941-71.

738 Pearson, John E. "Urban Housing and Population Changes in the Southwest, 1940-1960." SOCIAL SCIENCE QUARTERLY 44 (1964): 357-66.

Discusses the characteristics of population change in the United States for the years 1940 to 1960, suggests number of persons per room as a measure for aggregate housing which most readily promotes interurban comparisons, and applies this measure to Southwest urban centers. Establishes a person-per-room ratio (PPR) of 1.01 as the upper limit for housing adequacy.

739 Perry, David, and Watkins, Alfred J., eds. "The Rise of the Sunbelt

Cities." URBAN AFFAIRS ANNUAL REVIEW 14 (1978): 1-309.

> Contains twelve essays dealing with urban development, entrepreneurship and boosterism, public services, class conflict, and visions of the urban future in the Sunbelt.

740 Preston, Howard L. "The Automobile Business in Atlanta, 1909-1920: A Symbol of 'New South Prosperity.'" GEORGIA HISTORICAL QUARTERLY 58 (1974): 262-77.

> Discusses the interest of "New South" boosters in promoting the fortunes of Atlanta, and the promotional activities surrounding the National Association of Manufacturers automobile exhibition in 1909. Indicates the important, positive impact on business development in Atlanta provided by the growth of automobile retailing in that city.

741 Quiett, Glenn Chesney. THEY BUILT THE WEST: AN EPIC OF RAILS AND CITIES. New York: D. Appleton-Century Co., 1934. 569 p.

> Surveys the development of the West from an entrepreneurial perspective stressing the role of great men, visions and events. Individual chapters discuss the process of town building, and the establishing and early years of such cities as Denver, San Francisco, Los Angeles, San Diego, Portland, Tacoma, Seattle, and Spokane.

742 Rabinowitz, Howard R. "From Reconstruction to Redemption in the Urban South." JOURNAL OF URBAN HISTORY 2 (1976): 169-94.

> Examines the political activities of blacks, Republicans, and conservatives in the region's cities and the efforts of the latter to manipulate the state legislatures against racial equality in urban areas. Finds techniques similar to those used against the rise of immigrant political power in the North.

743 Rice, Herbert W. "Early Rivalry Among Wisconsin Cities for Railroads, 1836-1849." WISCONSIN MAGAZINE OF HISTORY 35 (1951-1952): 10-16.

> Describes competition among various Wisconsin communities to secure railroad service, noting the attitudes of promoters and boosters in established as well as nascent or projected settlements.

744 Rogers, Tommy W. "Net Migration Rates of the Eighty Standard Metropolitan Statistical Areas of the Census South, 1950-1960." LOUISIANA STUDIES 6 (1967): 135-48.

> Investigates the impact of ten independent variables in explaining observed differences in the migration patterns observed for

southern SMSAs between 1950 and 1960. Positive statistically significant correlations were observed for the variables of industrial change, median education, and 1940-50 net migration rates.

745   Ross, D. Reid, and Weister, C.W. "The Relationship Between Urban Growth and Transportation Development in the Cincinnati-Northern Kentucky Area." CINCINNATI HISTORICAL SOCIETY BULLETIN 21 (1963): 112-32.

    Contends that from its early history Cincinnati was a multifunction city with interindustry linkages, strategically situated for collection and distribution of goods and services for its hinterland. Analyzes the impact of various transportation modes on urban growth, from the traditional wagon roads of the 1790s to the development of commuter transportation during the years 1870 and 1940, concluding with a discussion of contemporary trends.

746   Rubin, Julius. CANAL OR RAILROAD: IMITATION AND INNOVATION IN RESPONSE TO THE ERIE CANAL IN PHILADELPHIA, BALTIMORE, AND BOSTON. Philadelphia: American Philosophical Society, 1961. 106 p.

    Compares the response of the three cities to the completion of the canal, focusing upon its economic impact.

747   _____. "Urban Growth and Regional Development." In THE GROWTH OF THE SEAPORT CITIES: 1790-1825, edited by David T. Gilchrist, pp. 3-21. Charlottesville: University of Virginia Press, 1967.

    Speculations on city growth as an aspect of more general processes of economic development, including discussions of interior town development and reasons for the differential experiences of northern and southern United States.

748   Scheiber, Harry N. "Urban Rivalry and Internal Improvements in the Old Northwest, 1820-1860." OHIO HISTORY 71 (1962): 277-339.

    Details the interplay of regional and local rivalries among urban centers at the state level by focusing on the history of Ohio's improvement policy. Contends that localism and regionalism proved so strong as to make any comprehensive, rational planning of a system of internal improvements impossible, both in the old Northwest and for the nation as a whole.

749   Schmid, Calvin F., and Schmid, Stanton E. GROWTH OF CITIES AND TOWNS--STATE OF WASHINGTON. Olympia: Washington State Planning and Community Affairs Agency, 1969. 176 p.

Regional Studies

Analyzes twentieth century urbanization in Washington, presenting overall population trends for the state, and its cities and towns. Includes a case study of the process of expansion in Seattle, as well as brief discussion of growth of such cities as Spokane and Tacoma.

750   Schnell, Christopher J., and Clinton, Katherine B. "The New West: Themes in Nineteenth Century Urban Promotion, 1815-1880." BULLETIN OF THE MISSOURI HISTORICAL SOCIETY 30 (1974): 75-88.

Contends that the "urban dream competed with the agrarian ideal as a symbol of opportunity for many pioneers" and delineates major themes of nineteenth century promotional literature.

751   Schnell, Christopher J., and McLear, Patrick E. "Why the Cities Grew: A Historiographical Essay on Western Urban Growth 1850-1880." MISSOURI HISTORICAL SOCIETY BULLETIN 28 (1972): 162-77.

Delineates the basic causes of urban growth in the trans-Mississippi West, stressing the impact of a variety of factors including technology, the transportation and agricultural revolutions, natural and geographical advantages, commercialism, urban promoters, and urban rivalries, and the increasing healthfulness of urban life.

752   Stewart, Peter C. "Railroads and Urban Rivalries in Antebellum Eastern Virginia." VIRGINIA MAGAZINE OF HISTORY AND BIOGRAPHY 81 (1973): 3-22.

Describes the three-cornered struggle for urban supremacy among Richmond, Norfolk, and Petersburg, in the three decades prior to the Civil War, and the way in which it affected the development of Virginia's railroads.

753   Still, Bayrd. "Patterns of Mid Nineteenth Century Urbanization in the Middle West." MISSISSIPPI VALLEY HISTORICAL REVIEW 28 (1941): 187-206.

Surveys nineteenth-century midwestern urban development focusing on the experiences of Buffalo, Cleveland, Detroit, Chicago, and Milwaukee, noting several shared characteristics, such as a limited conception of municipal functions, an expectation that citizens would promote the city's growth, the encouragement of manufacturing rather than trade, and replication, as a result of imitation, of tested forms of municipal practice and urban service.

754   Storey, Britt Allen. "William Jackson Palmer, Promoter." COLORADO MAGAZINE 43 (1966): 44-55.

Regional Studies

Discusses Palmer's activities as urban promoter in the West during the latter portion of the nineteenth century, focusing on the way in which he used his railroad, the Denver and Rio Grande, in conjunction with the founding of new towns in Colorado, and the impact this had on other towns in the area.

755 Tharp, Claude Roy. MICHIGAN CITIES AND VILLAGES: ORGANIZATION AND ADMINISTRATION, 1857-1951. Ann Arbor: University of Michigan Press, 1951. 40 p.

756 Vance, Rupert B., and Demerath, Nicholas J., eds. URBAN SOUTH. Freeport, N.Y.: Books for Libraries Press, 1971. 307 p.

Fourteen essays consider various aspects of southern urbanization organized into three main headings: the emergence and growth of southern cities, the city as a social organization, and the impact of the South's new urbanism on that section's future.

757 Wade, Richard C. SLAVERY IN THE CITIES: THE SOUTH, 1820-1860. New York: Oxford University Press, 1964. 340 p.

Traces the development of urban slavery and reconstructs the social existence of black slaves in the cities, emphasizing the ways in which slavery in the urban context differed from its rural counterpart. Notes that by 1860 in the cities slavery as an institution was languishing. Sees the nature of urban society as a causal agent, indicating the greater complexities in relationships it fostered, the presence of free blacks, the activities of churches, and urban retail economic pressures, all of which blurred lines more easily maintained in the countryside.

758 _____. THE URBAN FRONTIER: THE RISE OF WESTERN CITIES, 1790-1830. Cambridge, Mass.: Harvard University Press, 1959. 360 p.

Pioneer attempt to relate the development of western urbanism and to discuss the role of the city in the western experience. Contends that the rise of the cities was by 1830, "one of the dominant facts of Western life."

759 _____. "Urban Life in Western America, 1790-1830." AMERICAN HISTORICAL REVIEW 64 (1958): 14-30.

Surveys the growth of western towns and cities, indicating some of the reasons responsible for their development and the ways in which they provided for their inhabitants. Emphasizes the distinctive social and cultural developments that separated rural and metropolitan West, and the role of the cities in accelerating the West's transformation "from a gloomy wilderness to a richly diversified region."

760 Waring, George E., Jr., comp. REPORT ON THE SOCIAL STATISTICS OF CITIES. 2 vols. Part 1. THE NEW ENGLAND AND MIDDLE STATES. Part 2. THE SOUTHERN AND WESTERN STATES. New York: Arno Press, 1970.

Contains detailed descriptions of over two hundred American cities based upon data from the 1880 census, along with histories of several of the major cities.

761 Weiher, Kenneth. "The Cotton Industry and Southern Urbanization." EXPLORATIONS IN ENTREPRENEURAL HISTORY 14 (1977): 120-40.

Results of a systematic investigation of southern urbanization through the application of urban economic models indicates that the cotton South's urban system conformed to the concepts of central place theory, and that the cotton industry proved fundamentally responsible for "the location, size, and growth of the majority of southern cities on into the 1920s."

762 _____. "Southern Urbanization and Urban Growth: 1880-1930, An Application of Central Place Theory." Ph.D. dissertation, Indiana University, 1975. 173 p.

Analyzes the pace and pattern of southern urbanization using central place theory, stressing the key importance of the cotton industry in structuring the emergence of a multiordered urban network.

763 Weisel, Edward Berry. "City, County, State: Intergovernmental Relations in Texas, 1835-1860." Ph.D. dissertation, Rice University, 1975. 339 p.

Finds that the state legislature used state legal supremacy to enhance and strengthen local government's functional autonomy and that the local communities, in turn, attempted to use state power to further local economic development and population growth.

764 Wellenreuther, Hermann. "Urbanization in the Colonial South: A Critique (and a Reply from Joseph A. Ernst and H. Roy Merrens)." WILLIAM AND MARY QUARTERLY 31 (1974): 653-71.

Criticizes the thesis that the distributive function of urban centers played a major role in furthering diversification of the economy in the southern colonies as conceptually flawed in that it adopts a monocausal approach and is empirically inadequate, in that it generalizes overly from a single example. Stresses the need to consider a wide variety of factors, includ-

Regional Studies

ing economic functions and infrastructures, settlement patterns, economic behaviors, and political developments.

765 Wells, Eugene Tate. "St. Louis and Cities West, 1820-1880. A Study in History and Geography." Ph.D. dissertation, University of Kansas, 1951. 624 p.

Investigates the factors of city development in the trans-Mississippi West, emphasizing transportation, economics, geographical location and the interests of local inhabitants in the leading cities of the area: Cincinnati, Chicago, Memphis, and Kansas City.

766 Wheeler, Kenneth W. "Early Urban Development in Texas, 1836-1865." Ph.D. dissertation, University of Rochester, 1964. 331 p.

Presents a study of a neglected aspect of frontier history, the city, and profiles the development of Galveston, Houston, Austin, and San Antonio.

767 _____. TO WEAR A CITY'S CROWN: THE BEGINNINGS OF URBAN GROWTH IN TEXAS, 1836-1865. Cambridge, Mass.: Harvard University Press, 1968. 222 p.

Sees Texas as "the last urban frontier of the Old South," and describes and analyzes, within a comparative context, economic, municipal, social and cultural conditions in Galveston, Houston, Austin, and San Antonio.

768 Williamson, Jeffrey G. "Antebellum Urbanization in the American Northeast." JOURNAL OF ECONOMIC HISTORY 25 (1965): 592-608.

Presents confirmation regarding the scope and findings of an ongoing research project on northeastern urbanization in the nineteenth century which involved systematic analysis of urban population statistics in relation to economic growth and which employs a comparative approach over space.

769 Wotton, Grigsby H. "The New City of the South: Atlanta, 1843-1873." Ph.D. dissertation, Johns Hopkins University, 1973. 450 p.

Describes Atlanta's rapid urbanization growth between the years 1843 and 1873 from a city of social instability and disorder to a principal distribution center for food and manufactured products.

770 Wright, William C., ed. NEW JERSEY SINCE 1860: NEW FINDINGS AND INTERPRETATIONS. Trenton: New Jersey Historical Commission, 1972. 99 p.

Regional Studies

Includes four major articles: "The Historian's Passaic 1855-1912: A Research Model of New Jersey's Urban Past" by Michael Ebner, "The Black Experience in Newark" by Kenneth and Barbara Jackson, "The Impact of Industrialization in the New Jersey Legislature" by Joseph Mahoney, and "Politics and Economics in Frank Hague's Jersey City" by Richard Connors.

771 _____. URBAN NEW JERSEY SINCE 1870. Trenton: New Jersey Historical Commission, 1975. 116 p.

Contains four papers, dealing with blacks in Newark, boosterism in Newark, nativism in Jersey City, and Atlantic City as a middle-class playground, with an introduction by the editor and comments by Bayrd Still and Seth M. Scheiner.

772 Wunder, John, ed. TOWARD AN URBAN OHIO: A CONFERENCE TO COMMEMORATE THE BICENTENNIAL OF THE AMERICAN REVOLUTION. Ohio American Revolution Bicentennial Conference Series, no. 5. Columbus, Ohio: Ohio Historical Society, 1977. 44 p.

Booklet containing five brief essays providing chronologically ordered overview of urbanization in Ohio: Charles N. Glaab, "The Idea of the City and Early Ohio Growth"; Harry N. Scheiber, "Ohio's Transportation Revolution--Urban Dimensions, 1803-1870"; Melvyn Dubofsky, "Industrialization in Ohio's Gilden Age"; Zane L. Miller, "Ohio's Immigrants and the Rush to an Urban Setting: Ethnicity and Community in Historical Perspective"; and James F. Richardson, "The City in Twentieth-Century Ohio: Crisis in Stability and Services."

773 Zelinski, Wilbur. "Where the South Begins: The Northern Limit of the Appalachian South in Terms of Settlement Landscape." SOCIAL FORCES 30 (1951): 172-78.

Posits the "settlement landscape" as a device for establishing the precise limits of the South since it gauges "Southerners" in terms of cultural factors distinguishing southern house traits, towns, and the southern countryside.

Chapter 6
COLONIAL CITIES AND TOWNS

774 Abbott, Carl. "The Neighborhoods of New York, 1760-1775." HISTORY 55 (1974): 35-54.

    Questions the prevailing view that the walking city of colonial times was characterized by little functional specialization and differentiation of residential neighborhoods. Contends that New York, at least, was characterized by a series of concentric zones focused on an urban core.

775 Alexander, John A. "Urban American in the Revolutionary Era: Studies in the Neglected Period of American Urban History." JOURNAL OF URBAN HISTORY 5 (1979): 241-53.

    Reviews four recent works on the Revolution in American cities and finds that they, in the main, reinforce the view that the major cities of colonial America played a vital role in the independence movement. Urges urban historians to pay more attention to the Revolutionary era.

776 Alexander, John K. "The City of Brotherly Fear: The Poor in Late-Eighteenth-Century Philadelphia." In CITIES IN AMERICAN HISTORY, edited by Kenneth T. Jackson and Stanley K. Schultz, pp. 79-97. New York: Knopf, 1972.

    Examines the reasons and results of the fear of the city's poor which gripped Philadelphia's upper and middle classes in the period. Regards that fear to be, along with residential segregation and poverty, the most persistent elements in American urban life.

777 _____. "The Philadelphia Numbers Game: An Analysis of Philadelphia's Eighteenth-Century Population." PENNSYLVANIA MAGAZINE OF HISTORY AND BIOGRAPHY 98 (1974): 314-24.

    Argues that Sam Bass Warner's estimate of the city's pre-1790 population based upon the 1775 Constable's Returns was inaccurately low. Suggests a formula of 6.27 x the number of houses which produces a figure that is more than 20 percent higher.

778 Archdeacon, Thomas J. "The Age of Leisler: New York City, 1689-1710: A Social and Demographic Interpretation." Ph.D. dissertation, Columbia University, 1971. 345 p.

Utilizes demographic sources to examine the ethnic composition of New York City, noting the gradual exchange of power and numerical dominance from the Dutch to the English and French.

779 _____. NEW YORK CITY, 1664-1710: CONQUEST AND CHANGE. Ithaca, N.Y.: Cornell University Press, 1976. 197 p.

Uses census data, tax lists, land and probate records, and genealogical material to demonstrate the thesis that the English conquest of New Amsterdam brought sweeping socioeconomic and political changes that destroyed Dutch hegemony and substituted participatory, semidemocratic politics for deferential.

780 Archer, John. "Puritan Town Planning in New Haven." JOURNAL OF THE SOCIETY OF ARCHITECTURAL HISTORIANS 34 (1975): 140-49.

Examines the European and biblical origins of the town plan of New Haven and demonstrates how practical mercantile considerations produced alterations.

781 Barck, Oscar T., Jr. NEW YORK CITY DURING THE WAR FOR INDEPENDENCE. Ann Arbor, Mich.: University Microfilms, 1970.

Focuses upon the difficulties which British occupation posed to the residents of the city in peace-keeping, physical welfare, commerce and business, the provision of food and fuel, the press, churches, and schools.

782 Boyer, Lee R. "The Golden Hill and Naussau Street Riots: New York City, 1770." Ph.D. dissertation, University of Notre Dame, 1972. 221 p.

Calls the Golden Riot remarkably similar to the Boston Massacre which occurred forty-four days later. Attributes the riot largely to beliefs that the soldiers stole the employment of the poor and that the Quartering Act was responsible for high taxes.

783 Bridenbaugh, Carl. CITIES IN REVOLT. URBAN LIFE IN AMERICA, 1743-1776. New York: Knopf, 1966. 433 p.

Examines the impact of the building Revolution upon the

people of the five largest colonial cities and analyzes and describes the "public mind" of the citizenry. Regards the cities as vital in providing a locale where people, leadership, and events could interact.

784 _____. CITIES IN THE WILDERNESS. THE FIRST CENTURY OF URBAN LIFE IN AMERICA. New York: Knopf, 1964. 500 p.

Concentrates on its five largest cities--Boston, New York, Newport, Philadelphia, and Charleston--to develop a pattern of urban growth in colonial America in three stages of development: villages, towns, and cities. Stresses the differences between urban and rural life in the period.

785 _____. SEAT OF EMPIRE: THE POLITICAL ROLE OF EIGHTEENTH CENTURY WILLIAMSBURG. Charlottesville, Va.: Dominion Books, 1963. 85 p.

Presents Williamsburg as the setting for activities "which cleared away the rubbish of feudalism and monarchy, without which the great developments of democracy in the nineteenth and twentieth centuries could never have taken place." Gives great credit to Virginia's aristocrats for their adoption of republican values and ways.

786 Bridenbaugh, Carl, and Bridenbaugh, Jessica. REBELS AND GENTLEMEN: PHILADELPHIA IN THE AGE OF FRANKLIN. New York: Oxford University Press, 1962. 383 p.

Contends that Philadelphia became the primary unit for the reception and distribution of European culture because of its increasing importance as an urban center due to trade and immigration which encouraged the full and free interplay of people and ideas.

787 Brobeck, Stephen. "Revolutionary Change in Colonial Philadelphia: The Brief Life of the Proprietary Gentry." WILLIAM AND MARY QUARTERLY 33 (1975): 410-34.

Contends that the Revolution destroyed the cohesion of the non-Quaker gentry in the city and democratized the political institutions of the city and state, thus subjecting them to popular accountability. Pronounces the prerevolution gentry as a self-conscious power elite perpetuated through recruitment and arranged marriages.

788 Brown, Richard D. REVOLUTIONARY POLITICS IN MASSACHUSETTS: THE BOSTON COMMITTEE OF CORRESPONDENCE AND THE TOWNS, 1772-1774. Cambridge, Mass.: Harvard University Press, 1970. 282 p.

Stresses the ways in which urban life fostered the growth of a sentiment of independence in the colony and the manner in which the urban network facilitated the activities of the committee.

789 Bushman, Richard L. FROM PURITAN TO YANKEE: CHARACTER AND THE SOCIAL ORDER IN CONNECTICUT, 1690-1765. Cambridge, Mass.: Harvard University Press, 1967. 343 p.

Argues that Puritans became Yankees as the law and authority embodied in the former's governing institutions collapsed under the impact of urbanization and economic ambition, coupled with the Great Awakening. Explores the search for new methods of ordering society.

790 Carey, Matthew. A SHORT ACCOUNT OF THE MALIGNANT FEVER, LATELY PREVALENT IN PHILADELPHIA: WITH A STATEMENT OF THE PROCEEDINGS THAT TOOK PLACE ON THE SUBJECT, IN DIFFERENT PARTS OF THE UNITED STATES. 1794. Reprint. New York: Arno Press, 1970. 164 p.

Discusses the efforts of the city to organize measures designed to cope with one of the worst threats to the health of the residents of urban America in the eighteenth and nineteenth centuries.

791 Cook, Edward M., Jr. THE FATHERS OF THE TOWNS: LEADERSHIP AND COMMUNITY STRUCTURE IN EIGHTEENTH-CENTURY NEW ENGLAND. Baltimore: Johns Hopkins University Press, 1976. 273 p.

Develops a typology of New England towns based upon political behavior, taxation patterns, and population and posits a process of evolution from small, self-contained farming villages to urban centers.

792 Davis, Thomas J. "Slavery in Colonial New York City." Ph.D. dissertation, Columbia University, 1974. 255 p.

Focuses upon slavery as both a labor supply and a system of social control. Contends that free white workers eventually moved for its abolition as a labor system, but insisted upon the retention of discriminatory practices and laws to maintain social control.

793 Diamondstone, Judith. "Philadelphia's Municipal Corporation, 1701-1776." PENNSYLVANIA MAGAZINE OF HISTORY AND BIOGRAPHY 90 (1966): 183-201.

Finds that the corporation, although a powerful institution in England, was ineffectively transplanted to America and that it ran against the tide of popular government in colonial America, which was seated in the provincial assembly.

Colonial Cities and Towns

794   Dructor, Robert. "The New York Commercial Community: The Revolutionary Experience." Ph.D. dissertation, University of Pittsburgh, 1975. 778 p.

    Establishes the political, economic, and social characteristics of the commercial community, using account and letter books, diaries, church lists, and vice admiralty courts records, and analyzes the attitudes of its members toward the Revolution. Includes extensive appendices giving data on the community.

795   Earle, Alice Morse. COLONIAL DAYS IN OLD NEW YORK. 1890. Reprint. Detroit: Singing Tree Press, 1968. 312 p.

    Contains excerpts from records, diaries, and letters concerning life in the Dutch city of New Amsterdam, especially on education, child rearing, crime and punishment, religion, and recreation.

796   Earle, Carville, and Hoffman, Ronald. "Urban Development in the Eighteenth-Century South." PERSPECTIVES IN AMERICAN HISTORY 10 (1976): 7-80.

    Sees southern urbanization in the century as largely the produce of economic forces associated with certain staple crops. Finds three patterns of urban dominance over the hinterlands: that of the overseas ports, that divided between these and colonial ports, and that controlled exclusively by colonial ports.

797   Eckelberry, Roscoe H. THE HISTORY OF THE MUNICIPAL UNIVERSITY IN THE UNITED STATES. U.S. Office of Education, Bulletin, 1932. no. 2. Washington, D.C.: Government Printing Office. 213 p.

    Presents brief historical surveys of the eleven municipal universities in existence in 1932 and generalizes about the conditions which have led to their development and their characteristic features. Stresses the variety of experiences that have characterized their evolution.

798   Ehrlich, Jessica Kross. "A Town Study of Colonial New York: Newtown, Queens County (1642-1790)." Ph.D. dissertation, University of Michigan, 1974. 263 p.

    Contrasts Newtown to the prototype of the isolated, homogeneous, self-contained New England town and finds it to be, by 1790, a politically impotent, socially stratified village with little free land and a surplus of black and white landless labor.

799   Ernst, Joseph A., and Merrens, H. Roy. "'Camden's turrets pierce the

skies!': The Urban Process in the Southern Colonies during the Eighteenth Century." WILLIAM AND MARY QUARTERLY 30 (1973): 549-74.

> Uses merchants' letterbooks with their revelations about the development of trade and commerce, to elaborate a view of the urban process in southern colonies, especially North Carolina, Virginia, and Maryland. Contends that the subject of urbanization in the era is subordinate to that of the development of regional economic systems.

800 Feinstein, Estelle F. STAMFORD PURITAN TO PATRIOT: THE SHAPING OF A CONNECTICUT COMMUNITY, 1614-1774. Stamford, Conn.: Stamford Historical Society, 1976. 231 p.

> Finds eighteenth-century Stamford characterized by religious fragmentation, governmental lethargy, and increasing social stratification. Contends that the Revolution merely reinforced the town's "standing order."

801 Flexner, James Thomas. "The Great Columbian Federal City." AMERICAN ART JOURNAL 2 (1970): 30-45.

> Contends that Washington, and not Jefferson, hired and supported Pierre L'Enfant in his building of the nation's capital. Examines the struggle between proponents of the new federal city and those who wanted the capital to remain in Philadelphia or New York.

802 Foner, Philip S. LABOR AND THE AMERICAN REVOLUTION. Westport, Conn.: Greenwood Press, 1976. 257 p.

> Contends that mechanics, artisans, laborers, seamen, and other workers did more than any other segment of society to galvanize the urban population to accept independence and that they coupled their arguments for political autonomy with designs for a more equalitarian and democratic society.

803 Fries, Sylvia Doughty. THE URBAN IDEA IN COLONIAL AMERICA. Philadelphia: Temple University Press, 1977. 218 p.

> Examines Boston, Philadelphia, Williamsburg, and Savannah and finds that the colonial city was the product of an effort to reconstruct Old World society and to recreate the moral order of the countryside in the urban environment. Identifies that ambivalence as the source of antiurbanism and as a major cause of the urban crisis of modern times.

804 Garvan, Anthony N.B. ARCHITECTURE AND TOWN PLANNING IN COLONIAL CONNECTICUT. Ann Arbor, Mich.: University Microfilms, 1975. 166 p.

Colonial Cities and Towns

Attributes Connecticut town architecture to European precedents, but strongly tempered by the forces of change within both societies and by the chronological framework in which they were operating.

805 Goodfriend, Joyce D. "Too Great a Mixture of Nations: The Development of New York City Society in the Seventeenth Century." Ph.D. dissertation, University of California-Los Angeles, 1975. 339 p.

Explores the effect of ethnic diversity on communal life in New York City and suggests that the institutionalization of ethnic pluralism promoted stability and achieved communal equilibrium.

806 Haley, Jacquetta Mae. "Voluntary Organizations in Pre-Revolutionary New York City, 1750-1776." Ph.D. dissertation, State University of New York at Birmingham, 1976. 276 p.

Examines the characteristics of individuals involved in voluntary organizations and the projected goals and activities implemented to solve eighteenth-century urban problems.

807 Haller, William. THE PURITAN FRONTIER: TOWN-PLANTING IN NEW ENGLAND COLONIAL DEVELOPMENT, 1630-1660. New York: AMS Press, 1969. 119 p.

Examines the Puritan design for frontier development through the technique of town planting. Concentrates upon the physical growth of the towns and upon the problems inherent in accommodating a population which was increasingly characterized by ethnic and religious diversity.

808 Henretta, James A. "Economic Development and Social Structure in Colonial Boston." WILLIAM AND MARY QUARTERLY 22 (1965): 75-92.

Compares and analyzes Boston's tax lists for 1687 and 1771 in order to ascertain the magnitude of change in the city's social composition. Finds that society became more stratified and unequal, with "merchant princes" and proletarians at opposite ends of the social spectrum.

809 Hunt, James Barton. "The Crowd and the American Revolution: A Study of Urban Political Violence in Boston and Philadelphia, 1763-1776." Ph.D. dissertation, University of Washington, 1973. 543 p.

Deals with the social and economic structure of the upper class of Newport, details its function in politics, and assesses its civic and cultural contributions.

Colonial Cities and Towns

810 Innes, John H. NEW AMSTERDAM AND ITS PEOPLE: STUDIES, SOCIAL AND TOPOGRAPHICAL, OF THE TOWN UNDER THE DUTCH AND EARLY ENGLISH RULE. Port Washington, N.Y.: Friedman, 1969. 365 p.

> Deals largely with the process of immigration and with social mobility in a systematic, if largely impressionistic, manner.

811 Kelley, Joseph J., Jr. LIFE AND TIMES IN COLONIAL PHILADELPHIA. Harrisburg, Pa.: Stackpole, 1973. 256 p.

> Concentrates on the city's major institutions and practices, including the town plan, business and and commerce, theatre, music, painting, religion, taverns, sexual mores, newspapers, and politics. Focuses on the era from 1681 to 1776.

812 Kite, Elizabeth S., ed. L'ENFANT AND WASHINGTON, 1791-1792: PUBLISHED AND UNPUBLISHED DOCUMENTS BROUGHT TOGETHER FOR THE FIRST TIME. Baltimore: Johns Hopkins Press, 1929. Reprint. New York: Arno Press, 1970. 182 p.

> Contains letters and papers of L'Enfant, Washington, and Jefferson showing the interaction between aesthetics and politics that produced the nation's capital.

813 Lockridge, Kenneth A. A NEW ENGLAND TOWN THE FIRST HUNDRED YEARS, DEDHAM, MASSACHUSETTS, 1636-1736. New York: Norton, 1970. 208 p.

> Describes the development of a single New England town in an attempt to convey the essence of preindustrial village life, the changes it underwent and tries to identify those characteristics of the town that appear uniquely American as opposed to those derived from and shared with English agricultural common till. Asserts that those forces which proved most powerful in shaping Dedham's history also affected other towns and, generalizing from this case study, argues that "this part of colonial America was moving away from a powerful corporate impulse deeply indebted to the European past, toward an age of pluralism, individualism, and liberty," but that this process "was neither as rapid nor as direct as might be thought."

814 Lucas, Stephen E. PORTENTS OF REBELLION: RHETORIC AND REVOLUTION IN PHILADELPHIA, 1765-1766. Philadelphia: Temple University Press, 1976. 333 p.

> Argues that the political rhetoric of Philadelphia Whigs was vital in shifting public opinion to a position in favor of Independence, especially their "second-order" economic arguments which dealt with questions of social justice, advantage or disadvantage, and future economic prospects.

815 Lydon, James G. "Philadelphia's Commercial Expansion, 1720-1739."

PENNSYLVANIA MAGAZINE OF HISTORY AND BIOGRAPHY 91 (1967): 401-18.

> Uses customs house reports to identify sources and patterns of Philadelphia's commercial growth.

816 Mohl, Raymond A. "Poverty in Early America, a Reappraisal: The Case of Eighteenth-Century New York City." NEW YORK HISTORY 1 (1969): 5-27.

> A case study of New York City calls into question the traditional view of colonial America as a land of widespread economic opportunity, great social mobility, and little poverty, and suggests the need for additional studies of urban poverty.

817 Nash, Gary B. "City Planning and Political Tension in the Seventeenth Century: The Case of Philadelphia." PROCEEDINGS OF THE AMERICAN PHILOSOPHICAL SOCIETY 112 (1968): 54-73.

> Presents details of the tensions, misunderstandings, and rivalries on the part of both William Penn and the colonists which attended the founding of Pennsylvania during the years from 1681 to 1684.

818 _____. "Poverty and Poor Relief in Pre-Revolutionary Philadelphia." WILLIAM AND MARY QUARTERLY 33 (1976): 3-30.

> Argues that the modernization of the colonial economy during the eighteenth century "was accompanied by the evolution of poverty from an occasional to a systematic problem." Examines changing attitudes toward poverty and its alleviation among Philadelphia's elite.

819 _____. "The Transformation of Urban Politics, 1700-1765." THE JOURNAL OF AMERICAN HISTORY 60 (1973): 605-32.

> Contends that the experience of Boston, New York, and Philadelphia indicates the evolution of a "radical" mode of politics in colonial urban centers characterized by the politicization of lower-class elements and a political culture that proved "far from deferential, increasingly anti-authoritarian, occasionally violent, and often destructive of the very values which the political elite wished to preserve."

820 _____. "Up from the Bottom in Franklin's Philadelphia." PAST AND PRESENT 77 (1977): 57-83.

> Discusses the opportunities for socioeconomic mobility in late seventeenth- and eighteenth-century Philadelphia and identifies the last few decades of the colonial period as a time of increasing stratification, growing numbers of impoverished city people, constricted opportunity for lower strat inhabitants, and high rates of population turnover among the laboring poor,

testifying to a "silent transformation of urban life that involved occupational specialization, redistribution of wealth, spreading commercialization, decay of familiar institutions, legitimization of personal interest, and the creation of a market economy."

821 _____. "Urban Wealth and Poverty in Pre-Revolutionary America." JOURNAL OF INTERDISCIPLINARY HISTORY 6 (1976): 545-84.

Presents data on wealth distribution, inventoried wealth, poor relief, warnings out, and tax forgiveness of eighteenth-century New York, Boston, and Philadelphia, indicating the occurrence of a powerful transformation of life in these seaport cities, specifically, the growth of poverty, weakening economic leverage of the artisan and shopkeeper class, and a consolidation of wealth among merchants, lawyers, and land speculators.

822 Nash, Gary B., and Smith, Billy G. "The Population of Eighteenth-Century Philadelphia." PENNSYLVANIA MAGAZINE OF HISTORY OF BIOGRAPHY 99 (1975): 362-68.

Criticizes John K. Alexander's attempt (no. 777) to construct a population table for eighteenth-century Philadelphia for assuming constancy in the ratio of people per house throughout the century, and notes that his figures have little utility for gauging population prior to 1750. Suggests the number of taxables in the city would serve as a more reliable basis for population estimates and presents some population figures estimates derived in this manner.

823 Olton, Charles S. ARTISANS FOR INDEPENDENCE: PHILADELPHIA MECHANICS AND THE AMERICAN REVOLUTION. Syracuse, N.Y.: Syracuse University Press, 1975. 172 p.

Argues that the pursuit of profit, rather than any ideological commitment to independence or equality motivated Philadelphia artisans in their quest for independence. Insists that mechanics and artisans could already vote, were reasonably well-off economically, and mostly desired a bigger slice of the economic pie.

824 Papenfuse, Edward C. IN PURSUIT OF PROFIT: THE ANNAPOLIS MERCHANTS IN THE ERA OF THE AMERICAN REVOLUTION, 1763-1805. Baltimore: Johns Hopkins University Press, 1975. 288 p.

Discusses how the export of tobacco played a major role in mercantile opportunity, economic development, and urban growth during the latter half of the eighteenth century.

Colonial Cities and Towns

825 Paul, Charles L. "Colonial Beaufort." NORTH CAROLINA HISTORICAL REVIEW 42 (1965): 139-52.

Discusses the founding and early development of Beaufort, a seaport in North Carolina.

826 Peterson, Arthur, and Edwards, George W. NEW YORK AS AN EIGHTEENTH CENTURY MUNICIPALITY PRIOR TO 1731. New York: AMS Press, 1968. 352 p.

Presents detailed information of New York City's early days emphasizing the development of municipal institutions.

827 Peyer, Jean B. "Jamaica, Long Island 1656-1776: A Study of the Roots of American Urbanism." Ph.D. dissertation, City University of New York, 1974. 404 p.

Statistically analyzes changes and continuities in Jamaica, New York's social structure and organization. Emphasizes interrelationship of occupational groups, social stratification and mobility, population growth, family size, marriage patterns, and religious affiliations.

828 Powell, Sumner Chilton. PURITAN VILLAGE: THE FORMATION OF A NEW ENGLAND TOWN. Wesleyan, Conn.: Wesleyan University Press, 1963. 258 p.

Discusses the development of Sudbury, Massachusetts, through an examination of the town's founders and early leaders, as well as their formative debates and conflicts. Contends that the towns of New England differed from one another in origins and natures, and identifies as a key process for attention the change, transition, and stability of English local institutions across the Atlantic Ocean in the seventeenth century.

829 Rainbolt, John C. "The Absence of Towns in Seventeenth-Century Virginia." JOURNAL OF SOUTHERN HISTORY 35 (1969): 343-60.

Contends that Virginia's colonial leaders did wish to create towns to centralize economic and social activity, but failed to overcome the geographical barriers to urban growth, largely as a result of local political rivalries as well as the conflict between crown and burgesses as to the purpose of towns.

830 Rogers, George C., Jr. CHARLESTON IN THE AGE OF THE PINCKNEYS. Norman: University of Oklahoma Press, 1969. 187 p.

Traces Charleston's evolution from a colonial town in the mid-eighteenth century to a thriving commercial city just prior to the Civil War.

Colonial Cities and Towns

831   Rutman, Darrett. HUSBANDMEN OF PLYMOUTH: FORMS AND VILLAGES IN THE OLD COLONY, 1620-1692. Boston: Beacon Press, 1967. 100 p.

    Emphasizes changing life-styles and social relationships in the towns and villages of the colony and relates these to the formation of communities.

832   _____. "People in Process: The New Hampshire Towns of the Eighteenth Century." JOURNAL OF URBAN HISTORY 1 (1975): 262-92.

    Focuses on a sample of New Hamsphire towns, mainly for the eighteenth century, in an attempt to test and refine "morphology of societal evolution" suggested by James A. Heretta (THE EVOLUTION OF AMERICAN SOCIETY, 1700-1815 [1973]). Concludes that while there was in fact an ongoing demographic process in early New England towns, it seems best understood in terms of population density and levels of economic opportunity rather than age of "generative" implied by the morphology hypothesis.

833   _____. WINTHROP'S BOSTON: PORTRAIT OF A PURITAN TOWN, 1630-1649. Chapel Hill: University of North Carolina Press, 1965. 324 p.

    Assesses "the nature of the difference between the ideal which lay behind the Winthrop migration of 1630 and the reality of the settled community as reflected in institutional development." Concludes that despite Winthrop's ideals based upon medieval notions of community, Boston rather speedily reflected a "modern" society which displayed individualism, materialism, separation between church and state, including the withdrawal of the former from secular affairs, an associational nature of society, and a "Franklinesque" morality.

834   Ryerson, R.A. "Political Mobilization and the American Revolution: The Resistance Movement in Philadelphia, 1765 to 1776." WILLIAM AND MARY QUARTERLY 31 (1974): 565-88.

    Focuses on leadership recuitment in Philadelphia, detailing the emergence of new radical leadership, and presenting data regarding age, wealth, occupation, nationality, and religion of members of Philadelphia's resistance committees.

835   _____. THE REVOLUTION IS NOW BEGUN: THE RADICAL COMMITTEES OF PHILADELPHIA, 1765-1776. Philadelphia: University of Pennsylvania Press, 1978. 305 p.

    Demonstrates how the city's radicals gradually built momentum and broadened their support by appealing to a wide variety of occupational, social, religious and ethnic groups. Concludes that the members of the radical committees were "new men" who used hostility to Great Britain as a wedge for overthrowing the city's elite.

836   Sellers, Leila. CHARLESTON BUSINESS ON THE EVE OF THE AMERICAN REVOLUTION. New York: Arno Press, 1970. 259 p.

Argues that Charleston was the most significant city in the American South and that the British alienated much of the city's business elite by their political and economic policies.

837   Shaffer, Janet. "New London." VIRGINIA CAVALCADE 15 (1966): 22-29.

Discusses the importance of New London, the seat of Bedford County, Virginia, during the revolutionary era.

838   Singleton, Esther. SOCIAL NEW YORK UNDER THE GEORGES, 1714-1776: HOUSE STREETS, AND COUNTRY HOMES, WITH CHAPTERS ON FASHIONS, FURNITURE, CHINA PLATE, AND MANNERS. 1902. Reprint. Port Washington, N.Y.: Friedman, 1969. 407 p.

Recreates the daily life of the city's upper class, focusing upon the area described in the subtitle.

839   Still, Bayrd. "New York's Morality: The Formative Years." NEW YORK HISTORICAL SOCIETY QUARTERLY 47 (1963): 239-55.

Discusses the development of the mayoralty in seventeenth-century New York City, stressing that, despite its limited stated powers, the office held considerable importance in that the incumbent usually fulfilled a dual role, not only gaining favors for the local community but also winning community support for the provincial authority.

840   Teaford, Jon Christian. THE MUNICIPAL REVOLUTION IN AMERICA: ORIGINS OF MODERN URBAN GOVERNMENT, 1650-1825. Chicago: University of Chicago Press, 1975. 152 p.

Describes the transformation in the political structure, function, and external relationships of the American municipality between 1650 and 1825, the vital years in which Americans discarded the model of urban government inherited from medieval Europe and substituted an ideal which determined the course of municipal development up to the present, "an ideal which saw the municipality as a residential community governed for the good of all the city's inhabitants, rather than only serving its commercial interests."

841   Tepaske, John J. "Funerals and Fiestas in Early Eighteenth Century

St. Augustine." FLORIDA HISTORICAL QUARTERLY 44 (1965): 97-104.

> Notes the drab character of social life in Spanish Florida, and focuses on memorial funeral rites for deceased monarchs and celebrations on the accession of a new king in St. Augustine, the only two events which brought forth a display of "pomp and panoply."

842 Thompson, Marvin G. "Litchfield, Connecticut and an Analysis of Its Political Leadership, 1719 to 1784." Ph.D. dissertation, University of Connecticut, 1977. 196 p.

> Studies the political life of Litchfield and concludes its leaders were responsible, wealthy citizens who ran the local government smoothly.

843 Tolles, Frederick B. MEETING HOUSE AND COUNTING HOUSE: THE QUAKER MERCHANTS OF COLONIAL PHILADELPHIA, 1682-1763. New York: Norton, 1963. 292 p.

> Contends that the phenomenal growth of the city in the colonial area depended largely upon the ambition and the business acumen of Quaker merchants who combined religious fervor with common sense.

844 Walker, Paul K. "The Baltimore Community and the American Revolution, 1763-1783: A Study in Urban Development." Ph.D. dissertation, University of North Carolina-Chapel Hill, 1973. 405 p.

> Traces Baltimore's expansion of commercial activity, reveals the town's commercial leaders to be the leaders of protest against Britain and shows the positive effect of war on economic growth.

845 _____. "Business and Commerce in Baltimore on the Eve of Independence." MARYLAND HISTORICAL MAGAZINE 71 (1976): 296-309.

> Examines the nature of commercial activity in Baltimore, stressing that its businessmen followed the example of older eastern urban centers. Notes Baltimore's dependence on Philadelphia, but sees signs of increasing autonomy.

846 Walsh, W. Richard. CHARLESTON'S SONS OF LIBERTY: A STUDY OF THE ARTISANS, 1763-1789. Columbia: University of South Carolina Press, 1959. 166 p.

> Examines the contributions of Charleston's middle-class artisans and mechanics to the life of the city and to such revolutionary organizations as the Sons of Liberty.

Colonial Cities and Towns

847 Warden, G.B. BOSTON, 1689-1776. Boston: Little, Brown, 1970. 404 p.

>Traces Boston's development from the royalization of the colony to the Declaration of Independence, with emphasis on its emergence as the economic center of New England and the focal point of antimperial agitation.

848 _____. "The Distribution of Property in Boston, 1692-1775." PERSPECTIVES IN AMERICAN HISTORY 10 (1976): 81-130.

>Based on deeds and mortgages, concludes that property was distributed widely and frequently among a majority of Boston's adult population. Notes patterns of uncertainty, risk, and change in property transfers, suggesting that distinctions between rich and poor may have been "continually shifting, blurred, and confused."

849 _____. "Inequality and Instability in Eighteenth-Century Boston: A Reappraisal." JOURNAL OF INTERDISCIPLINARY HISTORY 6 (1976): 585-620.

>Presents a detailed critique of five basic propositions which seemingly underlie recent scholarly contentions that eighteenth-century Boston witnessed increased social stratification, political elitism and economic inequality. Asserts that they prove neither persuasive nor convincing because of faulty assumptions, failure to check collateral sources and data, and neglect of the wider context of the phenomena being analyzed. Contends further that instability rather than inequality proved responsible for the heightened mistrust and extremism that preceded the Revolutionary War.

850 Wiberley, Stephen E., Jr. "Four Cities: Public Poor Relief in Urban America, 1700-1775." Ph.D. dissertation, Yale University, 1975. 241 p.

>Compares public poor relief in Boston, New York City, Philadelphia, and Charles Town (now Charleston) and finds an emphasis on making the poor work for their room and board, but contends that there was no real indigent class because the numbers were small, included many women and children, and were in close contact with those above them on the social ladder.

851 Wilkenfeld, Bruce M. "The New York City Common Council, 1689-1800." NEW YORK HISTORY 52 (1971): 249-74.

>Analyzes occupation, tenure, family background and religion of several hundred members of New York City's Common Council and concludes that while throughout the colonial

Colonial Cities and Towns

period men from the upper occupational strata held a disproportionate share of council seats, certain changes are discernable. The years from 1734 to 1775 witnessed increased elite predominance, whereas after the Revolution this pattern was, to an extent, reversed.

852 _____. "The Social and Economic Structure of the City of New York, 1695-1796." Ph.D. dissertation, Columbia University, 1973. 270 p.

Studies the distribution of wealth and property, and geographic and economic mobility of New Yorkers during a period of great demographic and economic expansion. Compares findings with studies of other American communities.

853 Wilkins, Barratt. "A View of Savannah on the Eve of the Revolution." GEORGIA HISTORY QUARTERLY 54 (1970): 577-84.

Contends that Savannah in 1774 was a town of considerable maturity and progress, based on the development of an economic hinterland separate from that of Charles Town (now Charleston), and provides a brief description of the town.

854 Withey, Lynn E. "Population Change, Economic Development, and the Revolution: Newport, R.I., as a Case Study, 1760-1800." Ph.D. dissertation, University of California-Berkeley, 1976. 245 p.

Considers Newport in the late eighteenth century, detailing the nature of its population, including age and sex structure, family size and degree of geographical mobility, economic currents, including mercantile activities, and discusses the city's decline, analyzing the impact of the Revolution and more general factors.

855 Wolf, Stephanie Graumon. URBAN VILLAGE: POPULATION, COMMUNITY, AND FAMILY STRUCTURE IN GERMANTOWN, PENNSYLVANIA, 1683-1800. Princeton, N.J.: Princeton University Press, 1976. 361 p.

Argues that, despite its relatively small size, Germantown displayed a variety of urban characteristics in the eighteenth century, including an impressive amount of heterogeneity and mobility.

856 Zuckerman, Michael. PEACEABLE KINGDOMS: NEW ENGLAND TOWNS IN THE EIGHTEENTH CENTURY. New York: Knopf, 1970. 329 p.

Argues that consciousness of community remained a prime value of public life in the towns of Massachusetts at least until 1770, emphasizing the force and role of concord and consensus as an organizing force for political and social life.

Chapter 7

URBAN INSTITUTIONS

857 American Public Health Association. A HALF CENTURY OF PUBLIC HEALTH. New York: American Public Health Association, 1921. Reprint. New York: Arno Press, 1970. 461 p.

>Contains a history of the Association and studies on housing, sewage, water systems, food supplies, and child welfare. Stresses the importance of the germ theory for cities seeking to prevent disease and epidemics.

858 Atkins, Gordon. HEALTH, HOUSING AND POVERTY IN NEW YORK CITY 1856-1898. Philadelphia: Porcupine Press, 1977. 343 p.

>Divides the era under consideration into three periods, with the depression of the 1870s in the middle, and examines the interaction among health, housing and poverty in each. Concludes that great progress was made during the era, despite the setbacks of the depression years.

859 Bader, Louis. "Gas Illumination in New York City, 1823-1863." Ph.D. dissertation, New York University, 1970. 375 p.

>Finds that gas light played a major role in the transformation of the city's social and physical environment during the period. Concludes that customer dissatisfaction spawned demands for municipal ownership of the utility, and led to the formation of the Consumer's Gas Association.

860 Bagdadi, Mania Kleinburd. "Protestants, Poverty and Urban Growth: A Study of the Organizations of Charity in Boston and New York, 1820-1865." Ph.D. dissertation, Brown University, 1975. 358 p.

>Relates efforts to deal with poverty to urban growth and the rediscovery of community. Stresses the evolution from voluntarism to professionalism in the areas of welfare, sanitation, and child care.

861 Barnes, Joseph W. "The Arson Years: Fire Protection, Fire Insurance,

Urban Institutions

and Fire Politics 1908-1910." ROCHESTER HISTORY 38 (1976): 1-47.

> Illustrates how a rash of costly arson-originated fires in Rochester spurred significant improvements in the city's fire protection system and eventually contributed to the state's celebrated efforts to regulate the insurance industry.

862 Barrett, Paul. "Public Policy and Private Choice: Mass Transit and the Automobile in Chicago Between the Wars." BUSINESS HISTORY REVIEW 49 (1975): 473-97.

> Contends that public policy decisions, heavily influenced by the interplay between crisis and intellectual inertia, were the major reason why the automobile triumphed over mass transit in Chicago. Locates much of the difficulty in the unrealistic assumption that mass transit must pay for itself to be viable.

863 Barsness, Richard W. "Los Angeles' Quest for Improved Transportation, 1846-1861." CALIFORNIA HISTORICAL QUARTERLY 46 (1967): 291-306.

> Argues that southern California largely failed in its efforts to attract sufficient capital to build a serviceable transportation system prior to the Civil War. Concludes that the disastrous drought of the 1860s finally spurred the building of the first railroad.

864 Berrol, Selma C. "Education in New York City: 1900-1920." ILLINOIS QUARTERLY 35 (1973): 20-30.

> Shows that, during the period of heavy immigration into New York City, the public schools served an important role in the behavioral assimilation of immigrant children, thus minimizing social disorder, crime, and ethnic conflict, and therefore preserving the stability of the heterogeneous city.

865 Blake, John B. PUBLIC HEALTH IN THE TOWN OF BOSTON, 1630-1822. Cambridge, Mass.: Harvard University Press, 1959. 278 p.

> Traces the evolution of the public health system over the first two hundred years of the city's history, stressing the gradual displacement of private by public efforts.

866 Blake, Nelson M. WATER FOR THE CITIES: A HISTORY OF THE URBAN WATER SUPPLY PROBLEM IN THE UNITED STATES. Syracuse, N.Y.: Syracuse University Press, 1956. 341 p.

> Focuses upon the efforts of New York, Philadelphia, Boston, and Baltimore to develop an adequate water supply system between 1790 and 1860. Concludes with two chapters on the evolution of water supply problems in U.S. cities in the century after 1860.

Urban Institutions

867   Blasingame, Ralph. "The Public Library as an Urban Phenomenon." Ph.D. dissertation, Columbia University, 1973. 85 p.

     Views the public library as a product of urban-industrial society in latter part of the nineteenth century, one that was local rather than state controlled, governed by an elite board, bureaucratic in form, and monocratic in administrative style.

868   Bonelli, Vincent Francis. "The Response of Public and Private Philanthropy to the Panic of 1819 in New York City." Ph.D. dissertation, Fordham University, 1976. 255 p.

     Analyzes the role that public and private institutions played in alleviating New York City's social problems after the panic, the institutions' cooperative efforts in immediate relief, and the long-range solutions of which focused on emotional concern for the individual and his/her place in society.

869   Bonkowsky, Elizabeth Leitch. "The Church and the City: Protestant Concern for Urban Problems, 1800-1840." Ph.D. dissertation, Boston University, 1973. 251 p.

     Locates the origins of the latter-day Social Gospel in the efforts of pre-Civil War "city missionaries" to deal with the problems of the urban poor. Notes that they developed no coherent theology or ideology to guide their actions, but responded in an ad hoc manner.

870   Brace, C.L. "What the Cities Are Doing for the Children of the Poor." NEW ENGLAND MAGAZINE 25 (1901-1902): 63-73.

     Examines the efforts of private charitable organizations and of city agencies to provide disadvantaged urban children with recreation, education, housing, and other forms of welfare.

871   Brewer, Paul W. "Voluntarism on Trial: St. Louis' Response to the Cholera Epidemic of 1849." BULLETIN OF THE HISTORY OF MEDICINE 49 (1975): 102-22.

     Finds that the epidemic forced St. Louisians to reconsider their reliance upon voluntarism and to begin a halting movement toward public health measures. Questions whether a voluntaristic society can operate in an urban environment.

872   Brieger, Gert H. "Sanitary Reform in New York City: Stephen Smith and the Passage of the Metropolitan Health Bill." BULLETIN OF THE HISTORY OF MEDICINE 40 (1966): 407-29.

     Details the enactment of sanitary reform and calls it the first comprehensive health legislation of its kind in the United

Urban Institutions

States, one which served as a model for numerous cities and states. Also notes that it contributed to the overthrow of the Tweed Ring.

873   Brownell, Blaine A. "The Notorious Jitney and the Urban Transportation Crisis in Birmingham in the 1920s." ALABAMA REVIEW 25(1972): 105-18.

Identifies the jitney, large touring cars converted to provide space for five to seven paying passengers, as the most serious contributor to traffic congestion in the city. Concludes that when the jitney was ordered off the street in the interests of public safety, the continuing increase in the use of private automobiles added to the congestion level.

874   Bullough, William A. CITIES AND SCHOOLS IN THE GILDED AGE: THE REVOLUTION OF AN URBAN INSTITUTION. Port Washington, N.Y.: Kennikat Press, 1974. 183 p.

Traces the efforts of businessman and educators to turn the control of public urban education over to professionals and bureaucrats who would mold the schools into producers of workers needed in a technological, industrial economy.

875   _____. "'It's Better to Be a Country Boy': The Lure of the Country in Urban Education in the Gilded Age." HISTORIAN 35 (1973): 183-95.

Contends that many educators tried to reproduce rural conditions in the city through nature study, miniature farms, and recreated crossroads workshops, but that these proved to be neither adequate models nor effective solutions for urban education.

876   Cain, Louis P. "Raising and Watering a City: Ellis Sylvester Chesbrough and Chicago's First Sanitation System." TECHNOLOGY AND CULTURE 13 (1973): 353-72.

Finds that Chesbrough's innovations in water and sanitation were largely responsible for Chicago's unrestricted urban growth and freed the city from the limitations imposed by an unfavorable topography. Contends that Chicago was willing to pay the price to have pure water and effective sanitation.

877   _____. "Unfouling the Public's Nest: Chicago's Sanitary Diversion of Lake Michigan Water." TECHNOLOGY AND CULTURE 15 (1974): 594-613.

Examines the activities of the Chicago Sanitary District between 1889 and 1930 and the political, economic, geographical, and

Urban Institutions

technological constraints which inhibited effective sewage disposal. Lauds its conservative approach to technological change.

878 Calhoun, Richard B. "From Community to Metropolis: Fire Protection in New York City, 1790-1875." Ph.D. dissertation, Columbia University, 1974. 374 p.

Uses the development of a professional fire fighting service in New York City as a case study to indicate the antebellum involvement of local government in certain public services. Contends that unprecedented urban growth and the breakdown of traditional community structures and values forced governmental action, which should be seen, therefore, as a pragmatic response to changed conditions rather than as flowing from an ideology of activism.

879 _____. "New York City Fire Department Reorganization, 1856-1870: A Civil War Legacy." NEW YORK HISTORICAL QUARTERLY 60 (1976): 7-34.

Argues that the Civil War produced lessons in operational, managerial, and logistical efficiency which were applied to such civilian functions as the provision of fire protection. Suggests that such practical applications of martial knowledge and experience were probably common in northern cities of the era.

880 Cameron, Diane Maher. "Historical Perspective on Urban Police." JOURNAL OF URBAN HISTORY 5 (1978): 125-31.

Compares the view of police found in James F. Richardson's URBAN POLICE IN THE UNITED STATES (1974), with that put forth by George L. Mosse in POLICE FORCES IN HISTORY (1975), and finds that they are inextricably intertwined with the value system of the total society. Points up the need to study the backgrounds and attitudes of policemen as individuals, as well as examining the law enforcement institution.

881 Candeloro, Dominic. "The Chicago School Board Crisis of 1907." JOURNAL OF THE ILLINOIS STATE HISTORICAL SOCIETY 68 (1975): 396-406.

Examines the efforts of reform Mayor Edward F. Dunne to reform the Chicago system by upgrading the quality of the school board, fostering teacher unionization, and regulating the activities of the superintendent. Concludes that some of these reforms survived the efforts of the next administration to undo them.

882 Carwardine, Richard. "The Second Great Awakening in the Urban Centers: An Examination of Methodism and the New Measures." JOURNAL OF AMERICAN HISTORY 59 (1972): 327-40.

> Insists that there was already an indigenous revival movement in eastern cities, especially among the Methodists, before Charles Finney brought his message to them. Claims that many Protestant churches embraced revivalism as a remedy for urban problems.

883 Caye, James F. "Crime and Violence in the Heterogeneous Urban Community: Pittsburgh 1870-1890." Ph.D. dissertation, University of Pittsburgh, 1977. 276 p.

> Finds that crimes, especially those involving violence, became increasingly characterized by class and ethnic antagonisms in this period. Attributes this largely to the confusions and tensions that accompanied rapid and large-scale industrialization.

884 Cheape, Charles W. "The Evolution of Urban Public Transit, 1880-1912: A Study of Boston, New York and Philadelphia." Ph.D. dissertation, Dartmouth College, 1976. 407 p.

> Contends that these cities responded to the pressures of urban growth and the consequent need for mass transit by creating legal monopolies, building municipally owned subways, and establishing transit commissions. Concludes that mass transit also produced business consolidation and greater government responsibility for the economy.

885 Clement, Priscilla F. "The Response to Need, Welfare and Poverty in Philadelphia, 1800 to 1850." Ph.D. dissertation, University of Pennsylvania, 1977. 442 p.

> Examines the city's welfare system in the context of its wider social, political and economic development, and dates the emergence of a recognizable welfare bureaucracy from the crisis created by depression of the 1840s.

886 Cohen, Abby. "Public Health and Preventive Medicine in Providence, 1913." RHODE ISLAND HISTORY 36 (1977): 55-63.

> Briefly examines the Providence milk scandal of 1913 in the context of public health history, municipal corruption, and progressive reform.

887 Cohen, Ronald D. "Schooling in Early Nineteenth-Century Boston and New York." JOURNAL OF URBAN HISTORY 1 (1974): 116-23.

> Uses studies of Stanley K. Schultz (no. 1002) on Boston and Carl F. Kaestle (no. 944) on New York as a springboard for

the discussion of current historiographical interpretations regarding nineteenth-century urban education. Calls for further study of the impact of greater schooling upon the culture of the wider society.

888 _____. "Urban Schooling in the Gilded Age and After." JOURNAL OF URBAN HISTORY 2 (1976): 499-506.

Reviews the recent literature on urban education and finds that nearly all the authors agree that the major thrust of school reform was to rationalize the system, making it conform to economic, technological, social, and political change. Finds that they differ largely in their views of how the "victims" reacted to this trend.

889 _____. "Urban Schooling in Twentieth-Century America: A Frame of Reference." URBAN EDUCATION 8 (1974): 423-37.

Reviews the literature on the role of the urban school in providing educational opportunity and concludes that schools cannot reform until the wider society does. Calls for local case studies of city school systems to deepen our knowledge of the interaction between school and society.

890 Cohen, Sol. PROGRESSIVES AND URBAN SCHOOL REFORM: THE PUBLIC EDUCATION ASSOCIATION OF NEW YORK CITY, 1895-1954. New York: Bureau of Publications, Teacher's College of Columbia University, 1964. 273 p.

Focuses on the Public Education Association to illustrate the theses that progressive education was a manifestation of the larger reform impulse of the Progressive era and that educational policymaking is the result of a political process. Insists that progressive education also had an unsavory side.

891 Collins, Cherry Wedgwood. "Schoolmen, Schoolma'ams and School Boards: The Struggle for Power in Urban School Systems in the Progressive Era." Ph.D. dissertation, Harvard University, 1976. 329 p.

Analyzes the conflict between a coalition of businessmen, professionals, and school administrators, on the one hand, and classroom teachers, on the other. Feels that the former, aided by the antilabor and antifeminist sentiment of the 1920s, curtailed the growth of the teacher power movement and transformed superintendents from educators to business managers.

892 Corn, Jacqueline Karnell. "Community Responsibility for Public Health: The Impact of Epidemic Disease and Urban Growth on Pittsburgh." WESTERN PACIFIC HISTORICAL MAGAZINE 59 (1976): 319-39.

Focuses on the Pittsburgh Board of Health in the years 1851,

Urban Institutions

1872, and 1888 when the city council made significant alterations in the health code. Concludes that the period was characterized by limited, makeshift responses to emergencies rather than a comprehensive philosophy of public health.

893 ———. "Municipal Organization for Public Health in Pittsburgh, 1851-1895." Ph.D. dissertation, Carnegie-Mellon University, 1976.

Examines the evolution of the concept of community responsibility for public health through the agency of the board of health. Attributes the development to the pressures resulting from an expanding economy and rapid population growth.

894 Cosgrove, John J. HISTORY OF SANITATION. New York: Gordon Press, 1977. 125 p.

Traces the evolution of water and sewage systems from ancient times to the present.

895 Cox, Harvey. THE SECULAR CITY: SECULARIZATION AND URBANIZATION IN THEOLOGICAL PERSPECTIVE. New York: Macmillan Co., 1965. 244 p.

Analyzes the impact of urbanization and its resultant secularization upon American religious faith and practice. Seeks to portray these social changes as new conditions requiring adaptation by the church, rather than as disastrous or antagonistic.

896 Cross, Robert D., ed. THE CHURCH AND THE CITY, 1865-1910. Indianapolis: Bobbs Merrill, 1967. 359 p.

Contains nineteen essays or sermons by prominent clergymen of the era designed to demonstrate that institutionalized religion was responding creatively to the challenges of secularism, urbanization, industrialization, and immigration. Sees four general modes of response: transformations, transplantation, adaptations, and reintegrations.

897 Cutler, William W. III. "A Preliminary Look at the Schoolhouse: The Philadelphia Story, 1870-1920." URBAN EDUCATION 8 (1974): 381-99.

Examines the changing functions, both real and symbolic, of the urban schoolhouse and analyzes the reasons for Philadelphia's failure to solve the problem of overcrowding.

898 Dentler, Robert A.; Mackler, Bernard; and Warshauer, Mary Ellen, eds. THE URBAN R'S: RACE RELATIONS AS THE PROBLEM IN URBAN EDUCATION. New York: Praeger, 1967. 304 p.

Contains essays by twenty scholars, teachers and psychologists

Urban Institutions

organized around the broad categories of the urban context of education, intergroup relations of urban school children, programming education for urban minorities, and black children and youth in northern large cities.

899   Doyle, Don H. "The Social Functions of Voluntary Associations in a Nineteenth Century American Town." SOCIAL SCIENCE HISTORY 1 (1977): 333-55.

Examines the overt and covert functions of voluntary organizations in Jacksonville, Illinois, finding that they integrated individuals into the wider society and provided forms of discipline to supplement those of the family and church.

900   Duffy, John. A HISTORY OF PUBLIC HEALTH IN NEW YORK CITY, 1625-1866. New York: Russell Sage Foundation, 1968. 619 p.

Traces the evolution of efforts to deal with public health issues in New York City from the private, voluntary organizations of colonial days to the health boards and formal governmental agencies of the mid-nineteenth century. Attributes progress to a pragmatic approach based upon workability.

901   _____. "Hogs, Dogs, and Dirt: Public Health in Early Pittsburgh." PACIFIC MAGAZINE OF HISTORY AND BIOGRAPHY 87 (1963): 294-305.

Finds that Pittsburgh took steps to deal with sanitation and public health problems as early as 1800 and developed a public sanitary committee in 1832. Argues that urban conditions mandated public action far earlier than did rural ones.

902   _____. "The Impact of Asiatic Cholera on Pittsburgh, Wheeling, and Charleston." WESTERN PENNSYLVANIA HISTORY MAGAZINE 47 (1964): 199-211.

Finds that the first wave of cholera produced temporary boards of health in three cities, the second led to permanent local boards, and the third brought about state boards of health and city health departments, the latter just after the Civil War.

903   _____. "Medicine and Medical Practice in Early Pittsburgh." WESTERN PENNSYLVANIA HISTORY MAGAZINE 45 (1962): 333-43.

Investigates the quality of medical practice in the city and finds that physicians readily prescribed patent medicine advertised in the newspapers and that Pittsburgh residents generally considered that they had the best medical care available.

904   _____. "Nineteenth Century Public Health in New York and New Orleans: A Comparison." LOUISIANA HISTORY 15 (1974): 327-37.

Finds some similarities and many significant differences in the way in which the two cities handled public health, based mainly upon their cultural differences. Finds New Orleans to have been much more socially conscious.

905 _____. "Smoke, Smog, and Health in Early Pittsburgh." WESTERN PENNSYLVANIA HISTORY MAGAZINE 45 (1962): 93-106.

Contends that the city's water supply was largely responsible for Pittsburgh's good health record in the early nineteenth century, while physicians and city officials largely ignored the hazards of smoke and smog, which were more slow acting and subtle.

906 _____. SWORD OF PESTILENCE: THE NEW ORLEANS YELLOW FEVER EPIDEMIC OF 1853. Baton Rouge: Louisiana State University Press, 1966. 191 p.

Describes the impact of a devastating plague upon the population of the South's most important city in the antebellum period.

907 Duis, Perry R. "The Saloon and the Public City: Chicago and Boston, 1880-1920." Ph.D. dissertation, University of Chicago, 1975. 4,708 p.

Uses contrasting urban environments, Chicago and Boston, to examine the role the saloon played as an economic, political and legal institution and the public's response to it.

908 East, Dennis H. "Health and Wealth: Goals of the New Orleans Public Health Movement, 1879-1884." LOUISIANA HISTORY 9 (1968): 245-75.

Examines the various obstacles which prevented city health officials from taking effective action against yellow fever and the failure of the Auxiliary Sanitary Association to take necessary precautions to prevent epidemics.

909 Ellis, John H. "Memphis' Sanitary Revolution, 1880-1890." TENNESSEE HISTORICAL QUARTERLY 23 (1964): 186-92.

Demonstrates that Memphis underwent a massive campaign of sanitation reform in the 1880s, impelled by various epidemics in previous decades. Locates the major impetus in the enlightened self-interest of merchants and cotton brokers.

910 Ellis, John H., and Galishoff, Stuart. "Atlanta's Water Supply--1865-1918." MARYLAND HISTORIAN 8 (1977): 5-22.

Describes the difficulties encountered in attempts to keep Atlanta's water supply abreast of rapid population growth, and traces the important role of the city's businessmen and water officials in promoting the expansion of the municipal water works.

911 Erenberg, Lewis A. "Urban Night Life and the Decline of Victorianism: New York City's Restaurants and Cabarets, 1890-1918." Ph.D. dissertation, University of Michigan, 1974. 369 p.

> Asserts that the structure of the cabaret and its entertainment provided the desired environment for a society that was questioning traditional roles and values and seeking a more public social life.

912 Finkelman, Paul. "Class and Culture in Late Nineteenth-Century Chicago: The Founding of the Newberry Library." AMERICAN STUDIES 16 (1975): 5-22.

> Contends that the Newberry Library represented a reaction by the city's elite against urbanization, industrialization, and immigration and was intended to serve as a "cultural resort."

913 Fisher, Robert B. "The People's Institute of New York City, 1897-1934: Culture, Progressive Democracy, and the People." Ph.D. dissertation, New York University, 1974. 471 p.

> Follows the progressivism of the People's Institute of New York City, designed to upgrade the quality of life by educating the working class in the values and goals of "democratic humanism."

914 Flack, James K., Jr. "The Press in Detroit, 1880-1900." MICHIGAN HISTORY 50 (1966): 76-87.

> Asserts that the city's press functioned as responsible organs that provided reliable news, assured a hearing for widely divergent viewpoints, served as a medium for literary work, and functioned as the "community's diary."

915 Foster, Charles I. "The Urban Missionary Movement, 1814-1837." PENNSYLVANIA MAGAZINE OF HISTORY AND BIOGRAPHY 75 (1951): 47-65.

> Examines the efforts of evangelical Christians in the major cities of the era to provide education, charity, and opportunities for worship for the city's poor. Finds their efforts in direct contrast to the nation's espousal of individualism.

916 Galishoff, Stuart. SAFEGUARDING THE PUBLIC HEALTH: NEWARK, 1895-1918. Westport, Conn.: Greenwood Press, 1975.

Urban Institutions

Argues that the clamor of social reformers for improved public health usually "played second fiddle" to the maintenance of a healthy business climate that would attract new industry. Claims that the business-dominated board of health emphasized professional administration over humanitarian concerns.

917   Gardner, James F. "Microbes and Morality: The Social Hygiene Crusade in New York City, 1892-1917." Ph.D. dissertation, Indiana University, 1974. 439 p.

Describes the social hygiene movement as a "tenuous alliance between sanitarians and moralists" and examines the factors that influenced and determined the course of social hygiene in an urban environment.

918   Giglierano, Geoffrey. "The City and the System: Developing a Municipal Service, 1800-1915." CINCINNATI HISTORICAL SOCIETY BULLETIN 35 (1977): 223-48.

Contends that Cincinnati's Progressive era reformers conceived of the city's sewer system as an organic entity of which the necessary bureaucracies and properly oriented individuals were an integral part.

919   Ginsberg, Stephen F. "The History of Fire Protection in New York City, 1800-1842." Ph.D. dissertation, New York University, 1968. 371 p.

Discovers that fire protection was closely related to other urban services and problems, which increased in magnitude as the city expanded. Finds that volunteer firemen became a significant political force after the great fire of 1835.

920   _____. "The Police and Fire Protection in New York City: 1800-1850." NEW YORK HISTORY 52 (1971): 133-50.

Relates the evolution of municipal fire protection to developments in insurance, politics, urban disorders, the provision of an adequate water supply, and, most importantly, to police protection. Treats all of these as functions of urban growth.

921   Godfrey, Hollis. HEALTH OF THE CITY. Boston: Houghton, Mifflin, 1910. 372 p.

Discusses various aspects of urban public health, including noise, air, food, milk, water, sewerage, plumbing, and housing.

922   Gollson, Gordon. "Nineteenth Century New Orleans: Its Public Health Ordeal." LOUISIANA STUDIES 4 (1965): 87-100.

Examines the debate in the city over public health engendered by the yellow fever epidemics of 1853 and 1878. Finds that most articulate citizens denounced the local board of health as incompetent.

923   Greer, Colin. THE GREAT SCHOOL LEGEND: A REVISIONIST INTERPRETATION OF AMERICAN PUBLIC EDUCATION. New York: Basic Books, 1972. 206 p.

Argues that, contrary to widespread belief, public schools in the late nineteenth and early twentieth century actually branded the children of immigrants and the poor as inferior, forced many out prematurely, and made them economically inferior in adulthood.

924   Gregory, George Peter. "A Study in Local Decision Making: Pittsburgh and Sewage Treatment." WESTERN PENNSYLVANIA HISTORY MAGAZINE 57 (1974): 25-42.

Examines the city's first efforts at sewage treatment, the proposed alternatives, their possible effects, and the rationale of the final policy. Concludes that civic leaders relied upon short-term solutions because of their commitment to economy-minded, efficiency-oriented decision making in government.

925   Griffen, Clyde. "An Urban Church in Ferment: The Episcopal Church in New York City, 1880-1900." Ph.D. dissertation, Columbia University, 1960. 448 p.

Discovers that the church responded to developing class antagonisms and heavy immigration by establishing recreational, educational, and welfare activities, trade schools, settlement houses, and workingmen's clubs to promote sobriety, industry, thrift, and self-improvement.

926   Gusfield, Joseph; Kronus, Sidney; and Mark, Harold. "The Urban Context and Higher Education: A Delineation of Issues." JOURNAL OF HIGHER EDUCATION 41 (1970): 29-43.

Contends that nineteenth-century colleges and universities reflected the dominant rural political interests and were set in rural locales for the study of an agricultural curriculum. Proposes a series of changes to provide campuses with a more urban orientation.

927   Haller, Mark H. "Historical Roots of Police Behavior: Chicago, 1890-1925." LAW AND SOCIETY REVIEW 10 (1976): 303-24.

Attributes police behavior in the early twentieth century to four interrelated orientations: sensitivity to neighborhood

Urban Institutions

desires, involvement in the political system, involvement in the rackets as a means of earning additional income, and the development of an informal system of operation with its own subculture.

928 _____. "Police Reform in Chicago, 1905-1935." AMERICAN BEHAVIORAL SCIENTIST 13 (1970): 649-66.

Shows that while police leadership cooperated with reformers interested in administrative and technological efficiency, they generally did not cooperate with civic reformers concerned with vice, gambling, and liquor who frequently saw corruption and political control of police as the major problem.

929 Hardy, Bruce A. "American Privatism and the Urban Fiscal Crisis of the Interwar Years: A Financial Study of New York, Philadelphia, Detroit, and Boston, 1915-1945." Ph.D. dissertation, Wayne State University, 1977. 537 p.

Traces the urban fiscal crisis in these cities in the interwar years to markedly increased spending due to (1) growth in size and market power of private industries, (2) new technologies and extensive growth of urban services, and (3) deferred spending during World War I. Places the problem within the context of the growing interdependence of society.

930 Harkins, Michael J. "Public Health Nuisances in Omaha, 1870-1900." NEBRASKA HISTORY 56 (1975): 471-92.

Finds that Omaha's residents generally accepted such health hazards as garbage, pollution, patent medicine, prostitution, open privies, and body snatching as inevitable by-products of urban living and put little pressure upon the government or politicians to better conditions.

931 Heale, M.J. "Patterns of Benevolence: Associated Philanthropy in the Cities of New York, 1830-1860." NEW YORK HISTORY 57 (1976): 53-79.

Finds that philanthropic organizations responded to the increasing urbanization of the period by creating nonsectarian societies which differentiated between the deserving and the undeserving poor and sought to prevent the encouragement of pauperism by indiscriminate benevolence.

932 Henderson, Mary C. THE CITY AND THE THEATRE: NEW YORK PLAYHOUSES FROM BOWLING GREEN TO TIMES SQUARE. Clifton, N.J.: James T. White, 1974. 323 p.

Explores the relationship between the city and the theatre in five different phases of New York's growth: pre-1798; the park and the Bowery, 1798-1850; lower Broadway, 1850-70; Union Square, 1870-99; and Times Square, since 1900.

933   Hilton, George W., and Due, John F. ELECTRIC INTERURBAN RAILWAYS IN AMERICA. Palo Alto, Calif.: Stanford University Press, 1960. 463 p.

Details the building and technology of the interurbans, their passenger and freight traffic, financial history, and their final decline and abandonment. Also focuses individually on the more than three hundred separate interurban lines.

934   Hollander, Jacob Harry. "The Cincinnati Southern Railway: A Study in Municipal Activity." Ph.D. dissertation, Johns Hopkins University, 1886. 96 p.

Focuses on the reasons for the building of the railway, the legislation which created it, the construction and operation of the road, the litigation surrounding its financing, and its impact upon the city's indebtedness, tax levy, and commercial and financial possibilities.

935   Holt, Glen E. "The Changing Perception of Urban Pathology: An Essay on the Development of Mass Transit in the United States." In CITIES IN AMERICAN HISTORY, edited by Kenneth T. Jackson and Stanley K. Schultz, pp. 324-43. New York: Knopf, 1972.

Contends that residential movement away from the urban core to the suburban fringe antedated the development of mass transit. Argues that the tension caused by commuter crowding in mass transit gave a major impetus to increased use of the automobile.

936   Hopkins, Richard J. "Public Health in Atlanta: The Formative Years, 1865-1879." GEORGIA QUARTERLY 53 (1969): 287-304.

Feels that while the Atlanta Board of Health was not a truly effective force for the protection of public health in those years, neither was it a menace to the well-being of the inhabitants. Attributes its lack of achievement to the body's advisory status.

937   Huggins, Nathan I. PROTESTANTS AGAINST POVERTY: BOSTON'S WAR ON POVERTY 1870-1900. Westport, Conn.: Greenwood Press, 1970. 225 p.

Examines the efforts of Boston's Protestant reformers to apply their eighteenth century humanitarian philosophy to the urban, immigrant, industrial city and to develop forms and organizations that were at once voluntary and professional. Sees them as the forerunners of social workers.

Urban Institutions

938   Issel, William H. "Modernization in Philadelphia School Reform, 1882-1905." PENNSYLVANIA MAGAZINE OF HISTORY AND BIOGRAPHY 94 (1970): 358-83.

      Finds that upper-class members of the Public Education Association and the Civic Club led the move for reorganization of the schools which centralized all power in the hands of the Board of Public Education and placed all executive work in the hands of educational experts.

939   Jackson, Joy J. "Municipal Problems in New Orleans, 1880-1896." Ph.D. dissertation, Tulane University, 1961. 355 p.

      Compares New Orleans' administrative and political problems involved in providing urban services to those of other cities and finds many similarities and some important differences, based largely upon the Creole culture of the city.

940   Jamieson, Duncan R. "Cities and the AMA: The American Medical Association's First Report on Public Hygiene." MARYLAND HISTORIAN 8 (1977): 23-32.

      Describes the genesis, makeup, and findings of the American Medical Association's first report on public hygiene in 1848. Finds that the report was based upon the later discredited miasma theory of disease but still stimulated a cleanup of slum conditions which reduced mortality.

941   Johnson, David R. "The Search for an Urban Discipline: Police Reform as a Response to Crime in American Cities, 1800-1875." Ph.D. dissertation, University of Chicago, 1972. 254 p.

      Analyzes the evolution of the idea of a professional police force, the nature of the urban underworld, and urban crime patterns between 1840 and 1870. Focuses upon the efforts of reformers in the Civil War era to discipline both individual patrolmen and urban police forces.

942   Johnson, Scott R. "The Trolley Car as a Social Factor: Springfield, Massachusetts." HISTORICAL JOURNAL OF WESTERN MASSACHUSETTS 1 (1972): 5-17.

      Pronounces the trolley a profound social and economic factor between 1890 and 1930, one which helped to improve the standard of living, promoted educational opportunity, and provided access to recreation.

943   Jordan, Kevin E. "Ideology and the Coming of Professionalism: American Urban Police in the 1920s and 1930s." Ph.D. dissertation, Rutgers University, 1972. 228 p.

Urban Institutions

Concentrates on the activities of the leadership of the urban police departments and the widespread reform movement to professionalize and become the "fourth vital institution of society."

944   Kaestle, Carl F. THE EVOLUTION OF AN URBAN SCHOOL SYSTEM: NEW YORK CITY, 1750-1850. Cambridge, Mass.: Harvard University Press, 1973. 205 p.

Contends that the city's schools were an institutional response by the established to the threat of social fragmentation caused by population increase, poverty, and immigration, and that they were marked by bureaucracy, class bias, and racism.

945   Kalisch, Philip A. "The Black Death in Chinatown: Plague and Politics in San Francisco, 1900-1904." ARIZONA AND THE WEST 14 (1972): 113-36.

Contends that business interests and newspapers in the city deliberately downplayed the seriousness of the outbreak and condemned the actions of the city government and the federal health authorities in order to prevent publicity that might be bad for business.

946   Katz, Michael B. "The Emergence of Bureaucracy in Urban Education: The Boston Case, 1850-1884." HISTORY OF EDUCATION QUARTERLY 8 (1968): 155-88.

Concentrates upon the Boston school system and contends that in the years between 1850 and 1875 bureaucracies gained control of the educational process. Also illustrates some resistance to this trend among members of the elected school board.

947   Ketcham, George A. "Municipal Police Reform: A Comparative Study of Law Enforcement in Cincinnati, Chicago, New Orleans, New York and St. Louis, 1844-1877." Ph.D. dissertation, University of Missouri, Columbia, 1967. 297 p.

Insists that modernization of the police department in these cities lagged behind improvements in other urban services because of a residual fear that efficient law enforcement would lead to tyranny, and that it came about primarily from demands for "law and order" by vigilantes.

948   Knowles, Jane B. "Luxury Hotels in American Cities, 1810-1860." Ph.D. dissertation, University of Pennsylvania, 1972. 359 p.

Asserts that these hotels filled an important social function where the new cities were impotent and that they were symbolic of "palaces of the public" in a land of equal opportunity.

Urban Institutions

949 Lane, Roger. POLICING THE CITY BOSTON 1822-1885. Cambridge, Mass.: Harvard University Press, 1967. 299 p.

    Argues that the establishing of municipal police forces formed one portion of a larger problem generated by the growth of the nineteenth-century city: the need to develop new attitudes as well as institutions appropriate to change and changing conditions in the nation as a whole. Whereas the conventional political wisdom of postrevolutionary America warned of the dangers of powerful governments, the rise of cities demanded the exercise of competent authority. Hence, the development of urban police forces involved fundamental debate on the nature of "right and liberty, the proper scope of government, and the purpose of the law in a democracy."

950 Larsen, Lawrence H. "Nineteenth-Century Street Sanitation, A Study of Filth and Frustration." WISCONSIN MAGAZINE OF HISTORY 52 (1969): 239-47.

    Describes the sorry state of public sanitation in American cities and some of the factors responsible for the persistence of problems throughout the nineteenth century.

951 Lazerson, Marvin. ORIGINS OF THE URBAN SCHOOL: PUBLIC EDUCATION IN MASSACHUSETTS, 1870-1915. Cambridge, Mass.: Harvard University Press, 1971. 278 p.

    Focuses on the efforts of Massachusetts' school reformers to deal with the problems posed by urbanization, industrialization, immigration, and poverty. Contends that they eventually emphasized vocational education as a means of social control. Concludes that these trends led to educational segregation on the basis of curriculum, social class, and projected vocational role.

952 _____. "Urban Reform and the Schools: Kindergarten in Massachusetts, 1870-1915." HISTORY OF EDUCATION QUARTERLY 11 (1971): 115-42.

    Analyzes the disagreements among Massachusetts educators over how best to serve the needs of poor and immigrant stock children and concludes that they eventually agreed upon the goals of social control and Americanization as being the overriding concerns.

953 Lee, Robert, ed. CITIES AND CHURCHES: READINGS ON THE URBAN CHURCH. Philadelphia: Westminster Press, 1962. 366 p.

    Readings intended to serve as a text for courses, focuses on urban life and culture, religious conceptions of the city, the churches, urban sect and cult movements, urban church organization, community conflict and cooperation, and theology and the urban church.

954   Lerner, Monroe, and Anderson, Odin W. HEALTH PROGRESS IN THE UNITED STATES 1900-1960. Chicago: University of Chicago Press, 1963. 354 p.

Considers mortality trends, illnesses and impairments, economic aspects of health, and the social consequences of declining mortality. Based on government statistical data. One chapter (11, pp. 105-13) focuses specifically on urban health.

955   Levett, Allan Edward. "Centralization of City Police in the Nineteenth Century United States." Ph.D. dissertation, University of Michigan, 1975. 159 p.

Studies the emergence of city police departments, emphasizing the relationship of large scale social change to the political processes. Investigates the establishing of these new "politicized bureaucracies" and argues that "police centralization resulted from a politically concentrated demand to control a whole category of persons," whose behavior had to be defined as deviant.

956   Levine, Jerald Elliot. "Police, Parties, and Polity: The Bureaucratization, Unionization and Professionalization of the New York City Police 1870-1917." Ph.D. dissertation, University of Wisconsin, 1971. 538 p.

Explores the internal dynamics of the New York City Police and the external political pressure on them. Refutes the assumption that "the social change regarding the police was superimposed from above" and that Tammany Hall worked with the police to control municipal government.

957   Lewinski-Corwin, E.H. "The Dispensary Situation in New York City." MEDICAL RECORD 97 (1920): 181-85.

Provides a statistical and analytical survey of the operation of the free clinic system of New York City in 1920. Includes recommendations for decentralization of dispensaries into neighborhoods.

958   Lipman, Andrew. "The Rochester Subway: Experiment in Municipal Rapid Transit." ROCHESTER HISTORY 36 (1974): 1-23.

Discusses the subway system's rise and decline from early twentieth-century construction to the end of passenger service in 1956, ascribing its failure to the nature of residence patterns in Rochester.

Urban Institutions

959 Lucas, Paul R. "The Church and the City: Congregationalism in Minneapolis, 1840-1890." MINNESOTA HISTORY 44 (1975): 55-69.

> Investigates the impact of urbanization on the patterns of congregational order through case studies of three Congregational churches--First, Plymouth, and Second--and notes that despite similarities in origins, early development, and membership, the three churches "displayed surprisingly diverse reactions to growth and change in Minneapolis in the late nineteenth century."

960 Luckingham, Bradford Franklin. "Associational Life of the Urban Frontier: San Francisco, 1848-1856." Ph.D. dissertation, University of California, Davis, 1968. 247 p.

> Attributes "the growing pluralism and expansiveness of local society" to the rise of associational activity and sees these associations as contributing toward the urban maturity for the larger city.

961 Luscombe, Irving Foulds. "WNYC: 1922-1940--The Early History of a Twentieth Century Urban Service." Ph.D. dissertation, New York University, 1968. 388 p.

> Explores the political pitfalls and social advantages of a city owned radio station, whose purpose was to improve the services of the police and fire departments and to raise the general educational and cultural levels of the populace.

962 McCullough, David. THE GREAT BRIDGE. New York: Simon and Schuster, 1972. 636 p.

> Provides a comprehensive discussion of the construction of the Brooklyn Bridge, including questions of engineering and politics, traces its impact on the city's inhabitants, and discusses the attitudes and character of Washington Roebling.

963 McShane, C. Kelvin. "The 1918 Kansas City Influenza Epidemic." MISSOURI HISTORICAL REVIEW 63 (1968): 55-70.

> Argues that Kansas City's high death rate was due to the refusal of merchants to comply with closing orders, the use of questionable home remedies, and political feuding between officials of the two major health agencies.

964 _____. "American Cities and the Coming of the Automobile, 1870-1910." Ph.D. dissertation, University of Wisconsin, Madison, 1976. 344 p.

> Describes and analyzes innovation in urban transportation in an attempt to explain the favorable response--after a period

of initial resistance--the automobile, concluding that changed public attitudes toward "mechanically powered travel on city streets" proved a decisive factor. Analyzes the factors prompting this change, and surveys muncipal regulations on transportation related issues, and early forms of urban transportation.

965 _____. TECHNOLOGY AND REFORM: STREET RAILWAYS AND THE GROWTH OF MILWAUKEE, 1887-1900. Madison: State Historical Society of Wisconsin, 1974. 487 p.

Studies the impact of the street railway from a perspective which stresses its relationship to political affairs. Initial chapters provide an overview of the history and economic structure of street railways in America.

966 Magnuson, Norris. SALVATION IN THE SLUMS: EVANGELICAL SOCIAL WORK, 1865-1920. Metuchen, N.J.: Scarecrow Press, 1977. 299 p.

Discusses the development of popular evangelicalism, noting that the commitment of religiously motivated slum workers extended beyond the saving of souls to include a wide range of temporal social concerns, which led ultimately to their elaborating wide-ranging social service programs within the cities.

967 Marchiafava, Louis J. "Institutional and Legal Aspects of the Growth of Professional Urban Police Service: The Houston Experience, 1878-1948." Ph.D. dissertation, Rice University, 1976. 247 p.

Traces the progression of the Houston police department as it acquired institutional form characterized by the regulation of salaries and formalization of rules, and increased areas of responsibility climaxing with the passage of a Civil Service Law in 1948.

968 Masotti, Louis H., and Hadden, Jeffrey K., eds. SUBURBIA IN TRANSITION. New York: New Viewpoints, 1974. 345 p.

A collection of edited selections of NEW YORK TIMES articles that explore the changing dynamics of metropolitan America as reflected in the transformation occurring within the "outer city."

969 Massouh, Michael. "Innovations in Street Railways before Electric Traction: Tom L. Johnson's Contributions." TECHNOLOGY AND CULTURE 18 (1977): 202-17.

Focuses on the years between 1873 and 1888 and the activities of Tom L. Johnson, inventor and entrepreneur, who experi-

Urban Institutions

mented with various power sources and management techniques designed to increase the utility and profitability of street railways, including the farebox, singlefare transfer system, and the shallow conduit cable system.

970   May, Henry F. PROTESTANT CHURCHES IN INDUSTRIAL AMERICA. New York: Octagon Books, 1963. 297 p.

Concentrates on five major denominations, Presbyterian, Congregationalist, Baptist, Methodist and Episcopalian, and assesses the ways in which they responded and readjusted to the growing industrialization of the United States in the three decades following the Civil War as an important episode in American social thought. Emphasizes the urban areas of the East and Middle West which first experienced the impact of large-scale industrial development.

971   Mayer, John A. "Private Charities in Chicago from 1871-1915." Ph.D. dissertation, University of Minnesota, 1978. 599 p.

Describes the development of several private charities in the city during the period and analyzes their unsuccessful efforts at social control and the ways in which they served the needs of the middle and upper classes. Feels that these charitable efforts retarded demands for public welfare programs.

972   Meeker, Edward. "The Social Rate of Return on Investment in Public Health, 1880-1910." JOURNAL OF ECONOMIC HISTORY 34 (1974): 392-419.

A cost-benefit analysis which concludes that the investment in public health for the period 1880-1910 proved economically sound in that the social rate of return on that investment exceeded the market rate of return on capital.

973   Melosi, Martin V. "'Out of Sight, Out of Mind': The Environment and Disposal of Municipal Refuse, 1860-1920." HISTORIAN 35 (1973): 621-40.

Sees solid waste disposal as representative of problems magnified by urbanization, surveys some of the methods available, and indicates some of the philosophical and societal factors that militated against cities mounting a systematic attempt to deal with the problem.

974   Miller, Janet Ann. "Urban Education and the New City: Cincinnati's Elementary Schools, 1870-1914." Ed.D. dissertation, University of Cincinnati, 1974. 501 p.

Analyzes the forces which combined to change the city's schools into a complex system which provided a variety of

special programs and services in response to the culture of
the early twentieth-century urban community. Examines the
role played by organized labor, businessmen, women's organizations, and neighborhood groups.

975 Miller, Wilbur R. "The Legitimation of the London and New York
City Police, 1830-1870." Ph.D. dissertation, Columbia University,
1973. 418 p.

Compares the evolution of the two police forces and finds
them alike in that they arose from similar concerns for the
need for improved policing and aroused similar fears of possible police states. Concludes that they were strikingly
different with respect to structure and practice, especially
with regard to their attitudes toward sumptuary laws and the
lower orders.

976 Mohl, Raymond A. "Education as Social Control in New York City,
1784-1825." NEW YORK HISTORY 51 (1970): 219-237.

Asserts that "the schools of preindustrial New York City provided formal indoctrination in middle class morality," and that
in time of socioeconomic change, moral training for the poor
constituted a defense of the traditional structured community.

977 _____. "Humanitarianism in the Preindustrial City: The New York
Society for the Prevention of Pauperism, 1817-1823." JOURNAL OF
AMERICAN HISTORY 57 (1970): 576-99.

Argues that the orientation of the New York Society for the
Prevention of Pauperism displayed a growing emphasis on
social control and an ideology of moral stewardship, as a
reaction to the increasing incidence of social ills and general
disorder seemingly generated by immigration, urbanization,
and industrialization, and the shift away from earlier tenets
of Christian benevolence and enlightenment rationalism, a
characteristic which typified philanthropic reform.

978 _____. POVERTY IN NEW YORK, 1783-1825. New York: Oxford
University Press, 1971. 318 p.

Case studies of the social-welfare history of New York City
during a period of economic and social transformation, indicating an increasing incidence of poverty and the attitudes
and response of the public powers and private humanitarians.

979 _____. "Urban Education in the Twentieth Century: Alice Barrows
and the Platoon School Plan." URBAN EDUCATION 9 (1974): 213-37.

Focuses on the crucial role of Alice Barrows as promoter, publicist, and activist on behalf of the adoption of the Gary

Urban Institutions

Platoon plan by school systems throughout the nation in the 1920s and 1930s.

980 Murphy, Thomas P., and Warren, Charles R., eds. ORGANIZING PUBLIC SERVICES IN METROPOLITAN AMERICA. Lexington, Mass.: D.C. Heath, 1974. 245 p.

Twelve selections on various aspects of metropolitan reorganization including discussions of structural change, centralization and decentralization.

981 Murray, Constance. "Portland, Maine, and the Growth of Urban Responsibility for Human Welfare, 1830-1860." Ph.D. dissertation, Boston University Graduate School, 1960. 457 p.

Dispels the traditional view that the years from 1830 to the Civil War characterized the high point of individualism in America by presenting the picture of urban growth in Portland which led to restrictive laws and institutions.

982 Myers, Gustavus. HISTORY OF PUBLIC FRANCHISES IN NEW YORK CITY. New York: Arno Press, 1974. 206 p.

Provides an overview of public and private ownership of municipal services in New York City, Manhattan and the Bronx from colonial times on, with individual chapters on Ferry Franchises, water supply, gas works, street railways, rapid transit, and subways.

983 Newman, Harvey K. "The Vision of Order: White Protestant Christianity in Atlanta, 1865-1966." Ph.D. dissertation, Emory University, 1977. 208 p.

Stresses the role of white Protestant churches in joining with other social, economic, and political forces in Atlanta to promote the goal of an orderly community, and argues that with urban growth and revivalism, churches relaxed membership requirements and had less impact on the daily lives of their members. As such, Atlanta's religious organizations proved increasingly effective as conservers of order.

984 Olton, Charles S. "Philadelphia's First Environmental Crisis." PENNSYLVANIA MAGAZINE OF HISTORY AND BIOGRAPHY 98 (1974): 90-100.

Considers various environmental problems of Revolutionary era Philadelphia generated by increasing manufacturing and commercial development, and the attempts of the city's inhabitants at ameliorating these difficulties.

Urban Institutions

985   Parks, Arthur Lincoln. "Retail Consumers' Cooperatives in New York City: A History of Cooperative Activity, 1900-1950, with Case Studies of Selected Societies." Ph.D. dissertation, Columbia University, 1953. 407 p.

       Describes various attempts at establishing cooperatives, including case studies of both successes and failures, relating local and national factors which affected their development.

986   Powell, John H. BRING OUT YOUR DEAD: THE GREAT PLAGUE OF YELLOW FEVER IN PHILADELPHIA IN 1793. New York: Arno Press, 1970. 326 p.

       Uses city records, memoirs, and additional documents to reconstruct the dimensions of the epidemic which killed ten percent of the city's population. Shows how the city, aided by a group of extra-legal volunteers, eventually overcame the disaster.

987   Ravenel, Mazyck P., ed. A HALF CENTURY OF PUBLIC HEALTH. New York: Arno Press, 1970. 461 p.

       Nineteen essays by health field practitioners assess various aspects of public health development, including such urban related topics as water purification, sewage and solid refuse pollution, housing, and industrial hygiene.

988   Ravitch, Diane. THE GREAT SCHOOL WARS, NEW YORK CITY, 1805-1973: A HISTORY OF THE PUBLIC SCHOOLS AS BATTLEFIELD OF SOCIAL CHANGE. New York: Basic Books, 1974. 449 p.

       Views the public school in New York City as a "battleground where the aspirations of the newcomers and the fears of the native population met and clashed," and details the political history of these struggles, as related to the changing nature of the city's population, government style, and the rise of various currents of reform.

989   Reese, William J. "Progressive School Reform in Toledo: 1898-1921." NORTHWEST OHIO QUARTERLY 47 (1975): 44-59.

       Details key educational reform which brought Toledo the major elements of its modern public school system: kindergartens, playgrounds, manual training programs, Americanization classes, and special schools for handicapped children. Discusses the role of school officials and civic groups in creating these programs, and stresses the powerful impact of William B. Guitteau, the leader and major spokesman for reform after 1905.

990   Reichard, Maximilian. "The Origins of Urban Police: Freedom and

Urban Institutions

Order in Antebellum St. Louis." Ph.D. dissertation, Washington University, 1975. 376 p.

> Analyzes the contrast between persisting attitudes and changing social structure, and hypothesizes that the organization of the St. Louis police was dependent on a basic conflict between the values of freedom and order.

991 Rhines, Charlotte Cannon. "A City and Its Social Problems: Poverty, Health and Crime in Baltimore, 1865-1875." Ph.D. dissertation, University of Maryland, 1975. 506 p.

> Explores the ineffectiveness of Baltimore's city government, detailing the conflicts and confusions in dealing with social problems, and concludes that the dependence of the city council upon voluntary help proved worthless.

992 Richardson, James F. "THE NEW YORK POLICE: COLONIAL TIMES TO 1901. New York: Oxford University Press, 1970. 332 p.

> Explains how and why the community and its police agencies responded to the changing nature of New York City's need for establishing an urban discipline, exploring the impact of political, economic, and ethnic factors.

993 _____. "To Control the City: The New York Police in Historical Perspective." In CITIES IN AMERICAN HISTORY, edited by Kenneth T. Jackson and Stanley K. Schultz, pp. 272-89. New York: Knopf, 1972.

> Reviews the nineteenth-century administrative history of the police, stressing its strong links with the political process and political parties, and the concomitant prevalence of patronage, bribery, and corruption.

994 _____. URBAN POLICE IN THE UNITED STATES. Port Washington, N.Y.: Kennikat Press, 1974. 226 p.

> Overall history of the development of police forces in American cities from the English background to the present, concentrating especially on the years since 1950. Covers such processes as bureaucratization and professionalization, while documenting changing patterns of police administration. Argues that Americans typically have failed to reach a consensus as to the proper scope and function of the police, leading to conflicts which have molded police performance in a variety of ways.

995 Rosenberg, Carroll Smith. "Evangelicalism and the New City: A History of the City Mission Movement in New York, 1812-1870." Ph.D. dissertation, Columbia University, 1968. 475 p.

Urban Institutions

Follows the development of the city mission from the early part of the century through the 1860s. Several chapters discuss the growing urban problems of New York City and how they facilitated the evolution of these missions.

996 _____. RELIGION AND THE RISE OF THE AMERICAN CITY: THE NEW YORK CITY MISSION MOVEMENT, 1812-1870. Ithaca, N.Y.: Cornell University Press, 1971. 300 p.

Details the changing scope and methods of the city missions, stressing their transformation from purely religious bodies to instruments for dealing with social problems. Sees the city mission as a Jacksonian institution, but in a context that includes the evolution of philanthropic activity as a response to urban problems. Includes descriptions of the city, as well as of particular missions and their philosophies and activities.

997 Rosenberg, Charles E. THE CHOLERA YEARS: THE UNITED STATES IN 1832, 1849, and 1866. Chicago: University of Chicago Press, 1962. 257 p.

Contends that nineteenth-century Americans regarded cholera as an "urban" disease and that they failed to make significant progress against it until they stopped regarding the malady as a personal sin.

998 Schneider, John C. "Mob Violence and Public Order in the American City, 1830-1865." Ph.D. dissertation, University of Minnesota, 1971. 204 p.

Analyzes urban rioting from four case studies on New York City, Philadelphia, St. Louis, and Detroit, by focusing on the disposition and activity of urban authority. Suggests that the cities were outgrowing their institutional agencies of control, and that a more sophisticated commitment to the functioning of public order was necessary.

999 _____. "Public Order and the Geography of the City: Crime, Violence, and the Police in Detroit, 1845-1875." JOURNAL OF URBAN HISTORY 4 (1978): 183-208.

Studies the interaction of urban shape and form with problems of urban public order, contending that the nineteenth-century city's physical development "influenced the mercurial patterns of crime and violence, informed the drive toward professional policing, and helped define and expedite police policy."

1000 _____. "Urbanization and the Maintenance of Order: Detroit, 1824-1847." MICHIGAN HISTORY 60 (1976): 260-81.

Urban Institutions

Contends that the American tradition presents a tension between the need to maintain order and a belief in democratic individualism, which has affected the responses of urbanizing communities, like Detroit, to problems of crime and violence. Only after 1847 when increasing spatial differentiation and ethnic diversity produced a breakdown in public order did traditional attitudes toward policing break down and the development of a professional police occur.

1001 Schultz, Stanley K. "Breaking the Chains of Poverty: Public Education in Boston, 1800-1860." In CITIES IN AMERICAN HISTORY, edited by Kenneth T. Jackson and Stanley K. Schultz, pp. 306-23. New York: Knopf, 1972.

Contends that the nineteenth-century public school movement was a response to a perceived urban crisis, which included rising crime rates, increased incidence of juvenile delinquency, and floods of immigrants, and that city leaders supported education as a means to secure social order.

1002 _____. THE CULTURE FACTORY: BOSTON PUBLIC SCHOOLS, 1789-1860. New York: Oxford University Press, 1973. 394 p.

Sees Boston's schools as agencies of the city's elite for imposing order and morality upon the ethnic working class. Argues that the elite relied upon the schools as a socializing force but were unable to build them fast enough to keep up with population expansion.

1003 Sinclair, Bruce. PHILADELPHIA'S PHILOSOPHER MECHANICS: A HISTORY OF THE FRANKLIN INSTITUTE, 1825-1865. Baltimore: Johns Hopkins University Press, 1974. 353 p.

Avers that the institute gradually turned its attention from pure science to technology as the city became more and more industrialized, and provided much of the intellectual underpinning for the emergence of large-scale manufacturing in Philadelphia.

1004 Singleton, Gregory H. "Religion in the City of the Angels: American Protestant Culture and Urbanization, Los Angeles, 1850-1930." Ph.D. dissertation, University of California, Los Angeles, 1976. 441 p.

Analyzes the tradition of Protestant social forms which dominated the late nineteenth and early twentieth centuries. Includes analysis of life patterns associated with religious institutions, occupations, and social associations.

1005 Smith, Robert P. "Illusion and Reality in the Press and Other Contemporary Sources: Urban Recreation in Brooklyn, 1890-1898." Ph.D. dissertation, Indiana University, 1973. 295 p.

Urban Institutions

Systematically examines leisure activities in Brooklyn during a period of rapid industrialization and urbanization, revealing differences between idealized perceptions of recreational life and what activities were actually available.

1006   Smith, Stephen. THE CITY THAT WAS AND THE REPORT OF THE GENERAL COMMITTEE OF HEALTH, NEW YORK CITY, 1806. Metuchen, N.J.: Scarecrow Press, 1973. 301 p.

Issued by the New York Academy of Medicine, contains two reports on public health in New York City in the early nineteenth century, describing unhealthful conditions and discussing the legal, political, and medical barriers to improving them.

1007   Somers, Dale A. "The Leisure Revolution: Recreation in the American City, 1820-1920." JOURNAL OF POPULAR CULTURE 5 (1971): 125-47.

Documents and surveys the burgeoning enthusiasm for recreation and organized sports as a function of the shift from a rural-agrarian to an urban-industrial society. Contends that by 1920, the United States was well on its way to becoming a leisure-oriented country, and outlines some of the impacts of this ongoing revolution.

1008   Sorrels, William W. MEMPHIS' GREATEST DEBATE: A QUESTION OF WATER. Memphis, Tenn.: Memphis State University Press, 1970. 139 p.

Traces the development of the city's water system throughout the nineteenth century.

1009   Stambler, Moses. "The Effect of Compulsory Education and Child Labor Laws on High School Attendance in New York City, 1898-1917." HISTORY OF EDUCATION QUARTERLY 8 (1968): 189-214.

Contends that although the fundamental causes of the twentieth-century transformation of secondary schools from exclusive to inclusive institutions was the "rise of technological and urban society within the context of American middle class ideology," a New York case study indicates that compulsory education and child labor laws functioned as "more immediate and more significant short-range cause."

1010   Steiner, William F., Jr. "Philadelphia's Newspapers: Years of Revolution and Transition, 1764-1794." Ph.D. dissertation, University of Pennsylvania, 1972. 450 p.

Uses circulation, statistics and content analysis to demonstrate

Urban Institutions

that, no matter how much they differed politically or ideologically, the city's newspapers followed a similar course of development and shared such common concerns as how to make money, how to gather news, how to print a paper, and what role to play in Philadelphia.

1011 Surrency, Erwin C. "The Evolution of an Urban Judicial System: The Philadelphia Story, 1683-1968." AMERICAN JOURNAL OF LEGAL HISTORY 18 (1974): 95-123.

Surveys the historical development of the courts in Philadelphia County, discussing the colonial and early post-Revolutionary situation, and examining various institutions, such as the criminal courts, district court, trial court, and county court.

1012 Tarr, Joel A. "From City to Farm: Urban Wastes and the American Farmer." AGRICULTURAL HISTORY 49 (1975): 598-612.

Surveys the development of urban waste disposal practices in the nineteenth century and investigates factors affecting the usage of sewerage in farming, including debates over hygienic utility and economic practicality.

1013 _____. "Urban Pollution--Many Long Years Ago." AMERICAN HERITAGE 22 (1971): 65-69.

Notes that the horse became the target for sanitary officials and health reformers who saw it as a major polluter of city streets and contributing factor in epidemic disease.

1014 Taylor, George R. "The Beginning of Mass Transportation in Urban America, Parts I and II." SMITHSONIAN JOURNAL OF HISTORY 1 (1966): 35-50; 51-54.

Traces the growth in population and development of new modes of public transportation which encouraged the separation of work and residence and growth of outlying urban neighborhoods for the period 1820 through 1860.

1015 Tierno, Mark J. "The Search for Pure Water in Pittsburgh: The Urban Response to Water Pollution, 1893-1914." WESTERN PENNSYLVANIA HISTORICAL MAGAZINE 60 (1977): 23-36.

Stresses the importance of fears about epidemic diseases in causing the formation of a coalition of the city's business and financial elite with professionals in engineering, medicine, and public health to develop a municipal water system.

1016 Trachtenberg, Alan. BROOKLYN BRIDGE: FACT AND SYMBOL. New York: Oxford University Press, 1965. 182 p.

Urban Institutions

> Details the construction of the Brooklyn Bridge emphasizing its importance as a cultural symbol representing America's change from a predominantly rural to an urban and industrial society, since "as a major construction in America's leading city, it became the vehicle for ideas and feelings associated with the new conditions."

1017 Troen, Selwyn K. THE PUBLIC AND THE SCHOOLS: SHAPING THE ST. LOUIS SYSTEM, 1838-1920. Columbia: University of Missouri Press, 1975. 248 p.

> Discusses the transformations of St. Louis' public schools as reflecting the changing nature of the city, particularly its expanding and increasingly diverse population, thus emphasizing the mutuality of the interaction between school and society.

1018 Trolander, Judith A. SETTLEMENT HOUSES AND THE GREAT DEPRESSION. Detroit: Wayne State University Press, 1975. 216 p.

> Studies the changing role of the social settlement, identifying reasons for its decline as a leading agency of reform. Notes that the increasingly important role of the business-dominated Community Chests paralleled the demise of the settlement movement and that specialized, professionalized agencies preempted former settlement functions.

1019 Tyack, David B. THE ONE BEST SYSTEM: A HISTORY OF AMERICAN URBAN EDUCATION. Cambridge, Mass.: Harvard University Press, 1974. 353 p.

> Interpretive history stressing the changing institutional structure and ideology of education, stressing the transition from village school to urban system. Considers the emergence of an ideological and organizational consensus, the reform thrust of 1890 to 1920, and explores some of the major changes in urban education during the period from 1890 to 1940, as well as evolving criticisms of the system since that time.

1020 Urban, Wayne. "Organized Teachers and Educational Reform During the Progressive Era: 1890-1920." HISTORY OF EDUCATION QUARTERLY 16 (1976): 35-52.

> Focuses on attitudes of local teacher organizations toward educational reform in three major cities, noting the opposition of these groups to the centralization movement of the 1890s and the combination of efficient administration and pedagogical change early in the twentieth century. Concludes that organized teachers were neither educational nor political progressives, and that they acted primarily to protect their jobs and improve their economic status.

Urban Institutions

1021 Walch, Timothy. "Catholic Social Institutions and Urban Development: The View from Nineteenth-Century Chicago and Milwaukee." CATHOLIC HISTORICAL REVIEW 64 (1978): 16-32.

> Contends that since Chicago and Milwaukee in the 1890s were small towns whose few public institutions were overcrowded, the establishment of Catholic urban social institutions in those cities influenced both the Catholic and non-Catholic population and enjoyed public support and assistance. This contrasts with other areas, like the East, where public law and Protestant benevolent associations had established hospitals, schools, and asylums long before the advent of the Catholic Church.

1022 Walker, James B. FIFTY YEARS OF RAPID TRANSIT: 1864 TO 1917. New York: McDevitt-Wilson's, 1918. Reprint. New York: Arno Press, 1978. 291 p.

> Argues that New York City politicians were more responsible than technological difficulties in preventing the city from developing an adequate rapid transit system during the period.

1023 Walker, Samuel. A CRITICAL HISTORY OF POLICE REFORM: THE EMERGENCE OF PROFESSIONALISM. Lexington, Mass.: D.C. Health, 1977. 206 p.

> Examines police reform from the mid-nineteenth century through the end of the 1930s, focusing on the origins, development, and fruition of the concept of professionalization. Explores the experience of Cleveland, Cincinnati, Detroit, Milwaukee, Kansas City, and St. Louis, relating it to national patterns.

1024 Waring, Joseph I. "Charleston Medicine 1800-1860." JOURNAL OF THE HISTORY OF MEDICINE AND ALLIED SCIENCE 31 (1976): 320-42.

> Discusses the development of professional medical organizations and institutions in Charleston and provides information regarding public health procedures, mortality rates and epidemics in the city.

1025 Watts, Eugene J. "The Police in Atlanta, 1890-1905." JOURNAL OF SOUTHERN HISTORY 39 (1973): 165-82.

> Discusses Atlanta police life from 1890 to 1905, focusing on the structure of the department, the ordinary routine of police work, the composition of the force, and the influence of city politics on the police.

1026 Weidner, Charles H. WATER FOR A CITY: A HISTORY OF NEW

YORK CITY'S PROBLEM FROM THE BEGINNING TO THE DELAWARE RIVER SYSTEM. New Brunswick, N.J.: Rutgers University Press, 1974. 339 p.

> Surveys the development of New York's water system from a perspective which emphasizes technological and engineering issues along with political and economic factors structuring the system's construction.

1027 Wheelock, Lewis F. "Urban Protestant Reactions to the Chicago Haymarket Affair, 1886-1890." Ph.D. dissertation, State University of Iowa, 1956. 375 p.

> Claims that Protestant churches had remained faithful to and aware of their responsibilities to society, contrary to the assumption that crises, like the Haymarket riot, jolted Protestantism out of a period of supposed hostility toward working people.

1028 Wieder, Alan V. "Immigration, the Public Schools, and the Twentieth Century American Ethos: The Jewish Immigrant as a Case Study." Ph.D. dissertation, Ohio State University, 1977. 157 p.

> Uses data garnered from interviews with thirteen Jewish immigrants and their descendants to explore such questions as the reality of the American dream and the melting pot, the effect of public schools on immigrant children, and the relationship between schools and the alienation and fragmentation of urban life.

1029 Wilcox, Delos F. ANALYSIS OF THE ELECTRIC RAILWAY PROBLEM. New York: 1921. 789 p.

> Contains an analysis and commentary on information gathered by the Federal Electric Railways Commission of 1919 charged with investigation problems that the nation's street railway systems faced.

1029a Williams, Marilyn Thornton. "The Municipal Bath Movement in the United States, 1890-1915." Ph.D. dissertation, New York University, 1972. 235 p.

> Examines the background and need for public baths and compares those constructed at public expense in New York City, Boston, and Chicago with those built by private philanthropy in Philadelphia and Baltimore. Concludes with an analysis of the American Association for Promoting Hygiene and Public Baths and the "gospel of cleanliness."

1029b _____. "Philanthropy in the Progressive Era: The Public Baths of Baltimore." MARYLAND HISTORICAL MAGAZINE 72 (1977): 118-31.

Urban Institutions

>Argues that the movement for public baths in Baltimore succeeded only through the efforts of private philanthropy and flowed from a belief that improvements in the environment of the immigrant working class would make them upright, moral, middle-class citizens.

1029c Wood, Diane M. "A Case Study in Local Control of Schools: Pittsburgh, 1900-1906." URBAN EDUCATION 10 (1975): 7-26.

>Concludes that local control of schools varied in effectiveness according to the socioeconomic makeup of the community and that while controlization produced many necessary reforms it also destroyed a sense of responsiveness and community control on the part of the lower and lower middle class.

1029d Woods, Joseph G. "The Progressives and the Police: Urban Reform and the Professionalization of the Los Angeles Police." Ph.D. dissertation, University of California, Los Angeles, 1973. 665 p.

>Examines the efforts of urban reformers to professionalize police work through the introduction of civil service, the application of technology, and the separation of the police from politics. Doubts that these professionalized police departments have been any more effective in combatting urban crime than were the old, politically oriented ones, although they have proven to be much more expensive.

1029e Zarychta, Ronald M. "Municipal Reorganization: The Pittsburgh Fire Department as a Case Study." WESTERN PENNSYLVANIA HISTORICAL MAGAZINE 58 (1975): 471-86.

>Focuses on the development of Pittsburgh's Fire Department to explore the rationalization and systematization of governmental institutions during the second half of the nineteenth century.

Chapter 8

PLANNING, ARCHITECTURE, AND URBAN RENEWAL

1030 Abbott, Edith, and Breckinridge, Sophonisba, et al. THE TENEMENTS OF CHICAGO 1908-1935. New York: Arno Press, 1970. 505 p.

> Examines various aspects of tenement house life ranging from legal and financial arrangements to lack of light and ventilation. Proposes a four part program including slum clearance, new buildings, enforcement of tenement codes, and repair and reconditioning of old houses.

1031 Abrahamson, Julia. A NEIGHBORHOOD FINDS ITSELF. New York: Biblo and Tannen, 1971. 370 p.

> Examines the efforts of residents of the Hyde Park-Kenwood area of Chicago to stem the tide of urban decay and to create a stable, interracial community. Stresses the need for grass roots community involvement at all stages of the process.

1032 Abrams, Charles. THE CITY IS THE FRONTIER. New York: Harper and Row, 1965. 394 p.

> Focuses on housing as the key to urban problems, defines a set of objectives for renewal, and provides a blueprint for cities to meet those objectives. Suggests a new philosophy that takes a positive attitude toward cities and commits the nation to an all-out effort to improve conditions.

1033 _____. FORBIDDEN NEIGHBORS: A STUDY OF PREJUDICE IN HOUSING. Port Washington, N.Y.: Kennikat Press, 1971. 404 p.

> Examines housing patterns in Detroit, Chicago, and Miami, and the influence of realty codes, home-building and improvement associations, and government agencies. Concludes with a detailed program for action in the area of housing desegregation.

1034 _____. THE FUTURE OF HOUSING. New York: Harper and Brothers, 1946. 428 p.

Examines the various elements that comprise the nation's housing problem and the role played by a variety of government agencies in dealing with it. Provides an outline for a combined public and private program to promote adequate housing.

1035 Alexander, Robert L. "Baltimore Row Houses of the Early Nineteenth Century." AMERICAN STUDIES 16 (1975): 65-76.

Avers that row houses were a rational architectural response to the social and economic pressures of the American city and that they were built for and by several different classes in urban society in the early nineteenth century.

1036 Alonso, William. "Cities and City Planners." DAEDALUS 92 (1963): 824-39.

Locates the impetus for city planning in the mainstream architectural, reformist, and technological trends of the early twentieth century. Examines the current state of the profession and the dilemmas that it faces which were imposed by the gap between professional codes and political realities.

1037 Alves, William R., and Morrill, Richard L. "Diffusion Theory and Planning." ECONOMIC GEOGRAPHY 51 (1975): 290-304.

Applies diffusion theory to the evolution of the American city in the past, connects it to the planning process, and discusses some potentially valuable generalizations of the theory and its consequences for future planning.

1038 Anderson, Martin. THE FEDERAL BULLDOZER: A CRITICAL ANALYSIS OF URBAN RENEWAL, 1949-1962. New York: McGraw-Hill, 1967. 272 p.

Criticizes urban renewal programs for their haste to uproot and tear town, and for their impact on the residents of the affected areas.

1039 Andrews, Wayne. ARCHITECTURE IN CHICAGO AND MID-AMERICA. New York: Harper and Row, 1968. 186 p.

Selects and evaluates what the author regards as the outstanding examples of architecture in the region.

1040 _____. ARCHITECTURE IN NEW ENGLAND: A PHOTOGRAPHIC HISTORY. Brattleboro, Vt.: Stephen Greene Press, 1973. 202 p.

Contains numerous photographs of New England structures, with an emphasis on urban settings.

1041 _____. ARCHITECTURE IN NEW YORK: A PHOTOGRAPHIC HISTORY. New York: Harper and Row, 1973. 212 p.

Planning, Architecture, Urban Renewal

Uses hundreds of photographs to argue the theme that most of the city's distinguishing architecture is fast disappearing and being replaced by buildings that are undistinguished, boring, and insulting.

1042   Arnold, Joseph L. THE NEW DEAL IN THE SUBURBS: A HISTORY OF THE GREENBELT TOWN PROGRAM, 1935-1954. Columbus: Ohio State University Press, 1971. 272 p.

   Deals with the origins of the program, conflicts over its formation, land acquisition, planning, and construction, the debate over federal retention of ownership, tenant selection, and federal management. Concludes with the impact of World War II and the eventual decision to sell the Greenbelt towns to private developers.

1043   Attoe, Wayne, and Latus, Mark. "The First Public Housing: Sewer Socialism's Garden City for Milwaukee." JOURNAL OF POPULAR CULTURE 10 (1976): 142-49.

   Examines the efforts of the Hoan administration in the post-World War I Milwaukee to provide public housing in its Garden Homes project. Contends that the project failed because the residents preferred to own rather than lease and to profit by the sale of their homes.

1044   Bach, Ira J. "A Reconsideration of the 1909 Plan of Chicago." CHICAGO HISTORY 2 (1973): 132-41.

   Describes the recruitment of Daniel Burnham to design a city plan for Chicago. Even though not all of the plan was eventually implemented, its success spawned the commissioning of other city beautiful plans throughout the country, most of which never achieved the success of the 1909 "Plan of Chicago."

1045   Banfield, Edward C., and Grodzins, Morton. GOVERNMENT AND HOUSING IN METROPOLITAN AREAS. New York: McGraw-Hill, 1958. 177 p.

   Part of the ACTION Series in Housing and Community Development funded by a Ford Foundation grant to the American Council to Improve our Neighborhoods. This volume confronts two major questions: the impact of metropolitan governmental structure on housing and related community facilities; and the changes needed in that structure to improve housing. Concludes that even within the limits posed by external factors structural alterations in local government can in fact produce significant improvements.

Planning, Architecture, Urban Renewal

1046   Banham, Reyner. LOS ANGELES: THE ARCHITECTURE OF FOUR ECOLOGIES. New York: Penguin Press, 1971. 256 p.

     Deals with the architecture of four distinct southern California ecological regions: Surfurbia, Foothills, the Plains of Id, and Autopia. Concludes with a general proposal for an ecology for architecture.

1047   Barnes, William R. "A National Controversy in Miniature: The District of Columbia Struggle over Public Housing and Redevelopment, 1943-1946." PROLOGUE 9 (1977): 91-104.

     Sees the struggle over public housing and redevelopment in the District as a microcosm of the national struggle that has raged over the past three decades. Contends that private business interests used reformist rhetoric to undercut public housing.

1048   _____. "The Origins of Urban Renewal: The Public Housing Controversy and the Emergence of a Redevelopment Program in the District of Columbia, 1942-1949." Ph.D. dissertation, Syracuse University, 1977. 447 p.

     Examines the structure and functioning of the Washington, D.C., community in the 1940s, the racial, institutional, ideological, and economic factors which shaped federal public housing and urban renewal policies, and the latter's impact upon the city.

1049   Bassett, Edward M. ZONING: THE LAWS, ADMINISTRATION, AND COURT DECISIONS DURING THE FIRST TWENTY YEARS. New York: Arno Press, 1974.

     Examines twenty years of zoning board practice in New York City and describes the city's districts, nonconforming building and rises, boards of appeal, and court decisions.

1050   Bauer, Catherine. MODERN HOUSING. New York: Arno Press, 1974. 331 p.

     Compares U.S. housing in its larger cities with that in several European countries and concludes that the speculative nature of the American housing industry produced a chaotic and substandard situation. Predicts a housing crisis with the creation of a new standard of human environment and the technique for achieving it.

1051   Bauman, John F. "Black Slums, Black Projects: The New Deal and Negro Housing in Philadelphia." PENNSYLVANIA MAGAZINE OF HISTORY AND BIOGRAPHY 41 (1974): 311-38.

     Concludes that public housing was a deliberate effort to further

Planning, Architecture, Urban Renewal

delimit the housing opportunities of Philadelphia's black population. Argues that public housing failed to reach those blacks eligible for public assistance or work relief.

1052 _____. "Safe and Sanitary without the Costly Frills: The Evolution of Public Housing in Philadelphia, 1929-1941." PENNSYLVANIA MAGAZINE OF HISTORY AND BIOGRAPHY 101 (1977): 114-28.

Identifies two strains of thought among housing reformers: the professionals who saw slum eradication as a panacea for all urban ills and the communitarians who favored decentralization. Attributes the failure of public housing in Philadelphia to a confusion between these two outlooks.

1053 Bellush, Jewel, and Hausknecht, Murray, eds. URBAN RENEWAL: PEOPLE, POLITICS, AND PLANNING. Garden City, N.J.: Anchor, 1967. 542 p.

Contains numerous articles by a variety of scholars dealing with such aspects of urban renewal as antecedents; expectations and goals; politics, planning, and decision making; execution; overview; success or failure; and new directions. Argues that housing reform has suffered both from the confusion of its friends and power of its enemies.

1054 Berkman, Herman G. "The New Town and Urban Change Form." LAND ECONOMICS 48 (1972): 93-103.

Surveys the changes in the "new town" concept from the British origins of Ebenezer Howard through their adaptation in the United States. Pleads for sufficient funding to create viable urban regions.

1055 Blumenfeld, Hans. "Continuity and Change in Urban Form." JOURNAL OF URBAN HISTORY 1 (1975): 131-47.

Argues that the interplay between the decisions of the community and those of its individual or corporate constituents creates and recreates the form of the city. Feels that the natural site and notion of property lines are as important as buildings in determining the continuity of the city.

1056 _____. THE MODERN METROPOLIS: ITS ORIGINS, GROWTH, CHARACTERISTICS AND PLANNING. Cambridge, Mass.: Harvard University Press, 1967. 377 p.

Contains reprints of thirty-three essays on the origins, growth, and form of the metropolis, metropolitan and regional planning, transportation, residential areas, urban design, and the methodology of planning.

Planning, Architecture, Urban Renewal

1057   Brownell, Blaine A. "The Commercial-Civic Elite and City Planning in Atlanta, Memphis, and New Orleans in the 1920s." JOURNAL OF SOUTHERN HISTORY 41 (1975): 339-68.

> Argues that the elites of these southern cities were much more involved in the city planning movement of the era than they were in efforts to change the structure of urban government. Finds that it needed considerable sharpening as a tool of either social control or radical urban innovation.

1058   Burnham, Daniel H., Jr., and Kingery, Robert. PLANNING THE REGION OF CHICAGO. Chicago: Lakeside Press, Donnelley and Sons, 1956. 191 p.

> Traces the evolution of city planning and city expansion in Chicago from the plan of Daniel Burnham, Sr., in 1909 to the mid-1950s.

1059   Butler, Jeanne F. "Competition 1792: Designing a Nation's Capitol." CAPITOL STUDIES (Special Issue) 4 (1976): 15-96.

> Examines the various city plans for building Washington submitted by competing designers. Includes many visual representations.

1060   Cady, David B. "The Influence of the Garden City Ideal on American Housing and Planning Reform, 1900-1940." Ph.D. dissertation, University of Wisconsin, Madison, 1970. 415 p.

> Focuses upon the planning principles of Ebenezer Howard and his concept of decentralization of population and industry into self-contained units. Contends that the failure of American planners to build a garden city has obsured the merits of Howard's plan to provide urban growth limitation and urban-rural equilibrium.

1061   Capeci, Dominic J., Jr. "Fiorello H. La Guardia and the Stuyvesant Town Controversy of 1943." NEW YORK HISTORICAL SOCIETY QUARTERLY 62 (1978): 289-310.

> Sees La Guardia torn between his respective commitments to civil rights and public housing when the private developers of the Stuyvesant project sought to exclude blacks. Faults La Guardia for ignoring the civil rights issue and accepting a contract that was openly discriminatory.

1062   Chapman, Edmund H. "City Planning Under Mercantile Expansion: The Case of Cleveland, Ohio 1796-1865." THE JOURNAL OF THE SOCIETY OF ARCHITECTURAL HISTORIANS 10 (1951): 10-17.

> Contends that Cleveland's proper development was thwarted by the rigidity and inflexibility of its design, by the lack of planning vision, and by the pressures of real estate speculation.

Planning, Architecture, Urban Renewal

1063 Checkoway, Barry N. "Suburbanization and Community: Growth and Planning in Post-War Lower Bucks County, Pennsylvania." Ph.D. dissertation, University of Pennsylvania, 1977. 259 p.

> Analyzes the decisions and institutions involved in the urbanization of the county, the responses of suburban municipalities and their planners to accelerated urban growth, and their planning and growth control. Raises questions about citizen participation and local self-government.

1064 Colean, Miles. RENEWING OUR CITIES. Milwood, N.Y.: Kraus Reprint, 1975. 181 p.

> Traces the evolution of urban slums and analyzes the elements involved in urban renewal. Assesses the costs and issues involved in renewal and sets forth a specific nine-point program to revitalize cities.

1065 Collins, George R., ed. PLANNING AND CITIES IN THE NINETEENTH CENTURY. New York: Braziller, 1968. 336 p.

> Contains a wealth of photographs, maps, plans, and drawings to illustrate the text which surveys the activities of the planning profession in its early stages.

1066 Condit, Carl W. CHICAGO, 1910-1929: BUILDING, PLANNING, AND URBAN TECHNOLOGY. Chicago: University of Chicago Press, 1973. 354 p.

> Written as a technical biography of the city between the adoption of Daniel Burnham's plan for redeveloping Chicago and the onset of the Great Depression. Focuses on the building of the transportation network, the commercial structures, and the public edifices and parks and how well they served the needs of the people who lived and worked in Chicago.

1067 _____. CHICAGO, 1930-1970: BUILDING, PLANNING, AND URBAN TECHNOLOGY. Chicago: University of Chicago Press, 1974. 351 p.

> Carries his study of the planning and technology of Chicago's building program up to the near present, focusing upon the post-World War II era in the area of residential, commercial, and public building, urban renewal, transportation, rapid transit, railroads, airports, and waterways.

1067a _____. THE CHICAGO SCHOOL OF ARCHITECTURE. A HISTORY OF COMMERCIAL AND PUBLIC BUILDING IN THE CHICAGO AREA, 1875-1925. Chicago: University of Chicago Press, 1964. 238 p.

> An outgrowth of THE RISE OF THE SKYSCRAPER (no. 1068),

Planning, Architecture, Urban Renewal

which provides added material on "the technical and formal background of the Chicago work and on the structural details of the buildings themselves, on the genesis of the major buildings, the social, economic, and intellectual history of the city, and contemporary attitudes toward the work of the school."

1068 _____. THE RISE OF THE SKYSCRAPER. Chicago: University of Chicago Press, 1952. 235 p.

A definitive, and often highly critical history of the steel-framed skyscraper and its impact on urban life.

1069 Coolidge, John. MILL AND MANSION: A STUDY OF ARCHITECTURE AND SOCIETY IN LOWELL, MASSACHUSETTS, 1820-1865. New York: Russell and Russell, 1967.

Places the architecture of Lowell in a historical and social context. Stresses the differences between the paternalistic, utopia-like mill towns of this era and later industrial communities.

1070 Davis, J. Tait. "Middle Class Housing in the Central City." ECONOMIC GEOGRAPHY 41 (1965): 238-51.

Examines housing patterns in twelve cities between 1945 and 1960 and finds a substantial decrease in middle-class dwellings in the central city. Contends that the location of the central business district is closely related to the development of concentric or sector clusters of housing values.

1071 DeForest, Robert W., and Veiller, Lawrence, eds. THE TENEMENT HOUSE PROBLEM: INCLUDING THE REPORT OF THE NEW YORK STATE TENEMENT HOUSE COMMISSION OF 1900. 2 vols. New York: Arno Press, 1970. 470 p.; 516 p.

Details the living conditions in the city's tenements, provides a history of tenement house legislation and analyzes and evaluates the enforcement of the 1901 housing code resulting from the commission's findings.

1072 Dougherty, J.P. "Baroque and Picturesque Motifs in L'Enfant's Design for the Federal Capital." AMERICAN QUARTERLY 26 (1974): 23-36.

Concludes that L'Enfant's design appealed both to those who wanted a grandiose, centralized city in the manner of European capitals, and to those, like Jefferson, who wanted a city open to the landscape of the surrounding countryside.

1073 Doxiadis, Konstantinos Apostolou. EKISTICS: AN INTRODUCTION TO THE SCIENCE OF HUMAN SETTLEMENT. New York: Oxford University Press, 1968. 527 p.

Attempts to posit a universal theory of human settlement, based upon the author's understanding of historical processes and his projections based upon existing data.

1074 Dragos, Stephen F. "Privately Funded Mechanisms for Milwaukee Redevelopment." URBAN LAND 36 (1977): 15-23.

Surveys the city's thirty-five-year effort at development and attributes its relative success to a judicious mix of efforts by private enterprise, civic organizations, and public agencies. Emphasizes the need for excellence in both concept and execution.

1075 Dubovik, Paul. "Housing in Holyoke and its Effects on Family Life, 1860-1910." HISTORICAL JOURNAL OF WEST MASSACHUSETTS 4 (1975): 40-50.

Contends that housing in Holyoke was inadequate, unhealthy, and repulsive because manufacturers and investors regarded crowded tenements as the most economical way to house a work force that was underpaid.

1076 Durr, William T. "The Conscience of a City: A History of the Citizens' Planning and Housing Association and Efforts to Improve Housing for the Poor in Baltimore, Maryland, 1937-1954." Ph.D. dissertation, Johns Hopkins University, 1972. 559 p.

Chronicles the development and the deficiencies of the Citizens' Planning and Housing Association, including administrative and procedural problems that led to its ultimate failure and characterizes the nation's incompetency in distributing housing as a commodity to the poor.

1077 Fein, Albert. "Frederick Law Olmsted: His Development as a Theorist and Designer of the American City." Ph.D. dissertation, Columbia University, 1969. 376 p.

Locates the wellspring of Olmsted's urban thought in a neo-Jeffersonianism which sought to recreate the social leadership of the rural community in the city through widespread property ownership, public education, and devotion to social advancement. Argues that Olmsted regarded the public environment, rather than the school room, as the primary educative force.

1078 _____, ed. LANDSCAPE INTO CITYSCAPE: FREDERICK LAW OLMSTED'S PLANS FOR A GREATER NEW YORK CITY. Ithaca, N.Y.: Cornell University Press, 1967. 490 p.

Contains twelve documents and reports on Olmsted's plans for the city. Includes an introductory essay by Fein dealing with Olmsted's life and the evolution of his vision of New York City.

1079 Fisher, Robert M. TWENTY YEARS OF PUBLIC HOUSING: ECONOMIC ASPECTS OF THE FEDERAL PROGRAM. Westport, Conn.: Greenwood Press, 1975. 303 p.

Analyzes the results of the public housing program based upon the Housing Act of 1937 and discusses the issues involved in public housing in the late 1950s. Contains important statistical data.

1080 Fishman, Robert. URBAN UTOPIAS IN THE TWENTIETH CENTURY: EBENEZER HOWARD, FRANK LLOYD WRIGHT AND LE CORBUSIER. New York: Basic Books, 1977. 332 p.

Analyzes and evaluates the efforts of the three principals to deal with the urban crisis of their time by constructing models of ideal cities. Stresses that their concepts were utopian in the sense that each was a coherent program for action arising out of thought that transcends current outlooks.

1081 Fitch, James Morston. AMERICAN BUILDING: THE HISTORICAL FORCES THAT SHAPED IT. Boston: Houghton-Mifflin, 1972. 382 p.

Traces the history of changing architectural styles in American cities and relates them to the social, economic, and cultural milieu.

1082 Frieden, Bernard J. THE FUTURE OF OLD NEIGHBORHOODS. Cambridge, Mass.: Joint Center for Urban Studies, 1964. 209 p.

Investigates the reasons for the decline of American central cities by the 1950s, focusing on New York City, Los Angeles, and Hartford, and discusses possible strategies for rebuilding those cities, especially in the area of housing.

1083 Friedman, Lawrence M. GOVERNMENT AND SLUM HOUSING: A CENTURY OF FRUSTRATION. Chicago: Rand, McNally, 1968. 206 p.

Traces and evaluates the evolution of legislation regarding slum housing from the New York Housing Law of 1867 to the mid-1960s. Concludes that the most productive approach is to reduce the punitive aspect of legislation and increase the inducement for landlords to improve property.

1084 Friedman, Lawrence M., and Spector, Michael J. "Tenement House Legislation in Wisconsin: Reform and Reaction." AMERICAN JOURNAL OF LEGAL HISTORY 9 (1965): 41-63.

Planning, Architecture, Urban Renewal

Discusses the background, passage, and content of the 1907 Wisconsin Tenement House Law, including the role of Edessa Junz, assistant factory inspector in the Bureau of Labor and Industrial Statistics, and Charles E. Estabrook, Republican assemblyman most responsible for the bill's enactment. Concludes that the battle over legislation was largely a struggle for symbols and that the law was designed to placate the builders and the politicians.

1085 Frye, Mary Virginia. "The Historical Development of Municipal Parks in the United States: Concepts and their Applications." Ph.D. dissertation, University of Illinois, 1964. 304 p.

Traces the evolution of the municipal park movement from colonial times to the early twentieth century, stressing the eventual incorporation of the idea into broader schemes for national and state recreation areas.

1086 Goist, Park Dixon. "Lewis Mumford and 'Anti-Urbanism.'" JOURNAL OF THE AMERICAN INSTITUTE OF PLANNERS 35 (1969): 340-47.

Contends that Mumford is not an exponent of antiurbanism, but rather a perceptive idealist whose view of the city includes not only what exists but what is ideal and possible. Concludes that this complex view of the city makes his work seem antiurban.

1087 Grant, David R. METROPOLITAN SURVEYS: A DIGEST. Chicago: Public Administration Service, 1958. 256 p.

Examines the technique of metropolitan surveys and finds that most of the 112 areas surveyed suffered from the same problems but proposed a variety of solutions. Also abstracts the results of those 112 surveys from across the nation and Canada.

1088 Greer, Guy. YOUR CITY TOMORROW. New York: Macmillan, 1947. 210 p.

Locates the cause of the urban crisis of the 1940s in a lack of planning and the consequent inconsistency of efforts to deal with slums and housing. Examines the political and fiscal limitations, focuses on Boston's comprehensive urban renewal plan, and details a program for action.

1089 Greer, Guy, and Hansen, Alvin W. URBAN DEVELOPMENT AND HOUSING A PROGRAM FOR POST-WAR. Planning Pamphlet no. 10. Washington, D.C.: National Planning Association, 1941. 24 p.

Urges an integrated approach to public housing which places it in the larger perspectives of urban renewal and city replanning and calls for federal aid to finance both the necessary planning and the purchasing of slum and blighted area land as the preliminary step to redevelopment.

1090 Greer, Scott. URBAN RENEWAL AND AMERICAN CITIES: THE DILEMMA OF DEMOCRATIC INTERVENTION. Indianapolis: Bobbs, Merrill, 1965. 201 p.

    Criticizes the urban renewal program for materially reducing the supply of housing in American cities by 1962, at a cost of over three billion dollars. Asserts that the problem lies not with the people but with "the way the damned system works."

1091 Gruen, Victor. THE HEART OF OUR CITIES: THE URBAN CRISIS, DIAGNOSIS AND CURE. New York: Simon and Schuster, 1964. 368 p.

    Focuses on the crisis of the central business district, and blames its problems primarily on the "traffickists" who permit the automobile to dictate rather than serve the needs of the city and its people. Details a "cellular" plan for the regeneration of the central city.

1092 Haar, Charles M. FEDERAL CREDIT AND PRIVATE HOUSING. New York: McGraw-Hill, 1960. 408 p.

    Surveys the evolution of federal housing credit, analyzes the structure and operation of the system of 1960, points up the major problems and policy issues, and makes recommendations for changes. Ties in federal credit policy with larger issues of metropolitan land use.

1093 Hancock, John L. "John Nolen and the American City Planning Movement: A History of Culture Change and Community Response, 1900-1940." Ph.D. dissertation, University of Pennsylvania, 1964. 686 p.

    Locates the source of urban planning in the Progressive era reformers' campaigns against societal waste and in the New Deal's urban policies which left a three-fold legacy of a trained body of experts, renewal through regional recentralization, and government-business cooperation.

1094 _____. "Planners in the Changing American City." 1900-1940." JOURNAL OF THE AMERICAN INSTITUTE OF PLANNERS 33 (1967): 290-304.

    Surveys the evolution of the city planning profession from the late nineteenth century to 1940. Summarizes the major principles which have guided the profession, with an emphasis on democratic processes, humanism, regionalism, and environmentalism.

Planning, Architecture, Urban Renewal

1095   Heidrich, Robert W. "A Village in a Park: Riverside, Illinois." HISTORICAL PRESERVATION 25 (1973): 28-33.

    Discusses the plan of Frederick Law Olmsted to build a village without disturbing the natural environment.

1096   Hines, Thomas S. BURNHAM OF CHICAGO, ARCHITECT AND PLANNER. New York: Oxford University Press, 1974. 445 p.

    Focuses on Burnham's role in the Columbian Exposition and the Chicago Plan and on his contribution to the city plans of Washington, D.C., Cleveland, and San Francisco.

1097   _____. "The Paradox of 'Progressive' Architecture: Urban Planning and Public Building in Tom Johnson's Cleveland." AMERICAN QUARTERLY 25 (1973): 426-48.

    Sees Mayor Johnson's choice of Daniel H. Burnham to design Cleveland's face lifting as that of the typical Progressive who deferred too readily to the expert. As a result, instead of planning innovations that reflected the industrial, urban conditions of the twentieth century, Johnson and Cleveland followed Burnham in a retreat to classical patterns not adapted to the urban scene. The author sees that retreat as typical of Richard Hofstadter's "backward looking" progressives.

1098   Hoffman, Ronald. THE ARCHITECTURE OF JOHN WELLBORN ROOT. Baltimore: Johns Hopkins University Press, 1973. 263 p.

    Analyzes and evaluates the work of the late-nineteenth century architect who designed many notable buildings in Chicago and Kansas City.

1099   Horten, Loren N. "Town Planning, Growth, and Architecture in Selected Mississippi River Towns in Iowa, 1833-1860." Ph.D. dissertation, University of Iowa, 1978. 466 p.

    Examines town planning and architecture in Dubuque, Davenport, and Muscatine and compares them to other cities of the period. Argues that the urban frontier in Iowa preceded the rural frontier and that city buildings there were similar to those of most midwestern and eastern towns of the era.

1100   Hoyt, Homer. ONE HUNDRED YEARS OF LAND VALUES IN CHICAGO, 1830-1933. New York: Arno Press, 1970. 519 p.

    Surveys the changing structure of land values through five distinct periods: canal building, 1830-42; railroad building, 1843-62; from the Civil War through the Great Fire, 1863-77; the skyscraper era, 1878-98; and the post-World War I era. Relates the growth of the city to rises in land values.

1101   Huggins, Kay Haire. "City Planning in North Carolina, 1900-1929."
NORTH CAROLINA HISTORY 46 (1969): 377-97.

   Links the "City Beautiful" movement in the state to broader
reform currents of the Progressive era. Locates the center of
the beautification impulse in various women's organizations
and civic groups.

1102   Huggins, Koleen A.H. "The Evolution of City and Regional Planning
in North Carolina, 1900-1950." Ph.D. dissertation, Duke University,
1967. 251 p.

   Investigates the beginnings of the modern planning movements
in North Carolina and finds that the model of the "City
Beautiful" was gradually displaced by the "City Useful."
Concludes that planning without political savvy is futile.

1103   Hunter, Leslie Gene. "Greenbelt, Maryland: A City on a Hill."
MARYLAND HISTORICAL MAGAZINE 63 (1968): 105-36.

   Examines the intellectual and political origins of the Greenbelt project, focusing upon the influence which energized
Franklin D. Roosevelt and Rexford G. Tugwell. Finds that
the "new towns" succeeded partially in employing relief
workers and in providing a model city, but failed to provide
adequate housing for low-income families at reasonable cost.

1104   Jackson, Anthony. A PLACE CALLED HOME: A HISTORY OF LOW-
COST HOUSING IN MANHATTAN. Cambridge: MIT Press, 1976.
359 p.

   Traces the development of housing regulations and efforts to
provide low-cost housing from the 1850s to the present. Concludes that private enterprise is not interested in or capable
of providing adequate housing and a decent environment.

1105   Jensen, Rolf. "The Relevance of History in City Design and Planning."
In CITIES OF VISION, pp. 256-99. New York: John Wiley and
Sons, 1974.

   Contends that delving into the historical background of an
urban area may help modern designers to derive fundamental
aesthetic values or truisms which may be equally valid in
contemporary times.

1106   Johnston, Norman J. "The Frederick Law Olmsted Plan for Tacoma."
PACIFIC NORTHWEST QUARTERLY 66 (1975): 97-104.

   Examines Olmsted's unorthodox plan for remaking the city and
attributes its abandonment to the desire of boosters and promoters to get on with the business of buying and selling lots
and bringing their town into the "real world."

1107 Jordy, William H. "The Commercial Style and the 'Chicago School.'" PERSPECTIVES IN AMERICAN HISTORY 1 (1967): 390-400.

Uses a review of Carl Condit's CHICAGO SCHOOL OF ARCHITECTURE (no. 1067a) to discuss the themes of American urban architecture. Contends that the Chicago School will be recognized as the "culminating chapter in the history of nineteenth-century urbanism."

1108 Kantor, Harvey A. "Modern Urban Planning in New York City: Origins and Evolution 1890-1933." Ph.D. dissertation, New York University, 1971. 466 p.

Discovers a rich diversity of planning approaches undertaken by municipal government, civic organizations, and foundations. Attributes that largely to the difficulties inherent in guiding urban growth in such a massive, pluralistic democracy.

1109 King, Andrew J. "Law and Land Use in Chicago: A Prehistory of Modern Zoning." Ph.D. dissertation, University of Wisconsin, Madison, 1976. 454 p.

Finds that questions of zoning and land use remained in private hands until the inability of the system to provide adequate means of stabilizing and rationalizing land conflicts led to increased use of public law and political action. Also contends that public law has been increasingly subjugated to private ends.

1110 Knutson, Robert. "The White City: The World's Columbian Exposition of 1893." Ph.D. dissertation, Columbia University, 1963. 295 p.

Credits the exposition with being the impetus for the city planning movement, and particularly for the emergence of the Chicago School of Architecture and urban design.

1111 Kovisars, Judith F. "Planned Change in a Changing Urban Environment: A Social History of Urban Renewal in Trenton, New Jersey." Ph.D. dissertation, University of Pennsylvania, 1970. 253 p.

Argues that social planning is alien to the American cultural ethos and that urban renewal has sought economic rather than social change, been basically reactionary, and exacerbated the situation that it was supposed to alleviate.

1112 Loewenstein, Louis K., and McGrath, Dorn C., Jr. "The Planning Imperative in America's Future." ANNALS OF THE AMERICAN ACADEMY OF POLITICAL AND SOCIAL SCIENCE 405 (1973): 15-24.

Presents a brief overview of the nature of city planning in the United States from the "City Beautiful" movement of the 1890s through the 1960s.

Planning, Architecture, Urban Renewal

1113 Lowe, Jeanne R. CITIES IN A RACE WITH TIME: PROGRESS AND POVERTY IN AMERICA'S RENEWING CITIES. New York: Random House, 1967. 601 p.

> Presents case histories of urban renewal in diverse cities since the 1940s in an attempt to identify the various kinds of forces, pressures, and conflicts involved in such attempts, and the factors that tend to promote success or failure, and to apply these historical lessons to help devise effective strategies to cope with the urban crisis. Stresses the need for cooperative federalism and major changes in values if the problems of the cities are to be overcome.

1114 Lubitz, Edward. "The Tenement Problem in New York City and the Movement for its Reform, 1856-1867." Ph.D. dissertation, New York University, 1970. 601 p.

> Examines first the condition of tenement housing, using the findings of the first legislative investigation in 1856, and second the activities of reform groups that facilitated the first tenement law in 1857.

1115 Lubove, Roy. COMMUNITY PLANNING IN THE 1920S. Pittsburgh: University of Pittsburgh Press, 1963. 155 p.

> Examines the founding and activities of the Regional Planning Association of America, one of the nation's pioneer urban planning associations.

1116 _____. THE PROGRESSIVES AND THE SLUMS: TENEMENT HOUSE REFORM IN NEW YORK CITY, 1890-1917. Westport, Conn.: Greenwood Press, 1974. 284 p.

> Examines the issue of housing reform during the Progressive era, focusing particularly on the activities of Jacob Riis and Lawrence Veiller. Criticizes reformers for focusing on restrictive codes rather than on constructing public housing and for failing to understand the connection between bad housing and broader social conditions.

1117 _____, ed. THE URBAN COMMUNITY: HOUSING AND PLANNING IN THE PROGRESSIVE ERA. Englewood Cliffs, N.J.: Prentice-Hall, 1967. 148 p.

> Contains reports on housing reform and planning by several city, state, and federal agencies during the Progressive era, as well as by such individual reformers as Lawrence Veiller, John Brisben Walker, Daniel H. Burnham, Frederick C. Howe, and Frederick Law Olmsted, Jr. Includes an introduction by the editor.

1118 Lyon, Elizabeth Anne Mack. "Business Buildings in Atlanta: A Study in Urban Growth and Form." Ph.D. dissertation, Emory University, 1971. 585 p.

> Identifies four distinct periods of building activity and their characteristic urban forms spanning the years from 1865 to 1930, based on photographs, atlases, fire insurance maps, city directories, and building permits. Details the impact of transportation, public utilities, planning activities, and the nature of economic activities on the size and patterning of business buildings.

1119 McDonnell, Timothy L. THE WAGNER HOUSING ACT. Chicago: Loyola University Press, 1957. 470 p.

> Analyzes the complexities of the federal legislative process attending the lengthy struggle to enact into law the Housing Act of 1937, including the activities of lobbyists representing executive agencies, real estate organizations, labor unions, and welfare groups.

1120 McEntire, Davis. RESIDENCE AND RACE. Berkeley and Los Angeles: University of California Press, 1960. 409 p.

> The final report of a study of housing problems of rural and ethnic minorities conducted for the Commission on Race and Housing, national in scope and focused on inequality of housing opportunity.

1121 McGrath, Kristin S. "American Values and the Slums: A Chicago Case Study." Ph.D. dissertation, University of Minnesota, 1977. 373 p.

> Case studies the development of slums in Chicago since that city's inception, with major attention to the activities of the Metropolitan Housing and Planning Council in the period since 1934, in an attempt to analyze the interaction between reform values and urban renewal programs. Finds that reform ultimately failed.

1122 MacKaye, Benton. THE NEW EXPLORATION. New York: Harcourt Brace and Co., 1928. Reprint. Urbana: University of Illinois Press, 1962. 243 p.

> Pioneer essay on regional and urban planning emphasizing the need to maintain ecological balance while maintaining development, a geotechnics approach. Describes the forces promoting urban sprawl and suggests ways for managing unplanned growth and promoting harmonious and healthful development.

Planning, Architecture, Urban Renewal

1123 McKelvey, Blake. "Housing and Urban Renewal: The Rochester Experience." ROCHESTER HISTORY 27 (1965): 1-28.

Provides an historical perspective on housing problems in Rochester and an analysis of urban renewal efforts in the 1960s.

1124 _____. "Rochester's Near Northeast." ROCHESTER HISTORY 29 (1967): 1-23.

Discusses the development of and attempts to cope with urban problems in Rochester's near northeast district, an area which experienced considerable black unrest during the 1960s.

1125 Martin, Judith. "New Towns. In Town and Future Urban Growth: Some Preliminary Assessments." PROSPECTS 3 (1977): 573-98.

Contends that urban growth has always been a response to economic pressures thus creating most present day urban problems. Assesses the historical impact of urban renewal legislation on city life and speculates on the prospects for a reinvigoration of cities.

1126 Meyer, David R. "Interurban Differences in Black Housing Quality." ANNALS OF THE ASSOCIATION OF AMERICAN GEOGRAPHERS 63 (1973): 347-52.

Investigates the determinants of black housing quality using 1960 census tract data for 109 SMSAs. Concludes that income-related and supply factors are the best predictors of differences in quality of black housing, whereas social class and household structure are not important independent predictors. Also notes that large black communities have better housing than small ones and that racial discrimination tends to distort supply factors.

1127 Meyerson, Martin, and Banfield, Edward C. POLITICS, PLANNING, AND THE PUBLIC INTEREST: THE CASE OF PUBLIC HOUSING IN CHICAGO. New York: Free Press, 1964. 353 p.

Studies site selection for public housing projects from a public policy and decision-making perspective, using both empirical and theoretical materials. "Politics," "planning," and "the public interest" serve as key concepts for the organization and analysis of the case study.

1128 Millspaugh, Martin, and Breckenfield, Gurney. THE HUMAN SIDE OF URBAN RENEWAL. New York: Washburn, 1960. 233 p.

Examines the attitude changes that accompany urban rehabilitation through case studies of neighborhoods in Chicago,

Miami, New Orleans, and Baltimore. Concludes that rehabilitation does in fact produce positive changes in the attitudes, values and behavior of slum neighborhoods, but cautions that changes cannot be achieved without paying attention to ancillary nonhousing problems.

1129 Mohl, Raymond A., and Betten, Neil. "The Failure of Industrial City Planning: Gary, Indiana, 1906-1910." JOURNAL OF THE AMERICAN INSTITUTE OF PLANNERS 38 (1972): 202-15.

A study of the largest planned city of the Progressive era--Gary--founded in 1906 by the U.S. Steel Corporation. Concludes that the conflict between human needs and dominant cultural and business values compromised the public interest and eventually resulted in failure.

1130 Moore, Charles, ed. PLAN OF CHICAGO BY DANIEL H. BURNHAM AND EDWARD H. BENNETT. New York: De Capo Press, 1970. 164 p.

Reproduces the famous 1909 plan which formed the basis for the work of the Chicago School of Architecture and which gave tremendous impetus to urban planning in cities all over the United States.

1131 Morrison, Hugh Sinclair. LOUIS SULLIVAN, PROPHET OF MODERN ARCHITECTURE. Westport, Conn.: Greenwood Press, 1971. 391 p.

Chronicles the life and work of the man often regarded as a the father of modern American urban architecture.

1132 Mullin, John Robert. "American Perceptions of German City Planning at the Turn of the Century." URBANISM PAST AND PRESENT 3 (1976-1977): 5-15.

Argues that an absence of knowledge concerning the German planning milieu is an important missing link in developing a comprehensive analysis of the roots of American city planning, and examines and analyzes the relationship between American and German city planning for the years 1890 to 1916, focusing especially on Frankfurt.

1133 Nairn, Ian. THE AMERICAN LANDSCAPE: A CRITICAL VIEW. New York: Random House, 1965. 152 p.

Criticizes the architecture and the unplanned nature of American cities, based upon the author's frequent travels in the United States between 1940 and 1960.

1134 Naloli, Salvatore J. "Zoning and the Development of Urban Land Use Patterns." ECONOMIC GEOGRAPHY 47 (1971): 171-84.

Planning, Architecture, Urban Renewal

Analyzes the impact and efficacy of large area and spot rezoning on urban land use pattern, focusing on the experience of Worcester, Massachusetts, from 1925 to 1963. Sees zoning as exerting a variety of influences, most notably with the patterns of land use development.

1135 Nash, William. RESIDENTIAL REHABILITATION: PRIVATE PROFITS AND PUBLIC PURPOSES. New York: McGraw-Hill, 1959. 272 p.

Analyzes private market factors that promote the maintenance or restoration of existing dwelling structures in an attempt to provide a basis for public policies to improve the economic potentials of rehabilitation and define those areas in which public action must supplement private market forces.

1136 Parris, Ronald G. "The Black Community and Housing Strategy." In SOUTH ATLANTIC URBAN STUDIES, edited by Jack R. Censer and N. Steinert, pp. 18-30. Columbia: University of South Carolina Press, 1977.

Argues that urban problems, including housing, are sociostructural in nature and must be understood in terms of how goods, services, opportunities, and choices are distributed among the population. Calls upon the poor to mobilize themselves as an interest group.

1137 Pawley, Martin. ARCHITECTURE VERSUS HOUSING. New York: Praeger, 1971. 128 p.

Analyzes within a cross-culturual framework major patterns in the development of mass housing from the nineteenth century to the present, including discussions of the impact of architectural theory and changing values.

1138 Peterson, Jon A. "The City Beautiful Movement: Forgotten Origins and Lost Meanings." JOURNAL OF URBAN HISTORY 2 (1976): 415-34.

Contends that the "City Beautiful" movement was a complex cultural phenomenon with three distinct components--municipal art, civic improvement, and outdoor art--each with a different constituency. Locates its origin in elements of the middle and upper classes.

1139 Rapkin, Chester, and Grigsby, William G. RESIDENTIAL RENEWAL IN THE URBAN CORE. Philadelphia: University of Pennsylvania Press, 1960. 131 p.

Analyzes the demand for housing in the Washington Square East Redevelopment Project, encompassing the Society Hill area of

Planning, Architecture, Urban Renewal

Philiadelphia, to provide public officials with current data and projected trends and potentials within the residential real estate market. Concludes that the central core of Philadelphia, and perhaps of other large cities, will not attract households with children despite rehabilitation, but that it does hold considerable allure for small households of educated and relatively affluent adults.

1140 Reps, John W. THE MAKING OF URBAN AMERICA. Princeton, N.J.: Princeton University Press, 1965. 574 p.

Describes and assesses the planning of towns and cities in the United States from colonial settlement up to World War II. Also includes chapters on the European background of American city planning, and the colonial American towns of Spain and France, and presents over three hundred reproductions of urban maps, plans, and views.

1141 _____. TOWN PLANNING IN FRONTIER AMERICA. Princeton, N.J.: Princeton University Press, 1969. 473 p.

Concentrates on planning in the United States, especially in the earlier periods.

1142 Riis, Jacob A. HOW THE OTHER HALF LIVES: STUDIES AMONG THE TENEMENTS OF NEW YORK. Williamstown, Mass.: Corner House Publishers, 1972. 231 p.

Presents a highly personalized but penetrating account of slum life in late nineteenth-century New York, based upon Riis' twelve-year career as a police reporter. Ranks as a major document in arousing the public to the need for reform in the area of urban poverty and housing.

1143 Rodwin, Lloyd. HOUSING AND ECONOMIC PROGRESS: A STUDY OF THE EXPERIENCE OF BOSTON'S MIDDLE-INCOME FAMILIES. Cambridge, Mass.: Harvard University Press, 1961. 228 p.

Explores the housing experience of middle-income families from 1850 through the 1950s to support the hypothesis that "rising income and rising standards of demand, coupled with inadequate adjustments of housing supply in response to such rise in income and standards, are the sources of most of our vexatious problems of housing and neighborhood development." Analyzes income, rent levels and expenditure patterns, and presents an empirical history and theoretical discussion of residential growth, development, and structure.

1144 Roper, Laura Wood. F.L.O.: A BIOGRAPHY OF FREDERICK LAW OLMSTED. Baltimore: Johns Hopkins University Press, 1973. 555 p.

Planning, Architecture, Urban Renewal

Sees Olmsted as motivated largely by a desire to establish "communicativeness" between people of disparate occupations and backgrounds in the American city. Examines Olmsted's various city plans and finds each energized by a "grand idea."

1145   Scott, Mellier Goodin. AMERICAN CITY PLANNING SINCE 1890. Berkeley and Los Angeles: University of California Press, 1969. 745 p.

Sketches major phases in American city planning. Chapters include: "The Spirit of Reform"; "The Heyday of the City Beautiful"; "Science and the City Functional"; "City Planning in the Age of Business"; "The Urban Community in National Life"; "Defense, War, and the Struggle Against Blight"; "Responses to Urban Flux"; and "The Search for a New Comprehensiveness."

1146   Scully, Vincent. AMERICAN ARCHITECTURE AND URBANISM. New York: Praeger, 1969. 275 p.

Discusses the impact of the concept of urbanism on American architectural thought and focuses upon individual architects who have contributed to the urban experience.

1147   Smallwood, James. URBAN BUILDER: THE LIFE AND TIMES OF STANLEY DRAPER. Norman: University of Oklahoma Press, 1977. 334 p.

Biography of an urban planner who, after joining the Oklahoma City Chamber of Commerce in 1919, oversaw that city's transition from frontier town into a major metropolitan center.

1148   Smith, Margaret S. "Between City and Suburb: Architecture and Planning in Boston's South End." Ph.D. dissertation, Brown University, 1976. 469 p.

Traces the evolution of the South End, like the Back Bay a planned residential community of the mid-nineteenth century, through planning, realization, decline, and revival. Concludes that its development was inhibited by a preference for suburban living on the part of middle-class Bostonians.

1149   Staples, John H. "Urban Renewal: A Comparative Study of Twenty-Two Cities, 1950-1960." WESTERN POLITICAL QUARTERLY 23 (1970): 294-304.

Focuses on several demographic, economic, and political variables in comparing the experience with urban renewal of twenty-two cities ranging in size from Chester, Pennsylvania, with a population of 64,000, to New York City, in an attempt to remove the study of urban renewal from a problem-oriented and normative framework to a more scientific level of inquiry.

1150 Sternlieb, George. "Housing, Urban Development, and Rehabilitation." In SOUTH ATLANTIC URBAN STUDIES, vol. 1, edited by Jack R. Censer and N. Steinert, pp. 37-47. Columbia: University of South Carolina Press, 1977.

Feels that the federal government has played a steadily decreasing role in the rehabilitation of urban neighborhoods because it is reflecting the preference of most Americans for suburban living. Contends that shrinking investment capital for housing will force rehabilitation.

1151 _____. THE TENEMENT LANDLORD. New Brunswick, N.J.: Rutgers University Press, 1966. 269 p.

Focuses upon Newark, New Jersey, to illustrate the nature of the slums housing program and to find the proper balance of coercive legislation and incentive to improve conditions. Contends that cities face a "crisis of function," to which question of race and class are secondary.

1152 Stewart, Ian Robert. "Central Park 1851-1871: Urbanization and Environmental Planning in New York City." Ph.D. dissertation, Cornell University, 1973. 379 p.

Reviews the history of Central Park, considering the original objectives, the politics involved in its construction and the designer's perception of the changing role of the modern city in American society.

1153 Straus, Michael W., and Wegg, Talbot. HOUSING COMES OF AGE. New York: Oxford University Press, 1938. 259 p.

Discusses the procedures, problems, and achievements of the Housing Division of the Public Works Administration as the major vehicle for the New Deal's low-rent and slum-clearance housing program. Includes a brief survey of earlier efforts to provide low-cost dwellings for the urban poor and a listing of all Public Works Administration housing projects.

1154 Straus, Nathan, Jr. THE SEVEN MYTHS OF HOUSING. 2d ed. New York: Arno Press, 1974. 314 p.

Presents a concrete plan for a post-World War II housing program, identifying and debunking misconceptions regarding the causes and prevalence of slums, and the efficacy and cost of public housing. Also traces the earlier history of public housing in the United States.

Planning, Architecture, Urban Renewal

1155 Sussman, Carl, ed. PLANNING THE FOURTH MIGRATION: THE NEGLECTED VISION OF THE REGIONAL PLANNING ASSOCIATION OF AMERICA. Cambridge: MIT Press, 1976. 227 p.

Anthology of essays written by the Regional Planning Association of America members in the 1920s, including contributions by Lewis Mumford, Clarence Stein, and Henry Wright, as reactions to the then-emerging urban-industrial city form and attendant problems. Selections include discussions of regionalism, planning, garden cities, and the nature and direction of metropolitan civilization.

1156 Sutherland, John F. "A City of Homes: Philadelphia Slums and Reformers, 1880-1918." Ph.D. dissertation, Temple University, 1973. 324 p.

Attributes housing reform in Philadelphia to the efforts of middle-class settlement house workers. Contends that basic conservatism limited their programs to model houses and restrictive legislation and caused them to ignore public housing until the war produced a housing crisis.

1157 Sutton, Stephanne Barry, ed. CIVILIZING AMERICAN CITIES: A SELECTION OF FREDERICK LAW OLMSTED'S WRITINGS ON CITY LANDSCAPES. Cambridge: MIT Press, 1971. 310 p.

An anthology of printed documents selected and edited to elucidate Olmsted's views on urban society, landscapes, and city designs. Includes an introductory chapter discussing Olmsted's career.

1158 Swanson, B.E. "Public Efforts to Redevelop American Cities." AMERICAN JOURNAL OF ECONOMICS AND SOCIOLOGY 25 (1966): 365-78.

Focuses on the historical experience of New York City with public housing programs from the 1940s to the 1960s, stressing the shift from redevelopment to renewal and municipal government reorganization.

1159 Tager, Jack, and Goist, Park Dixon, eds. THE URBAN VISION. Homewood, Ill.: Dorsey Press, 1970. 310 p.

Contains essays by architects, social theorists, and city planners on the shape that the American city should take.

1160 Taylor, Graham R. SATELLITE CITIES: A STUDY OF INDUSTRIAL SUBURBS. New York: Arno Press, 1970. 333 p.

Comments on the state and possibilities of community planning by focusing on the process of suburbanization fostered by the progressive outward movement of factories. Discusses the experience of Pullman, Illinois, and Gary, Indiana.

1161 Topping, Mark B. "The Emergence of Federal Public Housing: Atlanta's Techwood Project." AMERICAN JOURNAL OF ECONOMICS AND SOCIOLOGY 32 (1973): 379-86.

>Focuses on the first "low rent housing and slum clearance projects" under the Public Works Administration, contending that in addition to forming an experiment in economic recovery, the project represented a social experiment designed to improve the quality of life for Techwood's residents.

1162 Trachtenberg, Alan. "The Rainbow and the Grid." AMERICAN QUARTERLY 16 (1964): 3-19.

>Posits the tension between differing concepts of urban existence as exemplified by Thomas Pope's graceful "Rainbow," in his TREATISE ON BRIDGE ARCHITECTURE (1811), and the gridiron street plan with its emphasis on efficiency, and discusses the character of nineteenth-century Brooklyn and Walt Whitman.

1163 Tunnard, Christopher. THE CITY OF MAN. New York: Scribner, 1970. 424 p.

>Suggests "ways in which art can be interwoven with our culture to produce a more desirable City of Man," culminating in a new approach to civic design. Provides information regarding the development of urban planning in Europe and the United States and the changing form and functions of cities.

1164 Tunnard, Christopher, and Reed, Henry Hope. AMERICAN SKYLINE: THE GROWTH AND FORM OF OUR CITIES AND TOWNS. New York: New American Library, 1956. 302 p.

>Argues that the physical community in America has been molded by a variety of economic, social, and political forces, and illustrates the changing aspects of cities as a reflection of such forces over time, including seven specific eras: the colonial pattern, 1607-1776; the young republic, 1776-1825; the romantic era, 1825-50; the age of steam and iron, 1850-80; the expanding city, 1880-1910; the city of towers, 1910-33; and the regional city, 1933-present.

1165 Twombly, Robert C. "Saving the Family: Middle Class Attraction to Wright's Prairie House, 1901-1909." AMERICAN QUARTERLY 27 (1975): 57-72.

>Sees Wright's Prairie House as an effort on the part of the upper middle class to protect their families from the real and

imagined forces of disintegration brought about by the economic uncertainties and social reorganization of the city.

1166 Vance, James E., Jr. "The Classical Revival and Urban-Rural Conflict in Nineteenth Century North America." CANADIAN REVIEW OF AMERICAN STUDIES 4 (1973): 149-68.

Discusses the development and persistence of antiurbanism in the American tradition, focusing particularly on the early nineteenth-century architectural vogue known as the classical revival and its implications for conceptions of the city. Contends that the revival began the myth of the parasitical city.

1167 Veiller, Lawrence. HOUSING REFORM: A HANDBOOK FOR PRACTICAL USE IN AMERICAN CITIES. New York: Charities Publication Committee, 1910. 213 p.

Written by the premier housing reformer of the era. Contains practical advice on how to start a better housing campaign, how to influence local politicians, and how to lobby in the legislature. Also presents a series of "don'ts" for the would-be reformer, as well as sample housing codes.

1168 Walker, Mabel L. URBAN BLIGHT AND SLUMS: ECONOMIC AND LEGAL FACTORS IN THEIR ORIGIN, RECLAMATION, AND PREVENTION. Cambridge, Mass.: Harvard University Press, 1938. Reprint. New York: Russell and Russell, 1971. 442 p.

Focuses on problems involved in the rehabilitation of blighted areas, including discussions of land values, zoning, taxation, financing, and construction.

1169 Walker, Robert A. THE PLANNING FUNCTION IN URBAN GOVERNMENT. 2d ed. Chicago: University of Chicago Press, 1969. 410 p.

Analyzes the composition of planning boards in the United States, seeking to discover why the Model City Planning Enabling Act failed to achieve greater success. Concludes that the planning commissions set up under this act consisted of nonprofessionals who had little time to devote to their work. Also notes the prevalence of political conflict as a cause of failure.

1170 Warner, Sam Bass, Jr., ed. PLANNING FOR A NATION OF CITIES. Cambridge, Mass.: Harvard University Press, 1966. 310 p.

An outgrowth of a 1964 Bicentennial Conference on Planning for the Quality of Urban Life at Washington University, St. Louis, this volume of sixteen essays, with sections of federal

Planning, Architecture, Urban Renewal

responsibility, work and the quality of urban life, responsive physical planning, and responsive urban service, focuses on the "gap between what a thoughtful citizen is entitled to expect from urban planning and public policy and the contemporary performance of American cities."

1171 Wilson, William H. THE CITY BEAUTIFUL MOVEMENT IN KANSAS CITY. Columbia: University of Missouri Press, 1964. 171 p.

Stresses that while the 1893 Columbian Exposition is traditionally viewed as the inception of the "City Beautiful" movement, the Kansas City experience indicates growing interest in urban improvement in the early 1870s. Argues in opposition to those who have criticized the formalistic and derivative nature of that movement, claiming that it proved "fundamentally important" to Kansas City and created a significant base for the work of later urban planners.

1172 _____. "More Almost Than the Men: Mira Lloyd Dock and the Beautification of Harrisburg." PENNSYLVANIA MAGAZINE OF HISTORY AND BIOGRAPHY 99 (1975): 490-99.

Details the efforts of Mira Lloyd Dock, who "epitomized the 'New Woman' in turn-of-the-century America," in the civic improvement campaign which sought to add Harrisburg to those cities touched by the "City Beautiful" movement. Contends that this movement attempted to answer real human needs and that its success rested on the dedicated involvement of public-spirited citizens.

1173 Winnick, Louis. RENTAL HOUSING: OPPORTUNITIES FOR PRIVATE INVESTMENT. New York: McGraw-Hill, 1958. 295 p.

Investigates the decline in equity investment in new private rental housing in the years following the Korean War, assesses the extent to which market forces will influence this trend in the future, and indicates what positive role public policies might play in expanding the volume of private rental construction.

1174 Winpenny, Thomas R. "The Nefarious Philadelphia Plan and Urban America: A Reconsideration." THE PENNSYLVANIA MAGAZINE OF HISTORY AND BIOGRAPHY 101 (1977): 102-13.

Challenges the critics of the gridiron plan on three points: (1) that the Philadelphia plan had a benign effect on many city dwellers, (2) that many modest income homeowners gained as well as did the rich, and (3) that aesthetic objections to right angles are based upon a limited view of the urban environment.

Planning, Architecture, Urban Renewal

1175 Wolner, Edward W. "Daniel Burnham and the Tradition of the City Builder in Chicago: Technique, Ambition and City Planning." Ph.D. dissertation, New York University, 1977. 343 p.

> Views the city builder as an ambitious adventurer who, bolstered by the power of technology, suspended conventions of everyday life, defined experiences wholly in his terms and tried to incorporate the whole world into his "imperial self."

1176 Wood, Edith Elmer. INTRODUCTION TO HOUSING. Washington, D.C.: United States Housing Authority, Federal Works Agency, 1940. 161 p.

> Designed to present basic "facts and principles" of housing for communities engaged in slum clearance and the development of low-cost housing. Provides, therefore, a description of the state-of-the-art of attitudes toward and knowledge of housing in the 1930s.

1177 Woodbury, Coleman, ed. THE FUTURE OF CITIES AND URBAN REDEVELOPMENT. Chicago: University of Chicago Press, 1953. 764 p.

> Surveys blighted areas and ongoing redevelopment programs to identify major operation problems and practices. Considers underlying factors in urban growth that have generated problems and "certain questions of objectives and values that underlie many of the actual program and policy interests."

1178 Wright, Carroll D. THE SLUMS OF BALTIMORE, CHICAGO, NEW YORK, AND PHILADELPHIA: SEVENTH SPECIAL REPORT OF THE COMMISSIONER OF LABOR. New York: Arno Press, 1978. 620 p.

> Presents a detailed statistical picture of life in the slums of major cities, especially housing rentals, costs, and the wages and hours of workers.

1179 Wright, Frank Lloyd. THE LIVING CITY. New York: Horizon Press, 1958. 222 p.

> Contains Wright's philosophy of urban design, concentrating upon his plans for Broadacre City where the lines between city and country were to be erased in the 1930s.

1180 Zucker, Paul. NEW ARCHITECTURE AND CITY PLANNING. Freeport, N.Y.: Books for Libraries, 1971. 694 p.

> Contains the results of a symposium on the subject held at the conclusion of World War II and illustrates the state of the art at that time.

Chapter 9
CLASS, ETHNICITY, AND RACE

1181   Abbott, Edith. THE TENEMENTS OF CHICAGO, 1908-1935. Chicago: University of Chicago Press, 1936. Reprint. New York: Arno Press, 1978. 505 p.

      Details housing conditions in the city of Chicago, with special reference to the living conditions of Jewish, Polish, Czech, German, Italian, and black residents. Summarizes many years of studies done by the School of Social Service Administration of the University of Chicago.

1182   Akin, Edward N. "When a Minority Becomes the Majority: Blacks in Jacksonville Politics, 1887-1907." FLORIDA HISTORICAL QUARTERLY 53 (1974): 123-45.

      Contends that black political leaders in Jacksonville were assertive and effective during the late nineteenth century and were defeated only when whites gerrymandered ward boundaries to sap their strength. Places the Jacksonville case in the wider context of post-Reconstruction and Progressive era politics in southern cities.

1183   Barton, Josef J. PEASANTS AND STRANGERS: ITALIANS, RUMANIANS, AND SLOVAKS IN AN AMERICAN CITY, 1890-1950. Cambridge, Mass.: Harvard University Press, 1975. 217 p.

      Focuses upon the impact that the urban environment had upon the village culture of Cleveland's immigrant communities, helping to forge them into self-consciousness ethnic groups with effective mechanisms for survival and advancement.

1184   Bayor, Ronald H. NEIGHBORS IN CONFLICT: THE IRISH, GERMANS, JEWS, AND ITALIANS OF NEW YORK CITY, 1929-1941. Baltimore: Johns Hopkins University Press, 1978. 232 p.

      Finds that ethnic conflict arises from "the interlocking and mutual reinforcement" of various factors rather than from irrational prejudice. Identifies several types of conflict based upon economic and political competition, foreign issues, and territorial disputes.

1185 Beasley, Jonathon. "Blacks--Slave and Free-Vicksburg, 1850-1860." JOURNAL OF MISSISSIPPI HISTORY 38 (1976): 1-32.

Uses Vicksburg as a test case for Richard Wade's thesis (no. 757) that slavery was disintegrating in southern cities in the 1850s while segration was increasing. Argues that the Vicksburg situation did not fit either of these patterns.

1186 Beirne, Daniel R. "Steadfast Americans: Residential Stability Among Workers in Baltimore, 1880-1930." Ph.D. dissertation, University of Maryland, 1976. 212 p.

Examines the relationship between local industries and residential stability in three Baltimore communities during the period and finds that two of them promoted residential stability through industrial paternalism while the third hired workers from a wider labor market.

1187 Berger, Bennett M. WORKING-CLASS SUBURB: A STUDY OF AUTO WORKERS IN SUBURBIA. Berkeley and Los Angeles: University of California Press, 1968. 143 p.

Based originally upon a 1957 survey of Ford assembly plant workers in a suburb of San Jose, California. Disputes many of the then prevailing popular views of suburban life.

1188 Betten, Neil, and Mohl, Raymond A. "The Evolution of Racism in an Industrial City, 1906-1940: A Case Study of Gary, Indiana." JOURNAL OF NEGRO HISTORY 59 (1974): 51-64.

Argues that racism did not arise accidentally out of housing patterns, but rather out of conscious policies of discrimination and segregation in education, housing, employment, public services, and recreation designed and implemented by business and government. Concludes that the racism of white ethnics was learned behavior as part of their Americanization process.

1189 Blackwelder, Julia Kirk. "Women in the Work Force: Atlanta, New Orleans, and San Antonio, 1930 to 1940." JOURNAL OF URBAN HISTORY 4 (1978): 331-58.

Compares the work experiences of Chicano, black, native white, and immigrant women in the three cities and examines the impact of proportion in the population, cultural preferences, race discrimination, and female head of household upon the employment structure.

1190 Blasingame, John W. "Before the Ghetto: The Making of the Black Community in Savannah, Georgia, 1865-1880." JOURNAL OF SOCIAL HISTORY 6 (1973): 463-88.

    Contends that urbanization gave blacks the preconditions for the emergence of an intelligent leadership class, a sense of unity, and the will and the economic means to fight against white oppression. Views their enclaves as "enduring communities" rather than as "enduring ghettos."

1191 _____. BLACK NEW ORLEANS, 1860-1880. Chicago: University of Chicago Press, 1973. 301 p.

    Concentrates upon the social history of the city's black community during the Civil War and Reconstruction eras, especially the family, churches, schools, and occupations.

1192 Bloomberg, Susan E. "Industrialization and Skilled Workers: Newark, 1826-1860." Ph.D. dissertation, University of Michigan, 1974. 341 p.

    Argues that the impact of industrialization on Newark workers was not as devastating as it was in the New England mill towns or larger cities, because conditions allowed both native-born and foreign-born workers to maintain traditional family life. Contends that it did destroy the city's artisan class.

1193 Bodnar, John E. "The Immigrant and the American City." JOURNAL OR URBAN HISTORY 3 (1977): 241-49.

    Reviews four books dealing with different ethnic groups and their adjustment to an urban environment and finds little commonality. Suggests a common conceptual framework stressing the interaction between the structural and industrial nature of the community and the premigration ways and experiences of the immigrant to reconcile the apparent contradictions.

1194 _____. IMMIGRATION AND INDUSTRIALIZATION: ETHNICITY IN AN AMERICAN MILL TOWN, 1870-1940. Pittsburgh: University of Pittsburgh Press, 1977. 213 p.

    Analyzes the survival strategy of the ethnic working class in Steelton, Pennsylvania, to adjust to an urban-industrial life and their efforts to preserve their national identity and culture through organization. Places the Steelton experience in the larger contexts of ethnic conflict and the tensions between urban and suburban dwellers.

1195 _____. "Socialization and Adaptation: Immigrant Families in Scranton, 1880-1890." PENNSYLVANIA HISTORY 43 (1976): 147-62.

    Focuses on the impact of the urban-industrial environment on working-class Welsh and Irish immigrant families in the coal mining town. Argues that the historical-cultural experiences of the two groups accounted largely for their differences in adaptation.

1196 _____. "Steelton's Immigrants: Social Relationships in a Pennsylvania Mill Town, 1870-1940." Ph.D. dissertation, University of Connecticut, 1975. 232 p.

Deals with response of old stock people and institutions to the influx of eastern European and black workers and with the efforts of the latter to create separate ethnic communities. Finds that second generation immigrants and blacks were equally insulated from mainstream institutions until they cooperated in the formation of the steelworkers union in the 1940s.

1197 Boskin, Joseph. URBAN RACIAL VIOLENCE IN THE TWENTIETH CENTURY. Beverly Hills, Calif.: Glencoe Press, 1976. 188 p.

Investigates the causes and nature of both race riots by whites and ghetto uprisings of blacks, as well as manifestations of racial violence in the 1970s. Holds that the race riots were extensions of racism, while the latter were reactions against it.

1198 Boxerman, Lawrence H. "St. Louis Urban League: History and Activities." Ph.D. dissertation, St. Louis University, 1968. 192 p.

Traces the evolution of the league from its foundation in 1917 to the late 1960s and examines its activity in integrating blacks into the city's industrial work force and in helping black homeowners improve their property.

1199 Bragaw, Donald H. "Status of Negroes in a Southern Port City in the Progressive Era: Pensacola, 1896-1920." FLORIDA HISTORICAL QUARTERLY 51 (1973): 281-302.

Claims that the economic and social status of most blacks in Pensacola actually declined during the Progressive era, due primarily to the pressure extended by an expanding white population and the changing nature of the city's economy.

1200 Brown, Bertram S. "Making It in Nineteenth Century Urban America." In NEW DIMENSIONS IN MENTAL HEALTH, pp. 3-7. Washington, D.C.: U.S. Department of Health, Education, and Welfare, 1976.

Summarizes many of the most important conclusions, to date, of the Philadelphia social history project and speculates upon implications. Concludes that the origins of today's urban stress lie in the social structures and social pressures of nineteenth-century cities.

Class, Ethnicity, and Race

1201   Brown, Letitia Wood. FREE NEGROES IN THE DISTRICT OF COLUMBIA, 1790-1846. New York: Oxford University Press, 1972. 226 p.

       Examines the structure of the free black community in the city and the manner in which it helped to undermine the slave system.

1202   Buell, Charles C. "The Workers of Worcester: Social Mobility and Ethnicity in a New England City, 1850-1880." Ph.D. dissertation, New York University, 1974. 204 p.

       Details the employment patterns of the Irish and Yankee workers during the major industrial and population growth of Worcester, which are representative of work force patterns elsewhere.

1203   Camarillo, Albert. "The Making of a Chicano Community: A History of the Chicanos in Santa Barbara, California, 1850-1930." Ph.D. dissertation, University of California, Los Angeles, 1975. 384 p.

       Traces the evolution of the Chicano community, the impact of urbanization and industrialization upon its basic institutions, the development of a working class, and the influx of large numbers of Mexicans in the early twentieth century. Concludes that the community contributed greatly to the local economy, but did not share in the resultant prosperity.

1204   Capeci, Dominic J. THE HARLEM RIOT OF 1943. Philadelphia: Temple University Press, 1977. 262 p.

       Views the Harlem riot, and similar outbreaks of the World II era, as a transition between the interracial or communal riots of previous times and the property-oriented or commodity upheaval of contemporary days. Focuses upon the interaction between the militantcy of Adam Clayton Powell's followers and the gradualism of Mayor La Guardia and the National Association for the Advancement of Colored People.

1205   Cassell, Frank A. "The Great Baltimore Riot of 1812." MARYLAND HISTORICAL MAGAZINE 70 (1975): 241-59.

       Presents the riot as the result of political and social differences among the city's diverse population and as an aspect of a growing urban-rural dichotomy. Concludes that it illustrated an unfortunate tendency to substitute violence for constitutional process.

1206   Chrisman, Noel J. ETHNIC INFLUENCE ON URBAN GROUPS: THE DANISH-AMERICANS. San Francisco: R and E Research, 1975. 115 p.

Examines the manner in which Danish Americans adapted urban voluntary institutions to meet their own ethnic needs. Focuses upon newspapers, lodges and clubs, and upon informal social networks which emerged.

1207 Chudacoff, Howard P. "A New Look at Ethnic Neighborhoods: Residential Dispersion and the Concept of Visibility in a Medium-Sized City." JOURNAL OF AMERICAN HISTORY 60 (1973): 76-93.

Uses Omaha as a case study to argue that urban neighborhoods generally have a mixture of ethnic groups, with one usually giving the area its dominant character because of its commercial, cultural, and social institutions. Also insists that spatial mobility characterized all urban groups, whatever their ethnicity.

1208 Clark, Dennis J. "The Adjustment of Irish Immigrants to Urban Life: The Philadelphia Experience, 1840-1870." Ph.D. dissertation, Temple University, 1970. 284 p.

Concludes that the Irish made a moderately successful adjustment to urban life in Philadelphia, experiencing modest residential and occupational mobility, developed important institutions, and constructed a subcultural network. Contrasts their experience with that of the Boston Irish who had fewer housing, employment, and educational opportunities.

1209 _____. "The Irish Catholics: A Postponed Perspective." In IMMIGRANTS AND RELIGION IN URBAN AMERICA, edited by Randall M. Miller and Thomas D. Marzik, pp. 48-68. Philadelphia: Temple University Press, 1977.

Focuses on the experience of Irish Catholics in Philadelphia and concludes that they produced a peculiarly Irish-American brand of Catholicism shaped by the forces of urban change and opportunity, influenced by the currents of American Protestantism, and led by bishops adept at the managerial ethics.

1210 _____. THE IRISH IN PHILADELPHIA: TEN GENERATIONS OF URBAN EXPERIENCE. Philadelphia: Temple University Press, 1974. 246 p.

Contends that the Irish made a successful adjustment to urban living in Philadelphia, measured in terms of property acquisition, occupational diversification, and institutional development. Argues that widespread home ownership gave Philadelphia's neighborhoods an autonomy and stability not found in other cities of similar size.

1211 Clark, Kenneth B. DARK GHETTO: DILEMMAS OF SOCIAL POWER. New York: Harper and Row, 1965. 251 p.

Examines the physical boundaries of the black ghetto, its social dynamics, its psychology, its pathology, its schools, and its power structure. Concludes with a strategy for change and discussion of the relationship between the ghetto and white liberals.

1212 Clark, T.N. "Irish Ethic and Spirit of Patronage." ETHNICITY: AN INTERDISCIPLINARY JOURNAL OF THE STUDY OF ETHIC RELATIONS 2 (1975): 305-59.

Presents a "patronage interpretation" to explain the existence of higher municipal budgets in cities with a high percentage of Irish residents. Considers data sets from 1880 to 1967-68 to explore and document the hypothesis that the Irish ethic of "nonideological particularism" legitimated and reinforced the spirit of patronage politics.

1213 Cole, Donald B. IMMIGRANT CITY: LAWRENCE, MASSACHUSETTS, 1845-1921. Chapel Hill: University of North Carolina Press, 1963. 248 p.

Traces the evolution of Lawrence from a Yankee mill town to a polyglot industrial city, focusing on the job competition among its various ethnic groups which culminated in the textile strike of 1912.

1214 Conot, Robert. URBAN POVERTY: A COMPARISON OF THE LATIN AMERICAN AND THE UNITED STATES EXPERIENCE. Vol. 11: URBAN POVERTY IN HISTORICAL PERSPECTIVE: THE CASE OF THE UNITED STATES. Los Angeles: University of California, School of Architecture and Urban Planning, 1975. 33 p.

Surveys the evolution of urban poverty from colonial times to the present, focusing upon the status of immigrants and minorities. Includes a critique by J. Eugene Grigsby stressing the self-interest of established urbanites in maintaining sizeable pockets of poverty.

1215 Contopoulos, Michael. "The Greek Community of New York City: Early Years to 1910." Ph.D. dissertation, New York University, 1972. 334 p.

Examines Greek immigration to America, the strong sense of nationality that created tension in the community, and the influence of urban New York on attitudes and occupational patterns.

1216 Conzen, Kathleen Neils. IMMIGRANT MILWAUKEE, 1836-1860: ACCOMMODATION AND COMMUNITY IN A FRONTIER CITY. Cambridge, Mass.: Harvard University Press, 1976. 300 p.

Class, Ethnicity, and Race

Asserts that the first generation of Milwaukee Germans were able to find a middle way between assimilation and alienation, due to their settlement patterns, the wide spectrum of socioeconomic groups within the community, and the institutional completeness of their voluntary associations. Cites diversity as both the greatest strength and weakness of the group.

1217 Cook, Adrian. THE ARMIES OF THE STREETS: THE NEW YORK CITY DRAFT RIOTS OF 1863. Lexington: University of Kentucky Press, 1974. 323 p.

Examines the complex physical, ethnic, socioeconomic, and political causes of the riots. Places much of the blame upon misinformation and the ineptitude and biases of law enforcement officials.

1218 Crimmins, Timothy J. "The Crystal Stair: A Study of the Effects of Caste and Class on Secondary Education in Late Nineteenth Century Atlanta, Georgia." URBAN EDUCATION 8 (1974): 401-21.

Contends that, contrary to the claims of education boosters, class and race were important factors in determining how much social mobility could be achieved through public education in this nineteenth-century city. Concludes that the system shifted from an elite to a middle-class ladder of social mobility, while retarding the progress of blacks and lower-class whites.

1219 Crowe, Charles. "Racial Violence and Social Reform--Origins of the Atlanta Riot of 1906." JOURNAL OF NEGRO HISTORY 53 (1968): 234-56.

Argues that whites promoted the Atlanta riot in order "to create caste behavior, to drive Negroes into subservient personal relationships with individual whites, and to make life difficult for those who remained outside the pale of protection."

1220 Cumbler, John T. "The City and Community: The Impact of Urban Forces on Working Class Behavior." JOURNAL OF URBAN HISTORY 3 (1977): 427-42.

Finds that the more centralized urban institutions were, the greater the degree of working class solidarity developed. Also discovers significant variation in the ability and willingness of the working class in Lynn and Fall River, Massachusetts, to integrate new immigrant workers into their institutions.

1221 _____. WORKING CLASS COMMUNITY IN INDUSTRIAL AMERICA: WORK, LEISURE, AND STRUGGLE IN TWO INDUSTRIAL CITIES, 1880-1930. Westport, Conn.: Greenwood Press, 1979. 283 p.

Concentrates on the working class of Lynn and Fall River, Massachusetts, and their efforts to adjust to the vagaries of urban-industrial life through the creation of communities and institutions. Also examines the impact of the configurations of the urban setting and the demands the work place and immigration patterns had upon their communities.

1222 Dancis, Bruce. "Social Mobility and Class Consciousness: San Francisco's International Workmen's Association in the 1880s." JOURNAL OF SOCIAL HISTORY 2 (1977): 75-98.

Compares the memberships of the city's International Workmen's Association to San Francisco's general working class and finds that IWA members were more prosperous and more stable by almost every possible test. Concludes that geographical stability promoted radicalism.

1223 Daniels, Douglas Henry. "Afro-San Franciscans: A Social History of Pioneer Urbanites, 1860-1930." Ph.D. dissertation, University of California, Berkeley, 1975. 544 p.

Contends that San Francisco's black population largely escaped the trauma of ghettoization by developing its own survival strategies and institutions. Emphasizes the complexity and resiliency of the city's blacks.

1224 Davis, Allen F., and Haller, Mark H., eds. THE PEOPLES OF PHILADELPHIA: A HISTORY OF ETHNIC GROUPS AND LOWER-CLASS LIFE, 1790-1940. Philadelphia: Temple University Press, 1973. 301 p.

Contains twelve original essays with an introduction and summary by the coeditors. Deals with a variety of urban themes in the context of lower-class life in Philadelphia including poverty, residential mobility, violence, fire protection, crime, housing, and the experience of such ethnic groups as the Irish, blacks, Poles, Italians, and Jews.

1225 Dawley, Alan. CLASS AND COMMUNITY: THE INDUSTRIAL REVOLUTION IN LYNN. Cambridge, Mass.: Harvard University Press, 1979. 301 p.

Focuses upon the city's shoemakers and their fight for social equality through unionization and class-oriented politics. Sees electoral politics, rather than faith in occupational success or property ownership, as the shoemakers' major mechanism in an urban-industrial society.

1226 De Graaf, Lawrence B. "The City of Black Angels: Emergence of the Los Angeles Ghetto, 1890-1930." PACIFIC HISTORICAL REVIEW 39 (1970): 323-52.

Distinguishes between ghetto and slum and asserts that the city's ghetto was largely formed in the four decades prior to 1930, but that it did not become a slum until another decade of residential segregation, depression, and massive in-migration.

1227 Deskins, Donald R., Jr. "Race, Residence, and Workplace in Detroit, 1880 to 1965." ECONOMIC GEOGRAPHY 48 (1972): 79-94.

Finds open parishes as urban subcommunities with defineable boundaries and indigenous institutions, which encompassed much of the life of their largely ethnic communicants. Relates the evolution of the church to the expansion of the city.

1228 Dolan, Jay P. THE IMMIGRANT CHURCH: NEW YORK'S IRISH AND GERMAN CATHOLICS, 1815-1865. Baltimore: Johns Hopkins University Press, 1975. 221 p.

Focuses upon parishes as urban subcommunities with defineable boundaries and indigenous institutions, which encompassed much of the life of their largely ethnic communicants. Relates the evolution of the church to the expansion of the city.

1229 Dowty, Alan. "Urban Slavery in Pro-Southern Fiction of the 1850s." JOURNAL OF SOUTHERN HISTORY 32 (1966): 25-41.

Contends that proslavery apologists avoided discussing urban slavery because the urban environment was incompatable with the image of plantation slavery that they sought to convey. Argues that the city made the slave either too contented or rebellious to make effective propaganda.

1230 Drake, St. Clair. "Urban Violence and American Social Movements." PROCEEDINGS OF THE ACADEMY OF POLITICAL SCIENCE 29 (1968): 13-24.

Compares urban rioting resulting from three great social movements: abolition, labor, and woman suffrage. Concludes that violence has served as a "cry for help" stimulating relief measures, rather than as a means of overthrowing the system.

1231 Drake, St. Clair, and Cayton, Horace R. BLACK METROPOLIS: A STUDY OF NEGRO LIFE IN A NORTHERN CITY. New York: Harcourt, Brace and Co., 1945. 809 p.

Examines the institutions and dynamics of Chicago's black community and its interaction with the wider city dominated by whites. Stresses the socioeconomic differences among the city's blacks and their varying life-styles.

1232 Eckert, William Albert. "Ethnicity, Reformism and Public Policy in

American Cities." Ph.D. dissertation, Florida State University, 1976. 138 p.

> Finds great variations among ethnic groups with regard to both preference of urban political forms and attitudes toward particular public policy areas. Examines the various factors that account for these differences.

1233 Ernst, Robert. IMMIGRANT LIFE IN NEW YORK CITY, 1825-1863. Port Washington, N.Y.: Kennikat Press, 1965. 331 p.

> Examines the experience of Irish and German immigration in adjusting to urban life, focusing upon their settlement patterns, living conditions, distribution in the work force, efforts to promote labor organization, the creation of religious, educational, fraternal, and cultural societies, and their political behavior.

1234 Esslinger, Dean R. IMMIGRANTS AND THE CITY: ETHNICITY AND MOBILITY IN A NINETEENTH CENTURY MIDWESTERN COMMUNITY. Port Washington, N.Y.: Kennikat Press, 1975. 155 p.

> Analyzes data from a sample of ten thousand immigrants to South Bend, Indiana, between 1850 and 1880, concentrating on geographic and social mobility. Finds a reasonably high degree of mobility.

1235 Fanning, Charles. FINLEY PETER DUNNE AND MR. DOOLEY: THE CHICAGO YEARS. Lexington: University Press of Kentucky, 1978. 286 p.

> Analyzes Dunne's commentaries upon the daily life of Chicago's Irish working-class community, the impact of that community on the assimilation process, and the influence of Bridgeport on the city's ward-based political system.

1236 Farley, Reynolds. "The Urbanization of Negroes in the United States." JOURNAL OF SOCIAL HISTORY 1 (1968): 241-58.

> Examines the process of black urbanization from colonial times to the 1960s and elucidates some of the push and pull factors producing the migration from the South to northern cities. Stresses economic and social reasons.

1237 Feldberg, Michael. THE PHILADELPHIA RIOTS OF 1844: A STUDY OF ETHNIC CONFLICT. Westport, Conn.: Greenwood Press, 1975. 209 p.

> Attributes the riots to a variety of causes including anti-Catholic, anti-Irish nativism, response to social change and economic dislocation, working-class suffering, and a powerful

tradition of street brawling. Sees the riots as a "social-bargaining process" on the part of the lower social orders.

1238 Femminella, Francis X. "The Immigrant and the Urban Melting Pot." In PERSPECTIVES ON URBAN AMERICA, edited by Melvin I. Urofsky, pp. 43-66. Garden City, N.Y.: Doubleday, 1973.

Examines the major theories regarding the assimilation and acculturation of immigrants and posits his own thesis of impact-integration to explain the accommodation of immigrants to the urban environment.

1239 Franklin, Vincent P. "The Philadelphia Race Riot of 1918." PENNSYLVANIA MAGAZINE OF HISTORY AND BIOGRAPHY 99 (1975): 336-50.

Concludes that this riot follows the pattern of racial violence in northern cities described by Allen Grimshaw (no. 1266a). Specifically the cause of the riot was competition for limited housing in an "ecologically contested area" resulted in black response to white violence followed by sporadic violence long after the riot ended.

1240 Freedman, Stephen. "The Baseball Fad in Chicago, 1865-1870: An Exploration of the Role of Sport in the Nineteenth-Century City." JOURNAL OF SPORT HISTORY 5 (1978): 42-64.

Contends that baseball appealed primarily to the urban middle class and was a symbolic expression of many of its most deeply held values. Concludes that baseball was incorporated into the middle-class conception of urban organization and function.

1241 Freeman, Rhoda G. "The Free Negro in New York City Before the Civil War." Ph.D. dissertation, Columbia University, 1966. 504 p.

Finds that the city's blacks suffered discrimination in public facilities, were hampered by property qualifications for voting, and lost economic ground to newly arriving immigrants. Sees a few bright spots in their access to public education and in the emergence of the Negro press.

1242 Galatioto, Rocco G., and Cordasco, Francesco. "Ethnic Displacement in the Interstitial Community: The East Harlem Experience." PHYLON 31 (1970): 302-12.

Takes issue with the notion of the Chicago school and its successors that ghettoes are necessarily typified by deterioration, shifting population, and cultural isolation. Finds that East Harlem does not conform to this model.

1243 Galford, Justin B. "The Foreign Born and Urban Growth in the Great Lakes, 1850-1950: A Study of Chicago, Cleveland, Detroit, and Milwaukee." Ph.D. dissertation, New York University, 1957. 388 p.

    Finds that each of the four cities possessed distinctive characteristics that attracted particular nationalities, including favorable employment opportunities for specialized skills, industrial recruitment, social and cultural considerations, and examples of successful settlement by kinsmen or countrymen.

1244 Gans, Herbert J. THE URBAN VILLAGERS: GROUP AND CLASS IN THE LIFE OF ITALIAN AMERICANS. Glencoe, Ill.: Free Press of Glencoe, 1962. 367 p.

    Uses the Italian-American community in Boston's West End to illustrate the general thesis that ethnic neighborhoods and small-scale institutions enable urban dwellers to avoid the impersonality and anomie supposedly resulting from metropolitan life.

1245 Garonzik, Joseph. "The Racial and Ethnic Make-Up of Baltimore Neighborhoods, 1850-1870." MARYLAND HISTORICAL MAGAZINE 71 (1976): 392-402.

    Argues that the city's heterogenous ethnic and racial mixture was stabilized by the degree of institutional completeness which existed in each of the city's various neighborhoods, regardless of the new immigration and spread of heavy industry destroyed the integrated character of the city's neighborhoods.

1246 _____. "Urbanization and the Black Population of Baltimore, 1850-1870." Ph.D. dissertation, State University of New York-Stoney Brook, 1974. 441 p.

    Attempts to obtain an understanding of the black community and its "institutional life" through measurement of the physical and demographic characteristics of "neighborhood" in mid-nineteenth-century Baltimore.

1247 Geffen, Elizabeth M. "Violence in Philadelphia in the 1840s and 1850s." PENNSYLVANIA HISTORY 36 (1969): 381-410.

    Attributes the rash of violence to industrialization, government protection of industry, the growing maldistribution of wealth, and the increasing frustration of the masses, and contends that the city's leaders offered them only individualism, laissez-faire, equalitarianism, optimism, romantic escapism, and sentimentality.

1248 Ghent, Joselyn Maynard, and Jaher, Frederic Cople. "The Chicago Business Elite, 1830-1930: A Collective Biography." BUSINESS HIS-

TORY REVIEW 50 (1976): 228-328.

>Examines a sample of 1,186 members of the city's business elite and finds that two-thirds of them made their own fortunes, especially in manufacturing, meatpacking, and railroads. Concludes that most came from middle-class origins, rather than going from "rags to riches."

1249 Glasco, Laurence A. "Ethnicity and Social Structure: Irish, Germans and Native-Born of Buffalo, New York, 1850-1860." Ph.D. dissertation, State University of New York at Buffalo, 1973. 366 p.

>Finds that the Irish lagged far behind the native born and the Germans in occupational level and residential status. Also concludes that demographic and family patterns and the preponderance of immigrant voters eased the accommodation of ethnic groups and undercut the nativist sentiment of the 1850s.

1250 _____. "The Life Cycles and Household Structure of American Ethnic Groups: Irish, Germans, and Native-Born Whites in Buffalo, New York, 1855." JOURNAL OF URBAN HISTORY 1 (1975): 339-64.

>Argues that immigrant girls who worked as domestic in native households acculturated more rapidly than any other segment of the foreign-born population, so that domestic service was as important as work and schooling in the acculturation process.

1251 Glazer, Nathan, and McEntire, Davis, eds. STUDIES IN HOUSING AND MINORITY GROUPS. Berkeley and Los Angeles: University of California Press, 1960. 228 p.

>Contains seven studies by various scholars organized around the general theme of whether ethnic and racial minorities should rather live in segregated communities or dispersed through the general housing supply. Focuses upon blacks in Atlanta, Birmingham, San Antonio, Houston, New Orleans, and Miami; Puerto Ricans in New York City; Japanese Americans in San Francisco; and a transitional neighborhood in Detroit.

1252 Glazer, Nathan, and Moynihan, Daniel P. BEYOND THE MELTING POT: THE NEGROES, PUERTO RICANS, JEWS, ITALIANS, AND IRISH OF NEW YORK CITY. Rev. ed. Cambridge: MIT Press, 1970. 363 p.

>Examines the culture and institutions of the city's five most distinctive ethnic groups and their role in the wider life of the city. Introduction to this edition corrects the emphasis of the 1963 volume which predicted the eventual demise of ethnicity.

Class, Ethnicity, and Race

1253   Golab, Carol Ann. "The Polish Communities of Philadelphia, 1870-1920: Immigrant Distribution and Adaptation in Urban America." Ph.D. dissertation, University of Pennsylvania, 1971. 480 p.

        Views immigrant adaptation as a function of spatial distribution and develops a methodology for analyzing the latter based upon the interplay of demographic, economic, and cultural factors. Sees employment as the crucial variable which led to the creation of ethnic subcommunities.

1254   Goldberg, Robert A. "The Ku Klux Klan in Madison, 1922-1927." WISCONSIN MAGAZINE OF HISTORY 58 (1974): 31-44.

        Argues that Klan activities were directed especially against the city's small Italian community and appealed primarily to those attracted by its fraternalism, secrecy, and ritual. Sees Klansmen as ordinary people bewildered by the impact of urbanization and immigration.

1255   Goldfield, David. "The Black Ghetto: A Tragic Sameness." JOURNAL OF URBAN HISTORY 3 (1977): 361-70.

        Compares the emergence of black ghettoes in Detroit, Cleveland, Chicago, and New York, with respect to residential segregation, class sturcture, and economic status. Finds striking similarities and discusses the relative merits of ghetto enrichment or ghetto dispersion as a remedy.

1256   Goldfield, David, and Lane, James B., eds. THE ENDURING GHETTO: SOURCES AND READINGS. Philadelphia: Lippincott, 1973. 258 p.

        Contains twenty selections written by scholars from a variety of fields and by writers of fiction. Traces the evolution of the ghetto from an immigrant enclave in the early 1800s to the black community of the present day, focusing upon its ecology, creativity, and ongoing efforts to reform it.

1257   Goldner, Norman. The MEXICANS IN THE NORTHERN URBAN AREA: A COMPARISON OF TWO GENERATIONS. San Francisco: R and E Research Associates, 1972. 123 p.

        Compares the impact of the process of urbanization on two generations of Mexican Americans.

1258   Goldstein, Sidney, and Mayer, Kurt. "The Impact of Migration on the Socio-Economic Structure of Cities and Suburbs." SOCIOLOGY AND SOCIAL RESEARCH 50 (1965): 5-23.

        Concludes that migrants into the central city and the suburbs resemble each other more closely than they do nonmigrants in those respective areas, but that migration contributes to the socioeconomic differentiation of cities from the suburbs because of the greater numerical flow into the suburbs and because of the preponderance of higher status areas there.

1259 _____. "Population Decline and Demographic Structure of an American City." AMERICAN SOCIOLOGICAL REVIEW 29 (1964): 48-54.

Concentrates upon Providence, Rhode Island, and the correlation between its population decline since 1940 and other socioeconomic and demographic characteristics. Attributes narrowing of class differences in the city to a general diminution of class differences in American society, rather than to migration and changes in population size.

1260 Goodman, Paul. "Ethics and Enterprise: The Values of a Boston Elite, 1800-1860." AMERICAN QUARTERLY 18 (1966): 437-51.

Avers that Boston's elite possessed a value system which cast themselves in the role as agents of civic improvement and that they defended their code against those who scorned them as materialistic hypocrites and against those whose ruthless pursuit of wealth transcended all rules and morals.

1261 Grant, Robert B. "The Negro Comes to the City: A Documentary History from the Great Migration to the Great Depression." Ph.D. dissertation, Columbia University, 1970. 442 p.

Deals with the causes, size and reactions to the "Great Migration," living conditions, restricted occupational opportunities, and with respective attitudes of whites and blacks toward the other race. Utilizes testimony before government committees, newspapers, speeches, reports of investigatory agencies, poems, and novels.

1262 Gredel, Stephen. "Immigration of Ethnic Groups to Buffalo Based Upon Censuses of 1850, 1865, 1875, and 1892." NIAGARA FRONTIER 10 (1963): 42-56.

Finds that there were over forty-two nationalities represented in the city's cosmopolitan population by 1892. Relies largely upon state census data corrected by contemporary sources.

1263 Greeley, Andrew M. NEIGHBORHOOD. New York: Seabury Press, 1977. 174 p.

Examines four Chicago neighborhoods--St. Angela's, Beverly, Bridgeport, and Stanislowowo--and analyzes their origins, enemies, and functions. Sees neighborhoods as vital to urban living and to the "ethnic miracle."

Class, Ethnicity, and Race

1264 Green, Constance McLaughlin. THE SECRET CITY: A HISTORY OF RACE RELATIONS IN THE NATION'S CAPITAL. Princeton, N.J.: Princeton University Press, 1967. 389 p.

> Traces the evolution of Washington, D.C.'s black community from the founding of the city in 1791 to 1960, focusing upon the interaction between it and the white community and on the political power struggle since the 1930s. Finds that black Washington, D.C., was psychologically segregated from the beginning, but became only physically so around World War I.

1265 Griffen, Clyde, and Griffen, Sally. "Family and Business in a Small City: Poughkeepsie, New York: 1850-1880." JOURNAL OF URBAN HISTORY 1 (1975): 316-38.

> Contends that the extended family, with its kinship networks and self-help patterns, played an important role in business entrepreneurship in the city of that era. Sees no grounds for believing that the rise of business enterprise led to the nuclear family.

1266 _____. NATIVES AND NEWCOMERS: THE ORDERING OF OPPORTUNITY IN MID-NINETEENTH-CENTURY POUGHKEEPSIE. Cambridge, Mass.: Harvard University Press, 1978. 291 p.

> Examines the relative occupational mobility of the native-born, blacks, immigrants, and women, and finds that Poughkeepsie generally conformed to current interpretation. Finds that changes in the scale of economic organization and in the division of labor significantly affect mobility patterns.

1266a Grimshaw, Allen D., ed. RACIAL VIOLENCE IN THE UNITED STATES. Chicago: Aldine Publishing Co., 1969. 553 p.

> Contains historically and theoretically oriented articles grouped under four major headings: "The History of Negro-White Violence in America," "Patterns in American Racial Violence," "Causation: Some Theoretical and Empirical Nations," and "The Changing Meaning of 'Racial' Violence."

1267 Groneman, Carol. "Working Class Immigrant Women in Mid-Nineteenth Century New York: The Irish Womens' Experience." JOURNAL OF URBAN HISTORY 4 (1978): 255-74.

> Examines the work, leisure patterns, and family life that constituted the cultural community of young, single, female, Irish immigrants of the era.

1268 Groves, Paul A., and Shaw, Edward K. "The Evolution of Black Residential Areas in Late Nineteenth Century Cities." JOURNAL OF HISTORICAL GEOGRAPHY 1 (1975): 169-92.

> Attributes the development of black residential areas in Washington and Baltimore to: (1) a large and rapid increase in black migration (2) the consequent worsening of racial relations, especially with respect to economic and residential discrimination. Concludes that border cities developed ghettoes in much the same fashion as did northern cities.

1269 Guest, Avery M., and Weed, James A. "Ethnic Residential Segregation: Patterns of Change." AMERICAN JOURNAL OF SOCIOLOGY 81 (1976): 1088-111.

> Examines residential patterns in Cleveland, Boston, and Seattle between 1930 and 1970 and finds little evidence of a decline in segregation. Finds that differences in residential segregation were directly related to social status, but that ethnic segregation would continue to exist even if social status differences among ethnic groups disappeared.

1270 Guignard, Michael J. "Ethnic Survival in a New England Mill Town: The Franco-Americans of Biddeford, Maine." Ph.D. dissertation, Syracuse University, 1976. 367 p.

> Analyzes Franco-American survival efforts in a New England community, the role of geography, of socioeconomic status, and of their own hyphenated institutions in maintaining identity and cultural distinctiveness, and their conflicts with nativists.

1271 Haebler, Peter. "Habitants in Holyoke: The Development of the French Canadian Community in a Massachusetts City, 1865-1910." Ph.D. dissertation, University of New Hampshire, 1976. 350 p.

> Argues against the accepted view of the French-Canadian migrants as "clannish, poorly educated, prolific reproducers" and unaccepting of the American life-style. Based on written records and oral interviews.

1272 Hammett, Theodore M. "Two Mobs of Jacksonian Boston: Ideology and Interest." JOURNAL OF AMERICAN HISTORY 62 (1976): 845-68.

> Compares the nativist mob which burned the Ursuline convent in 1834 with the one that stormed the Massachusetts Anti-Slavery Society the following year. Finds the origins and ideology of the two very complex and almost mutually exclusive.

1273 Handlin, Oscar. BOSTON'S IMMIGRANTS: A STUDY IN ACCULTURATION. Cambridge, Mass.: Harvard University Press, 1959. 230 p.

Concentrates upon the economic and physical adjustment of Irish immigrants to Boston between 1790 and 1865 and emphasizes their development of group consciousness in the face of prejudice and discrimination.

1274 _____. THE NEWCOMERS: NEGROES AND PUERTO RICANS IN A CHANGING METROPOLIS. Cambridge, Mass.: Harvard University Press, 1959. 171 p.

Establishes patterns of social economic mobility of immigrant groups in New York City from 1620 through 1928 and then compares the black and Puerto Rican experience to that model. Concludes that both have followed the general experience of earlier immigrants and that disadvantages based upon color will be temporary.

1275 Hanson, Robert C., and Simmons, Ozzie G. "The Role Path: A Concept and Procedure for Studying Migration to Urban Communities." HUMAN ORIGINS 27 (1968): 152-58.

Focuses upon the urbanization of rural, Spanish-speaking migrants to Denver, and argues that the best measurements of adjustment is the extent to which each migrant acquires attributes descriptive of his or her status role.

1276 Haraven, Tamara. "Family Time and Industrial Time: Family and Work in a Planned Corporation Town, 1900-1924." JOURNAL OF URBAN HISTORY 1 (1975): 365-89.

Contends that French-Canadian working-class families in Manchester, New Hampshire, were not passive recipients of social and economic change, but rather made the town's factories adjust their work schedules to accommodate family behavior. Sees families as the major buffer between the members and the dehumanizing effects of industrialization.

1277 _____. "The Laborers of Manchester, New Hampshire, 1912-1922: The Role of Family and Ethnicity in Adjustment of Industrial Life." LABOR HISTORY 16 (1975): 249-65.

Asserts that Manchester's new immigrant laborers were not the passive victims of urbanization and modernization, but rather active agents who tried to shape the system to their own needs and who exercised great collective strength.

1278 Harris, William. "Work and the Family in Black Atlanta, 1880." JOURNAL OF SOCIAL HISTORY 9 (1976): 319-30.

Argues that Atlanta's black families were no more matriarchal in composition than were those of Atlantans in general and that there were far less fatherless black families in 1880 proportionately than there are today. Feels that Atlanta's black families generally conformed to the accepted pattern for nineteenth-century urban families.

1279 Haynes, Robert V. A NIGHT OF VIOLENCE: THE HOUSTON RIOT OF 1917. Baton Rouge: Louisiana State University Press, 1976. 338 p.

Details the clash between a black infantry unit and an all-white police force which erupted into a riot. Examines the city's black community and attempts to place the riot into a context of other urban riots of the time.

1280 Hepler, Mark K. "Color, Crime and the City." Ph.D. dissertation, Rice University, 1972. 296 p.

Focuses upon the criminal justice system in New Orleans in the 1850s and attributes the black riots of the era to the court's ineffectiveness in protecting Negro rights and its relative effectiveness in promoting black disunity and an atmosphere of fear.

1281 Hershberg, Theodore, et al. "Occupation and Ethnicity in Five Nineteenth-Century Cities: A Collaborative Inquiry." HISTORY METHODS NEWSLETTER 7 (1974): 174-216.

Examines and compares sociostructural and demographic characteristics in Philadelphia; Hamilton, Ontario; and Kingston, Buffalo, and Poughkeepsie, New York, in 1860. Finds a high degree of similarity in the correlation between occupation and ethnicity.

1282 Hertzberg, Steven. "The Jewish Community of Atlanta from the End of the Civil War Until the Eve of the Frank Case." AMERICAN JEWISH HISTORICAL QUARTERLY 62 (1973): 250-85.

Finds that Jewish merchants were a vital and generally accepted part of Atlanta's economic resurgence as the premier city of the New South until the Leo Frank Case unleashed a burst of anti-Semitism in 1913.

1283 _____. "Unsettled Jews: Geographic Mobility in a Nineteenth Century City." AMERICAN JEWISH HISTORICAL QUARTERLY 67 (1977): 125-39.

Finds that Atlanta's Jews remained in Atlanta to a higher degree than did the general population because their opportunities for economic success were relatively greater there than they were anywhere in the South.

1284 Higham, John. SEND THESE TO ME: JEWS AND OTHER IMMIGRANTS IN URBAN AMERICA. New York: Atheneum, 1975. 259 p.

Focuses upon the experiences of Jews and other immigrants to American cities and their reactions to hostility and discrimination. Develops a model of "pluralistic integration" to describe the process of accommodation undergone by immigrants in an urban environment.

1285 Hill, Carole E. "Adaptation in Public and Private Behavior of Ethnic Groups in an American Urban Setting (Atlanta)." URBAN ANTHROPOLOGY 4 (1975): 333-48.

Finds that the city's ethnic groups have generally been accepted into the city's economic life, have not formed ethnic enclaves, and have become progressively less dependent upon their ethnicity in their public and private behavior.

1286 Hollingsworth, J. Roger, and Hollingsworth, Ellen Jane. "Expenditures in American Cities." In THE DIMENSIONS OF QUANTITIVE RESEARCH IN HISTORY, edited by William O. Aydelotte et al., pp. 347-89. Princeton, N.J.: Princeton University Press, 1972.

Studies the expenditures of 278 cities with populations ranging from 10,000 to 25,000 in the year 1903. Finds significant regional variations in spending volume, based largely upon the nature of the economy and characteristics of the population.

1287 Hopkins, Nicholas S., et al. "Brokers and Symbols in American Urban Life." ANTHROPOLOGICAL QUARTERLY 50 (1977): 65-76.

Examines four communities: an upper middle-class suburban area, an Italian-American working-class neighborhood, a black ghetto, and a Puerto Rican enclave--and focuses on the role of "cultural brokers" in manipulating symbols of collective and personal identities.

1288 Hopkins, Richard J. "Occupational and Geographic Mobility in Atlanta, 1870-1896." JOURNAL OF SOUTHERN HISTORY 34 (1968): 200-213.

Compares native white, blacks, and immigrants with respect to occupational and geographic mobility, and finds that blacks were the most geographically and occupationally stable, and that immigrants benefited both occupationally and geographically from the native whites' obsession with the race question.

1289 _____. "Patterns of Persistence and Occupational Mobility in a Southern City: Atlanta, 1870-1920." Ph.D. dissertation, Emory University, 1972. 216 p.

Finds that all workers in Atlanta, whether black, immigrant, or native white, achieved much more occupational persistence than did those identified in previous studies of Newburyport, Poughkeepsie, or Birmingham. Also concludes that all but black workers achieved at least limited degrees of occupational mobility and that the urbanization process and mobility are interrelated in important ways.

1290 _____. "Status, Mobility, and the Dimensions of Change in a Southern City: Atlanta, 1870-1910." In CITIES IN AMERICAN HISTORY, edited by Kenneth T. Jackson and Stanley K. Schultz, pp. 216-31. New York: Knopf, 1972.

Contends that constant movement and change characterized the occupations and habitats of almost all Atlantans in the period, making southern cities anything but unique. Finds that only the white occupational elite remained relatively stable.

1291 Howe, Barbara J. "Clubs, Culture and Charity: Anglo-American Upper Class Activities in the Late Nineteenth Century City." Ph.D. dissertation, Temple University, 1976. 705 p.

Explains how the upper class of three American cities (Philadelphia, Cincinnati, and Milwaukee) and one British city (Birmingham, England) utilized institutions to maintain control and to "establish channels for the transmission of acceptable values" to the rest of the residents.

1292 Hunter, Lloyd A. "Slavery in St. Louis, 1804-1860." BULLETIN OF THE MISSOURI HISTORICAL SOCIETY 30 (1974): 233-65.

Argues that St. Louis possessed all the elements that characterized the antebellum slavery system of the South and that the city's leaders were as emotionally and politically committed to slavery as were their counterparts farther down the Mississippi.

1293 Ingham, John N. "The American Urban Upper Class: Cosmopolitans or Locals?" JOURNAL OF URBAN HISTORY 2 (1975): 67-88.

Uses indexes of intermarriage among the iron and steel elites of Philadelphia, Pittsburgh, and Cleveland and finds that they remained essentially "locals" in that highly intimate aspect of life, despite the cosmopolitan nature of their economic and financial networks.

1294 Jackson, Kenneth T. THE KU KLUX KLAN IN THE CITY. New York: Oxford University Press, 1967. 326 p.

Examines Klan activities in several southern, midwestern and western cities; the background of its members; its fraternal, social, coercive, and charitable activities; its publications and its involvement in municipal and state politics. Finds it to be largely a lower middle-class movement in cities with high growth rates.

1295 Jacobs, Donald M. "The Nineteenth Century Struggle Over Segregated Education in the Boston Schools." JOURNAL OF NEGRO EDUCATION 39 (1970): 76-85.

Examines the efforts of Boston's free black leadership, aided by sympathetic white liberals, to end segregated education in the city in the 1850s.

1296 Jaher, Frederic. "Nineteenth-Century Elites in Boston and New York." JOURNAL OF SOCIAL HISTORY 6 (1972): 32-77.

Compares the elites of Boston with those of New York and finds significant differences due to the nature of each city's economy. Suggests that historians utilize public opinion polls in order to validate their data identifying urban elites.

1297 Janis, Ralph. "The Brave New World that Failed: Patterns of Parish Social Structure in Detroit, 1880-1940." Ph.D. dissertation, University of Michigan, 1972. 242 p.

Comparatively examines various urban ethnic and religious groups in Detroit as an examplary study of social segregation in America's parish communities.

1298 _____. "Flirtation and Flight: Alternatives to Ethnic Confrontation in White Anglo-American Protestant Detroit, 1880-1940." JOURNAL OF ETHNIC STUDIES 6 (1978): 1-18.

Asserts that the city's white Anglo-Saxon Protestants dealt with the vagaries of urban-industrial growth and the influx of immigrants and blacks by the "creative use of social distance," while acknowledging that the group also produced its share of Klansmen, demagogues, and vigilantes.

1299 Jeffrey, Kirk, Jr. "Family History: The Middle-Class American Family in the Urban Context, 1830-1870." Ph.D. dissertation, Stanford University, 1972. 288 p.

Contends that middle-class rural families who moved into large northeastern cities found it difficult to develop new ties similar to those of the village and hence developed a utopian notion of their home life and largely withdrew from urban governance and reform.

1300 Johnson, James Weldon. BLACK MANHATTAN. New York: Arno Press, 1968. 284 p.

Traces the evolution of the black community in the borough from Dutch colonial times until that date. Focuses heavily upon the cultural and political activities of Harlem.

1301   Johnson, Thomas R. "The City on the Hill: Race Relations in Washington, D.C., 1865-1885." Ph.D. dissertation, University of Maryland, 1975. 443 p.

Examines the progression of the black population from the first large-scale migration to Washington, D.C., through the failure of the Reconstruction experiment, to the final development of a cohesive, well-organized black community.

1302   Kantrowitz, Nathan. "Ethnic and Racial Segregation in the New York Metropolis, 1960." AMERICAN JOURNAL OF SOCIOLOGY 74 (1969): 685-95.

Focuses upon the New York-New Jersey standard consolidated area, and find that there has been only a minimal decline in interethnic segregation between 1930 and 1960, and based upon the 1960 census tract data argues that white resistance to racial integration may reinforce and strengthen the separation of ethnic populations from one another.

1303   Katzman, David M. BEFORE THE GHETTO: BLACK DETROIT IN THE NINETEENTH CENTURY. Urbana: University of Illinois Press, 1973. 254 p.

Examines patterns of housing, employment, and vertical and horizontal mobility of the city's blacks in the days before the "Great Migration."

1304   Katzman, M.T. "Urban Racial Minorities and Immigrant Groups." AMERICAN JOURNAL OF ECONOMICS AND SOCIOLOGY 30 (1971): 15-26.

Applies the authors economic performance model, originally designed for white urban immigrant groups, to six racial minorities--Negroes, Mexicans, Puerto Ricans, Chinese, Filipinos, and Japanese--and finds very little conformity. Attributes the differences largely to discrimination and to minority subculture.

1305   Katznelson, Ira. BLACK MEN, WHITE CITIES: RACE, POLITICS, AND MIGRATION IN THE UNITED STATES, 1900-1930, AND BRITAIN, 1948-1968. New York: Oxford University Press, 1973. 219 p.

Compares patterns of black urbanization in the cities of the two countries and finds significant parallels.

1306   Kellogg, John. "Negro Urban Clusters in the Post Bellum South."
        GEOGRAPHICAL REVIEW 67 (1977): 310-21.

        Examines the growth of postbellum black areas in Lexington,
        Atlanta, Durham, and Richmond. Finds that rural black
        migrants either added to existing black areas on the fringes
        of these cities or succeeded to housing abandoned by lower-
        class, but more residentially mobile, whites.

1307   Kessner, Thomas. THE GOLDEN DOOR: ITALIAN AND JEWISH
        IMMIGRANT MOBILITY IN NEW YORK CITY, 1880-1915. New York:
        Oxford University Press, 1977. 224 p.

        Compares the social and residential mobility, patterns of the
        two groups and finds that, while Jews fared better than
        Italians, both groups experienced significant progress over
        two generations. Also discusses similarities and differences
        between New York and other cities with regard to facilitat-
        ing mobility.

1308   Kleinberg, Susan J. "Technology and Women's Work: The Lives of
        Working Class Women in Pittsburgh, 1870-1900." LABOR HISTORY
        17 (1976): 58-72.

        Focuses upon those women who worked in their own homes
        and finds that the unequal distribution of municipal and
        domestic technology made them work long hours and rein-
        forced their isolation. Also contends that their unpaid labor
        helped sustain the entire urban-industrial system.

1309   Klopper, Ruth. "The Family's Use of Urban Space Elements of Family
        Structure and Function among Economic Elites: Atlanta, Georgia, 1880-
        1920." Ph.D. dissertation, Emory University, 1977. 301 p.

        Analyzes economic elite families in Atlanta in 1880, offering
        insights into questions of parental authority, the relationship
        between class and kinship, and the relationship between the
        family and community.

1310   Krause, Corinne Azen. "Urbanization without Breakdown: Italian,
        Jewish, and Slavic Immigrant Women in Pittsburgh, 1900 to 1945."
        JOURNAL OF URBAN HISTORY 4 (1978): 291-306.

        Contends that immigrant women in Pittsburgh were able to ad-
        just to the rigors of urban life with very few traumatic results,
        despite the culture shock and sense of alienation engendered
        by life in a major manufacturing center.

1311   Kusmer, Kenneth L. A GHETTO TAKES SHAPE: BLACK CLEVELAND,
        1870-1930. Urbana: University of Illinois Press, 1978. 305 p.

Argues that Cleveland's small black population enjoyed an "almost equal" status with whites prior to the 1870s, but suffered a serious decline due to the growth of the city, industrialization, the "Great Migration," and growing racism and discrimination.

1312 Lack, Paul D. "Urban Slavery in the Southwest." Ph.D. dissertation, Texas Technical University, 1973. 358 p.

Examines slavery in Galveston, Little Rock, Austin, and Shreveport, newer and smaller western towns than those focused on by Richard Wade in SLAVERY IN THE CITIES (no. 757). Concludes that while patterns of urban bondage in these younger towns shared some similarities with those of older cities, significant contrasts existed, most prominently the fact that slavery seemed relatively stable.

1313 Lammermeier, Paul J. "The Urban Black Family of the Nineteenth Century: A Study of Black Family Structure in the Ohio Valley, 1850-1880." JOURNAL OF MARRIAGE AND THE FAMILY 35 (1973): 440-56.

Uses data from manuscript census to investigate the origins of the present-day urban black family, particularly the lower-class "black matriarchy," by comparing all male- and female-headed families on a range of socioeconomic variables. Concludes that nineteenth-century urban black family structure was "basically a two-parent, male-headed family that showed little evidence of retaining structural characterists of the slave family," and that, from the 1870s on, the slow rise of female-headed households accompanied increasing residential segregation.

1314 Laurie, Bruce; Hershberg, Theodore; and Alter, George. "Immigrants and Industry: The Philadelphia Experience, 1850-1880." JOURNAL OF SOCIAL HISTORY 9 (1975): 219-48.

Argues that a prior occupational stratification scheme should not be used as the means to study of social mobility in the nineteenth century, and that producing a more satisfactory clarification requires deeper understanding of the ways in which nineteenth-century occupations actually were stratified. Suggests that the end of such study ought to be "the accurate stratitication of the nineteenth century occupational universe," the means for which might include "socioeconomic and demographic profiles of individual occupations over time and techniques of record linkage in order to reconstitute the actual careers of individuals."

1315 Leeds, Morton, and Gary, Lawrence E. "The Process of Cultural

Stripping and Reintegration: The Rural Migrant in the City." JOURNAL OF AMERICAN FOLKLORE 83 (1970): 259-69.

> Presents some indexes of the change process that occur as rural or small-town residents move into urban areas, comparing lower-class life in rural and urban areas and outlining both penalties and benefits of movement to the city.

1316 Levesque, George A. "White Bureaucracy, Black Community: The Content Over Local Control of Education in Antebellum Boston." JOURNAL OF EDUCATIONAL THOUGHT 11 (1977): 140-55.

> Examines the establishment of a separate school system in Boston, stressing the role of black people in fostering segregation as a means of controlling the education of their children, and details the major developments that led to the 1855 decision in Massachusetts to officially desegregate.

1317 Levine, David Allan. INTERNAL COMBUSTION: THE RACES IN DETROIT, 1915-1926. Westport, Conn.: Greenwood Press, 1976. 221 p.

> Focuses on the race question as part of larger processes, including the dramatic growth of Detroit as an industrial center, the fragmentation of an older order, and the need for a system of social control felt by Detroit Progressives. Contends that "efficiency and organization in the interest of profit and social control produced the Urban League to educate Blacks to the institutional expectations of northern life; delimitation of factory jobs by race to minimize nonproductive Black-white rivalry; residential restriction, sanctioned by the events."

1318 Lieberson, Stanley. ETHNIC PATTERNS IN AMERICAN CITIES. New York: Free Press of Glencoe, 1963. 230 p.

> Quantitative analysis, based on census tract data of ethnic segregation and assimilation for the period 1910 to 1950 in Boston, Buffalo, Chicago, Cincinnati, Cleveland, Columbus, Philadelphia, Pittsburgh, St. Louis, and Syracuse, which seeks to identify the relative importance of determinants of the differential assimilation of ethnic groups.

1319 Light, Ivan, and Wong, Charles Choy. "Protest or Work: Dilemmas of the Tourist Industry in American Chinatowns." AMERICAN JOURNAL OF SOCIOLOGY 80 (1975): 1342-68.

> Suggests that the Chinatown case does not completely support the cultural as opposed to institutional theory of urban poverty, and points to the industrial division of labor as "a fruitful place to seek a synthesis of cultural and institutional theories."

1320   Litwack, Leon F. NORTH OF SLAVERY: THE NEGRO IN THE FREE STATES, 1709-1860. Chicago: University of Chicago Press, 1961. 318 p.

Focuses upon the life of blacks in northern cities, their education, economic status, and churches, and the prevalence of discrimination and segregation against them, even in the abolitionist societies.

1321   Lyman, Stanford M. "Conflict and the Web of Group Affiliation in San Francisco's Chinatown, 1850-1910." PACIFIC HISTORICAL REVIEW 43 (1974): 473-99.

Argues that nineteenth-century Chinatown "was a complex, highly organized community whose associations were not in constant harmony with one another," and that both intra-community conflict and cooperation served to isolate the Chinese from the larger city.

1322   Lynch, Hollis R. THE BLACK URBAN CONDITION. New York: Crowell, 1973. 469 p.

Contains documents written by forty prominent black leaders and scholars on the urban conditions of blacks through the end of the Civil War.

1323   McConnell, John W. THE EVOLUTION OF SOCIAL CLASSES. Washington, D.C.: American Council on Public Affairs, 1942. 228 p.

A sociological analysis of social class in New Haven, Connecticut, focusing on the evolution of wage earner and white-collar groups, based on statistical data from the New Haven family survey of 1931 and 1933.

1324   McKelvey, Blake. "Cities as Nurseries of Self-Conscious Minorities." PACIFIC HISTORICAL REVIEW 39 (1970): 367-81.

Contends that a survey of America's urban history reveals a continuing process of minority groups struggling "to assert their identity and achieve expression and recognition." Focuses on immigrant experiences as background to contemporary disputes over participation of the needy and slum residents in poverty and urban renewal programs.

1325   Margavio, Anthony V., and Molyneaux, J. Lambert. "Residential Segregation of Italians in New Orleans and Selected American Cities." LOUISIANA STUDIES 12 (1973): 639-44.

Contends that while New Orleans' Italian colony largely conformed to the pattern observed for other American cities, it diverged in that it proved neither as centralized nor as enduring.

1326 Mariano, John Horace. THE SECOND GENERATION OF ITALIANS IN NEW YORK CITY. New York: Arno Press, 1975. 317 p.

Focuses upon the statistics of population, and population distribution, occupations, health, standard of living, literacy, citizenship, dependency and delinquency, psychological traits, social organization, and political involvement. Based upon one thousand responses to a questionnaire.

1327 Martinez, Oscar J. "Chicanos and the Border Cities: An Interpretive Essay." PACIFIC HISTORICAL REVIEW 46 (1977): 85-106.

Investigates, within a historical context, the function as "spring boards" and "receptacles" of the "twin-city" complexes along the U.S.-Mexican border, with particular emphasis on Ciudad Juarez-El Paso, for Chicanos living north of the international boundary.

1328 Maskin, Melvin R. "Black Education and the New Deal: The Urban Experience." Ph.D. dissertation, New York University, 1973. 373 p.

Examines how the emergency educational projects of the Works Progress Administration (WPA) functioned in three ghettos of the North: New York City's Harlem, Chicago's South Side, and the black wards of Philadelphia. Maintains that these projects were the product of the New Deal's commitment to the principle of equal educational opportunity.

1329 Meister, Richard J., ed. THE BLACK GHETTO: PROMISED LAND OR COLONY. Lexington, Mass.: D.C. Heath, 1972. 219 p.

A collection of nineteen essays which examine black Americans' perceptions of and response to the city. Broad topics include "The Making of the Ghetto," "The Ghetto as Promised Land," "The Promised Land Questioned," "The Impact of the Ghetto," and "Ghetto Revolt." Includes an introduction and bibliographical essay.

1330 Meyer, Douglas K. "Changing Negro Residential Patterns in Michigan's Capital, 1915-1970." MICHIGAN HISTORY 56 (1971): 151-67.

Traces the development of black clusters, dispersion, ghetto concentration and consolidation, culminating in a stage of concentration and decentralization. Points to discrimination constraints on housing choice as a major factor in ghetto information.

1331 _____. "Evolution of a Permanent Negro Community in Lansing." MICHIGAN HISTORY 55 (1971): 141-54.

Identifies the factors leading to the establishment of blacks in housing and traces the development of their residential pattern, focusing particularly on the latter half of the nineteenth century.

1332 Miller, Randall M., and Marzik, Thomas D., eds. IMMIGRANTS AND RELIGION IN URBAN AMERICA. Philadelphia: Temple University Press, 1977. 170 p.

Eight essays pertaining to the relationship between religion or religious beliefs and the ethnic experience in post-Civil War urban America, focusing on several eastern and midwestern urban communities and the experience of non-Protestant groups.

1333 Miller, Richard G. "Gentry and Entrepreneurs: A Socioeconomic Analysis of Philadelphia in the 1790s." ROCKY MOUNTAIN SOCIAL SCIENCE JOURNAL 12 (1975): 71-84.

Uses manuscript returns for Pennsylvania's septennial census for 1793 and 1800, as well as Philadelphia tax rolls, to analyze that city's social stratification. Concludes that the distribution of real wealth indicates the development by 1800 of a "well-defined differentiated society."

1334 Mitchell, J. Paul, ed. RACE RIOTS IN BLACK AND WHITE. Englewood Cliffs, N.J.: Prentice-Hall, 1970. 179 p.

Examines the nation's major urban race riots between 1863 and 1968 and develops a model based upon similar developments in each instance. Contains many contemporary accounts of each riot.

1335 Modell, John, and Hareven, Tamara K. "Urbanization and the Malleable Household: An Examination of Boarding and Lodging in American Families." JOURNAL OF MARRIAGE AND THE FAMILY 35 (1973): 467-69.

Explores the extent and functions of the institution of boarding within the family, notes that by the 1880s it had lost both its middle-class respectability and its social control functioning and had become identified as a lower-class practice, hence coming under attack by reformers as a threat to the family. Argues that this latter concern was mistaken, since the family proved not fragile, but malleable, and that boarding served positive social functions.

1336 Mohl, Raymond A., and Betten, Neil. "Paternalism and Pluralism: Immigrants and Social Welfare in Gary, Indiana, 1906-1940." AMERICAN STUDIES 15 (1974): 5-30.

Analyzes the ideologies and programs of several social agencies working with immigrants, noting the prevalence of paternalism and Americanization, save in the case of the city's International Institute which maintained a pluralistic orientation.

1337 Mondello, Salvatore. "The Italian Immigrant in Urban America, 1880-1920, as Reported in the Contemporary Periodical Press." Ph.D. dissertation, New York University, 1960. 266 p.

Discovers a generally negative attitude toward Italian immigrants in periodical literature, with criticism typically focusing on the Italians' working and living habits, the threat they posed to democracy and law and order, as well as the primacy of narrow economic reasons, as opposed to political or idealistic, for their migration. Contends that the forced Americanization movement retarded the adjustment of Italians to America by creating an ethic hostile to assimilation.

1338 Monkkonen, Eric H. THE DANGEROUS CLASS: CRIME AND POVERTY IN COLUMBUS, OHIO, 1860-1865. Cambridge, Mass.: Harvard University Press, 1975. 186 p.

Quantitatively studies the influence of urban and industrial growth on crime and poverty in nineteenth-century Columbus, concluding that the effects of urbanization upon the "dangerous class" of criminals were subtle rather than significant.

1339 Montgomery, David. "The Working Classes of the Pre-Industrial American City, 1780-1830." LABOR HISTORY 9 (1968): 3-22.

Examines the working classes in Boston, New York, Philadelphia, and Baltimore, focusing on "the sources, size, and character" of this labor supply as well as their attitudes, customs, and institutions.

1340 Moore, Joan W. "Mexican Americans and Cities: A Study in Migration and the Use of Formal Resources." INTERNATIONAL MIGRATION REVIEW 5 (1971): 292-308.

Data for Mexican-American men in Los Angeles, "do not support the theoretical notion that urbanization is associated with abandonment of primary-group resources."

1341 Mormino, Gary R. "The Hill Upon the City: An Italo-American Neighborhood in St. Louis, Missouri, 1880-1955." Ph.D. dissertation, University of North Carolina, 1977. 505 p.

Traces the evolution of an Italian immigrant neighborhood from its inception in 1852, stressing the development of associational life and the ways in which New World conditions altered Old World Italo-American behavior. Discusses economic patterns and political and religious developments.

1342 Nelli, Humbert S. "Ethnic Group Assimilation: The Italian Experience." In CITIES IN AMERICAN HISTORY, edited by Kenneth T. Jackson and Stanley K. Schultz, pp. 199-215. New York: Knopf, 1972.

    Presents an overview of the general patterning of Italian immigrant assimilation, with special reference to Chicago. Asserts that the immigrant ghetto provided an important preliminary introduction to American life, and notes that economic success furthered assimilation and movement away from the initial community.

1343 _____. ITALIANS IN CHICAGO, 1880-1930: A STUDY IN ETHNIC MOBILITY. New York: Oxford University Press, 1970. 300 p.

    Contends that Italian immigrants and their offspring made a successful accommodation to life in urban America, largely through the medium of transitional institutions, ethnic politics, and economic mobility. Feels that most Italians were fully integrated into the wider life of the city by 1930.

1344 _____. "Italians in Urban America: A Study in Ethnic Adjustment." INTERNATIONAL MIGRATION REVIEW 1 (1967): 38-55.

    Sees the immigrant community and its institutions as a "staging area," bridging the gap between rural Old World traditions and the new American urban world, thus providing immigrants with a supportive as well as socializing experience.

1345 Newell, Barbara Warne. CHICAGO AND THE LABOR MOVEMENT: METROPOLITAN UNIONISM IN THE 1930S. Urbana: University of Illinois Press, 1961. 288 p.

    Examines the sources of support and opposition to the unionization of Chicago's municipal work force, their ideological outlook, and their methods.

1346 Nielson, David G. "Black Ethos: The Northern Urban Negro, 1890-1930." Ph.D. dissertation, State University of New York, Binghamton, 1972. 309 p.

    Argues that the "ordinary" blacks of the urban North developed a distinct sense of community marked by a heightening of their racial consciousness, an acceptance of blackness that provided many of the spiritual and attitudinal roots of the contemporary civil rights revolution.

1347 Oboler, Gina, and Oboler, Leon. "Mothers and Daughters in a Blue-Collar Neighborhood in Urban America." In SOUTH ATLANTIC URBAN STUDIES, vol. 1, edited by Jack R. Censer and N. Steinert, pp. 170-97. Columbia: University of South Carolina Press, 1978.

Class, Ethnicity, and Race

Focuses upon the predominantly Polish, working-class community of Manayunk, Philadelphia, and finds that its residents live in matrilateral societies and in families which do not conform to the nuclear ideal, but that they are more residentially mobile than most authorities have alleged.

1348 Olson, James S. THE ETHNIC DIMENSION IN AMERICAN HISTORY. New York: St. Martin's Press, 1979. 440 p.

Regards ethnic diversity as the central theme of American history, and focuses upon the interaction of the nation's various ethnic groups and the mainstream, especially in an increasingly urban environment. Discusses the efforts of ethnic groups to preserve their identity and culture through the creation of urban institutions.

1349 O'Neill, Hugh. "The Growth of Municipal Employee Unions." PROCEEDINGS OF THE ACADEMY OF POLITICAL SCIENCE 30 (1970): 1-13.

Provides an historical overview of the development of municipal employee unions from the early craft unions of the nineteenth century through the 1960s, including discoveries of labor strife, repression and radicalism, and the proliferation of municipal unionism in the mid-fifties.

1350 Orleans, Peter, and Ellis, Russell, Jr. RACE, CHANGE, AND URBAN SOCIETY. Beverly Hills, Calif.: Sage Publications, 1971. 640 p.

Compares the urban condition of blacks and Puerto Ricans, focusing upon law enforcement, legal aid, education, and community structure.

1351 Osofsky, Gilbert. HARLEM: THE MAKING OF A GHETTO, NEGRO NEW YORK, 1890-1930. New York: Harper and Row, 1966. 258 p.

Traces the evolution of Harlem from a fashionable white middle-class community at the turn of the century to a black ghetto in the 1920s. Argues that Progressive era reformers were highly optimistic about aiding urban blacks, but eventually gave way to despair as the "Great Migration" overwhelmed their efforts.

1352 Ovington, Mary White. HALF A MAN: THE STATUS OF THE NEGRO IN NEW YORK. New York: Longmans, Green and Co., 1911. Reprint. New York: Hill and Wang, 1969. 128 p.

Summarizes the results of a seven-year study of the conditions of blacks in New York by a prominent settlement house worker and cofounder of the National Association for the Advancement of Colored People.

Class, Ethnicity, and Race

1353 Parot, Joseph. "The Racial Dilemma in Chicago's Polish Neighborhoods, 1920-1970." POLISH AMERICAN STUDIES 32 (1975): 27-37.

Focuses on thirteen target community areas, encompassing the original primary and major secondary Polish settlement areas in Chicago for the years from 1870 through 1970, to analyze the parameters of Polish-black contact. Contends that third- and fourth-generation Poles are suffering the cultural and psychological shock of Handlin's first-generation uprooted, as the pressure of incoming black and Latin groups causes violent shifts between the "dual legacies of neighborhood maintenance and escape."

1354 Parris, Guichard, and Brooks, Lester. BLACKS IN THE CITY: A HISTORY OF THE NATIONAL URBAN LEAGUE. Boston: Little, Brown, 1971. 534 p.

Examines the foundations of the organization, the factors which contributed to its successes and failures, and the evolution of its present status.

1355 Passi, Michael M. "Immigrants and the City: Problems of Interpretation and Synthesis in Recent White Ethnic History." JOURNAL OF ETHNIC STUDIES 4 (1976): 61-72.

Reviews three books: IMMIGRANTS AND THE CITY: ETHNICITY AND MOBILITY IN A NINETEENTH CENTURY MIDWESTERN COMMUNITY by Dean R. Esslinger (no. 1234); POLISH AMERICAN POLITICS IN CHICAGO, 1880-1940 by Edward R. Kantowicz (no. 1524); and PEASANTS AND STRANGERS: ITALIANS, RUMANIANS AND SLOVAKS IN AN AMERICAN CITY by Josef Barton (no. 1183), whose central theme is "the confrontation of immigrant cultures with American urban-industrial society, reconsidered in light of the new sensitivity to the history of non-elite groups, the new quantitative methods, and the revised theoretical assumptions about the nature of assimilation."

1356 Pearson, Ralph L. "The National Urban League Comes to Baltimore." MARYLAND HISTORICAL MAGAZINE 72 (1977): 523-34.

Argues that the league contributed much to the black community through its sociological studies of white and black attitudes and situations, but that its dispassionate, detached approach was unable to counter the emotionalist racism which dominated the city.

1357 Perdue, Robert E. THE NEGRO IN SAVANNAH, 1865-1900. New York: Exposition Press, 1973. 156 p.

Argues that urban blacks provided the political, social, educational, and religious leadership for Negroes in Georgia, that they established and sustained a diverse, lively social and cultural life, and that they worked hard to alleviate the problems resulting from slavery and discrimination.

1358 Pernicone, Carol G. "The 'Bloody Ould Sixth': A Social Analysis of a New York City Working-Class Community in the Mid-Nineteenth Century." Ph.D. dissertation, University of Rochester, 1973. 268 p.

Studies New York City's sixth-ward immigrant community in the 1850s, a long settled Irish working-class neighborhood, and concludes that their life-style was not the stereotypical one of moral depravity and social disintegration.

1359 Pessen, Edward. "The Egalitarian Myth and the American Social Reality in the 'Era of the Common Man.'" AMERICAN HISTORICAL REVIEW 76 (1971): 989-1034.

Draws on quantitative data on the distribution of wealth in Boston, New York, Brooklyn, and Philadelphia to critique the thesis of antebellum egalitarianism. Concludes that "the evidence on the backgrounds and wealth of the rich indicates that the second quarter of the nineteenth century was something other than an age of egalitarianism."

1360 _____. "The Lifestyle of the Antebellum Urban Elite." MID AMERICA 60 (1973): 163-83.

Tests the validity of the thesis that "antebellum America was marked by democratic social mingling against comprehensive evidence in the social behavior of the northeastern urban socioeconomic elite." Concludes that upper-class contacts with middle and lower groups remained restricted to those compelled by the pursuit of wealth, power, and social harmony and that in private affairs.

1361 _____. RICHES, CLASS, AND POWER BEFORE THE CIVIL WAR. Lexington, Mass.: D.C. Heath, 1973. 378 p.

Focuses primarily upon upper-class life in New York, Brooklyn, Boston, and Philadelphia, and analyzes the reasons for their dominance in the "age of the common man."

1362 _____. "A Social and Economic Portrait of Jacksonian Brooklyn: Inequality, Social Immobility, and Class Distinction in the Nation's Seventh City." NEW YORK HISTORICAL SOCIETY QUARTERLY 55 (1971): 318-53.

Focuses on the social and economic consequences of Brooklyn's expansion during the early nineteenth century based largely on tax assessment data. Concludes that the years from 1810 to

Class, Ethnicity, and Race

1841 witnessed an increase in inequality and an absence of significant social mobility.

1363 Peyer, Jean B. "Jamaica, Long Island 1656-1776: A Study of the Roots of American Urbanism." Ph.D. dissertation, City University of New York, 1974. 404 p.

Analyzes both changes and continuity in social structure and organization, emphasizing the "interrelationship of occupational groups, social stratification and mobility, population growth, family size, marriage patterns, and religious affiliations."

1364 Philpott, Thomas L. THE SLUM AND THE GHETTO: NEIGHBORHOOD DETERIORATION AND MIDDLE-CLASS REFORM, CHICAGO 1880-1930. New York: Oxford University Press, 1977. 428 p.

Argues that settlement-house workers failed to eliminate Chicago's slums and contributed to the growth of its black ghetto because, despite all their good will and honest effort, they accepted the structures of privatism and racism.

1365 Pozzetta, George E. "The Italians of New York City, 1890-1914." Ph.D. dissertation, University of North Carolina, Chapel Hill, 1971. 433 p.

Examines the acculturation of Italian immigrants in New York City, considering the settlement patterns, political, economic, and religious adjustments and the causes of immigration. Considers their impact on New York City and the changes resulting from their introduction.

1366 Rabinowitz, Howard N. "The Conflict Between Blacks and the Police in the Urban South, 1865-1900." HISTORIAN 39 (1976): 62-76.

Contends that friction between blacks and police proved common towards the end of the nineteenth century and that the origins of large-scale race riots rest on the resentments that surfaced in the emerging ghettoes of the postbellum South.

1367 _____. "From Reconstruction to Redemption in the Urban South." JOURNAL OF URBAN HISTORY 2 (1976): 169-94.

Concentrates on two basic questions: "what were the techniques of Redemption in the urban South and what difference dit it make to urban Blacks whether the Radicals or Redeemers controlled municipal governments?" Contends that while urban blacks remained better off than their rural counterparts, the Redeemer triumphs weakened gains that had occurred during the time of Radical rule.

Class, Ethnicity, and Race

1368 _____. "Half a Loaf: The Shift from White to Black Teachers in the Negro Schools of the Urban South, 1865-1890." JOURNAL OF SOUTHERN HISTORY 40 (1974): 565-94.

    Notes that black pressure resulted in the shift away from white instructors, but that increasingly this "half a loaf" compromise helped produce a segregated school system in which facilities for blacks proved highly unequal.

1369 _____. "The Search for Social Control: Race Relations in the Urban South, 1865-1890." Ph.D. dissertation, University of Chicago, 1973. 936 p.

    Deals with the lives of urban blacks during the transition period of the origin and development of segregation and uses Atlanta, Raleigh, Montgomery, Richmond, and Nashville as a microcosm in which to explore the larger questions of Reconstruction.

1370 Raymond, Richard. "Mobility and Economic Progress of Negro Americans." AMERICAN JOURNAL OF ECONOMICS AND SOCIOLOGY 28 (1969): 337-50.

    Examines changes in the relative economic status of blacks for the period 1940 to 1950, identifying a great improvement in that status nationally, with a still greater differential between North and South. Contends that the rapid rural to urban migration of these years might have been a necessary condition for improving blacks' economic conditions, but that it does not in itself provide a sufficient explanation.

1371 Reichard, Maximilian. "Black and White on the Urban Frontier: The St. Louis Community in Transition, 1800-1830." MISSOURI HISTORICAL SOCIETY BULLETIN 33 (1976): 3-17.

    Contends that the city's slaveowners were adapting the institution to urban society, largely through the imposition of stringent black codes against free and slave blacks alike. Argues that urban life gave blacks greater individual freedom but not economic opportunity or political voice.

1372 Renshaw, Patrick. "The Black Ghetto 1890-1940." JOURNAL OF AMERICAN STUDIES 8 (1974): 41-59.

    Focuses on the origins and development of the black ghetto, discussing the "Great Migration," exploring reasons for the failure of black business and capitalism, and examining the role of blacks in politics. Stresses distinctions between black and ethnic ghettoes, indicating the varying constraints that increasingly restricted the mobility of urban blacks.

Class, Ethnicity, and Race

1373   Richards, Leonard L. GENTLEMENT OF PROPERTY AND STANDING, ANTI-ABOLITION MOBS IN JACKSONIAN AMERICA. New York: Oxford University Press, 1970. 196 p.

        Examines riots in New York; Philadelphia; Cincinnati; and Utica, New York, and concludes that there were two types of mobs involved: groups of substantial citizens who directed their fire at white abolitionists and largely unorganized groups of lower-class people who attacked blacks.

1374   Ridgway, Whitman H. "A Social Analysis of Maryland Community Elites, 1827-1836: A Study of the Distribution of Power in Baltimore City, Frederick County, and Talbot County." Ph.D. dissertation, University of Pennsylvania, 1973. 628 p.

        Systematically studies power hierarchies in three Maryland communities: Baltimore City, Frederick and Talbot Counties during the Jackson era. Stresses and develops a discriminating approach for detecting methodological problems inherent in systematic analysis of community elites.

1375   Rischin, Moses. THE PROMISED CITY: NEW YORK'S JEWS 1870-1914. Cambridge, Mass.: Harvard University Press, 1962. 342 p.

        Deals largely with the development of group consciousness on the part of east European Jews, their involvement in the labor movement and socialism, and their interaction with settlement house workers and social reformers. Sees 1914 as the date of their emergence as a community.

1376   Rockaway, Robert A. "Anti-Semitism in an American City: Detroit, 1850-1914." AMERICAN JEWISH HISTORICAL QUARTERLY 64 (1974): 42-54.

        Explores various manifestations of anti-Semitism and the Jewish community's response. Contends that Detroit's German-Jewish leaders, after initially attempting to divorce themselves from the activities of their "less respectable" Russian coreligionists, ultimately came to realize that anti-Semitic elements did not make these fine distinctions.

1377   _____. "Ethnic Conflict in an Urban Environment: The German and Russian Jew in Detroit, 1881-1914." AMERICAN JEWISH HISTORICAL QUARTERLY 60 (1970): 133-50.

        Focuses on the cultural gap between German and eastern Jews, and the activities of Jewish philanthropic organizations and the Industrial Removal Office designed to facilitate the dispersal of Jews from East Coast cities and their resettlement in less-crowded urban centers.

1378 Romo, Ricardo. "Work and Restlessness: Occupational and Spatial Mobility among Mexicanos in Los Angeles, 1918-1928." PACIFIC HISTORICAL REVIEW 46 (1977): 157-80.

> Finds that low occupational status and limited upward mobility characterized Mexican workers in Los Angeles, in comparison to that of workers in Los Angeles and Boston. Suggests that this may partially explain the high spatial mobility of Mexican laborers who, due to discrimination, job security, and strong ties with their homeland, rarely remained in Los Angeles for long periods of time.

1379 Rosales, Francisco A. "Mexican Immigration to the Urban Midwest During the 1920s." Ph.D. dissertation, Indiana University, 1978. 257 p.

> Traces Mexican immigration to Chicago, Detroit, and other midwestern cities, examines their migratory experiences, and focuses upon the establishment of Mexican-American colonies in East Chicago, Indiana, from 1910 to 1945.

1380 Rose, Harold M. "The All-Negro Town: Its Evolution and Function." GEOGRAPHICAL REVIEW 55 (1965): 362-81.

> Traces the development in four stages of "all-Negro towns," defined as places with a population of 1,000 or more or when over 95 percent are nonwhite.

1381 Rosenbaum, Judy Jolley. "Black Education in Three Northern Cities in the Early Twentieth Century." Ph.D. dissertation, University of Illinois at Urbana-Champaign, 1974. 262 p.

> Investigates the discrimination against blacks in Chicago, Indianapolis, and Philadelphia, and the intentions of educators to perpetuate the existing inequality through the use of differentiated curriculum and tracking programs.

1382 Rudwick, Elliot M. RACE RIOT AT EAST ST. LOUIS, JULY 2, 1917. Carbondale, Ill.: World Publication, 1964. 300 p.

> Analyzes the forces leading to the race riot and the failure of authorities to control it. Attempts to discern a pattern which operated during race riots in East St. Louis, Chicago, and Detroit.

1383 Ryan, James G. "The Memphis Riots of 1866: Terror in a Black Community During Reconstruction." JOURNAL OF NEGRO HISTORY 62 (1977): 243-57.

> Focuses on the causes of the Memphis riots, contending that while both whites and blacks had responsibility for the initial

outbreak of violence, the city's white political leaders played an important role in heightening the dividers while the delay in declaring law left the city's black community at the mercy of armed white mobs.

1384   Sanders, James W. THE EDUCATION OF AN URBAN MINORITY: CATHOLICS IN CHICAGO, 1833-1965. New York: Oxford University Press, 1977. 278 p.

Describes and analyzes the growth of the Catholic education system in Chicago, including charitable activity, settlement houses, youth groups, and professional training, as well as formal institutions from the primary grades to universities. Stresses the relationship between the city's development and that of the parochial school system.

1385   Scheiner, Seth M. NEGRO MECCA: A HISTORY OF THE NEGRO IN NEW YORK CITY, 1865-1920. New York: New York University Press, 1965. 246 p.

Focuses upon evolution of Harlem and Bedford-Stuyvesant and the life of their inhabitants--occupation, residence, mobility, society, and politics. Sees a movement from conflict to cooperation in their dealings with the wider society of the city.

1386   Schnore, Leo F., and Sharp, Harry. "Racial Changes in Metropolitan Areas, 1950-1960." SOCIAL FORCES 41 (1963): 247-52.

Discusses basic shifts in the racial composition in cities and metropolitan areas, indicating regional variations. Notes that 60 percent of southern Standard Metropolitan Statistical Areas had lower proportions nonwhite in 1960 than in 1950, whereas an overwhelming majority of SMSAs in other regions recorded sizeable relative gains in the number of nonwhites.

1387   Schoenberg, Sandra, and Bailey, Charles. "The Symbolic Meaning of an Elite Black Community: The Ville in St. Louis." MISSOURI HISTORICAL SOCIETY BULLETIN 33 (1976): 94-102.

Finds that blacks were scattered throughout the city in dispersed clusters so long as their numbers were small, but that they were gradually forced into enclaves and ghettoes through restrictive covenants as their numbers increased. Examines the creation of a viable subculture in one of those enclaves.

1388   Schumacher, Carolyn S. "School Attendance in Nineteenth Century Pittsburgh: Wealth, Ethnicity and Occupational Mobility of School Age Children, 1855-1865." Ph.D. dissertation, University of Pittsburgh, 1977. 230 p.

Assesses the popular response to institutional schooling in a city experiencing the early stages of industrial change and describes the characteristics of the school children.

1389   Seller, Maxine. "The Education of Immigrant Children in Buffalo, New York, 1890-1916." NEW YORK HISTORY 57 (1976): 183-200.

Explores the educational aspirations of Polish, Italians, and Jewish immigrants in Buffalo and the motives of that city's educational reformers. Stresses that the native-born reformers established programs which reflected their own vision of America, basically one of middle-class values and patriotism, rather than the needs of the immigrants.

1390   _____. "The Education of the Immigrant Woman: 1900 to 1975." JOURNAL OF URBAN HISTORY 4 (1978): 307-30.

Finds that many urban, immigrant women were able to achieve a good education and even to organize their own educational programs, despite the common belief that education for women was superfluous or, at most, ought to be restricted to utilitarian subjects.

1391   Shannon, Lyle, and Shannon, Magdaline. MINORITY MIGRANTS IN THE URBAN COMMUNITY: MEXICAN-AMERICAN AND NEGRO ADJUSTMENT TO INDUSTRIAL SOCIETY. Beverly Hills, Calif.: Sage Publications, 1973. 351 p.

Based upon the results of two surveys over a ten-year period of minorities in Racine, Wisconsin, focusing upon their economic absorption, occupation, income, generational and intergenerational mobility, children and child-rearing practices, associations, and their interaction with community agencies.

1392   Shaw, Douglas V. "The Making of an Immigrant City: Ethnic and Cultural Conflict in Jersey City, New Jersey, 1850-1877." Ph.D. dissertation, University of Rochester, 1973. 273 p.

Focuses upon the efforts of the city's native-born Protestant elite to Americanize the Irish working class through moral uplift and to keep them from achieving political power by the device of an appointed commission form by the state legislature led to Irish takeover of city government.

1393   Shiloh, James A. "The 'Higher Life' in the American City of the 1890s: A Study of its Leaders and their Activities in New York, Chicago, Philadelphia, St. Louis, Boston, and Buffalo." Ph.D. dissertation, New York University, 1972. 434 p.

Examines the background and activities of a representative sample of 233 civic leaders of the decade and finds them to be largely old-stock Protestants concerned with a reintegration of society in an urban environment. Finds that most of their activities involved efforts to uplift the working class and ethnic minorities.

1394 Silvia, Philip T. "The Spindle City: Labor, Politics, and Religion in Fall River, Massachusetts, 1870-1905." Ph.D. dissertation, Fordham University, 1973. 908 p.

Examines the efforts of British and Irish-born textile workers to adapt to life in Fall River through labor and political activity and the Americanizing efforts of the Catholic Church. Finds that the older immigrants were generally inhospitable to the French-Canadian newcomers who succeeded them in the mills.

1395 Simon, Roger D. "Housing and Services in an Immigrant Neighborhood." JOURNAL OF URBAN HISTORY 2 (1976): 435-58.

Investigates the practice of Polish immigrants of postponing the installation of home services while realizing income from the taking in of a second family. Concludes that this combination caused health problems but achieved a stable, lower middle-class residential neighborhood.

1396 Sklare, Marshall. "Jews, Ethnics, and the American City." COMMENTARY 53 (1972): 70-77.

Discusses reasons for the highly successful accommodation of Jews to the American city and their positive preference for city life, including some commentary on their immigrant experience in New York during the late nineteenth and early twentieth centuries.

1397 Smith, Timothy L. "Native Blacks and Foreign Whites: Varying Responses to Educational Opportunity in America, 1880-1950." PERSPECTIVES IN AMERICAN HISTORY 6 (1972): 309-35.

Investigates the differential between immigrant and black responses to urbanization arising from presumed contrasts in social heritage. Contends that the widening gap in social and educational achievements between children of the "new immigrants" and those of the contemporaneous black immigrants to northern and border cities did not stem from the supposed heritage of slavery and concomitant distortions in self-image and family, for these black families were ambitious and their children enrolled in school in larger proportions than those of the immigrants.

1398 Sorkin, Alan L. THE URBAN INDIAN. Lexington, Mass.: D.C. Heath, 1978. 158 p.

Surveys the historical movement of American Indians into cities, their economic and social status, their institutions, and their rate of acculturation and adjustment. Also examines the efforts of social agencies to deal with the manpower, health, housing, and education of American Indians.

1399 Spear, Allan H. BLACK CHICAGO: THE MAKING OF A NEGRO GHETTO, 1890-1920. Chicago: University of Chicago Press, 1967. 254 p.

Explores the forces that lead to the creation of a separate black community in Chicago, and the impact of this development on black ideology. Sees a shift in race relations from a relatively fluid pattern to a rigid one marked by discrimination and segregation, and an alteration in the ideology of black leaders from militant abolitionism to the acceptance of a separate community.

1400 Stimson, Grace Heilman. RISE OF THE LABOR MOVEMENT IN LOS ANGELES. Berkeley and Los Angeles: University of California Press, 1955. 529 p.

Contends that organized labor had a series of special problems in Los Angeles because of its sprawling configuration and because of the presence of Chinese and Mexican laborers, both of which contributed to its reputation as an open shop city.

1401 Strickland, Arvarh E. HISTORY OF THE CHICAGO URBAN LEAGUE. Urbana: University of Illinois Press, 1966. 286 p.

Traces the evolution of the league from its foundations in the World War I era through the civil rights activism of the 1960s. Stresses the role of the league in orienting black migrants to urban life and its evolution from a conservative to an activist organization.

1402 Sullivan, Margaret. "St. Louis Ethnic Neighborhoods, 1850-1930: An Introduction." MISSOURI HISTORICAL SOCIETY--ST. LOUIS BULLETIN 33 (1977): 64-76.

Describes the locational patterns of St. Louis ethnic groups, noting the incidence of continuing intracity mobility and stressing the importance of studying new ethnic neighborhoods as well as original areas of settlement. Contends that while ethnic groups moved quickly, "The overall residential relationship between the groups remained remarkably similar" for the period under discussion.

1403 Taeuber, Karl E., and Taeuber, Alma F. "The Negro as an Immigrant Group: Recent Trends in Racial and Ethnic Segregation in Chicago."

AMERICAN JOURNAL OF SOCIOLOGY 69 (1964): 374-82.

> Presents a simple model demonstrating that only a small proportion of black residential segregation can be attributed to low economic status and provides comparisons between whites and nonwhites, as well as immigrants, for selected socioeconomic characteristics for the period 1930 to 1960.

1404 _____. NEGROES IN CITIES: RESIDENTIAL SEGREGATION AND NEIGHBORHOOD. Chicago: Aldine Publishing Co., 1965. 284 p.

> Uses quantitative methods to explore the development of residential segregation and neighborhood change in U.S. cities. Considers social and economic factors in residential segregation, black migration, and residential succession while presenting considerable statistical information for the years from 1940 to 1960.

1405 Taylor, David V. "Pilgrim's Progress: Black St. Paul and the Making of an Urban Ghetto, 1879-1930." Ph.D. dissertation, University of Minnesota, 1977. 303 p.

> Discusses black migration into Minnesota and slavery during the antebellum period, focusing on its social history and demography from 1870 to the Depression.

1406 Terkel, Studs. DIVISION STREET: AMERICA. New York: Pantheon, 1967. 381 p.

> An impressionistic view of one of Chicago's most polyglot neighborhoods, based upon Terkel's interviews with people from a variety of ethnic backgrounds.

1407 Thernstrom, Stephan. THE OTHER BOSTONIANS: POVERTY AND PROGRESS IN THE AMERICAN METROPOLIS, 1880-1970. Cambridge, Mass.: Harvard University Press, 1973. 345 p.

> Studies the common people of Boston, focusing on several critical questions about social structure and social processes. Investigates population growth, migration and turnover, economic opportunity, occupational career patterns and achievement and relates these to ethnicity and social class. Finds "definite rigidities in the occupational structure, a series of barriers that impeded mobility and perpetuated inequality," but notes that the strength of such barriers should not be overestimated.

1408 _____. POVERTY AND PROGRESS: SOCIAL MOBILITY IN A NINETEENTH CENTURY CITY. Cambridge, Mass.: Harvard University Press, 1964. 286 p.

> Examines the changing social position of unskilled manual

laborers and their families in Newburyport, Massachusetts. Finds limited social mobility and suggests that the findings have significance for nineteenth-century America as a whole.

1409 Thomas, Richard. "The Detroit Urban League: 1916-1923." MICHIGAN HISTORY 60 (1976): 315-38.

Examines the efforts of the Urban League to help the black, rural peasant adjust to northern industrial society. Stresses that while the league intended to focus on job placement and assimilation, it increasingly became a major organization in the eyes of both blacks and whites, for all matters asociated with the black community.

1410 _____. "From Peasant to Proletarian: The Formation and Organization of the Black Industrial Working Class in Detroit, 1915-1945." Ph.D. dissertation, University of Michigan, 1976. 329 p.

Uses the emergence of the black industrial working class and its connection with the larger black community to give insight into black urbanization in the twentieth century.

1411 Tuttle, William M., Jr. RACE RIOT: CHICAGO IN THE RED SUMMER OF 1919. New York: Atheneum, 1970. 305 p.

Details the anatomy of a race riot, its origin, course, and eventual resolution.

1412 Uberti, John K. "Men, Manners, and Machines: The Young Man's Institute in Antebellum Philadelphia." Ph.D. dissertation, University of Pennsylvania, 1977. 231 p.

Investigates the response of the city's elite to immigration, strikes, uprisings, and new political parties based on anxiety by founding mechanics institutes for the dual purposes of self-help and social control. Sees them as an effort to ameliorate the change from a mechanic-artisan economy to an industrial one.

1413 Varbero, Richard A. "Urbanization and Acculturation: Philadelphia's South Italians, 1918-1932." Ph.D. dissertation, Temple University, 1975. 414 p.

Discusses the experiences of a predominantly peasant immigrant group and their emergence into a complex urban society "bearing often the symbols of their old-world background."

1414 Vinyard, JoEllen McNergney. THE IRISH ON THE URBAN FRONTIER: NINETEENTH CENTURY DETROIT. New York: Arno Press, 1976. 446 p.

Studies and identifies the reciprocal impacts of the interaction between Irish immigrants and the city. Notes a higher level of occupational achievement for the Irish of Detroit as opposed to other cities, identifying economic growth, size, and rate of expansion, population characteristics, and religious composition as key factors.

1415 Watts, Eugene J. "Black Political Progress in Atlanta: 1868-1895." JOURNAL OF NEGRO HISTORY 59 (1974): 268-86.

Focuses on the direct representation of blacks in city government as the critical issue of race and politics in Atlanta, arguing that the appearance of black political progress largely was an illusion in that the white majority accepted blacks' exercise of the franchise only within carefully prescribed limits, and that it "always opposed a black voice in the actual administration of city affairs and representation in city offices."

1416 Weaver, Robert C. "The Suburbanization of America, or, the Shrinking of the Cities." CIVIL RIGHTS DIGEST 9 (1977): 3-11.

Discusses the long history of the process of suburbanization in the United States to show that "suburbia was not created in order to establish a haven for a racist middle class." Notes that after its creation, however, suburbia did increasingly come to fulfill that function.

1417 Weber, Michael P. "Residential and Occupational Patterns of Ethnic Minorities in Nineteenth Century Pittsburgh." PENNSYLVANIA HISTORY 44 (1977): 316-34.

Analyzes a sample of blue-collar workers in four industrial wards in Pittsburgh between 1880 and 1920 to ascertain the impact of economic conditions on social mobility. Finds that Pittsburgh's unskilled workers enjoyed greater mobility than that reported for three other cities from which comparable data exists, suggesting that local economic conditions and industrial patterns produced varying patterns of success for blue-collar workers.

1418 Webster, Janice Reiff. "Domestication and Americanization: Scandinavian Women in Seattle, 1888 to 1900." JOURNAL OF URBAN HISTORY 4 (1978): 275-309.

Contends that the dynamics of the city and the migration patterns of Scandinavian immigrants en route to Seattle caused these immigrant women to discard their traditional roles and responsibilities.

1419 Weinbaum, Paul O. "Mobs and Demagogues: The Response to Collective Violence in New York City in the Early Nineteenth Century." Ph.D. dissertation, University of Rochester, 1977. 282 p.

Sees the riots in the early eighteenth century as the basis for the mid-1830s riots and concludes that the latter are "best explained as part of a traditional society.

1420 Weinberg, Daniel E. "Ethnic Identity in Industrial Cleveland: The Hungarians 1900-1920." OHIO HISTORY 86 (1977): 171-86.

Used oral history techniques to document that Hungarians in Cleveland created a community which not only eased their entry into American society but established a context in which their ethnic values, preferences, and needs persisted and were preeminent.

1421 Weiss, Nancy J. THE NATIONAL URBAN LEAGUE, 1910-1940. New York: Oxford University Press, 1974. 402 p.

Sees the league, like the National Association for the Advancement of Colored People, as "an authentic product of the progressive era in which it was founded," tied to the larger reform currents of the day, both in tactics and personnel. Portrays the connections as paradoxical, including elements of both social justice and racism, but argues that the league and the National Association for the Advancement of Colored People "are among the most important institutional legacies of the era of reform."

1422 Whyte, William F. STREET CORNER SOCIETY. Chicago: University of Chicago Press, 1955. 366 p.

Classic study of the social structure of an Italian immigrant ghetto, "Cornerville," in an eastern city in the 1930s and 1940s.

1423 Wilkie, Jane Riblett. "The Black Urban Population of the Pre-Civil War South." PHYLON 37 (1976): 250-62.

Examines the urbanization of blacks for the period 1790 to 1860, concluding that the preference of blacks for cities has origins that predate the rural to urban shifts accompanying World War I, and noting that free blacks have a much higher rate of urbanization than both salves and the white population in the South.

1424 _____. "Social Status, Acculturation and School Attendance in 1850 Boston." JOURNAL OF SOCIAL HISTORY 11 (1977): 179-92.

Examines the relationship between educational opportunity and both social class and acculturation using census-collected school attendance data for Boston. Tentatively concludes that lower social status restricted educational opportunities principally for older children, but that cultural background proved far more important than social class in determining school attendance.

1425 Williams, Melvin R. "A Blueprint for Change: The Black Community in Washington, D.C., 1860-1870." RECORDS OF THE COLUMBIA HISTORICAL SOCIETY OF WASHINGTON, D.C. 1971-1972 48 (1973): 359-93.

Focuses on Reconstruction attempts to alter the condition of blacks, particularly with regard to public education, emancipation, and enfranchisement, documenting the inability of the nation's capital to proceed with a social revolution. Provides data on black residences, family organization, occupations, and religious, social, and benevolent organizations.

1426 Wintz, Cary D. "Black Writers in 'Nigger Heaven': The Harlem Renaissance." Ph.D. dissertation, Kansas State University, 1974. 388 p.

Sees the urban ghetto replacing the rural South as the primary environment of blacks in the country and credits the Harlem Renaissance as the major expression of black thought during the twenties and early thirties.

1427 Yans-McLaughlin, Virginia. FAMILY AND COMMUNITY: ITALIAN IMMIGRANTS IN BUFFALO, 1880-1930. Ithaca: Cornell University Press, 1977. 286 p.

Focuses on the family experience of working-class Italians in Buffalo, stressing the factors that promoted family cohesion. Sees the family as a flexible adaptive institution which, nonetheless, can retain traditional patterns.

1428 Zachary, Alan M. "Social Disorder and the Philadelphia Elite Before Jackson." PENNSYLVANIA MAGAZINE OF HISTORY AND BIOGRAPHY 99 (1975): 288-308.

Profiles the city's elite of the 1820s, indicating their attitudes and concerns and argues that "a continuing tradition of leadership, founded on service, reverence for the past, and maintenance of the Republican heritage characterized Philadelphia's leaders."

1429 Zachary, Wayne W., and Lichtenstein, Irvin. "Sociogeographic Boundaries and Personal Movement in the Manayunk Area of Philadelphia." In SOUTH ATLANTIC URBAN STUDIES, vol. 1, edited by Jack R. Censer and N. Steinert, pp. 198-228. Columbia: University of South Carolina Press, 1978.

Finds that Manayunk has successfully established and maintained for over two generations, quietly and independently, a stable environment for its racially and ethnically mixed populations. Examines the travel patterns of its residents both within the community and to other sections of metropolitan Philadelphia.

1430   Zunz, Oliver. "The Organization of the American City in the Late Nineteenth Century: Ethnic Structure and Spatial Arrangement in Detroit." JOURNAL OF URBAN HISTORY 3 (1977): 443-66.

Focuses on the spatial organization of late nineteenth-century Detroit to assess the degree of ethnic clustering. Concludes that the territorial divisions which existed did in fact reflect ethnic and class divisions.

Chapter 10

URBAN POLITICS AND GOVERNMENT

1431   Adrian, Charles. GOVERNING URBAN AMERICA. New York: McGraw-Hill, 1933. 452 p.

   Examines urban political theory, political processes, laws and forms of city government, administrative procedures and structures, and the provision of urban services. Predicts that urban reformers still have a long way to go in equipping the city to satisfy the needs of its citizens.

1432   Allswang, John M. A HOUSE FOR ALL PEOPLES: ETHNIC POLITICS IN CHICAGO, 1890-1936. Lexington: University Press of Kentucky, 1971. 253 p.

   The story of the role of various ethnic groups in the rise of the Democratic party in Chicago with particular emphasis on the period from the end of World War I to the election of President Franklin D. Roosevelt in 1932. Argues that it was not until the 1920s that the ethnics were sufficiently strong politically to influence elections significantly.

1433   _____. THE NEW DEAL AND AMERICAN POLITICS: A STUDY IN POLITICAL CHANGE. New York: John Wiley and Sons, 1978. 155 p.

   Argues, based upon county-level election data, that cities played a relatively lesser role in the electoral success of the New Deal than is generally supposed. Contends that cities remained more heavily Democratic than the rest of the nation after the New Deal was ended.

1434   Anderson, Alan D. THE ORIGIN AND RESOLUTION OF AN URBAN CRISIS: BALTIMORE 1890-1930. Baltimore: Johns Hopkins University Press, 1977. 143 p.

   Attributes Baltimore's urban crisis to a mix of private and governmental decisions that affected spatial and demographic growth. Argues that Progressive era reform efforts in the city were led by businessmen who defined the terms of the crisis and proposed reforms of primary benefit to their class.

1435 Arnold, Linda M. "Congressional Government of the District, 1800-1846." Ph.D. dissertation, Georgetown University, 1975.

Contends that Congress mismanaged the government of the District to the point where its citizens clamored for home rule and a retrocession of part of its territory to Virginia and Maryland, culminating in the return of Alexandria to Virginia in 1846. Focuses also on the efforts of abolitionists to attack the city's slaveholders through the mechanism of congressional rule.

1436 Banfield, Edward C. THE UNHEAVENLY CITY: THE NATURE AND FUTURE OF OUR URBAN CRISIS. Boston: Little, Brown, 1969. 308 p.

Asserts that the urban crisis is a function of class differences rather than racial ones. Looks to economic growth, demographic change, and the process of middle and upper classification, rather than to governmental policies, to solve current urban problems.

1437 _____, ed. URBAN GOVERNMENT: A READER IN ADMINISTRATION AND POLITICS. New York: Free Press of Glencoe, 1941. 718 p.

Contains numerous entries arranged around the categories of: urban government as a subject for study, urban government in the federal system; the machine and its reform, "good government," the trend of urban politics, influence and leadership, management problems, and policy formation.

1438 Banfield, Edward C., and Wilson, James Q. CITY POLITICS. Cambridge, Mass.: Harvard University Press, 1963. 363 p.

Discusses the nature and structure of city politics and examines several forms and styles of urban politics, including the machine, reform, nonpartisanship, and council-manager forms. Also looks at political roles of city employees, voters, and civic leaders.

1439 Bartolemeo, John S. "Public Debate and the Social Bases of Politics: Philadelphia, 1844." Ph.D. dissertation, University of Pennsylvania, 1977.

Finds that both major political parties were led by people who scored high on several indices of cosmopolitanism, including an inclination toward professionalism, an impersonal analytical approach to news coverage, and a preference for voluntary organizations based upon specialized skills and knowledge.

Urban Politics and Government

1440 Bauman, John F. "The City, the Depression, and Relief: The Philadelphia Experience, 1929-1939." Ph.D. dissertation, Rutgers University, 1969. 473 p.

> Analyzes federal social workers' belief in a "democratic relief program" and the reasons for its failure under the combined pressure of economic interest groups and partisan politics. Contends that New Deal relief policies failed to alter the city's political structure and process significantly.

1441 Beard, Charles A. AMERICAN CITY GOVERNMENT: A SURVEY OF NEWER TENDENCIES. New York: Arno Press, 1970. 420 p.

> Argues that the lines between city and state government were often so blurred and their responsibilities in urban affairs so ill defined that much of the reform legislation of the Progressive era often proved to be of very little effect.

1442 Berg, Barbara J. "The Remembered Gate: Origins of American Feminism." Ph.D. dissertation, City University of New York, 1976. 601 p.

> Refutes the accepted interpretation of the women's movement as emerging from the experiences of female abolitionists, and credits urban growth for the transformation of women's consciousness and the eventual sharing of experiences which led to the demand for expanded rights.

1443 Bernstein, Arthur I. "The Rise of the Democratic-Republican Party in New York City, 1789-1800." Ph.D. dissertation, Columbia University, 1964. 467 p.

> Attributes the party's success to its connections with the Irish Emigrant Society, the Tammany Society, and various workingmen's groups, while the rival Federalists were becoming almost totally dependent upon the business community.

1444 Betters, Paul V. CITIES AND THE 1936 CONGRESS. Washington, D.C.: U.S. Conference of Mayors, 1936. Reprint. New York: Arno Press, 1978. 27 p.

> Looks at congressional action with respect to cities from the standpoint of an urban mayor, focusing upon the impact of the municipal bankruptcy law, Wagner Housing Bill, the Resettlement Administration, Rural Electrification Administration, federal aid for crime prevention, and a federal water pollution bill.

1445 Betters, Paul V.; Williams, J. Kerwin; and Reeder, Sherwood L. RECENT FEDERAL CITY RELATIONS. Washington, D.C. U.S. Conference of Mayors, 1936. Reprint. New York: Arno Press, 1978. 145 p.

Deals largely with the attitude of the U.S. Conference of Mayors toward federal government action in the area of municipal finance, especially the Emergency Relief and Construction Act, Federal Municipal Debt Reconstruction bill, Home Owners Loan Corporation, Public Works Administration, and Federal Emergency Relief Administration.

1446   Blumberg, Barbara M. "The Works Progress Administration in New York City: A Case Study of the New Deal in Action." Ph.D. dissertation, Columbia University, 1974. 599 p.

Argues that the Works Progress Administration benefited about one-quarter of the city's population to some degree and aided significantly in urban renewal and in cultural and educational enrichment. Also shows how the New Deal's essential conservatism and the opposition of Republicans and rural Democrats seriously limited the program's effectiveness.

1447   Bonjean, Charles M., and Lineberry, Robert L. "The Urbanization-Party Competition Hypothesis: A Comparison of All United States Counties." JOURNAL OF POLITICS 32 (1970): 305-21.

Denies any real connection between urbanization and party competitiveness. Finds almost no connection between ecological-demographic variables and interparty competition.

1448   Bowers, John L., Jr. "Limitations on Municipal Indebtedness." VANDERBILT LAW REVIEW 5 (1951): 37-56.

Traces the movement to limit municipal indebtedness from the 1870s to the 1950s and discusses the various devices which cities have used to avoid the restrictions. Also speculates on the probabilities of success of various avoidance schemes.

1449   Braucher, Samuel C. "The Municipal Authority in Pennsylvania 1933-1950." PENNSYLVANIA BAR ASSOCIATION QUARTERLY 22 (1951): 292-303.

Examines the operation of the Municipal Authorities Act between 1933 and 1950 and finds that it has enabled 261 cities to provide a wide variety of municipal services.

1450   Bremer, William W. "New York City's Family of Social Servants and the Politics of Welfare: A Prelude to the New Deal, 1928-1933." Ph.D. dissertation, Stanford University, 317 p.

Develops the history of influential New York social servants who pioneeered unemployment programs to explain how ideas of collectivism were used to maintain the tradition of individualism in welfare programs.

Urban Politics and Government

1451 Buenker, John D. "Chicago's Ethnics and the Politics of Accommodation." CHICAGO HISTORY 3 (1974): 92-100.

   Examines the efforts of the city's various ethnic groups to use politics as a means of accommodating themselves to the urban environment, of obtaining material benefits, of gaining recognition and group esteem, and of preserving their identity and culture.

1452 _____. "The Dynamics of Chicago Ethnic Politics, 1900-1930." JOURNAL OF THE ILLINOIS STATE HISTORICAL SOCIETY 7 (1974): 175-200.

   Examines the bases and goals of ethnocultural politics in the Windy City, analyzes the factors which determined ethnic groups' success or failure, and provides an overview of ethnic political succession in the first three decades of the century.

1453 _____. "The Politics of Resistance: The Rural-Based Yankee Republican Machines of Connecticut and Rhode Island." NEW ENGLAND QUARTERLY 67 (1974): 212-37.

   Identifies hostility toward cities and their heavily immigrant stock working-class population as the major glue which held together the Roraback and Brayton political organizations in Connecticut and Rhode Island. Finds legislative malapportionment to be the most effective weapon in their arsenals.

1454 Capeci, Dominic J. "From Different Liberal Perspectives: Fiorello H. La Guardia, Adam Clayton Powell, Jr., and Civil Rights in New York City, 1941-1943." JOURNAL OF NEGRO HISTORY 62 (1977): 160-73.

   Contrasts La Guardia's "politics of reform" with Powell's "politics of resentment" and analyzes the reasons for the continual conflict, despite the fact that both, in their own way, were committed to making gains for their black East Harlem constituents.

1455 Caro, Robert A. THE POWER BROKER: ROBERT MOSES AND THE FALL OF NEW YORK. New York: Knopf, 1974. 1,246 p.

   Traces Moses' career from idealistic reformer to boss of the nation's largest bureaucracy to the last hurrah. Focuses upon Moses' uses and abuses of power in running the city and on his tremendous influence in shaping the development of metropolitan New York.

1456 Chalmers, Leonard. "Fiorello La Guardia, Paterfamilias at City Hall: An Appraisal." NEW YORK HISTORY 56 (1975): 210-25.

Praises La Guardia for his efforts in restoring the morale of the city's bureaucracy after the Seabury investigations and for making it run efficiently. Faults La Guardia for leaving no framework for a continuation of a good government beyond his own administration.

1457 Clubb, Jerome M., and Allen, Howard W. "The Cities and the Election of 1928: Partisan Realignment?" AMERICAN HISTORICAL REVIEW 74 (1969): 1205-20.

Contends that the alignment of urban, immigrant voters with the Democratic party probably resulted more from a "critical period" beginning in the mid-1920s rather than from a "critical election" of 1928. Finds significant difference between the presidential vote and that for lesser offices in 1928.

1458 Cobb, James Charles. "Politics in a New South City: Augusta, Georgia, 1946-1971." Ph.D. dissertation, University of Georgia, 1975. 243 p.

Traces political events from the overthrow of the Cracker party machine by the Independent party, the blacks' early political efforts and the eventual division of Augusta into a black ghetto core with an outlying white suburbia.

1459 Connery, Robert H., and Leach, Richard H. THE FEDERAL GOVERNMENT AND METROPOLITAN AREAS. Cambridge, Mass.: Harvard University Press, 1960. 275 p.

Surveys the various federal programs dealing with metropolitan areas, analyzes the representation of various urban interest groups in Washington and the role of Congress and the president, and discusses the pros and cons of a department of urban affairs.

1460 _____. "Southern Metropolis: Challenge to Government." JOURNAL OF POLITICS 26 (1964): 60-81.

Examines the growth of the metropolis in the South in the 1950s and analyzes the problems involved in providing adequate services and effective governance. Focuses upon annexation, experiments in regional government, and federal policy guidelines.

1461 Conzen, Kathleen Neils. "Precocious Reformers: Immigrants and Party Politics in Ante-Bellum Milwaukee." HISTORICAL MESSENGER OF THE MILWAUKEE COUNTY HISTORICAL SOCIETY 33 (1977): 44-56.

Acknowledges that Milwaukee's Germans participated in machinelike politics involving blind voting, corruption, and violence but insists that they also led a reform movement within the Democratic party. Finds them especially interested in an open primary and other efforts to open up the nomination process.

1462 Corty, Floyd L., and Havard, William C., Jr. "Rural-Urban Consolidation: The Baton Rouge Experiment." LABOR STUDIES 3 (1964): 196-209.

Examines the emergence of parish-wide metropolitan government in Baton Rouge, the problems leading to its adoption, the opposition to and complexities of the form, the process of consolidation, and evaluates its consequences. Concludes that the city received more positive benefits than did the hinterlands.

1463 Cronin, Bernard C. FATHER YORKE AND THE LABOR MOVEMENT IN SAN FRANCISCO, 1900-1910. New York: Irvington, 1972. 239 p.

Investigates the role played by Peter Yorke, the Irish-American labor priest, in the unionization movement and the political life of San Francisco. Focuses upon his role in waterfront and street car strikes, the graft prosecution, and the stabilization of the labor movement.

1464 Curran, D.J. "Social Change and Political Lag in Metropolitan Milwaukee." AMERICAN JOURNAL OF ECONOMICS AND SOCIOLOGY 25 (1966): 229-40.

Examines the economic changes that have taken place in the metropolitan area since the 1920s and finds that legal, political, and financial institutions have failed to adjust sufficiently to meet the needs of its residents. Attributes this inertia to intrametropolitan rivalry, a lack of area-wide outlook, and the attitude of the "haves" toward the "have-nots."

1465 Cutright, Phillips. "Urbanization and Competitive Party Politics." JOURNAL OF POLITICS 25 (1963): 552-64.

Using data from the 1940s and 1950s, finds that urbanization is positively associated with competitive party politics and is more significant than high degrees of manufacturing employment or religious homogeneity.

1466 Dahl, Robert A. WHO GOVERNS? DEMOCRACY AND POWER IN AN AMERICAN CITY. New Haven, Conn.: Yale University Press, 1961. 335 p.

Focuses upon the structure and operation of the political system of New Haven, looking at the distribution and patterns of influence, the distribution and use of political resources and the interaction between the forces of stability and those of change.

1467 Danforth, Brian J. "The Influence of Socioeconomic Factors upon Political Behavior: A Quantitative Look at New York City Merchants, 1828-1844." Ph.D. dissertation, New York University, 1974. 332 p.

Shows how the New York City merchants secured their wealth by becoming involved in the politics as well as the commerce of the city. Underscores the importance of viewing political behavior as determined by both social and economic factors.

1468 Degler, Carl N. "American Political Parties and the Rise of the City: An Interpretation." JOURNAL OF AMERICAN HISTORY 51 (1964): 41-59.

A new interpretation of political parties in light of urban industrialization in the 1880s and 1890s through the election of John Kennedy.

1469 _____. "Labor in the Economy and Politics of New York City, 1850-1860: A Study of the Impact of Early Industrialism." Ph.D. dissertation, Columbia University, 1952. 360 p.

Examines the impact of industrialization upon the labor force, the organization and tactics of unions, and the latter's political involvement. Concludes that workers generally supported the Democratic party and ignored the efforts of several labor parties.

1470 Dorsett, Lyle W. "Frank Hague, Franklin Roosevelt, and the Politics of the New Deal." NEW JERSEY HISTORY 94 (1976): 23-35.

Contends that Roosevelt continued to work with Hague so long as he delivered the vote for New Deal candidates, despite Hague's opposition to the Civil Works Administration, his police state tactics, and his unsavory reputation.

1471 _____. FRANKLIN D. ROOSEVELT AND THE CITY BOSSES. Port Washington, N.Y.: Kennikat Press, 1977. 134 p.

Examines the impact of the New Deal on the political organizations of James Michael Curley in Boston, Edward Crump in Memphis, Ed Flynn in the Bronx, Thomas J. Pendergast in Kansas City, Edward J. Kelly in Chicago, and Frank Hague in Jersey City, and denies that the federalization of welfare destroyed them. Finds that Roosevelt pursued an uneven policy toward urban machines.

1472 Drury, James W. HOME RULE IN KANSAS. Government Research

Series, no. 31. Lawrence: Governmental Research Center, University of Kansas, 1965. 88 p.

>Traces the evolution of the home rule movement in the state from 1854 to 1959, analyzes the constitutional amendment and the adoption process, and delineates its effects. Concludes that the amendment has changed the fundamental pattern of state-city relations in Kansas.

1473 Dunfee, Charles D. "Harold Burton, Mayor of Cleveland and Works Progress Administration, 1935-1937." Ph.D. dissertation, Case Western Reserve University, 1975. 387 p.

>Examines the operation of the Works Progress Administration (WPA) in Cleveland and finds that it was of immense assistance in relieving the cost of welfare and enabled cities to repair deteriorated facilities and to upgrade the delivery of municipal services.

1474 Dye, Thomas R. "Urban Political Integration: Conditions Associated with Annexation in American Cities." MIDWEST JOURNAL OF POLITICAL SCIENCE 8 (1964): 430-46.

>Examines the incidence of annexation in 213 urbanized areas during the 1950s and finds that the form of city government, the age of settlement, and the social class distance between city and suburb were the most important variables. Concludes that the legal difficulty of the annexation process was of little or no significance.

1475 Elazar, Daniel. CITIES OF THE PRAIRIE: THE METROPOLITAN FRONTIER AND AMERICAN POLITICS. New York: Basic Books, 1970. 514 p.

>Compares the governments of several midwestern cities and divided them into "representative oligarchies" and "organized polyarchies," both of which are fundamentally elitist. Scores the nation's "individualistic political culture" for being at the root of city corruption.

1476 _____. "Urban Problems and the Federal Government: A Historical Inquiry." POLITICAL SCIENCE QUARTERLY 82 (1967): 505-26.

>Examines federal-city relations prior to 1933 and finds that, prior to World War I, cities did not make specialized demands upon the national government. Identifies the era from 1913 to 1933 as the one that separated the large metropolitan areas from the rest of the nation in terms of their relationship to the federal government.

1477 Elkins, Eugene R. MUNICIPAL HOME RULE IN WEST VIRGINIA.

Morgantown: West Virginia University, 1965. 54 p.

Examines the home rule amendment and law, analyzes its residual powers, and discusses its provisions for adjustment in area and jurisdiction.

1478 Farkas, Suzanne. "The Federal Role in Urban Decentralization." AMERICAN BEHAVIORAL SCIENTIST 15 (1971): 15-35.

Assesses the impact of federal programs in urban decentralization since the 1930s and charges that these programs have contributed significantly to many of the problems which decentralization is designed to correct.

1479 Feinstein, Estelle F. STAMFORD IN THE GILDED AGE: THE POLITICAL LIFE OF A CONNECTICUT TOWN, 1868-1893. Stamford, Conn.: Stamford Historical Society, 1973. 319 p.

Traces the development of Stamford from a town of 10,000 in the 1870s to a city of over 110,000 a century later and emphasizes the politics of town meetings, school reform, public works, public health, and the control of poverty, vagrants, and liquor as these changed over time.

1480 Feldberg, Michael. "The Crowd in Philadelphia History: A Comparative Perspective." LABOR HISTORY 15 (1974): 323-36.

Sees riots as purposeful methods of direct action whereby ethnic groups vied for jobs or political power, antiabolitionists moved against alleged radicals, and laborers fought for higher wages. Holds that violence was inseparable from the process of social bargaining.

1481 Fox, Daniel M. "Social Policy and City Politics: Tuberculosis Reporting in New York, 1889-1900." BULLETIN OF THE HISTORY OF MEDICINE 49 (1975): 169-95.

Presents tuberculosis reporting as a political football in the struggle between Tammany Hall and the reform-minded fusionists. Claims that the city's "model" reporting program was more a skillful political response of concerned and ambitious men than a result of scientific progress.

1482 Furlow, John W. "An Urban State Under Siege: Pennsylvania and the Second Gubernatorial Administration of Gifford Pinchot, 1931-1935." Ph.D. dissertation, University of North Carolina, Chapel Hill, 1973. 596 p.

Studies Pennsylvania's reaction to the depression and cites Pinchot's attempt to devise an independent course of action, which ultimately failed because of his rural bias in policy making.

1483 Gelfand, Mark I. "A Nation of Cities: The Federal Government's Response to the Challenges of Urban America, 1933-1960." Ph.D. dissertation, Columbia University, 1972. 689 p.

> Reviews the origins of federal-municipal ties, their implementation through the New Deal, Eisenhower's retraction of support, and the revival of special attention in John Kennedy's presidential campaign.

1484 Gilbert, Charles E. "National Political Alignments and the Politics of Large Cities." POLITICAL SCIENCE QUARTERLY 79 (1964): 25-51.

> Dates the Democratic trend in city politics to ethnic and religious developments in the 1920s, exacerbated by the impact of the Great Depression. Argues that party preferences related to national politics seem to be controlling in city elections in the long run.

1485 Gilbert, Charles E., and Clague, Christopher. "Electoral Competition and Electoral Systems in Large Cities." JOURNAL OF POLITICS 24 (1962): 323-49.

> Examines data from mayoral and city council elections in the nation's twenty-four largest cities between 1945 and 1962 and identifies six distinct models of party competitiveness.

1486 Goldstein, Michael L. "Preface to the Rise of Booker T. Washington: A View from New York City of the Demise of Independent Black Politics, 1889-1902." JOURNAL OF NEGRO HISTORY 62 (1977): 81-99.

> Contends that blacks reacted to their decline in political status in the city by forming independent party organizations, but they failed to force Tammany Hall to grant them recognition or benefits. Concludes that they either had to participate in a segregated party structure or eschew politics altogether.

1487 Goodnow, Frank J. CITY GOVERNMENT IN THE UNITED STATES. 1910. Reprint. New York: Arno Press, 1978. 315 p.

> Examines the administrative history of American cities, concentrating upon public works, utility regulation, courts, and public welfare agencies. Written by a prominent urban, good government reformer of the Progressive era.

1488 Gordon, Daniel. "Immigrants and Municipal Voting Turnout: Implications for the Changing Ethnic Impact on Urban Politics." AMERICAN SOCIOLOGICAL REVIEW 34 (1970): 665-81.

> Based upon data from 268 cities, posits a high degree of cor-

relation between the presence of immigrants and the mayor-council form of municipal government.

1489 Gordon, Michael A. "The Labor Boycott in New York City, 1880-1886." LABOR HISTORY 16 (1975): 184-229.

Examines the Irish and other Old World origins of the boycott and analyzes its impact on the New York mayoral election of 1886 in which labor and working-class votes propelled radical Henry George into second place behind Abram Hewitt and ahead of Theodore Roosevelt.

1490 Gordon, Rita Werner. "The Change in the Political Alignment of Chicago's Negroes During the New Deal." JOURNAL OF AMERICAN HISTORY 56 (1969): 584-603.

Concludes that the New Deal was the principal cause of the shift to Democratic allegiance on the part of Chicago's blacks, even though the city's party machine made significant inroads prior to that.

1491 Greenberg, Irwin F. "The Philadelphia Democratic Party, 1911-1934." Ph.D. dissertation, Temple University, 1972. 625 p.

Traces the growth of the Democratic party from a mere "adjunct of the Republican Machine" in 1911 to its rejuvenation in 1933, which is attributed to the partisan realignment of the voters in 1932.

1492 Greer, Scott. GOVERNING THE METROPOLIS. New York: John Wiley, 1962. 153 p.

Surveys and synthesizes the existing literature on governing the metropolis. Stresses the "schizoid policy" of having an economically and ecologically integrated metropolis governed by a fragmented governmental system.

1493 Grele, Ronald J. "The Structural Development of Urban Liberalism in the Democratic Party of the Fourth Congressional District of New Jersey, 1930-1960." Ph.D. dissertation, Rutgers University, 1971. 557 p.

Contends that organized labor, liberal volunteer associations, ethnic communities, blacks, suburbanites, and Princeton intellectuals coalesced in support of Democrats committed to urban liberalism in Mercer and Burlington Counties. Also discusses the structural limitations inhibiting the development of liberalism.

1494 Haas, Edward F. THE ILLUSION OF REFORM: DELESSEPS S. MORRISON AND NEW ORLEANS POLITICS, 1946-1961. Baton Rouge:

Louisiana State University Press, 1974. 368 p.

> Demonstrates how major southern cities sought to create the impression of reform while largely ignoring the plight of their black citizens.

1495 _____. "New Orleans on the Half Shell: The Maestri Era, 1936-1946." LOUISIANA HISTORY 13 (1972): 283-310.

> Examines Maestri's rise to power and his economic and social policies, his tolerance of gambling, vice, and prostitution, and his relationship with the Roosevelt administration.

1496 Hamilton, Howard D. "The Municipal Voter: Voting and Non-Voting in City Elections." AMERICAN POLITICAL SCIENCE REVIEW 65 (1971): 1135-40.

> Utilizes data from various cities over a forty-year period. Concludes that, because of low voter turnout due largely to nonpartisan elections, the electorate on city elections is far less representative of the general populace than it is in presidential elections.

1497 Hammack, David C. "Participation in Major Decisions in New York City, 1890-1900: The Creation of Greater New York and the Centralization of the Public School System." Ph.D. dissertation, Columbia University, 1973. 484 p.

> Concludes that power in New York City was more concentrated than Wallace Sayre and Herbert Kaufman reported in GOVERNING NEW YORK CITY and discusses possible reasons for the greater concentration of the 1890s.

1498 Hanlon, Edward F. "Urban-Rural Cooperation and Conflict in the Congress: The Breakdown of the New Deal Coalition, 1933-1938." Ph.D. dissertation, Georgetown University, 1967. 462 p.

> Analyzes over 200 votes on a variety of urban-related issues to demonstrate that conflict between northern urban Democrats and southern rural ones was a fundamental cause for the breakup of the New Deal coalition. Documents increase in the urban support of the New Deal from 1934 to 1938.

1499 Harris, Carl V. POLITICAL POWER IN BIRMINGHAM, 1871-1921. Twentieth Century America Series. Knoxville: University of Tennessee Press, 1977. 318 p.

> Divides Birmingham's politically effective population into three economic interest groups and analyzes their interaction on three key issue categories: extraction of revenue, provision of services, and regulation of business. Concludes that the upper 1 percent exerted the greatest influence, largely due to the structure of the decision-making process.

1500 Havens, Murray C. "Metropolitan Areas and Congress: Foreign Policy and National Security." JOURNAL OF POLITICS 26 (1964): 758-74.

> Analyzes roll calls in the House on military appropriations, foreign aid, and international trade policy between 1945 and 1962 to determine if urbanization was an independent variable. Finds that it has relatively little influence compared to socioeconomic and other considerations.

1501 Hays, Samuel P. "The Changing Political Structure of the City in Industrial America." JOURNAL OF URBAN HISTORY 1 (1974): 6-38.

> Develops a conceptual framework for understanding the evolution of the city since the mid-nineteenth century which discards the traditional model of reformers versus reactionaries. In its place he suggests a constant tension between forces of decentralization and centralization in human relationships and institutions, between centrifugal and centripetal tendencies, and between social differentiation and social integration.

1502 _____. "Political Parties and the Community-Society Continuum." In THE AMERICAN PARTY SYSTEMS: STAGES OF POLITICAL DEVELOPMENT, edited by William N. Chambers and Walter D. Burnham, pp. 152-81. New York: Oxford University Press, 1967.

> Argues that urban political organization reflected the transition from community to society and that the corresponding evolution from localized political structures to centralized ones accounted for different levels of political participation on the part of different socioeconomic groups and favored the organized, upper middle class.

1503 Heale, M.J. "From City Fathers to Social Critics: Humanitarianism and Government in New York, 1790-1860." JOURNAL OF AMERICAN HISTORY 63 (1976): 21-41.

> Argues that the fragmented, overcrowded, heterogeneous city of the mid-nineteenth century led to a split between government and welfare, with the former controlled by party machines and the latter by evangelical missionaries and charity workers. Contends that the latter functioned as critics of municipal government and helped pave the way for later humanitarian reforms.

1504 _____. "Harbingers of Progressivism: Responses to the Urban Crisis in New York, c. 1845-1860." JOURNAL OF AMERICAN STUDIES 10 (1976): 17-36.

> Compares the antebellum reformers in New York City to the progressive profile sketched by the "status revolution" scholars of the Progressive era. Sees the reforms of both periods as being produced by a coalition of humanitarians and politicians.

1505 Healy, Patrick. THE NATION'S CITIES: CHANGE AND CHALLENGE.

New York: Harper and Row, 1974. 288 p.

> Surveys city government in the United States since the formation of the National League of Cities in 1924, focusing on its development, changing problems, programs, and structure; its ability to cope with burgeoning urban problems; and its prospects for the future.

1506 Hendrickson, Kenneth E., Jr. "George R. Lunn and the Socialist Era in Schenectady, New York, 1909-1916." NEW YORK HISTORY 47 (1966): 22-40.

> Attributes Lunn's success to consumer discontent with various city utilities and with General Electric, but concludes that arguments between Lunn and the local Socialist party prevented any really effective reforms.

1507 _____. "The Socialist Administration in Reading, Pennsylvania, Part I, 1927-1931." PENNSYLVANIA HISTORY 39 (1972): 417-42.

> Attributes the Socialists' success in the city to discontent among homeowners with rising property taxes and the former's pledge of "scientific assessment." Assigns that eventual defeat largely to the party's failure to cope with the Great Depression and to fusion of the two major parties.

1508 _____. "Triumph and Disaster: The Reading Socialists in Power and Decline, 1932-1939, Part II." PENNSYLVANIA HISTORY 40 (1973): 381-411.

> Contends that the Socialists returned to power in 1935 largely because of their effective criticism of the city's relief and recovery efforts and lost in 1939 due to a split in the party over popular front activities.

1509 Hennessey, Timothy, and Feen, Richard H. "Social Science as Social Philosophy: Edward C. Banfield and the 'New Realism' in Urban Politics." AMERICAN BEHAVIORAL SCIENTIST 17 (1973): 171-204.

> Compares Banfield's view of city reformers in THE UNHEAVENLY CITY (no. 1436) to that of William Graham Sumner and the nineteenth-century Social Darwinists. Contends that Banfield's "New Realism" is really a sophisticated exposition of laissez-faire economics and Social Darwinism.

1510 Hershkowitz, Leo. "New York City, 1834-1840, A Study in Local Politics." Ph.D. dissertation, New York University, 1960. 545 p.

> Finds that the Jacksonian Democrats based their strength primarily upon immigrants and workers and some merchants, while the Whigs attracted the majority of merchants, nativists, and old Federalists and National Republicans. Concludes that by 1840 the city had become essentially "Democratic."

1511 Heyda, Sister Marie. "The Urban Dimension and the Midwestern Frontier: A Study of Democracy at Ypsilanti, Michigan: 1825-1858." Ph.D. dissertation, University of Michigan, 1966. 362 p.

> Develops a predictive model for the emergence of democracy based upon the Ypsilanti experience and identifies the crucial variables as a time of critical problems, the presence of a spirit of egalitarianism, and the settlers' possession of some adeptness in the political traditions of western civilization.

1512 Hoffecker, Carol E. "The Politics of Exclusion: Blacks in Late Nineteenth-Century Wilmington, Delaware." DELAWARE HISTORY 16 (1974): 60-72.

> Contends that both major political parties agreed in excluding blacks, with the immigrant-based, labor-oriented Democrats denouncing them as tools of capitalism and the industrialist-dominated Republicans taking them for granted and refusing to accommodate blacks into the framework of economic issues.

1513 Holland, Reid. "The Civilian Conservation Corps in the City: Tulsa and Oklahoma City in the 1930s." CHRONICLES OF OKLAHOMA 53 (1975): 367-75.

> Emphasizes the work of the Civilian Conservation Corps in building urban parks in these Oklahoma cities. Concludes that the existence of the parks ultimately aided the recovery and continuing prosperity of Tulsa and Oklahoma City.

1514 _____. "Urban Frontier Leadership." Ph.D. dissertation, Oklahoma State University, 1972. 253 p.

> Examines the leadership in four Plains cities--Tulsa, Kansas City, Omaha, and Des Moines--in the early twentieth century and compares the social and political activity of the elites of each city.

1515 Holliday, Harold L., and Whipple, David. "Free Speech and the Right of Municipalities to Regulate the Use of Public Places, 1919-1951." UNIVERSITY OF KANSAS CITY LAW REVIEW 19 (1951): 191-204.

> Concentrates on the difficulties of balancing the right of free speech against the requirement of the municipality to protect the interests of its citizens. Concludes that prior restraint is always unconstitutional, but that the validity of imposing sanctions after the fact is more uncertain.

1516 Holt, Michael F. "Forging a Majority: The Formation of the Republican Party in Pittsburgh, Pennsylvania, 1848-1860." Ph.D. dissertation, Johns Hopkins University, 1967. 539 p.

Finds that local ethnic, religious, and economic divisions influenced party alignments more than did such national issues as slavery, with the Republicans drawing primarily from native, Protestant businessmen, and Protestant immigrants, while the Democrats appealed largely to the Catholic immigrants and the working class.

1517 Homel, Michael W. "The Politics of Public Education in Black Chicago, 1910-1941." JOURNAL OF NEGRO EDUCATION 45 (1976): 179-91.

Argues that the alleged arbitrariness, competition, and favoritism of Chicago machine politics actually worked in favor of black demands for better education when legalism, civil service, and democratic public opinion did not. Concludes that reliance upon white politicians in the upper echelons of the organization was ultimately harmful.

1518 Howard, Perry H.; Long, William J.; and Zdrazil, G.A. "An Ecological Analysis of Voting Behavior in Baton Rouge: From Strom Thurmond to George Wallace." SOCIAL FORCES 50 (1971): 45-52.

Divides Baton Rouge into three ecological areas based upon occupational level and race and analyzes the presidential election returns between 1948 and 1968. Finds that upper-white and labor-white voters were looking for a non-Democratic alternative while blacks were becoming progressively more committed to the Democrats.

1519 Hurst, Marsha. "Integration, Freedom of Choice and Community Control in Nineteenth Century Brooklyn." JOURNAL OF ETHNIC STUDIES 3 (1975): 33-55.

Finds that "reformers" favoring centralization of the school system and racial integration were mostly upper-class professionals while black leaders generally sided with the board of education and other professional politicians in maintaining local control.

1520 Jackson, Kenneth T. "Metropolitan Government Versus Political Autonomy: Politics on the Crabgrass Frontier." In CITIES IN AMERICAN HISTORY, edited by Kenneth T. Jackson and Stanley K. Schultz, pp. 442-62. New York: Knopf, 1972.

Finds that the struggle between centralization in the name of efficiency and local control in the name of democracy has been a constant feature of urban politics for over two hundred years. Argues that governing functions be divided among metropolitan and local governments according to their nature.

1521 Jeffries, John W. TESTING THE ROOSEVELT COALITION: CON-

NECTICUT SOCIETY AND POLITICS IN THE ERA OF WORLD WAR II. Knoxville: University of Tennessee Press, 1979. 312 p.

> Focuses largely upon the cities and suburbs and their response to Roosevelt, the New Deal, and World War II. Finds that the coalition of 1936 largely persisted despite shifts in its geographic, ethnic, and socioeconomic proportions.

1522 Jones, Gene D. "The Origins of the Alliance Between the New Deal and the Chicago Machine." JOURNAL OF THE ILLINOIS STATE HISTORICAL SOCIETY 67 (1974): 253-74.

> Argues that, like most urban political machines, the Kelly-Nash organization opposed Roosevelt's nomination in 1932 but was later won over to his side because the New Deal's provided enormous political benefits.

1523 Judd, Jacob. "The Administrative Organization of the City of Brooklyn, 1834-1855: Part I, II." JOURNAL OF LONG ISLAND HISTORY 5 (1965): 4-16, 39-50.

> Describes the features of Brooklyn's charter and its operation in the mid-nineteenth century and details the political struggles for control of the city which resulted from its organizational features.

1524 Kantowicz, Edward R. POLISH-AMERICAN POLITICS IN CHICAGO, 1888-1940. Chicago: University of Chicago Press, 1975. 260 p.

> Examines the structure of Chicago's Polonia and traces its political evolution from the turn of the century to the early 1970s. Discusses the reasons why Chicago's largest ethnic group has failed to elect a mayor.

1525 Kaplan, Barry J. "A Study in the Politics of Metropolitanization: The Greater New York City Charter of 1897." Ph.D. dissertation, State University of New York, Buffalo, 1975. 420 p.

> Analyzes the struggle between advocates and opponents of consolidation of the New York area, the leaders, including Andrew Green, and compares the process with other American cities faced with metropolitanization.

1526 Kaufman, Herbert. "Robert Moses: Charismatic Bureaucrat." POLITICAL SCIENCE QUARTERLY 90 (1975): 521-38.

> Takes some issue with the portrayal of Moses in Robert Caro's THE POWER BROKER (1974). Denies that Moses wielded as much power as Caro alleges, but styles him a charismatic bureaucrat who dominated certain facets of New York City government.

1527 Knight, Robert. INDUSTRIAL RELATIONS IN THE SAN FRANCISCO BAY AREA, 1900-1918. Berkeley and Los Angeles: University of California Press, 1960. 463 p.

   Examines the impact on the city and its environs of the conflict between industry and a powerful labor movement, which eventually produced a political party (Union Labor party) that controlled city government for several years.

1528 Kotler, Milton. "The Disappearance of Municipal Liberty." POLITICS AND SOCIETY 3 (1972): 83-116.

   Contends that Boston's municipal liberties were at their zenith prior to the revolution when the city had a highly democratic constitution based upon a general meeting of its inhabitants and contends that municipal liberties were eroded when the new constitution substituted the elective franchise and the mayor-council form of government for deliberative citizenship.

1529 Kremm, Thomas W. "The Rise of the Republican Party in Cleveland, 1848-1860." Ph.D. dissertation, Kent State University, 1974. 341 p.

   Analyzes the conditions in Cleveland that fostered the rise of the Republican party. Concludes that the growing split between Protestants and Catholics dominated the city's politics.

1530 Lanahan, Anna M. "Brooklyn's Political Life, 1898-1916." Ph.D. dissertation, St. John's University, 1977. 374 p.

   Traces the evolution of Brooklyn's Democratic political machine during the period and investigates the nature of its conflict with the more famous Tammany Hall organization of Manhattan. Concludes that the Brooklyn machine was "parochial in the extreme" and "anti-Tammny, anti-agrarian-progressive, and anti-hypocritical."

1531 Leggett, John C. "Class Consciousness and Politics in Detroit: A Study in Change." MICHIGAN HISTORY 48 (1964): 289-314.

   Develops a broad overview of the interaction between Detroit workmen's structural position and sense of class consciousness for the period 1900-60, noting the social forces that have facilitated or impeded the formation and maintenance of that sense of class identity.

1532 Leonard, Ira M. "New York City Politics, 1841-1844: Nativism and Reform." Ph.D. dissertation, New York University, 1965. 488 p.

   Asserts that popular displeasure with municipal government, seen as subordinated to narrow partisan political interests, rather than ethnic and religious prejudice, accounts for the victory of the nativist movement in New York City.

1533 _____. "The Politics of Charter Revision in New York City, 1845-1847." NEW YORK HISTORICAL QUARTERLY 62 (1978): 43-70.

Examines the efforts of reformers to systematize and rationalize New York City government. Contends that professional politicians and the hordes of voters who held municipal jobs headed the successful effort to sidetrack charter reform.

1534 Lewinson, Edwin R. BLACK POLITICS IN NEW YORK CITY. New York: Twayne, 1974.

Presents an overview of the roles of blacks in the political process in New York City, concentrating on the years since 1870, and analyzes the factors that have retarded or facilitated blacks gaining political power. Has chapters on two contemporary political figures, Adam Clayton Powell and J. Raymond Jones.

1535 Liebert, Roland J. DISINTEGRATION AND POLITICAL ACTION: THE CHANGING FUNCTIONS OF CITY GOVERNMENTS IN AMERICA. New York: Academic Press, 1976. 223 p.

Accounts for contemporary variations in the functional scope of American muncipal governments by examining the historical operation of three major forces shaping community development: local tradition, national trends toward bureaucratic complexity and interdependency, and the increased demand for services generated by population growth.

1536 Lindquist, John H. "An Occupational Analysis of Local Politics: Syracuse, New York, 1880-1959." SOCIOLOGY AND SOCIAL RESEARCH 49 (1965): 343-54.

Argues that businessmen and professionals have dominated office holding in the city and that lawyers, merchants, and manufacturers have led all others in both public and political party offices. Contends that blue-collar and white-collar workers have achieved virtually no political status.

1537 Lineberry, Robert L., and Fowler, Edmund P. "Reformism and Public Policies in American Cities." AMERICAN POLITICAL SCIENCE REVIEW 61 (1967): 701-16.

Examines the impact of political structures, both reformed and unreformed, on policymaking in American cities by treating policy choices on taxation and expenditure levels of cities as a dependent variable and relating them to socioeconomic characteristics of cities and to structural characteristics of their governments.

1538 London, Herbert I. "The Nativist Movement in the American Republican Party in New York City During the Period 1843-1847." Ph.D. dissertation, New York University, 1966. 411 p.

Considers two hypotheses: (1) nativism in the American Republican party was hastened by the influx of Catholic immigrants; and (2) the nativist movement in the American Republican party accelerated the assimilation of immigrants.

1539 Lowi, Theodore J. AT THE PLEASURE OF THE MAYOR: PATRONAGE AND POWER IN NEW YORK CITY, 1898-1948. New York: Free Press of Glencoe, 1964. 272 p.

Combines the historical-descriptive recruitment and community power relations approaches to investigate the problem of whether the mayor's patronage power results in a dynamic pluralist democracy or a static system of corporate privilege.

1540 Lupsha, Peter A. "The Politics of Urban Change." CURRENT HISTORY 55 (1968): 327-332, 365-66.

Historical perspective on the development of urban politics and its role in the contemporary urban crisis, with speculations on likely directions of future change.

1541 McBain, Howard Lee. AMERICAN CITY PROGRESS AND THE LAW. New York: Columbia University Press, 1918. 352 p.

Based on lectures presented in 1917, analyzes legal principles in regard to urban government, policies and problems. Includes discussions of home rule, municipal powers, police, planning, municipal ownership, recreation, and the promotion of commerce and industry.

1542 McCandless, Carl A. URBAN GOVERNMENT AND POLITICS. New York: McGraw-Hill, 1970. 517 p.

Locates conflict of various types--socioeconomic, ethnocultural, and geographical--at the center of urban politics and argues that the function of politics is to provide a setting in which those conflicts can be resolved and compromised to the satisfaction of all parties.

1543 McCarthy, Michael P. "'Suburban Power': A Footnote on Cleveland in the Tom Johnson Years." NORTHWEST OHIO QUARTERLY 45 (1972): 21-27.

Shows the importance of the growing middle class which, as it moved further from downtown Cleveland, continued to support Mayor Tom Johnson and suburban annexation. As faith in the future of the central city and government centralization declined after World War I, so too did middle-class support for annexation, leaving the city and its politics isolated.

1544   McCaughey, Robert. "From Town into City: Boston in the 1820s." POLITICAL SCIENCE QUARTERLY 88 (1973): 191-213.

Suggests that by the 1820s, anonymity, disorder, and conflict-oriented politics already had appeared in Boston, an interpretation which challenges the traditional view that the consensual community characterized Boston until the 1840s.

1545   Macchiarola, Frank J. "The State and the City." PROCEEDINGS OF THE ACADEMY OF POLITICAL SCIENCE 31 (1974): 104-18.

Provides a brief historical summary of relations between New York City, then focuses on the nature of that relationship during the years of Rockefeller's governorship. Argues that availability of state resources, process of state politics, and degree of recognition of the seriousness of the city's needs form the critical backdrop for assuring city-state relations.

1546   MacColl, E. Kimbark. THE SHAPING OF A CITY: BUSINESS AND POLITICS IN PORTLAND, OREGON, 1885-1915. Portland, Ore.: Georgian Press, 1976. 534 p.

Examines the role which organized business played in the reform movement of the period, especially with regard to the physical expansion of the city and periodic antivice drives.

1547   McKenna, William J. "The Negro Vote in Philadelphia Elections." PENNSYLVANIA HISTORY 32 (1965): 406-15.

Examines black voting patterns in Philadelphia, focusing mainly on the years since 1960, and discusses reasons for the black community's strong and continuous identification with the Democratic party.

1548   Madden, Daniel R. "City-State Relations in Wisconsin, 1835-1901: The Origins of the Milwaukee Home Rule Movement." Ph.D. dissertation, University of Wisconsin, 1972. 315 p.

Traces changes in municipal autonomy in Wisconsin by focusing upon Milwaukee's local legislation as a salient indicator of trends in urban self-rule and city-state relations.

Urban Politics and Government

1549 Madgwick, P.J. "The Politics of Urban Renewal." JOURNAL OF AMERICAN STUDIES 5 (1971): 265-80.

> Analyzes the various political factors that have contributed to the failure to achieve the housing goals established by the Housing Act of 1949.

1550 Mann, Arthur. LA GUARDIA: A FIGHTER AGAINST HIS TIMES, 1882-1933. Chicago: University of Chicago Press, 1969. 384 p.

> Concentrates upon the forces, ethnic, socioeconomic, geographic, and intellectual, which made La Guardia into an urban liberal and which made him a political maverick in Congress during the 1920s.

1551 _____. LA GUARDIA COMES TO POWER. Chicago: University of Chicago Press, 1969. 199 p.

> Analyzes the reasons for La Guardia's victory over Tammany Hall in 1933, focusing upon his coalition of regular Republicans, reformers, and discontented Jews, Italians, and other non-Irish ethnics.

1552 Martin, Roscoe C. THE CITIES AND THE FEDERAL SYSTEM. New York: Atherton Press, 1965. Reprint. New York: Arno Press, 1978. 200 p.

> Calls for an expanded partnership between cities and the federal government in a metro-urban society to bypass often hostile state governments and discusses its potential in such areas as airport development, urban renewal, and public housing.

1553 Merino, James A. "Cooperative Schemes for Greater Boston: 1890-1920." NEW ENGLAND QUARTERLY 45 (1972): 196-226.

> Describes continuing and unsuccessful attempts to extend the political limits of Boston by establishing an authoritative metropolitan government.

1554 _____. "A Great City and Its Suburbs: Attempts to Integrate Metropolitan Boston, 1865-1920." Ph.D. dissertation, University of Texas, Austin, 1968. 167 p.

> Traces the development of various ideas for metropolitan coordination and offers explanations for Massachusetts' failure to meet the challenge of metropolitan government.

1555 Merriam, Charles. CHICAGO, A MORE INTIMATE VIEW OF URBAN POLITICS. New York: Macmillan Co., 1929. Reprint. New York: Arno Press, 1970. 305 p.

Provides a description of Chicago politics during the first few decades of the twentieth century, providing information on city builders and leaders, and formal and informal political processes. Includes comments and descriptive material on race, religion, sex, and social class.

1556   Miller, Richard G. PHILADELPHIA, THE FEDERALIST CITY: A STUDY IN URBAN POLITICS, 1789-1801. Port Washington, N.Y.: Kennikat Press, 1976. 192 p.

Gives reasons for the development of political parties in Philadelphia, the socioeconomic background of their leaders, and how American democracy functioned in an urban environment.

1557   Millett, John D. THE WORKS PROGRESS ADMINISTRATION IN NEW YORK CITY. Chicago: Published for Committee on Public Administration of the Social Science Research Council by Public Administration Service, 1938. Reprint. New York: Arno Press, 1978. 228 p.

Analyzes the Works Progress Administration's impact upon the city from the local level, focusing upon the activities of the division of operations, women's and professional programs, finance and statistics, and employment.

1558   Moses, Robert. WORKING FOR THE PEOPLE: PROMISE AND PERFORMANCE IN PUBLIC SERVICE. New York: Harper and Brothers, 1956. 283 p.

Presents an account of some of Moses' activities and experiences as related to the pragmatic problems of public administration, based on an edited compilation drawn from reports, speeches, letters, and articles dealing with various controversial issues of policy or administration.

1559   Mullins, William H. "San Francisco and Seattle during the Hoover Years of the Depression, 1929-1933." Ph.D. dissertation, University of Washington, 1975. 213 p.

Examines the attitudes and methods of local government in attempting to frame a response to the varied economic problems generated by the Great Depression, stressing the enlarged role of the local community and increasing retreat from the "individual ethic" which characterized Hoover.

1560   Nodyne, Kenneth R. "The Role of De Witt Clinton and the Municipal Government in the Development of Cultural Organizations in New York City, 1803 to 1817." Ph.D. dissertation, New York University, 1969. 255 p.

Views the eighteenth-century concept of paternalistic municipal governments and the growth of the spirit of cultural nationalism, as the two forces that were responsible for New York fostering its cultural organizations.

1561 Peel, Roy V. THE POLITICAL CLUBS OF NEW YORK CITY. 1935. Reprint. Port Washington, N.Y.: Kennikat Press, 1968. 360 p.

Examines the role played by political clubs as neighborhood voluntary associations which do much of the day-to-day work of organizing and campaigning for both machine and reform organizations. Deals with their financing, clubhouses, objectives, leadership, and activities.

1562 Pessen, Edward. "Who Governed the Nation's Cities in the 'Era of the Common Man'?" POLITICAL SCIENCE QUARTERLY 87 (1972): 591-614.

Examines government policies and the wealth and social status of officeholders in New York City, Brooklyn, Philadelphia, and Boston, during the Jacksonian era, concluding that elite elements of the population, specifically substantial property holders, exercised great political influence.

1563 Reichley, James. THE ART OF GOVERNMENT: REFORM AND ORGANIZATION POLITICS IN PHILADELPHIA. New York: Fund for the Republic, 1959. Dubuque, Iowa: Brown Reprints, 1972. 128 p.

Based largely on interviews, analyzes the nature and impact of reform politics in Philadelphia for the period 1949-58. Contends that while the reform movement produced some worthwhile and permanent institutional change, its one real failure lay in not altering the practices of urban politics in any meaningful fashion.

1564 Reinders, Robert C. END OF AN ERA, NEW ORLEANS, 1850-1860. New Orleans: Pelican, 1964. 250 p.

Focuses on political developments at the grass roots level in the decade before the Civil War, detailing the issues that concerned the average citizen, the solutions proposed to deal with urban problems, and the origins of modern urban political organization.

1565 Rischin, Moses. "Sunny Jim Rolph: The First 'Mayor' of All the People." CALIFORNIA HISTORICAL QUARTERLY 53 (1974): 165-72.

Provides an overview of the life and political career of San Francisco's five-term mayor of the early twentieth century. Sees Rolph as the "first modern American mayor" and a symbol of the human and communal possibilities of the modern great city.

Urban Politics and Government

1566 Rodgers, Cleveland. ROBERT MOSES: BUILDER FOR DEMOCRACY. New York: Holt, 1952. 356 p.

    Laudatory biography of Robert Moses, stressing his contribution to urban planning and design in New York City, his philosophy of democratic government and its impact on Moses' political style, as well as his influence in urban design in other areas of the world.

1567 Ryan, Joseph F. "Abraham Lincoln and New York City, 1861-1865: War and Politics." Ph.D. dissertation, St. John's University, 1969. 363 p.

    Discusses the interdependent relationship between Lincoln and New York City resulting from the Civil War and the demands of party politics. Usually under attack by the city's Republicans, he was afforded unanimous support on all the important objectives of the war.

1568 Salisbury, Robert H. "Urban Politics: The New Convergence of Power." JOURNAL OF POLITICS 26 (1964): 775-97.

    Provides an historical investigation of the question of the structure of power, focusing on the big U.S. cities whose major growth occurred prior to World War I. Notes the developing bifurcation of power between economic and political elites as a function of the changing industrial and social order in the city and as a prelude to the contemporary situation characterized by a "new convergence."

1569 Scott, George W. "The New Order of Cincinnatus: Municipal Politics in Seattle during the 1930s." PACIFIC NORTHWEST QUARTERLY 64 (1973): 137-46.

    Discusses the issues animating municipal politics in Seattle, focusing on the reform efforts of Cincinnatus, an organization created by a Seattle attorney which ran various candidates for public office. For three years the organization functioned as a civic conscience, but it failed to make the transition between protest and the implementation of reform.

1570 Shover, John L. "The Emergence of a Two-Party System in Republican Philadelphia, 1924-1936." JOURNAL OF AMERICAN HISTORY 60 (1974): 985-1002.

    Examines ethnic and social-class voting patterns in Philadelphia to underscore the inadequacy of the critical election concept. Urges instead, the concept of a critical period, a model that focuses on processes.

1571 _____. "Ethnicity and Religion in Philadelphia Politics, 1924-1940."

AMERICAN QUARTERLY 25 (1973): 499-515.

> Presents empirical tests of the influence of persistent ethnic loyalties on voting behavior and concludes that ethno-religious political consciousness proved a potent factor.

1572 Shufro, Joel A. "Boston in Massachusetts Politics, 1730-1760." Ph.D. dissertation, University of Wisconsin, Madison, 1976. 393 p.

> Details the role of Massachusetts, Boston in particular, in pre-revolutionary politics and characterizes the opposition to the British interference as a "popular discontent" which formed the base to the opposition party.

1573 Shumsky, Neil L. "San Francisco's Workingmen Respond to the Modern City." CALIFORNIA HISTORY QUARTERLY 55 (1976): 46-57.

> Contends that as American cities modernized during the latter half of the nineteenth century, creating new economic, political, and social systems, they also created a new type of individual, the workingman, for whom the "very essence" of urban life was struggle, "social, political, and religious as well as economic." Develops this theme by focusing on the activities of the Working Man's party in San Francisco, which functioned as social club, fraternal organization, political machine, and church, and helped to mediate between the workingman and the modern city.

1574 Silver, Arthur M. "Jews in the Political Life of New York City, 1865-1897." Ph.D. dissertation, Yeshiva University, 1954. 241 p.

> Studies the political activities of the Jews of New York City and determines their political attitude and voting habits.

1575 Smith, Roland M. "The Politics of Pittsburgh Flood Control, 1936-1960." PENNSYLVANIA HISTORY 44 (1977): 3-24.

> Analyzes the role of Pittsburgh's business and professional elites in civic affairs. Focuses on their activities as members of the Citizens' Committee on Flood Control and of the Flood Commission of Pittsburgh, both agencies of the city's chamber of commerce.

1576 Sobczak, John N. "The Politics of Relief: Public Aid in Toledo, 1933-1937." NORTHWESTERN OHIO QUARTERLY 48 (1976): 134-42.

> Argues that such local political conditions as the patronage system and factionalism, obstructed relief efforts, significantly contributing to the inadequacies of relief in Toledo.

1577 Sparks, Frank M. GOVERNMENT AS A BUSINESS. Chicago: Rand McNally, 1916. 284 p.

Outlines fundamental principles of municipal government from a practical as opposed to a theoretical perspective. Includes discussions of various forms of city government, taxes, services, and franchises, and provides brief historical sketches on basic institutions and practices.

1578 Spaulding, Charles B. "Occupational Affiliations of Councilmen in Small Cities." SOCIOLOGY AND SOCIAL RESEARCH 35 (1950): 194-208.

Analyzes the occupational status and political alliances of city council members in the small cities of southern California using data collected for May and June, 1948, and then compared with data for 1933. Notes the "continuing and relatively undisputed dominance of the traditional propertied, business and professional groups."

1579 Stave, Bruce M. THE NEW DEAL AND THE LAST HURRAH: PITTSBURGH MACHINE POLITICS. Pittsburgh: University of Pittsburgh Press, 1970. 262 p.

Investigates the origins of the Pittsburgh Democratic machine, as rooted in the New Deal, arguing that Roosevelt's policies, rather than undermining the bosses "facilitated the transfer of urban political power from Republicans to Democrats."

1580 _____, ed. SOCIALISM AND THE CITIES. Port Washington, N.Y.: Kennikat Press, 1975. 212 p.

A series of seven essays introduced by the editor and concluding with an appendix of a reprinted 1913 letter from Walter Lippmann on municipal socialism. Essays by James R. Green, Sally Miller, Kenneth E. Hendrickson, Jr., Michael Ebner, and Garin Burbank, cover Milwaukee, Wisconsin; Reading, Pennsylvania; and Passaic, New Jersey, during the Progressive era.

1581 Stevens, Errol W. "Heartland Socialism: The Socialist Party of America in Four Midwestern Communities, 1898-1920." Ph.D. dissertation, Indiana University, 1978. 268 p.

Studies party activities in Milwaukee, Wisconsin; Canton, Illinois; and Elwood and Marion, Indiana. Locates its support primarily among skilled workers galvanized by economic crisis and finds that each local pursued reformist, rather than revolutionary, policies and that each was severely damaged by World War I.

1582 Stickle, Warren E. "Edward I. Edwards and the Urban Coalition of 1919." NEW JERSEY HISTORY 90 (1972): 83-96.

Urban Politics and Government

Discusses the applejack campaign of 1919 in New Jersey as the start of a political realignment which saw the creation of a new urban Democrat coalition, sparked by considerations of ethnicity as opposed to Americanization in regard to the issue of Prohibition.

1583 _____. "New Jersey Democracy and the Urban Coalition: 1919-1932." Ph.D. dissertation, Georgetown University, 1971. 664 p.

Details the gradual development of a newer American coalition in New Jersey based on the existence of common enemies and causes like the Ku Klux Klan and prohibition, which submerged former cleavages between "old" and "new immigrants" and stimulated ethnic pluralism and cultural liberalism. Stresses this development as occurring from the bottom up, flowing out from the wards and precincts of New Jersey's cities to state and national politics.

1584 Sullivan, Martin E. "'On the Dole': The Relief Issue in Detroit, 1929-1939." Ph.D. dissertation, University of Notre Dame, 1974. 255 p.

Uses Detroit to study the development of public assistance policies, the effects of New Deal relief activities on the economy during the thirties, and the political and economic consequences of unionization of the auto industry, especially during the 1937-38 recession.

1585 Syrett, Harold C. THE CITY OF BROOKLYN, 1865-1898: A POLITICAL HISTORY. New York: AMS Press, 1968. 293 p.

Focuses upon the political history of Brooklyn from the end of the Civil War to its incorporation into greater New York, the internal struggle between the professional politicians and the reformers of Seth Low, and the conflict with the state legislature in Albany over home rule.

1586 Teaford, Jon C. CITY AND SUBURB: THE POLITICAL FRAGMENTATION OF METROPOLITAN AMERICA, 1850-1970. Baltimore: Johns Hopkins University Press, 1979. 231 p.

Contends that many upper middle-class gentry of the 1920s and 1930s sought to refashion the urban structure of government in order to gain the benefits of both local control and centralization. Examines their concept of the "federative metropolis" and the reasons for its failure.

1587 Teska, Anona. "The Federal Impact on the Cities." In PERSPECTIVES ON URBAN AMERICA, edited by Melvin I. Urofsky, pp. 267-94. New York: Anchor, 1967.

Considers the ways in which federal programs not specifically designed to deal with urban problems, for example, the Public Works Administration, have powerfully affected America's cities.

1588   Thomas, Thaddeus P. "The City Government of Baltimore." Ph.D. dissertation, Johns Hopkins University, 1895. 51 p.

Focuses upon the administrative and legislative machinery of the city and the evolution of the commission form of government. Includes a critique of the commission form as increasing patronage and fragmenting vital functions.

1589   Thurner, Arthur W. "Polish Americans in Chicago Politics, 1890-1930." POLISH AMERICAN STUDIES 28 (1971): 20-42.

Discusses the evolution of ethnic politics among Chicago's Polish Americans and concludes that they failed to achieve the material benefits and recognition to which their numbers entitled them, largely because of Irish domination of the Democratic party.

1590   Trout, Charles H. BOSTON, THE GREAT DEPRESSION, AND THE NEW DEAL. New York: Oxford University Press, 1977. 401 p.

Discusses the impact of New Deal programs on Boston's economy, political traditions, and social life, noting the considerable degree to which pre-Depression legacies endured. Also stresses the ways in which the New Deal policies were altered by local forces, conditions, and political processes.

1591   U.S. National Resources Committee. URBAN GOVERNMENT. Washington, D.C.: Government Printing Office, 1939. Reprint. New York: Arno Press, 1978.

Contains articles by five leading urbanologists of the day on the development of urban government, federal-city relations, muncipal lobbying groups, and public safety.

1592   Van Valen, Nelson S. "Power Politics: The Struggle for Municipal Ownership of Electric Utilities in Los Angeles, 1905-1937." Ph.D. dissertation, Claremont Graduate School and University Center, 1964. 404 p.

Investigates the quarter-century-long dispute between the private utility companies and the city over who was to generate the power from the Owens' group project and who was to distribute it. Concludes that the civic forces prevailed because of the financial advantages in municipal ownership and effective political action.

Urban Politics and Government

1593 Vaughan, Philip H. "President Truman's Committee on Civil Rights: The Urban Implications." MISSOURI HISTORICAL REVIEW 66 (1972): 413-30.

    Sees the Civil Rights Committee as reflecting an egalitarian ethic and a determination to make cities safe. Notes that the goals of preserving America's cities and securing black rights provided a framework for subsequent presidential administrations.

1594 _____. "Urban Aspects of Civil Rights and the Early Truman Administration, 1946-1948." Ph.D. dissertation, University of Oklahoma, 1971. 178 p.

    Explores the attitudes of black intellectuals and white liberals who, in the 1940s, increasingly denounced the deplorable conditions confronting black urban dwellers and provided the impetus of a new civil rights movement. Focuses particularly on the Committee on Civil Rights established by Truman, and the President's commitment to securing black rights and preserving the nation's cities, as well as his recognition of the vital link between those two goals.

1595 Walker, Samuel E. "Terence V. Powderly: 'Labor Mayor': Workingmen's Politics in Scranton, Pennsylvania, 1870-1884." Ph.D. dissertation, Ohio State University, 1973.

    Investigates the insurgent workingmen's movements which stressed improved city government and efficient handling of municipal finances. Also examines the political career of local labor leader Terence Powderly, whose career illustrates the impact of the community environment on the outlook of workingmen.

1596 Watts, Eugene J. "Property and Politics in Atlanta: 1865-1903." JOURNAL OF URBAN HISTORY 3 (1977): 295-333.

    Develops and refines an analytical model of the several factors in urban elections, using multivariate statistical analysis. Concludes that larger property holdings were "a constant if not overriding correlate of political success," save in contests for councilmen where no attribute proved a good predictor of political performance.

1597 _____. THE SOCIAL BASES OF CITY POLITICS: ATLANTA, 1865-1903. Westport, Conn.: Greenwood Press, 1978. 188 p.

    Examines the qualifications of political candidates in Atlanta during the period and finds that substantial property holders formed a disproportionately large portion of the group. Suggests a model and methodology for similar studies in other cities.

1598 Wheeler, William B. "Urban Politics in Nature's Republic: The Development of Political Parties in the Seaport Cities in the Federalist Era." Ph.D. dissertation, University of Virginia, 1967. 507 p.

> Focuses on Philadelphia, New York, Baltimore, and Boston in an examination of the development and composition of the Federalist and the Republican political parties. Concludes that the Federalists offered opportunity in 1787, but it was the Republicans who by 1800 offered the "very promise of American life."

1599 Willis, Edmund P. "Social Origins of Political Leadership in New York City from the Revolution to 1815." Ph.D. dissertation, University of California, Berkeley, 1967. 393 p.

> Presents a career line study of New York City's elected office holders to examine the social origins of the political leaders and how the patterns of social characteristics varied and to discover if a continuity of political ideology existed from prewar to postwar times.

1600 Wolfinger, Raymond, and Field, John. "Political Ethos and the Structure of City Government." AMERICAN POLITICAL SCIENCE REVIEW 60 (1966): 306-26.

> Presents arguments indicating the need for substantial modifications in the ethos theory, which explains political patterns as a reflection of two differing conceptions of public interest, held by native middle class reformers and the immigrant. Research design is based on 1960 data, but implications and commentary relate to earlier historical periods.

Chapter 11
BOSSES, MACHINES, AND URBAN REFORM

1601 Addams, Jane. "Political Reform." In BOSSES AND REFORMERS, edited by Blaine A. Brownell and Warren E. Stickle, pp. 118-36. Boston: Houghton, Mifflin, 1973.

> Pronounces the village ideal of the machine politician more meaningful to ethnic neighborhoods than the negative and abstract prescriptions of reformers.

1602 _____. TWENTY YEARS AT HULL HOUSE. New York: Macmillan, 1966. 462 p.

> An autobiography which covers the first twenty years of Jane Addams at Hull House, including influences on her work, the founding of Hull House, work on labor legislation in Illinois, and efforts to help the immigrants and promote education.

1603 _____. "Why the Ward Boss Rules." THE OUTLOOK 58 (1898): 879-82.

> Attributes the success of the ward boss to his humanness and friendliness, to his ability to provide jobs for his immigrant constituents, and to his affecting of a life-style that made the latter envious.

1604 Alloway, David N. THE AGONY OF THE CITIES: URBAN PROBLEMS IN CONTEMPORARY AMERICA. Upper Montclair, N.J.: Montclair State College Press, 1969. 59 p.

> Examines the roots of the contemporary urban crisis and the reasons for the failure of the previous social reform movements. Urges solutions that involve both professional expertise and popular participation.

1605 Allswang, John M. BOSSES, MACHINES AND URBAN VOTERS: AN AMERICAN SYMBIOSIS. Port Washington, N.Y.: Kennikat Press, 1977. 157 p.

Analyzes the literature on urban political machines and the reasons for their success or failure in dealing with city problems and then compares the careers of William Marcy Tweed, Charles Francis Murphy, Big Bill Thompson, Anton Cermak, and Richard J. Daley.

1606   Armbruster, Timothy Deegan. "The American City, 1890-1920: A Search for Understanding and Control." Ph.D. dissertation, Case Western Reserve University, 1974. 225 p.

Focuses upon such middle-class urban reform agencies as the National Municipal League and upon its moral fervor which was both its fundamental strength and salient weakness. Links structural reform to antiurban ideology.

1607   Aronson, David Israel. "The City Club of New York: 1892-1912." Ph.D. dissertation, New York University, 1975. 670 p.

Insists that the City Club, which began as an elitist organization dedicated to the good government, mugwump type of reform, evolved into a more middle-class activist organization with an interest in social and economic issues. Pronounces it conservative and efficiency-oriented, but motivated by a genuine sense of civic mindedness.

1608   Baughin, William A. "Murray Seasongood: Twentieth-Century Urban Reformer." Ph.D. dissertation, University of Cincinnati, 1972. 1,176 p.

Contends that population stability and homogenity postponed reform in Cincinnati until 1923. Argues that, despite differences in leadership styles and goals, efficiency minded reformers eventually turned Cincinnati into the best governed city in America.

1609   Bean, Walton. BOSS REUF'S SAN FRANCISCO. Berkeley and Los Angeles: University of California Press, 1952. 344 p.

Examines Abe Reuf's political organization, his connection with the Union Labor party, and the graft prosecutions which gave rise to much other reformist activity in California. Accepts the standard boss-reformer dichotomy.

1610   Beirne, Charles J. "Jersey City's Experiment with Commission Government." NEW JERSEY HISTORY 82 (1964): 109-20.

A brief account of the passage of the Walsh-Leavitt bill in the state legislature, the campaigns in Jersey City for the adoption of the commission form of municipal government, and the reasons for the failure of the adopted reform to improve local government in any substantial way.

Bosses, Machines, Urban Reform

1611 Bernard, Richard M., and Rice, Bradley R. "Political Environment and the Adoption of Progressive Municipal Reform." JOURNAL OF URBAN HISTORY 1 (1975): 149-74.

    A quantitative study of over 150 cities to determine what variables correlated with adoption of either a commission or city manager form of municipal government. Concludes that advocates of such structural reforms were most likely to succeed in cities that were small, young, ethnically homogeneous, and which enjoyed relatively high socioeconomic status.

1612 Blackford, Mansel G. "Reform Politics in Seattle During the Progressive Era, 1902-1916." PACIFIC NORTHWEST QUARTERLY 59 (1968): 177-85.

    Holds the division between two groups of workingmen, the one native or "Old Immigrant," skilled homeowners and the other unskilled "New Immigrants," held the key to reform in Seattle. Argues that the former supported middle-class reform and grew increasingly conservative while the latter moved increasingly toward labor radicalism after 1914.

1613 Blassingame, Lurton W. "Frank J. Goodnow and the American City." Ph.D. dissertation, New York University, 1968. 179 p.

    Analyzes Goodnow's thought and develops two major themes: (1) his insistence upon separating politics and polity formulation from administration or execution of policy and (2) his attempt to transform the "boss" into a responsible party leader through open primaries, civil service, and tenure in office.

1614 Boyer, Paul. URBAN MASSES AND MORAL ORDER IN AMERICA, 1820-1920. Cambridge, Mass.: Harvard University Press, 1978. 387 p.

    Contends that the underlying assumption of three generations of urban reformers was that the city, despite its obvious differences from the village, should replicate the latter's moral order. Also argues that the reformers themselves differed over whether to create this moral order by coercive legislation or by improving the urban environment.

1615 Breckinridge, Sophonisba P., ed. THE CHILD IN THE CITY: A SERIES OF PAPERS PRESENTED AT THE CONFERENCES HELD DURING THE CHICAGO CHILD WELFARE EXHIBIT. Chicago: Manz Engraving Co., Hollister Press, 1912. Reprint. New York: Arno Press, 1978.

    Contains papers on various aspects of the life of children in the city by participants at the 1911 exhibit, including Breckinridge, Julia Lathrop, Lillian Wald, Jane Addams, Florence Kelly, and Charles Zueblin.

1616 Bremner, Robert H. "The Civic Revival in Ohio." AMERICAN JOURNAL OF ECONOMICS AND SOCIOLOGY 10 (1951): 185-206, 301-12, 417-29; 11 (1952): 99-100.

> Examines how Mayors Tom Johnson in Cleveland and "Golden Rule" Jones and Brand Whitlock in Toledo applied their theories of special privilege, taxation and municipal ownership to their respective cities; how they helped achieve home rule and initiative and referendum in 1912; and how they battled the special interests opposed to civic revival.

1617 Brown, A. Theodore. THE POLITICS OF REFORM: KANSAS CITY'S MUNICIPAL GOVERNMENT, 1925-1950. Kansas City, Mo.: Community Studies, 1958. 430 p.

> Contends that the municipal reform movement in Kansas was successful and long-lived because it refused to forego positive programs to improve city life and municipal services merely to save money or keep the tax burden low. Argues that the movement redefined politics rather than eliminated it.

1618 Brownell, Blaine A., and Stickle, Warren E., eds. BOSSES AND REFORMERS: URBAN POLITICS IN AMERICA, 1880-1920. Boston: Houghton Mifflin, 1973. 252 p.

> A book of readings, composed of fourteen selections by scholars and contemporaries grouped into three categories: (1) the city boss in the context of the urban political machine, (2) urban reform, and (3) the city boss and progressive reform. An introductory essay places the readings in historiographical context and emphasizes that the traditional boss-reformer dichotomy is not an accurate way of viewing progressive politics. (Individual selections are annotated under the authors' names.)

1619 Bryce, James. THE AMERICAN COMMONWEALTH. 3 vols. New York: AMS Press, 1973.

> Charges that bosses had no social value or redeeming features, were interested only in the material rewards of their positions, and manipulated ignorant ethnic voters at the expense of "good" citizens.

1620 Bullough, William A. "Hannibal versus the Blind Boss: The 'Junta,' Chris Buckley, and Democratic Reform Politics in San Francisco." PACIFIC HISTORICAL REVIEW 46 (1977): 181-206.

> Demonstrates that the coalition of businessmen, professional officeholders, and reformers which formed the Junta used the same tactics in ousting San Francisco Democratic political boss Christopher A. Buckley it accused him of using in the 1890s to gain and retain power.

1621 Callow, Alexander B., Jr. THE TWEED RING. New York: Oxford University Press, 1966. 351 p.

> Presents the ring as the first full-blown urban political machine in America and analyzes the sources of its power, its functions, and the reasons for its demise. Concludes that the reformers who destroyed Tweed never understood the reasons for his success and left the door open for the revival of Tammany Hall.

1622 _____, ed. THE CITY BOSS IN AMERICA: AN INTERPRETIVE READER. New York: Oxford University Press, 1976. 335 p.

> Contains selections by over two dozen urban analysts on the critical features of machine politics: the rise of the boss, running the machine, the boss and the immigrant, corruption, the boss and the reformer, and the modern machine. Includes introductory essays to each section by the editor.

1623 Calvert, Monte A. "The Manifest Functions of the Machine." In URBAN BOSSES, MACHINES, AND PROGRESSIVE REFORMERS, edited by Bruce M. Stave, pp. 45-55. Lexington, Mass.: D.C. Heath, 1972.

> Argues that the machine politicians were generalists with a broad developmental viewpoint that allowed them to provide necessary urban services at a cost that, even with the attendant graft, was less than that permitted by any viable alternative.

1624 Cerillo, Augustus, Jr. "Reform in New York City: A Study of Urban Progressivism." Ph.D. dissertation, Northwestern University, 1969. 286 p.

> Compares Progressive era reformers to the patrician reformers of the late nineteenth century and finds that the former were largely recruited from the professions and that they departed sharply from the practice of their predecessors by emphasizing research over reform, process over panacea, and administration over men and measures.

1625 _____. "The Reform of Municipal Government in New York City: From Seth Low to John Purroy Mitchel." NEW YORK HISTORICAL SOCIETY QUARTERLY 57 (1973): 51-71.

> Contrasts the late nineteenth-century New York reformers, who sought to promote reform by "turning the rascals out" and replacing them with good men, with reformers during the early part of the twentieth century who viewed reform as an administrative process, calling for reliance on experts, the

development of the Bureau of Municipal Research, and bureaucratic innovations.

1626 Chalmers, Leonard. "Fernando Wood and Tammany Hall: The First Phase." NEW YORK HISTORICAL SOCIETY QUARTERLY 52 (1968): 379-402.

Presents Wood as the prototype of the Tammany Hall boss who mastered the techniques of winning the support of the urban electorate, manipulating party machinery, and stealing elections. Finds that Wood failed to gain complete control of Tammany because he refused to share patronage with other sachems.

1627 _____. "Tammany Hall and New York City Politics, 1853-1861." Ph.D. dissertation, New York University, 1967. 258 p.

Contends that Tammany's General Committee owed its hegemony to its continuity, its use of the immigrant vote, dispensation of patronage, and its stamp of approval from the organization's sachems. Argues that its first "boss," Fernando Wood, advanced the Hall's influence through advocacy of home rule and expansion of executive power, but rent the party with factionalism by his blatant self-interest.

1628 _____. "Tammany Hall, Fernando Wood, and the Struggle to Control New York City, 1857-1859." NEW YORK HISTORICAL SOCIETY QUARTERLY 53 (1969): 7-33.

Locates Wood's success in his ability to appeal to the city's immigrant vote and to relate urban problems to politics. Regards Wood's use of municipal patronage as the inspiration for the Tweed Ring and the birth of the city's political machine.

1629 Clark, Geoffrey W. "The Progressives versus the Political Machine in Hoboken, 1911-1915." In HOBOKEN: A COLLECTION OF ESSAYS, edited by Edward Halsey Foster and Geoffrey W. Clark, pp. 63-79. New York: Irvington Publishers, 1976.

Examines the struggle between the business-oriented, WASP, upper-class reformers and the political machine backed by the Irish and Italian working class. Concludes that the latter won the struggle because it actually aided the ethnic working class in its fight for prosperity and dignity.

1630 Cline, Dorothy I. ALBUQUERQUE AND THE CITY MANAGER PLAN, 1917-1948. Albuquerque: University of New Mexico, 1951. 48 p.

Contends that the nonpartisan aspect of the city manager plan extracted the core from the democratic process, and left government to the jockeying of blocs, factions, and interests operating behind the scenes. Insists that political parties are essential to the operation of a metropolis in a democratic fashion.

1631 Cohen, Sol. PROGRESSIVES AND URBAN SCHOOL REFORM: THE PUBLIC EDUCATION ASSOCIATION OF NEW YORK CITY, 1895-1954. New York: Bureau of Publications, Teacher's College of Columbia University, 1964. 273 p.

Examines the efforts of school reformers to deal with the social problems posed by immigrant children and the slums and presents progressive education as part of a broader social reform effort which had its apex during the Progressive era.

1632 Colburn, David R., and Pozzetta, George E. "Bosses and Machines: Changing Interpretations in American History." HISTORY TEACHER 9 (1976): 445-63.

An historiographical essay tracing the changing interpretations of the political machine from the 1880s to the present. Places the role of Progressive era machines in the larger context of later interpretations of the period, highlighting works by Eric McKitrick, Richard Wade, J. Joseph Huthmacher, John Buenker, and Humbert Nelli.

1633 Collett, Kay G., and Alexander, Henry M. THE CITY MANAGER PLAN IN ARKANSAS. Fayetteville: University of Arkansas Division of Public Administration, 1966. 112 p.

Briefly surveys the outlines of the city manager system nationwide and focuses upon its structure and operation in the state. Also analyzes the sources of support and opposition to its adoption.

1634 Commons, John R. "Referendum and Initiative in City Government." POLITICAL SCIENCE QUARTERLY 17 (1902): 609-30.

Contends that cities have three distinct types of problems--technical, business, and political--and that these require both political and business organization. Calls for the separation of political and technical issues and a division of authority between the expert and the politician.

1635 Connors, Richard J. A CYCLE OF POWER: THE CAREER OF JERSEY CITY MAYOR FRANK HAGUE. Metuchen, N.J.: Scarecrow, 1971. 226 p.

Uses Hague as a case study of how American mayors achieve, exercise, and retain power. Argues that Hague tried to use his office to penetrate the city's formal and informal institutions, either tying them to his regime as satellites or neutralizing their power.

1636 Cornwell, Elmer E., Jr. "Bosses, Machines, and Ethnic Groups." ANNALS OF THE AMERICAN ACADEMY OF POLITICAL AND SOCIAL SCIENCES 353 (1964): 27-39.

> Discusses the symbiotic relationship between urban political machines and immigrants in the period before immigration restriction and the growth of government sponsored welfare services reduced the influence of political bosses. Since then, blacks and Puerto Ricans have become the new immigrants and they are gradually being absorbed by the urban party organizations, albeit in a somewhat different way than were earlier immigrants.

1637 Crooks, James B. POLITICS AND PROGRESS: THE RISE OF URBAN PROGRESSIVISM IN BALTIMORE, 1895 TO 1911. Baton Rouge: Louisiana State University Press, 1968. 259 p.

> Presents an "analysis of the Baltimore reform elite, an account of the sequence of the reformers' rise to power from 1885 to 1911, and a review of the Baltimore attempt to enact the progressive reform agenda."

1638 Culton, Donald R. "Charles Dwight Willard: Los Angeles City Booster and Professional Reformer, 1888-1914." Ph.D. dissertation, University of Southern California, 1971. 363 p.

> Traces Willard's evolution from city booster to professional reformer. Portrays him as representative of the city's business and professional elite and as demonstrating the continuity between the mugwumps of the 1880s and the conservative reformers of the Progressive era.

1639 Dahlberg, Jane S. THE NEW YORK BUREAU OF MUNICIPAL RESEARCH: PIONEER IN GOVERNMENT ADMINISTRATION. New York: New York University Press, 1966. 258 p.

> A study of the bureau from 1907 to 1921. The bureau attempted to bring order to public administration by standardized accounting and business procedures.

1640 Davis, Allen F. SPEARHEADS FOR REFORM: THE SOCIAL SETTLEMENTS AND THE PROGRESSIVE MOVEMENT, 1890-1914. New York: Oxford University Press, 1967. 322 p.

> Studies the ideas and actions of leaders of the settlement house movement in Boston, Chicago, and New York to gauge their impact on reform movements of the period.

1641 Deaton, Thomas Mashburn. "Atlanta During the Progressive Era." Ph.D. dissertation, University of Georgia, 1969. 478 p.

>Contends that, although all segments of Atlanta society contributed to reform, the business community generally took the lead while officeholders usually led the opposition. Focuses mainly on structural political reform and antivice crusades.

1642 De Lorme, Roland L. "The Shaping of a Progressive: Edward P. Costigan and Urban Reform in Denver, 1900-1911." Ph.D. dissertation, University of Colorado, 1965. 422 p.

>Traces the evolution of Costigan into the leader of an urban, middle-class reform movement in Denver which focused upon municipal ownership and political innovation. Argues that Costigan harmonized a concern for individual liberty with the need for government intervention to solve urban social problems.

1643 _____. "Turn-of-the-Century Denver: An Invitation to Reform." COLORADO MAGAZINE 45 (1968): 1-15.

>Reviews the corruption and impotence of Denver city government in dealing with taxes, public utilities' franchises, public transportation, gambling, and prostitution. These conditions bred the success of subsequent reformers to unite in a coalition that passed an impressive array of political, economic, and social legislation.

1644 Diner, Steven Jay. "A City and Its University: Chicago Professors and Elite Reform, 1892-1919." Ph.D. dissertation, University of Chicago, 1972. 314 p.

>A case study of professors and urban society which "places professors within the social structure of the city and shows how they became a potent force for change by making themselves part of an upper strata elite." Emphasizes the alliance with businessmen, professionals, and club women.

1645 Disbrow, Donald W. "Reform in Philadelphia under Mayor Blankenburg, 1912-1916." PENNSYLVANIA HISTORY 27 (1960): 379-96.

>Regards the Blankenburg administration as a progressive one because of its insistence upon better administrative procedures, economy, open bidding for city contracts, municipal planning, and inter-city cooperation against national monopolies. Feels that insurgency failed to last because of the city's overwhelming allegiance to Republicanism.

1646 Dorsett, Lyle W. BOSSES AND MACHINES IN URBAN AMERICA. St. Charles, Mo.: Forum Press, 1974. 16 p.

Examines the functions of urban political machines and asserts that they played a vital role in urban governance, even though acknowledging their corruption and venality.

1647 _____. "The City Boss and the Reformer." PACIFIC NORTHWEST QUARTERLY 63 (1972): 150-54.

Urges scholars to drop the "boss-reformer dichotomy" because their goals, accomplishments, and methods were similar. Charges that historians have often ascribed pure motives to reformers and opportunistic motives to bosses for doing much the same thing.

1648 _____. THE PENDERGAST MACHINE. New York: Oxford University Press, 1968. 163 p.

Examines the origins, functions, and growth of the Pendergast machine and its efforts to wield power at the state and national levels. Investigates its relationship to the New Deal and the scandals which led to its ultimate downfall.

1649 Dudden, Arthur P. "Lincoln Steffens' Philadelphia." PENNSYLVANIA HISTORY 31 (1964): 449-58.

A critical examination of Lincoln Steffens' muckraking article on municipal corruption in Philadelphia concludes that Steffens was usually correct in his major insights, but not as perceptive as James Bryce or local reform leaders. His importance lay in his journalistic ability to rouse public attention.

1650 Duffy, John J. "Charleston Politics in the Progressive Era." Ph.D. dissertation, University of South Carolina, 1963. 396 p.

Describes Charleston's efforts at reform as marred by three-way partisan Democratic politics, Protestant-Catholic antagonism, and consequent bitter struggles over prohibition. Demonstrates that middle-class, fiscally conservative reform eventually gave way to one more attuned to the needs of the working class and immigrants.

1651 Du Mont, Rosemary Ruhig. "The Large Urban Public Library as an Agency of Social Reform, 1890-1915." Ph.D. dissertation, University of Pittsburgh, 1975. 201 p.

Sees the emergence of the large urban public library as a response to southern and eastern European immigration and the economic and social changes wrought by industrialization and urbanization. Concludes that these conditions caused libraries to emphasize service as opposed to intrinsic educational worth.

1652 East, John P. COUNCIL-MANAGER GOVERNMENT: THE POLITICAL THOUGHT OF ITS FOUNDER, RICHARD S. CHILDS. Chapel Hill: University of North Carolina Press, 1965. 183 p.

Examines the foundations of Childs' philosophy and its crystallization in the short ballot and council manager forms of municipal government. Also provides a critique of Childs' governance model as a closed system and a static view of how cities operate.

1653 Ebner, Michael H., and Tobin, Eugene M., eds. THE AGE OF URBAN REFORM: NEW PERSPECTIVES ON THE PROGRESSIVE ERA. Port Washington, N.Y.: Kennikat Press, 1977. 213 p.

Collection of ten original essays on aspects of urban reform in a variety of cities, with an introduction by the editors. individual selections are Edward J. Kopf on the reform environment in Chelsea, Massachusetts; Harold L. Platt on the modernization of Houston; Michael P. McCarthy on the annexation movement in Chicago; Lee F. Pendergrass on the Municipal League of Seattle; Augustus P. Cerillo, Jr., on municipal reform in New York City; Martin J. Schiesl on public administrations in Los Angeles; John F. Bauman on the Philadelphia Housing Commission; Wayne J. Urban on the Atlanta school system; and Eugene M. Tobin on railroad reform in Jersey City.

1654 Elenbaas, Jack D. "The Boss of the Better Class: Henry Leland and the Detroit Citizens League, 1912-1924." MICHIGAN HISTORY 58 (1974): 131-50.

Identifies Leland and the Detroit Citizens League with upper- and upper middle-class attempts to reorganize urban government to better serve their needs and purposes and to curtail the influence of labor, workers, ethnic minorities, and professional politicians. Calls the league an upper-class machine and Leland an elite boss.

1655 _____. "Detroit and the Progressive Era: A Study of Urban Reform, 1900-1914." Ph.D. dissertation, Wayne State University, 1968. 240 p.

Contends that reform was a tool or weapon used by various interest groups in the city to build or destroy coalitions for political and economic gain. Business leaders were largely successful in promoting self-interested political and economic measures, in proclaiming them to be in the public interest, and in ignoring social questions.

1656 _____. "The Excesses of Reform: The Day the Detroit Mayor Arrested the City Council." MICHIGAN HISTORY 54 (1970): 1-18.

Contends that Detroit charter reformers, mostly social and business elites such as the Citizens League and the Board of Commerce, falsely accused many city councilmen of corruption in order to facilitate the elimination of the ward system.

1657 Everand, Wayne M. "Bourbon City: New Orleans, 1878-1900." LOUISIANA STUDIES 11 (1972): 240-51.

> Finds that New Orleans corresponded to the model of the New South city during the last two decades of the nineteenth century and that the Choctaw Ring, the dominant Democratic political machine, succeeded in harmonizing many diverse interest groups while coopting many of the ideals of reform groups.

1658 Finfer, Lawrence A. "Leisure as Social Work in the Urban Community: The Progressive Recreation Movement, 1890-1920." Ph.D. dissertation, Michigan State University, 1974. 326 p.

> Locates the recreation movement in the desire of a range of people from social workers to business booster groups to create an efficient, conflict-free society. Argues that, although they were presented as promoting community self-government, recreation centers were actually means of social control over lower-class people.

1659 Fisher, Robert B. "The People's Institute of New York City, 1897-1934: Culture, Progressive Democracy, and the People." Ph.D. dissertation, New York University, 1974. 471 p.

> Examines this organization's efforts to school the city's working-class population in the values of Democratic humanism and to support and promote reform legislation to restructure the urban environment. Notes that the institute was supported primarily by annual contributions from the city's wealthier citizens, and that these funds declined noticeably after World War I.

1660 Foster, Mark. "Frank Hague of Jersey City: 'The Boss' As Reformers." NEW JERSEY HISTORY 86 (1968): 106-17.

> Examines Hague's career prior to 1917 and his election as mayor, showing him as a political pragmatist who supported certain progressive reforms, even though he rejected progressivism after becoming mayor.

1661 Fox, Kenneth. BETTER CITY GOVERNMENT: INNOVATION IN AMERICA URBAN POLITICS, 1850-1937. Philadelphia: Temple University Press, 1977. 222 p.

> Applying the theory of "functional innovation," contends that a small group of federal bureaucrats in the census bureau developed the structural governmental reforms of the Progressive era. Takes issue with those who have focused on who governs as opposed to how they govern.

1662 Fragnoli Raymond R. "The Transformation of Reform: The Detroit Citizens League, 1912-1933." Ph.D. dissertation, University of Michigan, 1976. 405 p.

>Discusses the development and successes of the Detroit Citizen's League, a political reform organization, and its eventual incorporation into the city's administration as a "fact-finding agency."

1663 Fredman, L.E. "Seth Low: Theorist of Municipal Reform." JOURNAL OF AMERICAN STUDIES 6 (1972): 19-39.

>Contends that Low consistently advocated the same principles and programs from the mugwump period into the Progressive era and that this perspective formed one of several impulses in the latter era. Sees mugwump-like honesty, efficiency and economy as prerequisite to social reform.

1664 Frye, Robert J., and Dyer, John A. THE CITY MANAGER SYSTEM IN ALABAMA. University: University of Alabama Press, 1961. 45 p.

>Surveys the development of the system in Alabama, examines the operation of the system, and discusses the interaction between managers and various interest groups.

1665 Furer, Howard B. "The American City: A Catalyst for the Women's Rights Movement." WISCONSIN MAGAZINE OF HISTORY 52 (1969): 285-305.

>Argues that the rise of the city signaled the rise of women and served as a catalyst in helping women achieve equal rights. The adoption of the Nineteenth Amendment marked the decline of the agrarian myth and the emergence of a new status for women.

1666 Galvin, John T. "The Dark Ages of Boston City Politics." PROCEEDINGS OF THE MASSACHUSETTS HISTORICAL SOCIETY 89 (1977): 88-111.

>Examines the city's political life between 1880 and 1890 and the origins of the struggles that dominated the first half of the next century. Focuses on the efforts of Patrick J. Maguire to organize a city-wide machine and to forge alliances between the Yankees and the Irish.

1667 German, Richard Henry Lee. "The Queen City of the Savannah: Augusta, Georgia, during the Urban Progressive Era, 1890-1917." Ph.D. dissertation, University of Florida, 1971. 455 p.

>Attributes the reformist surge in Augusta to a business-led, broad-based coalition that included representatives of the working class and ethnic minorities. Assigns its demise to efforts

by the business efficiency leadership to deny the latter groups access to positions of responsibility.

1668 Gersman, Elinor Mondale. "Progressive Reform of the St. Louis School Board, 1897." HISTORY OF EDUCATION QUARTERLY 10 (1970): 3-21.

Argues that the chief concern of St. Louis reformers was "business efficiency and economy" and that they used the at-large method of electing members to the school board in order to gain power and promote their ideas.

1669 Gerz, Richard J., Jr. "Urban Reform and the Musser Coalition in the City of Lancaster, 1921-1930." JOURNAL OF THE LANCASTER COUNTY HISTORY SOCIETY 78 (1974): 49-110.

Analyzes the evolution of a coalition of prominent business and professional leaders, many of whom were Republicans, who felt the party machine stood in the way of needed reform. Together with Democrats they formed the Coalition party under the leadership of self-made businessman Frank C. Musser.

1670 Gillette, Howard, Jr. "Philadelphia's City Hall: Monument to a New Political Machine." PENNSYLVANIA MAGAZINE OF HISTORY AND BIOGRAPHY 97 (1972): 223-49.

Contends that the building of Philadelphia's City Hall in 1874 marked the emergence of a full-scale urban political machine which mastered the art of utilizing public power for private profit and which applied the lessons learned about patronage and favoritism to public works in general.

1671 Gleason, Bill. DALEY OF CHICAGO: THE MAN, THE MAYOR, AND THE LIMITS OF CONVENTIONAL POLITICS. New York: Simon and Schuster, 1970. 384 p.

Concludes that Daley succeeded in making the business community part of his governing coalition and that, in so doing, he lost a good deal of touch with the city's neighborhoods. Argues that Daley still had a chance in 1970 to be either the mayor of all the people or just another political boss.

1672 Gosnell, Harold F. MACHINE POLITICS: CHICAGO MODEL. Chicago: University of Chicago Press, 1968. 247 p.

Analyzes the operation of the Chicago Democratic organization in the 1930s, just after the triumph of the Kelly-Nash machine. Focuses on the ward boss, the precinct captain, the voter, the organization's handling of elections, and the relation of the press to voting.

1673 Gottfried, Alex. BOSS CERMAK OF CHICAGO: A STUDY OF POLITICAL LEADERSHIP. Seattle: University of Washington Press, 1962. 459 p.

> Traces Cermak's rise from the Czech-inhabited Lawndale section to mayor of the city of Chicago. Emphasizes the importance of Cermak's continuing ties to Lawndale and to the Czech community as factors in his success.

1674 Gould, Alan B. "Walter L. Fisher: Profile of an Urban Reformer, 1880-1910." MID-AMERICA 57 (1975): 157-72.

> Sees Fisher as an upper middle-class urban reformer who defies the traditional political and social stereotypes; who benefited from industrialization and urbanization; who served causes and not classes; who joined shifting coalitions around specific issues, such as municipal ownerships of utilities; yet who always focused upon the creation of a more predictable and orderly society.

1675 Greene, Lee S., ed. CITY BOSSES AND POLITICAL MACHINES. Philadelphia: American Academy of Political and Social Science, 1964. 217 p.

> Contains ten essays by a variety of scholars on various aspects of bosses, machines, and city politics. Of particular interest to urban historians are "The Changing Pattern of Urban Party Politics" by Fred I. Greenstein; "Bosses, Machines, and Ethnic Groups" by Elmer E. Cornwell, Jr.; "From Bossism to Cosmopolitanism: Changes in the Relation of Urban Leadership in a Large Manager City: The Case of Kansas City" by Stanley T. Gabis.

1676 Greenstein, Fred I. "The Changing Pattern of Urban Party Politics." THE ANNALS OF THE AMERICAN ACADEMY OF POLITICAL AND SOCIAL SCIENCES 353 (1964): 1-13.

> Traces the growth and change of the old-style politician and the urban machine from the 1880s to the 1950s, stressing their ability to survive and their historical value for studying in a comparative framework, other emerging industrial nations with growing urban areas.

1677 Griffith, Ernest S. A HISTORY OF AMERICAN CITY GOVERNMENT: THE CONSPICUOUS FAILURE, 1870-1900. New York: Praeger, 1974. 308 p.

> A comprehensive survey of the evolution of city government, and for the late nineteenth century, an examination of the relationship of the city to public opinion; the interrelations of growth, functions, and advances in applied science; state re-

lations; and education. Sees corruption as the conspicuous failure of the period, climaxing between 1880 and 1894.

1678 _____. A HISTORY OF AMERICAN CITY GOVERNMENT: THE PROGRESSIVE YEARS AND THEIR AFTERMATH, 1900-1920. New York: Praeger, 1974. 352 p.

A continuation of the survey of municipal reform by the "dean of students of the history of municipal government." Sees Progressives as pragmatists interested in making the cities efficient, honest, and humane. Suburban growth in the 1920s surrounded the cities and cut off their growth, thus cutting off related reform efforts.

1679 Grinder, Robert Dale. "The Anti-Smoke Crusades: Early Attempts to Reform the Urban Environment, 1893-1918." Ph.D. dissertation, University of Missouri, Columbia, 1973. 178 p.

Seeks to place the crusade against smoking in the larger context of efforts to clean up the urban environment. Contends that the movement was led by social and civic elites who often disagreed over motives and methods, and who received fluctuating support from the rest of the population.

1680 Haeger, John D., and Weber, Michael P., eds. THE BOSSES. St. Charles, Mo.: Forum Press, 1974. 82 p.

Contains eight essays on the nature of bossism by both turn-of-the-century bosses and critics and modern day observers. Includes brief introductory essays by the editors.

1681 Haller, Mark H. "Urban Vice and Civic Reform: Chicago in the Early Twentieth Century." In CITIES IN AMERICAN HISTORY, edited by Kenneth T. Jackson and Stanley K. Schultz, pp. 290-305. New York: Knopf, 1972.

Finds that antivice crusades were sponsored by a wide range of civic reformers, including social settlement workers, religious leaders, women's clubs, business organizations, and professional associations. Argues that the life of the city both fascinated and appalled them.

1682 Hamilton, Fred. RIZZO: FROM COP TO MAYOR OF PHILADELPHIA. New York: Viking, 1973. 209 p.

Traces Rizzo's rise from South Philadelphia's Little Italy to police commissioner to mayor. Stresses Philadelphia's character as a "loose confederation of separatist neighborhoods" each having distinct ethnic and income-related lifestyles and each commanding loyalty superior to that given the city as a whole.

1683 Hans, Lester F. "Community Action: Sunset Park and Woodlawn; Governing the City I; Governing the City II: Three Curriculum Units for Slow Learners." Ph.D. dissertation, Carnegie-Mellon University, 1972. 354 p.

> Includes a survey of the scholarship on the boss and the urban political machine indicating how scholarly opinion within the last two decades has come to stress the role of the machine in integrating immigrants into the political and social life of the city.

1684 Hays, Samuel P. "The Politics of Reform in Municipal Government in the Progressive Era." PACIFIC NORTHWEST QUARTERLY 55 (1964): 157-69.

> Sees progressive municipal reform largely as the effort of the business community and the upper class to alter traditional decentralized, less Democratic system which emphasized efficiency and support for the decision-making process of business and industry rather than of representative government.

1685 Henderson, Thomas M. TAMMANY HALL AND THE NEW IMMIGRANTS: THE PROGRESSIVE YEARS. New York: Arno Press, 1976. 314 p.

> Indicates that while Tammany Hall Irish leaders attempted to accommodate the new immigrants, that recognition was not extensive and it was distributed unevenly. Because Jews became voting citizens more quickly than Italians, they gained a disproportionate influence with Tammany Hall. Even so, political boundaries were drawn to mitigate both Jewish and Italian influence.

1686 Hershkowitz, Leo. TWEED'S NEW YORK: ANOTHER LOOK. Garden City, N.J.: Anchor Books, 1978. 408 p.

> Argues that Tweed was a victim of sensational journalism and that he and Tammany Hall did not really control New York City, let alone wield much influence in Albany and Washington. Insists that Tweed represented the interests of the city, especially the lower classes and that this made him fair game for nativists and antiurbanists.

1687 Holden, Arthur C. THE SETTLEMENT IDEA: A VISION OF SOCIAL JUSTICE. New York: Arno Press, 1970. 213 p.

> Traces the history of the settlement house movement from its British origins in 1884 to the post-World War I era when the country's hostility to immigrants threatened to dry up the settlement workers' sources of funding.

1688 Holli, Melvin G. REFORM IN DETROIT: HAZEN S. PINGREE AND

URBAN POLITICS. New York: Oxford University Press, 1969. 269 p.

> A study of Detroit Mayor Hazen S. Pingree's rise to power, his efforts to transform the Republican party to reflect his social reform orientation, and his own conversion from structural to social reformer during his years as mayor, 1890 to 1897. Concludes that Pingree took that same urban reformer orientation to the Michigan statehouse when he became governor.

1689 _____. "Urban Reform in the Progressive Era." In THE PROGRESSIVE ERA, edited by Lewis L. Gould, pp. 133-52. Syracuse: Syracuse University Press, 1974.

> Divides urban reform into a descriptive phase, from 1894 to 1897, and a prescriptive phase which split between structural and social programs. Focuses upon the concept of efficiency and its ramifications and concludes that municipal expenditures were more closely correlated with city size and growth than with governmental form.

1690 Holmgren, Daniel Marrin. "Edward Webster Bemis and Municipal Reform." Ph.D. dissertation, Case Western Reserve University, 1964. 372 p.

> Traces Bemis's career first as an academic at Vanderbilt University and the University of Chicago interested in the economics of public utility regulation. After his dismissal from Chicago, Bemis became active in Detroit on behalf of municipal ownership of the street railway lines, and then in Cleveland as superintendent of water works.

1691 Horowitz, Helen L. "Varieties of Cultural Experience in Jane Addams's Chicago." HISTORY OF EDUCATION QUARTERLY 14 (1974): 69-86.

> Contends that Jane Addams developed significant differences with Chicago's cultural philanthropists over the best way to deal with the city's problems, eventually embracing political action and interest group actions by working people as opposed to the voluntarism and civic mindedness of the philanthropists.

1692 Hosay, Philip M. "The Challenge of Urban Poverty: Charity Reformers in New York City, 1835-1890." Ph.D. dissertation, University of Michigan, 1969. 280 p.

> Finds that pre-Civil War charity reformers concentrated on integrating the poor into an ideal cohesive urban structure through moralistic reform, but that their nativist bias and the devastating impact of the depression of the 1870s led many to abandon the field to professional social workers.

1693 Howe, Frederic C. THE CONFESSIONS OF A REFORMER. New York: Times Books, 1973. 352 p.

> The partial autobiography of the attorney, writer, and reformer who popularized Cleveland Mayor Tom Johnson's reforms, emphasizing in particular Henry George's single-tax philosophy. His most famous book, THE CITY, THE HOPE OF DEMOCRACY (1905), was an optimistic statement of what a city could be.

1694 Huthmacher, J. Joseph. "Charles Evans Hughes and Charles Francis Murphy: The Metamorphosis of Reform." NEW YORK HISTORY 44 (1965): 28-34.

> Contends that Murphy allowed the younger members of his machine to support reform measures so long as they paid off in votes and patronage, and that he and Tammany were especially responsive to social and economic legislation in the interests of their constituents.

1695 _____. SENATOR ROBERT F. WAGNER AND THE RISE OF URBAN LIBERALISM. New York: Atheneum, 1968. 362 p.

> The first four chapters of this scholarly biography deal with Robert Wagner as a state senator and president pro tempore of the New York State Senate during the Progressive era and stress Wagner's early concern for social reform legislation that received national attention during the New Deal.

1696 _____. "Urban Liberalism and the Age of Reform." MISSISSIPPI VALLEY HISTORICAL REVIEW 49 (1962): 231-41.

> Contends that effective social reform from the Progressive era to the present depended largely upon the constructive collaboration, on specific issues, of the urban lower and middle classes, with the further cooperation, on some issues, of organized labor.

1697 Isaac, Paul E. "Municipal Reform in Beaumont, Texas, 1902-1909." SOUTHWESTERN HISTORICAL QUARTERLY 78 (1975): 409-30.

> Shows that municipal reform in Beaumont generally conformed to the pattern described by Samuel P. Hays: businessmen, interested more in efficiency than democracy, organized local government on a corporate model and centralized authority by reducing the number of elected officials. Chief opposition came from Democratic party regulars who opposed centralization as undemocratic.

1698 Issel, William. "Class and Ethnic Conflict in San Francisco Political

History: The Reform Charter of 1898." LABOR HISTORY 18 (1977): 341-59.

> Regards the 1898 charter as the first step whereby San Francisco's business and professional elite translated their corporate ideal into social reality at the expense of the ethnic working class. Emphasizes the complexity of the reformist process.

1699 Jentz, John B. "Artisans, Evangelicals, and the City: A Social History of Abolition and Labor Reform in Jacksonian New York." Ph.D. dissertation, City University of New York, 1977. 509 p.

> Finds a significant overlap between the labor and antislavery movements in the city and that New York artisans were the most significant segment of both reform movements.

1700 Johnson, Charles A. DENVER'S MAYOR SPEER. Denver: Bighorn Books, 1970. 255 p.

> A political biography based heavily on contemporary newspaper accounts of Robert Walter Speer who, except for two years, was mayor and political boss of Denver from 1905 to 1918.

1701 Johnson, Tom L. MY STORY. New York: AMS Press, 1970. 326 p.

> The autobiography of street-railroad operator, steel producer, congressman, and reform mayor who made Cleveland "the best governed city in America."

1702 Knerr, George F. "The Mayoral Administration of William L. Strong, New York City, 1895-1897." Ph.D. dissertation, New York University, 1957. 311 p.

> Attributes Strong's election to voter response to exposure of corruption and finds that he instituted many worthwhile reforms in street cleaning, refuse disposal, police administration, education, and charity. Links his defeat to his overreliance upon business principles and to his wavering between patronage and civil service.

1703 Komons, Nick Alexander. "Chicago, 1893-1907: The Politics of Reform." Ph.D. dissertation, George Washington University, 1962. 448 p.

> Believes reform during this period was limited because reformers were unwilling to form an alliance with the working class and were unable to reduce the political power of the business community. Even among reformers division existed between conservatives and radicals, making consensus on major issues nearly impossible.

1704 Kraus, Harry P. "The Settlement House Movement in New York City, 1886-1914." Ph.D. dissertation, New York University, 1970. 295 p.

> Identifies settlement house workers as Protestant, college educated men and women motivated by religious and ethical imperatives to aid the urban poor. Contends that they achieved significant success until population shifts, institutional change, the professionalization of social work and the competition of publicly administered programs undermined their effectiveness.

1705 Kurland, Gerald. SETH LOW: THE REFORMER IN AN URBAN AND INDUSTRIAL AGE. New York: Twayne Publishers, 1971. 415 p.

> Biography of the son of a wealthy New York commercial family who served as president of Columbia University and twice as municipal reform mayor of New York. Contends that Low was actually more liberal and sophisticated in his social outlook than is usually realized, particularly with respect to the rights of labor and the need for governmental regulation of industry.

1706 Kusmer, Kenneth L. "The Functions of Organized Charity in the Progressive Era: Chicago as a Case Study." JOURNAL OF AMERICAN HISTORY 60 (1973): 657-78.

> Traces the transformation of Chicago's Charity Organization Society from the attitudes of its founders, who thought society could be regenerated by reinfusing small-town values to those of its later members who saw it as an urban service whose chief function was helping individuals adjust to a modern industrial society.

1707 Lane, James B. JACOB A RIIS AND THE AMERICAN CITY. Port Washington, N.Y.: Kennikat Press, 1974. 267 p.

> Examines Riis's career and his philosophy of urban reconstruction which sought to use reason, progress, and morality to join the "two Americas" of rich and poor into an organic unity. Focuses on his advocacy of specific reforms and on his amiable working relationship with Theodore Roosevelt.

1708 Lebkuecher, Patricia Brewster. "The Urban Social Reform Movement: 1880-1900." Ph.D. dissertation, Middle Tennessee State University, 1975. 237 p.

> Studies the efforts of journalists, settlement house workers, religious spokesmen, and novelists and analyzes the origins of their reformist beliefs and their common concerns for certain types of reforms. Also considers the origins of opposition to reform, centering it in a belief in Social Darwinism and economic nationalism.

1709   Lewinson, Edward R. JOHN PURROY MITCHEL: THE BOY MAYOR OF NEW YORK. New York: Astra Books, 1965. 299 p.

> Portrays Mitchel as an efficiency-minded reformer who instituted many worthwhile changes in zoning laws and administration but failed to meet the real needs of the people of New York and expended his energies in economy and antivice reforms.

1710   Lewis, Michael. "The Reform of Urban Reform." In SOUTH ATLANTIC URBAN STUDIES, edited by Jack R. Censer and N. Steinert, pp. 3-17. Columbia: University of South Carolina Press, 1977.

> Contends that the professional approach to urban reform contributed to troubled quality of city life. Argues for "more realistic if impractical politics of redistributive reform."

1711   Lineberry, Robert L., and Fowler, Edmund P. "Reformism and Public Policies in American Cities." AMERICAN POLITICAL SCIENCE REVIEW 61 (1967): 701-16.

> Argues that middle-class reformers were largely successful in their efforts to eliminate parochial and class-inspired interests from urban government. Sees reformers as a "continuous variable" which makes government increasingly less responsive to popular input as each new change is added.

1712   Locke, David Stratton. "The Village Vision: Goals and Limits in Urban Reform, 1890-1914." Ph.D. dissertation, Brown University, 1972. 380 p.

> Traces much of the failure of municipal reform to the persistence of rural ideas and values in the face of urban-industrial life. Feels that reformers disagreed as to whether the solution lay in the home, the neighborhood, or the application of social science.

1713   Lowi, Theodore. "Machine Politics--Old and New." THE PUBLIC INTEREST 9 (1967): 83-92.

> Compares New York, a "reformed" city, with Chicago, a "machine" city, and finds that reform failed to improve the capability of urban governments to deal with socioeconomic and cultural problems.

1714   Lubove, Roy. "Frederic C. Howe and the Quest for Community in America." HISTORIAN 39 (1976): 270-91.

> Concludes that Howe's "urban liberalism" was inspired by the values of agrarian egalitarianism and small-town evangelical Protestantism which underlay his desire to restore a sense of

community and social cohesion to urban life. Discusses his growing disillusionment with the welfare state after World War I.

1715 _____. "The Twentieth-Century City: The Progressive as Municipal Reformer." MID-AMERICA 41 (1959): 195-209.

Believes that municipal reformers were united in a vision of the city as a social organism which, if properly managed, would enable men to attain the good life. Argues that reformers were unrealistic in ignoring class and ethnic differences that prevented the emergence of the social organism.

1716 McArthur, Benjamin. "The Chicago Playground Movement: A Neglected Feature of Social Justice." SOCIAL SERVICE REVIEW 49 (1975): 376-95.

Portrays the playground movement as a coalition of social welfare workers, civic organizations, and business and professional leaders seeking to promote social order by guarding the health and morals of children, solidifying the home, and inculcating a democratic ethos.

1717 McCarthy, Michael. "Businessmen and Professionals in Municipal Reform: The Chicago Experience, 1887-1920." Ph.D. dissertation, Northwestern University, 1970. 247 p.

Examines the attitudes and activities of the businessmen and professionals of the "'right wing' of Chicago progressivism," who spearheaded the drive for governmental reform and city planning. Sees the reform movement in Chicago as part of a large scale transformation in American society.

1718 _____. "On Bosses, Reformers, and Urban Growth: Some Suggestions for a Political Typology of American Cities." JOURNAL OF URBAN HISTORY 4 (1977): 29-38.

Contends that the bosses and machines developed in "working-class spread cities" as opposed to "middle-class spread cities," which usually supported reform efforts. Presents spatial patterns as a more rational explanation for the growth of machines than differences in ethnic or racial makeup.

1719 _____. "Politics and the Parks: Chicago Businessmen and the Recreation Movement." JOURNAL OF THE ILLINOIS STATE HISTORICAL SOCIETY 65 (1972): 158-72.

Argues that many sophisticated businessmen supported the parks program, largely as a means of controlling organized labor rather than repressing it. Finds that organized labor opposed the parks as being inaccessible to the average working man.

1720 _____. "Prelude to Armageddon: Charles E. Merriam and the Chicago Mayoral Campaign of 1911." JOURNAL OF THE ILLINOIS STATE HISTORICAL SOCIETY 67 (1974): 505-18.

> Locates the Chicago Progressive Republican movement in the city's professionals and intellectuals and analyzes the strategy which enabled them to wrest the mayoral nomination from the regulars.

1721 _____. "'Suburban Power': A Footnote on Cleveland in the Tom Johnson Years." NORTHWEST OHIO QUARTERLY 45 (1972-1973): 21-27.

> Describes the way in which Johnson managed to elaborate a platform that gained support not only from labor, but from the suburban middle class, indicating that "factory workers and middle class communities shared a wide range of mutual concerns."

1722 McKenzie, Roderick Duncan. THE NEIGHBORHOOD: A STUDY OF LOCAL LIFE IN THE CITY OF COLUMBUS, OHIO. Chicago: University of Chicago Press, 1923. Reprint. New York: Arno Press, 1970. 799 p.

> Contends that the saloon and the ward boss provided the only viable forms of stability and organization in the lives of the inhabitants of the central business district of Columbus and scores reformers who would destroy those connections without dealing with the root causes of social disorganization in the area.

1723 McKitrick, Eric L. "The Study of Corruption." POLITICAL SCIENCE QUARTERLY 72 (1957): 502-14.

> Sees urban political machines as dynamic institutions which adapted and absorbed most of the innovations of the reformers and remained in control of politics and government.

1724 Mandelbaum, Seymour J. BOSS TWEED'S NEW YORK. New York: John Wiley and Sons, 1965. 196 p.

> Contends that New York was so fragmented politically, ethnically, and geographically and so lacking in effective communications and transportation networks that "only a universal payment of benefits--a giant 'pay-off'--could pull the city together in a common effort."

1725 Marcus, Alan L. "Professional Revolution and Reform in the Progressive Era: Cincinnati Physicians and the City Election of 1897 and 1900." JOURNAL OF URBAN HISTORY 5 (1979): 183-208.

Contends that professionalism among the city's physicians was not a by-product of the efforts to solve social problems and to improve the physical well-being of their fellow citizens, but rather was a result of efforts to stop the decline in status which affected physicians with the onset of large-scale urbanization.

1726 Marks, Donald David. "Polishing the Gem of the Prairie: The Evolution of Civic Reform Consciousness in Chicago, 1874-1900." Ph.D. dissertation, University of Wisconsin, Madison, 1974. 224 p.

Focuses upon two upper-class reform groups, the Citizens Association and the Civic Federation, and delineates their progress from voluntarism to acceptance of positive government. Argues that these organizations maintained social leadership for their members but unintentionally promoted freer access to government by all classes of Chicagoans.

1727 Merton, Robert K. "The Latent Functions of the Machine." In BOSSES, MACHINES, AND PROGRESSIVE REFORMERS, edited by Bruce M. Stave, pp. 27-37. Lexington, Mass.: D.C. Heath, 1972.

Insists that bosses and machines emerged naturally from the context of urban America and provided a variety of services for a variety of subgroups. Chides reformers for engaging in "social ritual" rather than "social engineering."

1728 Miggins, Edward Michael. "Businessmen, Pedagogues, and Progressive Reform: The Cleveland Foundation's 1915 School Survey." Ph.D. dissertation, Case Western Reserve University, 1975. 371 p.

Investigates the philanthropic and business reform movements during the Progressive era, and concludes that the Cleveland Foundation helped the business community's attempt to control the social, economic, and political dislocations of modern urban society.

1729 Miller, Richard G. "Fort Worth and the Progressive Era: The Movement for Charter Revision, 1899-1907." In ESSAYS ON URBAN AMERICA, edited by Margaret Francine Morris and Elliot West, pp. 89-126. Austin: University of Texas Press, 1975.

Attributes the adoption of the commission form of government in Fort Worth to the efforts of efficiency-minded elites to centralize power and to curtail the influences of the working class and ward politicians. Discusses the naiveté of the electorate in being gulled by Democratic rhetoric while acquiescing in the loss of its own political influence.

1730 Miller, William D. MEMPHIS DURING THE PROGRESSIVE ERA, 1900-

1917. Madison, Wis.: American History Research Center, 1957. 243 p.

> Analyzes the social conditions that gave rise to the reformist impulse in Memphis, especially its high crime rate, the adoption of the commission form of government, and the ironic emergence of "Boss" Edward H. Crump as a strong political leader who accomplished many of the reformers' goals.

1731 _____. MR. CRUMP OF MEMPHIS. Baton Rouge: Louisiana State University Press, 1964. 373 p.

> Covers the period of Crump's mayoralty, his tenure as county trustee, and his career in Congress, emphasizing his tight control of Memphis politics and substantial influence throughout Tennessee as well as his commitment to honesty and efficiency in government.

1732 _____. "Rural Values and Urban Progress: Memphis, 1900-1917." MISSISSIPPI QUARTERLY 21 (1968): 263-74.

> Argues that it was not organized religion, but rather the efforts of political boss Edward H. Crump, that destroyed the institutionalized basis of the Memphis "sin-center myth" popularized by romantic agrarians.

1733 Miller, Zane L. "Boss Cox's Cincinnati: A Study in Urbanization and Politics, 1880-1914." JOURNAL OF AMERICAN HISTORY 54 (1968): 823-38.

> Argues that, contrary to contemporary views, George B. Cox and his machine helped to bridge racial and cultural differences dividing the city and "to bring positive and moderate reform government to Cincinnati and to mitigate the conflict and disorder which accompanied the emergence of the new city." This, in turn, created an atmosphere conducive to further reform.

1734 _____. BOSS COX'S CINCINNATI: URBAN POLITICS IN THE PROGRESSIVE ERA. New York: Oxford University Press, 1968. 301 p.

> An examination of social and political issues in Cincinnati from 1880 to 1913 and in particular the shifting coalitions of three geographically and socially distinct city and suburban groups who were vital to political success. Interprets reform as a move by the residents of the periphery of the city to overthrow the power of the George Cox machine, which drew its strongest support from the center.

1735 Mitchell, J. Paul. "Boss Speer and the City Functional: Boosters and Businessmen versus Commission Government in Denver." PACIFIC

NORTHWEST QUARTERLY 63 (1972): 155-64.

While the adoption of the commission form of city government is generally seen as a typical businessman's progressive reform designed to promote efficiency, such was not the case in Denver where the business community generally supported the boss rule of Mayor Robert Speer because they enjoyed influence with his machine and because Speer exemplified the city beautiful ideas of typical urban reformers.

1736 _____. "Municipal Reform in Denver: The Defeat of Mayor Speer." COLORADO MAGAZINE 45 (1968): 42-60.

Largely the story of how Henry J. Arnold, who won the election as county assessor in 1910 because of his nomination by Democratic supporters of party boss Mayor Robert W. Speer, later won election as mayor in 1912 on a citizens' reform ticket over Speer's hand-picked successor.

1737 _____. "Progressivism in Denver, the Municipal Reform Movement, 1904-1916." Ph.D. dissertation, University of Denver, 1966. 425 p.

Views reform in Denver as the result of a reform coalition of people of diverse orientations, backgrounds, and political affiliations united largely by opposition to the political machine of Mayor Robert W. Speer. Ironically their abortive efforts at commission government led to a stronger mayoral system headed by Speer, but did promote a civic regeneration program.

1738 Mohl, Raymond A. "Schools, Politics, and Riots: The Gary Plan in New York City, 1914-1917." PEDAGOGICA HISTORICA 15 (1975): 39-72.

Uses a case study of reform Mayor John Purroy Mitchel's attempt to introduce the duplicate school plan in New York to delineate some of the problems and issues attending urban progressive reform.

1739 Muccigrosso, Robert. "The City Reform Club: A Study in Late Nineteenth-Century Reform." NEW YORK HISTORICAL SOCIETY QUARTERLY 52 (1968): 235-54.

Analyzes the club as an upper middle-class reform organization created primarily to combat Tammany Hall, but which failed to meet the needs of the city's immigrant working class and eventually suffered defeat. Sees it as a forerunner of the City Club, Citizen's Union, and National Municipal League.

1740 Muraskin, Jack. "Municipal Reform in Two Missouri Cities." MISSOURI HISTORICAL SOCIETY 25 (1969): 213-28.

Although both Kansas City and St. Louis experienced municipal reform activity from the 1890s through the Progressive era and in both cases the business community actively supported urban reform, Kansas City emerged as a national model, while St. Louis appeared to stagnate.

1741 _____. "St. Louis Municipal Reform in the 1890s: A Study in Failure." BULLETIN OF THE MISSOURI HISTORICAL SOCIETY 25 (1968): 38-49.

Argues that the depression of 1893 undermined the efforts of the Civic Federation and Lee Meriwether to reduce ethnic and sectional hostilities through a reform program emphasizing efficiency and clean government. Although Meriwether lost the mayoral election to Republican Henry Ziegenhein, the 1897 campaign did focus attention on major municipal reforms which were adopted in the next decade.

1742 Mushkat, Jerome. TAMMANY: THE EVOLUTION OF A POLITICAL MACHINE, 1789-1865. Syracuse, N.Y.: Syracuse University Press, 1971. 476 p.

Contends that Tammany was neither unique nor reprehensible, but rather was a product of American civilization which presents in microcosm a study of how the nation adjusted to the major, social, economic, and political changes of the nineteenth century and how it carried out the everyday conduct of its political affairs. Focuses on the growth of New York City's Democratic party, the evolution of the machine, the role played by Tammany in both, and the Hall's operating political philosophy.

1743 Nelli, Humbert S. "John Powers and the Italians: Politics in a Chicago Ward, 1896-1921." JOURNAL OF AMERICAN HISTORY 57 (1970): 67-84.

Attributes the failure of Jane Addams and Hull House associates to unseat Powers to their middle-class orientation of politics as a struggle between good and evil and their consequent unwillingness to cooperate with neighborhood Italians who viewed politics as a source of obtaining jobs and community facilities.

1744 Nord, David. "The Experts versus the Experts: Conflicting Philosophies of Municipal Utility Regulation in the Progressive Era." WISCONSIN MAGAZINE OF HISTORY 58 (1974-1975): 219-36.

Finds that reformers divided between those who favored direct political influence upon utilities by consumers of their services and those who advocated regulation by state commission. Argues that efforts at grass roots democracy persisted until the 1930s.

1745 Nussbaum, Raymond O. "Progressive Politics in New Orleans, 1896-1900." Ph.D. dissertations, Tulane University, 1974. 228 p.

Portrays reform in New Orleans as a revolt which embraced the full range of white socioeconomic groups, led by the city's elite, against the established political machine. Concludes that the latter eventually regained control due to its superior organization and political skill.

1746 _____. "The Ring is Smashed!: The New Orleans Municipal Election of 1896." LOUISIANA HISTORY 17 (1976): 283-97.

Argues that the New Orleans experience fits none of the standard explanations of progressivism. While the political machine did assist the new Italian Catholic immigrants, many of the reform leaders were Catholics who received support from and nominated political candidates from nearly every social and economic group in the city.

1747 O'Connor, Len. CLOUT: MAYOR DALEY AND HIS CITY. Chicago: H. Regnery Co., 1975. 272 p.

Discusses the political career of Richard J. Daley, examining the basis of his power and longevity as mayor of Chicago. Largely descriptive and anecdotal, but provides the perceptive insights of a veteran Chicago newscaster into the nature of the city and its politics.

1748 Palmer, John Albert. "Some Antecedents of Progressivism: Buffalo in the 1890s." Ph.D. dissertation, State University of New York, Buffalo, 1967. 219 p.

Attributes much of the reformist impulse in Buffalo in the 1890s to the oversimplified notion on the part of many established citizens that the city's problems were caused by the presence of large blocs of unassimilated immigrants. This skewed outlook undermined the humanitarian viewpoint of many reformers and seriously hampered their ability to reform the city's political and socioeconomic systems.

1749 Parkhurst, Charles H. OUR FIGHT WITH TAMMANY. 1895. Reprint. New York: Arno Press, 1970. 296 p.

Presents the case of the Society for the Prevention of Crime in New York City against saloons, vice, gambling, the police, and Tammany Hall, charges which eventually led to the formation of the Lexow Commission and the temporary triumph of reform.

1750 Pease, Otis A. "Urban Reformers in the Progressive Era." PACIFIC NORTHWEST QUARTERLY 62 (1971): 49-58.

Believes that the principal thrust of progressivism and its legacy was the development of political pluralism through its efforts to professionalize government in order to regulate private capitalism, thus laying the foundations for the New Deal. Progressives accommodated both the old elite and aspirations of the newer ethnic minorities in an evolving welfare state.

1751 Pendergrass, Lee F. "The Formation of a Municipal Reform Movement: The Municipal League of Seattle." PACIFIC NORTHWEST QUARTERLY 66 (1975): 13-25.

Examines the motives and activities of the league and concludes that it contained elements to sustain most existing interpretations of municipal reform and it was able to bring together diverse groups under its auspices to promote collective identity through both formal and informal channels.

1752 _____. "Urban Reform and Voluntary Association: A Case Study of the Seattle Municipal League, 1910-1929." Ph.D. dissertation, University of Washington, 1972. 149 p.

Takes issue with the notion that progressive reform should be thought of as a series of shifting coalitions. Argues that, in Seattle at least, different interests worked together to promote a collective identity for a variety of motives. Attributes reform's disintegration to manifestations of intolerance and the worsening of economic conditions.

1753 Petskek, Kirk R. THE CHALLENGE OF URBAN REFORM: POLICIES AND PROGRAMS IN PHILADELPHIA. Philadelphia: Temple University Press, 1973. 336 p.

Analyzes the reasons for the success of the reform administration of Joseph Clark and Richardson Dilworth in the 1950s and 1960s, stressing the cooperation of private and public interests with the direction of city planners.

1754 Piott, Steven L. "Modernization and the Anti-Monopoly Issue: The St. Louis Transit Strike of 1900." BULLETIN OF THE MISSOURI HISTORICAL SOCIETY 35 (1978): 3-16.

Argues that corporate arrogance led to the transit strike and animated homeowners, housewives, workers, taxpayers, citizens, and merchants to unite with organized labor in favor of better service. Concludes that they were defending their community from the forces of modernization.

1755 Pivar, David J. PURITY CRUSADE: SEXUAL MORALITY AND SOCIAL CONTROL, 1868-1900. Westport, Conn.: Greenwood Press, 1973.

Traces the activities of the purity reformers within the cities, and their political alliance with municipal reformers, including discussions of vice commissions, social work and education, censorship, social hygiene, and industrial purification.

1756 _____. "Theocratic Businessmen and Philadelphia Municipal Reform, 1870-1900." PENNSYLVANIA HISTORY 33 (1966): 289-307.

Sees religion as a force promoting the emergence of civic consciousness and providing an ideological consensus among reformers, who emphasized the general moral outlook rather than the specific forms of religious worship. Contends that an "ideological reformation" which saw churches as the bulwark of the businessman's conception of civilization proved central to the development of municipal reform.

1757 Pratt, John W. "Boss Tweed's Public Welfare Program." NEW YORK HISTORICAL SOCIETY QUARTERLY 45 (1961): 396-411.

Focuses on various aspects of the Tweed organization's social welfare program, arguing that in the absence of a general commitment to public responsibility for the poor, this program served a beneficial and much needed purpose.

1758 Reese, William J. "The Control of Urban School Boards during the Progressive Era: A Reconsideration." PACIFIC NORTHWEST QUARTERLY 68 (1977): 164-73.

Contends that the switch from a ward-based to a city-wide school board resulted in control passing from a localized elite to a more metropolitan one, but did not change its socioeconomic makeup.

1759 Reynolds, George Miller. MACHINE POLITICS IN NEW ORLEANS, 1897-1926. New York: AMS Press, 1968. 245 p.

Analyzes the organization and operation of the New Orleans political machine known as the Choctaws or the Ring and its boss, Dr. Martin Behrman. Also discusses the efforts of independents to curb organization power and the reasons for their failure.

1760 Rice, Bradley R. PROGRESSIVE CITIES: THE COMMISSION GOVERNMENT MOVEMENT IN AMERICA, 1901-1920. Austin: University of Texas Press, 1977. 160 p.

Traces the rise of the commission form of government, first implemented as the Galveston Plan, as a popular progressive reform for small- and medium-sized cities and shows that the reform had various supporters, each with varying motives.

Attributes its general decline after 1917 to the rising popularity of the city manager plan.

1761 Rickard, Louise E. "The Politics of Reform in Omaha, 1918-1921." NEBRASKA HISTORY 53 (1972): 419-45.

Argues that there were two reform groups in Omaha--one emphasizing moral and sumptuary legislation and the other structural political change. The failure of reform was due primarily to the ineptness and inconsistency of the reformers themselves.

1762 Riess, Steven A. "The Baseball Magnates and Urban Politics in the Progressive Era: 1895-1920." JOURNAL OF SPORT HISTORY 1 (1974): 41-61.

Argues that several major league baseball franchises during the era were controlled by leaders of urban political machines who gave the teams preferential consideration and protection in exchange for favorable publicity, kickbacks, and jobs for their constituents.

1763 Rigenback, Paul T. "Discarding Rural Nostrums for City Problems: Moving Towards Urban Reform." ROCKY MOUNTAIN SOCIAL SCIENCE JOURNAL 10 (1973): 33-42.

Argues that only after appeals to the rural ethic failed to provide adequate solutions to the problems of congestion, pollution, poverty, and class tensions did many would-be reformers come to intellectual grips with the city and begin rudimentary thinking about the quality of urban life.

1764 Riordan, William L., ed. PLUNKITT OF TAMMANY HALL. Intro. by Arthur Mann. New York: E.P. Dutton, 1963. 98 p.

Contains series of observations on urban politics and the operation of bosses and political machines by one of Tammany Hall's most colorful sachems as recorded by a New York journalist.

1765 Ritchie, Donald A. "The Gary Committee: Businessmen, Progressives, and Unemployment in New York City, 1914-1915." NEW YORK HISTORICAL SOCIETY QUARTERLY 57 (1973): 327-47.

Contends that this committee of businessmen and social workers aided less than 4 percent of the city's unemployed while maintaining a large surplus in its treasury. Sees it as typical of the business efficiency approach to social reform.

1766 Rosenberg, Arnold S. "The New York Reformers of 1914: A Profile." NEW YORK HISTORY 50 (1969): 187-206.

Argues that reformers in New York City, "quite possibly the most important of the Progressive centers," included individuals representing diverse socioeconomic, ethnocultural, and religious backgrounds united to support a myriad of reform proposals.

1767 Royko, Mike. BOSS: RICHARD J. DALEY OF CHICAGO. New York: Dutton, 1971. 215 p.

Examines Daley's rise to power and his management of the city and the Democratic party. Written by a prominent Chicago journalist and critic of the Daley organization.

1768 Schiesl, Martin J. THE POLITICS OF EFFICIENCY: MUNCIPAL ADMINISTRATION AND REFORM IN AMERICA, 1880-1920. Berkeley and Los Angeles: University of California Press, 1977. 259 p.

Details the differences between those older elements of the middle class who sought to use urban governmental reorganization merely as a mechanism to elect good men and those newer professionals and bureaucrats who saw in it the emergence of a new form of positive government that would assume responsibility for the welfare of all its citizens. Locates the key to municipal reform in a desire for efficiency that animated professionals, businessmen, and politicians. Contends that these structural reformers developed more effective and fairer means of delivering urban services, but isolated city government from popular, democratic influences.

1769 ———. "Progressive Reform in Los Angeles Under Mayor Alexander, 1909-1913." CALIFORNIA HISTORICAL QUARTERLY 54 (1974): 37-56.

Studies progressivism in Los Angeles, seeing the years from 1909 to 1913 as a "crucial transition period in the city's politics and reform polity" in that the reform movement had led to increased executive power and administrative responsibility and had destroyed the machine's traditional functions in electoral politics.

1770 Scott, Anne Firor. "Jane Addams and the City." VIRGINIA QUARTERLY REVIEW 43 (1967): 53-62.

Pronounced Addams one of the earliest and most perceptive of urban theorists, based largely upon her Hull House experiences. Sketches the outline of her theories and the reforms that she supported as a result.

1771 Scott, James C. "Corruption, Machine Politics, and Political Change." AMERICAN POLITICAL SCIENCE REVIEW 63 (1969): 1142-58.

Places the interaction between machines and reformers in a

comparative, cross-cultural framework and relates it to economic change and the needs of the organization's constituents.

1772 Shapley, Rufus E. SOLID FOR MOLHOOLEY: A POLITICAL SATIRE. 1889. Reprint. New York: Arno Press, 1970. 210 p.

Presents the reformers' case against the Irish machine politician in satirical and undiluted form. Includes cartoons by the bane of the Irish politico's existence, Thomas Nast.

1773 Shelton, Brenda K. REFORMERS IN SEARCH OF YESTERDAY: BUFFALO IN THE 1890S. Buffalo: State University of New York Press, 1976. 245 p.

Examines the efforts of upper middle-class citizens to cope with the problems of poverty, housing, public health, education, immigration, and organized labor. Faults them for harboring moralistic and condescending attitudes toward minority groups and for failing to understand the real causes of the problems they sought to solve.

1774 Silverman, Robert A. "Nathan Matthews: Politics of Reform in Boston, 1890-1910." NEW ENGLAND QUARTERLY 50 (1977): 626-43.

Portrays Matthews as a Brahmin reformer with an unstinting commitment to efficiency and economy and a devotion to the corporate model of city government which severely limited his ability to govern the city.

1775 Skolnik, Richard S. "Civic Group Progressivism in New York City." NEW YORK HISTORY 51 (1970): 411-39.

Argues that the reform efforts of civic groups in New York, although falling far short of stated goals and expectations, did pressure machine politicians into a more receptive attitude toward reform and that they developed and normalized a new reform technique applicable to other cities.

1776 _____. "The Crystallization of Reform in New York City, 1890-1964." Ph.D. dissertation, Yale University, 1964.

Analyzes the rise in New York City of middle- and upper-class reformers who rejected the values of the professional politicians and contended that good government required honest and efficient public officials. Supporting an active municipal government which would play a role in modernizing the city, they ultimately formed civic organizations to exercise political leverage and to promote reform ideas in government.

1777 _____. "George Edwin Waring, Jr.: A Model for Reformers." NEW

YORK HISTORICAL SOCIETY QUARTERLY 52 (1968): 354-78.

> Contends that Waring, in contrast to most good government reformers in the William Strong administration, turned his sanitation department into a model which produced both efficiency and economy and adequate and equitable public service to all segments of New York society.

1778 Solomon, Noal. WHEN LEADERS WERE BOSSES. Hicksville, N.Y.: Exposition Press, 1975. 205 p.

> Discusses political machines and politics, providing case studies of Boston's James Michael Curley, Atlantic City's Nucky Johnson, Jersey City's Frank Hague, Kansas City's Thomas J. Pendergast, and Huey Long, Richard Daley, and Tammany Hall and a lengthy treatment of Dan O'Connell and his Albany machine. Other topics include political ethics, corruption, the legislative process, and corruption as related to the presence and practices of the machines.

1779 Speer, Michael S. "Urbanization and Reform: Columbus, Ohio, 1870-1900." Ph.D. dissertation, Ohio State University, 1972. 298 p.

> Contends that Columbus mirrored other cities in its efforts and failures at urban reform even though it lacked ethnic heterogeneity, heavy industry, great poverty, and chronic labor troubles, characteristics often considered essential to the reformist impulse. Focuses upon efforts to promote governmental efficiency, provide urban services, and enforce middle-class morality.

1780 Stave, Bruce M., ed. URBAN BOSSES, MACHINES, AND PROGRESSIVE REFORMERS. Lexington, Mass.: D.C. Heath, 1972. 158 p.

> Contains nineteen selections, including turn-of-the-century observations by James Bryce, Jane Addams, Lincoln Steffens, and George Washington Plunkitt, with the remaining contributions by recent scholars dealing with the themes of the machine and its functions, bosses and reformers, and businessmen, socialists, and municipal reform.

1781 Steffens, Joseph Lincoln. THE AUTOBIOGRAPHY OF LINCOLN STEFFENS. New York: Harcourt Brace Jovanovich, 1968. 884 p.

> Provides considerable information regarding politics and social conditions in New York, and Steffens's briefer comments on urban problems in several cities, including St. Louis, Minneapolis, Pittsburgh, Philadelphia, Cincinnati, and Chicago.

1782 _____. THE SHAME OF THE CITIES. New York: McClure, Phillips and Co., 1904. Reprint. New York: Hill and Wang, 1957. 214 p.

> Examines political corruption in several major cities and blames it largely on the business community and the commercial mentality of the average citizen, rather than upon machine politicians.

1783 Steinberg, Alfred. THE BOSSES. New York: Macmillan, 1972. 379 p.

> Presents a journalistic and often one-dimensional view of six of the nation's most famous and notorious city bosses--Frank Hague, James Michael Curley, Huey Long, Eugene Talmadge, Ed Crump, and Tom Pendergast.

1784 Stewart, Frank M. A HALF-CENTURY OF MUNICIPAL REFORM: THE HISTORY OF THE NATIONAL MUNICIPAL LEAGUE. Berkeley and Los Angles: University of California Press, 1950. 287 p.

> Traces the evolution of the National Municipal League from its inception in the 1890s to 1949, with particular emphasis on its model charter and its influence on the urban reform efforts of the Progressive era.

1785 Stillman, Richard J. III. THE RISE OF THE CITY MANAGER: A PUBLIC PROFESSIONAL IN LOCAL GOVERNMENT. Albuquerque: University of New Mexico Press, 1974. 170 p.

> Concerned mainly with the modern city manager and his values and performance, but traces the development of this office during the Progressive era and examines the "historical evolution of the managerial profession: its changing ideology, leadership, internal structure, and external support."

1786 Sutherland, John F. "A City of Homes: Philadelphia Slums and Reformers, 1880-1918." Ph.D. dissertation, Temple University, 1973. 324 p.

> Investigates conservative housing reform efforts in late nineteenth- and early twentieth-century Philadelphia, describing reformers' limited success as the result of misunderstood public housing problems.

1787 _____. "The Origins of Philadelphia's Octavia Hill Association: Social Reform in the 'Contented City.'" PENNSYLVANIA MAGAZINE OF HISTORY AND BIOGRAPHY 99 (1975): 20-44.

> Discusses the housing reform efforts of the Octavia Hill Association in the late nineteenth and early twentieth century, arguing that despite paternalism, this social reform group espoused important concepts like house reconstruction and neigh-

borhood rehabilitation while publicizing the plight of the poor and helping secure housing legislation for Pittsburgh as well as Philadelphia.

1788 Tarr, Joel A. A STUDY IN BOSS POLITICS: WILLIAM LORIMER OF CHICAGO. Urbana: University of Illinois Press, 1971. 376 p.

Stresses Lorimer's constructive role in providing needed services to a varied constituency and of integrating immigrants into the political process. Portrays Chicago's middle-class reform groups as elitist and out of touch with the real needs of the city's populace.

1789 _____. "The Urban Politician as Entrepreneur." MID-AMERICA 49 (1967): 55-67.

Pronounces the urban politician an entrepreneur who regarded politics as a business, used his power for personal and party gain, and who dealt in influence, laws, government grants, and franchises.

1790 _____. "William Kent to Lincoln Steffens: Origins of Progressive Reform in Chicago." MID-AMERICA 47 (1965): 48-57.

Traces the origins of the Chicago Municipal Voters League to Steffens's article on Chicago and demonstrates that Kent's response to the piece prompted the muckraker partially to revise his opinion of the Windy City.

1791 Taylor, Quintard. "The Chicago Political Machine and Black-Ethnic Conflict and Accommodation." POLISH AMERICAN STUDIES 29 (1972): 40-66.

Analyzes reasons for the continual success of the Chicago political machine for the period 1952 to 1972, focusing on the use of black-white ethnic conflict. Contends that the machine has used racial and ethnic tension to perpetuate its rule through manipulating fears and animosities, while making sufficient concessions to each group so as to keep the coalition supporting the "organization" intact.

1792 Thomas, Lately. "Tammany Picked an Honest Man." AMERICAN HERITAGE 18 (1967): 34-39, 94-98.

Focuses on the 1909 New York mayoral campaign in which Tammany Hall backed William Jay Gaynor, who after winning the election, proceeded to show an almost obsessive concern with civic responsibility.

1793 Tobin, Eugene M. "In Pursuit of Equal Taxation: Jersey City's Struggle

Against Corporate Arrogance and Tax-Dodging by the Railroad Trust." AMERICAN JOURNAL OF ECONOMICS AND SOCIOLOGY 34 (1975): 213-24.

> Examines the efforts of Mark Fagan, George L. Record, and their colleagues to use taxation to control the railroads and asserts that they failed because the voters were not prepared to accept the social reorganization necessary to overcome corporate opposition. Concludes that the railroads accepted regulation to avoid equal taxation.

1794 _____. "Mark Fagan and the Politics of Urban Reform: Jersey City 1900-1917." Ph.D. dissertation, Brandeis University, 1972. 448 p.

> Attributes the failure of reform in Jersey City to the failure of the Fagan administration to deal effectively with absentee land ownership, railroads, and utilities. Argues that voters ultimately preferred the security of machine politics, especially when reformers adopted machinelike tactics to hold power.

1795 _____. "The Progressive as Humanitarian: Jersey City's Search for Social Justice, 1890-1917." NEW JERSEY HISTORY 93 (1975): 77-98.

> Analyzes the unsuccessful efforts of Jersey City's social reformers to promote social welfare by both public and private means. Contends that these activities were largely native, middle-class, and Protestant, but that they were motivated more by a sense of community than by status anxiety.

1796 _____. "The Progressive as Politician: Jersey City, 1896-1907." NEW JERSEY HISTORY 91 (1973): 5-23.

> Sees Fagan as developing into a "reform boss" whose successes resulted from political know-how and an effective party organization. Contends that Jersey City's progressive movement proved a failure, and that the city emerged "as a symbol of municipal indifference."

1797 _____. "The Progressive as Single Taxer: Mark Fagan and the Jersey City Experience, 1900-1917." AMERICAN JOURNAL OF ECONOMICS AND SOCIOLOGY 33 (1974): 287-97.

> Contends that Jersey City reform Mayor Mark Fagan, like other urban reformers, came to espouse the single tax reform only after successive electoral defeats, fights with conservative state legislatures and courts, and other frustrations. Concludes that Fagan and his followers finally resorted to the single tax as the only fundamental reform solution to the ills they saw in urban society.

1798 Toulmin, Harry Aubrey, Jr. THE CITY MANAGER: A NEW PROFES-

SION. New York and London: D. Appleton and Co., 1916. Reprint. New York: Arno Press, 1978. 310 p.

> Reflects the conviction of Progressive era good government reformers that municipal administration required a "scientific" approach based upon college level training.

1799 Travis, Anthony R. "Mayor George Ellis: Grand Rapids Political Boss and Progressive Reformer." MICHIGAN HISTORY 58 (1974): 101-30.

> Contends that Ellis's political career suggests a type of urban politician who fits neither traditional nor revisionist interpretations of bossism and reform, since he was a left-wing progressive who was at once a machine politician and a social reformer.

1800 Trolander, Judith A. "Twenty Years at Hiram House." OHIO HISTORY 78 (1969): 25-37.

> Portrays Hiram House, Cleveland's first settlement house, as an effective force in working among the immigrant poor and of meeting the needs of the neighborhood it served, especially in the areas of kindergarten, home economics, and manual training classes.

1801 Tucker, Louis Leonard, ed. "The Life of the 'Boss of Cincinnati.'" CINCINNATI HISTORICAL SOCIETY BULLETIN 26 (1968): 137-57.

> Discusses the paucity of sources for historical investigations of George B. Cox, political boss of Cincinnati from 1886 to 1916, and presents an edited version of an autobiographical piece by Cox relating his rise to power and the reasons for his success which appeared in the NEW YORK WORLD on May 14, 1911.

1802 Turner, George Kibbe. "Galveston: A Business Corporation." NEW McCLURES MAGAZINE 28 (1906): 610-20.

> One of the classic statements of the corporate model of urban governance which denounces the aldermanic system as the source of all urban problems and claims that the solution lies only in adopting the form and practice of business.

1803 Urban, Wayne. "Organized Teachers and Educational Reform During the Progressive Era: 1890-1920." HISTORY OF EDUCATION QUARTERLY 16 (1976): 35-52.

> Investigates the attitudes of teachers' organizations in Atlanta, New York City, and Chicago, and concludes that they opposed the centralization of schools and pedagogical changes. Contends that teachers acted largely out of perceived self-interest, and occasionally supported educational reforms, but out of different motivations than those of middle- and upper-class reformers.

1804 Wade, Louise C. GRAHAM TAYLOR: PIONEER FOR SOCIAL JUSTICE, 1851-1938. Chicago: University of Chicago Press, 1964. 268 p.

> Presents the Chicago reformer, minister, and teacher as an organizer and propagandist for social justice, who translated the Social Gospel into a variety of practical reforms.

1805 _____. "The Heritage from Chicago's Early Settlement Houses." JOURNAL OF THE ILLINOIS STATE HISTORICAL SOCIETY 60 (1967): 411-41.

> Examines the activities of Chicago's settlement house workers, their involvement in ward politics, and their contributions to urban and national reform. Finds that professionalism and the climate of the 1920s ended their political and reformist efforts.

1806 Wald, Lillian D. THE HOUSE ON HENRY STREET. New York: Dover Publications, 1971. 317 p.

> Written by one of its most famous settlement workers, this volume describes the house's services for children, youth, and immigrants and discusses the social forces at work in Henry Street and New York.

1807 Walsh, George. GENTLEMAN JIMMY WALKER: MAYOR OF THE JAZZ AGE. New York: Praeger, 1974. 362 p.

> Focuses on the career of James J. Walker, providing a colorful political and anecdotal discussion of his tenure as mayor of New York City.

1808 Walsh, James P. "Abe Ruef Was No Boss: Machine Politics, Reform, and San Francisco." CALIFORNIA HISTORICAL QUARTERLY 51 (1972): 3-16.

> Argues that reformers succeeded in prosecuting Abe Ruef and in removing Mayor Eugene Schmitz from office, but not in locating and prosecuting the corporate bribe givers. By using promises of immunity prosecutors were able briefly to control the board of supervisors as effectively as had the bosses. Ironically, after the scandals the electorate returned Schmitz to office on the board of supervisors because he, like most of them, was an ethnic.

1809 Warren, Roland L.; Rose, Stephen M.; and Bergunder, Ann F. THE STRUCTURE OF URBAN REFORM. Lexington, Mass.: Lexington Books, 1974. 220 p.

> Analyzes the structure for initiating urban reform and the processes essential for sustaining it. Focuses upon the actions of community decision organization in instituting and continuing reform activities.

1810 Weinstein, James. "Organized Business and the City Commission and Manager Movements." JOURNAL OF SOCIAL HISTORY 28 (1962): 166-82.

    Argues that business supported the commission and city manager forms in order to rationalize and systematize urban life, and even sometimes favored planning and municipal ownership of utilities. Contends that Socialists opposed the former as destructive of localized control, but supported the latter as a prelude to socialism.

1811 Weiss, Nancy Joan. CHARLES FRANCIS MURPHY, 1858-1924: RESPECTABILITY AND RESPONSIBILITY IN TAMMANY POLITICS. Northampton, Mass.: Smith College, 1968. 139 p.

    This Edwin H. Land Prize winning essay supports J. Joseph Huthmacher's thesis that progressivism was more than a middle-class movement. Charles F. Murphy, for instance, cracked down on prostitution, worked to reform the police force, and supported other state and local reforms at the same time he used "honest graft" and patronage to his political advantage.

1812 Wendt, Lloyd, and Kogan, Herman. BIG BILL OF CHICAGO. Indianapolis: Bobbs-Merrill, 1953. 384 p.

    Descriptive, anecdotal, and popularized biography of William Hale Thompson, "Big Bill the Builder," focusing mainly on his reign as Mayor of Chicago, from 1915 to 1923 and 1927 to 1931.

1813 _____. BOSSES IN LUSTY CHICAGO: THE STORY OF BATH-HOUSE JOHN AND HINKY DINK. Bloomington: Indiana University Press, 1967. 384 p.

    This is a reissue of LORDS OF THE LEVEE, a biography of "Bathhouse John" Coughlin and "Hinky Dink" Kenna, joint bosses of Chicago's first ward from 1890 to 1940.

1814 West, Elliott. "Cleansing the Queen City: Prohibition and Urban Reform in Denver." ARIZONA AND THE WEST 14 (1972): 331-46.

    Shows that while Prohibitionists and Progressives frequently cooperated, their paths sometimes crossed, as in the general election of 1914. Argues that "local progressivism was never a unified movement, but an amalgam of interested groups."

1815 White, Leonard D. THE CITY MANAGER. Chicago: University of Chicago Press, 1927. Reprint. Westport, Conn.: Greenwood Press, 1969. 355 p.

    Compares the structure and functioning of urban government

before and after cities adopted the city manager form. Shows significant differences in the socioeconomic and ethno-religious makeup of city councils which switched from the ward system to at-large elections.

1816 Whiteaker, Larry H. "Moral Reform and Prostitution in New York City, 1830-1860." Ph.D. dissertation, Princeton University, 1977. 329 p.

Describes the "crusades" of New York's reformers and their four major reform associations: the New York Magdalene Society, New York Female Benevolent Society, American Society for Promoting the Observance of the Seventh Commandment, and New York Female Moral Reform Society.

1817 Wolfe, Margaret Ripley. "State and Municipal Food and Drug Control, 1908-1920: The Career of Lucius Polk Brown in Tennessee and New York City." Ph.D. dissertation, University of Kentucky, 1974. 293 p.

Uses Brown's work in the public health movement in an attempt to explain how reformers created bureaucracies and what made them grow and why they changed.

1818 Wolfinger, Raymond E. "Why Political Machines Have Not Withered Away and Other Revisionist Thoughts." JOURNAL OF POLITICS 34 (1972): 364-98.

Presents a definition of machine politics as "part of a typology of incentives for political participation," analyzes some of the inconsistencies in arguments that explain the incidence of such politics as a function of the socioeconomic composition of urban electorates, and points to contemporary geographical variations in political styles.

1819 Woods, Joseph G. "The Progressives and the Police: Urban Reform and the Professionalization of the Los Angeles Police." Ph.D. dissertation, University of California, Los Angeles, 1973. 665 p.

Describes the development of police "professionalization" as a method of reform in the Los Angeles Police Department, demonstrating its resulting ineffectiveness in crime reduction.

1820 Woods, Robert A. THE NEIGHBORHOOD IN NATION BUILDING: THE RUNNING COMMENT OF THIRTY YEARS AT THE SOUTH END HOUSE. New York: Houghton Mifflin Co., 1923. Reprint. New York: Arno Press, 1970. 348 p.

Contains essays and speeches by Woods over a thirty-year period on the problems, goals, and methods of settlement houses, with special reference to South End House.

Bosses, Machines, Urban Reform

1821 Woods, Robert A., and Kennedy, Albert J. THE SETTLEMENT HORIZON: A NATIONAL ESTIMATE. New York: Arno Press, 1970. 399 p.

    Written by two prominent settlement house workers. Examines the origins, organization and activities of the movement and its interaction with urban political machines and with other private and semiprivate agencies.

1822 Woods, Robert A., ed. THE CITY WILDERNESS: A SETTLEMENT STUDY BY RESIDENTS AND ASSOCIATES OF SOUTH END HOUSE. Boston: Houghton Mifflin Co., 1898. Reprint. New York: Arno Press, 1970. 319 p.

    Discusses the efforts of the workers at the Boston South End House to deal with unemployment, inadequate housing, and political corruption among its residents of Irish, Jewish, German, Italian, and black extraction.

1823 Woods, Robert A., and Kennedy, Albert J., eds. HANDBOOK OF SETTLEMENTS. New York: Charities Publication Committee, 1923. Reprint. New York: Arno Press, 1970. 326 p.

    Contains detailed information on the settlement house movement in the United States and on individual settlement houses.

1824 Wortman, Marlene Stein. "Domesticating the Nineteenth-Century American City." PROSPECTS 3 (1977): 531-72.

    Contends that historians have neglected the feminine characteristics of urban progressivism and that much of the reformist impulse flowed from a preoccupation with making the city, as a physical and social environment, conform to the demands of the ideal home environment. Explores the nineteenth-century evolution of that mind set.

1825 Zink, Harold. CITY BOSSES IN THE UNITED STATES: A STUDY OF TWENTY MUNICIPAL BOSSES. Durham, N.C.: Duke University Press, 1930. Reprint. New York: AMS Press, 1968. 371 p.

    A reprint of a classic study of urban bosses of the late nineteenth and early twentieth century, which summarizes their backgrounds, relationships, and activities, including their attitudes and roles in reform attempts of the era.

1826 Zolot, Herbert M. "The Issue of Good Government and James Michael Curley: Curley and the Boston Scene from 1897-1918." Ph.D. dissertation, State University of New York, Stony Brook, 1975. 635 p.

    Focuses upon Curley's struggles with fellow Irish-American Democrats and with the Yankee, Protestant Good Government

Association. Delineates the conflict between the latter's insistence upon scientifically managed, efficient, economical, and business-oriented government and the Irish machine politician's emphasis upon personal political favor and social services to the disadvantaged.

1827 Zueblin, Charles. AMERICAN MUNICIPAL PROGRESS. New York: Macmillan Co., 1916. Reprint. New York: Arno Press, 1978. 522 p.

Recounts the progress made by urban reformers in such areas as water supply, sewerage, public health, street paving, recreation, municipal ownership, and administration.

ADDENDUM

1828 Abbott, Carl. "Indianapolis in the 1850's: Popular Economic Thought and Urban Growth." INDIANA MAGAZINE OF HISTORY 74 (1978): 293-315.

   Finds that the booster literature reflected the consensus of the majority of Indianapolis' articulate residents that economic growth was the greatest desideratum. Also concludes that most of the city's inhabitants had a realistic view of their prospects and were not fooled by the grandiose claims of the boosters.

1829 Alexander, Elliott Bracken. "Middletown as a Pioneer Community." Ph.D. dissertation, Ball State University, 1978. 278 p.

   Uses techniques of the "new urban history" to analyze geographical and social mobility patterns in Muncie, Indiana, for the years 1850-80. Finds high rates of population turnover, but that upward mobility typified those who remained.

1830 Ardnt, R., et al. "Some Personal Thoughts about Cities." NATION'S CITIES 16 (1978): 6-25.

   Contains several highly personal assessments about urban life and growing up in the city by ten editors and writers for the journal, stressing what they value most about the cities in which they work.

1831 Arnold, Joseph L. "The Neighborhood and City Hall: The Origin of the Neighborhood Associations in Baltimore, 1880-1911." JOURNAL OF URBAN HISTORY 6 (1979): 3-30.

   Argues the importance of middle-class protective and improvement associations in the development of the U.S. city's contemporary neighborhood system as well as for understanding the dynamics of political power in the modern city.

1832 Baltzell, E. Digby. PURITAN BOSTON AND QUAKER PHILADELPHIA. Riverside, N.J.: Free Press, 1979. 640 p.

Addendum

Focuses upon two versions of the Protestant ethic and respective impact upon the spirit of class authority and leadership. Examines different patterns of wealth; education; thought; art and architecture; the medical, legal, and clerical professions; and governance.

1833 Barclay, Morgan J. "Reform in Toledo: The Political Career of Samuel M. Jones." NORTHWEST OHIO QUARTERLY 50 (1978): 79-89.

Argues that an examination of the careers of such early midwestern urban Progressives as Samuel Jones, Hazen Pingree, and Tom Johnson serves as a healthy corrective to interpretations of the Progressive era as a "triumph of conservatism" or a "search for order." Urges a focus on urban, rather than national, reform activities.

1834 Beirne, D. Randall. "Residential Growth and Stability in the Baltimore Industrial Community of Canton during the Late Nineteenth Century." MARYLAND HISTORICAL MAGAZINE 74 (1979): 39-51.

Attributes the residential stability of the Canton community in the face of general mobility to a variety of factors acting independently and in unison: paternalism, ethnicity, the family, and employment in local industry. Sees the key in the scale of local industry and the attitudes of local management.

1835 Berg, Barbara. THE REMEMBERED GATE: ORIGINS OF AMERICAN FEMINISM: THE WOMAN AND THE CITY, 1800-1860. New York: Oxford University Press, 1978. 343 p.

Argues that the burgeoning urban growth of this era had important impacts on women and the rise of feminism--as distinct from the more narrowly focused issues of women's rights--"at once heightening women's oppression and setting the stage for her future efforts at emancipation."

1836 Bilhartz, Terry David. "Urban Religion and the Second Great Awakening: A Religious History of Baltimore, Maryland, 1790-1830." Ph.D. dissertation, George Washington University, 1979. 422 p.

Examines "the urban and urbane aspects of the second great awakening by analyzing the size, social structure, and influence of Baltimore's church congregations between 1790 and 1830."

1837 Blaine, James G. II. "The Birth of a Neighborhood: Nineteenth-Century Charlestown, Massachusetts." Ph.D. dissertation, University of Michigan, 1978. 537 p.

Focuses on the efforts of Charlestown's residents to maintain a sense of community in the face of the rapid and enormous changes engendered by the expansion and industrialization of Boston. Devotes special attention to the Irish immigrants who inherited the neighborhood and who tried to build their own version of a community.

1838 Blumenfeld, H. "The Old City and the New Metropolis." In his METROPOLIS . . . AND BEYOND: SELECTED ESSAYS BY HANS BLUMENFELD, pp. 26-32. New York: John Wiley, 1979.

Focuses upon the experiences of Philadelphia and Toronto to illustrate the changing distributions of functions in the modern metropolis, the interaction between the center and the periphery, the movement of persons within the metropolitan area, and the costs and benefits of private and public transportation.

1839 Blutza, Steven J. "Oakland's Commission and Council-Manager Plans-- Causes and Consequences: An Historical and Analytical Study." Ph.D. dissertation, University of California, 1978. 565 p.

Attributes the enactment of charter reform during the Progressive Era to a coalition of small businessmen, professionals, and organized labor which triumphed over a combination of big businessmen and machine politicians. Finds that the latter dominated the first several commissions, however, and that several realignments eventually led to a city manager system in 1930.

1840 Briggs, John W. AN ITALIAN PASSAGE: IMMIGRANTS TO THREE AMERICAN CITIES, 1890-1930. New Haven, Conn.: Yale University Press, 1978. 348 p.

Examines the interaction between Italian immigrants and urban life in Rochester and Utica, New York, and Kansas City, Missouri. Focuses upon the transition from Italian to Italian American especially as it was reflected in their mutual benefit societies, education, businesses, politics, and the press.

1841 Brown, A.T., and Dorsett, L.W. K.C.: A HISTORY OF KANSAS CITY, MISSOURI. Boulder, Colo.: Pruett Publishing, 1978. 303 p.

Traces the evolution of the city from its origins as a fur trading center to its present status as a metropolis. Stresses the role played by various waves of urban reformers in trying to make the city more livable.

1842 Bunker, J.G. HARBOR AND HAVEN: AN ILLUSTRATED HISTORY OF THE PORT OF NEW YORK. Woodland Hills, Calif.: Windsor Publications, 1979. 302 p.

Traces the evolution of the New York City harbor from its seventeenth-century founding to the present, stressing the ex-

Addendum

periences of the people who passed through the port, both on the way in and out.

1843 Chamberlayne, Donald W. "The Politics of Urban Renewal in Holyoke, Massachusetts: 1957-1974." Ph.D. dissertation, University of Massachusetts, 1978. 474 p.

Examines the city's three major urban renewal projects and arrives at two basic conclusions: (1) that the city developed considerably greater technical and administrative capacity to plan and implement projects as appointed commissioners were supplanted by staff experts responsible to the mayor and, (2) that significant constraints were imposed upon the range of policy alternatives by aldermanic politics.

1844 Connolly, Harold X. A GHETTO GROWS IN BROOKLYN. New York: New York University Press, 1979. 248 p.

Traces the development of the Bedford-Stuyvesant area, beginning with black life in Brooklyn during the colonial period, through focusing mainly on public policy perspectives of the post-1940 ghetto problems.

1845 Cox, Richard J. "The Plight of the American Municipal Archives: Baltimore, 1729-1979." AMERICAN ARCHIVIST 42 (1979): 281-92.

Traces the evolution of efforts to establish an adequate city archives in Baltimore over two and one-half centuries. Finds the biggest inhibiting factor to be a lack of interest on the part of city government officials.

1846 Cuilier, J. "Mobility and the Social Organization of Urban Space in the United States, 1760-1820." INTERNATIONAL JOURNAL OF URBAN AND REGIONAL RESEARCH (London) 2 (1978): 270-86.

Attributes the reforms of the 1820s not to a growing egalitarianism, but rather as an effort by the urban ruling class to moderate possible class conflict. Sees the rational organization of urban social space as a response to modernization which divided the city into districts based upon function.

1847 Dalin, David G. "Jewish and Non-Partisan Republicanism in San Francisco, 1911-1963." AMERICAN JEWISH HISTORY 68 (1979): 492-516.

Outlines the prominent and active political role of the Jewish community, and the roots and causes of their persisting pattern of nonpartisan Republicanism.

1848 Daniels, Bruce C. THE CONNECTICUT TOWN: GROWTH AND DE-

VELOPMENT, 1635-1790. Middletown, Conn.: Wesleyan University Press, 1979. 288 p.

> Examines the process of town settlement and formation, the growth and distribution of population, the evolution of town-meeting government, the growth and governance of church societies, the proliferation of local institutions, the emergence of central places, and the role of urbanization in early New England society.

1849 Davis, Ronald L.F., and Holmes, Harry D. "Insurgency and Municipal Reform in St. Louis, 1893-1904." MIDWEST REVIEW 1 (1979): 1-18.

> Contends that the experience of St. Louis with municipal reform suggests three conclusions of wider applicability: (1) that the movement for municipal ownership encompassed people from many class or status groups, with blue-collar workers predominating; (2) that the city's social justice movement was clearly distinguished from that advocating honesty and efficiency in government, and; (3) that reform's ultimate failure was a consequence of its broad-based nature which enabled the propertied class to dominate the movement.

1850 Decker, Peter R. "Jewish Merchants in San Francisco: Social Mobility on the Urban Frontier." AMERICAN JEWISH HISTORY 68 (1979): 396-407.

> Summarizes the Jewish merchant experience in nineteenth-century San Francisco stressing the associational activity and in-group organization they established to protect themselves from "the excesses of laissez-faire capitalism" and established institutions. Asserts that much of the anti-Jewish prejudice of the early 1850s disappeared due to the accomplishments of San Francisco's Jewish community.

1851 Donagher, Richard J. "The Urban Bull Moose: A Case Study of Philadelphia and Pittsburgh." Ph.D. dissertation, Fordham University, 1979. 381 p.

> Finds that the Washington (Progressive) party in the state was largely supported by those who wished to break with the dominant Republican political machine, including reformers and Pittsburgh urban machine politicians. Concludes that Roosevelt received his greatest support in the "ring" wards of both cities, and managed to gain considerable support in the "core," immigrant working-class wards of Pittsburgh because of the efforts of machine politicians.

1852 Doris, Dawn Dwyer. "A Century of City-Building: Three Generations of the Kilgour Family in Cincinnati, 1789-1914." Ph.D. dissertation, Miami University, 1979.

Addendum

Analyzes the generative role played by the Kilgour family, the most prestigious members of Cinciannati's social and economic elite, in the city's urbanization. Notes changing notions of public and private role of the American urban upper class.

1853 Ehrlich, Richard L., ed. IMMIGRANTS IN INDUSTRIAL AMERICA, 1850-1920. Charlottesville: University Press of Virginia, 1977. 218 p.

Contains ten essays by a variety of scholars dealing with the impact of industry upon family life in Philadelphia, working women in New York City, family and work patterns in Buffalo, Italians in Buffalo, Irish political response to nativism in Jersey City, managerial reform, the Irish and the labor boycott in New York City, immigrants and industry in Philadelphia, ethnicity and occupation in Buffalo, and a comparison of Irish, German, and native-born workers in Poughkeepsie, New York.

1854 Ernest, William Joel III. "Urban Leaders and Social Change: The Urbanization Process in Richmond, Virginia, 1840-1880." Ph.D. dissertation, University of Virginia, 1978. 438 p.

Documents the response to growth from the perspective of changing notions of community and the need to redefine the public interest. Finds that the city's leaders proved reluctant to abandon "more traditional forms of community cohesion."

1855 Fischer, Joel. "Urban Transportation: Home Rule and the Independent Subway System in New York City, 1917-1925." Ph.D. dissertation, St. John's University, 1978. 395 p.

Focuses largely upon the political struggles and urban rural conflict which revolved around attempts to build the largest of New York City's three subway systems, the Independent Subway lines. Also uses census data for 1910 to 1940 to inform a subway-benefit theory.

1856 Fisher, Irving D. "Frederick Law Olmsted and the Philosophic Background to the City Planning Movement in the United States." Ph.D. dissertation, Columbia University, 1976. 429 p.

Examines the reasons for indifference or antagonism toward comprehensive city planning in nineteenth-century America and attributes them largely to the tendency to view land only as a speculative commodity, to residential mobility, and to antiurban bias. Credits Olmsted with uniting art and science to form a comprehensive urban plan which would meet the social and aesthetic needs of the entire community.

Addendum

1857 Flack, Irwin F. "Who Governed Cincinnati? A Comparative Analysis of Government and Social Structure in a Nineteenth Century River City: 1819-1860." Ph.D. dissertation, University of Pittsburgh, 1978. 326 p.

> Argues that Cincinnati was governed neither by immigrant-based machine politicians or by elites, but by a governing class which emerged out of a complex set of circumstances engendered by urban growth. Does agree that the city's elite ameliorated the impact of change and maintained the existing social order when other social-integrative mechanisms had broken down.

1858 Flowerdew, Robin. "Spatial Patterns of Residential Segregation in a Southern City." JOURNAL OF AMERICAN STUDIES 13 (1979): 93-107.

> Uses Memphis as a case study to develop a model of the spatial pattern of residential segregation appropriate to southern cities. Finds that black sections are not limited to the inner city as in the North but are located throughout and that the quality of social services varies among these sections.

1859 Foster, Mark. "City Planners and Urban Transportation: The American Response, 1900-1940." JOURNAL OF URBAN HISTORY 5 (1979): 365-96.

> Contends that the reasons for the failure of public transportation in American cities were enormously complex and did not result from any kind of organized conspiracy. Argues that the triumph of the automobile was evident before World War II, due to the changing dynamics of urban transportation.

1860 Funigiello, Philip J. THE CHALLENGE TO URBAN LIBERALISM: FEDERAL-CITY RELATIONS DURING WORLD WAR II. Knoxville: University of Tennesse Press, 1978. 273 p.

> Seeks to fill the knowledge gap of federal-city relations in the period between the New Deal and the Truman administration. Finds that an impressive beginning of federal-city cooperation in planning ultimately dissolved before the challenge of conservatives and the primacy of war-induced foreign policy issues.

1861 Gabaccia, Donna R. "Houses and People: Sicilians in Sicily and New York, 1890-1930." Ph.D. dissertation, University of Michigan, 1979. 368 p.

> Examines the housing and private lives of Sicilians in Italy and on the lower east side, focusing on residential choices

Addendum

and patterns and everyday activities to explore the relationship between public and private worlds and the impact of the physical environment on behavior.

1862 Gelfand, Mitchell. "Progress and Prosperity: Jewish Social Mobility in Los Angeles in the Booming Eighties." AMERICAN JEWISH HISTORY 68 (1979): 408-33.

Describes and analyzes occupational, residential, and property mobility for Los Angeles's Jewish population, noting various contrasts with patterns for the city as a whole and with other U.S. cities.

1863 Graves, John W. "Town and Country: Race Relations and Urban Development in Arkansas 1865-1905." Ph.D. dissertation, University of Virginia, 1978. 448 p.

Finds that Arkansas blacks made substantial gains in the state's cities during the period and that a black middle class eventually emerged, but that the hostility and prejudice of rural whites led to the enactment of disfranchisement and segregation statutes designed to counteract the liberating influence of urban life.

1864 Hamilton, Kenneth M. "Black Town Promotion and Development on the Middle Border, 1877-1914." Ph.D. dissertation, Washington University, 1978. 215 p.

Examines three black communities--Nicodemus, Kansas; Boley, Oklahoma; and Langston, Oklahoma--and finds that they developed within the same social, economic, and legal context as did white towns on the midwestern frontier, and that they were founded for the same reasons. Concludes that their exclusive racial character made them more attractive to blacks, but that otherwise there were few discernible differences.

1864a Hill, Carole E. "Ethnicity as a Factor in Urban Social Change." In SOUTH ATLANTIC URBAN STUDIES, vol. 3, edited by S.M. Hines, G.W. Hopkins, and A.M. McCandless, pp. 107-21. Columbia: University of South Carolina Press, 1979.

Discusses the changing nature of ethnicity in Atlanta, focusing largely on the present-day city and the changes generated by the arrival of large numbers of Latin Americans.

1865 Hines, Samuel M.; Hopkins, George W.; and McCandless, Amy M., eds. SOUTH ATLANTIC URBAN STUDIES. Vol. 3. Columbia: University of South Carolina Press, 1979. 400 p.

Presents ten essays from a variety of disciplinary perspectives,

Addendum

fifteen book review essays, and a symposium on "The Legacy of V.O. Key's 'Southern Politics.'"

1866 Hogan, David. "Education and the Making of the Chicago Working Class, 1880-1930." HISTORY OF EDUCATION QUARTERLY 19 (1978): 227-70.

    Argues that all ethnic groups tended to keep their children in school longer in order to increase their economic welfare and that ethnicity was not an independent variable which differentiated various groups but rather a cultural mediation of the class experience of immigrants.

1867 Hoover, Knight Eugene. "Organizational Networks and Ethnic Persistence: A Case Study of Norwegian American Ethnicity in the New York Metropolitan Area." Ph.D. dissertation, Columbia University, New York, 1979. 406 p.

    Examines the institutional factors responsible for the persistence of ethnicity as opposed to assimilation, focusing on both ethnic and Norwegian national organizations as "maintainers and creators of ethnic identity."

1868 Ingham, John N. THE IRON BARONS: A SOCIAL ANALYSIS OF AN AMERICAN URBAN ELITE, 1874-1965. Westport, Conn.: Greenwood Press, 1978. 242 p.

    Examines the social characteristics of the iron and steel entrepreneurial elites of Pittsburgh, Philadelphia, Bethlehem, Cleveland, Youngstown, and Wheeling. Concludes that they operated within the framework of family and class origins, functioned as members of elite clubs, were very community- and place-oriented, and established institutions with a great deal of continuity.

1869 Jablonski, James L. "Conscience and Commitment: William Dean Howells and Urban America." Ph.D. dissertation, Marquette University, 1978. 373 p.

    Finds that Howells was unique in his understanding and appreciation of the complexities of urban life in the late nineteenth century. Commends Howells for defining America's notion of community, and the sense of what constituted place and environment.

1870 Janis, Ralph. "The Decline and Fall of New York City: Popular Illusion or Historical Fact?" INDIANA ACADEMY OF THE SOCIAL SCIENCES, PROCEEDINGS 13 (1978): 109-13.

    Reports on efforts to acquaint undergraduate students with the reasons for the city's difficulties and to combat the stereotypes

Addendum

with which they approached the topic. Finds that a shrinking of the city's economic base was the major reason for its decline.

1871 Jordan, Lalyon Wayne. "Police Power and Public Safety in Antebellum Charleston: The Emergence of a New Police, 1800-1860." In SOUTH ATLANTIC URBAN STUDIES, vol. 3, edited by S.M. Hines, G.W. Hopkins, and A.M. McCandless, pp. 141-72. Columbia: University of South Carolina Press, 1979.

Focuses on the institutionalizing of a police service as a variation of the generally observed process in Western European and U.S. cities, whereby earlier ad hoc constabulary gave way to quasiprofessional police forces.

1872 Kasson, John F. AMUSING THE MILLION: CONEY ISLAND AT THE TURN OF THE CENTURY. New York: Hill and Wang, 1979. 120 p.

Portrays Coney Island as a case study of the growing cultural revolt against genteel standards of taste and conduct and the rise of mass culture. Finds that the amusement center lost its uniqueness when others adopted its popular culture emphasis.

1873 Kim, Illsoo. "Immigrants to Urban America: The Korean Community in the New York Metropolitan Area." Ph.D. dissertation, Columbia University, New York, 1979. 618 p.

Describes and analyzes "how national and international economic and political institutions and policies result in and effect the creation, operation and character of an ethnic community."

1874 Kocolowski, Gary P. "Louisville at Large: Industrial-Urban Organization, Inter-City Migration, and Occupational Mobility in the Central United States, 1865-1906." Ph.D. dissertation, University of Cincinnati, 1978. 212 p.

Contends that industrialization and metropolitanization after 1880 reduced the transiency of urban migration, especially in inland cities such as Louisville, and that mobility is due more to changes in economic and family structure than to individuals seeking upward mobility.

1875 _____. "Stabilizing Migration to Louisville and Cincinnati, 1865-1901." CINCINNATI HISTORICAL SOCIETY BULLETIN 37 (1979): 23-40.

Argues that the Ohio River cities displayed more population stability than that found by Stephan Thernstrom, Peter Knights, and Howard Chudacoff in other cities. Finds the key to the stability of foreign stock populations in the presence of familial group relationships, ethnic organizational activities, and secure industrial or ethnic retail business employment.

1876 Lane, Roger. VIOLENT DEATH IN THE CITY: SUICIDE, ACCIDENT, AND MURDER IN NINETEENTH-CENTURY PHILADELPHIA. Cambridge: Harvard University Press, 1979. 193 p.

Uses data on violent deaths in Philadelphia to take issue with the interpretations of the Chicago school of sociology regarding the connection between urban growth and the increase of violence. Insists that the city was at least partially successful in imposing its demands for order upon its expanding population and that we have yet to find a functional substitute for the industrial city as a social system.

1877 Leashore, Bogart R. "Interracial Household in 1850-1880 Detroit, Michigan." Ph.D. dissertation, University of Michigan, 1979. 242 p.

Develops a typology of interracial households: blacks living in white households, whites living in black households, and interracial marriages.

1878 Light, Dale B. "Class, Ethnicity, and the Urban Ecology in a Nineteenth Century City: Philadelphia's Irish, 1840-1890." Ph.D. dissertation, University of Pennsylvania, 1979. 259 p.

Identifies some of the "behaviorally significant subgroups" among Philadelphia's Irish population and relates such internal differentiation to "the development of a self-conscious Irish ethnic community in the city." Discusses the relationship among class, ethnicity, and urban ecology.

1879 Livingston, John. "The Industrial Removal Office, the Galveston Project and the Denver Jewish Community." AMERICAN JEWISH HISTORY 68 (1979): 434-58.

Investigates the response of Denver's German-Jewish community to the influx of Eastern European Jews characterizing the way in which the Industrial Removal Office and the Galveston Plan as evidence not of hostility between American Jews and recent coreligious immigrants, but as designed to help the integration of Eastern Europeans into American society while also "resolving some of the difficulties created by the concentration of the immigrant population in the port cities of the Northeast."

1880 Lubove, Roy. "Planning and Pluralism in American Society." In SOUTH ATLANTIC URBAN STUDIES, vol. 3, edited by S.M. Hines, G.W. Hopkins, and A.M. McCandless, pp. 85-106. Columbia: University of South Carolina Press, 1979.

Addendum

Traces the development of different community types in colonial America, stressing the "conflict between planning ideals and pluralistic culture." Argues that planning has proved most successful in those community types which were of small size, had relatively homogeneous populations, and where some central consensus or authority prevailed.

1881 McDonald, Terence Joseph. "Urban Development, Political Power, and Municipal Expenditure in San Francisco, 1860-1910: A Quantitative Investigation of Historical Theory." Ph.D. dissertation, Stanford University, 1979. 285 p.

Uses annual per capita municipal expenditure to test the "demand theory" of urban government development and policy formulation. Finds the idea of government responding to demands generated by the urbanization process essentially accurate, but incomplete in that it fails to consider the type of political regime in power.

1882 McShane, Clay. "Transforming the Use of Urban Space: A Look at the Revolution in Street Pavements, 1880-1924." JOURNAL OF URBAN HISTORY 5 (1979): 279-307.

Concludes that changes in paving surfaces during the era resulted primarily from a demand for technological solutions to such social problems as high mortality rates and the middle classes' desire for residential segregation. Finds that late nineteenth-century urbanites sought technological solutions in the absence of effective social organizations.

1883 Melvin, Patricia M. "Neighborhood in the 'Organic' City: The Social Unit Plan and the First Community Organization Movement, 1900-1920." Ph.D. dissertation, University of Cincinnati, 1978. 506 p.

Relates the social unit theory of Wilbur C. Phillips with its emphasis on neighborhoods as "nations in miniature" forming part of an organic whole, with the efforts of community organizers to translate that belief into a workable system or a public policy. Finds that Phillips' theory enjoyed much currency during the Progressive era. It declined drastically in the 1920s with the rise of "fragmented metropolis."

1884 Morgan, Myfanwy, and Golden, Hilda H. "Immigrant Families in an Industrial City: A Study of Households in Holyoke, 1880." JOURNAL OF FAMILY HISTORY 4 (1979): 56-67.

Uses 1880 census data to derive a sample to investigate household size and composition, the characteristics of heads of household, the presence of nonrelatives, and family types. Finds significant variations between foreign-born and native-born households.

Addendum

1885 Nobel, Richard A. "Paterson's Response to the Great Depression." NEW JERSEY HISTORY 96 (1978): 87-98.

Deals largely with Paterson's efforts to deal with the massive unemployment engendered by depression in a highly industrialized city. Concludes that its record of public relief assistance was minimal and threatened by constant demands to cut back, but was nevertheless adequate due largely to generous state financial aid.

1886 Noel, Thomas J. "The City and the Saloon: Denver, 1858-1916." Ph.D. dissertation, University of Colorado, 1978. 294 p.

Views the saloon as a crucial urban institution which provided a wide spectrum of goods and services to various segments of society. Contends that reformers and prohibitionists dealt a serious blow to the urban, ethnic working class when they abolished the saloon without making any provision for the vital functions which it served.

1887 O'Donnell, Charles Patrick. "Capitalism and Cities: A Critical Examination of the Rise of Industrial Capitalism and the Making of the First Modern Cities in America." Ph.D. dissertation, University of California, Berkeley, 1978. 701 p.

Argues the need for a new urban theory which will relate the development of city problems to overall processes of capitalist development, and provide a functional, statistical, and impressionistic analysis of mid-nineteenth-century cities which suggest that these were the first "truly modern U.S. cities," pointing to the presence and interplay of four critical urban sectors: production, social reproduction, infrastructure, and state.

1888 Papaleo, Ralph Joseph. "The Democratic Party in Urban Politics in New York State, 1933-38." Ph.D. dissertation, St. John's University, 1978. 623 p.

Details the myriad factors undermining the Democratic party's power in New York State, citing as the most damaging factor the party leadership's inability to resolve the issue of reapportionment in the state legislature to secure greater representation for New York City.

1889 Patton, Thomas Warren. "An Urban Congressional Delegation in an Age of Reform: The New York County Democratic Delegation to the House of Representatives, 1901-1917." Ed.D. dissertation, New York University, 1978. 292 p.

Finds that the Democratic delegation was composed largely of "undistinguished" politicians who remained either indifferent or opposed to those issues generally seen as the major reform agenda of the Progressive era.

Addendum

1890 Peihl, Mel. "Urban Catholicism and American Culture." INDIANA ACADEMY OF THE SOCIAL SCIENCES PROCEEDINGS 13 (1978): 101-8.

> Contends that, contrary to prevailing wisdom, urbanization did not result in a diminution of religious activities, at least among Catholics. Attributes this phenomenon to the church becoming more extroverted and activist, but also to its ability to ameliorate those tendencies in urban Protestantism.

1891 Pencake, William. "The Social Structure of Revolutionary Boston: Evidence from the Great Fire of 1760." JOURNAL OF INTERDISCIPLINARY HISTORY 2 (1979): 266-78.

> Indicates ways in which memorials used to secure compensation by those who suffered losses in the great fire can aid in uncovering patterns of poverty and wealth in prerevolutionary Boston, especially as a corrective to biases in other documentation, like tax records tend to underrepresent inequality and poverty.

1892 Peterson, Jon A. "The Impact of Sanitary Reform Upon American Urban Planning, 1840-1890." JOURNAL OF SOCIAL HISTORY 13 (1979): 83-103.

> Discusses the relationship between advances in understanding infectious disease and the growing sense of social problems created by rapid urban development, and the ways these created a "virtual city planning agenda for nineteenth-century American cities."

1893 Pickering, John R. "Blueprint of Power: The Public Career of Robert Speer in Denver, 1878-1918." Ph.D. dissertation, University of Denver, 1978. 247 p.

> Contends that Speer served as a vital cohesive force in Denver society at a crucial period in the city's development and was a leader of vision who provided for the city's future growth. Sees him as a broker who harmonized diverse interests, a centralizer who pulled together the diffuse strands of city government, a ritualist who eschewed moral reform, and an idealist who sought to create the "city beautiful" as well as the "city functional."

1894 Potts, James H. "The Evolution of Municipal Accounting in the United States: 1900-1935." BUSINESS HISTORY REVIEW 52 (1978): 518-36.

> Discusses the relative merits of applying standard commercial accounting techniques to cities and efforts to develop new philosophies of accounting based upon the city's unique place in society. Finds that cities have oscillated between the two

approaches and that commercial techniques designed for profit-making enterprises many have more applicability to the urban situation than has been generally supposed.

1895 Ralph, Raymond M. "The City and the Church: Catholic Beginnings in Newark, 1840-1870." NEW JERSEY HISTORY 96 (1978): 105-18.

Focuses upon the efforts of Irish and German immigrants to the city to build their parish churches and schools over the objections of various nativist groups. Deals mostly with the social and political manifestations of ethnoreligious conflict.

1896 Rose, Mark H., and Clark, John G. "Light, Heat, and Power: Energy Choice in Kansas City, Wichita, and Denver, 1900-1935." JOURNAL OF URBAN HISTORY 5 (1979): 340-64.

Argues that the wants and needs of consumers were the primary forces shaping energy choices in the three cities. Concludes that by 1935 the three had become energy intensive places with a series of reshaped indoor and outdoor environments as a result of a mixture of new technologies, old and new values, and public and private decisions.

1897 Rousey, Dennis C. "The New Orleans Police, 1805-1889: A Social History." Ph.D. dissertation, Cornell University, 1978. 367 p.

Finds that the role of the police in New Orleans was defined by their relationship to the dominant political machine and to the ethnic and working-class origins of most patrolmen. Concludes that the New Orleans police contributed greatly to the city's high crime rate through misfeasance and malfeasance by their increasing bureaucratization.

1898 Ryan, Dennis P. "Beyond the Ballot Box: A Social History of the Boston Irish, 1845-1917." Ph.D. dissertation, University of Massachusetts, 1979. 202 p.

Focuses on a variety of topics including the Irish's institutional response to poverty, parochial school experiences, career patterns, relations with other ethnic and racial groups, women's roles and associational and leisure activities.

1899 Silver, Christopher. "A New Look at Old South Urbanization: The Irish Worker in Charleston, South Carolina, 1840-1860." In SOUTH ATLANTIC URBAN STUDIES, vol. 3, edited by S.M. Hines, G.W. Hopkins, and A.M. McCandless, pp. 141-172. Columbia: University of South Carolina Press, 1979.

Argues that historians have overstressed the uniqueness of the urban Old South, and suggests that the Irish experience in antebellum Charleston "closely approximated the situation found in most American cities at that time."

Addendum

1900 Smith, Douglas L. "The New Deal and the Urban South: The Advancement of a Southern Urban Consciousness during the Depression Decade." Ph.D. dissertation, University of Southern Mississippi, 1978. 509 p.

> Finds that the New Deal's basic conservatism and decentralized administrative apparatus allowed southern political leaders maintain the status quo, but that it did profoundly influence regional urban development. Concludes that by 1940 southern municipalities were beginning to recognize, define, and increasingly deal with urban problems through central, community institutions.

1901 Spletstoser, Frederick M. "Back Door to the Land of Plenty: New Orleans as an Immigrant Port, 1820-1860." Ph.D. dissertation, Louisiana State University, 1978. 466 p.

> Focuses upon New Orleans as a port of entry and area of first settlement for over fity thousand Irish and German immigrants. Finds that they were largely destitute, engendered nativist feelings, suffered the most from inadequate urban services, burdened local and state welfare agencies, and engendered political and social ferment.

1902 Staples, Robert. "Land of Promise, Cities of Despair: Blacks in Urban America." BLACK SCHOLAR 10 (1978): 2-10.

> Examines the particular problems which face blacks in the inner city, speculates on the possibility of a political solution, and sketches the "changing face of racism." Contends that industry wants to maintain a reserve pool of unemployed black labor in order to protect private ownership of the means of production.

1903 Starr, Dennis J. "The Nature and Uses of Economic, Political, and Social Power in Trenton, New Jersey, 1880-1917." Ph.D. dissertation, Rutgers University, 1979. 357 p.

> Focuses on the domination of Trenton by a cohesive "Patrician" upper class, and explores the ways in which they maintained social control.

1904 Steiner, Henry M. CONFLICT IN URBAN TRANSPORTATION: THE PEOPLE AGAINST THE PLANNERS. Lexington: Lexington Books, 1978. 124 p.

> Investigates the conflict between planners and urban populations over the Mo Pac Expressway in Austin, Texas, Interstate 40 in Memphis, the Los Angeles International Airport, the San Francisco BART system, and bus mass transit in Watts, Houston, and Seattle. Abstracts common elements regarding philosophical and economic issues, environmental aspects, and social questions.

Addendum

1905 Tarr, Joel A. "The Separate vs. Combined Sewer Problem: A Case Study in Urban Technology Design Choice." JOURNAL OF URBAN HISTORY 5 (1979): 308-39.

> Finds that conflicting scientific theories about disease etiology and municipal budget constraints dictated that larger cities usually built sewerage systems which combined the functions of storm water removal and household waste disposal. Concludes that this resulted in pollution and health hazards, especially to downstream cities and towns.

1906 Tichnor, Thomas J. "Motor City: The Impact of the Automobile Industry upon Detroit, 1900-1975." Ph.D. dissertation, University of Michigan, 1978. 356 p.

> Examines the impact of the automobile industry of the city's economic, cultural, demographic, and spatial decentralization and its role in portraying Detroit as a working-class metropolis. Finds that the city's single industry orientation has been a mixed bag, causing both high wages and high unemployment.

1907 Toll, William. "Mobility, Fraternalism, and Jewish Cultural Change: Portland, 1910-1930." AMERICAN JEWISH HISTORY 68 (1979): 459-91.

> Examines the relationship between members in voluntary associations and social mobility, focusing on the B'nai B'rith Building Lodge no. 65, noting that Portland's Jewry proved an especially secure ethnic enclave with high rates of persistence and thus retained considerable cultural continuity.

1908 Tygiel, Jules. "Housing in Late Nineteenth-Century American Cities: Suggestions for Research." HISTORICAL METHODS 12 (1979): 84-96.

> Delineates the sources available for a study of housing and its impact upon people and makes suggestions for the study of the physical and social consequences of urbanization. Urges quantitative and qualitative analysis of bureau of labor statistics reports, census manuscript materials, investigative hearings, and labor journals.

1909 Vance, J.E. INSIDE THE MINNESOTA EXPERIMENT: A PERSONAL RECOLLECTION OF EXPERIMENTAL PLANNING AND DEVELOPMENT IN THE TWIN CITIES METROPOLITAN AREA. Minneapolis: University of Minnesota, Center for Urban and Regional Affairs, 1977. 117 p.

> Results from forty years of Vance's experience with the Twin Cities Metropolitan Council. Deals with the origin of the planning movement in the 1920s, its institutionalization in the 1950s, and the evolution of the council's research efforts, its program for land use and transportation planning, and its role in governmental reorganization.

Addendum

1910 Walsh, James P., ed. THE SAN FRANCISCO IRISH, 1850-1976. San Francisco: Irish Literary and Historical Society, 1978. 150 p.

> Contains ten essays by Walsh and seven other scholars on individual San Francisco Irish-Americans, on their early settlement, on their role in machine politics and reform and on their current status in the life of the city. Insists that, despite a great deal of assimilation and acculturation, the difference between the Irish and the rest of the city's population remain significant.

1911 Wolniewicz, Richard. "Northeast Minneapolis: Location and Movement in an Ethnic Community." Ph.D. dissertation, University of Minnesota, 1979. 250 p.

> Investigates several hypotheses related to "the development of an ethnic area and intraurban migration from 1905-1945," focusing on the Polish community.

AUTHOR INDEX

In addition to authors, this index includes all editors, compilers, and contributors to works cited in the text. References are to entry number and alphabetization is letter by letter.

A

Abbott, Bernice 466
Abbott, Carl 337, 467-68, 671, 774, 1828
Abbott, Collamer M. 672
Abbott, Edith 1030, 1181
Abrahamson, Julia 1031
Abrams, Charles 126, 1032-34
Abramson, Alan V. 127
Abramson, Mark 128
Adams, John S. 129, 469
Addams, Jane 1601-3
Adkins, Howard G. 673
Adler, Ronald 1
Adrian, Charles 1431
Aikman, Duncan 470
Ainsley, William F., Jr. 130
Akin, Edward N. 1182
Alexander, Elliott Bracken 1829
Alexander, Henry M. 1633
Alexander, John A. 775
Alexander, John K. 776-77
Alexander, Robert L. 1035
Algren, Nelson 471
Allen, Howard W. 1457
Allen, James B. 674
Alloway, David N. 1604
Allswang, John M. 1432-33, 1605
Alonso, William 1036
Alter, George 1314

Alves, William R. 1037
American Public Health Association 857
Anderson, Alan D. 131, 1434
Anderson, Guy G. 675
Anderson, Jack 338
Anderson, Martin 1038
Anderson, Nels 339
Anderson, Odin W. 954
Andrews, Wayne 472, 1039-41
Angell, Robert C. 132
Angle, Paul M. 133
Anton, Thomas J. 134
Archdeacon, Thomas J. 778-79
Archer, John 780
Ardnt, R. 1830
Aries, Philippe 340
Armbruster, Timothy Deegan 1606
Armstrong, Edward G. 135
Armstrong, Thomas F. 676
Arnold, Joseph L. 1042, 1831
Arnold, Linda M. 1435
Aronson, David Israel 1607
Atkins, Gordon 858
Attoe, Wayne 1043
Axelrod, Bernard 473
Aydelotte, William O. 1286

B

Bach, Ira J. 474-75, 1044

Author Index

Bader, Louis 859
Bagdadi, Mania Kleinburd 860
Bailey, Charles 1387
Bain, Donald E., Jr. 136, 476
Baltzell, E. Digby 137, 1832
Banfield, Edward C. 1045, 1127, 1436-38
Banham, Reyner 1046
Barck, Oscar T., Jr. 781
Barclay, Morgan J. 1833
Barnes, Joseph W. 477-78, 861
Barnes, William R. 1047-48
Barrett, Paul 862
Barrows, Robert G. 479
Barsness, Richard W. 480, 863
Barth, Gunther 138
Bartolemeo, John S. 1439
Barton, Josef J. 1183
Barton, Thomas F. 481
Bass, Herbert 463
Bassett, Edward M. 1049
Bauer, Catherine 1050
Baughin, William A. 1608
Bauman, John F. 1051-52, 1440
Bayor, Ronald H. 1184
Beals, Ralph L. 139
Bean, Walton 1609
Beard, Charles A. 1441
Beasley, Jonathon 1185
Beaudet, Paul 482
Bebout, John E. 677
Bedford, Henry F. 341
Beime, Daniel R. 1186
Beirne, Charles J. 1610
Beirne, D. Randall 1834
Belcher, John C. 140
Belcher, Wyatt W. 678
Bellush, Jewel 1053
Bender, Thomas 342-43
Benjamin, Philip S. 483
Berg, Barbara J. 344, 1442, 1835
Berger, Bennett M. 1187
Bergunder, Ann F. 1809
Berkman, Herman G. 1054
Bernard, Richard M. 1611
Berns, Walter 345
Bernstein, Arthur I. 1443
Bernstein, Barton J. 310
Berrol, Selma C. 864
Berry, Brian J.L. 141-42

Beshers, James M. 143-44
Betten, Neil 96, 123, 1129, 1188, 1336
Betters, Paul V. 1444-45
Bigelow, Martha C. Mitchell 484
Bilhartz, Terry David 1836
Binford, Henry 145
Bingham, Robert F. 28
Blackford, Mansel G. 1612
Blackwelder, Julia Kirk 1189
Blaine, James G. II 1837
Blake, John B. 865
Blake, Nelson M. 866
Blasingame, John W. 1190-91
Blasingame, Ralph 867
Blassingame, Lurton 1613
Blood, Robert O., Jr. 146
Bloomberg, Susan E. 147, 1192
Blumberg, Barbara M. 1446
Blumenfeld, Hans 1055-56, 1838
Blumin, Stuart M. 148-50, 430
Bluoin, Francis X. 679
Blutza, Steven J. 1839
Bodnar, John E. 1193-96
Bogue, Donald J. 151
Bolding, Gary 485
Bonelli, Vincent Francis 868
Bonfield, Edward C. 1436-38
Bonjean, Charles M. 1447
Bonkowsky, Elizabeth Leitch 869
Booth, Alan 152
Borchert, John R. 680
Boskin, Joseph 1197
Bowden, Martyn J. 153
Bowers, John L., Jr. 1448
Boxerman, Lawrence H. 1198
Boyer, Lee R. 782
Boyer, Paul 1614
Brace, C.L. 870
Bragaw, Donald H. 1199
Braucher, Samuel C. 1449
Breckenfield, Gurney 1128
Breckinridge, Sophonisba 1030, 1615
Breemen, Richard R. 431
Bremer, William W. 1450
Bremner, Robert H. 1616
Brenneman, Bill 486
Brewer, Paul W. 871
Bridenbaugh, Carl 783-86

Author Index

Bridenbaugh, Jessica 786
Brieger, Gert H. 872
Briggs, John W. 1840
Broadman, Anthony E. 154
Brobeck, Stephen 787
Bromley, David G. 155
Brook, Anthony 487
Brooks, Lester 1354
Brown, A. Theodore 11, 1617, 1841
Brown, Bertram S. 1200
Brown, Letitia Wood 1201
Brown, Richard D. 681, 788
Brownell, Blaine A. 12, 346, 682-87, 873, 1057, 1061, 1618
Brumberg, George D. 156
Brunner, Edmund De Schweinitz 157
Bryant, Keith L., Jr. 688
Bryce, James 1619
Buder, Stanley 488
Buehler, Alfred G. 489
Buell, Charles C. 1202
Buenker, John D. 1451-53
Bullough, William A. 874-75, 1620
Bunker, J.G. 1842
Burchard, John 88
Burgess, Ernest W. 347, 396, 490
Burnell, Peter C. 107
Burnham, Daniel H., Jr. 1058
Burnham, Walter E. 1502
Burt, Nathaniel 491
Burton, Ian 158
Bushman, Richard L. 789
Butler, Edgar W. 159
Butler, Elizabeth B. 559
Butler, Jeanne F. 1059
Butler, Tod J. 492
Byington, Margaret F. 559

C

Cable, Mary 493
Cady, David B. 1060
Cahill, Susan 72
Cahnman, Werner J. 160, 168
Cain, Louis P. 876-77
Calhoun, Daniel 113
Calhoun, Richard B. 878-79
Callahan, Helen 494
Callow, Alexander B., Jr. 73-74, 1621-22

Calvert, Monte A. 1623
Camarillo, Albert 1203
Cameron, Diane Maher 880
Candeloro, Dominic 881
Capeci, Dominic J., Jr. 1061, 1204, 1454
Carey, Matthew 790
Caro, Robert A. 1455
Carpenter, Charles G. 689
Carpenter, David G. 40-41
Carpenter, Niles 161
Carter, Harold 162
Cartwright, Walter J. 282
Carwardine, Richard 882
Cassell, Frank A. 1205
Caye, James F. 883
Cayton, Horace R. 1231
Censer, Jack R. 135-36, 217, 331, 1136, 1150, 1347, 1429, 1710
Cerillo, Augustus, Jr. 1624-25
Chaffee, Eugene B. 495
Chalmers, Leonard 1456, 1626-28
Chamberlayne, Donald W. 1843
Chamberlin, Everett 496
Chambers, William N. 1502
Chapin, F. Stuart 163
Chapman, Edmund H. 497, 1062
Cheape, Charles W. 884
Checkoway, Barry N. 1063
Chrisman, Noel J. 81, 1206
Chudacoff, Howard P. 2, 164, 1207
Clague, Christopher 1485
Clark, Dennis J. 165, 498, 1208-10
Clark, Geoffrey W. 524, 1629
Clark, John G. 348, 499-501, 1896
Clark, Kenneth B. 1211
Clark, Norman H. 502
Clark, T.N. 1212
Clark, Thomas D. 690
Clark, W.A.V. 166
Clement, Priscilla F. 885
Cline, Dorothy I. 1630
Clinton, Katherine B. 750
Clubb, Jerome M. 1457
Cobb, James Charles 691, 1458
Cochran, Lillian T. 167

Author Index

Cohen, Abby 886
Cohen, Ronald D. 887-89
Cohen, Sol 890, 1631
Cohn, Raymond L. 692
Colburn, David R. 1632
Cole, Donald B. 1213
Colean, Miles 1064
Collett, Kay G. 1633
Collins, Cherry Wedgwood 891
Collins, George R. 1065
Comhaire, Jean 168
Commons, John R. 1634
Condit, Carl W. 169, 1066-68
Conk, Margo Anderson 693
Connery, Robert H. 1459-60
Connolly, Harold X. 1844
Connors, Margaret E. 503
Connors, Richard J. 1635
Conot, Robert 1214
Contopoulos, Michael 1215
Conway, Alan 504
Conzen, Kathleen Neils 432, 1216, 1461
Conzen, Michael P. 170-72, 694
Cook, Adrian 1217
Cook, Ann 3
Cook, Edward M., Jr. 791
Cook, Philip L. 505
Coolidge, John 1069
Cooper, Michele F. 72
Cordasco, Francesco 1242
Corn, Jacqueline Karnell 892-93
Cornwell, Elmer E., Jr. 1636
Corty, Floyd L. 1462
Cosgrove, John J. 894
Cox, Harvey 895
Cox, Richard J. 349, 1845
Crimmins, Timothy J. 329, 1218
Cronin, Bernard C. 1463
Crooks, James B. 1637
Cross, Robert D. 896
Crowe, Charles 1219
Crowther, Simeon J. 695
Cullier, J. 1846
Culton, Donald R. 1638
Cumbler, John T. 1220-21
Cunningham, Lynn C. 506
Curran, Donald J. 4, 433, 1464
Curry, Leonard P. 696-98

Curtis, James Robert 507
Cutler, Irving 508
Cutler, William W. III 897
Cutright, Phillips 1465

D

Dahl, Robert A. 1466
Dahlberg, Jane S. 1639
Daley, C.U. 417
Dalin, David G. 1847
Dancis, Bruce 1222
Danforth, Brian J. 509, 1467
Daniels, Bruce C. 1848
Daniels, Douglas Henry 1223
Davies, Edward J. 173
Davis, Allen F. 1224, 1640
Davis, J. Tait 1070
Davis, John 174
Davis, Kingsley 102
Davis, Lenwood G. 434
Davis, Ronald L.F. 699, 1849
Davis, Stephen R. 510
Davis, Thomas J. 792
Davis, Walter G. 5
Dawley, Alan 1225
Daws, Gavan 511
Dawson, Cole P. 512
Deaton, Thomas Mashburn 1641
Decker, Peter R. 175-76, 1850
DeForest, Robert W. 1071
Degler, Carl N. 1468-69
De Graaf, Lawrence B. 1226
De Lorme, Roland L. 1642-43
Demerath, Nicholas J. 756
Dentler, Robert A. 898
Deran, Elizabeth 6
Deskins, Donald R., Jr. 1227
Dewey, Richard E. 114
Diamondstone, Judith 793
Dickens, Charles 7
Diner, Steven Jay 1644
Disbrow, Donald W. 1645
Doherty, Robert 700
Dolan, Jay P. 1228
Donagher, Richard J. 1851
Donaldon, Scott 350
Doris, Dawn Dwyer 1852

Author Index

Dorsett, Lyle W. 75, 513, 1470-71, 1646-48, 1841
Dougherty, J.P. 1072
Douglas, Harlan P. 177
Douglass, Truman B. 351
Downs, Anthony 76
Dowty, Alan 1229
Doxiadis, Konstantinos Apostolou 351, 1073
Doyle, Don H. 178, 899
Dragos, Stephen F. 1074
Drake, St. Clair 1230-31
Dructor, Robert 794
Drury, James W. 1472
DuBick, Michael A. 128
Dubovik, Paul 1075
Dudden, Arthur P. 1649
Due, John F. 933
Duffy, John 900-906, 1650
Duis, Perry R. 907
Du Mont, Rosemary Ruhig 1651
Dunbar, Willis 701
Duncan, Beverly 179-80
Duncan, Otis D. 181
Dunfee, Charles D. 1473
Dunn, Frederick R. 115
Dupree, Marguerite 331
Durr, William T. 1076
Dyckman, John W. 352
Dye, Thomas R. 182, 1474
Dyer, John A. 1664
Dykstra, Robert R. 353

E

Eames, Edwin 183
Earle, Alice Morse 795
Earle, Carville 796
Earle, Clarke 184
Earnest, Grace E. 702
East, Dennis H. 908
East, John P. 1652
Eastman, Crystal 559
Ebner, Michael H. 514, 1653
Eckelberry, Roscoe H. 797
Eckert, William Albert 1232
Edwards, George W. 613, 826
Ehrlich, Jessica Kross 798
Ehrlich, Richard L. 1853
Eistenhold, John S. 703

Elazar, Daniel J. 354, 1475-76
Eldredge, H. Wentworth 77, 519
Elenbaas, Jack D. 1654-56
Elkins, Eugene R. 1477
Ellis, John H. 909-10
Ellis, Roy 515
Ellis, Russell, Jr. 1350
Erenberg, Lewis A. 911
Ericksen, Eugene P. 516
Ericson, William 336
Ermisch, John 185
Ernest, William Joel III 1854
Ernst, Joseph A. 799
Ernst, Robert 1233
Ershkowitz, Herbert 435
Esslinger, Dean R. 1234
Everand, Wayne M. 1657

F

Fahey, John 517
Fanning, Charles 1235
Farkas, Suzanne 1478
Farley, Reynolds 186, 1236
Farrell, Richard T. 518
Feagin, Joe R. 78
Feen, Richard H. 1509
Fein, Albert 1077-78
Feinstein, Estelle F. 800, 1479
Feiss, Carl 519
Feldberg, Michael 1237, 1480
Femminella, Francis X. 1238
Ferdinand, Theodore N. 520
Field, John 1600
Fine, David M. 355
Fine, Sidney 521
Finfer, Lawrence A. 1658
Finkelman, Paul 912
Finster, Jerome 79, 436
Firey, Walter 187
Fischer, Claude S. 188, 356
Fischer, Joel 1855
Fisher, Irving D. 1856
Fisher, Robert B. 913, 1659
Fisher, Robert M. 1079
Fishman, Robert 1080
Fitch, J.A. 559
Fitch, James Morston 1081
Fitzharris, Joseph C. 189
Flack, Irwin F. 1857

Author Index

Flack, James K., Jr. 914
Fleisch, Sylvia 327
Fleming, William F. 522
Flexner, James Thomas 801
Flowerdew, Robin 1858
Fogelson, Robert M. 523
Folk, Patricia A. 704
Folsom, Burton W. 190
Foner, Philip S. 802
Fortune Magazine 80
Foster, Charles I. 915
Foster, E.C. 116
Foster, Edward Halsey 524, 1629
Foster, Mark S. 525, 1660, 1859
Fowler, Edmund P. 1537, 1711
Fowler, Richard B. 549
Fox, Daniel M. 336, 1481
Fox, Kenneth 1661
Fox, Mary F. 147
Fox, Richard G. 191
Fragnoli, Raymond R. 1662
Franklin, Vincent P. 1239
Fredman, L.E. 1663
Freedman, Stephen 1240
Freeman, Rhoda G. 1241
Friedel, John 81
Frieden, Bernard J. 82, 1082
Friedman, Lawrence M. 1083-84
Fries, Sylvia Doughty 803
Frisch, Michael 192
Frye, Mary Virginia 1085
Frye, Robert J. 1664
Funigello, Philip J. 193, 1860
Funnell, Charles E. 526
Furer, Howard B. 357, 527, 1665
Furlow, John W. 1482
Futterman, Robert A. 8

G

Gabaccia, Donna R. 1861
Galatioto, Rocco G. 1242
Galfont, Blanche H. 9
Galford, Justin B. 1243
Galishoff, Stuart 910, 916
Gallery, John A. 668
Galvin, John T. 1666
Gans, Herbert J. 1244
Gardner, James F. 917

Garner, John Sturdy 194, 528
Garofalo, Charles 529
Garonzik, Joseph 1245-46
Garvan, Anthony N.B. 804
Gary, Lawrence E. 1315
Gates, Grace H. 530
Gazell, James Albert 531
Geen, Elizabeth 83
Geffen, Elizabeth M. 1247
Gelfand, Mark I. 1483
Gelfand, Mitchell 1862
German, Richard Henry Lee 532, 1667
Gersman, Elinor Mondale 1668
Geruson, Richard T. 10
Gerz, Richard J., Jr. 1669
Ghent, Joselyn Maynard 1248
Giannini, Ralph 533
Giglierano, Geoffrey 918
Gilbert, Charles E. 1484-85
Gilchrist, David T. 705
Gillette, Howard, Jr. 1670
Gilmore, Harlan 195
Ginsberg, Stephen F. 919-20
Gittell, Marilyn 3
Glaab, Charles N. 11, 84, 196-97, 437
Glasco, Laurence A. 1249-50
Glazer, Nathan 1251-52
Gleason, Bill 1671
Glen, Grave A. 534
Godfrey, Hollis 921
Goheen, Peter G. 198, 358
Goist, Park Dixon 105, 359-62, 1086, 1159
Golab, Carol Ann 1253
Goldberg, Robert A. 1254
Golden, Hilda H. 1884
Goldfield, David R. 12, 117, 535, 687, 706-7, 1255-56
Goldin, Claudia Dale 708
Goldman, Mark 536
Goldner, Norman 1257
Goldstein, Michael L. 1486
Goldstein, Sidney 199, 1258-59
Gollson, Gordon 922
Gong, Alfred 537
Goodall, Elizabeth J. 538
Goode, Judith Gravich 183

Author Index

Goodfriend, Joyce D. 805
Goodman, Paul 1260
Goodnow, Frank J. 1487
Gordon, Daniel 1488
Gordon, Michael A. 1489
Gordon, Rita Werner 1490
Gosnell, Harold F. 1672
Gottfried, Alex 1673
Gottman, Jean 85, 200, 709
Gould, Alan B. 1674
Gould, Lewis L. 1689
Gould, Peter 227
Graff, Harvey J. 201
Grant, David R. 1087
Grant, Robert B. 1261
Graves, John W. 1863
Greb, Gregory A. 539
Gredel, Stephen 1262
Greeley, Andrew M. 1263
Green, Constance McLaughlin 13-14, 438, 540-43, 1264
Green, Martin 363
Green, Mary Fulton 544
Greenberg, Irwin F. 1491
Greene, Lee S. 1675
Greenleaf, Richard E. 545
Greenstein, Fred I. 1676
Greer, Colin 923
Greer, Guy 1088-89
Greer, Scott 86, 1090, 1492
Gregory, George Peter 924
Grele, Ronald J. 677, 1493
Griffen, Clyde 202-3, 925, 1265-66
Griffen, Sally 203, 1265-66
Griffin, C.W. 364
Griffith, Ernest S. 1677-78
Grigsby, William G. 1139
Grimshaw, Allen D. 1266a
Grinder, Robert Dale 1679
Groneman, Carol 1267
Groszins, Morton 1045
Groth, Philip 710-11
Groves, Paul A. 1268
Gruen, Victor 365, 1091
Guest, Avery M. 204-6, 1269
Guignard, Michael J. 1270
Gusfield, Joseph 926
Guteman, Stanley S. 366
Gutman, Robert 87, 439

H

Haar, Charles M. 1092
Haas, Edward F. 1494-95
Hadden, Jeffrey K. 253
Haebler, Peter 1271
Haeger, John Denis 367, 546, 712, 1680
Hagood, Margaret J. 207
Haig, Robert M. 208
Haley, Jacquetta Mae 806
Haller, Mark H. 927-28, 1224, 1681
Haller, William 807
Halverson, Eva H.T. 15
Halverson, Frank D. 15
Hamilton, Fred 1682
Hamilton, Howard D. 1496
Hamilton, Kenneth M. 1864
Hammack, David C. 368, 1497
Hammett, Theodore M. 1272
Hancock, John L. 369, 1093-94
Handlin, Oscar 88, 1273-74
Hanlon, Edward F. 1498
Hans, Lester F. 1683
Hansen, Alvin W. 1089
Hansen, Gladys 547
Hanson, Robert C. 1275
Haraven, Tamara 209, 440, 1276-77, 1335
Hardy, Bruce A. 929
Harkins, Michael J. 930
Harper, Frank C. 548
Harper, Robert A. 85, 200
Harris, Carl V. 1499
Harris, Neil 384
Harris, William 1278
Hart, John F. 210
Harvey, David 211
Haskell, Henry C. 549
Hassler, F.L. 212
Hatt, Paul K. 89
Hauser, Philip M. 90, 370, 437
Hausknecht, Murray 1053
Havard, William C., Jr. 1462
Havens, Murray C. 1500
Hawes, Joseph M. 16
Hawley, Amos H. 213
Haynes, Robert V. 1279
Hays, Samuel P. 214, 1501-2, 1684

Author Index

Heale, M.J. 713, 931, 1503-4
Healy, Patrick 1505
Heibrun, James 215
Heidrich, Robert W. 1095
Henderson, J.V. 216
Henderson, Mary C. 932
Henderson, Thomas M. 1685
Hendrickson, Kenneth E., Jr. 1506-8
Hennessey, Timothy 1509
Henretta, James A. 808
Henry, Nicholas 217
Hepler, Mark K. 1280
Herbert, D.T. 218
Hershberg, Theodore 441, 1281, 1314
Hershkowitz, Leo 1510, 1686
Hertzberg, Steven 1282-83
Hessler, Sherry O. 550
Heyda, Sister Marie 1511
Hicks, John D. 219
Higgs, Robert 220-21
Higham, John 1284
Hill, Carole E. 1285, 1864a
Hillhouse, A.M. 17
Hilton, George W. 933
Hines, Samuel M. 1864a-65, 1871, 1880, 1899
Hines, Thomas S. 1096-97
Hirch, Werner Z. 416, 423
Hodes, Frederick A. 551
Hodges, Margaret 552
Hoffecker, Carol E. 553, 1512
Hoffman, Ronald 796, 1098
Hogan, David 1866
Holborn, Frederick L. 381
Holden, Arthur C. 1687
Holland, Reid A. 222, 1513-14
Hollander, Jacob Harry 934
Holli, Melvin G. 1688-89
Holliday, Harold L. 1515
Hollingsworth, Ellen Jane 223, 1286
Hollingsworth, J. Rogers 223, 1286
Holmes, Harry D. 699, 1849
Holmgren, Daniel Martin 1690
Holt, Glen E. 658, 935
Holt, Michael F. 1516
Holtan, Orley I. 371
Homel, Michael W. 1517
Hoover, Dwight W. 442-44
Hoover, Edgar M. 224, 714

Hoover, Knight Eugene 1867
Hopkins, George W. 1864a-65, 1871, 1880, 1899
Hopkins, Nicholas S. 1287
Hopkins, Richard J. 715, 936, 1288-90
Horowitz, Daniel 372
Horowitz, Helen Lefkowitz 554, 1691
Horowitz, Irving L. 18
Horten, Loren N. 1099
Hosay, Philip M. 1692
Howard, Perry H. 1518
Howe, Barbara J. 1291
Howe, Frederick C. 372-74, 1693
Hoyt, Homer 225-26, 1100
Huang, Jui-Cheng 227
Hudson, John 228
Huggins, Kay Haire 1101
Huggins, Koleen A.H. 1102
Huggins, Nathan I. 937
Hughes, James W. 91
Hughes, Paul J.L. 375
Hughes, Sarah S. 716
Hunt, James Barton 809
Hunter, Albert 229-30
Hunter, Floyd 231
Hunter, Leslie Gene 1103
Hunter, Lloyd A. 1292
Hurst, Marsha 1519
Hutchinson, William R. 555
Huth, Mary Jo 232, 376
Huthmacher, J. Joseph 1694-96

I

Ingham, John N. 1293, 1868
Innes, John H. 810
Isaac, Paul E. 1697
Issel, William H. 938, 1698

J

Jablonski, James J. 1869
Jackson, Anthony 1104
Jackson, Dorothy B. 556
Jackson, Joy J. 939
Jackson, Kenneth T. 92, 220, 577, 776, 935, 993, 1001, 1290, 1294, 1520, 1681

Author Index

Jacobs, Donald M. 1295
Jacobs, Jane 19, 223
Jaher, Frederic Cople 1248, 1296
James, D. Clayton 557
Jamieson, Duncan R. 940
Janis, Ralph 1297-98, 1870
Jeffrey, Kirk, Jr. 1299
Jeffries, John W. 1521
Jensen, Rolf 1105
Jentz, John B. 1699
Johnson, Charles A. 1700
Johnson, David R. 941
Johnson, James Weldon 1300
Johnson, Scott R. 942
Johnson, Thomas R. 1301
Johnson, Tom L. 1701
Johnston, Norman J. 1106
Johnston, R.J. 218, 234
Jonas, Franklin 446
Jones, Emrys 235
Jones, Gene D. 1522
Jordan, Kevin E. 943
Jordan, Lalyon Wayne 1871
Jordy, William H. 1107
Judd, Jacob 1523
Juliani, Richard N. 236

K

Kaestle, Carl F. 944
Kail, Thomas E. 377
Kalisch, Philip A. 945
Kantor, Harvey A. 1108
Kantowicz, Edward R. 1524
Kantrowitz, Nathan 1302
Kaplan, Barry J. 1525
Karp, David A. 237
Kasperson, Roger E. 238
Kassarda, John D. 239
Kasson, John F. 1872
Katz, Michael B. 946
Katzman, David M. 348, 1303
Katzman, M.T. 1304
Katznelson, Ira 1305
Kaufman, Herbert 1526
Keiser, John H. 558
Kelley, Joseph J., Jr. 811
Kellogg, John 1306
Kellogg, Paul U. 559

Kennedy, Albert J. 1821, 1823
Kessner, Thomas 1307
Ketcham, George A. 947
Keyes, Scott 118
Kim, Illsoo 1873
King, Andrew J. 1109
King, Moses 560
Kingery, Robert 1058
Kipp, Samuel M. III 717
Kirker, Harold 561
Kirker, James 561
Kirkland, Edward C. 718
Kirschner, Don S. 378
Kite, Elizabeth S. 812
Klebanow, Diana 119, 379-80, 446
Klein, Milton M. 562
Klein, Philip 563
Kleinberg, Susan J. 1308
Klopper, Ruth 1309
Knapp, Vertie 564
Knerr, George F. 1702
Knight, Oliver 719
Knight, Robert 1527
Knights, Peter R. 240, 311
Knowles, Jane B. 948
Knutson, Robert 1110
Kocolowski, Gary P. 1874-75
Kogan, Herman 1812-13
Komons, Nick Alexander 1703
Kopf, Edward J. 565
Kotler, Milton 1528
Kouwenhoven, John A. 566
Kovisars, Judith F. 1111
Kramer, Carl 567
Kramer, Paul 381
Kraus, Harry P. 1704
Krause, Corinne Azen 1310
Krazberg, Melvin 241
Kremm, Thomas W. 242, 1529
Kristol, Irving 382
Kronus, Sidney 926
Kurland, Gerald 1705
Kusmer, Kenneth L. 1311, 1706
Kuznets, Simon S. 20

L

Lack, Paul D. 1312
Lafore, Lawrence 568

Author Index

LaGory, Mark E. 243
Lammermeier, Paul J. 1313
Lampard, Eric E. 244-47, 447-48
Lanahan, Anna M. 1530
Landesman, Alter F. 569
Landis, Paul H. 720
Lane, James B. 1256, 1707
Lane, Roger 949, 1876
Lantz, Herman 570
Larsen, Lawrence H. 197, 721, 950
Latus, Mark 1043
Laurie, Bruce 1314
Lazerson, Marvin 951-52
Leach, Christopher 7
Leach, Richard H. 1459-60
Leashore, Bogart R. 1877
Lebkuecher, Patricia Brewster 1708
Lee, Lawrence B. 571
Lee, Robert 953
Leech, Margaret 572
Leeds, Morton 1315
Leggett, John C. 1531
Leiby, James 21
Lemon, James T. 722
Leonard, Ira M. 446, 1532-33
Lerner, Monroe 954
Levesque, George A. 1316
Levett, Allan Edward 955
Levine, David Allan 1317
Levine, Jerald Elliot 956
Lewinski-Corwin, E.H. 957
Lewinson, Edward R. 1543, 1709
Lewis, Michael 1710
Lichtenberg, Mitchell Palmer 120
Lichtenstein, Irvin 1429
Lieberman, Richard K. 248
Lieberson, Stanley 180, 1318
Liebert, Roland J. 1535
Light, Dale B. 1878
Light, Ivan 1319
Lindquist, John H. 1536
Lindsay, George D. 723
Lineberry, Robert L. 1447, 1537, 1711
Lipman, Andrew 958
Lippincott, Sarah Lee 568
Litchfield, Norman 573
Litwack, Leon F. 1320
Livingood, James W. 249

Livingston, John 1879
Lloyd, Anne 65, 121
Locke, David Stratton 1712
Lockridge, Kenneth A. 813
Loewenstein, Louis K. 1112
Loftin, Bernadette Kuehn 724
Lofton, Paul F., Jr. 574
Lohmann, Karl Baptiste 725
London, Herbert I. 1538
Long, William J. 1518
Longstreet, Stephen 575
Lorant, Steffen 576
Lotchin, Roger W. 577-78
Lowdon, Wingo, Jr. 244
Lowe, George D. 250
Lowe, Jeanne R. 83, 1113
Lowenstein, Louis K. 307
Lowi, Theodore 1539, 1713
Lubitz, Edward 1114
Lubove, Roy 1115-17, 1714-15, 1880
Lucas, Paul R. 959
Lucas, Stephen E. 814
Luckingham, Bradford Franklin 726, 960
Lupsha, Peter A. 1540
Luscombe, Irving Foulds 961
Lydon, James G. 815
Lyman, Stanford M. 1321
Lynch, Hollis R. 1322
Lyon, Elizabeth Anne Mack 1118

M

McArthur, Benjamin 1716
McBain, Howard Lee 1541
McCandless, Amy M. 1864a-65, 1871, 1880, 1899
McCandless, Carl A. 1542
McCarthy, Michael P. 122, 1543, 1717-21
McCaughey, Robert 1544
McCausland, Elizabeth 466
Macchiarola, Frank J. 1545
McClelland, John M., Jr. 579
McClymer, John F. 580
MacColl, E. Kimbark 1546
McComb, David G. 581
McConnell, John W. 1323
McCullough, David 962

Author Index

MacDonald, Norbert 727
McDonald, Terence Joseph 1881
McDonnell, Timothy L. 1119
McElrath, Dennis 383
McEntire, Davis 1120, 1251
McGrath, Dennis 10
McGrath, Dorn C., Jr. 1112
McGrath, Kristin S. 1121
Mack, Herb 3
MacKaye, Benton 1122
McKee, James B. 449
McKelvey, Blake 22-25, 450-53, 582-89, 1123-24, 1324
McKenna, William J. 1547
McKenzie, Roderick Duncan 26, 396, 1722
McKeown, James E. 93
McKinzie, Richard D. 348
McKitrick, Eric L. 1723
Mackler, Bernard 898
McLaughlin, Glenn E. 27
McLear, Patrick E. 590, 728, 751
MacMichael, Stanley L. 28
McMullin, Thomas A. 591
McShane, Clay Kelvin 963-65, 1882
Madden, Daniel R. 1548
Madgwick, P.J. 1549
Magnuson, Norris 966
Mandelbaum, Seymour J. 1724
Mann, Arthur 384, 1550-51
Marchiafava, Louis J. 967
Marcus, Alan L. 1725
Margavio, Anthony V. 1325
Margon, Arthur 385
Mariano, John Horace 1326
Mark, Harold 926
Marks, Donald David 1726
Marsh, Margaret Sammartino 251
Marshall, Leon S. 252
Martin, Judith 1125
Martin, Robert R. 729
Martin, Roscoe C. 1552
Martinez, Oscar J. 1327
Marx, Leo 386
Marzik, Thomas D. 1209, 1332
Maskin, Melvin R. 1328
Masotti, Louis H. 253, 968
Massouh, Michael 969
Matthews, Fred H. 387

Maurice, Arthur B. 592
Mawn, Geoffrey P. 730
May, Henry F. 970
Mayer, Harold M. 593
Mayer, John A. 971
Mayer, Kurt 1258-59
Mazzi, Francis J. 594-95
Meadows, Paul 94
Meeker, Edward 972
Meister, Richard J. 1329
Melosi, Martin V. 973
Melvin, Patricia M. 1883
Merino, James A. 1553-54
Merrens, H. Roy 799
Merriam, Charles 1555
Merriam, Paul G. 596
Merton, Robert K. 1727
Messmer, Charles 597
Meyer, David R. 731, 1126
Meyer, Douglas K. 1330-31
Meyerson, Martin 1127
Michel, Jerry B. 254
Miggins, Edward Michael 1728
Miller, Janet Ann 974
Miller, Randall M. 1209, 1332
Miller, Richard G. 255-56, 1333, 1556, 1729
Miller, Rita S. 598
Miller, Roberta Balstad 731a
Miller, Wilbur R. 975
Miller, William D. 599, 1730-32
Miller, Zane L. 29, 454, 1733-34
Millett, John D. 1557
Mills, Edward S. 257
Millspaugh, Martin 1128
Mitchell, Bruce 732
Mitchell, George L. 30
Mitchell, J. Paul 1334, 1735-37
Mitchell, Robert B. 258
Mizruchi, Ephraim H. 94
Modell, John 1335
Mohl, Raymond A. 95-96, 123, 816, 976-79, 1129, 1188, 1336, 1738
Molotch, Harvey 259
Molyneaux, J. Lambert 1325
Mondello, Salvatore 1337
Monkkonen, Eric H. 388, 1338
Montgomery, David 1339

Author Index

Moore, Charles 1130
Moore, Joan W. 1340
Morgan, E. 389
Morgan, Helen M. 600
Morgan, Myfanwy 1884
Mormino, Gary R. 1341
Morrill, Richard L. 1037
Morris, James 31
Morris, Margaret Francine 97, 1729
Morrison, Hugh Sinclair 1131
Moses, Leon 260
Moses, Robert 1558
Mosse, George L. 880
Mowry, George E. 32
Moynihan, Daniel P. 390, 1252
Muccigrosso, Robert 1739
Muirhead, James F. 33
Muller, Dorothea R. 391
Muller, Edward K. 733-34
Muller, Peter O. 261
Mullin, John Robert 1132
Mullins, William H. 1559
Mumford, Lewis 34, 392-93
Muraskin, Jack 1740-41
Murphy, Raymond E. 262
Murphy, Thomas P. 980
Murray, Constance 981
Mushkat, Jerome 1742
Myers, Gustavus 982
Myhra, Thomas J. 601

N

Nadeau, Remi A. 602, 735
Nairn, Ian 1133
Naloli, Salvatore J. 1134
Napier, Rita G. 736
Nash, Gary B. 817-22
Nash, Gerald D. 737
Nash, William W. 82, 1135
National Resources Committee 263
Natoli, Salvatore J. 264
Naumes, Margaret Jane Oyaas 265
Neff, Frank A. 35
Neill, Peter 107
Nelli, Humbert S. 1342-44, 1743
Nevins, Allan 394
Newcomb, Charles 490
Newell, Barbara Warne 1345
Newman, Harvey K. 983

Newmark, Helen 36
New York Historical Society 603
Nielson, David G. 1346
Nobel, Richard A. 1885
Nodyne, Kenneth R. 1560
Noel, Thomas J. 1886
Nord, David 1744
Nordstrom, Carl 604
Norris, Joe L. 615
Noyes, Richard 605
Nussbaum, Raymond O. 1745-46

O

Oboler, Gina 1347
Oboler, Leon 1347
O'Connor, Len 1747
O'Donnell, Charles Patrick 1887
Ogburn, William F. 395
O'Kane, James M. 167
Older, Mrs. Fremont [Cora Older] 606
Olson, James S. 1348
Olton, Charles S. 823, 984
O'Neill, Hugh 1349
O'Riordan, Timothy 174, 397
Orleans, Peter 1350
Osofsky, Gilbert 1351
Osterweis, Rollin G. 607
Ottensmann, John R. 266
Ovington, Mary White 1352
Owen, Wilfred 37

P

Palmer, John Albert 1748
Papaleo, Ralph Joseph 1888
Papenfuse, Edward C. 824
Park, Robert E. 396
Parker, Margaret Terrell 608
Parkhurst, Charles H. 1749
Parkins, Almon 609
Parks, Arthur Lincoln 985
Parot, Joseph 1353
Parraga, Charlotte Marie Nelson 610
Parris, Guichard 1354
Parris, Ronald G. 1136
Passi, Michael M. 1355
Paterson, John 397

Author Index

Patton, Thomas Warren 1889
Paul, Charles L. 825
Pawley, Martin 1137
Peal, Ethel 38
Pearson, John E. 738
Pearson, Ralph L. 1356
Pease, Otis A. 1750
Peek, Charles W. 250
Peel, Roy V. 1561
Peihl, Mel 1890
Pencake, William 1891
Pendergrass, Lee F. 1751-52
Penna, Anthony N. 611
Perdue, Robert E. 1357
Perloff, Harvey S. 244
Pernicone, Carol G. 1358
Perry, David 739
Pessen, Edward 267-68, 1359-62, 1562
Petersen, William J. 612
Peterson, Arthur E. 613, 826
Peterson, Jon A. 1138, 1892
Petskek, Kirk R. 1753
Peyer, Jean B. 827, 1363
Philpott, Thomas L. 1364
Pickering, John R. 1893
Pierce, Bessie L. 614-15
Piott, Steven L. 1754
Pivar, David J. 1755-56
Platt, Harold L. 269
Pomerantz, Sidney 616
Popenoe, David 87, 439
Porter, Philip W. 617
Posadas, Barbara Mercedes 618
Potts, James H. 39, 1894
Powell, John H. 986
Powell, Sumner Chilton 828
Pozzetta, George E. 1365, 1632
Pratt, Edward E. 619
Pratt, John W. 1757
Pred, Allan 270-74
Preston, Howard L. 275, 740
Preston, Richard E. 276-77
Pursell, Carroll, Jr. 241
Putman, S.H. 278

Q

Quandt, Jean B. 279, 398, 620

Queen, Stuart A. 40-41
Quiett, Glenn Chesney 741

R

Rabinowitz, Howard R. 742, 1366-69
Radford, John P. 621
Rainbolt, John C. 829
Raleigh, J.H. 399
Ralph, Raymond M. 622, 1895
Rammelkamp, Julian S. 623
Rannells, John 280
Rapkin, Chester 258, 1139
Ratajczak, Donald 302
Ravenel, Mazyck P. 987
Ravitch, Diane 988
Raymond, Richard 1370
Redfearn, George V. 239
Reed, Henry Hope 1164
Reed, Marvin E., Jr. 400
Reed, Merl E. 624
Reeder, Sherwood L. 1445
Reese, William J. 989, 1758
Reeve, Kay A. 625
Reichard, Maximilian 990, 1371
Reichley, James 1563
Reid, Bill G. 401
Reinders, Robert C. 1564
Reiss, Albert J. 89
Renshaw, Patrick 1372
Reps, John W. 1140-41
Reynolds, George Miller 1759
Rhines, Charlotte Cannon 991
Rhoda, Richard 281
Ricciotti, Dominic 402
Rice, Bradley R. 1611, 1760
Rice, Herbert W. 743
Richards, Ira D. 626
Richards, Leonard L. 1373
Richardson, James F. 42, 95-96, 98, 282, 880, 992-94
Rickard, Louise E. 1761
Rickert, John E. 283
Rickey, Don 627
Ridgway, Whitman H. 1374
Riess, Steven A. 403, 1762
Rigenback, Paul T. 1763

Author Index

Riis, Jacob A. 1142
Riordan, William L. 1764
Rischin, Moses 1375, 1565
Ritchie, Donald A. 1765
Robson, William A. 43
Rockaway, Robert A. 1376-77
Rodgers, Cleveland 1566
Rodwin, Lloyd 1143
Roebuck, Janet 44
Rogers, George C., Jr. 830
Rogers, Tommy W. 744
Romo, Ricardo 1378
Roper, Laura Wood 1144
Rosales, Francisco A. 1379
Rose, Harold M. 1380
Rose, Mark H. 1896
Rose, Stephen M. 1809
Rose, William G. 628
Rosenbaum, Judy Jolley 1381
Rosenberg, Arnold S. 1766
Rosenberg, Carroll Smith 995-96
Rosenberg, Charles E. 997
Rosenwaike, Ira 629
Ross, D. Reid 745
Rossi, Peter H. 45
Rousey, Dennis C. 1897
Royko, Mike 1767-69
Rubin, Julius 746-47
Rudwick, Elliot M. 1382
Russell, James M. 630
Rutman, Darrett 831-33
Ryan, Dennis P. 1898
Ryan, James G. 1383
Ryan, Joseph F. 1567
Ryerson, R.A. 834-35

S

Sale, Roger 631
Salisbury, Neil E. 210
Salisbury, Robert H. 1568
Sanders, James W. 1384
Sarver, Phillip M. 632
Scharf, Thomas J. 633
Scheiber, Harry N. 748
Scheiner, Seth M. 1385
Schiesl, Martin J. 1768
Schlegel, Marvin W. 665
Schlereth, Thomas J. 634
Schlesinger, Arthur M. 46
Schmid, Calvin F. 635, 749

Schmid, Stanton E. 749
Schmitt, Peter J. 404
Schneider, John C. 405, 998-1000
Schnell, Christopher J. 750-51
Schnitzer, Henry R. 636
Schnore, Leo F. 90, 99-101, 437, 455, 1386
Schoenebaum, Eleanore W. 637
Schoenberg, Sandra 1387
Schultz, Charles 638
Schultz, Frederick M. 456
Schultz, Stanley K. 92, 220, 577, 776, 935, 993, 1001-2, 1290, 1520, 1681
Schumacher, Carolyn S. 1388
Scientific American 102
Scott, Anne Firor 1770
Scott, George W. 1569
Scott, James C. 1771
Scott, Mellier Goodin 1145
Scully, Vincent 1146
Seller, Maxine 1389-90
Sellers, Leila 836
Sennett, Richard 106, 406
Shaffer, Janet 837
Shambaugh, Benjamin F. 639
Shane, Allen J. 47
Shannon, Lyle 1391
Shannon, Magdaline 1391
Shapley, Rufus E. 1772
Sharp, Emmit F. 207
Sharp, Harry 1386
Sharpless, John B. 295-97, 457
Shaw, Douglas V. 1392
Shaw, Edward K. 1268
Shelton, Brenda K. 1773
Shideler, James H. 407
Shiloh, James A. 1393
Shortridge, Ray M. 297
Sheen, Ivan D. 48
Shover, John L. 1570-71
Shufro, Joel A. 1572
Shumsky, Neil L. 1573
Siegel, Adrienne 408-9
Silver, Arthur M. 1574
Silver, Christopher 1899
Silverman, Robert A. 1774
Silvia, Philip T., Jr. 640, 1394
Simmons, James W. 142
Simmons, Ozzie G. 1275
Simon, Roger D. 298, 641, 1395

Author Index

Simonds, Thomas C. 642
Sinclair, Bruce 1003
Singleton, Esther 838
Singleton, Gregory H. 1004
Sirjamaki, John 299
Sjoberg, Gideon 300
Sklare, Marshall 1396
Skolnik, Richard S. 1775-77
Sly, David F. 199
Smallwood, James 1147
Smith, Billy G. 822
Smith, Douglas L. 1900
Smith, Everett G., Jr. 210
Smith, James B. 301
Smith, Joel 155
Smith, Margaret S. 1148
Smith, Page 410
Smith, Robert P. 1005
Smith, Roland M. 1575
Smith, Stephen 1006
Smith, Timothy L. 1397
Smith, Wilson 103
Smolensky, Eugene 302
Sobczak, John N. 1576
Solomon, Noal 1778
Somers, Dale A. 643, 1007
Sorkin, Alan L. 1398
Sorrels, William W. 1008
Sparks, Frank M. 1577
Spaulding, Charles B. 1578
Spear, Allan H. 1399
Spector, Michael J. 1084
Speer, Michael S. 1779
Speizman, Milton D. 104
Spletstoser, Frederick M. 1901
Stambler, Moses 1009
Staples, John H. 1149
Staples, Robert 1902
Starr, Dennis J. 1903
Stave, Bruce M. 458, 1579-80, 1727, 1780
Steen, Ivan D. 644
Steffens, Joseph Lincoln 1781-82
Steglich, W.G. 282
Stein, Maurice P. 411
Steinberg, Alfred 1783
Steiner, Henry M. 1904
Steiner, William F., Jr. 1010
Steinert, N. 135-36, 217, 331, 1136, 1150, 1347, 1429, 1710

Stephenson, Charles 303
Sternlieb, George 1150-51
Stevens, Errol W. 1581
Stewart, Frank M. 1784
Stewart, Ian Robert 1152
Stewart, Peter C. 752
Stewart, Roy P. 645
Stickle, Warren E. 1582-83, 1601, 1618
Still, Bayrd 49-50, 119, 459, 646-55, 753, 839
Stillman, Richard J. III 1785
Stimson, Grace Heilman 1400
Stone, Gregory P. 237
Storey, Britt Allen 754
Straus, Michael W. 1153
Straus, Nathan, Jr. 1154
Strauss, Anselm L. 51
Strickland, Arvath E. 1401
Strickler, Carolyn J. 656
Strong, Josiah 412
Stroud, Rosemary 304
Sullivan, Margaret 1402
Sullivan, Martin E. 1584
Surrency, Erwin C. 1011
Sussman, Carl 1155
Sutherland, John F. 1156, 1786-87
Sutter, Ruth E. 52
Suttles, Gerald D. 305
Sutton, Stephanne Barry 1157
Swanson, B.E. 1158
Swanson, Joseph A. 306, 329a
Syrett, Harold C. 1585
Szuberla, Guy 413

T

Taeuber, Alma F. 308, 1403-4
Taeuber, Irene B. 307
Taeuber, Karl E. 308, 1403-4
Tager, Jack 105, 1159
Tarr, Joel A. 1012-13, 1788-90, 1905
Taylor, David V. 1405
Taylor, George R. 309, 1014
Taylor, Graham R. 1160
Taylor, Quintard 1791
Teaford, Jon Christian 840, 1586
Tennant, Robert J. 142

Author Index

Tepaske, John J. 841
Terkel, Studs 1406
Teska, Anona 1587
Tharp, Claude Roy 755
Thernstrom, Stephan A. 106, 310-11, 460-61, 657, 1407-8
Thomas, Brinley 312
Thomas, John L. 414
Thomas, Lately 1792
Thomas, Lewis F. 41
Thomas, Richard 1409-10
Thomas, Thaddeus P. 1588
Thomlinson, Ralph 53
Thompson, Marion Brackenridge 124
Thompson, Marvin G. 842
Thompson, Westcott 633
Thompson, Wilbur R. 313
Thurner, Arthur W. 1589
Tichnor, Thomas J. 1906
Tierno, Mark J. 1015
Tietze, Frederick I. 93
Tilly, Charles 462
Tobin, Eugene M. 1653, 1793-97
Toll, Seymour I. 54
Toll, William 1907
Tolles, Frederick B. 843
Topping, Mark B. 1161
Toulmin, Harry Aubrey, Jr. 1798
Trachtenberg, Alan 107, 1016, 1162
Travis, Anthony R. 1799
Troen, Selwyn K. 658, 1017
Trolander, Judith A. 1018, 1800
Trollope, Anthony 55
Trout, Charles H. 1590
Tucker, Louis Leonard 659, 1801
Tunnard, Christopher 56, 1163-64
Turner, George Kibbe 1802
Turner, Howard E. 605
Turner, Ralph E. 415
Tuttle, William M., Jr. 1411
Twombly, Robert C. 1165
Tyack, David B. 1019
Tygiel, Jules 1908
Tyler, Elaine 314

U

Uberti, John K. 1412
Ullmann, John E. 304

U.S. Department of Housing and Urban Development, Office of International Affairs 57
U.S. National Resources Committee 1591
U.S. National Resources Committee. Research Committee on Urbanism 58
Urban, Wayne 1020, 1803
Urofsky, Melvin I. 364, 1587

V

Vadasz, Thomas P. 660
Vance, James E., Jr. 315-17, 1166, 1909
Vance, Rupert B. 756
Van Valen, Nelson S. 1592
Varbero, Richard A. 1413
Vaughan, Philip H. 1593-94
Veiller, Lawrence 1071, 1167
Vernon, Raymond 59, 714
Vinyard, JoEllen McNergney 1414

W

Wade, Louise C. 1804-5
Wade, Richard C. 60, 318, 416-17, 463-64, 593, 757-59
Wakstein, Allen M. 108
Walch, Timothy 1021
Wald, Lillian D. 1806
Walker, Charles R. 661
Walker, James B. 1022
Walker, Kenneth 83
Walker, Mabel L. 1168
Walker, Paul K. 844-45
Walker, Richard A. 319
Walker, Robert A. 1169
Walker, Robert H. 418, 465
Walker, Samuel E. 1023, 1595
Walsh, George 1807
Walsh, James P. 1808, 1910
Walsh, W. Richard 846
Ward, David 320-23
Warden, G.B. 847-49
Ware, Caroline F. 662
Waring, George E., Jr. 760
Waring, Joseph I. 1024

Author Index

Warner, Robert M. 147
Warner, Sam Bass, Jr. 61-62, 147, 324-27, 384, 457, 1170
Warren, Charles R. 980
Warren, Roland L. 109, 1089
Warshauer, Mary Ellen 898
Watkins, Alfred J. 739
Watson, Wreford J. 174
Watts, Eugene J. 1025, 1415, 1596-97
Weaver, Robert C. 63, 1416
Weber, Adna F. 64
Weber, Max 419
Weber, Michael P. 125, 154, 663, 1417, 1680
Weber, Michael R. 65
Webster, Janice Reiff 1418
Weed, James A. 1269
Wegg, Talbot 1153
Weidner, Charles H. 1026
Weiher, Kenneth 761-62
Weimer, David R. 420
Weimer, Howard R. 66
Weinbaum, Paul O. 1419
Weinberg, Daniel E. 1420
Weiner, Howard R. 421
Weiner, Ronald R. 664
Weinstein, James 1810
Weisel, Edward Berry 763
Weiss, Nancy Joan 1421, 1811
Weiss, Shirley F. 163
Weiss, Thomas 67, 185
Weister, C.W. 745
Wellenreuther, Hermann 764
Wells, Eugene Tate 765
Wendt, Lloyd 1812-13
Wertenbaker, Thomas J. 665
West, Elliot 97, 1729, 1814
Whebell, C.F.J. 328
Wheeler, Kenneth W. 766-67
Wheeler, Thomas C. 110
Wheeler, William B. 1598
Wheelock, Lewis F. 1027
Whipple, David 1515
White, Dana F. 329, 422, 465
White, Leonard D. 1815
White, Lucia 424
White, Morton 423-24
Whiteaker, Larry H. 1816

Whyte, William F. 1422
Wiberley, Stephen E., Jr. 850
Wiebe, Robert H. 425
Wieder, Alan V. 1028
Wilcox, Delos F. 68, 1029
Wilkenfeld, Bruce M. 851-52
Wilkie, Jane Riblett 1423-24
Wilkins, Barratt 853
Willbern, York 111
Williams, J. Kerwin 1445
Williams, Marilyn Thornton 1029a-29b
Williams, Melvin R. 1425
Williamson, Harold F., Jr. 260
Williamson, Jeffrey G. 69, 306, 329a, 768
Willis, Edmund P. 1599
Wilson, James Q. 112, 1438
Wilson, Theodore A. 348
Wilson, William H. 70, 666, 1171-72
Wilson, Wreford J. 397
Winfield, Gerald F. 330
Winnick, Louis 1173
Winpenny, Thomas R. 1174
Wintz, Cary D. 1426
Wirth, Louis 426
Wise, David O. 331
Withey, Lynne E. 332, 854
Wohl, R. Richard 427, 667
Wolf, Stephanie Graumon 855
Wolfe, Margaret Tipley 1817
Wolfinger, Raymond 1600, 1818
Wolner, Edward W. 1175
Wolniewicz, Richard 1911
Wong, Charles Choy 1319
Wood, Diane M. 1029c
Wood, Edith Elmer 1176
Woodbury, Coleman 1177
Woods, Joseph G. 1029d, 1819
Woods, Robert A. 1820-23
Woodward, C. Vann 464
Wortley, Lady Emmeline S. 71
Wortman, Marlene Stein 1824
Wotton, Grigsby H. 769
Wright, Carroll D. 1178
Wright, Frank Lloyd 1179
Wright, William C. 770-71
Wunder, John 772
Wurman, Richard S. 668

Author Index

Y

Yancey, William L. 516
Yans-McLaughlin, Virginia 1427
Yearley, Clifton K. 428
Yeates, Maurice H. 333
Yoels, William C. 237
Young, James Sterling 669

Z

Zachary, Alan M. 1428
Zachary, Wayne W. 1429
Zangrando, Joanna Schneider 429
Zarychta, Ronald M. 1029e
Zdrazil, G.A. 1518
Zelinski, Wilbur 773
Zimmer, Donald T. 334
Zink, Harold 1825
Zolot, Herbert M. 1826
Zorbaugh, Harvey W. 670
Zucker, Paul 1180
Zuckerman, Michael 856
Zueblin, Charles 1827
Zunz, Oliver 335-36, 1430

TITLE INDEX

This index includes all titles of books cited in the text. In some cases titles have been shortened. References are to entry numbers and alphabetization is letter by letter.

A

Age of Urban Reform, The 1653
Agony of the Cities, The 1604
Albuquerque and the City Manager Plan, 1917-1948 1630
American Architecture and Urbanism 1146
American Building 1081
American Cities in the Growth of a Nation 13
American City, The (Queen and Carpenter) 40
American City, The (Weber and Lloyd) 65
American City: A Documentary History, The 84
American City: An Urban Geography, The 262
American City: A Rank and File History 661
American City: Historical Studies, The 98
American City Government 1441
American City Novel, 1900-1940, The 9
American City Planning since 1890 1145
American City Progress and the Law 1541
American Commonwealth, The 1619
American Landscape, The 1133

American Municipal Progress 1827
American Notes 7
American Skyline 1164
American Urban History 73
American Urban History. 2d ed. 74
American Urbanization 22
American West in the Twentieth Century, The 737
Amusing the Million 1872
Analysis of the Electric Railway Problem 1029
Anatomy of a Metropolis 714
Antebellum Natchez 557
Anthropology of the City 183
Architecture and Town Planning in Colonial Connecticut 804
Architecture in Chicago and Mid-America 1039
Architecture in New England 1040
Architecture in New York 472, 1041
Architecture of John Wellborn Root, The 1098
Architecture Versus Housing 1137
Armies of the Streets, The 1217
Artisans for Independence 823
Art of Government, The 1563
As City upon a Hill 410
As Others See Chicago 615
At the Edge of Megalopolis 605
At the Pleasure of the Mayor 1539

Title Index

Autobiography of Lincoln Steffens, The 1781
Automobile Age of Atlanta 275

B

Back to Nature 404
Before the Ghetto 1303
Being Urban 237
Better City Government 1661
Beyond the Melting Pot 1252
Big Bill of Chicago 1812
Biography of Frederick Law Olmsted, A 1144
Black Chicago 1399
Black Ghetto 1329
Black Manhattan 1300
Black Men, White Cities 1305
Black Metropolis 1231
Black New Orleans, 1860-1880 1191
Black Politics in New York City 1534
Blacks in the City 1354
Black Urban Condition, The 1322
Born Grown, an Oklahoma City History 645
Boss: Richard J. Daley of Chicago 1767
Boss Cermak of Chicago 1673
Boss Cox's Cincinnati 1734
Bosses, The (Haeger and Weber) 1680
Bosses, The (Steinberg) 1783
Bosses, Machines and Urban Voters 1605
Bosses and Machines in Urban America 1646
Bosses and Reformers 1618
Bosses in Lusty Chicago 1813
Boss Reuf's San Francisco 1609
Boss Tweed's New York 1724
Boston, 1689-1776 847
Boston, the Great Depression, and the New Deal 1590
Bring Out Your Dead 986
Brooklyn, U.S.A. 598
Brooklyn Bridge 1016
Bullfinch's Boston, 1787-1817 561
Burnham of Chicago, Architect and Planner 1096

C

Canal or Railroad 746
Census Data of the City of Chicago, 1920, 1930 490
Challenge of the City, 1860-1910, The 75
Challenge of Urban Reform, The 1753
Challenge to Urban Liberalism, The 1860
Changing Economic Function of the Central City, The 59
Changing Metropolis, The 93
Changing of Metropolitan America 213
Changing Spatial Structure of American Cities, The 266
Charles Francis Murphy, 1858-1924 1811
Charleston Business on the Eve of the American Revolution 836
Charleston in the Age of the Pinckneys 830
Charleston's Sons of Liberty 846
Chicago, A More Intimate View of Urban Politics 1555
Chicago: An Intimate Portrait of People, Pleasures, and Power, 1860-1919 574
Chicago: City on the Make 471
Chicago: Growth of a Metropolis 593
Chicago: Metropolis of the Mid-Continent 508
Chicago, 1910-1929 1066
Chicago, 1930-1970 1067
Chicago and Its Suburbs 496
Chicago and the Labor Movement 1345
Chicago on Foot 474
Chicago School of Architecture, The 1067a
Child in the City, The 1615
Children in Urban Society 16
Cholera Years, The 997
Church and the City, 1865-1910, The 896
Cities (Hoover) 442

Title Index

Cities (Morris) 31
Cities, The 60
Cities: Their Origins, Growth, and Human Impact 102
Cities and Churches 953
Cities and Immigrants 320
Cities and Schools in the Gilded Age 874
Cities and Society 89
Cities and the Federal System, The 1552
Cities and the 1936 Congress 1444
Cities and Towns of Illinois 725
Cities and Urbanization 10
Cities in American History 92
Cities in a Race with Time 1113
Cities in Revolt 783
Cities in the Motor Age 37
Cities in the Wilderness 784
Cities of Our Past and Present 103
Cities of the Nation's Historic Metropolitan Core 469
Cities of the Prairie 1475
City: American Experience, The 107
City: A Study of Urbanism in the United States, The 41
City: The Hope of Democracy, The 373
City and Country 378
City and Country in America 420
City and Hinterland 731a
City and Suburb 1586
City and the Theatre, The 932
City Beautiful Movement in Kansas City, The 1171
City Bosses and Political Machines 1675
City Bosses in the United States 1825
City Boss in America, The 1622
City-Building Process, The 298
City Government in the United States 1487
City Growth and Values 28
City Growth in the United States, England and Wales 1820-1861 296
City in American History, The 23
City in American Life, The 381
City in History, The 34
City in Southern History, The 687
City Is the Frontier, The 1032

City Life, 1865-1900 3
City Makers 735
City Manager, The 1815
City Manager Plan in Arkansas, The 1633
City Manager: A New Profession, The 1798
City Manager System in Alabama, The 1664
City Moves West, The 729
City of Brooklyn, 1865-1898, The 1585
City of Man, The 1163
City of the Future, A Narrative History of Kansas City, 1850-1950 549
City Politics 1438
City That Was and the Report of the General Committee of Health, New York City, 1806, The 1006
City Ways 81
City Wilderness, The 1822
Civic History of Kansas City, Missouri, A 515
Civilizing American Cities 1157
Class and Community 1225
Classic Essays on Cultural Cities 406
Cleveland: Confused City on a Seesaw 617
Cleveland, The Making of a City 628
Cleveland: Village to Metropolis 497
Clout: Mayor Daley and His City 1747
Colonial Days in Old New York 795
Columbia Historical Portrait of New York, The 566
Coming of Age 70
Community and Social Change in America 342
Community in Search of Itself, A 570
Community Planning in the 1920s 1115
Community Power Structure 231
Company Town in the American West, The 674

Title Index

Comparative Atlas of America's Great Cities, A 1
Confessions of a Reformer, The 1693
Conflict in Urban Transportation 1904
Connecticut Town, The 1848
Contemporary Metropolitan America 469
Core of the City, The 280
Council-Manager Government 1652
Critical History of Police Reform, A 1023
Culture and the City 554
Culture Factory, The 1002
Culture of Cities, The 392
Cycle of Power, A 1635

D

Daley of Chicago 1671
Dangerous Class, The 1338
Dark Ghetto 1211
Death and Life of Great American Cities, The 19
Denver's Mayor Speer 1700
Diary of Philip Hone, 1828-1851 394
Dilemmas of Urban America 63
Dimensions in Urban History 223
Disintegration and Political Action 1535
Division Street 1406

E

Eclipse of Community, The 411
Economic Rivalry between St. Louis and Chicago, 1859-1880, The 678
Economy of Cities, The 233
Education of an Urban Minority, The 1384
Ekistics 1073
Electric Interurban Railways in America 933
Emergence of Metropolitan America, 1915-1966, The 24
End of an Era, New Orleans, 1850-1860 1564
Enduring Ghetto, The 1256
Essays on Urban America 97
Ethnic Dimension in American History, The 1348

Ethnic Influence on Urban Groups 1206
Ethnic Patterns in American Cities 1318
Evolution of American Urban Society, The 2
Evolution of an Urban School System, The 944
Evolution of Social Classes, The 1323
Exploding Metropolis, The 80

F

Factories in the Valley 197
Falling Apart 389
Family and Community 1427
Family and Kin in Urban Communities, 1700-1930 209
Fathers of the Towns, The 791
Father Yorke and the Labor Movement in San Francisco, 1900-1910 1463
Federal Bulldozer, The 1038
Federal Credit and Private Housing 1092
Federal Government and Metropolitan Areas, The 1459
Fifty Years of Rapid Transit 1022
Finley Peter Dunne and Mr. Dooley 1235
Forbidden Neighbors 1033
Fortunes and Failures 175
Fragmented Metropolis 523
Franklin D. Roosevelt and the City Bosses 1471
Frank Murphy 521
Free Negroes in the District of Columbia, 1790-1846 1201
From Commonwealth to Commerce 367
From Farm to Factory to Urban Pastoralism 731
From Main Street to State Street 361
From Puritan to Yankee 789
From Village to Industrial City 622

Title Index

Frontier Elements in a Hudson River Village 604
Frontier Farming in an Urban Shadow 171
Future of Cities and Urban Redevelopment, The 1177
Future of Housing, The 1034
Future of Old Neighborhoods, The 1082
Future of Our Cities, The 8

G

Gentleman Jimmy Walker 1807
Gentlemen of Property and Standing, Anti-Abolition Mobs in Jacksonian America 1373
Ghetto Grows in Brooklyn, A 1844
Ghetto Takes Shape, A 1311
Gold Coast and the Slum, The 670
Golden Door, The 1307
Governing the Metropolis 1492
Governing Urban America 1431
Government and Housing in Metropolitan Areas 1045
Government and Slum Housing 1083
Government as a Business 1577
Graham Taylor 1804
Great Bridge, The 962
Great Cities in America 68
Great Cities of the World 43
Great School Legend, The 923
Great School Wars, New York City, 1805-1973, The 988
Greenwich Village: A Brief Architectural and Historical Guide 649
Greenwich Village, 1920-1930 662
Growth of American Manufacturing Areas 27
Growth of Cities and Towns-State of Washington 749
Growth of Cities in the 19th Century, a Study in Statistics, The 64
Growth of Los Angeles in Historical Perspective, The 657
Growth of the Seaport Cities, 1790-1828, The 705
La Guardia: A Fighter against His Times 1550
La Guardia Comes to Power 1551

H

Half a Man 1352
Half-Century of Municipal Reform, A 1784
Half Century of Public Health, A (Ravenel) 987
Half Century of Public Health, A (American Public Health Association) 857
Handbook of Settlements 1823
Harbor and Haven 1842
Harlem: The Making of a Ghetto, Negro New York, 1890-1930 1351
Harlem Riot of 1943, The 1204
Health, Housing and Poverty in New York City 1856-1898 858
Health of the City 921
Health Progress in the United States 1900-1960 954
Heart of Our Cities, The 365, 1091
Historian and the City, The 88
Historical Geography of Detroit, The 609
History and the Role of the City in American Life 384
History of American City Government: The Conspicuous Failure, A 1677
History of American City Government: The Progressive Years and Their Aftermath 1678
History of Chicago, A 614
History of Kansas City, Missouri, A 1841
History of Naugatuck, Connecticut 540
History of Philadelphia 1609-1884 633
History of Public Franchises in New York City 982
History of Public Health in New York City, 1625-1866, A 900
History of Sanitation 894
History of Social Welfare and Social Work in the United States, A 21
History of South Boston 642

Title Index

History of the Chicago Urban League 1401
History of the Municipal University in the United States, The 797
History of Urban America, A 11
History of Urban Growth and Development, A 434
Hoboken 524
Holyoke, Massachusetts 541
Home Rule in Kansas 1472
Homestead's Households 559
House for All Peoples, A 1432
House on Henry Street, The 1806
Housing and Economic Progress 1143
Housing Comes of Age 1153
Housing Reform 1167
How Cities Grew 168
How the Other Half Lives 1142
Human Consequences of Urbanization, The 141
Human Side of Urban Renewal, The 1128
Husbandmen of Plymouth 831

I

Illusion of Reform, The 1494
Images of the American City 51
Immigrant Church, The 1228
Immigrant City 1213
Immigrant Life in New York City, 1825-1863 1233
Immigrant Milwaukee, 1836-1860 1216
Immigrants and the City 1234
Immigrants in Industrial America, 1850-1920 1853
Immigration and Industrialization 1194
Industrial Causes of Congestion of Population in New York City 619
Industrial Relations in the San Francisco Bay Area, 1900-1918 1527
Industrial Urban Community, The 339
Influence of the Foreign Heritage on the American City, The 57
In Pursuit of Profit 824
Inside the Minnesota Experiment 1909
Instant Cities 138
Intellectuals Versus the City, The 424
Internal Combustion 1317

Introduction to Housing 1176
Irish in Philadelphia, The 1210
Irish on the Urban Frontier, The 1414
Iron Barons, The 1868
Italian Passage, An 1840
Italians in Chicago, 1880-1930 1343

J

Jacob A. Riis and the American City 1707
John Purroy Mitchel 1709

K

Kansas City and the Railroads 196
King's Handbook of New York City, 1893 560
Ku Klux Klan in the City, The 1294

L

Labor and the American Revolution 802
Land of Contrasts, The 33
Landscape into Cityscape 1078
Land Use in Central Boston 187
Language of Cities, The 126
L'Enfant and Washington, 1791-1792 812
Life and Times in Colonial Philadelphia 811
Living City, The 1179
Long's Planned City 579
Los Angeles: From Mission to Modern City 602
Los Angeles: The Architecture of Four Ecologies 1046
Louis Sullivan, Prophet of Modern Architecture 1131
Lowell: A Study of Industrial Development 608

M

Machine in the Garden, The 386
Machine Politics 1672
Machine Politics in New Orleans, 1897-1926 1759

Title Index

Madison, Indiana 1811-1860 334
Making of Urban America, The 1140
Making of Urban History, The 458
Man and the Modern City 83
Man-Made Philadelphia 668
Measurements for Social History 324
Measurement of Urbanization and Projection of Urban Population, The 199
Meeting House and Counting House 843
Megalopolis 709
Memphis during the Progressive Era, 1900-1917 1730
Memphis' Greatest Debate 1008
Men, Cities, and Transportation 718
Metropolis and Region 181
Metropolis and Region in Transition 180
Metropolis on the Move 85, 200
Metropolitan Community, The 26
Metropolitan Enigma, The 112
Metropolitan Financing 4
Metropolitan Surveys 1087
Mexicans in the Northern Urban Area, The 1257
Michigan Cities and Villages 755
Migration and Urban Development 312
Mill and Mansion 1069
Mill Town 502
Milwaukee, The History of a City 651
Minority Migrants in the Urban Community 1391
Miracle on Cherry Creek 486
Mirror for Gotham 653
Mobile Americans 164
Modern American City, The 56
Modern City and Its Problems, The 374
Modern Housing 1050
Modern Metropolis, The 1056
Mr. Crump of Memphis 1731
Municipal Bonds 17
Municipal Finance 35
Municipal Home Rule in West Virginia 1477
Municipal Revolution in America, The 840
My Story 1701

N

National Archives and Urban Research, The 79, 436
National Urban League, 1910-1940, The 1421
Nation's Cities, The 1505
Natives and Newcomers 1266
Negroes in Cities 1404
Negro in Savannah, 1865-1900, The 1357
Negro Mecca 1385
Neighborhood 1263
Neighborhood: A Study of Local Life in the City of Columbus, Ohio, The 1722
Neighborhood, City, and Metropolis 87
Neighborhood Finds Itself, A 1031
Neighborhood in Nation Building, The 1820
Neighbors in Conflict 1184
New Amsterdam and Its People 810
New Architecture and City Planning 1180
Newcomers, The 1274
New Deal and American Politics, The 1433
New Deal and the Last Hurrah, The 1579
New Deal in the Suburbs, The 1042
New England Town the First Hundred Years, Dedham, Massachusetts, 1636-1736, A 813
New Exploration, The 1122
New Jersey since 1860 770
New Orleans, 1718-1812 500
New Orleans and the Railroads 624
New Urban History, The 99
New World of Urban Man, The 351
New York: An American City, 1783-1803 616
New York: The Centennial Years 1676-1976 562
New York as an Eighteenth Century Municipality 613
New York as an Eighteenth Century Municipality Prior to 1731 826
New York Bureau of Municipal Research, The 1639

391

Title Index

New York City, A Student's Guide to Localized History 654
New York City, 1664-1710 779
New York City during the War for Independence 781
New York in Fiction 592
New York in the Thirties 466
New York Police, the 992
Next Place You Come To, The 52
Night of Violence, A 1279
Nineteenth Century Cities 106
Nineteenth Century Inland Centers and Ports 469
Nineteenth Century Ports 469
Norfolk: Historic Southern Port 665
North America 55
North of Slavery 1320

O

Old New York in Early Photographs, 1835-1901 603
On Cities and Social Life 426
One Best System, The 1019
One Hundred Years of Land Values in Chicago, 1830-1933 1100
Organizing Public Services in Metropolitan America 980
Origin and Resolution of an Urban Crisis, The 1434
Origin of Cities of the United States 15
Origins of the Urban School 951
Other Bostonians, The 1407
Our Cities: Their Role in the National Economy 58, 263
Our Fight with Tammany 1749

P

Peaceable Kingdoms 856
Peasants and Strangers 1183
Pendergast Machine, The 1648
People of Jacksonian City, The 435
Peoples of Philadelphia, The 1224
Perspectives on the American Community 109
Philadelphia, The Federalist City 1556
Philadelphia: The Unexpected City 568
Philadelphia-Baltimore Trade Rivalry, The 249
Philadelphia Gentlemen 137
Philadelphia Quakers in the Industrial Age, 1865-1920, The 483
Philadelphia Riots of 1844, The 1237
Philadelphia's Philosopher Mechanics 1003
Pittsburgh: Forge of the Universe 548
Pittsburgh: The Story of an American City 576
Pittsburgh District Civic Frontage, The 559
Pittsburgh Survey, The 559
Place Called Home, A 1104
Plain People of Boston, 1830-1860, The 240
Planning and Cities in the Nineteenth Century 1065
Planning for a Nation of Cities 1170
Planning Function in Urban Government, The 1169
Planning the Fourth Migration 1155
Planning the Region of Chicago 1058
Plan of Chicago by Daniel H. Burnham and Edward H. Bennett 1130
Plunkitt of Tammany Hall 1764
Police Forces in History 880
Policing the City Boston 1822-1885 949
Polish-American Politics in Chicago 1524
Political Clubs of New York City, The 1561
Political Power in Birmingham, 1871-1921 1499
Politics, Planning, and the Public Interest 1127
Politics and Progress 1637
Politics of Efficiency, The 1768
Politics of Reform, The 1617
Population History of New York City 629
Population Redistribution and Economic Growth, United States 1870-1950 20

Title Index

Portents of Rebellion 814
Poverty and Progress 1408
Poverty in New York, 1783-1825 978
Power Broker, The 1455
Preface to Urban Economics, A 313
Preindustrial City, Past and Present, The 300
Private City, The 61
Problem of Boston, The 363
Progressive Cities 1760
Progressives and the Slums, The 1116
Progressives and Urban School Reform 890, 1631
Protestant Churches in Industrial America 970
Protestants against Poverty 937
Public and the Schools, The 1017
Public Health in the Town of Boston, 1630-1822 865
Pullman 488
Puritan Boston and Quaker Philadelphia 1832
Promised City, The 1375
Puritan Frontier, The 807
Puritan Village 828
Purity Crusade 1755

Q

Queen City, The 513
Quest for an American Sociology 387

R

Race, Change, and Urban Society 1350
Race Riot 1411
Race Riot at East St. Louis, July 2, 1917 1382
Race Riots in Black and White 1334
Racial Violence in the United States 1266a
Railroad and the City, The 169
Rail Routes South 696
Rebels and Gentlemen 786
Recent Federal City Relations 1445
Reformers in Search of Yesterday 1773
Reform in Detroit 1688
Religion and the Rise of the American City 996

Remembered Gate, The 344, 1835
Renewing Our Cities 1064
Rental Housing 1173
Report on the Social Statistics of Cities 760
Residence and Race 1120
Residential Rehabilitation 1135
Residential Renewal in the Urban Core 1139
Reveille in Washington, 1860-1865 572
Revolutionary Politics in Massachusetts 788
Revolution Is Now Begun, The 835
Riches, Class, and Power before the Civil War 1361
Rise of Sports in New Orleans, 1850-1900, The 643
Rise of the City, 1878-1898, The 46
Rise of the City Manager, The 1785
Rise of the Labor Movement in Los Angeles 1400
Rise of the Skyscraper, The 1068
Rise of Urban America, The 14
Rizzo 1682
Robert Moses 1566
Rochester: An Emerging Metropolis, 1925-1961 587
Rochester: The Quest for Quality, 1890-1925 587
Rochester on the Genesee 588
Rural-Urban Migration in Wisconsin, 1940-1950 207

S

Safeguarding the Public Health 916
Salvation in the Slums 966
San Francisco: Magic City 606
San Francisco: The Bay and Its Cities 547
San Francisco 1846-1856 578
San Francisco Irish, 1850-1976, The 1910
Satellite Cities 1160
Search for Order, 1877-1920, The 425
Season in New York, 1801, A 600

Title Index

Seat of Empire 785
Second Generation of Italians in New York City, The 1326
Secret City, The 1264
Secular City, The 895
Selected Bibliography of the American City, A 456
Senator Robert F. Wagner and the Rise of Urban Liberalism 1695
Send These to Me 1284
Seth Low 1705
Settlement Horizon, The 1821
Settlement Houses and the Great Depression 1018
Settlement Idea, The 1687
Seven Myths of Housing, The 1154
Shame of the Cities, The 1782
Shaping an Urban Future 82
Shaping of a City, The 1546
Shaping of Urban Society, The 44
Short Account of the Malignant Fever, Lately Prevalent in Philadelphia, A 790
Slavery in the Cities 757
Slum and the Ghetto, The 1364
Slums of Baltimore, Chicago, New York, and Philadelphia, The 1178
Social Area in Cities 218
Social Bases of City Politics, The 1597
Social Change in an Industrial Town 663
Social Characteristics of Cities 395
Social Construction of Communities, The 305
Socialism and the Cities 1580
Social Justice and the City 211
Social New York under the Georges, 1714-1776 838
Social Saga of Two Cities, The 635
Social Science and the City 100
Social Study of Pittsburgh, A 563
Society and Power 700
Sociology of Cities, The 299
Sociology of City Life 161
Solid for Molhooley 1772
South Atlantic Urban Studies 1865
Spatial Dynamics of U.S. Urban-Industrial Growth, 1800-1914, The 272

Spearheads for Reform 1640
Stamford in the Gilded Age 1479
Stamford Puritan to Patriot 800
Steel Workers, The 559
Streetcar Suburbs 326
Street Corner Society 1422
Structure and Growth of Residential Neighborhoods in American Cities, The 226
Structure of the Metropolitan Community, The 151
Studies in Housing and Minority Groups 1251
Study in Acculturation, A 1273
Study in Boss Politics, A 1788
Study of Urban Geography, The 162
Study of Urbanization, The 90
Suburbanization Dynamics and the Future of the City 91
Suburban Myth, The 350
Suburban Trend, The 177
Suburbia in Transition 968
Sword of Pestilence 906

T

Taming Megalopolis 77
Taming of the Frontier, The 470
Tammany 1742
Tammany Hall and the New Immigrants 1685
Technology and Reform 965
Technology in Western Civilization 241
Tenement House Problem, The 1071
Tenement Landlord, The 1151
Tenements of Chicago, 1908-1935, The 1181
Testing the Roosevelt Coalition 1521
They Built the West 741
Three Centuries of New Haven, 1638-1938 607
Three Generations in Twentieth Century America 348
Three Iron Mining Towns 720
Toward an Understanding of the Metropolis 208
Toward an Urban Ohio 772

Title Index

Toward an Urban Vision 343
To Wear a City's Crown 767
Town into City 192
Town Planning in Frontier America 1141
Towns and Cities 235
Transportation and the Growth of Cities 195
Travels in the United States during 1849 and 1850 71
Trouble Downtown 341
Tweed Ring, The 1621
Tweed's New York 1686
Twentieth Century Cities 469
Twentieth Century City, The 412
Twenty Years at Hull House 1602
Twenty Years of Public Housing 1079

U

Unheavenly City, The 1436
Urban America: A History with Documents 50
Urban America: From Downtown to No Town 12
Urban America in Historical Perspective 96
Urban America in the Twentieth Century 104
Urban and Regional Studies at United States Universities 118
Urban Anthology 191
Urban Blight and Slums 1168
Urban Bosses, Machines, and Progressive Reformers 1780
Urban Builder 1147
Urban Crowding and Its Consequences 152
Urban Development and Housing a Program for Post-War 1089
Urban Economics and Public Policy 215
Urban Ethos in the South, 1920-1930, The 683
Urban Frontier: The Rise of Western Cities, 1790-1830, The 758
Urban Government 1591
Urban Government: A Reader in Administration and Politics 1437
Urban Government and Politics 1542
Urban Growth and Circulation of Information 273
Urban Growth Dynamics in a Regional Cluster of Cities 163
Urban Growth in the Age of Sectionalism 706
Urban Habitat, The 376
Urban Idea in Colonial America, The 803
Urban Indian, The 1398
Urbanism, Urbanization, and Change 94
Urbanization of America, The 108
Urbanization of America, 1860-1915, The 25
Urban Community 347
Urban Community: Housing and Planning in the Progressive Era, The 1117
Urban Experience, The 356
Urban Experience: Themes in American History, The 95
Urbanization of Modern America, The 29
Urbanization of the Suburbs, The 253
Urbanization of the Upper Midwest, 1930-1960 680
Urban Legacy 446
Urban Masses and Moral Order in America, 1820-1920 1614
Urban Nation, 1920-1960, The 32
Urban New Jersey since 1870 771
Urban Police in the United States 880, 994
Urban Poverty 1214
Urban Problems and Prospects 76
Urban Racial Violence in the Twentieth Century 1197
Urban Reader, The 72
Urban Renewal 1053
Urban Renewal and American Cities 1090
Urban R's, The 898
Urban Scene: Human Ecology and Demography, The 101
Urban Scene: Myths and Realities, The 78

Title Index

Urban Slavery in the American South 1820-1860 708
Urban Social Structure 143
Urban Sociology 159
Urban South 756
Urban South in the Twentieth Century, The 684
Urban Structure 53
Urban Structure and Population Growth 243
Urban Threshold, The 150
Urban Traffic, A Function of Land Use 258
Urban Utopias in the Twentieth Century 1080
Urban View, The 86
Urban Village 855
Urban Villagers, The 1244
Urban Vision, The 1159
Urban Vision: Selected Interpretations of the Modern American City, The 105
Urban West at the End of the Frontier, The 721
Urban Wilderness, The 62

V

Vanishing America, A 110
Violent Death in the City 1876

W

Wage Earning Pittsburgh 559
Wagner Housing Act, The 1119
Washington: Capital City, 1879-1950 542
Washington: Village and Capital, 1800-1878 543
Washington Community, 1800-1828, The 669
Water for a City 1026
Water for the Cities 866
Water Power City, 1812-1854, The 587
When Leaders Were Bosses 1778
Where Cities Meet 677
Who Governs? 1466
Winthrop's Boston 833
Withering Away of the City 111
Women and the Trades 559
Work Accidents and the Law 559
Working Class Community in Industrial America 1221
Working-Class Suburb 1187
Working for the People 1558
Works Progress Administration in New York City, The 1557

Y

Your City Tomorrow 1088

Z

Zoned American 54
Zoning 1049

SUBJECT INDEX

This index is alphabetized letter by letter and references are to entry numbers. Major areas of emphasis within a subject have been underlined.

A

Abolitionism 1320, 1373
  in Cincinnati 512, 638
  in New York City 1699
  riots resulting from 1230
  in Philadelphia 1480
  in Washington, D.C. 1435
Accounting, evolution of municipal systems of 39, 1894
Acculturation. See Assimilation and acculturation
Addams, Jane 1602, 1691, 1743, 1770
  concept of community of 362
Advertising, sense of community expressed in 361
Age, social mobility and 154
Agrarianism 350, 401, 403, 414, 420, 750, 1714
  myths of southern 698
  in poetry 418
  role of in Memphis 599
  See also Rural areas
Agricultural societies, in Virginia 707
Agriculture
  economic ramifications of 215
  in Illinois 725
  impact on city growth 309, 751
  influence of neighboring cities on 171, 330
  use of sewerage in 1012

Airports
  Los Angeles 1904
  politics of development of 1552
Alabama, city manager system in 1664
Albany, N.Y.
  comment by travelers on 71
  family and community life in 503
  politics of 1778
Albuquerque
  government of 1630
  history of 545
Alcohol, consumption of as an indicator of life-style 250. See also Liquor; Prohibition
Alexander, George 1769
Alexander, John K. 822
Alger, Horatio, Jr. 388
Alienation 366, 371, 565, 625
  education and 1028
  of immigrant women 1310
  of Milwaukee Greeks 1216
  myths of 354
Alviso, Calif. 507
American Association for Promoting Hygiene and Public Baths 1092a
American Fur Company 546
American Indians 1398
Americanization. See Assimilation and acculturation

Subject Index

American Medical Association, report on public hygiene 940
Amherst, N.Y., history of 476
Anchorage, founding 666
Anderson, Sherwood, concept of community of 362
Annapolis, Revolutionary War in 824
Annexation 155, 290, 1474
   in Chicago 618, 1653
   in Cleveland 1543
   in Indianapolis 479
   in the South 1460
Anniston, Ala., history of 530
Anomie, urbanization and 190
Anti-Semitism
   in Atlanta 1282
   in Detroit 1376
Architecture 3, 105, 1081, 1098, 1131, 1133, 1137, 1146, 1180
   of Boston 1148
   of Chicago 634, 1039
   classical revival 1166
   of colonial Connecticut 804
   of Iowa 1099
   of Los Angeles 1046
   of Lowell, Mass. 1069
   of New England 1040
   of New York City 472, 560, 649, 1041
   of Rochester, N.Y. 582
   of southern railway stations 688
   terminology connected with 126
   use of house facades in determining period of construction 283
   use of the past in dealing with urban 329
   See also Chicago School of Architecture; Housing
Archives
   development of municipal 1845
   use of resources found in 193
   See also U.S. National Archives
Arizona, the saloon in territorial 699
Arkansas
   city manager plan in 1633
   race relations in 1863
Armenian Americans 1209
Arnold, Henry J. 1736

Arson 861
Art 72
   in colonial Philadelphia 811
   Coney Island as a symbol in 349
   images of the city in 402
Asia, cities of 43
Assimilation and acculturation 2, 100, 139, 1238, 1318, 1336, 1355
   of American Indians 1398
   of British Americans 1394
   domestic service as an aid to 1250
   education and 864
   failure of as a threat to social order 352
   of German Americans 1250
   of Greek Americans 1217
   of Irish Americans 1195, 1235, 1250, 1273, 1392, 1394
   of Italian Americans 1337, 1342, 1344, 1365, 1413
   of Norwegian Americans 1867
   of Polish Americans 1253
   of Scandanavian Americans 1418
   school attendance and 1424
   of Spanish-speaking Americans 1275
   spatial aspects of 1253
   of Welsh Americans 1195
Atlanta
   business buildings of 1118
   class, ethnicity, and race in 1251, 1278, 1282-85, 1288-90, 1309, 1369, 1415, 1864a
   education in 1653, 1803
   history of 329, 469, 529, 630
   impact of the automobile on 275, 740
   police in 1025
   politics and reform in 1415, 1596-97, 1641, 1803
   Protestant Church in 983
   public health in 936
   public housing in 1161
   riots in 1219
   urbanization of 769
   urban planning in 1057
   water supply of 910

Subject Index

Atlantic City
  politics of 1778
  as a resort area 526, 771
Atlases, comparative 1
Atomization, urbanization and 190
Augusta
  flood of 1888 in 494
  history of 532
  politics and reform in 1458, 1667
Austin, Tex.
  history of 766-67
  slavery in 1313
  transportation study of 1904
Australia, cities of 43
Authors. See Blacks, as authors; Novelists
Automobile industry 1906
  unionization of 1584
Automobiles 80, 224, 935, 964, 1859
  in Birmingham 873
  in Chicago 862
  choice of for transportation in the 1920s 331
  in decline of the city center 204, 1091
  impact of 60, 275
    on job distribution 714
  in Los Angeles 525
  need to curb the dominance of 365
  retail trade in Atlanta and 740
  the urban crisis and 8
Auxiliary Sanitary Association (New Orleans) 908

B

Balance of payments, influence on migration 312
Baltimore
  automobile use in 331
  class, ethnic, and race in 1186, 1205, 1245-46, 1268, 1339, 1356, 1374
  Dickens on 7
  history of 13, 249, 469, 844-45
  institutional studies of 866, 991
    public baths 1029a-29b
    religion 1836
  lumber trade in 703

mobility in 1834
municipal archives of 1845
patterns of service demands in 131
planning, architecture, and urban renewal in 1035, 1076, 1178
politics and reform in 1434, 1588, 1598, 1637, 1831
response to the Erie Canal by 746
Banfield, Edward C. 1509
Bankruptcy, law of 1444
Banks and banking 172
  in Boston 679
Barrows, Alice 979
Baseball 1762
  appeal to the middle class 1240
  cultural myths concerning 403
Baths, public. See Public baths
Baton Rouge, La., politics in 1462, 1518
Beaufort, N.C., history of 825
Beaumont, Tex., municipal reform in 1697
Behavior, human. See Social relations and behavior
Behrman, Martin 1759
Bellamy, Edward 414
Bemis, Edward Webster 1690
Bennett, Edward H. 1130
Berkeley, Calif., history of 36
Bethlehem, Pa. 1868
Bicentennial Conference on Planning for the Quality of Urban Life 1170
Biddeford, Maine, Franco-Americans in 1270
Billings, Mont., history of 381
Biographies, urban, bibliography on 437
Birmingham, Ala.
  the automobile in 873
  black housing in 1251
  history of 484, 556, 682
  politics of 1498
Birmingham, Engl., upper-class control of 1291
Birthplace, relationship to nineteenth-century family demographics 147

Subject Index

Birthrate
 impact of urbanization on rural 140
 industrialization and 167
 See also Fertility
Bismarck, N.D., history of 601
Blacks 95, 97, 676, 1211, 1236, 1255, 1287, 1304-5, 1320, 1322, 1329, 1346, 1350, 1372, 1380, 1404, 1864, 1902
 in Arkansas 1863
 in Atlanta 1278, 1288, 1415
 in Augusta 1458
 as authors 1426
 in Baltimore 1246, 1268, 1356
 in Baton Rouge, La. 1518
 bibliography on 434
 in Boston 1822
 in Chicago 1181, 1231, 1364, 1399, 1401, 1403, 1490, 1517, 1791
 in Cleveland 1311
 criminal justice for 1280
 in Detroit 1298, 1303, 1317, 1409-10, 1877
 education of 1316, 1328, 1368, 1381, 1397, 1517
 employment of female 1189
 exclusion from civic affairs 467
 family of 1278, 1313
 historiographical studies on 457
 housing and residential areas of 1051, 1126, 1136, 1181, 1239, 1251, 1268, 1330-31
 in Jacksonville, Fla. 1182
 in Lansing, Mich. 1330-31
 in Los Angeles 1226
 in Memphis 1858
 migration by 70, 1261
 mobility of 1266, 1274, 1288, 1370
 in New Jersey 770-71, 1493
 in New Orleans 1191, 1280, 1494
 in New York City 1241, 1252, 1274, 1300, 1351-52, 1385, 1454, 1486, 1519, 1534, 1844

 in Pensacola, Fla. 1199
 in Philadelphia 1051, 1224, 1239, 1547
 police and 1366
 political studies of 742, 1182, 1415, 1454, 1458, 1486, 1490, 1493-94, 1512, 1517-19, 1534, 1547, 1636, 1791
 in Poughkeepsie, N.Y. 1266
 Protestant reactions to 1298
 in Racine, Wis. 1391
 in St. Louis 1371, 1387
 in St. Paul 1405
 in San Francisco 1223
 in Savannah 1190, 1357
 in the South 742, 1182, 1306, 1366-69, 1423
 standard of living of 716
 in Steelton, Pa. 1196
 in Virginia 716
 in Washington, D.C. 1201, 1264, 1268, 1301, 1425
 in Wilmington, Del. 1512
 See also Riots; Slavery; Urban League
Blankenburg, Rudolph 1645
Blooming Grove, Wis., influence of Madison on 171
Boarders and boarding 1335
Boise, Idaho, history of 495
Boley, Okla. 1864
Bonds, municipal 17
Boston 33, 68, 363
 class, ethnicity, and race in 322, 1143, 1208, 1244, 1260, 1269, 1272-73, 1295-96, 1316, 1318, 1339, 1359, 1361, 1393, 1407, 1423, 1666, 1891, 1898
 comment by travelers on 7, 71
 crime and violence in 520, 809
 dependency and child development in eighteenth century 201
 economic studies of (development, poverty, wealth, etc.) 323, 821, 847-48, 850, 929
 history of 13, 469, 561, 642,

Subject Index

784, 788, 803, 808-9, 821, 833, 847-50
institutional studies of 860, 907, 939, 1029a
   education 887, 946, 1001-2, 1295, 1316
   police 949
   public health and sanitation 865-66
   transportation 321, 326
land use in 187
planning, architecture, and urban renewal in 1088, 1148
politics and reform in 819, 1471, 1528, 1544, 1553-54, 1562, 1572, 1590, 1598, 1640, 1666, 1774, 1778, 1822, 1826
population studies of 240
response to the Erie Canal by 746
urbanization of 679
Boston Committee of Correspondence 788
Brayton, Charles R. 1453
Bridgeport, Conn., comment by travelers on 71
Bridges
   of Boston 642
   design of as a cultural phenomenon 429
   See also Brooklyn Bridge
British Americans in Fall River, Mass. 1394
Brooklyn, N.Y.
   history of 534, 569, 573, 598, 637, 1162
   politics in 1519, 1523, 1530, 1562, 1585
   socioeconomic studies of 1359, 1361-62
Brooklyn Bridge 962, 1016
Brown, Lucius Polk 1817
Bryce, James 368, 1649
Buckley, Christopher A. 1620
Bucks County, Pa., growth and planning of 1063
Buffalo, N.Y. 536
   class, ethnicity, and race in

1249-50, 1262, 1281, 1318, 1389, 1393, 1427, 1853
politics and reform in 1748, 1773
suburbanization of 136, 482
urbanization of 753
Building codes 507
Buildings 19
   of Atlanta 1118
   of Chicago 1066-67a
   See also Architecture; Skyscrapers
Burgess, E.W. 225
Burke, Thomas 732
Burner, Henry C. 377
Burnham, Daniel H., Sr. 1044, 1058, 1066, 1096-97, 1117, 1130
Burton Harold 1473
Business and commerce 37, 273
   of Baltimore 844-45
   black 1372
   of Charleston 539
   of Chicago 671
   of Cincinnati 518
   of Illinois 725
   impact on urbanization 210, 286, 309, 313, 681
   influence of cities on foreign 1500
   of New Orleans 485, 624
   of New York City 613, 1467
   nineteenth century 367
   of Norfolk 665
   of Philadelphia 786, 811, 815, 843, 984
   of Portland 1546
   promotion of 1541
   of St. Louis 623, 627
   of seaport cities 705
   of the South 799
   urban dominance and (1890) 128
   See also Industry
Businessmen and merchants
   of Annapolis in the Revolutionary War 824
   of Augusta 1667
   of Baltimore 1434

Subject Index

    of Chicago 1248, 1671, 1703, 1717, 1719
    of Denver 1735
    Jewish in San Francisco 1850
    of New York City 1511, 1765
    of Oakland, Calif. 1839
    of Philadelphia 255, 1756
    of Pittsburgh 1516
    in politics and reform 1434, 1511, 1516, 1536, 1546, 1667, 1671, 1703, 1717, 1719, 1735, 1756, 1768, 1810, 1839
    social orientation of 182
Bus lines, in Los Angeles 1904

C

Cabarets, in New York City 911
Cahan, Abraham, analysis of his tenement fiction 355
Cairo, Ill., history of 570
California, role of the railroad in southern 735
Cambridge, Mass., influence of commuting on 145
Canton, Ill., socialism in 1581
Capital
    in development of the frontier 712
    importance to urban growth 173, 306
        in St. Louis 623
    See also Investment
Capitalism 1887
    black 1372
    regulation of in the Progressive era 1750
    value of land under 317
Catholic Church 1890
    Americanization of immigrants by 1394
    bias against in Philadelphia 1237
    in Newark, N.J. 1895
    in New York City 1228
    social institutions of 1021
Catholic education
    in Boston 1898
    in Chicago 1384
Censorship 1755

Census data
    for Chicago 490
    dimensions of errors in 297
    in studying religious preference 242
    for the study of occupations in New Jersey 693
Central city district 153, 162, 288
    of Cleveland 1722
    decline of 1082
        automobile in 204
        land values and 333
    development of immigrant ghettoes in 322
    economics of 59
    growth and development of 213
        in Boston 323
        in Spokane 517
    impact of the elevated railway on 335
    lack of middle-class housing in 1070
    migration to 1258
    of Philadelphia 280
    polarity with the suburbs 18
    renewal of 1091, 1139
Central Labor Union 631
Central Park (New York City) 1152
Cermack, Anton 1605, 1673
Charity 870, 915, 1291
    in Boston 860
    British comment on American 48
    in Chicago 971, 1384, 1706
    in New York City 860, 1503, 1692, 1702
    Protestantism and 860
Charleston
    history of 13, 538-39, 621, 784, 830, 836, 846, 850
    Irish Americans in 1899
    lumber trade in 703
    police in 1871
    politics in 1650
    poor relief in 850
    public health and medicine in 902, 1024
Charlestown, Mass. 1837

Subject Index

Chelsea, Mass.
   Progressive reform in 1653
   social order in 565
Chesbrough, Ellis Sylvester 876
Cheyenne, Wyo., history of 470
Chicago 31, 33, 43, 68, 670, 1681
   census data of 490
   civic pride in 337
   class, ethnicity, and race in 62, 294, 1181, 1231, 1235, 1243, 1248, 1255, 1263, 1328, 1342-43, 1353, 1364, 1379, 1381-82, 1384, 1393, 1399, 1401, 1403, 1406, 1411, 1451-52, 1490, 1517, 1524, 1589, 1673, 1743, 1866
   community structure in 618
   cultural conflict in 471
   economic studies of 260, 546, 671, 678, 712
   geography of 508
   history of 13, 29, 62, 469, 531, 554, 558, 575, 590, 593, 614, 634, 648, 765
   institutional studies of 531, 641, 907, 971, 1029a
      education 115, 881, 1328, 1381, 1384, 1517, 1803
      libraries 912
      police 927-28, 947
      public health and sanitation 876-77
      religion 555, 1021
      trade unions 1345
      transportation 862
   land values in 333, 1100
   poetry about 397
   politics and reform in 1355, 1451-52, 1471, 1490, 1517, 1522, 1524, 1555, 1589, 1640, 1644, 1653, 1671-73, 1691, 1703, 1713, 1716-17, 1719-20, 1726, 1743, 1747, 1767, 1778, 1781, 1788, 1790-91, 1803-5, 1812-13
   prohibition in 341
   promotion of 728
   suburbs of 496
   travelers' impressions of 615
   urban ecology of 229
   urbanization of 753
   urban problems of 370
   walking tours of 474
Chicago Charity Organization 1706
Chicago Historical Society, American city prints collection of 133
Chicago School of Architecture 1067a, 1107, 1110, 1130
Chicago School of "Human Ecology" 360
Chicago School of Sociology 387, 396, 426, 1876
Child care and rearing 860
   of migrants and minorities 1391
Child development, patterns of in nineteenth-century Boston 201
Child labor laws, and education in New York 1009
Childs, Richard S. 1652
Child welfare 857, 1615
Chimayo, N. Mex. 110
Chinese Americans 1304, 1319
   in Los Angeles 1400
   in San Francisco 945, 1321
Cholera 902, 997
   1949 St. Louis epidemic 871
Choteau, Mont. 110
Chudacoff, Howard 445
Church and state, in colonial Boston 833
Churches
   of blacks 1320
   of Boston 642
   evolution of in Detroit 1227
   as New York City ethnic sub-communities 1228
   records of as historical data 236, 242
   relationship of location to housing patterns 165
   urban slavery and 757
   See also Religion
Cincinnati
   class, ethnicity, and race in 1291, 1318, 1373, 1852, 1875

Subject Index

comment on by travelers 7, 47
economic rivalry with Louisville 696
education in 974
history of 13, 29, 169, 518, 550, 638, 765
influence of New England on 512
manufacturing in 671
police in 947, 1023
politics and reform in 1608, 1725, 1733-34, 1801, 1857
riots of 704
sewer system in 918
transportation in expansion of 281, 745
urban problems of 1781
Cincinnati Southern Railway 492, 934
Cities
   attitudes toward 51, 70, 338, 345, 354, 371-72, 377, 380, 390, 421, 423-24, 537, 552
   boosterism and promotion of 133, 467, 494, 529, 541, 611, 625, 639, 671-72, 676, 699, 728, 730, 732, 739-40, 743, 750-51, 753-54, 771, 1106, 1828
   diffusion in 227
   documents pertinent to 23, 84
   function of 99
   future of 64, 72, 78, 86, 91, 288, 508
   historiography of 96
   interrelationships between 26
   lack of beauty in 390
   in literature, film, and art 9, 71-72, 107, 355, 371, 385-86, 397, 399, 402, 408-9, 418, 422, 471, 592, 600, 615, 644, 650, 702, 1229
   location and settlement of 161, 168, 174, 210, 497, 508, 545, 754, 764, 1074
   methodology of research on 347
   relations with rural areas 18, 52, 149, 353, 378, 407, 423-24, 707, 1166, 1855
   with states 42, 1545, 1548, 1585
   with suburbs 60, 1194
   with the federal government 24, 58, 70, 79, 436, 1444-45, 1459, 1476, 1478, 1483, 1552, 1587, 1591, 1860
   role of in American thought 337-465
   sizes and types of 216, 234-35, 295-96, 366, 392
   statistics on 760
   See also Central city district; Towns and villages; Urbanization; names of cities
Citizen participation 109, 1324
Citizens Association (Chicago) 1726
Citizenship, of Italian Americans in New York City 1326
Citizens' Planning and Housing Association (Baltimore) 1076
Citizen's Union (New York City) 1739
"City Beautiful" movement 1138, 1145
   in Denver 1735
   in Harrisburg, Pa. 1172
   in Kansas City 1171
   in North Carolina 1101-2
City Club (New York City) 1607, 1739
City councils, occupations of members on 1578. See also Mayor-council form of government
City life 237, 395, 751, 953, 1162, 1830
   benefits of 354
   decentralization of 213
   hazards of 3
   in the Old South 702
   quality of 1170
City manager form of government 1630, 1633, 1664, 1785, 1810, 1815, 1839
City planning. See Urban planning

Subject Index

City Reform Club (New York City) 1739
City-state relations. See State government, relations with the city
Civic Federation 1726, 1741
Civil rights movement
 in Montgomery, Ala. 341
 in New York City 1454
 in the Truman administration 1593-94
Civil service
 in New York City 1702
 police and 1029d
Civil Service Law (Houston, 1948) 967
Civil War
 cities during 55, 103
  Iowa City, Iowa 639
  Washington, D.C. 572
 draft riots in New York City 1217
 See also Secession
Clark, Joseph 1753
Clergy, reform ideas of 1708
Cleveland
 city planning in 664, 1062, 1096-97
 class, ethnicity, and race in 1183, 1243, 1255, 1269, 1293, 1311, 1318, 1420, 1868
 history of 497, 617, 628
 neighborhood status in 205
 police in 1023
 politics and reform in 1473, 1529, 1543, 1616, 1693, 1700, 1721, 1800
 religious preferences in 242
 urbanization of 753
Cleveland Foundation 1728
Clinics. See Public health
Clinton, De Witt 1560
Cluster concept 12
Coalition party (Lancaster, Pa.) 1669
Colleges. See Community colleges; Universities and colleges
Colonial period 73-74, 96, 103, 431, <u>774-856</u>, 1891. See also Revolutionary War
Colorado
 cooperative communities in 699

 founding of new towns in 754
Columbia, S.C., history of 544, 574
Columbian Exposition (1893) 1096, 1110, 1171
Columbus, Ohio 267
 crime and poverty in 1338
 ethnic groups in 1318
 neighborhoods in 1722
 politics and reform in 1779
Commission form of government 1735, 1760, 1810
Communication(s) 178, 241
 comparative atlas of 1
 effect of urbanization on 2
 impact on urbanization 681
 in New York City 1724
 urban dominance (1890) and 128
 See also Information, circulation of; Newspapers
Community; community life 109, 279, 342, 354, 361-62, 396, 400, 419, 860, 1714, 1869
 in Albany, N.Y. 503
 black 1346, 1350
 change in 229, 348, 411
 in Charlestown, Mass. 1837
 in Chicago 618
 in colonial Boston 833
 in colonial New England 791, 856
 consciousness of 108
 control of 78
 decline of 340
 formation of 150
 in Greenwich Village 620
 historiographical studies of 431-32, 446
 influences on workingmen's outlooks 1595
 institutions of 305
 in Jersey City, N.J. 1795
 in Minneapolis-St. Paul 635
 in New York City 1519
 in Ohio 772
 Park's theory of 359
 political control in 1519
 portrayed in film 371
 power in 45, 231
 in the Progressive era 398, 1795

Subject Index

    rediscovery of 237
    relationship to family 1309
    in Richmond, Va. 1854
    in small-town America 110
    in Springfield, Mass. 192
    structure of 151
    traditional concept of 428
    transformation of 111
    See also Neighborhoods
Community centers, as a means of reviving small-town values 398
Community Chest 1018
Community colleges, urban history at 121
Community development
    comparative study of 134
    historiographical study of 448
Community planning, in Illinois 725
Commuters and commuting 145, 216
    the automobile and in the 1920s 331
Company towns 194, 528, 674
Compulsory education. See Education, compulsory
Computer mapping. See Mapping, computer
Concentric circle theory 225, 360, 516, 1070
Coney Island 1872
    as an urban art symbol 349
Congregational Church, in Minneapolis 959
Connecticut
architecture and town planning in 804
    history of 469, 789, 1848
    political studies of 1521
    urbanization of 220, 731
Conservatism
    the Progressive era as an example of 1833
    southern 742
Construction industry, technology in 241
Consumer's Gas Association 859
Consumption
    influence on migration 312
    influence on the "urban mind" 32

Cooperatives
    in Colorado 699
    in New York City 985
Corporate model of government 1802
Corruption 1475, 1622-23, 1677, 1723, 1771, 1778, 1782
    in Boston 1822
    in Chicago 927-28
    in Denver 1643
    in Detroit 1656
    in Milwaukee 1461
    in New Orleans 1897
    in New York City 993
    in Philadelphia 1649
    in Providence, R.I. 886
    in San Francisco 1808
Cotton industry, impact on southern urbanization 761-62
Coughlin, John 1813
Council manager form of government 1652
Courts 1487
    blacks in New Orleans 1280
    development of in Philadelphia 1011
Costigan, Edward P. 1642
Cox, George 1733-34, 1801
Cracker party 1458
Crane, Stephen, analysis of his tenement fiction 355
Credit, facilities for in Boston 679
Crime and violence 68, 112, 161, 390, 1266a
    bibliography of recent scholarship on 435
    in Birmingham 484
    in Boston 520
    in Columbus, Ohio 1338
    in Detroit 999-1000
    in Memphis 599
    in New York City 795
    origin and consequences of 417
    in Philadelphia 405, 1224, 1247, 1876
    in Pittsburgh 883
    political 1461
    See also Riots; Vice

Subject Index

Crime prevention, federal aid for 1444
Cross, Whitney 156
Crowds and mobs 405
   bibliography of recent scholarship on 435
   in Boston 1272
   in the Revolutionary War era 809
   See also Riots
Crump, Edward 1471, 1730-32, 1783
Culture; cultural life and activities 191, 246, 392, 406, 416, 430, 953
   of Birmingham 484, 682
   bridge design as 429
   of Charleston 621
   of Chicago 471, 558
   of Detroit 1906
   development of an urban 25
   ethnic and immigrant 426, 1183, 1194, 1233, 1252, 1270, 1348, 1355
   on the frontier 648
   of Houston 581
   the New Deal and 1446
   of New Mexico 625
   of New York City 600, 616, 1233, 1560
   of Philadelphia 644, 786
   of poverty 81
   school attendance and 1424
   stages of urban 384
   of Texas 767
   urban dominance and (1890) 128
   See also Assimilation and acculturation; Popular culture
Curley, James Michael 1471, 1778, 1783, 1826
Czechoslovakian Americans 1209
   in Chicago 1181, 1673

D

Daley, Richard J. 1605, 1671, 1747, 1767, 1778
Dallas, history of 469
Danish Americans 1206
Davenport, Iowa, architecture and city planning in 1099
Debt, municipal 1448
Decision making 163
   in city planning 664
   in communities 231
   control of 736
Dedham, Mass., history of 510, 813
Delaware, urbanization of 722
Democracy 382, 1511, 1556
   social 403
Democratic party 1433
   in Baton Rouge, La. 1518
   in Beaumont, Tex. 1697
   blacks in 1490, 1512, 1518, 1547
   in Boston 1826
   in Chicago 1432, 1490, 1589, 1767
   in Denver 1736
   immigrants and 1457
   Irish Americans in 1589
   labor support of 1469
   in Milwaukee 1461
   in New Jersey 1493
   in New York City 1469, 1530, 1742
   in New York State 1888
   in Philadelphia 97, 1491, 1547
   in Pittsburgh 1516, 1579
   in San Francisco 1620
   in Wilmington, Del. 1512
Democratic Republican party, in New York City 1443
Demographic studies 11, 90, 101, 147, 292-93
   bibliography on 118
   of Detroit 1906
   of the frontier 721
   of the post-World War II era 304
   of the South 686
   of urban renewal 1149
   use of as indicator of urbanism 282
   See also Population
Denver 33, 138
   history of 13, 178, 470, 473, 486, 513, 741
   Jewish Americans in 1879
   politics and reform in 1700, 1735-37, 1893

Subject Index

public utilities in 1896
the saloon in 1886
socioeconomic status in 468
Spanish-speaking Americans in 1275
Denver and Rio Grande Railroad 754
Depression (1870s) 1692
Depression (1929)
  in Columbia, S.C. 574
  in Detroit 341
  in New York City 466
  in Paterson, N.J. 1885
  in Pennsylvania 1482
  in Reading, Pa. 1507
  in San Francisco 1559
  in Seattle 1559
  settlement houses and 1018
  socialism in 1507
Des Moines, Iowa, leadership in 1514
Detroit
  automobile industry in 1906
  class, ethnicity, and race in 1227, 1243, 1252, 1255, 1297-98, 1303, 1317, 1376-77, 1379, 1382, 1409-10, 1414, 1430, 1531, 1877
  crime and police in 998-1000, 1023
  depression and World War II in 341
  fiscal problems of 929
  history of 13, 55, 469, 521, 609
  housing in 1033, 1251
  politics and reform in 1531, 1584, 1654-56, 1662, 1688, 1690
  population and land use study of 336
  press in 914
  urbanization of 753
Detroit Citizens League 1654, 1656, 1662
Developing countries, cities and urbanization in 102, 383
Dickens, Charles, on American cities 7
Dilworth, Richardson 1753

Disaggregated Residential Allocation Model 278
Divorce, urban-industrial life and 314
Dock, Mira Lloyd 1172
Domestic service, as an aid to acculturation 1250
Dos Passos, John, analysis of the fiction of 9
Draft. See Military conscription
Drama 72
Draper, Stanley 1147
Drieser, Theodore, analysis of the fiction of 9
Dubuque, Iowa
  architecture and city planning in 1099
  history of 612
Dunne, Edward F. 881
Dunne, Finley Peter 1235

E

Eau Claire, Wis., politics in 223
Ecology. See Urban ecology
Economic nationalism 1708
Economic studies 11, 14, 20, 58, 72, 99, 101, 108, 163, 170, 208, 215, 233, 244-46, 260, 263, 295, 313, 317, 329a, 392, 410, 416, 505, 1164
  of the American Indian 1398
  of Annapolis 824
  of Anniston, Ala. 530
  of Augusta 532
  bibliography on 118
  of Birmingham 484, 682
  of blacks 1231, 1255, 1370
  of Boston 679, 808, 847-49, 1590
  of Buffalo, N.Y. 536
  of Cairo, Ill. 570
  of the central city area 59
  of Charleston 621
  of Chicago 508, 546, 558, 614, 1231
  of Cincinnati 518, 704
  of Columbia, S.C. 544, 574
  comparison of rural and urban areas 149

Subject Index

of Denver 513
of Detroit 1414, 1584, 1655, 1906
fertility rates in 167
of frontier towns 721
of Greensboro, N.C. 717
of Houston 581
of immigrants and minority groups 1341, 1365, 1391, 1414
of Indianapolis 1828
of Jersey City, N.J. 770
of Los Angeles 523
metropolitan spending in 131
of migration 312, 1258, 1874
of Milwaukee 651
of Newark, N.J. 622
of New Bedford, Mass. 591
of New Hampshire towns 832
of New Haven, Conn. 607
of New Orleans 499-500
of Newport, R.I. 854
of New York City 616, 695, 779, 794, 992, 1026, 1365, 1870, 1467
of Norfolk, Va. 535, 665
of the Northeast 768
of Ohio 734
of Philadelphia 633, 695
of Pittsburgh 559
politics in 1467, 1568, 1590
public housing in 1079
of Racine, Wis. 699, 1391
regional 320
of Rochester, N.Y. 587
of St. Louis 1341
of San Francisco 578
of the seaport cities 705
of the southern states 683, 686, 764
of the suburbs 253
of Texas 729, 763, 767
urban renewal in 1149
of the western states 765
See also Capitalism; Income; Standard of living
Economists, attitude toward the city 421
Education 72, 76, 83, 93, 95, 112, 874-75, 888-91, 979, 1019, 1677, 1755

in Atlanta 1653
in Birmingham 484
of blacks 1191, 1241, 1316, 1320, 1328, 1350, 1368, 1381, 1397, 1425, 1517
in Boston 642, 887, 944, 1001-2, 1295, 1316
British comment on American 48
in Buffalo, N.Y. 1389, 1773
in Chicago 648, 881, 1517
in Cincinnati 512, 974
comparative atlas of 1
compulsory 1009
in Denver 468
influence of European on American 57
of the urban environment on 113, 115
in Jersey City, N.J. 636
in Massachusetts 951-52
the New Deal and 1446
in New Haven, Conn. 607
in New Orleans 1191
in New York City 598, 795, 864, 887, 913, 923, 944, 976, 988, 1009, 1233, 1241, 1446, 1631, 1702, 1738
in Philadelphia 897, 938
in Pittsburgh 563, 1029c
politics of 1517
poor and 915, 923, 952
in the Progressive era 890-91, 1020, 1631, 1653, 1668, 1758, 1803
race relations and 898
in St. Louis 1017, 1668
segregation in 951, 1295
social control and 42, 951-52, 976-77, 1001-2
social mobility and 1218
in Stamford, Conn. 1479
in Toledo, Ohio 989
the trolley car in aiding opportunities for 942
in urban history 113-25
urban sprawl and 85, 200
of women 1390
of the working class 913, 1002

Subject Index

YMCA schools 115
See also Catholic education; Home economics; School attendance; Teachers; Universities and colleges; Vocational education
Educators, attitude toward the city 421
Edwards, Edward I. 1582
Eisenhower, Dwight S., the city and 1483
Elections, municipal 1484-85, 1496
  in Baton Rouge 1518
  blacks in 1547
  immigrant turnout in 1488
  in Philadelphia 1547, 1570
  See also Franchise
Electronics 241
Elizabeth City County, Va., economic and social structure of 716
Ellis, George 1799
El Paso, Tex.
  history of 470
  Mexican Americans in 1327
Elwood, Ind., socialism in 1581
Emergency Relief and Construction Act 1445
Employment 320
  of blacks in Detroit 1303
  in city growth and development 313, 516
  comparative atlas of 1
  distribution of in New York City 714
  of Philadelphia Poles 1253
  spatial relationships of 316
  of women 1189, 1853
  See also Unemployment
Environment. See Urban environment
Epidemics. See Cholera; Plague; Yellow fever
Episcopal Church, in New York City 925
Equality and inequality 69. See also Social justice
Erie Canal 746
  in the development of central New York State 731a
Estabrook, Charles E. 1084

Ethnic groups; Ethnicity 98, 384, 1318, 1348, 1393
  in Baltimore 1245
  in Boston 1407, 1898
  in Buffalo, N.Y. 1853
  as a cause of civil disorder 417, 883
  change in community structure and 251
  in Chicago 1406, 1432, 1451-52, 1866
  conflict among 1353
  in Denver 468
  in Detroit 1297, 1430
  dynamics of 91
  historiographical studies of 448, 461
  housing and neighborhoods 218, 1120, 1207, 1251, 1269, 1325, 1417
  industrialization and 1194
  in Lawrence, Mass. 1213
  in Los Angeles 523
  migration and mobility of 154, 1207, 1875
  in New Bedford, Mass. 591
  in New Jersey 1493
  in New York City 647, 778, 805, 902, 1252, 1302, 1417, 1724
  occupation and 1281, 1853
  in Philadelphia 1429, 1570-71
  in Pittsburgh 559, 563
  in politics 1212, 1232, 1432, 1451-52, 1493, 1570-71, 1574, 1583, 1601, 1619, 1629, 1636, 1673, 1675, 1698, 1741, 1750, 1772
  in St. Louis 1402, 1741
  in San Francisco 1698
  social change and 1864a
  social class and 1430
  See also names of specific ethnic groups (e.g., Italian Americans)
Europe
  cities of 43
  influence on America 57
  municipal finance in 35
  urbanization of in Western 34

Subject Index

urban planning in 376, 1163
See also France; Germany; Great Britain
Evangelicalism 915, 966, 995
Eveleth, Minn., impact of the mining industry on 720
Everett, Wash., history of 502
Expressways, impact on distribution of the work force 714

F

Fagan, Mark 1793-94, 1796-97
Fall River, Mass.
   immigrants and working class in 1220-21, 1394
   textile industry of 640
Family; family life 106, 147, 332, 340, 395, 503, 827, 855
   bibliography on 440
   black 1191, 1278, 1313, 1425
   in business entrepreneurship 203, 1265
   dependency on 201
   effect of crowding on 152
   of housing on 1072, 1165
   French-Canadian 1276-77
   immigrant 1889
   impact of urbanization on 146, 209
   industrialization and 1276-77, 1853
   influence on migration 1874-75
   Irish 1267
   Italian-American 1427
   middle-class 1165, 1299
   rural-urban differences in the structure of 149
   Polish-American 1347
   relationship to community 1309
   size 827, 1363
   upper-class 1309
   See also City life
Fargo, N.D., economic rivalry in 675
Federal government
   housing and redevelopment activities of 1089, 1092, 1150
   influence on Washington, D.C. 543
   relations with the cities 24, 58, 70, 79, 1444-45, 1459, 1476, 1478, 1483, 1552, 1587, 1591, 1860
   bibliography on 436
Federalist party 1598
   in New York City 1510
Federal Municipal Debt Reduction bill 1445
Feminist movement 344, 357, 1442, 1665, 1835
Fertility 324
   correlation with economic growth 167
   decline of after 1783 334
   impact of urbanization on 209
   rural-urban differences in 149
   See also Birthrate
Festivals, of colonial Florida 841
Fiction, the city in 9, 72, 107, 355, 385, 388, 399, 409, 471, 592, 1229.
   See also Novelists
Filipino Americans 1304
Film, image of the city in 30, 66, 371
Finance, municipal 112, 288, 929, 1286
   in Europe 35
   federal government and 1445
   in Kansas City 515
   in Milwaukee 4
   in New York City 616
   in Scranton, Pa. 1595
   in slum clearance 1168
   urban dominance and (1890) 128
   urban renewal and 1089
   See also Accounting; Bonds, municipal
Financial institutions, of seaport cities 705. See also Banks and banking
Fire fighting services
   in New York City 878-79, 919-20
   in Philadelphia 1224
   in Pittsburgh 1029e
   in Rochester, N.Y. 861
Fisher, Walter J. 1674
Flood control, politics of in Pittsburgh 1575

Subject Index

Florida, social life of colonial 841
Flynn, Ed 1471
Folkways 41
Food and drugs, control of 1817
Food supply 857
Foreign aid and policy, influence of
    cities on 1500
Forks, Wash. 110
Fort Worth
    history of 469
    politics and reform in 97, 1729
France, urban policy and planning
    in 285
Franchise
    in Arkansas 1863
    blacks and the 1241, 1425,
        1863
    desire to limit by property quali-
        fication 380
    impact on urbanization 681
    in New York City 1241
    riots resulting from 1230
    in Washington, D.C. 1425
    See also Elections, municipal
Franchises, public 982, 1577, 1643
Franco-Americans, in Biddeford,
    Maine 1270
Frank, Leo 1282
Franklin Institute 1003
Frederick County, Md. 1374
Fredericksburg, Va. 676
Freedom. See Liberty
Free speech 1515
French Canadians
    in Fall River, Mass. 1394
    in Holyoke, Mass. 1271
    in Manchester, N.H. 1276-77
Friends, Society of. See Quakers
Friendship, urban life in limiting 366
Frontier
    cultural life on 648
    eastern capital on 712
    housing on 1141
    influence on the urban crisis 364
    Turner's thesis of applied to the
        Hudson Valley 604
    See also West, The
Fuller, Henry Blake 413
Funeral rites, of colonial Florida
    841

Fur trade
    in Detroit 609
    in Santa Fe 610
    See also American Fur Company

G

Galveston
    history of 766-67
    politics in 1802
    slavery in 1312
Galveston Plan 1760, 1879
Gambling
    in Denver 1643
    in New York City 1749
Game theory, in teaching urban
    history 122
Gangs, in Chicago 531
"Garden city regionalism" theory
    360
Gary, Ind. 487
    city planning in 1129, 1160
    immigrant social welfare in
        1336
Gary Platoon School Plan 979
    in New York City 1738
Gas lighting, in New York City
    859
Gaynor, William Jay 1792
Geneva, N.Y. 156
Geographic mobility. See
    Mobility
George, Henry 414, 1489, 1693
German Americans 1209
    in Boston 1822
    in Buffalo, N.Y. 1249-50
    in Chicago 1181
    in Milwaukee 1216
    in Newark, N.J. 1895
    in New Orleans 1901
    in New York City 1184, 1228,
        1233
    in Poughkeepsie, N.Y. 1853
Germantown, Pa., history of 855
Germany, city planning in 1132
Germ theory of disease 857
Gerrymandering 1182
Ghettoes. See Slums and ghettoes
Gladden, Washington 377
Godkin, E.L. 379-80

Subject Index

Good Government Association
  (Boston) 1826
Government. See Federal government; Politics and government; State government
Government spending, municipal
  impact of the political structure on 1537
  in San Francisco 1881
  as a stimulation for economic growth 131
Grand Rapids, Mich., politics and reform in 1799
Great Awakening, destruction of Puritanism and 789
Great Britain
  city growth in 295-60
  comments on American cities from 47-48, 702
  Industrial Revolution of compared to America's 252
  migration to and from 312
  urban policy and planning in 285
Greek Americans, in New York City 1215
Green, Andrew 1525
Green, Constance McLaughlin 458
Green Bay, Wis., politics in 223
Greenbelt, Md. 1103
Greenbelt town program 1042
Greensboro, N.C., urbanization of 717
Greenwich Village
  architecture of 649
  sense of community in 620
Griffith, D.W. 30, 66
Guitteau, William B. 989

H

Hague, Frank 770, 1470-71, 1635, 1660, 1778, 1783
Hale, Edward Everett 375, 377
Hamilton, Ont., occupation and ethnicity in 1281
Handlin, Oscar 458
Harbors. See Ports and harbors
Harlem. See New York City
Harlem Renaissance 1426

Harrisburg, Pa.
  "City Beautiful" movement in 1172
  Dickens on 7
Hartford, Conn.
  central city area of 1082
  Dickens on 7
Haymarket Affair, Protestant reactions to 1027
Hays, Samuel P. 458
Health 102
  in Birmingham 484
  effect of crowding on 152
  of Italian Americans in New York City 1326
  of Polish Americans 1395
  nineteenth century urban 64
  See also Public health
Heroes, decline of in fiction 385
Hewitt, Abram 1489
Hibbing, Minn., impact of the mining industry on 720
Hill, James J. 502
Historians, the city and 73-74, 88, 107, 421
Hoboken, N.J.
  effect of World War I on 527
  history of 524
  politics of 1629
  as a resort area 509
Holly Springs, Miss. 110
Holyoke, Mass.
  French Canadians in 1271
  history of 13, 541
  immigrants in 1884
  tenements of 1075
  urban renewal in 1843
Home economics 1800
Hone, Philip 394
Honolulu 31
  history of 511
Hoover, Herbert 1559
Hopedale, Mass. 194
Horses, as a source of urban pollution 1013
Hotels 948
  British comments on American 48
  of Philadelphia 644

Subject Index

Housing (cont.)
    of San Francisco 594-95
Housing 37, 58, 60, 72, 76, 79, 82, 112, 218, 857, 921, 987, 1034, 1050, 1088, 1117, 1137, 1176, 1908
    in Baltimore 1076
    bibliography on 436
    black 1126, 1136, 1239, 1303
    in Boston 1822
    in Buffalo, N.Y. 1773
    comparative atlas of 1
    costs of related to intraurban migration 166
    in Detroit 1303
    economic ramifications of 215
    federal credit policy for 1092
    government and 1045
    immigrant and minority 1251, 1395, 1861
    influence on growth of the suburbs 265
    as the key to urban problems 1032
    laws and regulations 1083
    in measuring social status 248
    middle income 1143
    in Milwaukee 298, 641
    in Minneapolis-St. Paul 635
    in New York City 858, 1861
    in Philadelphia 1224, 1239, 1653
    reform and rehabilitation of 1135, 1150, 1156, 1167
    in Rochester, N.Y. 1123
    segregation in 218, 776, 1033, 1269, 1313, 1317, 1325, 1403-4, 1858, 1882
    in the Southwest 738
    supply and demand of 1090
    terminology of 126
    See also Architecture; Building codes; Public housing; Residential patterns; Row houses; Slums and ghettoes; Tenements
Housing, low-income 1103, 1176
    in the New Deal 1153
    in New York City 1104
    See also Public housing
Housing, rental 226, 1173
Housing Act (1937) 1079, 1119
Housing Act (1937) 1079, 1119
Housing Act (1949) 1549
Housing Law (1867, New York) 1083
Houston
    black housing in 1251
    history of 269, 581, 766-67
    mass transit in 1904
    police in 967
    progressive reform in 1653
    riots in 1279
Howard, Ebenezer 1054, 1060, 1080
Howe, Frederick C. 1117, 1714
Howells, William Dean 1869
Hudson Valley (N.Y.), family and household structure in nineteenth century 149
Hughes, Charles Evans 1694
Hungarian Americans
    in Cleveland 1420
    in Hoboken, N.J. 527
Huthmacher, J. Joseph 1811

I

Ice industry, in Philadelphia 564
Ideology
    as a factor in city decline 570
    impact on urbanization 681
    of the New England town 410
    as a threat to social order 352
Illinois, cities of 725
Imagery, of the New England town 410
Immigrants and immigration
    in Atlanta 1285
    attitudes toward 368
    in Baltimore 1029b
    bibliography on 437
    in Boston 240, 937
    in Buffalo, N.Y. 1262, 1389, 1748, 1773
    in Chicago 1788
    in Cincinnati 1857
    in Cleveland 1800
    conflicts among 1184
    in Connecticut 1453
    in Detroit 1298
    education of 864, 1389-90, 1397, 1631

Subject Index

historiographical studies of 457, 461
history of 92
in Holyoke, Mass. 1884
housing and residential areas of 228, 320, 1181
industrialization and 1194-95
integration into the institutional network 1220
mobility of 165, 208, 663, 1234, 1266, 1288-90, 1307, 1314
in New Orleans 504
in New York City 394, 864, 925, 1510, 1685
in Ohio 772
in Philadelphia 165, 786, 1412, 1851, 1853
in Pittsburgh 1516
politics and 1453, 1457, 1488, 1510, 1516, 1524, 1551, 1589, 1600, 1603, 1622, 1627-28, 1683, 1685, 1739, 1743, 1746, 1748, 1751, 1857
in Poughkeepsie, N.Y. 1266
poverty of 1214
religion and 896, 925, 1228, 1298, 1332
in Rhode Island 1453
social relationships of first and second generation 1196
social welfare and 1336
in South Bend, Ind. 1234
women 1189
See also Ethnic groups; Nativism; names of immigrant groups (e.g., Italian Americans)
Income 257, 468
importance to establishment of a consumer economy 692
of minority, migrant groups 1391
relationship to intraurban migration 166
See also Wealth
Income tax
evolution of municipal 6
in Philadelphia 489
Incorporation 15
Independent party, in Augusta 1458

Indiana Historical Society Lectures (1971-72) 384
Indianapolis 671, 1828
civic chauvinism and rivalry in 479
education of blacks in 1381
Indians. See American Indians
Individualism 371, 385, 981
abandonment of by scholarly writers dealing with urban problems 421
in colonial Boston 833
of Hoover 1559
nineteenth century 367
urbanization and 190
Industrial accidents, the law and 559
Industrial health 987
Industrial Workers of the World 502, 631
Industry; industrialization 20, 22, 27, 37, 44, 58, 74, 96, 112, 198, 245-46, 324, 339, 358, 415
in Anniston, Ala. 530
birthrates and 167
blacks and 1902
in Boston 323
breakdown of the old order and 425
in Charleston 538, 621
in Chicago 260
in Cincinnati 518, 671
in Cleveland 664, 1311
comparative studies of 252
in Detroit 1298
divorce rates and 314
effect on worker status 663
the family and 1276, 1853
in Holyoke, Mass. 541
in Houston 581
in Illinois 725
the immigrant and 1195-96, 1276, 1355, 1853
importance to city growth 286, 309
in Kansas City 515
in Louisville 1874
in Lowell, Mass. 608
mobility and migration and 154, 1874

Subject Index

models of 272-73
in Newark, N.J. 1192
in New Bedford, Mass. 591
in New Jersey 770
in New York City 1469
in Ohio 772
in Pennsylvania 190
in Philadelphia 984, 1003, 1247, 1853
politics of 1568
promotion of 753, 1541
racism and 1311
response of religion to 896, 970, 1298
in St. Louis 623
in seaport cities 705
in southern segregation 710
spatial and locational aspects of 260, 270-72, 692
urban problems and 664, 1247
in Warren, Pa. 663
in Wilkes-Barre, Pa. 173
in Wisconsin 197
See also Business and commerce; names of industries (e.g., Steel industry)
Influenza, in Kansas City 963
Information, circulation of 273-74. See also Communication(s)
Inland water transportation 678. See also Mississippi River; Steam boats
Institutions. See Urban institutions
Insurance industry 920
regulation of in Rochester, N.Y. 861
Intellectual life
of Boston 363
the city in 397
nineteenth century 343
urban dominance and (1890) 128
Intellectuals, in New Jersey politics 1493
Interest groups, impact on urbanization 681
Internal improvements, in the Old Northwest 748
International Institute 1336
International Workmen's Association 1222

Interpersonal relations. See Social relations and behavior
Inventions, urbanization based on the number of 220
Investment
influence on migration 312
slums as discouragers of 319
See also Capital
Iowa, migration in 694
Iowa City, Iowa, history of 639
Irish Americans 1209, 1212, 1772
in Boston 1208, 1273, 1666, 1822, 1826, 1898
in Buffalo, N.Y. 1249-50
in Chareston 1899
in Charlestown, Mass. 1837
in Chicago 1235, 1589
in Detroit 1414
in Fall River, Mass. 1394
in Hoboken, N.J. 1629
in Jersey City, N.J. 1392, 1853
in Newark, N.J. 1895
in New Orleans 1901
in New York City 1184, 1228, 1233, 1252, 1358, 1489, 1853
in Philadelphia 1208, 1210, 1224, 1237, 1878
in politics 1212, 1772
in Poughkeepsie, N.Y. 1853
in San Francisco 1910
in Scranton, Pa. 1195
women 1267
in Worcester, Mass. 1202
Irish Emigrant Society 1443
Iron industry. See Steel industry
Isolation. See Social isolation
Italian Americans 1210, 1287, 1337, 1344, 1355, 1365, 1840
in Boston 1244, 1822
in Buffalo, N.Y. 1389, 1427
in Chicago 670, 1181, 1342-43, 1743
in Cleveland 1183
in Hoboken, N.J. 527, 1629
importance of church records to the study of 236
in New Orleans 1325, 1746

Subject Index

in New York City 1184, 1252, 1307, 1326, 1365, 1551, 1685, 1861
in Philadelphia 1224, 1413
in Pittsburgh 1310
in St. Louis 1341
social structure of 1422

J

Jacksonian period
   married women in 38
   in New York City politics 1510
Jacksonville, Fla., blacks in the politics of 1182
Jacksonville, Ill., voluntary associations in 899
Jamaica, N.Y. 1363
   history of 827
Janesville, Wis., politics in 223
Japanese Americans 1304
   in San Francisco 1251
Jefferson, Thomas 801, 812, 1072
Jersey City, N.J.
   class, ethnicity, and race in 771, 1392, 1853
   history of 636, 770
   Irish Americans in 1392
   politics and reform in 1470-71, 1610, 1635, 1660, 1778, 1793-97
   railroads in 1653
Jewish Americans 1209, 1284, 1396
   in Atlanta 1282-83
   in Boston 1822
   in Buffalo, N.Y. 1389
   in Chicago 1181
   in Denver 1879
   in Detroit 1376-77
   education of 1028
   in Los Angeles 1862
   mobility of 1850, 1862, 1907
   in New York City 1184, 1252, 1307, 1326, 1375, 1551, 1574, 1685
   in Philadelphia 1224
   in Pittsburgh 1310
   in Portland 1907
   in San Francisco 1847, 1850
   See also Anti-Semitism
Johnson, Nucky 1778

Johnson, Tom L. 969, 1097, 1543, 1616, 1693, 1700, 1721, 1833
Jones, J. Raymond 1534
Jones, Samuel M. 1616, 1833
Journalism, sense of community expressed in 361. See also Press
Journalists, reform ideas of 1708
Journals. See Periodicals
Junior colleges. See Community colleges
Junz, Edessa 1084
Justice. See Equality and inequality; Social justice
Juvenile delinquency 16
   of Italian Americans in New York City 1326

K

Kansas 699
   "City Beautiful" movement in 1171
   politics of 1472
   urban diffusion in 227
Kansas City
   architecture of 1098
   formulation of transportation policy in 196
   history of 372, 470, 515, 549, 667, 765, 1841
   influenza epidemic in 963
   Italian Americans in 1840
   police in 1023
   politics and reform in 1471, 1514, 1617, 1648, 1675, 1740, 1778
   public utilities in 1896
Kelly, Edward J. 1471, 1522, 1672
Kenna, "Hinky Dink" 1813
Kennedy, John F., the city and 1483
Kent, William 1790
Kentucky, transportation in the development of 745
Kilgour family 1852
Kindergarten, in Cleveland 1800
Kingston, N.Y. 178
   occupation and ethnicity in 1281

Subject Index

Kingstown, N.Y. 150
Kinship 294
Knights, Peter 445
Korean Americans, in New York City 1873
Ku Klux Klan 1254, 1294, 1298, 1583

L

Laboring class 415, 1339
  the American Revolution and 802, 823
  attitude toward urban slavery 792
  in Baton Rouge, La. 1518
  in Birmingham 484
  blacks as 1410
  in Chicago 1866, 1719
  in Cleveland 1721
  composition and distribution of 20, 67
  in Detroit 1410, 1531, 1906
  education of 913, 1002, 1866
  in Hoboken, N.J. 1629
  impact of industrialization on 1469
  influence on city growth 296
  institutional studies of 1220-21
  mobility of 1417
  in Newburyport, Mass. 1408
  in New York City 1443, 1469, 1489, 1510, 1699
  in Philadelphia 1480
  in Pittsburgh 559, 1417, 1516
  in politics 1225, 1443, 1469, 1480, 1489, 1510, 1516, 1518, 1531, 1536, 1573, 1581, 1595, 1612, 1629, 1718, 1721
  prohibition and 1886
  residential stability of in Baltimore 1186
  riots of 1230, 1480
  in San Francisco 1573
  in Scranton, Pa. 1595
  in Seattle 1612
  in Syracuse, N.Y. 1536
  suburbs of 1187
  versus the middle class 428
  in Virginia 707
  women of 1267, 1308

  in Worcester, Mass. 1202
  See also Employment; Trade unions; Unemployment
Labor laws and legislation, in Illinois 1602. See also Child labor laws; Industrial accidents, the law and
Labor-management relations
  as a cause of civil disorder 417
  in Everett, Wash. 502
  in Naugatuck, Conn. 540
  in Passaic, N.J. 514
  in Philadelphia 1412
  in Pullman, Ill. 488
  in the South 689
  See also Trade unions
La Guardia, Fiorello H. 1061, 1204, 1454, 1456, 1550-51
Laissez-faire 1509, 1850
Lampard, Eric 458
Lancaster, Pa., politics in 1669
Land use 19, 37, 58, 62, 162, 241, 276-77, 317, 330
  bibliography on 118
  in Boston 187
  changes in 226
  in Chicago 1109
  in Cleveland 664
  comparative atlas of 1
  economic ramifications of 215
  influence of cities on agricultural 171
  in Minnesota 1909
  in Norfolk, Va. 130
  relationship to city traffic 258
  sampling techniques for the study of 336
  simulation games in teaching about 122
  terminology of the economics of 126
  in Worcester, Mass. 264, 1134
Land values
  the automobile and 331
  in Chicago 333, 1100
  factors affecting 28
  lowering of by investors 517
  in slum clearance 1168
Langston, Okla. 1864
Lansing, Mich., blacks in 1330-31

Subject Index

Las Vegas 699
Law and urban areas 93
    industrial accidents and 559
    public health and 1006
    terminology of 126
    See also Child labor laws; Labor laws and legislation
Law enforcement. See Police
Lawrence, Mass.
    immigrants in 1213
    textile strike (1912) in 341
Lawyers 1536
    control of Philadelphia socioeconomic life by 255
Leadership 163, 1393, 1437, 1675, 1832
    in colonial New England 791
    development of in a pioneer community 196
    on the frontier 1514
    influence on city growth 334
    in Philadelphia 1428
    in the South 686
Leavenworth, Kans., creation and growth of 736
Leclaire, Ill., history of 528
Le Corbusier, Charles E.J. 1080
Leeds, Engl., effect of transportation on suburban growth of 321
Legal aid, blacks and 1350
Leisure
    of the Boston Irish 1898
    comparative atlas of 1
    of Irish working class women 1267
    localization of urban 40
Leland, Henry 1654
L'Enfant, Pierre 801, 812, 1073
Levittown, N.J., community development in 134
Lexow Commission 1749
Liberalism 1695-96, 1714
    in Chicago 555
    in the Democratic party 1493
Liberty 364, 1528
Libraries. See Public libraries
Life-styles 3, 72, 237, 1360
    alcohol consumption as an indicator of 250
    of blacks in Chicago 1231
    development of new 383

    impact of urbanization on rural 140
    of the Irish in New York City 1358
    in Plymouth Colony 831
    See also Quality of life
Lincoln, Abraham 1567
Lincolnwood, Ill., community development in 134
Liquor, control of in Stamford, Conn. 1479. See also Alcohol; Prohibition
Lippman, Walter 1580
Litchfield, Conn., colonial politics in 842
Literacy, of Italian Americans in New York City 1326
Literary colonies, in New Mexico 625
Literary societies, in Cincinnati 512
Literature
    the city in 72, 386, 408
    in frontier Chicago 648
    New York City in 537
    Pittsburgh in 552
    sense of community expressed in 361
    See also Fiction; Periodicals; Poetry; Travel literature
Little Rock, Ark.
    history of 626
    slavery in 1312
Lloyd, Henry Demarest 414
Lobbying 1591
Local history 438
London, police in 975
Long, Huey 1778, 1783
Longview, Wash. 579
Los Angeles 43, 86
    airport of 1904
    architecture and urban renewal in 1046, 1082
    class, ethnicity, and race in 1226, 1340, 1862
    divorce in 314
    history of 62, 381, 469-70, 523, 525, 602, 656, 741
    municipal ownership in 1592

Subject Index

police in 1029d, 1819
politics and reform in 1638, 1653, 1769, 1819
port of 480
religion in 1004
riots in 341
trade unions in 1400
transportation in 863
Louisville
  Dickens on 7
  economic rivalry with Cincinnati 696
  history of 567, 597
  migration and mobility in 1874-75
  travelers' comments on 71
Low, Seth 1585, 1625, 1663, 1705
Lowell, Mass. 316
  architecture of 1069
  comment by the British on 47
  industrial development of 608
Low-income groups
  community institutions of 305
  participation in social programs 1324
  social orientation of 182
  See also Poverty
Ludlow Massacre 674
Lumber industry
  influence on city growth 301
  planned cities created by 579
  in the South 703
Lunn, George R. 1506
Lyceum movement, in Chicago 648
Lynchburg, Va. 676
Lynn, Mass. 267
  immigrants and working class in 1220-21, 1225

M

McGee family (Kansas City) 667
McKelvey, Blake 444, 458
Madison, Ind., history of 334
Madison, Wis.
  influence on agricultural areas 171
  Ku Klux Klan in 1254
Maestri, Robert S. 1495
Magazines. See Periodicals
Maguire, Patrick J. 1666

Maine on St. Croix, Minn. 110
Manchester, N.H., French Canadians in 1276-77
Manifest destiny, the city during the period of 74
Manufacturing. See Industry
Mapping, computer 222
Marion, Ind., socialism in 1581
Marketing patterns, in the Boston area 679
Marketing techniques, role of in the decline of Cincinnati 492
Market place (urban form) 12
Marriage
  interracial in Detroit 1877
  patterns of in Jamaica, N.Y. 827, 1363
  social mobility and status of 154
  See also Divorce
Massachusetts
  colonial towns of 856
  education in 951-52
  urbanization of 681
Massachusetts Anti-Slavery Society 1272
Mass production, influence on the "urban mind" 32
Mass transit 884, 935, 1014, 1904
  in Chicago 862
  in New York City 1022
  See also types of mass transit (e.g., Subways)
Materialism
  in colonial Boston 837
  nineteenth century 367
Matthews, James B. 377
Matthews, Nathan 1774
Mayer, Harold 430
Mayor-council form of government
  in Boston 1528
  immigrant participation in 1488
  See also City councils
Mechanization, impact of urbanization on 140
Medicine and medical practice
  in Charleston 1024
  in Pittsburgh 903
  See also Public health

Subject Index

Megalopolis, concept of 77, 105
Memphis, Tenn.
   city planning in 1057
   history of 381, 599, 765
   politics and reform in 1471, 1730-32
   residential segregation in 1858
   riots in 1383
   water supply and sanitation in 909, 1008
Meriwether, Lee 1741
Merriam, Charles E. 1720
Methodism 882
Mexican Americans 1257, 1304, 1340
   in El Paso, Tex. 1327
   employment of female 1189
   in Los Angeles 1378, 1400
   in the Midwest 1379
   in Racine, Wis. 1391
   in Santa Barbara, Calif. 1203
Miami
   black housing in 1251
   history of 469
   housing patterns in 1033
   urban renewal in 1128
Michigan
   demographic history of families in 147
   influence of lumbering on 301
   organization and administration of cities in 755
   urbanization of 701
Middle ages, cities in the 44, 168, 299, 317
Middlebury, Vt. 110
Middle class 78
   appeal of baseball to 1240
   in Chicago 294, 1743, 1788
   in Columbus, Ohio 1779
   crime and in Boston 520
   family of 1299
   housing of 1143, 1165
   in Jersey City, N.J. 1795
   lack of in the central city 1070
   mobility of 175
   politics and reform and 1711, 1721, 1739, 1743, 1773, 1776, 1788, 1795, 1831
   response of to urban problems 476
   search for order by 425
   social orientation of 182
   suburbanization and 136, 319, 1287, 1416
   versus the working class 428
   women of the Jacksonian period 38
Midwestern states
   manufacturing in 692
   Mexican Americans in 1379
   politics of 1475
   promotion of 728
   urbanization of 680, 1753
   See also Old Northwest
Migrants
   assimilation of 2
   disorientation of 426
Migration 112, 307, 310, 324, 390
   by blacks 70, 1236, 1261, 1404
   in Boston 1407
   changing patterns of 20
   in Cincinnati 1875
   economic aspects of 312
   impact on socioeconomic structures 1258
   on urbanization 184
   intermetropolitan 127
   intraurban 64, 127, 129, 218
   in Milwwukee 166
   in Iowa 694
   in Louisville 1874-75
   of Mexican Americans 1379
   of Minneapolis Poles 1911
   rural-urban 207, 219, 1315
   measurement of 199
   role of popular literature in 409
   in the South 744
   in Syracuse, N.Y. 731a
Military, influence on San Antonio 523
Military conscription, riots as a result of 1217
Miller, Zane L. 444
Milwaukee 267, 1074
   Catholic social institutions of 1021

Subject Index

class, ethnicity, and race in 1216, 1243, 1291, 1461
finance in 4
history of 55, 432-33, 459, 641, 646, 650-52
housing, population, and services in 266, 298, 1043
intraurban migration in 166
police in 1023
politics in 1461, 1464, 1581
street railways in 965
urbanization of 753
Mining industry, impact on boom towns 720
Minneapolis
Congregational Church in 959
history of 469, 635
model of growth for 189
planning and development in 1909
Polish Americans in 1911
urban problems of 1781
Minorities 72, 1324
assimilation of 100
historiographical studies of 448'
housing of 1251
poverty among 1214
See also Ethnic groups; Immigrants and immigration; names of minority groups (e.g., Blacks)
Missionaries, urban 869, 915, 995-96, 1503
Mississippi, urban retardation in 673
Mississippi River, influence on New Orleans 485, 501, 624
Mitchel, John Purroy 1625, 1709, 1738
Mobile, Ala. 724
lumber trade in 703
Mobility 58, 98, 106, 267-68, 310-11, 390, 622, 1856
in Baltimore 1834
of blacks 1303, 1370, 1372, 1385
in Boston 240, 1407
in Chicago 294, 1343
in Detroit 1303
factors affecting 154
historiographical studies of 445, 461
history of 92

of immigrant and ethnic groups 165, 1207-8, 1218, 1222, 1234, 1266, 1274, 1288-90, 1307, 1314, 1343, 1347, 1378, 1391, 1402, 1417, 1850, 1862, 1907
in Jamaica, N.Y. 827, 1363
in Los Angeles 1378, 1862
in Massachusetts 700
in Muncie, Ind. 1829
in Newburyport, Mass. 1408
in Newport, R.I. 854
in New York City 816, 852, 1274, 1307, 1385
in Omaha, Nebr. 164, 1207
in Philadelphia 148, 820, 1208, 1224
in Pittsburgh 1417
in Portland 1907
in Poughkeepsie, N.Y. 203, 1266
in Racine, Wis. 1391
role of the Alger novels in achieving 388
in St. Louis 1402
in San Francisco 175-76, 1222, 1850
Soundex Indexes in studying 303
in South Bend, Ind. 1234
in Warren, Pa. 663
of white higher status individuals 308
of the working class 1408, 1417
Model Cities programs 58
Model City Planning Enabling Act 1169
Mohl, Raymond A. 444
Montgomery, Ala.
blacks in 1369
civil rights movement in 341
Moorhead, Minn., economic rivalry in 675
Morality 7, 132, 1612
colonial 803
Boston 833
education in maintaining 1002
in municipal reform 1756, 1779
in New York State 713
nineteenth century 64, 75
See also Sexual behavior; Values; Vice

Subject Index

Morrison, Delesseps S. 1494
Mortality, church records in determining infant 236
Moses, Robert 1455, 1526, 1558, 1566
Motion pictures. See Film
Mt. Tabor, N.J., environmental history of 287
Movies. See Film
Mugwumps 1638, 1663
Mumford, Lewis 1086
Muncie, Ind., mobility patterns in 1829
Municipal Authorities Act 1449
Municipal ownership 1541, 1616, 1642, 1690, 1810, 1827, 1849
    of public utilities 373, 571, 859, 1592, 1674
Municipal Reform League (Seattle) 1653, 1751-52
Municipal Voters League (Chicago) 1790
Murder 1876
Murphy, Charles Francis 1605, 1694, 1811
Murphy, Frank 521
Muscatine, Iowa, architecture and city planning in 1099
Music 72, 634, 811
Musser, Frank C. 1669

N

Nacogdoches, Tex. 110
Nash, Patrick 1522, 1672
Nashville, blacks in 1369
Nassau County, N.Y., growth of after World War II 304
Nast, Thomas 1772
Natchez, history of 557
National Association for the Advancement of Colored People 1204, 1421
National Association of Manufacturers 740
Nationalism. See Economic nationalism
Nationality, concepts of American 384

National League of Cities 1505
National Municipal League 1606, 1739, 1784
National Republican party, in New York City 1510
National Resources Committee, 1937 report of 18
Nativism
    in Biddeford, Maine 1270
    in Boston 1272
    in Buffalo, N.Y. 1249
    in Jersey, N.J. 771, 1853
    in Newark, N.J. 1895
    in New York City 1510, 1532, 1538, 1686, 1692
    in Philadelphia 1237
    Republican party and 1538
Nature
    exploitation of 364
    need to return to 404
Naugatuck, Conn., history of 13, 540
Nebraska, urban diffusion in 227
Neighborhoods 19, 162, 288, 1056, 1883
    in Baltimore 1245-46, 1268, 1831
    in Boston 1244
    in Buffalo, N.Y. 536
    change of 91
    characteristics of 218
    in Chicago 294, 1263, 1406
    in Columbus, Ohio 1722
    cities as a collection of 354
    in Detroit 1251
    ethnic and immigrant 320, 1207, 1210, 1244-46, 1251, 1268, 1402, 1404, 1406
    improvement associations in 1831
    influence of total city growth on 226
    in New York City 774
    in Omaha 1207
    in Philadelphia 1210
    in St. Louis 1402
    small town values and 398
    status of 205-6
    in Washington, D.C. 1268
    See also Community

Subject Index

Newark, N.J.
  blacks in 770-71
  Catholic Church in 1895
  history of 622
  industrialization in 1192
  public health in 916
  tenements in 1151
New Bedford, Mass., industrialization and social change in 591
Newberry Library (Chicago) 912
Newburyport, Mass., social position of unskilled workers in 1408
New communities 63, 82. See also New towns
New Deal
  blacks and 1328, 1490
  in Boston 1590
  in Chicago 1490, 1522
  city planning in 1093
  in Connecticut 1521
  in Detroit 1584
  in Kansas City 1648
  in New York City 1497
  in Philadelphia 1440
  politics of 1433, 1440, 1470-71, 1483, 1490, 1497, 1521-22, 1584, 1590, 1648, 1750, 1900
  slum clearance in 1153
  social reform in 1695
  in the South 1900
  See also Depression (1929)
New England
  architecture of 1040
  influence on Cincinnati 512
  leadership and community in eighteenth century 791
  promotion of southern industry by 672
  the town in 410, 807
  transportation change in 718
New Hampshire, eighteenth-century towns in 832
New Harmony, Ind. 110
New Haven, Conn.
  Dickens on 7
  evolution of social class in 1323
  history of 372, 607, 780
  politics in 1466
New Jersey
  boosterism and promotion in 771
  divorce in 314
  politics in 1493, 1582-83
  urbanization of 677, 770-71
  use of occupational census data in studying 693
New London, Va., history of 837
New Orleans
  city planning in 1057
  class, ethnicity, and race in 504, 1191, 1251, 1280, 1325, 1746, 1901
  comment by travelers on 47, 71
  development of sports in 643
  history of 13, 469, 485, 499-501, 624
  institutional studies of 939
  police 947, 1897
  public health 904, 906, 908, 922
  politics and reform in 1494-95, 1564, 1657, 1745-46, 1759
  urban renewal in 1128
Newport, R.I., history of 493, 784, 854
Newspapers
  of Chicago 648
  of Philadelphia 84, 1010
  role of St. Louis' in secession 597
  spatial aspects of information circulation in 274
  See also Journalism; Press
New towns 376, 754, 1054, 1103, 1125. See also New communities
New York City 31, 33, 43, 68, 172
  class, ethnicity, and race in 805, 816, 821, 850, 1184, 1204, 1215, 1217, 1227, 1233, 1241-42, 1251-52, 1255, 1267, 1274, 1296, 1300, 1302, 1307, 1326, 1328, 1339, 1352, 1358-59, 1361, 1365, 1373, 1375, 1385, 1393, 1396, 1419, 1486, 1534, 1844, 1853, 1861, 1867, 1873

Subject Index

comments by travelers on 7, 47, 71, 537, 600
economic studies of 852, 929
history of 13, 55, 62, 381, 394, 466, 469, 562, 566, 603, 613, 616, 629, 647, 653-55, 774, 778-79, 781-82, 784, 792, 794-95, 798, 805-6
institutional studies of 858, 860, 868, 977-78, 985, 995-96, 998, 1029a, 1692, 1867
    education 864, 887, 913, 976, 1009, 1328, 1631, 1738, 1803
    firefighting and police services 878, 919-20, 947, 956, 975, 992-93
    public health and sanitation 866, 872, 900, 904, 917, 956, 1006, 1026
    public utilities and franchises 859, 982
    recreation and entertainment 911, 932, 1005
    religion 925, 1228
    transportation systems 355, 1022, 1855
in literature 397, 592
neighborhoods of 248, 774
planning, architecture, and urban renewal in 472, 560, 1041, 1049, 1071, 1078, 1082, 1104, 1108, 1114, 1116, 1142, 1152, 1158, 1178, 1251
politics and reform in 819, 839, 851, 1443, 1446, 1450, 1454-56, 1467, 1469, 1471, 1481, 1486, 1489, 1497, 1503-4, 1510, 1525-26, 1532-34, 1538-39, 1545, 1551, 1557-58, 1560-62, 1566-67, 1574, 1598-99, 1607, 1621, 1624-28, 1639-40, 1653, 1685-86, 1694, 1699, 1702, 1705, 1709, 1713, 1724, 1738-39, 1742, 1749, 1757, 1764-66, 1775-78, 1781, 1792, 1803, 1806-7, 1811, 1816-17, 1855, 1889
population studies of 619, 714
slavery in 792
urbanization of 695
zoning law of (1913) 54
See also Brooklyn, N.Y.; Coney Island; Greenwich Village
New York Female Benevolent Society 1816
New York Female Moral Reform Society 1816
New York Magdalene Society 1816
New York Society for the Prevention of Pauperism 977
New York State
    philanthropy and morality in 713, 931
    politics in 1888
Nicodemus, Kans. 1864
Nolen, John 1093
Norfolk, Va.
    history of 467, 665
    land use in 130
    lumber trade in 703
    urban rivalry and railroads in 752
    yellow fever in (1855) 535
Northampton, Mass. 700
North Carolina, city planning in 1101-2
Northeastern states, urbanization of 709, 768
Northwest Territory. See Old Northwest
Norton, Charles Eliot 363
Norwegian Americans, in New York City 1867
Novelists, reform ideas of 1708. See also Fiction
Nyack, N.Y., history of 604

O

Oakland, Calif., politics and reform in 1839
Occupations 395, 1363
    of blacks 1191, 1385
    of city councilmen 1578
    correlation with wealth 255

Subject Index

of ethnic groups and immigrants 1215, 1249, 1281, 1288-90, 1314, 1326, 1378, 1391, 1414, 1417, 1853, 1899
mobility among 148, 154, 164, 240, 445, 1266, 1288-90, 1314
patterns of 112, 1215, 1407
relationship to the nineteenth-century family 147
statistics on 693
status of 468
O'Connell, Dan 1778
Ogden, Utah, history of 470
Ogden, William Butler 590
Ohio
blacks in 1313
history of 469
internal improvements in 748
urbanization of 734, 772
Oklahoma City, Okla.
Civilian Conservation Corps in 1513
history of 645
Old Northwest, internal improvements in 74
Olmstead, Frederick Law 1077-78, 1095, 1106, 1144, 1157, 1856
Olmstead, Frederick Law, Jr. 1117
Omaha, Nebr.
ethnic neighborhoods 1207
leadership in 1514
mobility in 164, 1207
politics and reform in 1761
public health in 930
Oral history 458
Ostrogorski, Moisei 368

P

Palmer, William Jackson
Panama City, Fla. 724
Panic of 1819, public and private responses to 868
Panic of 1837, in Chicago 590
Panic of 1857 639
Panic of 1873 618
Park, Robert, concept of the city by 362, 387

Parks 19, 1085
of Chicago 1066, 1719
of Illinois 725
of Oklahoma 1513
Parochial education. See Catholic education
Parsons, Talcott 203
Passaic, N.J., history of 514, 770
Paternalism, toward immigrants 1336
Paterson, N.J., Depression (1929) in 1885
Patronage, political
Irish Americans and 1212
in New York City 993, 1539, 1626, 1628, 1702
in Philadelphia 1670
in Toledo, Ohio 1576
Pelham, Mass. 700
Pendergast, Thomas J. 1471, 1647, 1778, 1783
Penn, William 817
Pennsylvania
economic and social order during industrialization in 190
politics in 1449, 1482
urbanization of 722
Pensacola, Fla.
blacks in 1199
lumber trade in 703
People's Institute of New York City 913, 1659
Periodicals
the city in (1865-1900) 422
suitable for urban education 114
Personality, urban 356
Petersburg, Va., urban rivalry and railroads in 752
Philadelphia 68, 249, 491, 568, 722
central city area of 280
civic order in 405
class, ethnicity, and race in 137, 148, 165, 236, 255, 776, 816, 818, 820-21, 850, 1208, 1210, 1224, 1237, 1239, 1247, 1253, 1281, 1291, 1293, 1314, 1318, 1328, 1333, 1339, 1347, 1359, 1361, 1373,

Subject Index

    1381, 1393, 1412-13, 1428-29, 1547, 1853, 1868, 1878
  comment by travelers on 7, 71, 644
  commercial growth of 815
  community change in 251
  fiscal problems of 929
  history of 13, 61, 97, 325, 469, 483, 498, 633, 668, 776-77, 784, 786-87, 790, 793, 803, 808-10, 814-15, 817-23, 834-35, 850
  income tax in 489
  industry in 489
  influence on its suburbs 265
  institutional studies of 885, 984, 998, 1029a
    education 897, 938, 1328, 1381
    fire fighting services 1224
    legal system 1011
    press 1010
    public health and sanitation 866, 986
    transportation 258
  municipal authority in 723
  planning, architecture, and urban renewal in 817, 1051-52, 1139, 1156, 1174, 1178, 1653, 1786-87
  politics and reform in 793, 809, 819, 834-35, 1439-40, 1480, 1491, 1547, 1556, 1562-63, 1570-71, 1598, 1649, 1670, 1682, 1753, 1756, 1786-87, 1851
  population and housing studies of 278, 516, 777, 822
  Quakers in 483, 843
  response to the Erie Canal by 746
  urbanization of 695
  urban problems of 1781
  violence in 809, 1876
Philanthropy
  in Baltimore 1029b
  in Chicago 554
  in Cleveland 1728
  the construction of public baths through 1029a-29b
  in Detroit 1377
  in New York City 868, 996
  in New York State 713, 931
  See also Charity
Phillips, Wilbur C. 1883
Phoenix, founding of 730
Physical engineering, as a solution to urban problems 351
Pinchot, Gifford 1482
Pine Grove, Pa. 110
Pingree, Hazen S. 1688, 1833
Pittsburgh
  attitudes toward by authors 7, 552
  class, ethnicity, and race in 1293, 1308, 1318, 1388, 1417, 1868
  consolidation activities in 289
  crime and violence in 883
  development of social order in 214
  history of 27, 29, 469, 547, 559, 576, 580
  institutional studies of 563
    education 1029c, 1388
    fire fighting services 1029e
    public health 892-93, 901-3, 905, 924, 1015
  political studies of 15-16, 1575, 1579, 1851
  society and social services of 563
  twentieth-century promotional efforts in 611
  urban problems of 1781
Plague, among the Chinese of San Francisco 945
Plunkitt, George Washington 1764
Plymouth Colony, social history of 831
Poetry, the city in 107, 397, 418
Police 95, 880, 955, 994, 1541
  in Atlanta 1025
  blacks and 1350, 1366
  in Boston 949
  in Charleston 1871
  in Chicago 927
  in Detroit 999-1000
  in Houston 967
  in Los Angeles 1029d, 1819
  in New Orleans 1897

Subject Index

   in New York City 920, 947, 956, 992-93, 1702, 1749
   reform and professionalization of 941, 943, 956, 967, 999-1000, 1023, 1029d, 1749, 1819
   in St. Louis 990
   in the South 1366
Polish Americans 1209
   in Buffalo, N.Y. 1389
   in Chicago 1181, 1353, 1524, 1589
   housing and services for 1395
   in Minneapolis 1911
   in Philadelphia 1224, 1253, 1347
Political clubs, in New York City 1561
Political ethics 1778. See also Corruption
Political parties 1447, 1465, 1468, 1484-85, 1502, 1675-76
   in Albuquerque 1630
   in Milwaukee 1461
   in Philadelphia 1556
   See also names of political parties (e.g., Democratic party)
Political patronage. See Patronage, political
Political scientists, attitude toward the city by 421
Politicians
   occupations of local 1578
   social origins and status of 1596-97, 1599
Politics and government 3, 25, 37, 43, 68, 72, 74-75, 83, 86, 100, 106, 108, 182, 268, 310, 410, 416, 819
   in Albuquerque 1630
   in Alviso, Calif. 507
   in Atlanta 1596-97, 1641
   in Augusta 532, 1458
   in Baltimore 1205, 1588, 1637
   in Baton Rouge, La. 1462
   in Beaumont, Tex. 1697
   bibliography on 118
   in Birmingham 484, 682, 1498
   blacks and 1182, 1372, 1385, 1454, 1458, 1486, 1490, 1494, 1512, 1534, 1547
   in Boston 849, 1528, 1544, 1553-54, 1572, 1590, 1666, 1774, 1826
   in Cairo, Ill. 570
   as a cause of civil disorders 417
   of urban problems 374
   in Charleston 1650
   in Chicago 614, 634, 1235, 1343, 1355, 1451-52, 1522, 1524, 1555, 1589, 1644, 1671-73, 1703, 1713, 1717, 1720, 1743, 1767, 1788, 1791, 1805, 1812-13
   in Cincinnati 638, 1608, 1733-34, 1801, 1857
   in the Civil War 55
   in Cleveland 617, 1473, 1529, 1543, 1616, 1693, 1700
   in Columbus, Ohio 1722
   community 231
   in Connecticut 1521
   in Denver 513, 1700, 1735-37, 1893
   in Detroit 1531, 1654-56, 1662, 1688
   of education 988
   ethnic groups and immigrants and 589, 1212, 1232-33, 1235, 1326, 1341, 1343, 1365, 1392, 1394, 1451-52, 1488-89, 1524, 1551, 1570-71, 1574, 1582, 1600-1601, 1603, 1612, 1619, 1622, 1627-29, 1636, 1666, 1675, 1683, 1685, 1698, 1739, 1741, 1743, 1746, 1748, 1772, 1788, 1822, 1826, 1851, 1857, 1878
   in Fall River, Mass. 1394
   in Fort Worth, Tex. 97, 1729
   geography of 238
   in Grand Rapids, Mich. 1799
   history of 11
   in Hoboken, N.J. 524, 1629
   impact of urbanization on 382
   inefficiency of 8
   interaction with city dwellers 29

in Jacksonville, Fla. 1182
in Jersey City, N.J. 770, 1392, 1610, 1635, 1660, 1793-97
in Kansas City 515, 1472, 1617, 1648, 1675
in Lancaster, Pa. 1669
in Litchfield, Conn. 842
in Los Angeles 523, 1769
in Lynn, Mass. 1225
machines, bossissm, and reform in 60, 70, 95, 97, 1437-38, 1461, 1601-1827, 1910
in Memphis 1730-32
middle-class withdrawal from 1299
in Milwaukee 646, 651, 965, 1461, 1464
in Natchez 557
nationalization of 318
in Newark, N.J. 622
the New Deal and 1433, 1440, 1470-71, 1483, 1490, 1497, 1521-22, 1584, 1590, 1648, 1750, 1900
in New England 791
in New Haven, Conn. 1466
in New Orleans 1494-95, 1564, 1657, 1745-46, 1759, 1897
in New York City 600, 613, 616, 779, 794, 839, 851, 988, 992-93, 1006, 1026, 1152, 1217, 1233, 1326, 1365, 1385, 1454-56, 1467, 1469, 1481, 1489, 1497, 1503-4, 1510, 1525-26, 1530, 1532-34, 1538-39, 1545, 1551, 1557-58, 1560-61, 1566-67, 1585, 1599, 1607, 1621, 1624-28, 1639, 1685-86, 1694, 1702, 1705, 1709, 1713, 1724, 1742, 1749, 1757, 1764, 1775-76, 1792, 1807, 1811, 1855, 1889
in New York State 1888
in Oakland, Calif. 1839
in Omaha, Nebr. 1761
in Philadelphia 498, 633, 787, 811, 1412, 1439, 1480, 1491, 1649, 1670, 1682, 1753, 1851
in a pioneer community 196
in Pittsburgh 289, 1516, 1575, 1579, 1851
police departments and 1029d
in Portland 1546
psychology of 188
of public health 1006
of public housing 1127
public opinion of 202
in Reading, Pa. 1507-8
relationship of street railways to 965
in Rhode Island 1453
in Rochester, N.Y. 587
in St. Louis 1292, 1341, 1849
in San Francisco 578, 1527, 1559, 1573, 1609, 1620, 1698, 1808, 1847, 1881, 1910
in Schenectady, N.Y. 1506
in Scranton, Pa. 1595
in Seattle 1559, 1612
shifts and changes in 93, 110
slavery and 1292
social and economic forces in 223
in the South 742, 764, 1461, 1900
in Stamford, Conn. 1479
suburban 253
in Syracuse, N.Y. 1536
terminology of 126
in Toledo, Ohio 1616, 1833
of urban planning and development 14, 82, 352, 1088, 1102, 1149, 1152, 1169, 1549, 1843
in Washington, D.C. 1264
of water supply 1026
in Wisconsin 1548
See also Corruption; Democracy; Elections, municipal; Franchise; Leadership; Power; Socialism
Pollution and pollution control 112, 987, 1013, 1444, 1755, 1763, 1905
Pope, Thomas 1162
Popular culture, agrarian and urban ideas in 346

Subject Index

Population 79, 102, 184, 198, 243, 291, 299, 324, 395, 1535
  bibliography on 436
  of Boston 240, 1407
  of the central city 59
  of Chicago 370
  of Cincinnati 492
  of Cleveland 664
  of Columbia, S.C. 544
  comparative atlas of 1
  decompression of 383
  density of 142, 245
    crowding and congestion problems 64, 152, 216, 619, 1763
  of Detroit 1414
  of Elizabeth City County, Va. 716
  of ethnic and racial groups 60, 1326, 1414
  of Germantown, Pa. 855
  historiographical studies of 461
  of Hoboken, N.J. 524
  of Illinois 725
  impact on urbanization 681
  influence on municipal spending 1286
  of Jamaica, N.Y. 827, 1363
  of Minneapolis-St. Paul 635
  of Muncie, Ind. 1829
  of Newark, N.J. 622
  of New England towns 791
  of New Hampshire towns 832
  of Newport, R.I. 854
  of New York City 619, 629, 714, 1326
  of Philadelphia 325, 777
  of Pittsburgh 893
  of Providence, R.I. 1259
  sampling techniques in 336
  of San Francisco 578
  of seaport cities 705
  of Seattle 727
  social change and 335
  of the South 710, 738
  spatial patterning of 266, 676
  statistics 64, 768
  structure of community and 151
  of Texas 763
  transportation and 1014
  trends 26, 58
  the urban crisis and 370
  of Vancouver 727
  of Washington (state) 749
  of Washington, D.C. 519
Portland, Maine 981
Portland, Oreg.
  history of 470, 596, 741
  politics in 1546
Ports and harbors 705
  of Los Angeles 480
  of New York City 1842
  of Norfolk 665
  of St. Louis 627
  of the South 796
Poughkeepsie, N.Y.
  family and business in 203, 1265
  mobility in 1266
  occupation and ethnicity in 1281, 1853
Poverty 78, 93, 95, 112, 161, 821, 915, 966, 1324, 1763
  in Baltimore 1076
  in Boston 937, 1898
  in Buffalo, N.Y. 1773
  comparative atlas of 1
  in Columbus, Ohio 1338
  culture of 81
  immigrant and minority 1214
  in New York City 858, 977-78
  in Philadelphia 776, 816, 818, 1224
  in Stamford, Conn. 1479
  theory of 1319
  See also Charity; Low-income groups; Public housing; Social welfare
Powderly, Terence V. 1595
Powell, Adam Clayton 1204, 1454, 1534
Power; power structures 268, 700, 736, 1539, 1543, 1568, 1635, 1747, 1759, 1789
  distribution of 1374
  measurement of 254
  stratification of 237
  theory of held by social reformers 368

Subject Index

utilization of 1670
See also Politics and government
Powers, John 1743
President, the cities and the 1459
Presidential election (1928) 1457
President's Committee on Civil Rights 1593-94
Press
  in Chicago 634
  in Detroit 914
  influence of in Virginia 707
  New York City black 1241
  See also Newspapers; Periodicals
Pressure groups 563
Prices 69
Private interests; Privatism 61-62, 156, 929, 1364
Production; productivity 257
  influence on migration 312
Profit; profit motive 317, 487-88
  impact on cities 42
  urbanization as a response to 220
Prohibition
  in Charleston 1650
  in Chicago 341, 531
  in Denver 1814, 1886
  in New Jersey 1582
Promoters and promotion. See Cities, boosterism and promotion of
Property
  distribution of in colonial Boston 848
    in colonial New York City 852
  held by candidates for office 1596-97
Prostitution
  in Denver 1643
  in New York City 1816
Protestant ethic 1832
Protestantism 1714
  in Atlanta 983
  importance to the future of cities 412
  response to the Haymarket Affair 1027
    to industrialization and immigration 970, 1027
    to urban problems 860, 869, 937
  social reform by in Jersey City, N.J. 1795

  in Los Angeles 1004
Providence, R.I.
  population and class in 1259
  public health in 886
Psychology
  political 188
  of social welfare 100
  of urban life 356
  See also Personality, urban
Public administration, terminology of 126
Public baths 1029a-29b
Public Education Association 890, 938, 1631
Public health 857, 902, 921, 940, 954, 987, 1817, 1827
  in Atlanta 936
  in Boston 865
  in Buffalo, N.Y. 1773
  in Charleston 1024
  comparative atlas of 1
  cost-benefit analysis of 972
  in Newark, N.J. 916
  in New Orleans 904, 906, 908, 921
  in New York City 858, 900, 904, 917, 957, 1006
  in Omaha, Nebr. 930
  in Philadelphia 986
  in Pittsburgh 563, 892-93, 901-2, 905
  in Providence, R.I. 886
  in St. Louis 871
  in Stamford, Conn. 1479
  See also Health; Medicine and medical practice
Public housing 1089, 1154
  in Atlanta 1161
  in Chicago 1127
  economics of 1079
  in Milwaukee 1043
  in New York City 1061, 1116, 1158
  in Philadelphia 1051-52, 1156, 1786-87
  politics of 1552
  in Washington, D.C. 1047-48
  See also Housing, low-income
Public libraries 867
  as agencies of social reform 1651

Subject Index

See also Newberry Library
(Chicago)
Public opinion 563
as a guarantor of civic order 405
regarding urban politics 202
Public policy, economic ramifications
of 215
Public safety 1591. See also Fire
fighting services; Police
Public services. See Social and
public services
Public utilities 68, 1896
franchises 1643
municipal ownership of 373, 571,
859, 1592, 1674
regulation of 1487, 1690, 1744
Public welfare. See Social welfare
Public works 1487
in Stamford, Conn. 1479
Pueblo, Colo., history of 632
Puerto Rican Americans 1287, 1304,
1350, 1637
in New York City 1251-52, 1274
Puget Sound, Wash., promotion of
732
Pullman, Ill.
history of 475, 488
planning of 1160
Puritanism
communal-religious orientation of
367
decline of 789
town planning and planting in
780, 807

Q

Quakers, role of in the development
of Philadelphia 483, 843
Quality of life 61, 248. See also
Life-styles

R

Race 63, 78, 98, 112, 126, 324
change in community structure and
251
changing composition of 101
dynamics of 91
social mobility and 1218

Race relations; racism 76, 1266a,
1902
in Arkansas 1863
in Chicago 1364
in Cleveland 1311
education and 898, 944
in employment 1189
evolution of 1188
in the South 742, 1369
the urban crisis and 8
in Washington, D.C. 542,
1264, 1301
See also Riots
Racine, Wis.
minority, migrant groups in 1391
social and economic change in
699
Radial center (urban form) 12
Radicalism
geographical aspects of 1222
labor 1612
Radio broadcasting 961
Railroads
in Chicago 678
in Cincinnati 550
development of cities and 169
in Jersey City, N.J. 1653,
1793
in Kansas City 195
in Los Angeles 863
in New Orleans 504, 624
role of in southern California
735
in the South 696
in Syracuse, N.Y. 731a
taxation of 1793
in Virginia 752
in Wisconsin 743
See also Cincinnati Southern Railway; Denver and Rio Grande
Railroad; Southern Pacific
Railroad; Western and
Atlantic Railroad
Railroads, electric 933, 1029.
See also Street railroads;
Trolley cars
Railroads, elevated, influence on
the central city 335
Railway stations, architecture of
southern 688

Subject Index

Raleigh, N.C., blacks in 1369
Rapid transit. See Mass transit
Raw materials, importance to the growth of Terra Haute, Ind. 481
Reading, Pa., socialism in 1507-8
Real estate 126
    1920s boom in Los Angeles 525
    See also Property
Real estate brokers, role in development of railroad policy 196
Reclamation of land 57
Record, George L. 1793
Recreation and entertainment 1007, 1541, 1658, 1827
    in Birmingham 484
    in Chicago 1716, 1719
    in Jersey City, N.J. 636
    in New York City 616, 795, 911, 925, 1005
    in Philadelphia 644
    the trolley car in aiding access to 942
    See also Coney Island; Leisure
Red Bluff, Calif. 110
Referendum and initiative 1634
Reformers. See Urban reform
Regionalism 25, 235, 420, 1056
    in city planning 1094, 1122
    North Carolina 102
    importance of the automobile to 204
    model of urbanization in 733
    in the South 685, 1460
Regional Planning Association of America 1115, 1155
Religion 95, 410, 953
    in Baltimore 1836
    in Birmingham 484
    of blacks 1191, 1425
    in Detroit 1297, 1414
    effect of urbanization on 895-96
    immigrants and 1233, 1332, 1341, 1365, 1414
    in Jamaica, N.Y. 827, 1363
    liberal in Chicago 555
    in municipal reform 1756
    in New Haven, Conn. 607
    in New Orleans 1191
    in New York City 600, 795, 1233, 1365
    in New York State's burned over district 156
    in Philadelphia 498, 811, 1571, 1756
    in politics 1571
    in St. Louis 1341
    social mobility and 154
    in Stamford, Conn. 800
    study of preferences for in Cleveland 242
    in Washington, D.C. 1425
    See also Catholic Church; Church and state; Churches; Clergy; Congregational Church; Great Awakening; Episcopal Church; Methodism; Missionaries, urban; Protestantism; Puritanism
Republican party 1598
    blacks in 1512
    in Chicago 1720
    in Cleveland 1529
    in Detroit 1688
    nativism and 1538
    in New York City 1538, 1567
    in Philadelphia 1851
    in Pittsburgh 1516, 1851
    in the South 742
    in Wilmington, Del. 1512
Residential areas. See Neighborhoods
Residential patterns 106, 179, 266, 1033, 1269
    of Baltimore laboring classes 1186
    of blacks 1330-31, 1385
    in the central city 1070
    change in community structure and 251
    in Charleston 621
    as a determinant of urban growth 516
    of ethnic groups and immigrants 1385, 1417
    of Lansing, Mich. 1330-31
    in New York City 1365, 1385, 1861
    in Philadelphia 278
    in Pittsburgh 1417
    relationship to the nineteenth-century family

Subject Index

in rental areas 226
in St. Louis 551
work place location and 316
See also Housing; Mobility
Resorts
Atlantic City as 526, 771
Hoboken, N.J. as 509
Newport, R.I. as 493
Resource allocation, model of 257
Restaurants, in New York City 911
Retail trade
urban slavery and 757
within communities 151
Reuf, Abe 1609, 1808
Revolutionary War 783
Annapolis during 824
Baltimore during 844-45
Boston during 809
Charleston during 836, 846
impact on urbanization 681
laborers and 802
Newport, R.I. during 854
New York City during 781, 794
Philadelphia during 97, 787, 809, 814, 823, 834-35
role of cities in 775
Stamford, Conn. during 800
Rhode Island, household structure in 332
Richardson, James F. 444
Richmond
blacks in 1369
Dickens on 7
land use in 276-77
urbanization in 1854
urban rivalry and railroads in 752
Riis, Jacob 1116, 1707
Riots 112, 998, 1197, 1334, 1366, 1373
in Atlanta 1219
in Baltimore 1205
causes of 1230, 1237
in Chicago 1411
in Cincinnati 704
in Houston 1279
in Los Angeles 341
in Memphis 1383
in New Orleans 1280
in New York City 782, 1204, 1217, 1419

in Philadelphia 1237, 1239, 1480
in St. Louis 1382
Riverside, Ill. 1095
River travel. See Inland water transportation; Mississippi River; Steam boats
Rizzo, Frank 1682
Rochester, N.Y.
fire fighting services in 861
historiographical essay on 451
history of 477-78, 582-89
housing problems in 123-24
Italian Americans in 1840
subways in 958
Rockefeller, John D. 497
Roebling, Washington 962
Rolph, Jim 1565
Roosevelt, Franklin 1103, 1470-71, 1521-22
Roosevelt, Theodore 1707, 1851
in New York politics 1489
search for a sense of community by 400
Root, John Wellborn 1098
Roraback, J. Henry 1453
Rotary Clubs 227
Row houses, in Baltimore 1035
Rumanian Americans 1355
in Cleveland 1183
Rural areas
distribution of the labor force in 67
economic study of 233
growth of 284
housing problems of 1120
impact of urbanization on 140, 146
influence on urban areas 185
life styles in 250
migration from 199, 207, 219, 409, 1315
nineteenth-century physical and moral health in 64
relations with cities 18, 52, 149, 353, 378, 407, 423-24, 707, 1166, 1855
social structures in 332
See also Agriculture
Rural-urban fringe areas 162

Subject Index

S

Sacramento, history of 36
St. Louis 68, 86
  class, ethnicity, and race in 1292, 1318, 1341, 1371, 1382, 1393, 1402
  Dickens on 7
  economic rivalry with Chicago 678
  education in 1017, 1668
  history of 13, 55, 469, 551, 623, 627, 699, 765
  police in 947, 990, 1023
  politics and reform in 1668, 1740-41, 1754, 1849
  public health in 871
  riots in 998
  social problems of 1781
  Urban League in 1198
St. Paul
  blacks in 1405
  history of 469-70, 635
  model of growth for 189
  planning and development in 1909
Salem, Mass. 700
Salem, N.H., history of 605
Saloons. See Taverns, inns, etc.
San Antonio
  black housing in 1251
  history of 470, 522, 766-67
San Diego, history of 302, 571, 741
San Francisco 31, 33, 138
  city planning in 1096
  class, ethnicity, and race in 175-76, 945, 1222-23, 1251, 1321, 1698, 1850, 1910
  history of 36, 78, 469-70, 547, 577-78, 594-95, 606, 741
  institutional studies of 960
  transportation 1904
  politics and reform in 1463, 1527, 1559, 1565, 1573, 1609, 1620, 1698, 1808, 1847, 1881, 1910
  Union Labor party in 533
San Jose, Calif., as a working-class suburb 1187
Sanitation 860, 950, 1892
  in Memphis 909
  in New York City 872
  See also Sewers and sewage disposal; Wastes and waste disposal
Santa Barbara, Calif., Mexican Americans in 1203
Santa Fe, history of 610, 625
Savannah
  blacks in 1190, 1357
  history of 853
  lumber trade in 703
  urbanization of 803
Scandinavian Americans, in Seattle 1419
Schenectady, N.Y., socialism in 1506
Schmitz, Eugene 1808
School attendance
  in Pittsburgh 1388
  social status and acculturation and 1424
Science, impact on approaches to studying cities 217
Scranton, Pa.
  immigrants in 1195
  politics in 1595
Seattle
  history of 13, 469, 631, 699, 741
  mass transit in 1904
  politics and reform in 1559, 1569, 1612, 1751-52
  population growth and change in 727
  promotion of 732
  residential segregation in 1269
  Scandinavian Americans in 1418
  urbanization of 749
Secession
  in Louisville 597
  reaction of Natchez to 557
Sectionalism, in Virginia 706-7
Secularization; secularism 895-96
Segregation 776, 1033, 1318, 1320, 1882
  in Arkansas 1863
  black ghettoes and 1255
  in Chicago 1399, 1403
  comparative atlas of socioeconomic 1

Subject Index

in Detroit 1297, 1317
in education 951
Boston 1295, 1316
of ethnic groups and immigrants
 218, 1033, 1269, 1313,
 1317, 1325, 1403-4
in New Orleans 1325
in New York City 1302
in St. Louis 1403
in the South 711, 1185, 1369,
 1858
Service industries, distribution of
 the labor force in 67.
 See also Social and public
 services
Settlement houses 1375, 1640,
 1687, 1708, 1820-21,
 1823
in Boston 1822
in Chicago 1384, 1805
in Cleveland 1800
in the Depression (1929) 1018
failures of 1364
housing reform by workers in
 1156
as a means of reviving small-town
 values 398
in New York City 924, 1375,
 1704, 1806
Sewers and sewage disposal 857,
 894, 921, 987, 1012,
 1827, 1905
in Chicago 876-77
in Cincinnati 918
in Milwaukee 641
in Pittsburgh 924
See also Sanitation; Wastes and
 waste disposal
Sexual behavior, in colonial Philadelphia 811. See also
 Morality
Shepherd, Alexander 543
Shoemaking and trade, in Lynn,
 Mass. 1225
Shreveport, La., slavery in 1312
Sidewalks 19. See also Streets
 and roads
Single tax 1797
Skyscrapers 85, 200, 1068
Slavery 708, 757, 1312

the lumber trade and 703
in New York City 792
in prosouthern fiction 1229
reaction of Natchez to 557
in St. Louis 1292
in Vicksburg, Miss. 1185
See also Abolitionism
Slovak Americans 1209, 1355
in Cleveland 1183
in Pittsburgh 1310
Slums and ghettoes 78, 80, 93,
 1064, 1088, 1178, 1255-
 56, 1287, 1329, 1366,
 1372
Boston immigrant 322
causes and prevalence of 1154
in Chicago 1121, 1364, 1399
in discouraging investment 319
housing law and 1083
in Los Angeles 1226
in New York City 1242, 1351,
 1844
in Philadelphia 1156, 1786
rehabilitation and clearance of
 1121, 1128, 1153, 1156,
 1161, 1168, 1176
in St. Paul 1405
See also Tenements
Smith, Page 156
Smith, Stephen 872
Smoking, crusade against 1679
Social and public services 288,
 395, 857, 1029, 1535,
 1577, 1623, 1768, 1779
in Baltimore 131
in Birmingham 556
British comment on American 48
in Columbia, S.C. 544
cost of in 1900 5
in creation of financial problems
 929
on the frontier 721
in Houston 269
impact of privatism on 61
impact on segregation 711
in Kansas City 515
in the Midwest 753
in Milwaukee 298
in mining towns of Minnesota 720
in New York City 613, 616,
 1777

Subject Index

in Ohio 772
in Pennsylvania 1449
in Pittsburgh 563
in the South 711, 739, 1460
within communities 151
See also specific types of services (e.g., Police)
Social behavior. See Social relations and behavior
Social change 245, 342, 407, 722
in Atlanta 1864a
as a cause of rioting 1237
ethnicity and 1864a
failure of urban renewal to achieve 1111
in Milwaukee 1464
population renewal and 335
in Racine, Wis. 699
in Richmond, Va. 1854
role of cities in 40
sense of community as a response to 359
in the South 717
suburban growth and 304
Social class and status 98, 101, 106, 268, 299, 1360, 1763, 1846
of the American Indian 1398
in Atlanta 1290
in Baltimore 1205
blacks and 1231, 1255, 1320
in Boston 849, 1244, 1407, 1832, 1891
in Buffalo, N.Y. 1249
as a cause of crime and violence 883
change in community structure and 251
in Detroit 1430, 1531
Episcopal Church's response to antagonisms involving 925
as a factor in educational bias 944
historiographical study of 461
housing as a measurement of 248
of immigrants and ethnic groups 1205, 1244, 1249, 1270, 1430

in Jamaica, N.Y. 827
migration and 308
of neighborhoods 205-6
in New Bedford, Mass. 591
in New Haven, Conn. 1323
in New York City 925, 1362
in Philadelphia 255, 820, 1333, 1570, 1832, 1878
of physicians 1725
politics and 1502, 1531, 1537, 1562, 1570, 1599, 1698
in Providence, R.I. 1259
relationship to kinship 1309
in Rhode Island 332
in St. Louis 623
in San Francisco 1222, 1698
school attendance and 1424
social mobility and 1218
in the South 686, 739
in Stamford, Conn. 800
in the suburbs 186, 253
urban problems and 1436
on the western frontier 596
See also Laboring class; Low-income groups; Middle class; Upper class
Social control 41, 161, 1755
city planning as 1058
Detroit Progressives and 1317
education as a means of 42, 951-52, 976-77
in Philadelphia 1412
recreation as 1658
in the South 1369
in Trenton, N.J. 1903
upon abolition of slavery 792
See also Social order
Social Darwinism 1509, 1708
Social differentiation 87, 159, 320
impact of migration on 1258
Social engineering 580
Social Gospel 869, 1804
Social integration 403
Socialism 1580, 1810
Jews and 1375
in Reading, Pa. 1507-9
in Schenectady, N.Y. 1506
Social isolation 565. See also Alienation
Socialist party of America 1581

437

Subject Index

Social justice 211, 1795, 1804, 1849
Social mobility. See Mobility
Social order 425
  in Atlanta 983
  in Boston 100-102
  in Chelsea, Mass. 565
  in Chicago 1716
  in Detroit 1000
  education and 100-102
  historiographical study of 449
  maintenance of in the South 683
  in Philadelphia 405, 1876
  in Pittsburgh 214
  politics of 1568
  Puritan Connecticut and 789
  upsetting of by urban growth 352
  See also Social control
Social organization. See Social structure and organization
Social planning 1111
  in solution of urban problems 351
  See also Urban planning
Social problems. See Urban problems
Social reform. See Urban reform
Social relations and behavior 81, 87, 102, 144, 159, 415
  the environment and 1861
  in Plymouth Colony 831
Social sciences, use of in urban history 455, 460
Social services. See Social and public services
Social structure and organization 143-44, 159, 168, 237, 317, 354, 392, 410, 1200
  of Boston 520, 808, 1407
  of Charleston 621
  civil disorders and 417
  of Columbus, Ohio, neighborhoods 1722
  in Detroit 1297
  effect of crowding on 152
  of Houston 269
  impact of migration on 1258
  of Italian Americans 1422

  in New York City 1326
  of Jamaica, N.Y. 827, 1363
  of Minneapolis-St. Paul 635
  of the preindustrial city 300
  urban dominance and (1890) 128
  urbanization and in Pennsylvania 190
  of Warren, Pa. 663
Social studies, use of urban history in 120
Social welfare 385, 860, 1488
  in Cincinnati 512
  conflict with private interests 61
  in the Depression (1930) and New Deal 1440, 1885
  in Detroit 1584
  in Gary, Ind. 1336
  history of 21
  in New York City 978, 1450, 1503, 1757
  in Philadelphia 885, 1440
  politics of 1576, 1584, 1636
  social psychology of 100
  terminology used in 126
  in Toledo, Ohio 1576
  See also Poverty
Social work 1755
  history of 21
  sense of community expressed in 361
Society; social life 1157
  of Augusta 532
  of Birmingham 682
  of blacks 1385, 1425
  of Boston 1590
  of Cairo, Ill. 570
  of Chicago 558
  of colonial Florida 841
  of Columbia, S.C. 574
  on the frontier 721
  of Houston 581
  impact of urbanization on migrant 426
  influence of urban areas on 430
  of Jersey City, N.J. 636
  of Los Angeles 523
  of Massachusetts 700
  of Milwaukee 646, 651
  of Natchez 557
  of New York City 600, 779, 794, 805, 1385

Subject Index

of Philadelphia 633
of Pittsburgh 559, 563
of Rochester, N.Y. 587
of the South 683
of Texas 767
of Washington, D.C. 1425
Society for the Prevention of Crime in New York City 1749
Society of Friends. See Quakers
Sociologists, attitude toward the city 421
Sociology. See Urban sociology
Somerville, Mass., influence of commuting on 145
Soundex Indexes, evaluation of 303
South Bend, Ind., mobility of immigrants in 1234
Southern Pacific Railroad, monopolization of the Los Angeles port by 480
Southern states 739
    blacks in 1366-69, 1423
    in British travel literature 702
    labor conflict in 689
    manufacturing in 692
    migration rates in 744
    New Deal in 1900
    New England entrepreneurs in 672
    northern limits of defined 773
    police in 1367
    politics in 742, 1460, 1865
    railway architecture in 688
    urbanization of 683-87, 690-91, 697-98, 710-11, 715, 717, 756, 761-62, 764, 796, 799
    urban slavery in 708, 757
Space; spatial relationships 12, 159, 211, 218, 229, 266, 270, 272, 278, 320, 1882
    in Detroit 1430, 1906
    in explaining political machine growth 1718
    as a factor in city growth 295-96
    in immigrant adaptation 1253
    impact of industrialization on 323
    in information circulation 274
    intraurban transportation and 281

of land values 333
in Memphis 1858
in New Bedford, Mass. 591
in Northeast urbanization 768
in residential segregation 1858
role of social and cultural values in 187
in St. Louis 623
of work place and residence 316
Spanish-speaking Americans
    in Atlanta 1864a
    in Denver 1275
    See also Mexican Americans; Puerto Rican Americans
Speer, Robert Walter 1700, 1735-37, 1893
Spokane
    history of 517, 741
    urbanization of 749
Sports, development of in New Orleans 643. See also Baseball
Springfield, Mass. 192
    the trolley car in 942
Stamford, Conn.
    history of 800
    politics in 1479
Standard Metropolitan Statistical Areas (SMSAs), comparative atlas 1
Standard of living
    in Elizabeth City County, Va. 716
    of Italian Americans in New York City 1326
    the trolley car in raising 942
State government, relations with the city 42, 1545, 1548, 1585
Staunton, Va. 676
Steam boats, social significance of 601
Steel industry 1868
    in Pittsburgh 559
    See also U.S. Steel Corp.
Steelton, Pa., immigrants and ethnic groups in 1194, 1196
Steffens, Lincoln 1649, 1781, 1790
Still, Bayrd 444, 458
Street railroads 969
    in Detroit 1690

Subject Index

influence on Boston 326
in Milwaukee 965
See also Railroads, electric; Railroads, elevated; Trolley cars
Streets and roads 1827, 1882
of Boston 642
of Illinois 725
of Milwaukee 641
of Philadelphia 644
of Rochester, N.Y. 583, 586
See also Expressways; Sidewalks
Stress (physiology), effect of crowding on 152
Strong, Josiah 391
Strong, William L. 1702, 1777
Suburbs; suburbanization 70, 91, 93, 95, 177, 288, 319-20, 356, 358, 968
beginning of 319
of Bucks County, Pa. 1063
of Buffalo, N.Y. 136, 482
of Chicago 496
of Cleveland 1721
density and growth patterns of 228
of Denver 468
effect of local transportation on 321, 326
failures of 371
geographical interpretation of 261
influence of 395
interaction with cities 18, 60, 1194
of Los Angeles 523
middle class 1287, 1416
migration to 1258
myths concerning 78, 350
of New Jersey 1493
of Philadelphia 251, 265
planning in 1160
in politics 1493, 1586, 1721
Progressive era reform and 1678
socioeconomic status of 101, 186, 239, 290, 304, 468
urbanization of 253
of Venice, Calif. 506
working-class 1187
Subways
in New York City 1855

in Rochester, N.Y. 958
Sudbury, Mass., history of 828
Suffolk County, N.Y. growth of after World War II 304
Suffrage. See Elections, municipal; Franchise
Suicide 1876
Sullivan, Louis 1131
Sumner, William Graham 1509
Superior, Wis., history of 699
Swanson, Joseph 221
Swing, David 555
Symbolism 1287
Brooklyn Bridge as 1016
Coney Island as an example of urban 349
the town as an example of community 361
Syracuse, N.Y.
ethnic groups in 1318
politics in 1536
regional development of 731a

T

Tacoma, Wash.
city planning in 1106
history of 741
urbanization of 749
Talbot County, Md. 1374
Talmadge, Eugene 1783
Tammany Hall 956, 1481, 1486, 1530, 1551, 1621, 1626-28, 1685-86, 1694, 1739, 1742, 1749, 1764, 1778, 1792, 1811
Tammany Society 1443
Taos, N. Mex., history of 625
Taverns, inns, etc. 907
of colonial Philadelphia 811
of Denver 1886
of New York City 1749
of territorial Arizona 699
See also Alcohol; Liquor; Prohibition
Taxation 1577, 1616
in Denver 1643
impact of political structures on 1537
in Jersey City, N.J. 1793
of mining companies 720

Subject Index

patterns of New England 791
of the railroads 1793
reform of 373
for refurbishing cities 19
in slum clearance 1168
See also Income tax; Single tax
Taylor, Graham 1804
Teachers
black 1368
organization of 1020, 1803
See also Education
Technology 83, 88, 241, 291, 415
in agriculture 330
in creation of municipal finance problems 929
failure of New Orleans to respond to 485
history of 11
impact on central city areas 335
on job distribution 714
on the growth of cities 286, 334, 622, 751
on the frontier 721
influence of European 57
lag of 260
response of the South to 686
role of in the decline of Cincinnati 492
urban problems and 664
use of in Philadelphia 498
use of by police departments 1029d
Telluride, Colo. 110
Tenement House Law (Wisconsin) 1084
Tenements
of Chicago 1030, 1181
of Fall River, Mass. 640
of Holyoke, Mass. 1075
of Newark, N.J. 1151
of New York City 1071, 1114, 1142
of Wisconsin 1084
Tennessee, food and drug control in 1817
Terra Haute, Ind., history of 481
Texas
intergovernmental relations in 763

urbanization of 729, 766-67
Textile industry, in Fall River, Mass. 640. See also Cotton industry
Theater
in Chicago 648
in colonial Philadelphia 811
in Jersey, N.J. 636
in New York City 932
in San Francisco 594-95
Thernstrom, Stephan 445, 458
Thompson, William Hale 1605, 1812
Ticknor, George 363
Tobacco industry, in colonial Annapolis 824
Toledo, Ohio
education in 989
politics and reform in 1576, 1616, 1833
Toronto 1838
Towns and villages 109-10, 235, 410
absence of in early Virginia 829
black 1864
growth of 157
sense of community in 361
See also names of towns and villages
Trade. See Business and commerce
Trade unions
in Buffalo, N.Y. 1773
in Chicago 1345
in Detroit 1584
in Fall River, Mass. 640, 1394
immigrants and 1225, 1375
in Los Angeles 1400
in Lynn, Mass. 1225
municipal 58, 1349
in New Jersey 1493
in New York City 1233, 1375, 1469
in Pittsburgh 563
in politics 1493, 1584
in San Francisco 1463
Traffic flow 258
Transportation 37, 58, 76, 79, 102, 112, 212, 241, 283, 320, 1056, 1838, 1859, 1904

Subject Index

bibliographies on 118, 436-37
   in Boston 679
   in Chicago 508, 862, 1066-67
   in Cincinnati 281, 492, 745
   comparative atlas of 1
   in Denver 1643
   economics of 215, 260, 507
   effect on suburban growth 321
   in Illinois 725
   influence on settlement patterns 174
   in Kansas City 515
   in Los Angeles 863
   in Milwaukee 641
   in Minnesota 1909
   in New England 718
   in New York City 1724
   nineteenth-century 3, 178
   in Ohio 734, 772
   in St. Louis 1754
   Superior, Wis. as a center of 699
   technology in 198
   terminology of 126
   in Terra Haute, Ind. 481
   urban dominance and (1890) 128
   urban growth and 196, 289, 309
   See also Automobiles; Bus lines; Inland water transportation; Mass transit; Railroads; Steam boats; Street railroads; Subways; Trolley cars
Travel literature 47-48, 71
   Chicago in 615
   Milwaukee in 650
   New York City in 600
   Philadelphia in 644
   southern states in 702
Trenton, N.J.
   class, ethnicity, and race in 1903
   urban renewal in 1111
Trolley cars 942
Truman, Harry 1593-94
Trumbull, Harriet and Maria 600
Tuberculosis, as a political issue 1481
Tugwell, Rexford G. 1103
Tulsa, Okla.
   Civilian Conservations Corps in 1513
   leadership in 1514
Turkey, urban policy and planning in 285
Turner, Frederick Jackson 604
   attitude toward urbanization 338
Tweed Ring 872, 1621, 1628, 1686, 1724, 1757

U

Unemployment
   aid of in the Progressive era 1765
   Boston settlement houses and 1822
   in the Depression (1929) 1885
   in Detroit 1906
   See also Employment
Union Labor party 533, 1527, 1609
U.S. Census Bureau 693. See also Census data
U.S. Civilian Conservation Corps 1513
U.S. Civil Works Administration 1470
U.S. Conference of Mayors 1445
U.S. Congress
   the cities and 1444, 1459, 1500
   government of Washington, D.C. by 1435
U.S. Department of the Interior, development of Anchorage by 666
U.S. Federal Electric Railways Commission 1029
U.S. Federal Emergency Relief Administration 1445
U.S. Home Owners Loan Corp. 1445
U.S. National Archives 79, 436
U.S. Public Works Administration 1161, 1445, 1587
   Housing Division 1153
U.S. Resettlement Administration 1444
U.S. Rural Electrification Administration 1444
U.S. Steel Corp. 1129
   influence on Gary, Ind. 487

Subject Index

U.S. Works Progress Administration 1328
  in Cleveland 1473
  in New York City 1446, 1557
Universities and colleges 926
  municipal 797
  urban studies programs at 114, 118-19
Upper class 1293, 1361, 1852, 1868
  of Atlanta 1309
  "back to nature" movement and 404
  of Boston 1260, 1296
  evolution of in Philadelphia 137
  importance to urban economic growth 173
  integration into 310
  maintenance of control by 1291
  neighborhoods of 206
  of New York City 1296
  in politics and reform 1502, 1518-19, 1586, 1776
  social orientation of 182
  in Trenton, N.J. 1903
  See also Wealth
Urban anthropology 183
Urban design 112, 1056, 1077, 1105, 1110, 1157, 1163, 1179, 1905
  in New York City 560, 1566
Urban ecology 10, 29, 53, 87, 101, 105, 168, 204, 229, 243, 299, 360, 396, 443, 446, 1878
  of Chicago 230
  cultural aspects of 187
  of the ghetto 1256
  of the preindustrial city 300
  relationship to the eighteenth-century family 147
  in urban planning 1122
  See also Urban environment
Urban environment 72, 83, 87, 102, 291, 369, 396, 507, 625
  attempts to improve on the frontier 721
  comparative atlas of 1
  of Connecticut 731
  of Houston 269

  importance to urban history 441
  influence on behavior 1861
    on child dependency 201
    on city growth 334
    on education 113, 115
    on the immigrant 1183, 1193, 1195
  interaction of urban dwellers with 2
  man's relationship to 376
  of Milwaukee 641
  of Mt. Tabor, N.J. 287
  of New York City 1152
  of Philadelphia 984, 1429
  transportation policy and 1904
  urban planning and 1094, 1152
  See also Urban ecology
Urban form 1055, 1155, 1163
  in Atlanta 1118
Urban geography 162, 262, 315, 319-20, 1818
  of Cincinnati 704
  historical studies of 609-10
  of New York City 1724
  politics in 238
  suburbanization and 261
  of the West 751, 765
  See also Mapping, computer
Urban history 537-565, 1828-1911
  bosses, machines, and urban reform 1601-1827
  class, ethnicity, and race 1181-1430
  colonial period of 774, 856
  general studies 1-125
    readers 72-112
    teaching materials 113-25
    textbooks 1-71
  historiography of 430-65
  institutional studies 857-1029e
  planning, architecture, and urban renewal 1030-1180
  politics and government 1431-1600
  regional studies 671-773
  single city studies 466-670
  social role of 384
  the urbanization process 126-336
  See also Cities; names of cities
Urban institutions 41, 214, 218,

Subject Index

    256, 269, 428, 513, 515,
    531, 544, 563, 578, 591,
    614, 644, 787, 820, <u>857-
    1029</u>, 1577
American Indian 1398
as a cause of urban problems 374
control of by the upper classes
    1291
function of in the Revolutionary
    War 97
immigrant and ethnic 1206, 1252,
    1270, 1343, 1348
nineteenth-century 25, 343
twentieth-century 32
the working class and 1220-21
See also subheading "institutional
    studies" under names of
    cities; types of urban insti-
    tutions (e.g. Police)
Urbanization; urban growth
accelerated 383
bibliography on 434
comparative atlas of 1
differentials in 210
documents pertinent to 50
factors affecting 28, 40, 286,
    295-96, 309, 312-13,
    321, 334, 516
historiographical study of 463
history of 25, 42, 49, 50, 60,
    64, 184, 328
measurement of 199
models of 189, 270-73, 733
the process of 126-336
research materials and methodol-
    ogies in 193
statistics on 64, 178
terminology of 94, 126
See also Cities; names of specific
    cities
Urban landscape 1157
Urban League 1354, 1421
    of Baltimore 1356
    of Chicago 1401
    of Detroit 1317, 1409
    of St. Louis 1198
Urban planning 42-43, 53, 58, 62,
    70, 78, 85, 87-88, 93,
    95, 100, 102, 105, 159,
    200, 360, 376, 579,
    1036-37, 1056-57, 1060,
    1063, 1065, 1088-89, 1093-

    94, 1096, 1105, 1112, 1115,
    1117, 1122, 1133, 1140,
    1144-45, 1147, 1155,
    1163, 1169-70, 1180,
    1541, 1810, 1856, 1859,
    1880, 1892
in Boston 1148
in Chicago 1044, 1058, 1066-
    67a, 1130, 1175
in Cleveland 664, 1062, 1097
in colonial Connecticut 780,
    804
on the frontier 1141
on Gary, Ind. 1129
in Germany 1132
in Iowa 1099
lack of 8
in Milwaukee 652
in Minnesota 1909
in New York City 1108, 1152
in North Carolina 1101-2
in Philadelphia 817, 1174,
    1753
principle and values for 19
in Pullman, Ill. 488
sense of community expressed in
    361
terminology of 126
use of the past in 329
See also Community planning
Urban problems 24, 26, 37, 42,
    63, 68, 72, 259, 291,
    370, 373, 389-90, 454,
    1088, 1155, 1505, 1604,
    1763, 1781, 1892
of Baltimore 991, 1434
bibliography on 442
of Birmingham 682
causes of 374, 619, 1200
class differences in 1436
of Cleveland 664
of Denver 138
failure to solve 364
government intervention in 421
of Hoboken, N.J. 527
housing as the key to 1032
middle class responses to 476
of Milwaukee 652
of New Orleans 1564
of New York City 619, 806,
    995-96, 1628

Subject Index

of Passaic, N.J. 514
politics of 1434, 1460, 1541, 1564, 1628
Protestant response to 868
of Rochester, N.Y. 588
of San Francisco 138
sociostructural nature of 1136
solution of 345, 351
of the South 684, 1460, 1505, 1540
suburbanization as a reaction to 136
use of the past in solving 329
Urban reform 92, 103-5, 374-75, 1441, 1601-1827, 1846, 1853, 1883
  in Atlanta 1641
  in Augusta 532, 1667
  in Baltimore 1433, 1637
  in Beaumont, Tex. 1697
  blacks and 1182, 1199, 1317, 1351
  in Boston 1774, 1826
  in Buffalo, N.Y. 1748
  in Charleston 1650
  in Chicago 1644, 1681, 1703, 1706, 1717, 1720, 1726, 1747, 1778, 1790, 1804-5
  in Cincinnati 918, 1608, 1725, 1733-34, 1801
  in Cleveland 1701, 1728
  in Denver 1642-43, 1700, 1734-37, 1814, 1893
  in Detroit 1317, 1654-56, 1662, 1688
  in Fort Worth, Tex. 97, 1729
  in Grand Rapids, Mich. 1799
  in Hoboken, N.J. 524, 1629
  historiographical study of 457
  housing reform in 1114, 1116-17
  in Jacksonville, Fla. 1182
  in Jersey City, N.J. 1610, 1793-97
  in Kansas City 1617, 1740, 1841
  in Lancaster, Pa. 1669
  the library in 1651
  in Los Angeles 1029d, 1638, 1769, 1819
  in Memphis 1730-32

  middle-class withdrawal from 1299
  in New Orleans 1494, 1657, 1745-46, 1759
  in New York City 1375, 1481, 1503-4, 1607, 1624-25, 1631, 1639, 1659, 1685, 1692, 1699, 1702, 1704-5, 1709, 1713, 1738-39, 1749, 1757, 1765-66, 1775-77, 1792, 1806, 1811, 1817, 1889
  in Oakland, Calif. 1839
  in Ohio 1616
  in Omaha, Nebr. 1761
  in Philadelphia 1645, 1753, 1756, 1786-87
  philanthropy and 1029b
  Protestants in 860, 869, 937, 1004, 1795
  in Providence, R.I. 886
  in Pullman, Ill. 488
  in St. Louis 1668, 1740-41, 1754, 1849
  in San Francisco 1609, 1620, 1698, 1808
  in Seattle 1612, 1751-52
  theory of political power in 368
  in Toledo 1833
  utility regulation in 1744
  women and 1824
Urban renewal 63, 72, 1032, 1038, 1053, 1064, 1082, 1088-91, 1113, 1125, 1128, 1149, 1177
  in Chicago 1031, 1067, 1121
  in Holyoke, Mass. 1843
  in New York City 1446
  participation of the poor in 1324
  in Philadelphia 1139
  politics of 1549, 1552, 1843
  in Rochester, N.Y. 1123-24
  in Trenton, N.J. 1111
Urban sociology 14, 20, 29, 40-41, 47, 90, 105, 108-9, 135, 160-61, 168, 267, 299, 356,

Subject Index

376, 392, 416, 443, 1163
approaches to and research techniques in 159
historiographical study on 449
Park's impact on 387
politics in 223, 1467
sense of community in 361
Urban sprawl 80, 85, 200, 1122
intraurban transportation in creating 281
Urban studies programs 119, 439
bibliographies on 114, 118
U.S. See United States
Utica, N.Y.
riots in 1373
Italian Americans in 1840
Utopias 393, 1080
Pullman, Ill. as 488
Zion City, Ill. as 505

V

Vagrancy 1479
Values 83
the agrarian myth and 599
attempt of middle class to dominate 425
attractiveness of Indian and Spanish-American 625
in the "back to nature" movement 404
impact of urbanization on 382
need to revive small-town 398
role of in spatial differentiation 187
See also Morality
Vancouver, population growth and change in 727
Veiller, Lawrence 1116-17
Venezuela, urban policy and planning in 285
Venice, Calif. 506
Vice 68, 161
crusades against 1755
in Atlanta 1641
in Chicago 1681
in New York City 1749
See also Gambling; Prostitution
Vicksburg, Miss., slavery and segregation in 1185
Villages. See Towns and villages

Virginia
absence of towns in early 829
railroads in urban rivalry of 752
urbanization of 706
urban-rural relations in 707
Virginia, Minn., impact of the mining industry on 720
Vital fringe (urban form) 12
Vocational education
in Cleveland 1800
as a means of social control 951
Voluntary associations and organizations 405, 860
in Boston 642
impact on urbanization 681
in institutionalizing class lines 175
in Jacksonville, Ill. 899
of Milwaukee Greeks 1216
in New Jersey politics 1493
in New York City 806
in Philadelphia politics 1439
of Portland Jews 1907
in St. Louis 871

W

Wade, Richard 430, 458, 1185
Wagner, Robert F. 1695
Wagner Housing Bill 1444
Walker, James J. 1807
Walker, John Brisben 1117
Walsh-Leavitt Act (New Jersey) 1610
Ware, Mass. 700
Waring, George Edwin, Jr. 1777
Warner, Sam Bass, Jr. 156, 430, 444, 458
Warren, Pa. 267
economic growth of 154
history of 663
Washington, Booker T. 1486
Washington, D.C. 31, 33, 68, 519
blacks in 1201, 1264, 1268, 1301, 1425
bridges of 429
comment by travelers on 7, 71

Subject Index

governance of 1435
history of 13, 55, 469, 542-43, 668
impact of the Civil War on 572
planning, architecture, and urban renewal in 801, 812, 1047-48, 1059, 1072, 1096
urbanization of 749
Washington, George 801, 812
Wastes and waste disposal 330, 973, 987, 1702. See also Sewers and sewage disposal
Water pollution. See Pollution and pollution control
Water rights 545
Water supply and systems 857, 866, 894, 987, 1827
 in Atlanta 910
 in Chicago 876
 in Memphis 1008
 in Milwaukee 641
 in New York City 920, 1026
 in Pittsburgh 1015
Wealth 390
 distribution of 255, 700, 821-22, 852, 1333, 1359
 as a cause of violence 1247
 means by which New York City merchants secured 1467
 See also Income; Upper class
Webb (Walter Prescott) Memorial Lectures (1974) 97
Welfare state 1714, 1750
Welsh Americans, in Scranton, Pa. 1195
Wenatchee Valley, Wash. 732
West, The 719, 726, 737, 741
 company towns in 674
 importance to the growth of cities 286
 New Orleans and 485
 promotion of 750
 settlement of 52
 social class in 596
 urbanization of 721, 751, 758-59, 765
 See also Frontier
Western and Atlantic Railroad 630
West Virginia, politics in 1477

Wheeling, W. Va.
 iron and steel industry in 1868
 public health in 902
White, William A. 377
Whitlock, Brand 377, 1616
Whitman, Walt 1162
Wholesale trade 151
Wichita, Kans.
 history of 13
 public utilities in 1896
Wilkes-Barre, Pa., growth and development of 173
Willard, Charles Dwight 1638
Williamsburg, Va., history of 785, 803
Williamson, Jeffrey 221
Wilmington, Del.
 blacks in 1512
 history of 553
 lumber trade in 703
 politics in 1512
Winthrop, John 833
Wirth, Louis 366
Wisconsin
 industrialization of 197
 influence of lumbering on 301
 politics in 1548
 rivalry for railroads in 743
 rural-urban migration in 207
 tenements in 1084
Women
 education of immigrant 1390
 employment of 1189, 1853
 the franchise and 1230
 Irish American 1267, 1898
 in the Jacksonian period 38
 occupational mobility of 1266
 Progressive reform movement and 1824
 Scandinavian American 1418
 in the trades of Pittsburgh 559
 working class in Philadelphia 1308
 in Pittsburgh 1310
 See also Feminist movement
Wood, Fernando 1626-28
Worcester, Mass. 700
 Dickens on 7
 land use and zoning in 264, 276-77, 1134
 workers of 1202

Subject Index

Working Man's party 1573
Workingmen's clubs, of the New York City Episcopal Church 925
World War I
  in creation of municipal finance problems 929
  effect on Hoboken, N.J. 527
  influence on socialism 1581
World War II
  Detroit and 341
  federal-city relations during 1860
  impact on the Greenbelt town program 1042
  political responses to 1521
Wright, Frank Lloyd 1080, 1165
Wright, John Stephen 728
Writers. See Blacks, as authors; Novelists

Y

Yellow fever
  in New Orleans 906, 908, 922
  in Norfolk, Va. 535
  in Philadelphia 986
Yorke, Peter 1463
Young Men's Christian Association, schools of the Chicago 115
Youngstown, Ohio
  iron and steel industry in 1868
  land use in 276-77
Ypsilanti, Mich., politics in 1511

Z

Ziegenheim, Henry 1741
Zion City, Ill., history of 505
Zoning 54
  in Alviso, Calif. 507
  in Chicago 1109
  in New York City 1049, 1709
  slum clearance and 1168
  in Worcester, Mass. 264, 1134